UNDERSTANDING WILLIAMS SYNDROME

Behavioral Patterns and Interventions

UNDERSTANDING WILLIAMS SYNDROME

Behavioral Patterns and Interventions

ELEANOR SEMEL
Boston University

SUE R. ROSNER
University of Iowa

Routledge
Taylor & Francis Group
New York   London

First published by Lawrence Erlbaum Associates, Inc., Publishers
10 Industrial Avenue
Mahwah, New Jersey 07430

Reprinted 2009 by Routledge

Routledge

270 Madison Avenue
New York, NY 10016

2 Park Square, Milton Park
Abingdon, Oxon OX14 4RN, UK

Cover design by Kathryn Houghtaling Lacey

Library of Congress Cataloging-in-Publication Data

Semel, Eleanor Messing.
Understanding Williams syndrome : behavioral patterns and interventions / Eleanor Semel, Sue R. Rosner.

p. cm.

Includes bibliographical references and index.

ISBN 0-8058-2617-3 (alk. paper)
ISBN 0-8058-2618-1 (pbk. : alk paper)
1. Williams syndrome. I. Rosner, Sue R. II. Title.
RJ506.W44 S45 2002
618.92'0042—dc21

2002029475

10 9 8 7 6 5 4 3 2

This book is dedicated to Eleanor's husband, Allan Frankle,
and Sue's husband, Lawrence M. Stolurow,
for their encouragement, patience, inspiration, and love.

This book could not have been written
without their continuing support.

List of Figures

List of Tables

Contents

Foreword

Ursulla Bellugi
Director, Laboratory for Cognitive Neuroscience
The Salk Institute for Biological Studies

Twenty-five years ago Williams syndrome was almost completely unknown in the United States, although cited earlier in Europe under other names. Increasingly over the past decade, Williams syndrome is becoming more widely recognized and better understood. An intriguing behavioral profile, a host of medical difficulties, groundbreaking discoveries in neurogenetics, and the collaborative efforts of scientists representing disciplines from cognitive neuroscience to brain imaging and molecular genetics are providing the impetus for a flourishing field of research endeavors. The insights, dedication, and commitment of parents and educators have played a vital role in this process.

Questions as to the universality, uniqueness, and the distinctiveness of the behavioral characteristics of the syndrome are under intense investigation. Issues regarding the generality of the cognitive profile and the underlying bases for the unusual profile of peaks and valleys of abilities are being examined in depth. The consistency and variability in levels of performance within and between cognitive domains is under scrutiny by scientists in research institutions in various countries. The exciting task of investigating the relationships between behavior, underlying neurobiology, and genetics is now underway.

At the same time, there is growing recognition of the multiple problems that individuals with Williams syndrome and their families, teachers, and other professionals face in dealing with this condition: developmentally, socially, academically, vocationally, and personally, at all points in the life cycle. Challenges include handling the learning difficulties, behavior problems, and deficient life skills often associated with the syndrome, as well as knowing how to use the positive strengths to advantage within the classroom and other situations. This involves capitalizing on their skills and strengths in areas such as language, storytelling, music, face recognition, and sociability.

Both the advances in research knowledge and recognition of the challenges involved in dealing with Williams syndrome have resulted in an extensive, ever expanding literature. There is a proliferation of articles in scientific journals, papers, and symposia presented at meetings and conferences, book chapters, monographs, and occasional reviews of the research. Other major contributions are the informative pamphlets, newsletters, and helpful booklets with advice for parents and teachers published by the Williams Syndrome Associations in the United

States and the United Kingdom. But such references have up to now been scattered. Some are unavailable or hard to find, others may be inappropriate for readers with one or another level of expertise or field of interest. The book, *Understanding Williams Syndrome: Behavioral Patterns and Interventions*, is designed to remedy this state of affairs.

This book is the first comprehensive source book on the behavioral patterns of individuals with Williams syndrome. Not only does it summarize and analyze the research literature, it also provides problem-specific interventions, general guidelines for addressing problems, and innovative techniques for developing the potential of many individuals with Williams syndrome. It captures essential features of the syndrome by combining research findings with real-life examples, clinical observations, and anecdotal reports. It goes beyond generalities by describing variation among individuals with the syndrome—behavioral, physical, educational, and cognitive variation—as well as subgroups within the syndrome. Comparisons with other conditions and other groups, both disabled and normally developing, are consistently made in the review of the literature and in the description of intervention strategies.

Eleanor Semel and Sue Rosner are the ideal people to pull these strands together, both with respect to research and to intervention. Dr. Semel is Professor Emerita at Boston University, where she received her doctorate and taught for many years. Acclaimed nationally and internationally for her pioneering work in the field of learning disabilities, she has created and authored many innovative educational and remedial programs for learning disabled children, and conducted extensive research in language, learning disabilities, and many other areas. Her writings include research articles and college-level textbooks and she is the senior author of one of the most comprehensive language and concept assessments available anywhere, the *Clinical Evaluation of Language Functions* (Semel, Wiig, & Secord, 1995). And she is also profoundly knowledgeable about Williams syndrome. In fact, Dr. Semel was the National Education Director for the Williams Syndrome Association for many years, where she established a "hotline" enabling parents to talk with her and seek her advice on therapies and interventions for their children. I know very many families who are deeply grateful to her for her wealth of information, ideas, and understanding of Williams syndrome.

Sue R. Rosner received her PhD in experimental psychology at the University of Connecticut. Her special fields of interest include developmental psychology, cognitive development, and the relation between child and clinical psychology. She has authored numerous publications in scientific journals, presented papers at professional meetings, supervised doctoral students, and has done considerable research in the field of memory in children. She was Associate Professor of Psychology, Acting Dean of the Faculties, Director of Summer Sessions, and Acting Dean of the College of Nursing at the University of Iowa. In 1989-1990 she served as consultant to the Salk Institute—Laboratory for Cognitive Neuroscience. Since that time Dr. Semel and Dr. Rosner have been working together on Williams syndrome.

In this book, Dr. Semel and Dr. Rosner identify some of the prototypic behavioral features of Williams syndrome based on their rate of occurrence and the consistency with which they are reported in the literature. Other relevant topics include discussion of physical features, medical conditions, and cutting-edge discoveries in the field of neurobiology and genetics, trends in research and treatment, educational applications, and care delivery systems for individuals with the syndrome.

The research literature is thoroughly summarized, analyzed, and synthesized within each of the major areas represented in this book. The areas include: Language Skills and Problems—acquisition, speech, syntax, semantics, pragmatics, and discourse; Perceptual-Motor Performance—visual-spatial perception, motor functioning, visual-motor integration, tactile defensiveness, and auditory hypersensitivity; Specific Aptitudes—sociability and empathy, curiosity for special topics and objects, memory functioning, and musicality; and Maladaptive Behaviors—fears and anxieties, distractibility, impulsivity, poor adaptability, low frustration tolerance, and atypical activity patterns. It also discusses clinical disorders, such as ADHD, autistic behaviors, mood disorders, depression, and obsessive-compulsive disorder that may sometimes be exhibited by individuals with Williams syndrome.

Consistencies and discrepancies in the research literature are highlighted in tables that present the frequency of behavioral characteristics at various age levels, and the relative strength of such behaviors compared to those of other groups, such as Down syndrome, Prader-Willi syndrome, Fragile X, autism, learning disability, and normal controls. An integral part of the research literature covered in the book consists of parent questionnaire data collected and analyzed by the authors, namely the Utah Survey as well as use of the Williams Syndrome Association (WSA) Checklist for new registrants in the association. Never before published, these surveys provide in-depth analyses, with descriptions and observations, of the 74 children included in the Utah Survey and the 225 children with Williams syndrome included as registrants in the WSA.

Although research on Williams syndrome is now abundant, there is still an acute need for practical methods of intervention. This book fulfills that need by providing a variety of approaches that may help individuals with Williams syndrome and their families. Discovering which interventions are effective with these special individuals can provide new insights into the mechanisms underlying their behavioral characteristics.

The authors have successfully gathered together extremely useful, highly readable yet insightful information on the behavioral patterns of individuals with Williams syndrome for parents, teachers, professionals, clinicians, researchers, the media, and general public. Crucially, the book also offers strategies designed to map onto the behavioral patterns and specific aptitudes of individuals with Williams syndrome to help parents, teachers, professionals, therapists, and clinicians address their multiple needs.

Drs. Semel and Rosner have provided the first book on this fascinating syndrome and it will be of critical importance to a wide audience of readers. This handbook combines breadth and depth, scholarly analysis with practical information on this intriguing genetically based disorder. The authors have reviewed the exciting explosion of research in this new field, taking into account research in several different countries and combining the results with their own research. Most importantly, the book provides invaluable information on interventions and practical implications to help individuals with Williams syndrome as well as those with other learning disorders reach toward their fullest potential. *Understanding Williams Syndrome: Behavioral Patterns and Interventions* offers readers a balanced presentation, an integrated framework, and much to think about and apply. It is a groundbreaking and important book that will have a wide audience of readers, and applications far beyond Williams syndrome itself. Indeed, the interventions and applications, which are the significant contributions of the authors, are relevant to the clinicians, professionals, and parents dealing in the far broader field of individuals struggling with other types of problematic conditions.

In the early 1990s, Dr. Semel was quoted in an article in *Discover Magazine* about Williams syndrome. In the article, she said: "Educators are confused because the Williams syndrome child tests like a retarded child, talks like a gifted child, behaves like a disturbed child, and functions like a learning-disabled child." Each of these terms has a specific meaning in the world of special education, yet none seems to fit the characteristic peaks and valleys in Williams syndrome. The result is that children with Williams syndrome are generally not well served by most schools.

And now, in this first book addressing research findings and a wealth of significant interventions, Dr. Semel and Dr. Rosner provide some answers to these puzzles—answers that will enable children with Williams syndrome to be better served by schools, by their parents and peers, and by the world. Even more, this book provides an intriguing foray into the world of special education in general, and an insightful perspective on what it means to be growing up different.

Preface

Back in the early 1990s, we began to write a single chapter to be included in a reference work on Williams syndrome. Initially, we focused on responses to our parent questionnaires on the behavioral characteristics of children with Williams syndrome, the related literature, and interventions appropriate for children with this condition in the areas of language, perceptual-motor performance, aptitudes, maladaptive behaviors, and academic skills.

Over the past decade, our venture underwent one metamorphosis after another as we continued on our own personal odyssey toward "Understanding Williams Syndrome." One chapter became several and then an entire book, reflecting many of the major developments in the field of Williams syndrome. These include the emergence of significant topics, issues, and trends; identification of various problems and skills of individuals with Williams syndrome within each survey area; and the complex interaction between research and clinical practice.

Generally, progress begins with observations and comments by parents, teachers, other professionals and researchers that lead to the development of laboratory studies, testing procedures, and relevant interventions. This is epitomized in the enormous effort exerted to determine the level of ability displayed in the various components of language by children with Williams syndrome. Such findings suggested new ways to help them. Discovery of their narrative talents and love of performing led us to use storytelling, puppetry, and improvisation as psycho-educational techniques for the teaching of social skills. The receptiveness of many children with Williams syndrome to verbal reasoning and explanations inspired us to introduce "problem analysis" as an intervention strategy, especially in the area of maladaptive behavior. Their grasp of semantic relatedness influenced our use of association cues and simple metaphors as learning tools; their language and memory skills convinced us early on that self-talk is a very potent form of verbal mediation and behavioral control.

The "empathy" of individuals with Williams syndrome is another cogent example of how observations and parent reports, including responses to one item in our Utah Survey, have been extended by laboratory studies of empathy, as well as ways of channeling such sensitivities into adaptive kinds of behavior.

The saga of musicality provides a classic example of these connections between research and practice. Initial reports concerning the musical interests and talents of individuals with Williams syndrome were crucial to efforts to provide opportunities for the development and recognition of their musical skills. These efforts, in turn, led to laboratory studies examining such abilities as absolute pitch, rhythmic sensitivity, composing, and memory for music. They have also brought attention to the importance of providing appropriate forms of music instruction and using music as a valuable resource for many individuals with Williams syndrome.

Sometimes clinical awareness of problems foreshadows research findings and contributes to them. For example, clinical experience and emerging trends in practice led us to increase our coverage of language pragmatics, that is, the communicative functions of language, from descriptions of a few representative problems involving mainly conversational style to discussion of thirteen problems. Many of these were previously unreported problems, such as difficulty accepting restrictions or expressing negative feelings, that needed to be addressed even though we were "sticking our necks out" in doing so.

Likewise, reports of several kinds of mental disorder have sensitized mental health providers to the possibility of their occurrence and the relation between certain symptoms and age level in individuals with Williams syndrome. These reports have also led to studies of the incidence of such problems and consideration of alternative methods of treatment, such as adapted forms of psychotherapy and psychopharmacology. We felt compelled to add this information to our previous discussion of behavior problems and the general effectiveness of psycho-educational strategies.

Coverage of the clinical aspects of the visual and motor problems of individuals with Williams syndrome was expanded as a result of the increased involvement of professionals, such as physical therapists, occupational therapists, and sensory integration therapists. Techniques for successfully treating such conditions also needed to be included.

Additional areas that should be studied clinically and in the laboratory include auditory perceptual processing problems, gross motor problems, difficulty with spatial orientation, and sensitivity to tactile stimulation in individuals with Williams syndrome.

Other important trends reflect changes in the demographics of Williams syndrome. The diversity of the racial, ethnic, and national backgrounds of the affected population is becoming increasingly recognized and with it some interest in determining whether such factors may affect performance and treatment.

We have also experienced an age shift from initially dealing almost exclusively with children of school age to a major broadening of the age levels of individuals that are studied, treated, and considered representative of Williams syndrome. Thus, we have included information on developmental milestones, patterns of acquisition, and age trends over the life span in a number of domains, such as language, perceptual-motor functioning, and socioemotional development.

Increased attention to age level also has implications for the number and types of interventions that should be provided. Early stimulation programs for young children; tutoring, clubs, and development of skills for children of school age; social opportunities, leisure activities (i.e., camps, tours), and educational programs (i.e., workshops, sometimes community college) for teenagers and adults, are some examples. There are also issues of vocation and employment, sexuality, independent living, and financial planning for many adults with Williams syndrome.

In addition, research designs are being scrutinized to determine what types of methods and comparison groups are best suited to reveal the properties of Williams syndrome. Initial studies generally focused on descriptions of the characteristics of children with Williams syndrome, sometimes compared to individuals with Down syndrome or other forms of mental retardation. Now, a much broader range of syndromes and groups are represented in efforts to evaluate and pinpoint the critical features of this disorder. In an attempt to deal with this wealth of information, we have constructed summary tables of research findings that appear throughout the book.

As more fine-grained research is conducted, there is irrefutable evidence of individual differences in performance, such as level of cognitive ability, even among those of similar age and background, as well as striking evidence of diagnostic subgroups, like those with the features of both Williams syndrome and autism.

We have not yet mentioned significant advances taking place in neurogenetics, such as the use of MRI (neuroimaging) techniques, chromosomal analyses, and the discovery of the gene(s) for Williams syndrome. There has also been progress in understanding medical conditions associated with Williams syndrome from the early days, when mainly aortic stenosis and failure to thrive were considered, to current-day guidelines for screening and examination of a variety of systems and possible defects. These areas, too, had to be included, or at least mentioned where appropriate in our book.

Readers will appreciate our quandary! An overabundance of intriguing, significant material, and too many pages. Therefore, the need to CUT, CUT, CUT. Revision after revision, addition after addition, pauses for other commitments, updating, and a patient editor, led us to the realization that some culling of content was absolutely necessary. After much thought, and with great regret, we decided that we must exclude the vast majority of our work on educational issues—the evaluation, placement, and management of students with Williams syndrome; their academic skills and problems; specific strategies for the teaching of reading, writing, spelling, and arithmetic—and the development of life skills; the management of family life; and vocational options. Wherever possible, we incorporated some of this material in this book.

Concerns about length also required the use of certain stylistic devices. For the sake of brevity, we have adopted the convention of using abbreviations to refer to frequently mentioned syndromes (e.g., WS for Williams syndrome, DS for Down syndrome, AUT for autism, P-W for Prader-Willi, Frag X for Fragile X syndrome). We also follow the convention of using suffixes, like "s," "c," and "a" to refer to group members, such as "WSs" for individuals with Williams syndrome, "WSc" to refer to children with Williams syndrome, and "Wsa" to refer to adolescents and adults with Williams syndrome. This notation is similarly applied to members of other groups, such as DSs, DSc, and so forth. Without the use of such devices, the flow of information becomes quite awkward and very repetitive. It goes without saying that the use of these abbreviations is not intended to stereotype individuals with Williams syndrome or undermine in any way the critical importance of regarding them as individuals and treating them with dignity and respect.

More indicative of our perspective on the individuality of WSs are the changes we made over the years in our working title of this manuscript. Initially, we used the term *behavioral characteristics,* but this implied a disconnectedness between behaviors that we do not espouse. This was followed by our use of the term *behavioral profile* to signify the generality of the portrayal and comparison of multiple features, but this had flaws, too. Finally, we settled on the present subtitle *behavioral patterns* to convey the pliability, interconnectedness, and individual variations in the attributes displayed by WSs.

So, now as our project nears completion, we are resisting the temptation to revise, edit, or add updated material on important interventions or groundbreaking discoveries. Instead, we close our work on this book with the hope that it will stimulate further progress in *Understanding Williams Syndrome* and serve as a guide to *Behavioral Patterns and Interventions* for those many people—parents, teachers and other educators, physicians, therapists, other professionals, researchers, and most of all, individuals with Williams syndrome (WSs)—for whom this book is written.

—Eleanor Semel
—Sue R. Rosner
La Jolla, California

Acknowledgments

First, we wish to express our deep appreciation to Dr. Ursula Bellugi for sharing with us her knowledge and insights about Williams syndrome, providing us the opportunity to interact with many Williams syndrome children and adults, and for encouraging and inspiring us to write this book.

We also want to recognize the valuable contributions of many individuals with Williams syndrome and their devoted families and teachers in revealing to us their experiences, difficulties, and triumphs.

We thank the Williams Syndrome Association for its pivotal role in providing leadership, information, resources, and support for individuals with Williams syndrome and all those closely involved with them, including parents, teachers, professionals, and researchers.

We would also like to thank those parents who kindly granted permission for us to include photographs of their Williams syndrome children in the cover design of our book. We are especially grateful to Professor Howard Lenhoff for having allowed us to reproduce pictures from the photo album on the Web site of the Williams Syndrome Foundation.

We also wish to recognize the significant contribution of our dedicated editors at Lawrence Erlbaum Associates, Susan Milmoe, Sondra Guideman, and Art Lizza, in the development, production, and publication of this book.

In addition, Dr. Semel would like to personally express her gratitude to the Williams Syndrome Association for the valuable experience she gained while serving as their National Education Director and for supporting her efforts in making the ground-breaking video, " Jenny," a story about a child diagnosed with Williams syndrome. During this period, she was able to establish the Williams Syndrome Hotline and wants to extend her appreciation to the many anonymous callers who consulted her over the years on the Williams Syndrome Hotline. They confided their problems, tried out her suggestions, and let her know when they worked and when they did not.

Finally, we would be remiss if we did not acknowledge the patience and loyalty of our many friends, children, grandchildren, and other family members who stood by us and understood when we were not able to be with them because we were so involved in writing this book. We are very pleased they are welcoming us back now that the book is finally finished.

1

Introduction

The frustrated efforts of five blind men trying to picture an elephant by exploring its separate parts are like the perplexed experts from various fields, each from their own perspective, trying to identify the critical features of Williams syndrome (WS). How is it possible to conceptualize a group of children who test as though retarded, speak as though gifted, behave sometimes as though emotionally disturbed, and function like the learning disabled? This is one of the enigmas that parents, teachers, professionals, and researchers face as they try to rear, teach, treat, and study individuals with WS.

On a more optimistic note, many of the puzzling features of WS are being demystified by research on the physical, medical, genetic, psychological, neurobiological, and psycho-educational aspects of WS. Investigation of the linkage between genes, brain, and behavior is particularly timely as the medical and scientific communities have become increasingly interested in the genome project and the problems of genetic disorders like WS (Bellugi, Wang, & Jernigan, 1994; Harris, 1995b; Lenhoff, Wang, Greenberg, & Bellugi, 1997).

But, just what is WS? How does it manifest itself? How is it related to other developmental disorders? And what types of intervention approaches are successful in dealing with the unusual profile that characterizes WS? These are the basic issues addressed in this book.

I. BACKGROUND ON WILLIAMS SYNDROME

Historical Overview

Initially identified as a condition involving a heart defect (supravalvular aortic stenosis, SVAS, or narrowing of major blood vessels), mental retardation, and stereotypic facial features, Williams syndrome is named after J. C. R. Williams, a cardiologist in New Zealand (Williams, Barrett-Boyes, & Lowe, 1961). It is also known as Williams–Beuren syndrome (WBS), after Dr. Beuren, mainly in Germany and on the continent (Beuren, 1972; Martin, Snodgrass, & Cohen, 1984). Some early articles associated the syndrome with idiopathic infantile hypercalcaemia, IIH (a type of retardation involving abnormal calcium metabolism), and a distinctive set of behaviors (Beuren, Apitz, & Harmanz, 1962; Jones & Smith, 1975; von Arnim & Engel, 1964). Since the mid-1980s, significant gains have been made toward understanding the neuropsychological, neurobiological, and psycho-educational features of WS (e.g., Arnold, Yule, & Martin, 1985; Bellugi, Marks, Bihrle, & Sabo, 1988; Morris, Demsey, Leonard, Dilts, & Blackburn, 1988).

Insight into the nature of WS culminated in the mid-1990s with its classification as a genetic disorder occurring in an estimated 1 in 20,000 to 50,000 births and involving a highly unusual set of characteristics (Mervis, Morris, Bertrand, & Robinson, 1999). These characteristics include distinctive facial and physical features, a unique cognitive profile, a singular mix of personality attributes, and an intriguing pattern of neurobiological findings. Despite its rarity, WS has captured the attention of researchers, professionals, and the media, including Oliver Sacks, probably due in part to its theoretical significance and practical implications. This is further motivated by the extraordinary charm of many individuals with WS (WSs), the exceptional dedication of numerous families, teachers, and others involved with them, and the impetus provided by the Williams Syndrome Association (WSA) of parents and professionals.

A. Distinctive Physical Features

Typically, children with WS (WSc) are very petite, "cute," and attractive individuals with a "pixie-like" appearance. They are inclined to share many physical features, usually resembling each other more than members of their own families. Unlike children with other developmental disorders, WSc tend to lack physical stigmata. Instead, they often evoke positive responses from adults.

Facial Characteristics. WSs, particularly youngsters, tend to show a distinctive pattern of craniofacial or morphological features that is sometimes referred to as "elfin, or pixie," facies (Jones & Smith, 1975; Lenhoff et al

1997). Characteristics may include a broad forehead, prominent eyes, full cheeks, a wide mouth, a short-upturned nose, and large ears. Their eyes tend to be set slightly closer together than average, with fullness (periorbital) around the eyes, and a small (epicanthal) fold of skin that overlaps the inner corner of the eye. The blue eyes of many WSs often feature a striking white pattern in the iris that looks like a lacy starburst (stellate iris).

WSc often have prominent lips, an elongated space between the upper lip and the nose (a long philtrum), a pointed nose (anteverted nares) with a full or bulbous tip, and a depressed nasal bridge. They may display down turning of the corners of the mouth and an open mouth posture. Frequently, these individuals have prominent ears that are low placed and somewhat pointed rather than rounded. Many WSc have a small head, a long neck, and sloping shoulders.

Despite their unusual characteristics, the facial features of WSc epitomize the prototype of an attractive juvenile. This undoubtedly contributes to their appeal.

Medical and Dental Conditions. Unfortunately, individuals with WS are subject to numerous health problems, many of which can be extremely serious, some life threatening. Even the typical conditions of most WSs require frequent medical, dental, and related types of checkups, tests, procedures, and treatment programs. Such problems and treatment can undermine the quality of life and impose burdens on the everyday functioning of WSs and their families.

Infancy is usually a traumatic period for child and family. From birth, WSc often have medical problems, including overt cardiac deficits (e.g., supravalvular aortic stenosis and heart murmurs). Such cardiac problems are frequent and often require surgery. WSc are also prone to incapacitating digestive and feeding difficulties (e.g., disordered sucking, swallowing, tongue thrusting, gagging, and gastrointestinal reflux), prolonged colic, eliminative disorders (e.g., constipation and rectal prolapse), and incessant crying. Metabolic problems (e.g., vitamin D sensitivity, impaired calcitonin secretion, and Infantile hypercalcaemia) are implicated in a general "failure to thrive." Hernias, renal abnormalities, and other kidney problems are common from infancy into adulthood (Hagerman, 1999; Morris et al., 1988; Pankau, Partsch, Winter, Gosch, & Wessel, 1986).

Small stature and a slight build are characteristic of WSc (Pankau, Partsch, Gosch, Opperman, & Wessel, 1992). Progressive joint limitation is often evident, initially hypotonic with joint laxity; contractures may occur later. Other skeletal problems may include angulation of the big toe (hallux valgus), a bent fifth finger (clinodactyly), or depression of the chest (pectus excavation).

Many WSc have dental abnormalities, such as small, "bud"-shaped, widely spaced, pointed teeth (microdonite); a poor bite (malocclusion); endentation; and delayed dental eruption. Eye problems, such as strabismus and hyperopia, and ear infections are frequent in WSc. In adulthood, WSs have a high incidence of hypertension, gastrointestinal problems, and urinary tract problems.

In order to deal with the various health problems of WS, baseline evaluation, continual monitoring of conditions of risk, and application of effective treatment are recommended from infancy on (Hagerman, 1999; Morris et al., 1988). For example, the digestive and elimination problems common in infancy (i.e., hypercalcaemia, reflux, and oral motor coordination difficulties) may need to be addressed by physicians, pediatricians, and other professional specialists (Hagerman, 1999).

A group of physicians experienced in treating WSs have prepared guidelines as to the types of examinations, tests, and procedures that should be routinely administered to WSs (Morris et al., WSA Newsletter, March, 1999, Vol. 16(1), pp. 4–6). Among the laboratory and radiology tests that physicians recommend are (a) blood chemistry, urinalysis, thyroid function, and FISH genetic tests for 7q11.23 deletion; (b) cardiology examination, including echocardiography, Doppler flow studies, and blood pressure measured in all four limbs; and (c) assessment of the genitourinary system, including ultrasound test of bladder and kidneys and urine analysis. In addition, many health professionals and researchers advise regular evaluation of the musculoskeletal, visual, auditory, dental, neurological, and behavioral status of WSs (e.g., Morris et al., 1999).

B. Developmental Problems

Developmental Delays. The majority of WSc are significantly delayed in attaining most developmental milestones, including speech and language, learning to walk and run, and learning to read and write. In language, WSs often make later strides that may result in a relative catch-up by late childhood, adolescence, or early adulthood (WSa). In other areas, like visual-spatial-motor skills, marked deficits remain throughout life. Many WSs experience sleep disturbance, eating problems, and an extreme sensitivity to certain sounds. They are also prone to particular kinds of behavioral problems, such as distractibility, impulsivity, rigidity, and atypical activity. Some WSs exhibit specific forms of behavior disturbance: attention deficit disorder with hyperactivity (ADHD) or without hyperactivity (ADD), phobias, or depression.

Cognitive Limitations. In terms of overall cognitive ability, most WSs score within the moderately retarded or mildly retarded range on intelligence tests, although some are in the severely retarded or borderline normal range (i.e., often earning an IQ between 40 and 90 on the Wechsler Intelligence Scale for Children–Revised, WISC–R). This is consistent across decades and continents (e.g., Einfeld, Tonge, & Florio, 1997; Udwin, Yule, & Martin, 1987). In general, mildly retarded adults reach an adult mental age (MA) of from 8;3 to 18;9 years (yrs) and are considered educable; moderately retarded adults reach an adult MA of 5;6 to 8;3 years and are considered trainable.

The IQ scores of WSs, however, may not accurately reflect their true intellectual potential. IQ tests comprise a number of subtests that tap different types of abilities. WSs typically exhibit marked unevenness across the various subtests of most IQ tests, with striking peaks and valleys of abilities across cognitive domains. For example, individuals may achieve relatively high scores on verbal tests, and low scores on performance tests. These individuals may also have difficulties with distractibility, eye–hand coordination, following directions, or retrieving the correct answer, which may confound obtaining an objective measure of their cognitive ability. To minimize these kinds of bias, special care should be taken in the selection and administration of tests (Levine, 1993, 1994).

C. Paradoxical Behavioral Profile

Recent studies of WS and other syndromes have focused on the "behavioral phenotype," that is, patterns of behavior that are reliably identified in a group of children with a known genetic disorder. The behavioral phenotype of WSs includes a unique cognitive profile and unusual socioemotional and personality attributes. As this constitutes a major focus of this book, only the highlights are mentioned in this introductory chapter.

Cognitive Incongruities. In the cognitive domain, proficient and creative use of special aspects of language coexists with mental retardation. WSs are noted for their well-developed vocabulary, relatively complex and syntactically correct sentences, and their ability to spin a good tale. In contrast, their reasoning usually remains at a preoperational or preschool level (e.g., Bellugi, Wang, & Jernigan, 1994), and they typically have difficulty grasping cause–effect relations (Semel & Rosner, 1991a). Even within the language domain, there are problems, such as difficulty in maintaining a topic of conversation.

Visuospatial difficulties and deficits in visuomotor functioning abound. These interfere with activities of daily living, such as cutting food, getting dressed, walking down stairs, and writing and drawing. When the visual stimuli involve faces, however, WSc and WSa are often comparable to normals in visual perception, recognition, and discrimination of faces. Inconsistencies are evident in the area of audition, too. Although most WSs react with strong aversion to certain common sounds (e.g., a motor running), mu-

6

sic is generally an area of intense enjoyment. Many WSs sing or play a musical instrument with some skill.

Socioemotional Contrasts. In the area of socioemotional development,
most WSs exhibit an intriguing profile. They tend to be extremely outgoing
and friendly, even with strangers, to the point of being called hypersocial.
Still, most become fearful and anxious when placed in an unfamiliar situation or when confronted with unanticipated change. Distractibility interferes with their performance on numerous tasks, everyday and school
related, yet their attention can be intensely focused on topics of special interest for long periods of time.

Academic Inconsistencies. Academic performance is exemplified by
several distinguishing contrasts: surprising ability to learn how to read; unanticipated skills in phonetically based oral spelling; poorly executed, painstaking, and sometimes illegible handwriting; an unexpected talent for storytelling, and extremely impaired number knowledge and usage. Although
it may take years, many WSs eventually learn basic reading but may not
know the number of pennies in a nickel. This puzzling mix of characteristics
may lead teachers into expecting unrealistic levels of performance, which is
frustrating to both teachers and WS students.

D. Neurobiological Factors

In the areas of neuroanatomy and neurophysiology, studies of brain organization in WSs often yield paradoxical results.

Neuroanatomical and Neurophysiological Research. Despite the fact
that language functioning is usually represented in the left hemisphere of
the brain and visuospatial functioning in the right, there are no indications
of lesions or other gross abnormalities in the brains of WSs that may be related to their language/visuospatial profile (Bellugi, Wang, & Jernigan, 1994;
Harris, 1995b). More detailed analyses of the structures of WSs' brains reveal, however, specific differences from those of normally developing individuals and groups with other types of developmental disorder. Consistent
with their behavioral phenotype, the frontal cortex of WSs is relatively
larger than their posterior (visual) cortex, and their visual cortex indicates
an abnormal clustering of cells. Other consistencies include relatively
spared structures in the limbic system of the temporal lobes that may be
associated with memory and emotionality; a relatively large cerebellum, especially in certain parts of the neocerebellum, which may have a language
function; and enlarged sections of the temporal lobe and planum temporale, which may provide a basis for their musical ability (Lenhoff et al.,

1997). In neurophysiological studies, WSs tend to exhibit hyperexcitability and less hemispheric specialization than most subjects when stimulated by certain auditory probes, such as sentences that are anomalous in meaning (Bellugi et al., 1994; Harris, 1995b).

Such research reveals some of the subtlety of the brain-behavior linkage in WSs and the oversimplicity of some of the earlier theories regarding the relation between localization of brain function, language, and cognition.

Genetic Research. In 1993, a dramatic discovery was announced: "WS is caused by a mutation, or change, in a single gene" (Morris, WSA National Newsletter, 1993, *10*(1), p. 3). This ended years of speculation about the etiology of WS (K. L. Jones, 1990): whether it is due to lack of calcium and vitamin D, difficulty in metabolizing calcitonin (CT), or a calcitonin-gene-related product (CGRP). It also led to intensified study of the WS molecular genetic profile and the extraordinary conclusion that WS arises from a microdeletion of DNA in a single copy region of chromosome 7, 7q11.23 (Ewart, Morris, Ensing et al., 1993).

The primary, first deleted gene identified for the region is the elastin gene (ELN), which causes supravalvular aortic stenosis (SVAS) in individuals with WS as well as those with SVAS but without other WS features. This finding has led to a search for adjacent, WS-linked genes in the surrounding area of 7q11.23. Thus far, somewhere between 16 and 20 genes have been implicated. Some seem to be related, at least for awhile, to certain behavioral aspects of WS, such as LIMK1 with visuospatial deficits, or the length of the deletion with low IQ (Bellugi, Lichtenberger, Mills, Galaburda, & Korenberg, 1999; Korenberg, WSA National Newsletter, 1999, *16*(2), pp. 4–5; Morris & Mervis, WSA National Newsletter, 1999, *16*(2), p. 3; Tassabehji, Metcalfe, Karmiloff-Smith et al., 1999).

Thus, use of the microdeletion technique permits linking the genetic origins of WS to certain aspects of the behavioral and physical phenotype of WS, such as specific cognitive functions, facial features, sociability, and spatial deficits (Bellugi et al., 1999; Morris & Mervis, 1999; Tassabehji et al., 1999). Advances in the human genome project will undoubtedly sharpen the process. At the same time, research with WSs may contribute to the current understanding of the human genome.

II. OVERVIEW OF BOOK

This book deals with the "what," "why," and "how" of the behavioral characteristics of WS. Designed as a handbook for parents, teachers, psychologists, researchers, and other professional specialists concerned with WS, it

provides a comprehensive analysis of the strengths, difficulties, and variations among WSs and practical guidelines for dealing with them. Technical
terms are defined, and theories and mechanisms are cited when appropriate. Comparisons between WSs and relevant groups (e.g., individuals with
Down syndrome, Prader–Willi syndrome, nonspecific mental retardation,
autism, ADD, ADHD, learning disability, and normally developing children)
are consistently drawn.

The book also features a variety of intervention approaches that are
grounded in the unusual properties of the WS behavioral profile and its
range of expression. Intervention strategies are based on clinical experience with WSs and other developmental disorders; reports of families,
teachers, professional specialists, and colleagues; as well as publications
and clinical studies where available. Special attention is given to identifying
procedures that are particularly effective with WSs in contrast to those for
other groups.

Thus, the two objectives of this book are complementary. The behavioral profile of WSs determines, in large part, the types of interventions that
are most successful with WSs, whereas the efficacy of various forms of intervention provides further insight into the features and processes that
may underlie the WS profile.

A. Research on Behavioral Characteristics

Informational Resources. Over the years since this book was begun,
there has been a virtual "knowledge explosion" about WS in the United States,
Canada, and abroad. Studies of WS are reported in professional journals,
scholarly books, chapters, other publications, and at conferences, meetings,
and other gatherings. Personal impressions of parents, teachers, professionals, and researchers provide another valuable source of information, along
with WSA links on the Internet and consultation on the WSA Hotline. Some
studies are easy to access, others less so, and clinical observations and personal accounts are seldom made known to many of those who may benefit.
This has required summarizing, integrating, and organizing numerous research studies and clinical accounts—some consistent, others inconsistent—
on a variety of topics.

To cut through the informational maze, the book presents both quantitative data and qualitative descriptions of WS. Research on the frequency or
prevalence of various characteristics in WSs is presented, as is information
concerning the intensity or predominance of these characteristics in WSs
and other groups when available. Surveys that use items based on parents'
observations—in particular, the Utah Survey and WSA Checklist—are often

cited (Semel & Rosner, 1991a).[1] The theoretical implications of the research in areas such as neuroscience, medicine, genetics, psycholinguistics, psychometrics, cognitive science, and developmental and clinical psychology are often noted.

Informational Aids. Tables summarize the research reported in the text, including the frequency of occurrence and predominance of a particular attribute, the age levels involved, and comparisons with other groups where applicable. These tables reveal the commonality with which WSs exhibit particular characteristics, the extent to which WSs' behavior differs from that of other groups, and the reference for each finding. Some characteristics are exhibited by nearly all WSs, others are concentrated at certain age levels, and still others are displayed less often overall. Thus, there are both developmental and individual differences among WSs, as well as a core of common characteristics evident by late childhood in what may be called the WS prototype.

Importantly, the WS profile tends to differ markedly from that of other developmentally challenged groups on specific distinguishing features, such as high verbal fluency, sociability, emotionality, empathy, and musicality, even though WSs often perform similarly to groups matched on relevant variables such as intelligence (IQ or mental age, MA) on other attributes.

To further illustrate the uniqueness of WSs behavior patterns, the book provides real-life examples and personal anecdotes. Some are based on the clinical experience of various kinds of professionals—including specialists in child clinical psychology, learning disability, speech and language therapy, mental health, and mental retardation—and consultation about many types of problems on the WSA Hotline. Parents, teachers, and others involved with WSs have also contributed their personal experiences, impressions, and interactions with WSs, as well as detailed accounts of interventions that may be appropriate for them.

---

[1]The Utah Survey (Semel-Rosner) consists of 75 behavioral items completed by parents or caregivers of 74 WSs (34 males, 40 females) at the 1988 Williams Syndrome Association (WSA) meeting. The WSA Checklist consists of 13 behavioral items as well as physical and educational items completed by parents of 225 WSs (131 males, 94 females) upon enrollment in the WSA. Both surveys contain items dealing with 5 major topics: language, perception and motor performance, specific aptitudes, behavioral problems, and academic skills. Subjects in both surveys, Utah (U) and Checklist (CH), represent 5 age levels: infants, 1–3 yrs (U, n = 10, CH, n = 114); toddlers, 4–6 yrs (U, n = 14, CH, n = 50); younger children, 7–10 yrs (U, n = 24, CH, n = 28); older children, 11–14 yrs (U, n = 15, CH, n = 22); and adolescents, 15–22 yrs (U, n = 11, CH, n = 11).

B. Intervention Needs

On a par with its discussion of behavioral characteristics, the book addresses the intervention needs of WSs. Information on alternative approaches is provided for the various problem areas that WSs typically display. Guidance in the selection and application of various remedial measures is also provided. This includes capitalizing on the strengths of WSs, as well as trying to reduce or circumvent many of the difficulties associated with WS.

Parents and Family Members. Most parents vividly remember the moment they were told: "Your child has Williams Syndrome." For virtually all these parents, this is a momentous event. Yet, its impact varies considerably, as it is affected by the age and condition of the child when diagnosed, how the information is conveyed, and the availability of support and treatment services. Parents usually need to adjust their expectations and accept the fact that they have a child who has a unique and special condition.

One mother "cried a river" (when told that her 11-month-old daughter had WS) "because [she] couldn't understand how [she] could have a child with so many troubles" (WSA Newsletter, Summer 1993, pp. 13–14). Other parents respond with relief. Because, as one couple put it, the diagnosis is "helpful in describing his delays and prescribing action. . . . The education specialist gave us hope for the future" (WSA Newsletter, Fall 1993, p. 24).

Regardless of developmental shifts in WSs abilities, problems, and needs and changes in the surrounding environment, most WSs require a great deal of support and special care. Informing parents of the intervention approaches and resources that may be available to them may assist in reducing some of the anxiety in the beginning. Helping parents establish an appropriate behavioral and educational program for their WSc is another important step. Many WSs benefit from early therapeutic interventions. Most require multiple kinds of treatment and supportive programs throughout their lives.

Parent organizations, such as the Williams Syndrome Association (WSA; founded in the United States in 1988) and the Infantile Hypercalcaemia Foundation (founded in Great Britain in 1979 by Sir George and Lady Cynthia Cooper), provide information and support for families and professionals, and encourage researchers interested in WS. In this capacity, they sponsor research and organize national, regional, and local meetings, conferences, and gatherings for families and professionals. Newsletters, such as the WSA Newsletter, provide a forum for families to share personal concerns, problems, and helpful suggestions with others and for professionals and researchers to inform parents and other interested parties about research findings, as well as medical, social policy, and educational information. Countries throughout the world have parent groups for WS, many with their own Web sites. For example, Argentina, Australia, Canada, France, Germany, Hungary, Ireland, Israel, Italy, Mexico, Portugal, Spain, and Sweden have parent groups (WSA National Newsletter, 2000, *17*, September, p. 32). Clinics experienced with WS are found in many cities with medical centers in the United States, such as Boston, Chicago (Park Ridge), Cincinnati, Cleveland, Philadelphia, San Diego, and New Hyde Park, New York (WSA National Newsletter, 2000, *17*, June, p. 4).

Professionals and Researchers. Information about intervention techniques may also be of value to professionals and researchers. Specialists in many fields may be unfamiliar with WS and not know how to best apply their expertise to WSs. Teachers generally find that the prototypical behavioral profile of WSs requires modification of customary teaching practices. Even special education techniques that usually benefit children with other forms of developmental disorder are not ordinarily effective with most WSs.

Similarly, specialists in other areas, such as speech and language therapy, physical and occupational therapy, social work, and clinical psychology, as well as medical specialists in pediatrics, cardiology, psychiatry, genetics, and internal medicine, may be uninformed about the special conditions associated with WS and how to address those treatment needs. Generally, some alteration in approach or technique is necessary. Specifics are discussed throughout the book.

Likewise, researchers in fields such as neuropsychology, neurobiology, genetics, psycholinguistics, cognitive psychology, personality, and behavior disturbance are often perplexed by the behavioral phenotype of WS, its fit with major theories, and how to interpret results obtained with WSs, even in their own field. Obtaining accurate, unbiased measures of WS performance may also be a challenge that requires becoming familiar with some of the aspects of WS and the application of relevant psychoeducational techniques.

C. Intervention Approaches

This book addresses these concerns by offering recommendations for dealing with the behavioral patterns of WSs, especially those that interfere with their functioning or disturb others. Organized by type of behavior, techniques designed to address those problems and cultivate the special aptitudes of WSs are clearly described. Alternative treatment approaches, suitable for use by parents, teachers, and other professionals, are presented.

Because of their unique profile, WSs often benefit from the professional services of a wide range of specialists. From time to time, this may include speech and language therapists, occupational therapists, physical therapists, audiologists, learning specialists, psychologists, and mental health professionals, in addition to various kinds of physicians (e.g., pediatricians, cardiologists, geneticists, ophthalmologists, internists).

Drawing on the skills and aptitudes of WSs and clinical experience with WSs and other developmental disorders, specific psycho-educational techniques are described. These include the use of verbal mediation, self-instruction, problem analysis, control mechanisms, and environmental controls. Application of such techniques is determined, of course, by the particular kind of problem and individual with WS.

D. Chapter Content

This book examines the strengths and weaknesses of WSs in four major areas of performance—language, perceptual-motor functioning, specific aptitudes, and behavior problems—as well as pivotal therapeutic methods designed to facilitate their functioning in these areas. Individual and subgroup variations among WSs in their behavioral characteristics and their reactions to various types of intervention are identified, although the emphasis is on the prototypical profile and psycho-educational strategies appropriate for it. The material is divided into eight chapters, six of which deal directly with a particular content area.

Chapter 2, "Language Skills and Problems," describes many of the strengths and weaknesses of WSs in various language areas, including language acquisition, semantics, syntax, pragmatics, discourse, and storytelling.

Chapter 3, "Intervention Approaches for Language Problems," discusses ways in which the language problems commonly displayed by WSs may be addressed. Some therapeutic techniques are intended mainly for use by speech language therapists; others can be applied by teachers, professional specialists, and parents, particularly with the guidance of therapists.

Chapter 4, "Perceptual and Motor Performance," focuses on the visuo-spatial deficits and strengths, motor deficiencies, and visuomotor integration problems of WSs, as well as their auditory hypersensitivity, tactile hypersensitivity, and skills in these areas. Interventions are discussed within the context of each separate area. This includes a description of relevant medical specialties. In particular, information is provided for occupational and physical therapists as to approaches that have been found to be especially effective with WSs. This chapter may also provide useful background information for parents, teachers, and other professionals. In addition, suggestions on the use of psycho-educational techniques (e.g., verbal strategies, task management, and environmental controls) may be helpful in coping with WS problems of visuomotor deficiency, and auditory and tactile hypersensitivity.

Chapter 5, "Specific Aptitudes," deals with four areas of specialized skills associated with WS: sociability including empathy, curiosity, memory, and musicality. The chapter also offers a variety of methods relevant to developing the skills and addressing the difficulties often exhibited in each area.

Chapter 6, "Maladaptive Behaviors," describes six kinds of behavior problems that are often manifested by WSs: anxieties and fears, distractibility and attentional problems, impulsivity, poor adaptability, low frustration tolerance, and atypical activity. It also describes other types of clinical disorder that are sometimes presented by WSs.

Chapter 7, "Intervention Approaches for Maladaptive Behaviors," describes the major types of treatment approaches applicable to WSs and the application of these interventions to specific types of behavior problems. It also provides a brief summary of procedures for the evaluation and diagnosis of problem behaviors in WSs as well as the treatment options of psychotherapy and/or psychopharmacology for more serious disorders.

Finally, chapter 8, "Summary and Conclusions," summarizes material from previous chapters on the behavioral characteristics of WS and considers how it may be synthesized into an integrated, overall profile of WS. Likewise, the treatment and intervention approaches of previous chapters are reviewed and condensed into a set of general guidelines that encompass the special procedures found to be helpful with WSs. Finally, recommendations for maximizing the educational and life skill potential of WSs are offered, based on implications of the behavioral phenotype and intervention guidelines discussed earlier.

E. Uses for This Book

Through its parallel emphasis on behavioral characteristics and interventions, this book aims to serve the needs and interests of multiple audiences: parents, families, caregivers, teachers, other educators, physicians, professional specialists, researchers, and those who are simply fascinated by WS. Discussion of the roles of various disciplines may encourage mutual exchange and foster cooperation among professionals and other groups.

Specifically, the background on WS characteristics may assist parents in understanding the attributes and range of variation of WSs. Researchers and physicians may want to use the book as a resource for information and references to the substantial literature on WS. It may also aid professionals in understanding the WS prototype and its variations.

Because this book contains considerable hands-on information, it provides both practical advice and research and theoretical background. Many parents and educators will want to read it thoroughly from cover to cover, whereas others may select sections that are particularly relevant to them at the time.

Likewise, the various professional specialists who find themselves providing diagnostic services and interventions to WSs may find it useful as a "how to do it" manual. In fact, the book offers valuable information for professionals on how to interact appropriately with WSs, in addition to special measures that may be helpful in treating WS problems. These may aid in addressing the skills, talents, problems, deficits, and difficulties often presented by WSs.

All those who are highly committed to WSs may benefit from the informational and practical aspects of the book. To these constituents—scholars, researchers, physicians, therapists, teachers, educators, and other professionals—but especially to the parents and teachers of WSc, WS poses a challenge. This book aims to address that challenge.

CHAPTER

2

Language Skills and Problems

Researchers describe WS language as "remarkable," "surprisingly well preserved," "unusual and picturesque," "relatively spared," "irrelevant and perseverative," "developmentally delayed," "non-intact," "gifted," and "engaging" (Bellugi, Lichtenberger, Jones, Lai, & St. George, 2000; Bellugi et al., 1994; Karmiloff-Smith, Grant, Berthoud, Davies, Howlin, & Udwin, 1997; Karmiloff-Smith, Klima, Bellugi, Grant, & Baron-Cohen, 1995; Semel, 1988; Semel & Rosner, 1991b; Udwin & Yule, 1990).

Most individuals with WS (WSs) are verbally fluent, articulate, and extremely interested in conversing with others. Their speech is usually grammatically complex, generally correct, but with some exceptions (discussed later). They are noted for having an extensive vocabulary, impressive storytelling skills, and being able to use their language abilities for their own purposes.

Despite striking individual differences in language competence and variation across subareas in ability, language stands as an area of surprising strength for most WSs relative to their cognitive limitations in intelligence test scores, Piagetian tasks, and general information, as well as marked visual–spatial-motor deficits (Bellugi et al., 2000; Mervis & Klein-Tasman, 2000). Parents report that 67% of children with WS (WSc) (n = 64, 4–22 yrs) have "highly developed language abilities," and 98% report that their WSc "can talk" (Utah Survey, Semel & Rosner, 1991a, 1991b).[2]

---

[2]Information regarding number and age of subjects is provided only the first time a particular research study is cited. ("yr" = years rounded to the next year, "mo" = months).

At the same time, WSs' speech can be repetitive, unfocused, and annoying in some respects (Levine, 1993; Semel & Rosner, 1991b, 1994; Udwin & Yule, 1988, 1989, 1990). A few are inarticulate or "nonverbal." Problems in some aspects of comprehension of language are commonplace, although the severity and frequency of these problems differ among WSs and across language areas.

This intriguing mix of features has stimulated the interest of many researchers throughout the world (e.g., Bellugi & colleagues; Borghgraef, Fryns, & Plissart; Carey, Levine, & Tager-Flusberg; Gosch, Pankau, & colleagues; Karmiloff-Smith & associates; Mervis & colleagues; Morris, Greenberg, & Keating; Udwin & Yule; Volterra, Vicari, & colleagues). Their efforts provide insight into the language commonalities and individual differences of WSs, as well as a framework, or "prototype," for comparing WSs with other groups (e.g., Bellugi et al., 1994; Bellugi et al., 2000; Mervis et al., 1999). It also has implications for theoretical issues concerning the unity or fractionalization of language, the modularity or distinctiveness of language as an area of human behavior, and the neurobiological underpinnings of WS language that challenge some of the long-held tenets of psycholinguistics, developmental psychology, neurobiology, neuropsychology, and language pathology (Bellugi et al., 1994; Karmiloff-Smith et al., 1997).

Although studies of WS language continue, a great deal of information has been revealed about the strengths and weaknesses of WSs in six language areas: language acquisition, speech and voice, semantics, syntax, language pragmatics, and discourse and narration.

This chapter describes findings in each of these areas. Chapter 3 describes various types of interventions that may be used to optimize and utilize the language skills of WSs and address their language problems.

I. LANGUAGE ACQUISITION

The early language development of most WSs generally follows an interesting pattern. It begins with early language delay, then there is a language spurt, followed by continued language growth that usually dominates other areas in most WSs. However, this is not true of all WSs. A few are not so fortunate in that they tend to experience more severe problems in acquiring language than most other children with WS (WSc).

A. Early Language Delay

There is abundant evidence—from early case studies, parental reports, and formal research studies—that most WSc are substantially language delayed (Bellugi, Sabo, & Vaid, 1988b; Jarrold, Baddeley, & Hewes, 1998; Mervis &

Bertrand, 1994; Plissart & Fryns, 1999; Thal, Bates, & Bellugi, 1989; Udwin & Yule, 1998b; von Arnim & Engel, 1964). Normally developing children typically say their first words at 1 year of age and full sentences at 2 years; the median age for first words in WSc is 2 years and for first sentences it is 3 years (Utah Survey, Semel & Rosner, 1991a, 1991b). Thus, although there is considerable variation, language milestones are usually reached much later by WSc. The time of acquisition of first words ranges from 6 months to more than 4 years, and of sentences from 12 months to beyond 14 years (Utah Survey). Over 80% of parents report that their WSc is "language delayed" on the WSA Checklist (n = 111, 4–22 yrs, Semel & Rosner, 1991a, 1991b).

Consistent with these observations, WSc lag an average of 20 months behind nonhandicapped peers on norms of expressive language (Singer-Harris, Bellugi, Bates, Jones, & Rossen, 1997). These norms are based on parents' reports of their WSc's early words (both production, i.e., expression, and comprehension, i.e., understanding), their production of gestures, and their production and comprehension of early sentences on the Infant Version of the MacArthur Communicative Development Inventory (CDI; Fenson, Dale, Reznick, Bates, Thal, & Pethick, 1994). Other findings are more surprising.

Contrary to expectation, WSc (n = 54) and children with Down syndrome (DSc, n = 39), ranging in age from 12 to 76 months, are similarly delayed in their acquisition of words (Singer-Harris et al., 1997). This is in marked contrast to the well-established vocabulary advantage of adolescents with WS (WSa) over adolescents with Down syndrome (DSa) (e.g., Bellugi et al., 1994). In fact, both groups fall well below the 10th percentile of normally developing infants on the CDI.

Along the same line, a study on the effects of naming on infants' tendency to look preferentially at named versus unnamed objects reveals no difference between infants with WS (n = 15 WSc, M = ~30 mo) and those with DS (Paterson, Brown, Gsodl, Johnson, & Karmiloff-Smith, 1999). Both groups show a looking preference for named objects but significantly less than that of control groups of normal infants matched on chronological age (CA) or mental age (MA).

To complicate the picture, WSc perform higher on language items (i.e., word production and comprehension) than nonlanguage cognitive items (e.g., reaching for a hidden object, using blocks), and DSc show the reverse pattern on the Bayley Scales of Infant Development (n's = 6, CA ~ 28 mo) (Mervis & Bertrand, 1994, 1997). In addition, 2-year-olds with WS (n = 24) are reported to exceed 2-year-olds with DS on the expressive vocabulary checklist of the Words and Sentences scale of the CDI (Mervis & Robinson, 2000). This advantage may be limited to language production, however, given the comparability of WSc and DSc on Paterson et al.'s (1999) naming comprehension task.

How can such inconsistencies be explained? Researchers point to the marked variability of young WSc and methodological differences in the CDI studies (Mervis & Robinson, 2000). On balance, however, it is clear that very young children with WS do not generally perform at a relatively high level on language kinds of skills or activities. This makes the later language progress of WSc even more remarkable, especially when considered in the context of other language delayed groups of children, such as children with DS, Fragile X syndrome (Frag X), or autism (AUT), who tend to be more limited than WSs in language skills as older children and adults (Schoenbrodt & Smith, 1995).

B. Language Growth

Having established that most WSs are initially substantially delayed in the acquisition of words and sentences, attention turns to examining their subsequent language development and how it compares to that of other groups.

Syntactic Spurt. Research reveals that onset of syntax is a critical factor in language growth of WSc (Jones, Singer, Rossen, & Bellugi, 1993; Mervis et al., 1994). Although WSc begin at the same low vocabulary level as DSc, they precede DSc in the emergence of grammar. And, once WSc begin to acquire syntax, they surpass DSc in the rate of vocabulary growth (WS n = 56, 3–22 yrs; DS n = 18, 8–21 yrs) (Jones et al., 1993). Thus, at the early level of sentence formation, the vocabulary productivity of WS toddlers begins to "spurt" (Mervis & Bertrand, 1997).

The difference between WSc and DSc in sentence structure, as well as sentence length (i.e., mean length in morphemes), is particularly striking. Compare the following sentences of a WSc and a DSc—both 3 years of age and at the same level of word production (~600 words)—for sentence quality and quantity:

WSc: "Mamma, need to pick up toys, vacuum floor," and "I go my room get one book bring out here."

DSc: "Gonna go car," and "Matt want bottle."

Moreover, the rate at which WSc develop syntax is similar to that of nonhandicapped children, but DSc are much lower than the norms in rate and level of syntactic development (Singer-Harris et al., 1997). This is consistent with previous research indicating that DSc develop relatively faster in vocabulary than in syntactic skills (Miller, 1988).

C. Early Language and Cognition

Besides differences between WSc and DSc in rate and type of language development, they differ in respective rates of development in the language versus nonlanguage areas of cognition (Goodman, 1994; Mervis et al., 1994). On measures of gesture communication, such as pointing, showing, or giving objects, WSc score lower than other child groups, namely, normally developing subjects, language-impaired subjects, and DSc, even though the groups are matched on language at the single word level (Goodman, 1993, 1994). At the word combination stage, the gestural disadvantage of WSc persists. They produce fewer schemes and pretend action sequences like play-drinking than any of the other groups, whereas DSc produce significantly more gestures than either WS or normal children and exceed even their own level of language comprehension and production (Singer-Harris et al., 1997).

In addition, WSc fail to show some of the lexical-cognitive linkages generally displayed by nonhandicapped and DS children. Although WSc usually produce their first words before they use pointing, in most groups pointing precedes first words. WSc also show a dissociation between a spurt in vocabulary verses the slower emergence of spontaneous sorting, that is, classification and exhaustive sorting of objects by type. Most groups acquire the two skills semi-simultaneously, whereas WSc tend to lag considerably behind in sorting skills (Mervis & Bertrand, 1997; Mervis et al., 1994).

Generally, language surpasses cognitive development in most WSc. Even before 4 years of age, WSc (n = 14, 5–48 mo) typically show a profile in which expressive language exceeds language comprehension and fine motor skills (Plissart & Fryns, 1999). Between the ages of 4 and 8 years, WSc (n = 41) also tend to score higher on communication skills than in daily living and motor skills on the Vineland Adaptive Behavior Scales–Interview Edition (Mervis, Klein-Tasman, & Mastin, 2001).

D. Nonverbal WS Children

Although most WSc acquire language skills after a period of early delay and some speech language intervention, a few are extremely delayed. This is demonstrated in the case of "Becky," a WSc who was still in the single-word stage at 5 years, 6 months of age (Thal et al., 1989). Other WSc remain nonarticulate and nonfluent; some are unable to speak.

In fact, a significant minority of WSc is not relatively skilled in language; they lag considerably behind other WSc. Seventeen percent of WSc over 4 years of age are not yet producing full sentences; the mean is 38 months. The norm for normals is 24 months (Utah Survey, Semel & Rosner, 1991a, 1991b).

Along the same line, Frank (1983) observed that 20% of WSc (n = 10, 4–17 yrs, M = 8;8 yrs)[3] lack the "high level and complex syntactical development" evident in others. In fact, one subject used hand signs for communication. Udwin and Yule (1990) reported that 16% of WSc (n = 43, 6–16 yrs, M = 11;6 yrs) do not display "fluent, well articulated speech." In fact, a subset of WSs shares many of the characteristics of autism, including severe language delay and impairment (Gillberg & Rasmussen, 1994).

Although there is increasing recognition that WSs range widely in language ability, from severely impaired to relatively gifted (e.g., Bellugi et al., 2000; Jarrold et al., 1998; Mervis & Klein-Tasman, 2000), many families, teachers, professionals, and researchers still need to become more aware of these individual differences in language skill and how to deal effectively with them.

II. SPEECH AND VOICE

One reason that WS language seems so impressive is because it "sounds so good" (Greer, Brown, Pai, Choudry, & Klein, 1997; Kataria, Goldstein, & Kushnick, 1981). WS speech is usually clear, easy to understand, and extremely expressive. At the same time, problems sometimes arise and individual differences are evident in articulation, rate of speech, fluency, and voice quality.

A. Oral-Motor Problems

Intelligible speech requires oral-motor capabilities. Parents, speech language therapists (SLTs), and other professionals report that WS infants and toddlers often have difficulty developing oral-motor skills, such as sucking, chewing, and swallowing (Ward, 1994). The severity of such oral-motor problems and tactile defensiveness sometimes requires the use of feeding tubes (AG or N/O tube) due to weak sucking reflexes and/or refusal to eat (written comments WSA Checklist Survey, Semel & Rosner, 1991a, 1991b).

In contrast to the normal oral-motor sequence of strong reflexes in sucking and swallowing at 0–4 months, voluntary tongue movements at 4–6 months, chewing at 8 months, and controlled biting of food at 12 months, WSc's feeding behaviors are more characteristic of children with motor disabilities (Wolery & Smith, 1989). Some WS infants and toddlers are observed to have insufficient lip closure. This often results in their chewing with lips open, forming a poor lip seal on the nipple or rim of a cup, and ex-

---

[3]The notation "8;8 yrs" indicates 8 years, 8 months of age, in accord with the conventional use of ";" to indicate "yrs;mo."

hibiting a generally "messy" eating pattern. These difficulties may involve low muscle tone, as well as problems in motor planning and perhaps impact speech production later on.

Pediatricians' records indicate that 71% of WSc have "early feeding difficulty" (Morris et al., 1988), over 60% of WSc (n = 111, 4–22 yrs) are reported to be "Picky Eater(s)"/have a "Self-Imposed Diet," and more than 25% of a wide age range of WSc (n = 225, 0–22 yrs) "Refused to Teethe or Place Objects in Mouth During Normal Teething Period" (WSA Survey, Semel & Rosner, 1991a, 199b).

Oral tactile defensiveness and difficulty with feeding and speech production is typically present in children with Frag X (Schoenbrodt & Smith, 1995).

B. Speech Articulation and Fluency

Adequate speech production requires rapid, smooth, sequential movements of the articulators combined with timed and appropriately coordinated respiration and phonation. WSc of preschool age generally display the same kinds of articulatory patterns and errors as normally developing children of the same mental age. By the school-age years, the articulation of most WSc is age appropriate and quite good (Dilts, Morris, & Leonard, 1990; Meyerson & Frank, 1987). Generally, they avoid common errors of misarticulation, such as "My mover hurt her fumb," "do" instead of "dog," or "wight" for "light." Eighty-four percent of WSc (n = 43, 6–15;9 yrs, M = 11;6 yrs) are said to display "fluent, well articulated speech" (Udwin & Yule, 1990).

Phonological Skills. Reportedly, mentally retarded children tend to make pronunciation errors. These include slurring of words and disorders of rhythm apparent in DSc (Carroll, 1986). However, it appears that the articulation characteristics of most WSc are more like those of normally achieving children than other groups of mentally handicapped children. In fact, WSs generally surpass other child groups in the areas of articulation and phonological memory (Vicari, Carlesimo, Brizzolara, & Pezzini, 1996).

To illustrate, parents report that young German children with WS (n = 25, 4–10 yrs) tend to articulate more clearly and are less likely to lisp than a matched group of mentally retarded children (MRc) with nonspecific disabilities (Gosch, Pankau, & Stading, 1994; Gosch, Stading, & Pankau, 1994). WSc also tend to have better articulatory skills than other syndrome groups known for their language skills, such as children with Fragile X syndrome (Schoenbrodt & Smith, 1995). Likewise, French-speaking children with WS (n = 10, 9–21 yrs) are better able to repeat novel nonwords than are normal controls (Karmiloff-Smith, 1992; Karmiloff-Smith, Grant, & Berthoud, 1993).

Anecdotal accounts of researchers testify to the word production skills of some WSc. For example, a 4-year-old WSc was reportedly able to accurately repeat difficult multisyllable words like "encyclopedia" with precision but had no understanding of their meaning (Bellugi et al., 2000). On the other hand, WSs may be vulnerable to certain kinds of articulatory problems.

Articulatory Problems. In some WSc, phonological accuracy may fluctuate under certain circumstances. Some WSs may have only occasional problems, such as mispronouncing tricky multisyllabic words like "electricity," "Episcopal," "aluminum," "successful," "nickelodeon," or "cinnamon," or phrases such as "bingle jells" for "jingle bells." Short utterances may be clearly expressed, but lengthy remarks may occasionally suffer articulatory breakdown. This can make it difficult for the listener to understand what is being said.

The infrequent individual phoneme errors or articulatory sequencing errors sometimes heard in the connected speech of WSs do not seem to be due to peripheral articulation factors such as dysarthria. It appears, instead, to be related to verbal dyspraxia or disruption in the planning of voluntary movement (i.e., motor planning problems) rather than specific phoneme errors.

Speech Fluency. Most WSc appear to be fluent speakers (Udwin et al., 1987), but some have dysfluencies. Clinical observation suggests that some WSc tend to speak unusually rapidly when excited or under stress. Under these circumstances, there can be a breakdown in articulation, or "cluttering"—that is, disintegration of clear articulation during rapid speech. It tends to occur in the production of polysyllabic words, in rapidly articulated, connected speech, in imitation of nonreduplicative (puh-tuh-kuh) syllables and in occasional dysfluencies involving repetition of sounds, syllables and words, false starts, and so on. Some of these problems are manifest in a tendency to use circumlocutions or roundabout ways of expression (see Section III, C on "Word-Finding Problems").

WSc seem to be unaware of their occasional cluttering and do little to avoid certain situations, sounds, or words as stutterers often do. Instead, WSs tend to engage in perseverative speech by overusing automatic phrases or dwelling on certain topics (see later section, V, B on "Topic Perseveration"). Children with other syndromes, such as Frag X and learning disability (LD), may also exhibit "cluttering."

Other Problems. Stuttering has been identified in a few children with WS. These cases seem to involve "frank" stuttering with a clonic or tonic spasm as opposed to "simple" cluttering. In addition, a few WSs have been reported to have hearing loss and concomitant voice and articulatory problems.

Tongue-tie is also occasionally evident. This can contribute significantly to articulatory problems, besides being unattractive physically. Whenever possible, despite the minor medical risks involved, seek medical support to cut the frenum. Speech therapy may also be helpful.

C. Hoarseness

A "hoarse" voice is featured as a prototypical characteristic of WS and a diagnostic sign in medical studies that deal with WS (e.g., Mervis et al.,1999). Some cardiologists describe all of their WS patients as having the "same deep somewhat metallic voice" (Beuren, Schulze, Eberle, Harmjanz, & Apitz, 1964). It is also one of the features used to distinguish between the genotype of WSs who display the classical WS profile and those with suspected WS (e.g., Joyce, Zorich, Pike, Barber, & Dennis, 1996).

The reported incidence of hoarse voice in WSs ranges between 20% and 100% in various studies (Beuren et al., 1964; Jones & Smith, 1975; Meyerson & Frank, 1987; Morris et al., 1988; Pagon, Bennett, LaVeck, Stewart, & Johnson, 1987). Sixty-seven percent of parents in the Utah Survey reported that their WSc has a "hoarse voice" (Semel & Rosner 1991a, 1991b). WSc are more likely to have their voices described as "deep, hoarse, or rough" by their German mothers than are children with other forms of developmental disability (Gosch et al., 1994). Although children with Frag X also display hoarseness (Schoenbrodt & Smith, 1995), their hoarseness sounds qualitatively different than WSs. An early article (Frank, 1983) reports a rather high incidence of hypernasality (60%) in a small sample of WSc.

Despite the suspected widespread occurrence of hoarseness in WSc, its physiological basis has not been identified or extensively researched. Possibly, it is linked to the deletion of the gene for elastin on chromosome 7 in WSs (Ewart, Morris, Atkinson et al., 1993; Morris, 1994; Morris, Thomas, & Greenberg, 1993). Elastin affects the connective tissue of the vocal folds.

D. Prosody

WSc are noted for their very effective use of prosody (i.e., intonational patterning, pauses, pitch) in conversation and storytelling (see Section IV, B, p. 61).

III. SEMANTICS

Most WSs have a "gift for gab" that impresses clinicians, researchers, family members, teachers, and professionals alike. This is due partly to their fascination with words and to their grasp of semantics, that is, the meaning of words, sentences, and their relation to the world.

The semantics of WSs is typically rich in meaning and intriguing as a field of study. They are noted for their use of unusual words, unfamiliarity with some relational terms, fluency in the production of category members, comprehension and use of metaphor, and concrete analogies. Creativity and affect in the social uses of language are other strengths.

A. Vocabulary Skills

WSs are noted for their relatively good vocabularies (Levine, 1993) and their "adeptness and enjoyment of words . . . [which] contributes to the impression that they are smarter than they really are" (von Arnim & Engel, 1964). Parents report that 87% of WSc (*n* = 64, 4–22 yrs) have a "sophisticated vocabulary" (Utah Survey, Semel & Rosner, 1991a, 1991b). Laboratory studies substantiate the relatively high level of WS vocabulary as well as some limitations.

Comprehension Tests. Many studies document the proficiency of WSa and their superiority over adolescents with DS (DSa) on formal tests of vocabulary, such as the Peabody Picture Vocabulary Test–Revised (PPVT–R). This is a comprehension test in which a target word is presented aurally and the subject is asked to point to the corresponding item in a four picture array. Examples of PPVT–R items correctly identified by WSa (*n* = 3, 11–16 yrs) are: "peninsula," "slumbering," "dissecting," "hoisting," "canine," "archaeologist," "cubical," "gnawing," "cornea," "spherical," "abrasive," and "tranquil" (Bellugi, Marks, Bihrle, & Sabo, 1988a).

Transforming the PPVT–R scores of WSa into age-equivalent (AE) values results in scores that are significantly higher than their mental age (MA) scores but less than their chronological (CA) in a number of studies (e.g., Bellugi et al., 1994, *n* = 10).

This contrasts markedly with the results of DSa: Their age-equivalent PPVT–R scores are less than their MA scores and significantly lower than the age-equivalent PPVT–R scores of WSa (e.g., WSa *M* = 8.4, DSa *M* = 5.3; Bellugi, Bihrle, Neville, Jernigan, & Doherty, 1992).

The surprisingly high performance of WSs is replicated in other studies. For example, 42% of WSs (*n* = 123, 4–49 yrs) score within the range of normally developing individuals on the PPVT–R, even though almost all of them fall within the range of the mentally retarded on intelligence tests (Mervis et al., 1999). Likewise, WSa (*n* = 12, 4;3–30;5 yrs, *M* = 21;11 yrs) score higher (*M* = 10;6) on the British Picture Vocabulary Scale (BPVS), a test similar to the PPVT–R, than on an abstract nonverbal reasoning test of intelligence (*M* = 6;4), the Raven Coloured Matrices, using spatial figures (Tyler et al., 1997).

Production Tests. Generally, WSa perform at a similar level on production and comprehension tests of vocabulary. Their scores on formal tests requiring word responses, such as the Gardner Expressive One Word Vocabulary Test (EOWPVT) are roughly equivalent to their PPVT–R scores (Rossen, Klima, Bellugi, Bihrle, & Jones, 1996). These are also higher than their overall mental age (MA) and the vocabulary production scores of DSa (Rossen et al., 1996).

Nonetheless, WSa tend to produce responses that are "lengthy and descriptive" and "somewhat tangential anecdotes" (Bellugi et al., 1988a). Responses to the TOLD item "sad" are illustrative: " 'Sad' is when someone dies; someone is hurt, like when you cry"; " 'Sad' means that someone hurts your feelings, or when someone starts crying." These kinds of answers fall short of the type required to be scored "correct," that is, a single precise definition (e.g., an emotion related to loss) or mention of two primary characteristics.

Intelligence Tests of Vocabulary. Tests of general ability often include subtests of word knowledge and lexical meaning as indicators of intelligence. Surprisingly, WSa do not tend to score well on intelligence tests of vocabulary. In fact, WSa score as low as DSa on the Vocabulary subtest of the WISC–R even though these same WSa surpass the DSa on the PPVT–R, a formal test of vocabulary comprehension, and tests of syntax (e.g., the TROG) and category fluency (Bellugi, Bihrle, Jernigan, Trauner, & Doherty, 1990).

In explaining the apparent discrepancy in results, Bellugi et al. (1992) pointed out that the WISC–R vocabulary test requires subjects to "produce a well-formed definition, a cognitive, not linguistic skill." Also, no credit or only partial credit is given for responding with exemplars or expansive descriptions of the term, the typical "style" of many WSa. For example, a WSa defines the word "hazardous" as follows: "Hazardous means that you have trash and the air is not clean" (Bellugi et al., 1992, p. 206). Because the scoring requires succinct, definitive answers to be counted as "correct," these kinds of WS responses are scored no higher than the clearly inadequate responses of DSa to the word "hazardous" (e.g., "I don't know," "Don't touch books not belong to you"). Thus, WSc can earn low scores on vocabulary tests even though they may be able to demonstrate some understanding by providing items related to the target word or using the target word correctly in a sentence. WS's word-finding problems contribute to the difficulty in obtaining an unbiased estimate of their vocabulary abilities.

This difficulty is similar to the problem exhibited on TOLD production tests: Only the test items and WISC–R scoring criteria differ. Perhaps the underestimation of WS vocabulary skills may be mitigated by allowing partial credit for para-responses as to "hazardous" or administering posttest vocabulary items. These alternatives should be considered, given the significant educational implications of intelligence test scores on crucial decisions like school placement.

Vocabulary of WSc. Generally, WSc of preschool and grade school age are less impressive than WSa on vocabulary tests. For example, the PPVT–R scores of 9- and 10-year-old WSc do not differ significantly from DSc matched on general ability (Klein & Mervis, 1999) although WSa routinely exceed DSa on such tests (e.g., Bellugi et al., 1994). Moreover, young Italian children with WS (n = 17, 4;10–15;3 yrs, M = 9;8 yrs) fall within, not above, the range of normal controls matched on nonverbal MA on the PPVT–R (Volterra, Capirci, Pezzini, Sabbadini, & Vicari, 1996).

Thus, the vocabulary skills of WSc do not appear to be as remarkable as those of WSa. This seems to reflect developmental changes in WS vocabulary, namely, the "consistent growth in vocabulary size [PPVT–R] during childhood and maintenance of this level in adulthood" (Mervis et al., 1999, p. 80). It is also noted that WSc (n = 56, 3–23 yrs) do not begin to clearly exceed DSc (n = 18, 7+ –22+ yrs) in PPVT–R vocabulary until "early adolescence" (Rossen et al., 1996).

B. Unusual Word Choice

Another striking aspect of WSc's expressive language is their unusual choice of words in spontaneous conversation (Bellugi, Sabo, & Vaid, 1988; Bellugi, Wang, & Jernigan, 1994a; Scheiber, 2000). It is so exceptional that researchers themselves search for the "right" word to describe the phenomenon, including "rare," "baroque," "sophisticated," and "picturesque."

Examples of WSa's use of atypical words are: "The bees abort the beehive" for "they leave the hive" (Bellugi et al., 1994, p. 32), and "I'll put the earrings in and you can buckle them" for "fasten" (Rossen et al., 1996, p. 384). Such word choices are slightly off the mark semantically, although they are often contextually and semantically appropriate. Some researchers refer to this type of word choice as "erudite" and attribute its use of closely related words to "lexical underspecification"; that is, the words of WSc may lack certain features (Karmiloff-Smith et al., 1993). It may also reflect their dysnomia (Scheiber, 2000).

Another indication of the unusual lexical predilections of WSs may be found in their responses to homonyms: words with two distinct meanings that are spelled and pronounced alike, such as "ear," "arm," or "bank" (Rossen et al., 1996). In situations where the particular meaning of the homonym is unspecified, most people tend to interpret the homonym in its dominant sense (i.e., body part, not vegetable, for "ear"), whereas WSs may be just as likely to select the secondary meaning (Rossen et al., 1996). When asked to provide both definitions of items in a homonym list, WSa, DSa, and normal fourth-grade controls are all able to give the primary meaning, but WSa are significantly more likely to access the secondary meaning than either of the other groups.

WSa are also more likely than normal controls to select the secondary rather than the primary meaning of a target homonym (e.g., "Bank") among alternatives in a forced-choice task (e.g., "Bank-River-Money") (Rossen et al., 1996). Possibly, WSs are less sensitive than others to the frequency characteristics of words (i.e., high frequency, commonly used words vs. low frequency, less commonly used words; see Tyler et al., 1997), although differences in semantic organization (structure) or processing operations (search, retrieval, or lexical constraints) may also be involved.

C. Word-Finding Problems

Although most people experience temporary lapses in their ability to remember something or find the right word (i.e., "tip of the tongue" phenomenon), clinical experience suggests that this condition is more extreme in WSs. In fact, it seems symptomatic of a more pervasive problem of WSs, referred to here as word-finding problems (Levine, 1994; Semel & Rosner, 1991a). These are manifest in a number of interesting, sometimes subtle ways.

Substitutions. When unable to think of a word, WSs may engage in word substitutions. These may take the form of semantically associated words or phoneme formulation errors. Semantic substitutions may include *semi-synonyms*, or words close in meaning, such as "evacuate" for "empty," or "rim" for "top" (of a stomach); *antonyms*, like "floor" for "ceiling"; or *lexical substitutions* involving category membership, like "escalator" for "elevator," "scissors" for "knife," or "oar" for "paddle" (Volterra et al., 1996).

Sometimes semantic errors are more distantly related, as in "branch" for "arm," "flower" for "mushroom," or "rein" for "string." Semantic relations may also be used to retrieve the correct word: "We went to a 'Chinese,' 'Japanese,' no, I mean a 'Vietnamese' restaurant." Occasionally, novel words are used, like "word machine" for "telephone."

Sometimes phoneme formulation and sequencing errors are heard: "tacus" for "cactus," "aminal" for "animal," "hopsital" for "hospital," or "emeny" for "enemy." Occasionally, word part sequencing errors are observed, such as "walk side" for "sidewalk," "flutter by" for "butterfly," or "tie neck" for "necktie." These types of paraphrases are observed in learning disabled children as well (Wiig & Semel, 1984).

Circumlocutions. Circumlocutions are roundabout ways of expressing a target word. The functional, visual, or another characteristic may substitute for the word, as with the semantic paraphrases noted by Volterra et al.

(1996), for example, "to hang up clothes" for "coat hanger." "Definitional statements" may also be used, as in the following personally observed example of a WSc struggling to define the word "shovel": "Well, you go out into the yard, and there's a lot of dirt, you know, and you move it around and you dig it. . . . It's like a broom, but you dig with it."

Word Starters or Carrier Phrases. Stereotypical verbal starters, lead-ins, or phrases are other ways in which WSc try to cover up their difficulty in remembering a word or to stall for time. Examples include starters like: "Well," "Now," "Look," "But," "And then," "Let me see," "Then," "And," "You know," and "You see." Verbal lead-in phrases may include:

"The name of that is ___."
"I presume that that's a ___."
"It's like a ___."
"I know just what you are talking about."

Fillers. Evasive verbalizations include interjections or fillers like "Ah . . . Um . . . Er . . . Uhm . . . Er . . . ," "Wow," "Boy," or "Oh"; semantically empty placeholders like "thingamajig," "You know," "Whatever you call it," "What'cha ma call it," "Whatever it is"; and the use of indefinite terms like "stuff," "it," "junk," "thing," "somebody," "that guy," "somewhere," "sometime," or "anytime" (Lucas, 1980, p. 178; Wiig & Semel, 1984).

Irrelevant topics, like personal reference (e.g., "I have one like that, too"), flattery ("that's a pretty dress"), or topical discontinuity, may reflect word-finding problems.

Children who are language learning disabled also tend to overuse these types of evasive verbalizations, circumlocutions, word substitutions, para-phrases, irrelevant topics, and verbal starters and fillers as they struggle with word-finding and dysnomic difficulties (Wiig & Semel, 1984).

Mechanisms. WS difficulties with word-finding could reflect "response blockage" or problems in accessing or retrieving information, such as the name of an object that the person knows (Scheiber, 2000). Alternatively, these problems may be a sign of problems in confrontation naming, irregu-larities in semantic structure, organization, or processing (e.g., decision making). They may also arise from lexical and conceptual difficulties with certain words, such as semantic relational terms. Whatever the cause, such problems may contribute to WSs' use of unusual words, that is, when they cannot "find" the target word they want to use, although it may be on the "tip of the tongue," they may substitute a semi-correct word or phrase, perseverate, or use circumlocutions or fillers to cover up their word-finding problems or to just keep the conversation going.

In any event, WSs often handle their word-finding problems in ways that are difficult to detect or diagnose as such. In test situations, word-finding problems may be interpreted as ignorance or lack of knowledge. In fact, it is difficult to obtain an unbiased measure of WS ability because performance can be confounded by word-finding problems on many kinds of tests: language tests, intelligence tests, ability tests, aptitude tests, achievement tests, and classroom tests and quizzes (Levine, 1993).

D. Semantic Relational Terms

Despite vocabulary strengths, it is not unusual for WSc to have difficulty using and understanding certain seemingly simple words and concepts (Scheiber, 2000). Reports of parents, teachers, professionals, and personal experience in clinical settings suggest that WSc often have difficulty dealing with semantic relational terms that refer to concepts such as the following:

Spatial—"in," "on"; "above," "below"

Directional—"right," "left"; "up," "down"

Positional—"top," "middle," "bottom"; "high," "low"

Temporal—"before," "after"

Ordinal—"first," "last"

Comparative—"bigger," "smaller"

Quantitative—"more," "less"

Causal—"because," "since"

Conditional—"if" . . . "then," "unless"

Equality—"same," "different"

Inclusion/Exclusion—"all," "some," "none," "any"; "except," "but not." (Wiig & Semel, 1984)

Research indicates that WSs (n = 20, 8;4–34;10 yrs, M = 18;7) are prone to make errors on dimensional words (e.g., "long," 10%; "tall," 25%) and comparative sentences (e.g., "The knife is longer than the pencil," 25%; "The box is bigger than the cup," 35%) on the TROG (Test for Reception of Grammar) (Karmiloff-Smith et al., 1997). Along the same lines, WSa pilot subjects (n = 7) tested at the Salk Institute (personal communication, 1990) seem particularly vulnerable to spatial and temporal errors despite their overall good performance on two semantic tests, Word Classes and Semantic Relations, of the Clinical Evaluation of Language Fundamentals–Revised (CELF–R; Semel, Wiig, & Secord, 1987).

Further evidence of particular difficulty with spatial terms is demonstrated in the production and comprehension errors of WSs on a task specifically designed to test their knowledge of spatial prepositions, such as "between," "above," and "in front of" (Bellugi et al., 2000). WSs ($n = 28$, $M = 19$ yrs, 10–41 yrs) selected the wrong picture referent for aural prepositions 11.5% of the time, as compared to 0.2% for normal, younger controls. They also produced erroneous spatial descriptions of target pictures 30% of the time, as compared to a significantly lower error rate for normal MA controls (Bellugi et al., 2000).

Likewise, WSc are often confused by temporal or ordinal terms, especially when expressed as a series (e.g., "first," "second," "last") or in serial relations (e.g., "he was fourth in line"). Such confusions and uncertainties about the use of spatial terms like "on," "under," "over," and "between" may contribute to the difficulty WSs often have in following directions. Similarly, some WSs may be confused by the concepts and terms for "left" and "right." Reportedly 38% of WSc do not know their left from right (Utah Survey, Semel & Rosner, 1991a, 1991b). Such deficiencies can severely limit the ability of WSs to function adequately in perceptual–motor and educational tasks (see chap. 4).

Furthermore, problems with semantic relations may extend beyond lexical items into inadequate use as sentence constituents. This is exemplified by WSs' difficulty with adverbial clauses ("after," "before," "because," "if") and prepositional phrases (e.g., saying, "He threw the ball *at* the window," not "*through* the window"; or "I put the box *below* the bed," not "*under* the bed"; see Section IV, "Syntax").

Similarly, WSs' use of causal relational terms, like "if . . . then" and "when . . . then," seems to be both disjointed or deleted in speech and poorly understood. Eighty-four percent of WSc are said to have "difficulty in seeing cause and effect relationships" (Utah Survey, Semel & Rosner, 1991a, 1991b). On the other hand, WSa often include correctly formed causal sentences in their production of stories in the "Frog" storytelling task (Reilly, Klima, & Bellugi, 1990).

Other semantic terms that are particularly troublesome include quantitative relations, such as "more than" or "less than," and comparative relationships like "older than." Inclusion kinds of relations ("all, some, any . . . except") and class exclusion relations ("not, none, neither . . . nor," "but not") may also present problems.

Kinship terms and concepts can pose difficulty, too, especially second-order relations like brother-in-law or sister-in-law or mother's baby versus baby's mother. Some WSc need help with these types of language relations, others do not. In this respect, WSc resemble children with learning disability who may also have problems with semantic relational terms.

E. Category Concepts

Another aspect of semantics involves the use and understanding of category concepts, including category fluency or production, knowledge of the properties of categories, and the establishment of abstract category concepts.

Category Production

The ability to access language concepts such as taxonomic categories is often studied by administering fluency tests like the category production task. This involves asking subjects to name as many items as they can from a category like "Animals," "Food," "Furniture," or "Clothing" within a specified period of time.

In tests involving category fluency, WSa produce significantly more category items than DSa. Their output also tends to be higher than expected from their scores on intelligence tests (Bellugi et al., 1994). Interestingly, WSa tend to produce a rather high proportion of nonprototypical, unusual responses, when asked to tell the names of animals (e.g., "sea lion," "chihuahua," "koala bear," "anteater"), as well as many common items (e.g., "lion," "tiger," "elephant," "dog"). In contrast, DSa are less likely than WSa to produce atypical responses and they are more likely than WSa to include repetitions and extra-category responses as well as fewer items. Compared to normal second-graders, WSa are high in the number of atypical responses produced, even though the groups are equivalent in total output (Bellugi et al., 1994). This suggests that the semantic networks or the processing characteristics of WSa are qualitatively and quantitatively different from that of other groups.

There are limitations, however, in the generalizability of these results. Even in the case of WSa, response word frequency does not differ significantly from that of DSa or normal control subjects ($n = 9$, 10–11 yrs) except during the latter part of a recall trial of category items (Rossen et al., 1996). Perhaps unconstrained production, by its very nature, differs among subject samples and age groups.

Category Production in WSc. Once again there are age-related differences in performance as grade school age children with WS fail to show the unusually high category fluency of WSa (Mervis et al., 1999; Scott et al., 1994; Volterra et al., 1996). For example, Italian-speaking WSc tend to fall within the range of normal MA matched controls—not higher—in number of category responses produced (Volterra et al., 1996).

Moreover, the category production of 9- and 10-year olds with WS (n = 18) is comparable to that of DSc matched on age and MA and to normal controls matched on MA (Scott et al., 1994). Furthermore, all three groups score significantly lower than a fourth group of normally developing children, CA matched controls of the WSc, on total output as well as typicality (i.e., goodness of example) and word frequency of the words produced (Scott et al., 1994). This suggests that CA, not MA, is the dominant factor at this age level (i.e., 9–10 yrs) of WS.

Clarification of age-related differences in word fluency (i.e., category production) is evident in the steep rise in output of WSs (n = 84, 5–40 yrs) at around age 11 (Bellugi et al., 2000).

At the same time, the category knowledge and production of WSs should not be minimized. Other studies indicate that WSa (n = 10) are comparable to "normal," academically achieving subjects matched on MA in their ability to generate the names of animals (i.e., category production). They are also knowledgeable about animal properties, responding correctly to questions such as "Do birds breathe?" (Carey, Johnson, & Levine, 1994; Johnson, Carey, & Levine, 1994). More importantly, WSa resemble normal MA controls in their ability to induce similarity based inferences, such as: Given that humans have the anatomical property "omentum," then other animals would have it too (Carey et al., 1994; Johnson & Carey, 1998; Johnson et al., 1994).

In addition, WSa (n = 12, 14;3–30;5 yrs, M = 22 yrs) perform similarly to control adults on priming tests of category structure. Presentation of taxonomic (category) or related word pairs (i.e., "lettuce-cabbage," "coat-hat," "broom-floor") result in faster responding than unrelated words. These results are interpreted as suggesting that WSa possess a semantic system that is organized and accessed in a normal manner (Tyler et al., 1997). It is nevertheless possible that more sensitive tests of semantic structure and automatic processing may indicate otherwise.

Lexical Constraints. Interestingly, WSs appear to use some but not all the lexical constraints used by normal children in word learning (Stevens & Karmiloff-Smith, 1997). Two previously reported constraints of young WSc (Mervis & Bertrand, 1993, 1994; Mervis et al., 1999) are displayed by WSs (n = 14, 7;5–31;5 yrs, M = 20 yrs). These are *fast mapping*, by which children map novel words onto objects for which they do not already have a name, and *mutual exclusivity*, which is the premise that a familiar object can have no more than one name. So an unknown word would be attached to the object for which no word was available. However, two other constraints are not observed by WSs: the *whole object constraint* in which a novel word heard in the presence of a novel object refers to the whole object rather than a part, and the *taxonomic constraint*, which occurs when in response to the request for "another 'X,' " the subject selects category coordinates, not perceptually or functionally similar objects (Stevens & Karmiloff-Smith, 1997).

Both results are intriguing. Problems with the whole object constraint are consistent with the "distinctive processing style" of WSa in which they display a predilection for the parts rather the whole of objects in studies of visuospatial cognition (Bellugi et al., 1990; Bellugi et al., 1992; Bellugi et al., 1994; see also chap. 4).

More relevant to issues of category structure, the fact that WSs may not be bound to taxonomic constraints in word learning suggests that their category boundaries may be more extended or less constrained than those of most people. This is consistent with the atypical, low frequency responses sometimes produced by WSa in category fluency (Bellugi et al., 1994; Rossen et al., 1996) and homonym tasks.

Explanatory Concepts

Despite the relative strength of WSa in tasks involving category production and knowledge of category properties (Carey et al., 1994; Johnson & Carey, 1998; Johnson et al., 1994), limitations are evident in their use of explanatory or "change" concepts in which major transformations in the exemplars and properties of concepts occur (Carey et al., 1994; Johnson & Carey, 1998). For example, WSs often define "death" as going away or sleeping rather than a "breakdown or cessation of the bodily machine." They may have problems, too, with the concept "animism"; some WSs seem to believe that some "inanimate" things, such as machines or the wind, are alive. They often fail to grasp the notion that a superset of "living thing" encompasses "plants" and "animals." WSs also appear to have difficulty with the concept of "identity": They often claim that an animal's species is changed when it wears a mask or costume that depicts another species (Johnson & Carey, 1998).

Thus, WSa may be able to perform as well as MA matched controls (CA = 10 yrs) on "factual knowledge" tasks, but they are most definitely impaired, usually responding at a preschool level on "explanatory" types of knowledge (Carey et al., 1994; Johnson & Carey, 1998). These results are not surprising because "explanatory" concepts involve transformations, and most WSa have difficulty performing simple transformational tasks (i.e., Piagetian number or mass conservation problems), whereas nonhandicapped children are usually able to solve such problems by age 7 (Bellugi et al., 1988a).

Nevertheless, the explanatory concept responses of WSs would not be mistaken for those of preschoolers. Consider, for example, the following response of a 32-year-old WSa to the question about what happens to people when they die: "They go to heaven, depending upon their quest in life, how they made their decisions and how they felt about other people and how much they have given. . . . To me when a person dies it's not the same as when they're alive. It's a different part of life" (Johnson & Carey, 1998, p. 192). Note the fluency and excellent use of words and grammar, but the speech also indicates little understanding that death is intrinsically different from life (Johnson & Carey, 1998).

F. Figurative Speech

Figurative speech goes beyond the literal meaning of words (vocabulary) and word categories in its use of word forms like metaphor, analogies, similes, personification, proverbs, irony, and idioms. These forms require "stretching" one's imagination with a semantic transformation and are often used in humor and sarcasm (Gardner, Winner, Bechhofer, & Wolf, 1978).

Figurative language is another area in which WSs vary widely in ability. There are reports that some WSa are able to produce dramatic figures of speech, such as ". . . Chocolate World and you might melt to the ground like melted butter" (Reilly et al., 1990, p. 371). Similes may also be generated spontaneously during conversation, for example, "The bridesmaids [at a wedding] looked like angels" (personal communication, WSa to SRR, Summer 1990).

Formal tests of WS figurative language demonstrate the variability of WSs (Bertrand, Mervis, Armstrong, & Ayers, 1994a; Karmiloff-Smith, 1992). Slightly more than one half of WSa subjects ($n = 12$) are able to provide acceptable explanations for metaphors, and about one half are significantly above chance in interpreting figurative sentences (e.g., "It's like talking to a brick wall"; Bertrand et al., 1994a). Interestingly, there is a link between ability to solve simple number conservation problems and use of figurative language (Bertrand et al., 1994a).

Likewise, some WSa are able to interpret statements of metaphor or irony correctly (Karmiloff-Smith, 1992). For example, a story about a boy named Robert who couldn't make up his mind ends with the metaphoric statement, "Robert, you're a real ship without a captain," or the ironic statement, "So, if you want a quick decision, ask Robert!" (Karmiloff-Smith, 1992). Several WSa, all with IQs above 50, were reportedly skilled at explaining metaphors (e.g., ". . . it means he doesn't know what he wants"). Some even succeeded on the ironic statements.

Comparing the performance of WSc ($n = 11$, 9–23 yrs) and children with autism (Karmiloff-Smith et al., 1995), half of the WSc pass both the metaphor items (e.g., "your head's made of wood") and the sarcasm items (e.g., "now that's a clever thing to do"). In contrast, only 20% of the children with autism succeed on metaphor, none on sarcasm, even though their IQ levels are higher than those of the WSc (Karmiloff-Smith et al., 1995).

Clinical experience suggests, as well, that many WSc are able to appreciate and use certain analogies, metaphors, similes, certain idioms, and other instances of figurative language satisfactorily. Some appear to collect commonly used "catch" phrases or cliches, and often use stereotypic phrases and colloquialisms appropriately in conversation.

On the other hand, most WSc seem to have problems with words with multiple or ambiguous meanings and interpreting implied meaning, idioms, and ambiguities. Oftentimes, they cannot determine the proper allusion when presented with a potentially problematic statement. An apt example is "She fell apart," which WSa are likely to either take literally or be mystified by its interpretation. Commonplace idioms can be interpreted properly, but problems arise in comprehending more complex ones (Semel, 1988).

Thus, WS individuals seem able to deal very well with word meaning and concepts that are relatively concrete but they are likely to have difficulty with more complex forms of figurative language and concepts that are abstract or transformational. But, even in the domain of figurative language, WSs frequently exceed what would be expected from their general level of cognitive abilities (e.g., IQ or MA) or the poorer performance associated with other forms of developmental disability.

Summary. Table 2.1 provides a research summary of the articles and papers on WS semantics cited earlier.

Examination of Table 2.1 brings into stark relief the capabilities and limitations of WSs in the area of semantics. Vocabulary strength is demonstrated by WSs' test scores (e.g., PPVT–R, BPVS, EOWPUT) surpassing their own MA and IQ (spatial intelligence test and WISC–R) scores, as well as the vocabulary scores of DSs (Bellugi et al., 1988a; Bellugi et al., 1994; Rossen et al., 1996; Tyler et al., 1997). Over 40% of WSs fall within the normal range on the PPVT–R (Mervis et al., 1999).

The superiority of WSs over DSs is not, however, evident until adolescence (Rossen et al., 1996). That is certainly a key factor in explaining the nonexceptional performance of WSs in the childhood years. WSc, unlike WSa, are comparable, sometimes even poorer—but not better—than normal MA controls or DSc on vocabulary tests like the PPVT–R and Boston Naming Test (Klein & Mervis, 1999; Rossen et al., 1996; Volterra et al., 1994, 1996).

At all ages studied, WSs almost always lag behind CA controls in vocabulary, as well as on virtually all tests of language and cognitive abilities. Other vocabulary limitations include difficulty with spatial prepositions, temporal terms, terms of quantity, and cause–effect relations (Bellugi et al., 2000; Semel & Rosner, 1991a, 1991b). Similar difficulties with semantic relational terms are almost completely ignored in the WS research literature.

TABLE 2.1
Research on Semantics of WSs

Type of Test or Performance	Result	Source or Reference
"sophisticated vocabulary"	WSc 87%	Semel & Rosner, Utah Survey
Peabody Picture Vocabulary	WSa AE scores > MA	Bellugi et al., 1988a
Test-Revised (PPVT-R)[#]	WSa AE scores < CA	
PPVT-R[#]	WSa > DSa	Bellugi et al., 1990
		Bellugi et al., 1992; Bellugi et al., 1994b
PPVT-R[#]	WSs 42% in normal range	Mervis et al., 1999
British Picture Vocabulary	WSa scores > spatial intelli-	Tyler et al., 1997
Scale (BPVS)[#]	gence scores	
PPVT-R[#]	WSa scores > WISC-R (IQ)	Rossen et al., 1996
	WSa > DSa	
Expressive One Word	WSa scores > WISC-R	
Vocabulary Test (EOWPVT)[#]	WSa > DSa	
PPVT-R[#]	WSc = DSc until adolescence	Rossen et al., 1996
WISC-R Vocabulary Subtest[#]	WSa = DSa	Bellugi et al., 1990
PPVT-R[#]	WSc = normal MA controls	Volterra et al., 1994, 1996
Boston Naming Test[#]	WSc < normal MA controls	Volterra et al., 1994, 1996
PPVT-R[#]	WSc = DSc	Klein & Mervis, 1999
Secondary Meaning of	WSa > normal MA controls	Rossen et al., 1996
Homonyms[#]	WSa > DSa	
Spatial Prepositions[#]	WSs < normal MA controls	Bellugi et al., 2000
Production, Comprehension		
Difficulty with Cause-Effect	WSc 84%	Semel & Rosner, Utah Survey
Relations		
Category Production[#]	WSa > DSa	Bellugi et al., 1994
Infrequent Responses	WSa > DSa	
	WSa > normal controls	
Category Production[#]	WSa > DSa	Rossen et al., 1996
	WSa = normal CA controls	
	DSa = normal MA controls	
Infrequent Responses	WSa = DSa	
	WSa = normal child controls	
Category Production[#]	WSc = DSc, MA normal con-	Scott et al., 1994
	trols < CA controls	
Response Typicality	WSc = DSc & MA normal	
	controls < CA controls	
Category Production[#]	WSc − normal MA controls	Volterra et al., 1996
Category Production	WS steep rise at ~ 11 yrs	Bellugi et al., 2000
(Fluency)[#]		
Category Production[#]	WSa = normal MA controls	Carey et al., 1993, 1994
Category Properties and Con-	WSa = normal MA controls	Carey et al., 1993, 1994
crete Inferences[#]		
Priming of Taxonomic Coordi-	WSa = normal adult controls	Tyler et al., 1997
nates & Functional Prop-		
erties[#]		

(Continued

TABLE 2.1
(Continued)

Type of Test or Performance	Result	Source or Reference
Lexical Constraints[#]:		
Fast Mapping	WSs = normal child MA	Stevens & Karmiloff-Smith, 1997
Mutual Exclusivity	controls	
Whole Object Constraint	WSs < normal child MA	
Taxonomic Constraint	controls	
Explanatory Category	WSs < normal MA controls	Johnson et al., 1994; Johnson &
Concepts[#]		Carey, 1998
Figurative Sentences		Bertrand et al., 1994a
Metaphor Explanations	WSa ~50%	
Correct Interpretations	WSa ~50%	
Metaphor and Sarcasm	WSc > AUTc	Karmiloff-Smith et al., 1995
Items[#]		

Note: % = percent of subjects; # = subject scores; WSa = WS adolescents &/or adults; WSc = WS children; DS = Down syndrome; "a" = adolescents/adults; AE = age-equivalent score; MA = mental age; CA = chronological age; AUT = people with autism.

On the other hand, the category production skills of WSa are well documented in terms of consistently producing significantly more category items than DSa (Bellugi et al., 1994) and performing at a level similar to MA normal controls (Carey, Johnson, & Levine, 1993; Carey et al., 1994). Once again, there are developmental trends with a steep rise in category fluency at about age 11 (Bellugi et al., 2000) and children with WS not always surpassing those with DS (Scott et al., 1994; Volterra et al., 1996). WSc generally perform similarly to normal MA controls, but not CA normal controls (Scott et al., 1994; Volterra et al., 1996).

Knowledge of category properties by WSa is at the level of normal MA controls, a very provocative finding, but this does not extend to explanatory, more abstract concepts like "animate" (Carey et al., 1993, 1994; Johnson & Carey, 1998; Johnson et al., 1994). Moderate understanding of concrete figurative language is evident, especially in some WSa, although generally better than that of individuals with autism (Bertrand et al., 1994; Karmiloff-Smith et al., 1995).

Distinctive properties of WSs semantics are often observed in their unusual use of words, documented in their proclivity for secondary meanings of homonyms (Rossen et al., 1996). Other phenomena like word-finding problems deserve further study.

In conclusion, the importance of the vocabulary and category strengths of WSs should not be minimized. Consistent comparability to normal MA controls, and scores higher than their own IQ, is noteworthy in individuals with biogenetic syndromes or developmental disabilities at the level of WSs.

IV. SYNTAX

The syntactic expertise of WSs can best be conveyed by allowing three WSa to "speak for themselves." Samples of their own speech include: "Isn't she going to come over here and talk with us?"; "When I got up next morning, I talked but couldn't say anything so my mom had to rush me to the hospital"; "The dog was chased by the bees"; "Then before they climbed over, they saw baby frogs"; and "If it got really infected they would have taken my toe off" (Bellugi et al., 1988a, pp. 183–184). Their spontaneous use of nonsimple sentence forms—questions, negations, relative clauses, passives, and conditionals—is impressive and syntactically advanced even though there are some errors of generalization and syntactic structure (Bellugi et al., 1988a). But, do these sentences sound as though they were produced by retarded individuals with IQs between 40 and 60? They were!

Buttressed by these kinds of observations and laboratory tests, researchers generally agree that the syntax of adolescents and adults with WS (WSa) is, overall, remarkably and relatively spared (Bellugi, Bihrle, Neville, Jernigan, & Doherty, 1992; Bellugi et al., 1994). "Syntax" refers to the implicit and explicit rules of grammar applied in the expression and reception of language. "Remarkably spared" refers to the structural complexity and correctness of the sentences that WSs typically use. "Relatively spared" refers to the fact that WS syntax is vulnerable to certain kinds of errors and it is generally less well developed than that of their normally developing age-mates (CA controls).

Recent research has challenged some of these conclusions by calling into question the level of syntactic competence WSs typically achieve and the consistency of the results obtained. This has important theoretical implications because it bears directly on issues concerning the modularity or independence of language as a human activity. That is, whether language is separate from other areas of cognition, and in the case of WSs, superior to their performance in other realms of behavior. Arriving at a realistic appraisal of the syntactic skills and problems of WSs is vital, too, in terms of being able to identify their strengths and weaknesses and convey accurate information to parents, teachers, and others involved with WSs. In particular, speech language therapists (SLTs) linguists, and educators, among others, may benefit from information about the syntactic capabilities of WSs, individual differences in those capabilities, and how they compare with those of other groups, including developmental disorders and normally developing age-mates. This is often necessary for the selection and formulation of effective language strategies by SLTs, parents, teachers, and others.

The following sections seek to provide such information in order to clarify the general level of syntactic abilities that is characteristic of most WSs.

This includes describing the results of tests of syntactic abilities, common types of morphosyntactic errors, and comparing syntactic to other kinds of test performance and skills.

A. Tests of Syntactic Ability

Consistent with the syntactic complexity of the spontaneous statements quoted previously, WSa ($n = 3$, 11–16 yrs) score at about 80% correct on formal tests of comprehension and production. These comprehension tests include the Test for Reception of Grammar (TROG), the Test of Language Development–Subtest 3: Grammatic understanding (TOLD), and the Clinical Evaluation of Language Functions–Subtest 1: Processing Word and Sentence Structure (CELF); the Sentence Completion Test is a test of production (Bellugi et al., 1988a). Whereas performance is quite good overall, it is not perfect and the age-equivalent (AE) values of the test scores do not reach anywhere near the chronological age of these three WSa (Bellugi et al., 1988a). However, they do exceed their mental age (MA) (5+, 7+, 8+ yrs, respectively), on the Wechsler Intelligence Scale for Children–Revised, WISC–R). These and other test results are presented in Table 2.2 (see p. 00).

Interestingly, the TROG results (Bellugi et al., 1988a) are replicated almost exactly, 82% correct, in a large sample of WSs ($n = 20$, 8;4–34;10 yrs, $M = 18;7$ yrs) (Karmiloff-Smith et al., 1997), and the mean test age (AE), 6;6 years (Karmiloff-Smith et al., 1997), is comparable to the median test age of 7+ for the WSa in Bellugi et al. (1988a).

Despite the similarity in results, the interpretations differ. Bellugi et al. (1988a) stated that WSa perform better than expected on the comprehension tests, and described their expressive language as syntactically complex and correct except for occasional errors. Karmiloff-Smith et al. (1997) emphasized the WSs' types of errors and the discrepancy between their CA and TROG AE. Central to the argument is the "non-intactness" of WSs' morphosyntax, meaning that they are not proficient at upper levels of syntactic complexity nor for certain kinds of morphemes such as plural word endings (see Section B, "Types of Morphosyntactic Errors").

Comparison with Other Groups. Comparisons between WSa and DSa matched on age, gender, and IQ (FIQ, WISC–R) further demonstrate the superiority of WSa on various syntactic tests (Bellugi et al., 1990; Bellugi et al., 1994). This difference is dramatically illustrated in the ability of WSa, but not DSa, to complete tag questions like "John and Mary like apples, ___ (don't they)." Proper use of such constructions requires application of numerous syntactic rules, such as subject–verb inversion, proper auxiliary verb, correct pronoun, and affirmation/negation. Although most WSa are able to correctly complete tag questions, DSa are not (Bellugi et al., 1994).

Moreover, WSa's scores are usually at least double those of DSa on the Sentence Completion Test (production) and the Sentence Correction Test (metalinguistics), which assess proper use of passives, negations, conditionals, and sentence correction.

Importantly, WSa approximate the performance of normal 7-year-olds on tests of passives, negations, conditional grammar, and sentence correction (Bellugi et al., 1994). This is important because most normally developing children are able to pass Piagetian tests of reasoning, such as conservation and seriation, by age 7, whereas almost all WSa are unable to do so (Bellugi et al., 1988a; Bertrand, Mervis, Armstrong, & Ayers, 1994a). This suggests that WSa are markedly impaired in reasoning, although relatively skilled syntactically, or both.

Difficult Syntactic Constructions. Contrary to previous reports of relative strength in grammatical comprehension, Mervis et al. (1999) observed that WSc (n = 77, 5–52 yrs) tend to perform poorly on certain constructions of the TROG. Only 17% pass the test block that assesses comprehension of relative clauses and just 3% pass items testing right branching or center-embedded sentences.

Error analysis of WSs' responses on the TROG provides further insight into the extreme difficulty that WSs (n = 20, 8;3–34;1 yrs, M = 18;8 yrs) usually experience with embedded sentences (Karmiloff-Smith et al., 1997). For example, 93% fail the item, "The boy the dog chases is big," and 71% fail the item, "The circle the star is in is red." A construction like "but not" is much more difficult when it is center embedded, as in the sentence "The box but not the chair is red," with a 56% error rate, than when it is right embedded as in the sentence "The cat is big but not black," with a 6% error rate. Thus, WSs show "comprehension problems with a number of grammatical structures, in particular embedded structures that normals with comparable vocabulary levels find easy" (Karmiloff-Smith et al., 1997, p. 248). Learning disabled children (LDc) have similar problems with embedded and passive sentences (Wiig & Semel, 1984).

Interestingly, the error rate for reversible passive constructions, such as "The elephant is chased by the boy," is 21%. This is similar to the 27.5% rate for simple comparative sentences, such as "The knife is longer than the pencil," which contain semantic relational terms (Karmiloff-Smith et al., 1997). This underscores the problems WSs have with spatial, comparative language forms.

Another study of reversible sentences confirms the poor performance (24% error rate) of WSs (n = 8, 15–35 yrs, M = 21 yrs) compared to the near perfect performance of normal adult controls (n = 18, 19–29 yrs) (Karmiloff-Smith et al., 1998). This contrasts markedly with the previously reported success rate of ~90% for WSa (n = 10, 10–20 yrs) on passive constructions (Bellugi et al., 1994). Note that the comparison group in earlier studies of WSa's sentence(s) (Bellugi et al., 1994) is matched on mental age (MA), not CA as in Karmiloff-Smith et al. (1998). Possibly, the disparity in results reflects differences in the confusability of the reversible sentences (e.g., "The clown photographs the policeman") and the difficulty of the picture foils (e.g., reversible roles or participants engaged in another act) in the "off-line" Birkbeck Sentences Test in the latter study (Karmiloff-Smith et al., 1998).

Other studies support the position that syntax is a relative strength. Mervis et al. (1999) reported that 57% of WSs (n = 77, 5–52 yrs) score in the normal range on the TROG even though almost all of them score in the mentally retarded range on a general abilities test (Differential Ability Scales, DAS). Also, a number of studies indicate that WSs do not differ significantly from normal MA matched controls or children with other syndromes in syntactic ability. For example, WSs (n = 30, ~7;6–39 yrs, M = 17 yrs) are comparable to normal MA controls (n = 26, M = 6.9 yrs) on the Grammatical Morphemes and Elaborated Sentences subtests of the Test of Auditory Comprehension of Language–Revised (TACL–R) (Wang, Ennis, & Namey, 1997).

Syntactic Abilities of Williams Syndrome Children

Research consistently shows that WSc are generally comparable to, not relatively better than, mentally retarded and normal MA subject controls. For example, the language output of WSc (n = 20, 6–15;9 yrs) does not differ significantly from that of a group of mentally retarded children (MRc) matched on verbal IQ on measures such as MLU (mean length of an utterance in morphemes) and mean pre-verb utterance length. The WSc are superior to the controls only on grammatical completeness of utterances (Udwin & Yule, 1990).

Similar results obtain in studies comparing WSc with other syndromes. For example, WSc (n = 37, M = 7;9 yrs) do not differ significantly from IQ and MA matched children with Prader–Willi syndrome (PWc) on the CELF (Tager-Flusberg, Sullivan, Boshart, & Guttman, 1997).

Likewise, German-speaking WSc (n = 25, 4–10 yrs) do not differ significantly from a matched control group of MRc on various measures of the Heidelberg Language Development Test except for their ability to produce correct singular-plural forms (Gosch et al., 1994).

Along the same lines, English-speaking WSc (n = 31, 5–10 yrs) produce significantly more morphological errors and less complex syntax than normal CA controls in a storytelling task, although individual WSc perform within the normal range (Losh, Reilly, Bellugi, Cassady, & Klima, 1997). This demonstrates the marked variability of young WSc noted by other investigators (Semel & Rosner, 1991a, 1991b; Udwin & Yule, 1990; Volterra et al., 1996).

In several other studies, WSc show no advantage over control groups. In an extensive study of language skills, Italian-speaking WSc (n = 17, 4;10–15;03 yrs, M = 9;8 yrs) do not compare favorably to normal controls matched on nonverbal intelligence (Leiter Matrices) on several measures of syntax (Volterra et al., 1994; Volterra et al., 1996). In fact, the WSc are significantly poorer than the controls on the TROG, although many of the older WSc are well within the norms of normal controls on the comprehension items used in the Token Test. Interestingly, the distribution of TROG errors is similar for the two groups, namely, reversible passives ~35% (sic), prepositions ~16%, and gender errors ~16%, despite marked differences in overall performance level. Both of the latter are morphosyntactic constructions (see Section B).

On the Sentence Repetition test, the majority of WSc are below the minimum expected score for their MA, and the remaining one third are at, not above, the mean. Finally, on the Story Description tasks, which are used to obtain and analyze expressive language samples, the mean length of utterances (MLU) of most WSc are within the range expected for their MA, although a few are far above it.

Significantly, the scores of WSc of higher CA or MA are generally within or above the range of scores expected for their MA, whereas those of lower MA are often at the bottom of the range of control group scores (Volterra et al., 1994; Volterra et al., 1996). This supports the researchers' contention that the relatively poor performance of their subjects is attributable primarily to age level, that is, their subjects are younger than the adolescents studied by Bellugi and colleagues.

Interestingly, WSc errors on the Sentence Repetition test of grammatical production and the Story Description task deviate from those of normally developing children (Volterra et al., 1996). The younger WSc, in particular, are prone to make unusual word order errors and preposition errors as well as substitutions of function or inflected forms. For instance, the Italian version of the sentence "Luca puts the ball on the table" is repeated in Italian as "put Luca on the table," or "Luca on the ball on the table," or "put Luca on the table on the ball." These types of errors suggest that the younger WSc in this study are unable to comprehend these syntactic structures or have sequencing difficulties.

Age appears to play a critical role in accounting for some of the mixed results in studies of WSs' grammatical competence, although other factors (e.g., size of sample, subject variability, language spoken, the particular comparison group, the type of test, and the specific test demands) may contribute to the results.

Some of these influences are clarified in a broad-scale study of the grammatical performance of WSs (Mervis et al., 1999). Testing a large sample of WS subjects (n = 77, 5–51 yrs) on the TROG, performance increases steadily over the childhood years and is maintained during adulthood. Grammatical comprehension scores on the TROG indicate that syntax is a relative strength of WSs across this age range despite the occurrence of certain types of grammatical and morphosyntactic errors (discussed later).

Focusing on young WSc (n = 39, 2;6–12 yrs), performance is at the 3;6-year-old level on a standardized test of syntactic production, the Index of Productive Syntax (IPSyn), even though their mean CA is 7 years (Mervis et al., 1999). Importantly, the age-related increase in MLU on the IPSyn is accompanied by an increase in syntactic complexity (Mervis et al., 1999).

Thus, the syntax of these young WSc is appropriate for the length of their sentences, even for long sentences. This contrasts markedly with the results of children with other syndromes (i.e., Down syndrome, DS; Fragile X syndrome, Frag X; autism, AUT) in which increases in sentence length are not matched by corresponding increases in syntactic complexity. At the same time, the IPSyn scores of WSc are comparable rather than higher than their composite mental ability scores (Mervis et al., 1999).

Similarly, a study of language development (Bellugi et al., 2000) shows that WSc (n = 29) perform similarly to children with language impairment (n = 24) and early focal (FL) brain lesions (n = 14) on a sentence-repetition task, the Carrow Elicited Language Inventory (CELI), across the age range from 4 to 12 years. Although all groups show an age-related increase in their ability to repeat sentences, normal CA controls (n = 86) exceed the other groups at all age levels (Bellugi et al., 2000).

Table 2.2 presents a summary of research dealing with the syntactic test abilities of WSs. It also refers to studies on the morphosyntactic skills and errors of WSs. These are discussed in the next section.

B. Types of Morphosyntactic Errors

Morphosyntactic errors refer to problems in the grammatical use of morphemes, that is, the smallest units of meaning, such as articles ("a," "the"), auxiliary verbs, verb endings, and other function words. In even the earliest studies of WS language, researchers noted certain kinds of morphological and syntactic errors in their performance on formal tests and in their spontaneous utterances (Bellugi et al., 1988a). Errors include failure to use the possessive marker (e.g., "daddy chair" instead of "daddy's chair"), incorrect tense markings (e.g., "falled" instead of "fell"), and incorrect usage of personal pronouns (e.g., "his" instead of "hers") and reflexive pronouns (e.g., "himself," "herself") on the TROG. Production errors on the Sentence Completion test involve overgeneralization and problems of interpretation at the clausal level (Bellugi et al., 1988a).

Studies described later focus on morphosyntactic forms that are considered potentially difficult for WSs. These include prepositions (Rubba & Klima, 1991), inflections of English plural nouns and past tense verbs (Bromberg, Ullman, Marcus, Kelley, & K. Levine, 1994; Clahsen & Almazan, 1998), gender of French articles and word endings (Karmiloff-Smith, Grant, & Berthoud, 1993; Karmiloff-Smith et al., 1997), and pronoun reversals and errors (Kelley & Tager-Flusberg, 1994). Problems in comprehending wh-question words have also been identified clinically.

Prepositions. An in-depth analysis of prepositional usage in WSa focuses on the spontaneous language productions of one subject, Crystal, in her spontaneously generated story of the "Chocolate Princess" (Rubba & Klima, 1991) and her retelling of the "Frog Story" (see Section VI, "Discourse and Narration").

Along with the many correct uses of prepositions, 19% of Crystal's prepositions are judged to be divergent (25 of 130 exemplars). These are mainly erroneous substitutions, such as using "through" instead of "in" or "to" (e.g., "I looked *through* my pocket"), and omissions, such as deletions of the preposition "to," especially when referring to a change in color (e.g., "change a different color" where the preposition "to" is omitted). Errors are said to reflect difficulty in encoding situations or in processing the various meanings of a given term. Either way, these are problems involving semantic meaning.

Plurals and Past Tense Inflections. Regarding the use of inflectional forms, WSa ($n = 6$, $M = 18$ yrs) perform significantly better on regular than irregular forms of both plural nouns (e.g., "boys" vs. "feet") and past tense verbs (e.g., "walked" vs. "fell") (Bromberg et al., 1994). Pictures were used to elicit plural terms (e.g., "Here is a *book*. Here are three __"). Sentence probes were used to elicit past tense forms (e.g., Everyday I *drive a* Ford. Yesterday, I __ a Ford"). As expected from previous research, WSs made more errors on irregular forms than the regular forms. These are errors of overgeneralization (see Bellugi et al., 1988a; Bellugi et al., 1994b).

Similar results are obtained in a study comparing WSc ($n = 4$) and language-impaired children (Llc) on inflections and other syntactic tasks (Clahsen & Almazan, 1998). The WSc were unimpaired on both the syntactic tasks and regular inflections, whereas irregular inflections resulted in many errors. The Llc showed the reverse pattern: poor performance on regular inflections and syntactic tasks, good performance on irregular inflections.

WSs' pattern of overregularization extends to their exclusive use of "-er" suffixes to mark comparative adjectives and their failure to use the term "more" (e.g., "more open") and irregular forms (e.g., " good") appropriately, like normal MA controls (Clahsen & Temple, 2002).

Gender Rules. Use of gender rules by French-speaking WSs (*n* = 14, 9;0–22;6 yrs, *M* = 15;9 yrs) is surprisingly poor when compared to that of normal, younger controls (*n* = 18, 4;6–5;11 yrs, *M* = 5;1 yrs) in a task involving generalization of gender knowledge to nonce (nonword) exemplars of article-noun-adjective terms (Karmiloff-Smith et al., 1997). These results agree with reports regarding the difficulty that young Italian-speaking WSc have with gender terms (Volterra et al., 1996), as well as the difficulty that English-speaking WSa have with the gender terms of personal and reflexive pronouns (Bellugi et al., 1988a).

Pronoun Errors. Within clinical settings, English-speaking WSc have been observed to make pronoun gender errors as well as pronoun number errors. These are made at all levels, namely: first person—subjective "I," "we"; objective "me," "us"; possessive "my," "our"; third person—subjective "he," "she," "it," "they"; objective "him," "her," "it," "them"; or possessive "his," "her," "its," "their." The most frequent errors involve gender forms of the third person (i.e., "he/she," "him/her," "his/her or hers"). Sometimes, the pronoun "myself" is used where a reflexive is not indicated. On the other hand, pronoun reversals involving "I" and "you" are not usually observed in young WSc (*n* = 20, 3–8 yrs, *M* = 5;9 yrs) (Kelley & Tager-Flusberg, 1994).

Comprehending Wh-Questions. In addition, Volterra et al. (1996) noted that WSc often have a difficult time following the questions that experimenters ask them. Clinical observation also indicates that some WSc may have problems in understanding questions that begin with "wh" words, like "what," "who," "when," "where," "which," or "whose," as well as "why" or "how." At times, WSc may become confused by such questions and give answers that are incorrect or inappropriate. For example, a WSc responded to the question "When did Christopher Columbus discover America?", with "Nina, Pinto, Santa Maria." Learning disabled children also have wh-question comprehension problems (Wiig & Semel, 1984).

Interestingly, the same WSc who have difficulty understanding wh-questions seem to have less difficulty formulating wh-questions. When they themselves make inquiries, they often use the appropriate wh-question word to ask for information about a person, object, or location (i.e., "who," "what," "where"). The difference between research accounts of WSs' skill with questions and clinical observations of WSc's difficulty (Bellugi et al., 1994; Harrison, Reilly, & Klima, 1994; Kelley & Tager-Flusberg, 1994; Reilly et al. 1990) may be due to a number of factors, including the type of question form ("Yes/No" or "wh-"), the age and cognitive level of the WSs, sentence complexity (i.e., active declarative questions vs. passive negative questions), and the language context.

Summary. Table 2.2 provides a summary of research studies dealing with the syntactic abilities, and a few of the morphosyntactic forms of WSs.

Relative strength in syntax is clearly demonstrated by WSa in their 80% rate of correct responding on various tests of comprehension (CELF–R, TOLD, and TROG) and their age-equivalent scores being comparable to their MA, although not their CA, on the TROG (Bellugi et al., 1988a; Karmiloff-Smith et al., 1997). WSs perform similarly to normal MA controls on the TACL–R, and 50% of WSs score in the normal range on the TROG (Mervis et al., 1999; Wang et al., 1997).

WSa perform very well on production tests too, with 88% correct and a MLU higher than their MA or DSa on a Sentence Completion and Sentence Correction (metalinguistics) test (Bellugi et al., 1988a; Bellugi et al., 1993, 1994). However, WSa are not comparable to CA controls on reversible sentences or gender rules (Karmiloff-Smith et al., 1997; Karmiloff-Smith et al., 1998).

With age, performance on syntactic tests improves, with WSc scoring lower than WSs on the TROG, a comprehension test (Mervis et al., 1999). Children with WS are similar to mentally retarded controls (MRc) in terms of MLU production and pre-verb length of sentences (Udwin & Yule, 1990), similar to children with PW in comprehension on the CELF (Tager-Flusberg et al., 1997), and to MRc on the Heidelberg Language Development Test (Gosch et al., 1994). Sometimes WSc present mixed results. They are comparable to normal MA controls on a production test, and on only one of two comprehension tests (Volterra et al., 1996).

Interestingly, WSc exceed MRc on a few measures of production, namely, grammatical completeness (Udwin & Yule, 1990) and proper use of singular and plural forms (Gosch et al., 1994). Likewise, the complexity of sentences produced by WSc increases as a function of increases in sentence length (MLU), unlike the limitations shown by children with DS, Frag X, and AUT (Mervis et al., 1999). WSc also resemble children with language impairment and early focal lesions, but are poorer than CA controls in terms of their production on the CELI, their syntactic complexity and morphological correctness in a storytelling task (Bellugi et al., 2000; Losh et al., 1997).

Finally, the rulelike quality of WS syntax is demonstrated in the overregularization they exhibit when dealing with regular and irregular forms of plurals, past tenses, and comparatives where they perform better on regular versus irregular forms (Bromberg et al., 1994; Clahsen & Almazan, 1998; Clahsen & Temple, in press).

TABLE 2.2
Research on Syntactic Abilities of WSs

Type of Test or Performance	Result	Source or Reference
CELF—Subtest 1 (Comp)	WSa 80% Correct (Md)	Bellugi et al., 1988a
Word & Sentence Structure	AE 12 yr (Md)	
TOLD—Subtest 3 (Comp)	WSa 80% (Md)	
	AE 8 yr (Md)	
TROG (Comp)	WSa 80% (Md)	
CA	15 yr (Md)	
MA	7 yr (Md)	
Sentence Completion (Prod)	WSa 88% Correct (Md)	
MLU	10 yr (Md)	
TROG (Comp)	WSs ~82% correct	Karmiloff-Smith et al., 1997
	AE 6.9 yr	
TROG (Comp)[#]	WSs 57% normal range	Mervis et al., 1999
Sentence Completion Test	WSa = Normal Controls > DSa	Bellugi et al., 1992; Bellugi et
(Prod)[#]		al., 1994
Sentence Correction Test	WSa > DSa	
(Metalinguistics)[#]		
Reversible Sentences (Prod)[#]	WSa < Normal CA Controls	Karmiloff-Smith et al., 1998
MLU (Prod)[#]	WSc = MRc	Udwin & Yule, 1990
Pre-verb Length (Prod)[#]	WSc = MRc	
Grammatical Completeness[#]	WSc > MRc	
Heidelberg Language	WSc = MRc	Gosch et al., 1994
Development Test[#]		
Singular/Plural (Prod)[#]	WSc > MRc	
Storytelling Task (Prod)		
Morphological Errors	WSc > normal CA controls	Losh et al., 1997
Syntactic Complexity	WSc < normal CA controls	
TROG (Comp)[#]	WSc < Normal MA Controls	Volterra et al., 1996
Token Test (Comp)[#]	WSc = Normal MA Controls	
Sentence Repetition (Prod)[#]	WSc = Normal MA Controls	
TACL—R (Comp)[#]	WSs = Normal MA Controls	Wang et al., 1997
Grammatical Morphemes[#]	WSs = Normal MA Controls	
Elaborated Sentences[#]	WSs = Normal MA Controls	
CELF (Comp)[#]	WSc = PWc	Tager-Flusberg et al., 1997
TROG (Comp)[#]	WSc < WSs	Mervis et al., 1999
IPSyn (Prod)[#]	WSc < CA	Mervis et al., 1999
Complexity (f) MLU (Prod)[#]	WSc, not DSc, Frag Xc, AUTc	
Carrow Elicited Language	WSc = LIc & FLc,	Bellugi et al., 2000
Inventory (Prod)[#]	< Normal CA Controls	
Gender Rules	French WSa < Normal MA	Karmiloff-Smith et al., 1997
	Controls	
Inflections:	WSa: Regular > Irregular	Bromberg et al., 1994
Regular & Irregular[#]		
Inflections:	WSc: Regular > Irregular	Clahsen & Almazan, 1998
Regular & Irregular[#]	LIc: Irregular > Regular	

Note: Md = Median score; WSc = WS children; WSa = WS adolescents or adults; DSa = DS adults; DSc = DS children; AE = age-equivalent score; CA = chronological age; MA = mental age; Comp = Comprehension test; Prod = Production test; PWc = Prader–Willi children; Frag X = Fragile X syndrome; AUT = autism; LI = language impaired; FL = early focal lesions.

In sum, WSs exhibit a good basic understanding and usage of the fundamentals of grammar. They tend to be comparable to other types of MR or normal groups matched on verbal measures, like MA, but they reach their limits in dealing with the less regular or more complex and embedded rules of syntax.

V. PRAGMATICS OF LANGUAGE

"Pragmatics" is the performance aspect of language, that is, the social, communicative use of language (Bates, 1976; Fromkin & Rodman, 1988). It includes rules of language performance, such as speech acts and conversational postulates (Bates, 1976), as well as functions of communication, such as ritualizing, informing, controlling, and feeling (Wells, 1973, cited in Wiig & Semel, 1984). The field is broad in scope and complex in its relation to other areas. Although research on the language pragmatics of WSs is rather fragmented and incomplete, certain kinds of skills and problems have been identified (Scheiber, 2000; Udwin & Yule, 1998b).

Most WSc are enthralled by conversation and delight in using it in social interactions (Semel, 1988). Researchers note that WSs have "impressive" conversational skills (Karmiloff-Smith, 1992), mastery of conversational routines (Volterra et al., 1994), and relative strength in expressive language (Morris et al., 1988). Many respond well to "reasoning." They can often be "talked out" of behaving inappropriately, "talked into" conforming to acceptable standards of behavior, and "talked through" the establishing of new or improved forms of behavior.

Researchers have also noted vulnerabilities in certain areas of language pragmatics (Levine, 1993; Meyerson & Frank, 1987; Semel and Rosner, 1991a, 1991b; Udwin & Yule, 1990). Some problems are serious, others less so; likewise, some are pervasive, others more limited. Many are related to their difficulties in other areas, namely, socioemotional and behavioral problems.

The pragmatics of WS language is described next within the framework of functions of communication: ritualizing, informing, controlling, and feeling. Table 2.3 summarizes how the specific skills and problems of WSs map onto these functions (see p. 59).

A. Ritualizing Functions of Communication

WSs sometimes engage in incessant, inappropriate greeting behaviors and requests for attention, which are two of their more annoying behaviors.

Inappropriate Greeting Behaviors. Professionals frequently observe WSs as they enthusiastically greet everyone they meet, including almost all strangers with whom they come in contact. The compulsive greeting behavior of WSc is pervasive and unlimited. It can occur anywhere, including the park, classroom, public building, or on the street. This is a clear-cut breach in pragmatic rules that specify how and when to express various forms of greeting. It can be an annoyance and disturbance to others. It may also compromise the safety of WSs.

On a more positive note, many WSs are able to introduce themselves appropriately, although they may use overfamiliar forms. They can give their first and last name on request, and many can provide their address (number, street, and town). Some can give their telephone number or should be taught to do so, and more importantly, should be taught about to whom they may properly give it.

WSs may also need instruction in proper use of the telephone, including ways to introduce themselves, how to provide and request relevant information, and ways to end the call politely. They often need help in determining who is appropriate to call, what kinds of things are appropriate to discuss, how long to talk, and how often to phone people.

Inappropriate Requests for Attention. Most WSc seem to have difficulty in knowing how or when to request attention. Some remain quiet in formal situations like the classroom. Many others are too talkative. This may be shown in various contexts, such as not requesting permission to make a comment, to use classroom materials, to leave or change their seat, or to ask or answer a question. Many WSs are so skilled at making requests that they can control and manipulate situations.

The uninhibited calling out of WSs, like their greeting behavior, is usually compulsive, unrestrained, and disruptive. In certain respects, it resembles the compulsive calling out behaviors of individuals with Tourette syndrome, a neurological disorder with involuntary motor and vocal tics. It differs, however, in that the language used is not offensive or taboo as it is in Tourette syndrome (Schoenbrodt & Smith, 1995).

B. Informing Functions of Communication

The informing functions of communication include the rules of conversation and the offering and requesting of information.

Many WSs seem to have particular difficulty with five types of informing functions: talkativeness, topic relevance, turn-taking, answering of questions, and informational exchange.

Talkativeness

Excessive talkativeness is often considered a hallmark of WS (Arnold et al., 1985; Bellugi et al., 1988a; Dilts et al., 1990; Harris, 1995a, p. 135; Meyerson & Frank, 1987; Von Arnim & Engel, 1964). Eighty-two percent of parents state that their WSc "chatters" away (Utah Survey, Semel & Rosner, 1991a, 1991b). Other terms used by researchers, clinicians, and family members include "loquacious," "hyperlalia," and "motor mouth."

Cocktail Party Speech. Whereas the WS propensity to talkativeness has been described as "cocktail party chatter" (i.e., superficial and lacking in content; Jones & Smith, 1975; Scheiber, 2000; Udwin & Yule, 1990), this may not accurately describe relevant features of WS speech. Research comparing the language samples of WSc and developmentally disabled children suggests that WS speech may also serve "complex communicative purposes." That is, it is "by no means meaningless, repetitive, or superficial," although it is sometimes irrelevant or tangential (Udwin & Yule, 1990), as well as limited conceptually (Johnson & Carey, 1998).

Thus, the overabundant speech of WSc may be explained as a tendency to get "off-track." This may sometimes be due to problems of word finding, impulsivity, conceptual limitations, or to an overwhelming need to "keep the conversation going."

Topic Closure. Much of the verbosity of WSs seems to reflect problems of "topic closure," that is, determining the boundaries between utterances and structuring the content of messages in terms of ideas or topics (Lucas, 1980, p. 67). Without such markers, children may tend to rephrase and reiterate their verbalizations in ways that are frustrating to the listener. This may be as difficult to deal with as other children's lack of language skill.

Topic Relevance

The conversational postulates of dialogue require speakers to follow the rules of topic relevance—that is, offering only information assumed to be new and relevant to the listener, and requesting only information they really want (Bates, 1976). Related issues are topic maintenance and perseverating on a single topic.

WSs generally show wide variation in these skills. They are usually able to advance a conversation by making comments appropriate to the speaker's remarks. Some WSc are able to make repairs when a conversation breaks down, others are not able to do so. They are usually able to maintain the central topic and introduce topically related comments. Others need help. Comments of WSc may often be informative, but they may also be too long and convoluted.

Research Studies. Surveys support these observations. Tharp (1986) noted that WSc ($n = 63$, 4–29 yrs, $M = 10;11$ yrs) often have problems getting "their point across." Parents report that 90% of WSc "sometimes talk about irrelevant topics," 69% talk "incessantly about topically related subjects," and 57% "usually stay on a topic of conversation" (Utah Survey, Semel & Rosner, 1991a).

Similarly, Meyerson and Frank (1987) pointed out that WSs (n = 10, 8 children, 2 adults) show poor topic maintenance. Udwin and Yule (1990) reported that WSc are more likely than MRc to produce "fillers," that is, language with little content.

On the other hand, biographical interviews and related studies suggest that some WSa are capable of "at least a low-level capacity for active and analytical reflection about a conversational topic" (Harrison, Reilly, & Klima, 1994; Reilly et al., 1990).

Contributing Factors. Some WS individuals may have an intense desire to prolong a conversation beyond their knowledge of the topic. Sometimes WSc use seemingly inappropriate changes in topic to camouflage their word-finding problems. Problems of topic maintenance may reflect WSs' reluctance to ask for clarification or repetition of information. Social and personality factors may also play a role.

Tangential Speech. Sometimes tangential speech may be used as a defense. Parents report that 72% of WSc try to get out of uncomfortable situations by talking their way out, 78% use clever ways to disguise that they do not understand something (Utah Survey, Semel & Rosner, 1991a, 1991b). In any event, WSs' attempts to sidestep a topic of conversation can create at least momentary confusion for the listener.

Other Child Groups. Children with other forms of developmental disorder may also display problems of topic relevance, topic maintenance, and turn-taking. In individuals with ADHD, such difficulties are attributed to impulsivity (Schoenbrodt & Smith, 1995). The topic maintenance problems of children with Frag X (Schoenbrodt & Smith, 1995) seem to be more acute than those observed clinically in WSc.

Topic Perseveration

Topic perseveration is a related problem for many WSs (Udwin & Yule, 1998a, 1998b). "Perseveration" is a general term used to describe inappropriate and frequent repetitions in any area of performance, including writing, drawing, motor habits, or problem solving. Within the field of language pathology, perseveration usually refers to the repetition of words, phrases, or topics when they are no longer appropriate, although they might have been previously.

WS conversations may often center on areas of special interest (e.g., flags, insects, plants, rocks, or motors; see chap. 5, Section II, "Curiosity"). WSc may turn repeatedly to certain topics because they feel confident talking about them or to preserve their reputation of being a "good" talker (Levine, 1993; Semel & Rosner, 1991a).

Sometimes WSc perseverate on topics that are anxiety provoking, such as objects that have engines or make loud noises (Levine, 1993), or on traumatic experiences they have had.

WSc may perseverate on cliches, stereotyped phrases, and favorite conversational topics (Levine, 1983; Semel, 1988; Udwin et al., 1987). Use of phrasal perseveration and semantically empty placeholders (e.g., "You know," "now, er," "Whatchever you call it") may allow WSc to "hold the floor" while they try to produce an acceptable comment, novel, or humorous remark. Perseverative expressions and topical repetitions may also be used to disguise their word retrieval difficulties or as a defense against WSs revealing that they are unable to meet task demands (Lucas, 1980, p. 178).

Regardless of the reasons for the topical, word, and phrasal perseverations of WSs, parents attest to their undesirable frequency and the compulsivity of these forms of behavior (Discussion comments, Lenhoff, Levinson, in Wang, 1994).

Other Child Groups. Perseveration may co-occur with echolalia (i.e., immediate repetition of the other person's speech) in children with other types of disorder, such as autism and Fragile X syndrome (Schoenbrodt & Smith, 1995). Echolalia is seldom observed clinically in WSc, however. Similarly, echo shadowing, or repetition within a conversational dyad of what the speaker has just said, is not characteristic of WSc, although they occasionally "talk to themselves" or "self-interrupt."

Turn-Taking

The principles of dialogue also require skill in conversational turn-taking and turn-yielding (Bates, 1976). There are some reports of "poor turn-taking" in WSs (Meyerson & Frank, 1987; Scheiber, 2000). Other studies do not necessarily support this conclusion.

A preliminary study of young WSc ($n = 20$, 3–6 yrs) indicates appropriate length of conversational turns (Kelley & Tager-Flusberg, 1994). In another study, grade school age children with WS do not differ significantly from mentally retarded control subjects in their number of words or utterances per turn (Udwin & Yule, 1990).

Nevertheless, problems with turn-yielding or giving up the floor are observed clinically and mentioned sometimes by parents. Such difficulty seems to reflect the child's impulsivity or need for attention rather than inadequate knowledge of the "rules" of conversation. In fact, speaking out of turn tends to be a general problem (see earlier discussions of compulsive greeting behavior and inappropriate requests for attention, pp. 48–49).

LANGUAGE SKILLS AND PROBLEMS

Answering of Questions

WSc often have difficulty answering certain kinds of questions appropriately. Their answers can be long-winded, extremely delayed, off target, or completely wrong. Sometimes they give a correct answer to a slightly different question. These tendencies may reflect insufficient knowledge of the material, or difficulty comprehending the question, staying on track, retrieving or formulating the answer, or giving a brief answer. Parents report that 97% of WSc speak about tangential topics when they are unable to answer questions. They may also resort to using distractors (e.g., flattery) rather than saying "I don't know."

Bailly, Meljac, Calmette, and Lemmel (1994) indicated that French-speaking children with WS (n = 20, 6;8–14;4 yrs) often respond to tests of cognitive ability (WISC–R, Kaufman ABC, and Piagetian tasks) with "attempts to sidestep such confidential questions posed by an association of ideas with irrelevance, details, or various language tricks," such as "assonance" or the use of similar sounds or partial rhymes.

On the other hand, WSa are said to respond sensibly to examiner's questions in biographical interviews, free conversational sessions, and informal social interactions. In these situations, WSa tend to exceed DSa in their ability to solicit information from the examiner. They are also much more likely than DSa to expand on their requested responses with added information and extensive replies (Harrison et al., 1994; Reilly et al., 1990).

In testing and classroom situations, questions requiring a one-word answer (e.g., "Who invented the light bulb?") are often more difficult for WSs to deal with than sentence completion questions (e.g., "The earth revolves around the ___?") or open-ended questions.

Informational Exchange

"Information exchange" refers to the providing of information and requesting of information in conversational and instructional settings.

WSs are usually quite informative when asked to describe their physical condition or internal or mental state—like being cold, hungry, scared, or distressed by a sudden loud sound. Sometimes, however, they seem unaware of their own reaction in problem areas like visuospatial cognition or tactile defensiveness (see pp. 114 and 166).

Generally, WSs are able to form a simple question, make a statement, or express a problem adequately. They often need assistance, however, in knowing how and when to ask others to clarify or repeat information. Such difficulty with repair strategies can undermine topical continuity.

Following Instructions. Instructions and explanations may also pose serious problems. It has been observed clinically that most WSs have difficulty in following simple one-, two-, or three-step directions, especially those related to simple construction tasks (i.e., school or household tasks, block construction, jigsaw puzzles, arts and crafts, as well as writing letters and numbers). This can be a source of frustration, conflict, and failure for WSs, as well as their parents, teachers, specialists, employers, and others in many situations (home, family, treatment, school, formal testing, research studies, employment, community and group activities; see chap. 6, Section I.D.).

The inverse is also true. Most WSs experience inordinate difficulty in trying to explain concisely and clearly how to make or do something. (See chap. 4, Section I, "Visual-Motor Performance").

C. Controlling Functions of Communication

WSs place much importance on social interaction and relationships, so it is not surprising that they display both multiple difficulties and strengths in the area of pragmatic language behaviors that relate to influencing others and being influenced by others (i.e., the controlling functions of communication).

Persistent Questioning. Most WSs tend to engage in persistent questioning, that is, a tendency to ask the same question over and over again even though they have already received a reasonable answer to that question on at least one previous occasion. Persistent questioning may be focused on anxiety-related issues, such as changes in plans, routines, or anticipated activities (Dilts et al., 1990; MacDonald & Roy, 1988; Semel, 1988; Udwin et al., 1987). Also the health of themselves or others, imagined disasters, upcoming medical visits, or traumatic experiences in the past are extremely upsetting to most WSc (see chap. 6, p. 000). They also get into patterns of persistent questioning about anxiety-provoking appointments, like going to visit the doctor, dentist, hair stylist, or an unusual place. Thus, persistent questioning seems to reflect difficulty with the "controlling" and "feeling" aspects of communication functions more than problems of topic relevance per se.

Parents report that 82% of WSc ask "persistent questions," and 90% are said to "sometimes get into patterns of persistent questioning" (Utah Survey, Semel & Rosner, 1991a, 1991b). The following are examples of commonly asked questions: "When are we going to leave, when are we going to Grandma's?" "When are we going to get there?" "Are we there yet?"

Repeated, reiterative asking of exactly the same question often tries the patience of family members, teachers, and others involved with WSs. Asking WSs to refrain from persistent questioning is usually ineffective. The urge or necessity to keep asking is so compelling that it may overcome ordinary attempts to dissuade or discuss this problem. See chapter 3 for suggested interventions.

Conversational Distractors. Many WSs are quite adept at using language as a defense or distraction when a task or topic is beyond their capability. Many WSs are able to do this with such skill that it may be difficult to detect.

One way is through the use of flattery. They may comment on the clothing, jewelry, or social or body language cues of their conversational partner. WSc also tend to use flattery somewhat indiscriminately as a way to initiate or maintain a conversation or social contact with recent or casual acquaintances, as well as people they know very well (Levine & Wharton, 2000). It can be used also as a diversionary tactic to avoid an unpleasant task, awkward silent period, or the possibility of failure. In fact, widespread use of flattery may be a uniquely Williamesque feature.

Changing the subject of conversation or referring to a topic of special interest is another way in which WSs may try to control the conversation and distract others. They may launch into a discourse about their feelings, beliefs, or a personal experience. If asked to name major holidays, they may get off track by recounting in detail their Thanksgiving holiday (i.e., their travel to the dinner, who was at the dinner, what they ate, etc.), getting farther and farther away from the topic.

Asking questions of an examiner or conversational partner is another tactic. The questions are often personal but posed in a very disarming manner. Sometimes WSs are so eager to enter into or prolong a social conversation and interaction that they try to converse on subjects they know little about. Some have been known to resort to lying to keep the conversation going.

Direct and Indirect Requests. Clinical observation suggests that many WSc are rather adept at making requests for additional information, particularly of adults. Simple one-step directives are generally initiated and responded to appropriately by many WS children. Taking notice of such skill and praising WSc for their ability can serve as a reinforcer.

Many WSs may also be able to comprehend "indirect speech acts," or the implied use of a sentence (e.g., "It is very cold" may be a request to shut the window or to go into another room). This ability is consistent with their special sensitivity and empathy for others. Most have difficulty, however, understanding indirect requests that are more complex.

Accepting Restrictions. Whereas WSs usually respond favorably to simple direct commands, they may not be as receptive to warnings and prohibitions. Potentially, this resistance to restrictions or prohibitions can place the WS individual and others in danger. At the least, it can be an annoyance or nuisance.

Likewise, many WSs often have difficulty knowing how to respond appropriately when their requests for permission are denied. Some of their requests are like those of most children, such as asking to borrow someone's belongings, to receive a special gift like a pet, or to attend a certain event. Other requests of WSs may be less typical, such as asking to listen to the air conditioner, or to watch a fan go around and around. Still other requests may be somewhat idiosyncratic—at times even risky—such as asking to go up in a glider.

Denial of requests for permission to engage in disapproved activities may provoke resentment and anger. It is not uncommon for them to perseverate on their request—to sulk, nag, and stay angry for a prolonged period of time. Prohibiting WSs from doing things like watching a building under construction, continually entering a neighbor's yard, or riding a bicycle on a busy road can elicit a temper tantrum or other undesirable behaviors. Generally, they tend to overreact to denials of permission; their degree of upset may seem extreme. This may reflect their poor frustration tolerance.

Avoidance of Responsibility. Accepting responsibility, blame, and criticism for undesirable kinds of actions is difficult and requires a certain level of maturity. Many WSs have problems in this area. When confronted with tasks or situations they are unable to perform or would rather decline, WS individuals often have problems saying "No." Possibly, they do not know how to say "No" in a tactful manner or they may lack the ego strength. Or, maybe they are reluctant to disappoint others or to risk disapproval, rejection, and social isolation.

WSs may also try to avoid taking responsibility for having engaged in undesirable acts, such as accidentally breaking something, wandering away, or misbehaving in some other way. This is a difficult situation as many WSs have problems accepting blame.

In a similar vein, WSs often have trouble accepting criticism—even legitimate, tactful criticism—with equanimity, nondefensiveness, and a constructive attitude. The contributing factors seem to be, once again, fear of social rejection and disapproval, acute sensitivity, a fragile ego, and low self-esteem.

Receptivity to Reasoning. Most of the time, WSc are able to profit from the use of verbal reasoning if care is taken to adapt the level of discourse to their level and analogies are used to concretize and personalize the rationale. They tend to respond better when they understand the consequences of their own behavior, such as not walking around the classroom when other students are working because it bothers them. Sometimes, authoritative types of statements like "You may not walk around the room, sit down" may be effective, other times they may be unsuccessful.

Parents report that 78% of WSc can be "talked out of [performing undesirable] behaviors" (Utah Survey, Semel & Rosner, 1991a, 1991b). Oftentimes, WSc are able to express agreement and disagreement in a communicatively effective way.

It should be noted WSs' receptivity to "reasoning," verbal rationales, and analogies are real strengths that are unusual for people with their level of developmental disability. This can help to lay the groundwork for effective intervention and behavioral controls.

D. Feeling Functions of Communication

The feeling function of communication involves the verbal expression and monitoring of attitudes and feelings as well as responses to them. Paradoxically, WSs display a number of skills and difficulties in this area.

Social Sensitivity

Most WSs appear to excel in some areas of social sensitivity. WSc are generally adept at using eye contact to initiate and maintain a focus of joint attention between speaker and listener. This differs markedly from the gaze avoidance and avoidance of eye contact of individuals with Fragile X syndrome (Frag X), autism (AUT) (Schoenbrodt & Smith, 1995), and other forms of retardation.

WSc are usually sensitive to nonverbal cues, such as gestures, facial expressions, and body language, and often skilled in their use in verbal contexts. During conversation, WSs will give frequent nonverbal feedback by smiling, nodding the head, and using gestures to express their reaction. They may provide verbal feedback with appropriate comments, such as "yes," "sure," "oh," or "really." Such responses often indicate that WSs are really listening to what the speaker is saying, and an actual dialogue is taking place. WSs may also make humorous comments that are consistent with the speaker's remarks.

In addition, most WSc are able to adapt their speech style to the communication needs of the listener. WSc are known to change their use of grammar, vocabulary, and speech style depending on whether they are speaking to a doctor, the school principal, a younger child, or a baby. The way in which older WSc adapt their speech when telling "ghost" stories to younger WSc is a compelling example of this ability.

Some problems may arise, however, in the hypersensitivity that many WSs have in regard to the feelings of others. Combined with their limited ability in being able to alleviate the distress of others in certain situations, WSs may become quite upset and need special help in knowing how to handle their own feelings, too.

There are also reports that they have problems in "reading" body language and in understanding nonverbal language, for example, signs of a listener's boredom (Scheiber, 2000, pp. 42, 55). At present, there is no apparent explanation for the distinction between these reports and the previously described observations of WS abilities in this areas. Perhaps situational context is important, or perhaps age or the WSs' overpowering desire for social interaction obscures their ability to respond appropriately to nonverbal cues. Research is needed for clarification.

Communication of Feelings. Generally, WSs convey positive states and emotions, such as affection, appreciation, pleasure, and happiness, either appropriately or too profusely (Levine & Wharton, 2000). They are usually adept in making supportive statements or comments and verbally comforting others. Negative emotions or attitudes seem to be more difficult for them to express or convey appropriately except when prohibited from doing something. Then they can brew up a storm of anger (Levine & Wharton, 2001). Most WSs are able to make their wants known, but complaints are another matter. In a similar vein, WSs often have difficulty in accepting criticism as well as expressing criticism of others.

Protesting the actions of others is also a difficult area for many WSs. Most WSs tend to have problems in asking others to discontinue actions that displease them. Denying the requests of others to provide favors or use their property are other areas of difficulty. It is important for WSs to receive special help in assertiveness training and developing the communication skills necessary for dealing with these issues.

Table 2.3 presents a summary of WSs' specific skills and problems in the area of language pragmatics.

VI. DISCOURSE AND NARRATION

The pièce de résistance of expressive language for WSs is their ability to engage in meaningful discourse and produce interesting, attention capturing stories (Scheiber, 2000). Several research studies and clinical observation suggest that WSa tend to exhibit impressive ability and creativity in the areas of discourse and narration or storytelling.

TABLE 2.3
WS Language Pragmatics: Skills and Problems

Ritualizing Functions of Communication
  Inappropriate Greeting Behavior*
  Inappropriate Requests for Attention*
Informing Functions of Communication
  Talkativeness*
  Topic Relevance*
  Topic Perseveration*
  Turn-Taking*
  Answering of Questions*
  Informational Exchange*
Controlling Functions of Communication
  Persistent Questioning*
  Conversational Distractors*
  Direct and Indirect Requests*
  Accepting Restrictions*
  Avoidance of Responsibility*
  Receptivity to Reasoning[b]
Feeling Functions of Communication
  Social Sensitivity[a/b]
  Communication of Feelings[a/b]

---

* = Interventions presented in chap. 3
a = Interventions discussed in other chapters
b = Clinically observed as an area of relative strength

On the other hand, younger, school-age WSc may not be so gifted, and even WSa may be able to benefit from further shaping of their skills in this area. Reported weaknesses of WSc and WSa in the informing functions of language pragmatics support this contention.

A. Characteristics of WS Discourse

"Discourse" refers to the combining of sentences to express complex thoughts or ideas in linguistic units that are longer than sentences (Fromkin & Rodman, 1988). It deals with the cohesiveness, rhetorical force, verbal fluency, and the topic/subtopic structure of paragraphs or stories in written and spoken languages.

An oft-quoted example conveys the discourse skills of a WSa in describing her life aim to be a writer: "You are looking at a professional bookwriter. My books will be filled with drama, action, and excitement. And everyone will want to read them. . . . I am going to write books, page after page, stack after stack . . ." (Rossen, Klima, Bellugi, Bihrle, & Jones, 1996, p. 367).

This quote illustrates several features of good discourse: coherence (i.e., the statements "hang together"), thematic structure (i.e., subjects and predicates indicate what one is talking about and what is being said about it), "old" and "new" information is properly sequenced, and "frame and insert" (i.e., it provides a framework and its content). Utterance "flow" or fluency is exemplary, syntax is excellent, and word choice is appropriate. Despite the high level of discourse, this WSa had an IQ of 49 at the time of her statement. It seems likely that conventional intelligence tests may be missing something important about WS.

B. Narration and Story-Telling of WSs

Another talent of WSa is the ability to "weave vivid stories of imaginary tales" (Bellugi et al., 1994). This is illustrated in the following spontaneously generated story of a WSa (Reilly, Klima, & Bellugi, 1990):

> The story is about chocolate. Once upon a time, in Chocolate World there used to be a Chocolate Princess. She was such a yummy princess. She was on her chocolate throne and then some chocolate man came to see her. . . . The man said to her, "Please, Princess Chocolate, I want you to see how I do my work. And it's hot outside. Chocolate World and you might melt to the ground like melted butter. And if the sun changes to a different color, then the Chocolate World and you won't melt." (p. 371)

As these segments demonstrate, the story has coherence, structure, orientation of characters and setting, and a resolution of the problem.

These qualities are also apparent in the stories WSa generate from a wordless picture book, "Frog, Where Are You?" (Bellugi et al., 1994; Mayer, 1969). The book depicts a series of events, starting with a pet frog climbing out of his jar while a boy and his dog are sleeping. Distressed with the loss, they go to seek the frog. After many adventures, the boy and his dog discover a family of frogs and take a baby frog home. Subjects are asked to look at the pictures and tell a story about the boy, dog, and frog (e.g., Reilly et al., 1990).

A comparison of the stories of WSa and DSa is interesting. DSa tend to use simple, active declarative statements mostly in the present tense and few morphemes, whereas WSa tend to use advanced syntactic forms, such as compound sentences, tense marker morphemes, and subordinate clauses that set off "new from given" elements of the sentence. Coherence is evident in the sentences produced by WSa but not those of DSa (n = 4, Reilly et al., 1990; n = 10, Reilly, Harrison, & Klima, 1994).

The contrast is dramatically illustrated by quoting the opening statement of the first subject in each group:

DSa: "He looks in the bowl. He . . . sleep. . . ."

WSa: "Once upon a time there was this boy who had a dog and a frog. And it was night time. . . ." (Reilly et al., 1990)

Differences in story structure and use of expressive devices are also apparent. WSa stories are markedly higher in story form and content than those of DSa. All of the WSa provide an orientation to their stories by specifying time, characters, and states, as do all of the normal MA matched controls (7-8 yrs), but none of the DSa do so. DSa are more likely, however, to include content that is irrelevant (e.g., "The clothes is lying there"). Importantly, the problem or complication (searching for the frog) is mentioned repeatedly during the narration of all four of the WSa, as well as all the normal controls, but only two of the four DSa. Likewise, resolution of the story (i.e., finding the frogs and bringing one home) is mentioned by all WSa, by all normal controls, but by just one half of the DSa.

Thus, the stories of DSa are mostly at the "descriptive" level of narration (i.e., the level of normal 3- and 4-year-olds) in which each picture is described as a separate entity, whereas the stories of WSa are at the "structured" level of normal 7- and 8-year-olds.

Importantly, the WSa's expression of affect through the use of language is exceptional. WSa tend to exhibit voice changes in pitch and volume, vocalic lengthening, and stress changes to dramatize their storytelling. They are much more likely than DSa to use devices like whispering, or filling in of details, like "the next day being sunny" or "the boy being sad when he found that the frog was gone" (Reilly et al., 1990; Reilly et al., 1994).

In fact, WSa use affective expression more than any other comparison group. Only when older normal children—10- and 11-year-olds—tell the story to preschoolers do they match WSa in the use of affective language. The narrative emotionality of WSa is actually extreme. In repeated renditions of the same story, they continue to use vocal devices and affective enhancers to such a degree that it appears aberrant (Reilly et al., 1990).

In addition, young WSc ($n = 30$, 5-10 yrs) greatly exceed normal control children matched on CA or MA and gender in their use of elaboration and evaluative devices in telling the Frog story (Jones et al., 2000; Losh et al., 1997). Consistent with the aforementioned results (Reilly et al., 1990; Reilly et al., 1994), the WSc's stories contained a great deal of lexically coded evaluation (i.e., inferred affective and mental states), character speech and sound effects, and phrases and exclamations to capture listener attention, suggesting that WSs use evaluative devices from an early age on to engage listeners.

In fact, WSc's use of such devices exceeds that of normal control subjects at each CA level studied (5-6, 7-8, and 9-10 yrs). At the same time, the WSc showed unmistakable signs of language delay because their use of syntax was less complex and they made more morphological errors than their normal age-mate controls. In addition, normal controls produced proportionately more cognitive evaluation devices consisting of inferences of causality, character motivation, and mental or emotional states than WSc, whereas WSc produced proportionately more social engagement devices, such as exclamatory phrases, character speech, or sound effects, than the controls (Jones et al., 2000).

Further research on WSs' narration and discourse abilities is sorely needed to verify and extend the present findings so that skills and problems in these areas may be better addressed.

VII. SUMMARY AND CONCLUSIONS

The language skills and problems of WSs are dissimilar, not homogeneous, across language areas and individuals with WS. Differences in overall strength and weakness clearly emerge when areas are viewed from a comprehensive perspective. Differences in the amount of research conducted in the various areas are also clearly apparent in that some sections of this chapter are longer than others.

Extrapolating from present research studies and clinical observations, the areas may be ordered as follows in terms of their usual level of proficiency. Vocabulary vies with narrative storytelling as the area of greatest strength; next are syntax, articulation, and prosody; then the widespread problems of early language delay and troublesome aspects of some pragmatic functions; and, finally, the complex aspects of syntax, abstract concepts of semantics, and explication of discourse that stymie most WSs.

Concomitantly, there are many correspondences and reciprocal relations between areas. Possibly, there may be a common basis for certain semantic and syntactic problems, such as prepositions, clausal interpretations, or sentences with multiple transformations. There may also be some correspondence between speech dysfluencies and word-finding problems exhibited in behaviors such as hesitations, fillers, cluttering, and circumlocutions or between pragmatic language problems in the answering of questions and difficulties with some complex syntactic structures.

Comparing language ability with performance in other areas, WSs are usually markedly superior in language relative to the visual-spatial-motor domain, and WSa tend to score higher or similarly in language relative to scores on tests of intelligence, reasoning, and problem solving, although there are exceptions, particularly for younger WSc. At the same time, limitations in other areas, namely socioemotional difficulties, behavior problems, and restrictions in general ability and information, in particular, may impact WSs' ability to utilize their language potential. Additional areas of strength that may help to buttress WSs' language skills are discussed in later chapters. These may include their sociability, face recognition, empathy, musicality, curiosity, and certain types of memory processing. Likewise, the mechanisms involved in WSs' language proficiencies and deficiencies are related to other domains (notably, neurobiology), and there are multiple socioemotional, communicative, and educational aspects of language. Language does not exist in a vacuum.

Furthermore, the constellation of language skills and problems seems unique to WS. Although other groups may exhibit some of the language characteristics of WSs, these usually involve a few elements, not the entire configuration of language strengths and weaknesses of WSs. For example, most WSs progress beyond many other groups with comparable language delay in their subsequent level of achievement in areas such as vocabulary, figurative speech, syntactic complexity, articulation and prosody, narration and discourse, and the feeling functions of language pragmatics.

Finally, the vital role of numerous factors, such as age level, individual and subject sample differences, the criteria used for evaluating performance such as the characteristics of the comparison group, type of test, and test demands should be carefully considered in drawing conclusions about the level of WSs' language skills. It is also important to point out that there is a clear disparity between clinically based, phenomenological impressions of remarkable language skills and empirical findings of nonremarkable language test performance, such as failure to obtain a syntactic advantage of WSs over matched MA controls, MRc, or normal children. Indeed, researchers have sometimes remarked that they themselves are surprised that their WS data do not reveal higher scores that would be more in keeping with their own expectations.

Possibly, there is a "halo" effect involved in personally conversing with WSs due to their relatively sophisticated vocabulary, use of fairly complex syntactic structures, social orientation, ingratiating manner, and use of expressive devices. It is also possible that formal language tests may underestimate WSs' actual knowledge due to the tests themselves, the testing situation, or WSs' test-taking difficulties (e.g., word-finding problems). In any event, interventions for many of the language limitations of WSs should be considered as a worthwhile effort in order to strengthen an area with the potential for greater strength.

3

Intervention Approaches
for Language Problems

This chapter presents intervention approaches designed to maximize the language skills and help manage the language problems of WSs. Drawing on clinical experience with the unusual language profile of WS, many intervention procedures are provided for each of the problem areas described in chapter 2.

I. OVERVIEW OF INTERVENTION APPROACHES

Because WS is characterized by language delay and a number of other language problems, speech language therapy (SLT) is recommended for virtually all children with WS (Levine, 1993; Morris et al., 1988; Scheiber, 2000). Earlier parent surveys indicate that between 53% and 73% of WSc receive treatment (Gosch & Pankau, 1996a; Tharp, 1986). More recent surveys report that 100% of WSc have been referred to speech and language services (Grejtak, 1996c).

Speech language therapists (SLTs) occupy a key position in providing interventions for language-related problems. In contrast to the usual practice of providing therapy first to individuals who are most impaired, WSs with better language skills may benefit as much, if not more, than those who are severely impaired. Besides trying to remediate specific language problems and develop language skills, SLTs can help WSs use language as a tool to strengthen their performance in other areas. Parents, teachers, other specialists, and individuals involved with WSc may also play a role in the interventions recommended by SLTs.

Within the intervention process, SLTs generally serve five essential functions: assessment of language abilities, formulation of intervention plans, administration of treatment, supervision of others, and monitoring the intervention program. They may also provide demonstration lessons for classroom teachers, speech educators, and others, as well as diagnostic teaching when appropriate.

A. Assessment of Language Abilities

Because of the marked variability of WSs and the importance of language, the language abilities of WSs should be assessed by a qualified professional. Intensive evaluation of language skills and other abilities is important in designing an effective treatment program and establishing individual educational plans (IEPs), and in making decisions about school placement (Foreman, cf. WSA National Newsletter, 1991 Summer, p. 10).

Assessment may include examining WSs' abilities in semantics, syntax, pragmatics, discourse, and narration, as well as articulation, voice quality, and fluency. Formal tests are usually administered. Some language tests are comprehensive, others focus on a particular aspect of language functioning.[4]

But, formal tests alone are insufficient partly because they often fail to detect some of the distinctive capabilities and problems of WSs' language, such as storytelling skills or problems with compulsive greeting behavior. Tests may also underestimate WSs' language competence because of confounding factors, such as their difficulty with visual-spatial-motor tasks,

---

[4]Many kinds of language tests may be appropriate for WSs. These may include the CELF-R (Semel, Wiig, & Secord, 1987) to evaluate the overall syntactic and memory comprehension skills of WSs, the Clinical Evaluation of Language Fundamentals–Preschool (CELF-P, Wiig, Secord, & Semel, 1992) to measure semantics, grammar, and phonology in WSc, and the Test of Early Language Development (Hresko, Reid & Hammill, 1981) for subtests involving grammar, semantics, syntax and phonology.

In addition, the Token Test for Children (DiSimoni, 1978) assesses various aspects of language comprehension. The Boehm Test of Basic Concepts–Preschool Version (BTBC-PV) (Boehm, 1986a) or Revised (BTBC-R) (Boehm, 1986b) may be particularly useful for younger WS children. The Test of Auditory Comprehension of Language–Revised (Carrow-Woolfolk, 1985) may be used for all ages.

Vocabulary tests like the WORD Test (Jargensen, Barrett, Huisingh, & Zachman, 1981) and the Peabody Picture Vocabulary Test-Revised (Dunn & Dunn, 1981) are useful, as are tests for assessment of auditory discrimination skills: Wepman's Auditory Discrimination Test (2nd ed.; Wepman, 1987); the Goldman–Fristoe–Woodcock Auditory Skills Test Battery (Woodcock, 1976), the Screening Test of Auditory Perception (STAP; Kimmell & Wahl, 1981), and the Staggered Spondaic Word Test (SSW; Katz, 1962) for auditory dysfunction. Word-finding skills and disorders may be assessed with the Test of Word Finding (German, 1989), and narrative skills may be checked with the Bus Story Language Test (Renfrew, 1994).

word-finding problems, lack of familiarity with test content, test anxiety, behavior problems like distractibility, and the rigidity of standard scoring procedures.

Other important sources of information include interviews with parents, teachers, and the WS individual, as well as collecting a language sample from the WS, and observing the individual in the classroom or other group context. General information about Williams syndrome and information about the specific individual—strengths, weaknesses, cognitive abilities, areas of interest, and optimal methods of reinforcement—can facilitate program planning and treatment.

An initial period of diagnostic teaching may also be helpful in determining the individual's level of language functioning and target areas for intervention.

B. Types of Intervention Approaches

Intervention strategies should be designed to meet the needs of the individual WS. Flexibility should be used in deciding whether to sequence treatment according to the normal developmental pattern of acquisition (i.e., developmental model) or target specific problems or language functions for intervention (i.e., remedial model) (Rosenberg & Abbeduto, 1993). Research indicates that WSc typically exhibit irregular acquisition, such as an extended period of delay followed by a normal rate of language development (Singer-Harris et al., 1997).

As for type of intervention, WSs usually benefit from a four-pronged approach of structured therapy, mediational strategies, naturalistic approaches, and control mechanisms. In many cases, individual therapy may be better suited for the early stages of language acquisition, and group therapy for more advanced forms of treatment like the pragmatics of language (Friel-Patti & Lougeay-Mottinger, 1994).

Table 3.1 provides a summary description of the four approaches of intervention suggested for WSs. This is followed by a short discussion of each approach.

Structured Therapy

Due to cognitive limitations, most WSs respond best to specific training and guided learning experiences. Learning may be facilitated by using an appropriate mode of input (i.e., auditory, visual, or tactile-kinesthetic) and mode of output (i.e., oral or forced choice response). Comprehension may be facilitated by integrating the material to be presented in an organized way, interpreting it so that its significance is understood, and internalizing

TABLE 3.1
Language Intervention Approaches for WSs

Intervention Approach	Application
Structured Therapy	Adjust input and output mode
	Organize, interpret, and mediate material
Mediational Strategies	Use labeling, rehearsal, demonstration, dramatization, and self-instruction where applicable
Naturalistic Approaches	Devise naturalistic settings to evoke target language structures and functional activities to stimulate language usage
	Provide verbal feedback
Control Mechanisms	Use appropriate forms of reinforcement, direct instruction, and rechanneling strategies to motivate performance and redirect difficult or deficient behaviors

it through the application of mediation strategies. Where appropriate, formal language programs can provide structured instructional material.

Mediational Strategies

Mediational strategies may be used to help most WSs with adequate language skills to understand the input that is being presented, the output being trained and, most importantly, the relation between input and output. Mediational strategies may also assist with problems of following directions, comprehension of abstract concepts, and application of self-help procedures. Aside from verbal labeling, the strategies include rehearsal, demonstration, and self-instructional techniques.

Rehearsal Techniques. Effective rehearsal of language and other desired behavior usually involves having the WS individual engage in three successive steps: immediate reproduction of input; repetition of the reproduction, first aloud then silently; and reiteration of input to another person or surrogate at some later time (Semel & Rosner, 1991a, 1991b).

Demonstration Techniques. Alternative forms of demonstration include modeling, role-play, scenarios, vignettes, and videotaping of responses. Storytelling, playacting, and puppetry can also help to dramatize the difference between appropriate and inappropriate forms of language and behavior. Essential elements include concrete depiction of target responses, differentiation of correct and incorrect modes of response, and discussion of the difference.

Self-Instructional Techniques. Some WSs can be taught to self-administer verbal routines, such as self-instruction, self-reinforcement, and self-monitoring. Such training must be situation specific, administered step by step, explained thoroughly, practiced repeatedly, and its benefits made very clear.

Naturalistic Approaches

Naturalistic settings can provide a realistic milieu for language interaction, a wide range of language models, and spontaneity and flexibility in language usage. It also allows for greater generalizability of language learning than formal, structured instruction (Rosenberg & Abbeduto, 1993).

For most WSs, naturalistic applications may be used in three ways: to provide an environmental context for eliciting language forms in need of practice; to draw on functional activities, like household tasks or games, that provide a context for language usage and learning; and to provide the opportunity to use language feedback strategies, such as "acknowledging" (what the WS individual is saying), "expanding" (what is in need of correction), and "commenting" (on what is said) (McDade & Varnedoe, 1994).

Control Mechanisms

In many situations, WSs require direct instruction or rechanneling strategies to guide their behavior. Regardless of type of intervention or language problem, most WSs require reinforcement for their efforts. For most WSc, a verbal-social response, like "good talking!", "great!", or a nod or smile may be all that is needed, and it is often truly deserved. Socially based rewards, like the opportunity to talk with people, spend time with the teacher, sit next to the bus driver, or other nonverbal cues like a smile, nod, or approving gesture are also highly valued. Stickers of smiling faces and materials related to the WSc's topic of special interest (e.g., books, pictures, or sample items like flags or coins) may be effective, but other concrete material rewards—like candy, prizes, or tokens—generally have less incentive power. Taking WSc out to buy candy and sitting with them often has higher reward value than the candy itself. In this respect, WSc differ from children with many other forms of developmental disability.

Reinforcement should be administered immediately after the response and directed clearly to the WSc. A partially correct response, cooperative spirit, or overall progress may be noted and used to justify some type of reinforcement.

C. Participation of Parents, Teachers, and Others

Besides providing assessment and treatment of language problems, SLTs can serve a critical function by encouraging, advising, and supervising the intervention efforts of parents, teachers, and others.

At the same time, parents and teachers can play an active role by providing important information about the language abilities and difficulties, the environment, and other relevant characteristics of the WS individual. Ability to learn the words of a song, remember a list of words, categorize subordinates and superordinates, or engage in discourse and storytelling are skills of interest.

Parents and teachers can also participate in the therapy process by serving as models for language learning and providing WSs with opportunities to practice their emerging skills in real situations. It is important for them to administer appropriate forms of intervention and use effective methods of language feedback, such as acknowledgment, expansions, and comments. Many intervention strategies suggested for use by parents, teachers, and others are adaptations of those used by SLTs.

Finally, the SLT should monitor WS progress, making changes as needed in the intervention plan after conferring with others involved with the WS.

D. Application of Interventions

In the following sections, the four intervention approaches are applied to the six major language problem areas of WSs by SLTs. The problem areas include language delay, speech and voice, semantics, syntax, language pragmatics, and discourse and narration.

II. INTERVENTIONS FOR PROBLEMS OF LANGUAGE DELAY

Early language delay is typical of most WSc, but for some the delay may be more extensive. A few appear to be "nonverbal" in that speech is lacking or severely limited. Each type of language delay has its own treatment approaches.

A. Early Language Delay

In cases where WSc lag more than $1\frac{1}{2}$ to 2 years behind the typical age of 1 year for first words, 2 years for full sentences, professional assistance should be sought. By the age of 24 months, it is possible to determine whether or not a child is significantly slow in developing expressive language (Paul, 1996).

Oral-Motor Problems and Treatment. Some WS infants exhibit severe oral-motor problems that interfere with their feeding behavior and speech and language development. The muscles and structures involved in speech and voice production are the same as those used in chewing, sucking, and swallowing. WSc who have serious difficulty eating should be referred to a speech language pathologist (SLT) or an experienced occupational therapist with sensory integration (SI) or neurodevelopmental training (NDT) for assessment of oral-motor functioning. Assessment should include examination of the oral structures and interviews with parents about the child's eating behaviors (Wolery & Smith, 1989, pp. 458–464). Formal tests are available for assessing prespeech behaviors and feeding behaviors (Wolery & Smith, 1989).

A speech language therapist may work with an experienced occupational therapist to provide prespeech/feeding training for infants with severe oral-motor problems, tactile defensiveness around the mouth, and language delay with prespeech/feeding training (Meyerson & Frank, 1987; Udwin & Yule, 1988; Ward, 1994). For information about oral-motor problems, see Section III, "Speech and Voice" (also see chap. 4).

B. Facilitation of Language Learning

Most WSc with early language delay are observed to proceed through three stages of language development: beginning, intermediate, and advanced. Three corresponding levels of language stimulation are recommended to help them acquire language.

Beginning Level

The beginning level is designed for language-delayed WS children who are just beginning to talk. At the pre-speech level, interventions feature skills like learning to respond to one's name, point to objects, and repeat the naming of objects (Scheiber, 2000). Other training includes teaching the child to follow directions, basic concepts, and vocabulary (Cole & Cole, 1989).

Structured Therapy. Production of basic names and labels should be taught first: "mama," "dada," WSc's own name, names of siblings, caretakers, and so on. In teaching the labels for objects, the SLT, parent, or other adult first establishes whether the WSc is familiar with the target stimulus, like a truck or car. If not, the adult should provide opportunities for the WSc to explore and manipulate the object. Then, it may be presented along with its name.

In interactive chaining, question–answer dialogues are used to encourage WSc to attend to target stimuli and compare their features. For example, the SLT says: "This is a cat." "This is a dog." (Points to the dog) "Is this the cat?" "Where is the cat?" "Show me the cat." "Show me the dog."

At first, the adult requests nonverbal responses, such as pointing, showing, or giving. Most young children point to things they want when they are not yet able to use words, whereas WSc tend to be delayed in finger-pointing (Mervis & Bertrand, 1997; Scheiber, 2000). The adult provides training by pointing to objects and producing their names (Scheiber, 2000; Udwin & Yule, 1998b). "Yes–No" responses may precede WSc's use of one-word responses.

Mediational Strategies. Many WSc have a predilection to imitate speech, especially socially oriented speech and phrases. Songs may also help WSc to acquire words (Scheiber, 2000). At the pre-sentence stage, WSc may be asked to repeat a model of the target structure, word, or sentence. Allowing WSc to play with objects they accurately name can aid the learning process (Udwin & Yule, 1998b). Adults can provide models of correct speech (Scheiber, 2000).

Repetition can aid memorization. If the WSc's response is not totally correct, some part of it may still qualify for reinforcement.

Naturalistic Approaches. Combining object labeling and concrete inter action within realistic contexts may help WSc acquire early language and inspire vocabulary building. For example, a target item can be presented or demonstrated while saying its name within a sentence frame. Once object names are acquired, then object properties may be specified and learned.

It is important for the adult to speak slowly, clearly, and enthusiastically, and to establish eye contact with the WSc while referring to a target item or event. Repetition of the naming routine of labeling, looking, and showing is often necessary.

Intermediate Level

At the intermediate level, comprehension of basic concepts, use of vocabulary, and simple linguistic structure are emerging. Language may be stimulated by asking questions and giving simple verbal directions (Udwin & Yule, 1998b).

The semantic aspects of target structures may be introduced through use of the following techniques: classification, absurdities, sentence completion, or response formulation.

Classification. As the lexicon is expanded into a larger repertoire of words for objects and actions, the WSc learns to make finer distinctions between objects and ideas. Classification tasks may involve item grouping, category identification, naming of category members, and establishing subordinate and superordinate relations.

For many WSc, classification tasks are an area of language and cognitive strength.

Absurdities. Absurdities take advantage of the often reported good sense of humor of WSc by adding a bit of levity to lessons. This is done by asking WSc to resolve inconsistencies in absurd agent–action–object relations and suggesting choices for the correct answer (Scheiber, 2000; CLIP-Semantic Worksheets, Semel & Wiig, 1991).

For example, the WSc can be asked: "Do cats bark?" "Do trucks sleep?", or "Can you sit on a book?" "Can you read a chair?"

Detection of phonological absurdities can also be included, such as pointing to a cat and asking "Is this a 'cat' or a 'cap'?" This can help WSc become aware of finer auditory distinctions in a humorous, "nondrill" manner.

Sentence Completion. Sentence completion tasks require children to insert an omitted word at the end of a sentence. For example: "This says meow. It is a ____(cat)." "This says bow-wow. It is a ____(dog)."

If the response is incorrect, totally or partly, the error should be noted, then a model of the correct response provided and efforts made to elicit it from the WS youngster through the use of language facilitation cues. For example, the therapist could say "This is not a cat, it says 'bow-wow,' it's a 'd...o...g,'" where the sound *d* is said slowly as a hint to the WSc. Learning to integrate the segmented sounds is a useful skill.

Response Formulation. As the WSc's communication competence increases, use of cues is phased out. In response formulation, the SLT/instructor provides a series of informational statements and asks the WSc to restate and expand the information. For example, the adult says: "A car has wheels. A car has seats. A car has a steering wheel. You can go for a ride in a car. You can sit in a car." Then the adult says, "Tell me about cars."

Alternatively, the adult may pose eliciting kinds of questions. Gradually, the WSc is encouraged to increase utterance length and structure, from two-word sentences like "car go," "bye bye car," and "daddy car," to three-word sentences like "car go ride," "ride in car," "go bye bye car," to short simple sentences like "we ride in a car." Provide a model for correct speech (Scheiber, 2000). After developing target structures with supportive cues, the WSc can be asked to formulate words, sentence structures, or concepts independently.

Naturalistic approaches may also be used to elicit language and help WSc incorporate the target structures and concepts into their daily language usage (see examples of practical activities later).

Advanced Level

Interventions at the advanced level provide additional opportunities for WSs to practice linguistic structures and vocabulary items they do not use spontaneously. They also assist with higher language functions that are usually difficult for WSs, such as certain forms of language pragmatics, types of semantic concepts, and syntactic and morphosyntactic forms. Interventions for other language areas are included within each area.

Naturalistic Approaches. The WSc's acquisition of language concepts and conversational rules may be stimulated by providing structured language experience within the context of everyday activities. Such activities may also serve socioemotional functions by providing opportunities for social interaction and bolstering the WSc's self-esteem through tangible accomplishment.

Various types of activities may be used, such as cooking and kitchen tasks games, telephoning, TV "reporting," and making conversation at mealtime (Scheiber, 2000; CLIP-Preschool, Semel & Wiig, 1997). Selection of activity may depend on the family situation.

Kitchen activities provide an example of how practical activities may aid in learning language concepts and terms, such as the names of specific kinds of foods (e.g., "cookie") and food classes (e.g., "desserts"), basic terms of weights and measurements (e.g., cups, pints), geometric shapes (e.g., "round" or "square" pan), actions (e.g., "cut," "pour"), and properties of objects and substances (e.g., "hard," "sweet"). This may also provide practice in following directions, see CLIP-Preschool (Semel & Wiig, 1997).

Prolonged Language Delay

For WSs who remain at the early levels of language acquisition, able to speak, but with difficulty, formal speech language therapy should be continued throughout childhood along with other measures of early intervention and/or alternative methods of communication.

C. Interventions for Nonverbal WSs

Although most WSc are able to overcome initial language delays and difficulties, occasionally spoken communication remains a significant problem for a few. Those who are severely language delayed and do not progress through the stages of development described earlier should not be allowed to continue slipping behind. They usually respond well when treated as "severely language impaired" by SLTs. Some may be diagnosed as having dual disorders, autism, a pervasive developmental disorder involving social and language aberrations, as well as WS (see chap. 6). Two approaches may be helpful in treating nonverbal WSs: a modified version of a program of behavior modification and alternative modes of "total communication."

Behavior Modification Programs

Behavior modification programs usually combine structured reinforcement with modeling, shaped imitation, and controlled language responses. This approach entails consulting a professional, behaviorally trained SLT, psychologist, early childhood specialist, or special educator for clinical evaluation, program planning, administration of treatment, monitoring of treatment, and treatment supervision.

Target behaviors are identified and reinforcements that are meaningful to the WSc are selected. Reinforcements are administered to the child either immediately after each target response according to a predetermined schedule, or after the child has accumulated a predetermined number of reinforcers (e.g., smiling face stickers) or tokens if a token economy is established. The conditions for reinforcement are communicated to the participant and performance is tracked.

This technique has several advantages. It may be applicable to children who have little or no verbal skills or children unreachable by other means. It may be programmed so that the child is rewarded for making successive approximations of the target response. It often serves best WSs who are autistic or have autistic tendencies.

Its disadvantages are the preprogrammed, inflexible, and nonadaptive nature of the typical treatment plan. It may be difficult to identify specific target behaviors or decide whether a certain response has particular characteristics. There may be problems in selecting appropriate types of rewards or tokens, deciding on an optimal schedule of reinforcement, and adhering to that schedule. Use of tokens may be too difficult and abstract for younger, language delayed WSc who have cognitive problems. Also, tracking all aspects of the program may be tedious, and arranging for implementation of the program in multiple settings (e.g., school, home, day care) can be difficult at best, sometimes impossible.

Most importantly, many WSc do not respond well to behavior modification programs. In this respect, they differ markedly from children with autism and attention deficit hyperactivity disorder (ADHD) for whom behavioral modification programs are "very effective in the short term and, in the long term, may be more effective than drug treatment in controlling impulsivity, interpersonal behavior (including self-control skills), as well as academic performance" (Schoenbrodt & Smith, 1995, p. 27).

Alternative Forms of Communication

For WSc who are nonverbal or extremely delayed, alternative forms of communication—such as gesturing, signing, total communication (signing combined with speech), other communication systems, and communication boards—may offer a viable option or treatment of choice (Scheiber, 2000; Udwin & Yule, 1998b).

Total communication and/or sign language may be especially effective in cases where structured reinforcement and adapted behavior modification programs are unsuccessful. Combining signing with speaking (total communication) appears to help some WSc with severe language delay to "break the code," that is, to make the necessary connection between "words" (i.e., vocal sounds) and real objects, actions, events, and feelings. This can lead to better use of oral language. In a small number of cases, total communication may serve as an alternative to speech throughout childhood.

In the most severe cases, augmented speech materials, language picture boards, and computer touch windows are useful aids when all other measures fail. Picture boards contain arrays that depict common objects such as "bread" and "milk," as well as action sequences such as "go to store." Inarticulate children are able to communicate their needs, wishes, or feeling states by pointing to or selecting the appropriate picture(s). Technological devices, such as the Touchtalker system, have been effectively used by at least one young nonverbal WS child who was unable to use sign language (WSA Newsletter, 1991, Summer, pp. 24–25). Suitably designed computer programs have proven to be successful aids for some WSc with very limited verbal abilities.

Children with other handicapping conditions have benefited from use of language picture boards and signing or the combination of the two during the early childhood years. There are reports that very young nonverbal children with Fragile X syndrome are able to use signs as cues for grammatical morphemes when the child begins to acquire these forms (Schoenbrodt & Smith, 1995, pp. 85–86).

III. TREATMENT OF SPEECH AND VOICE PROBLEMS

A sine quo non for easy speech production and being easily understood is clear articulation and fluent speech. Without such skills, the language potential of WSs is markedly weakened. Fortunately, articulation and speech are generally spared, although problems sometimes occur. Articulatory disorders are relatively infrequent and often minor except for early problems with oral–motor functioning and widespread hoarseness. It is important to treat these problems in order to provide the opportunity for those affected to develop their other language skills.

A. Treatment of Oral–Motor Problems

The oral-motor problems of WSs require evaluation and often treatment administered by qualified SLTs or occupational therapists. SLTs who treat WSc report having to attend to their oral-motor problems before being able to elicit speech sounds (Ward, 1994). It should also be noted that low muscle tone in the tongue, lips, and cheeks may reduce speech intelligibility by decreasing the force and precision of articulatory contacts.

Assistance is often needed in feeding, including use of feeding tubes, to provide adequate nourishment in clinically acceptable ways. Parents often need to be cautioned to avoid tipping the child's head backward and dropping liquids or food into the child's mouth. They must also be told of the need to develop oral–motor skills because they are important in both speech production and functions related to eating (e.g., sucking, chewing, and swallowing). Many of the same mechanisms are used for eating and talking (Ward, 1994).

Some materials that may be useful for parents are: *An Approach to Pediatric Therapy* (Blanche, Botticelli, & Hallway, 1995); *Parent Articles About NDT* (Erhardt, 1999); *SI for Early Intervention* (Inamura, 1998); *An Introduction to Sensory Integration* (Arkwright, 1998); and *SenseAbilities* (Trott, Laurel, & Windeck, 1993).

B. Treatment of Problems of Articulation and Fluency

Articulation. The minority of WSc with articulatory problems can be treated with the same techniques as other individuals with these problems.

Some WSc exhibit problems of "cluttering," that is, disintegration of precise articulation during rapid speech. The following are examples of cluttering kinds of misarticulation: "cimamon" for "cinnamon," "nucular" for "nuclear," "condominiumumum" for "condominium," and "pasgetti" for "spaghetti." Although problems of cluttering are generally difficult to treat, several types of structured therapy may be tried with WSs.

One approach is elaborated echoing in which the SLT repeats the mispronounced word and says it correctly. This reassures WSc that they were understood and provides a verbal model for them to imitate. Later, variations of the modeled word may be introduced by changing its rate of presentation or pitch. A list of the misarticulations is helpful. Tape-recording both the mispronounced and correctly pronounced version of misarticulated words provides additional opportunities for WSc to imitate the correct model. It may also help them discriminate between correct and incorrect forms.

Alternatively, the SLT can model the correct version multimodally. A mirror may be used during language practice, particularly when the therapist and child are practicing words that are difficult to enunciate clearly. The WSc and therapist can look together in the mirror as they say the target word or the WSc's hand can be placed on the therapist's mouth or throat to feel the way the sounds are made. This allows WSc to both feel and see how sounds are formed. The sounds can then be imitated along with self-feedback. Using tactile or kinesthetic cues to supplement visual cues—that is, "motor kinesthesia"—is particularly helpful with WSc. In this way, they can learn that similar sounds require similar types of oral formation.

To provide practice, WSc can be asked to insert troublesome target words within preselected sentence frames or repeat sentences that contain the target words. Also, target forms can be carried over into naturalistic contexts by creating open language situations that require correct articulation of the target words.

Speech Fluency. When problems of speech rate are evident, the nature and severity of the disturbance and the child's reaction to it should determine the extent to which direct intervention is used. Often these problems can reflect difficulties in the area of language pragmatics or semantics, like problems with word finding or feature specification.

Sometimes, modification of the environmental factors that provoke or intensify the child's fluency problems is indicated. One may suspect that such factors could be operating if the WSc's fluency is good in some situations, inhibited in others. Consultation with a SLT may be useful in this situation. In other cases, establishing correct speech behaviors through modeling, shaping, and working to maintain them may be more appropriate (Scheiber, 2000).

Other Problems. A few WSs may have problems with stuttering, hearing loss, or tongue-tie that can affect their articulation, fluency, or rate of speech. When stuttering is present, a behavioral psychologist and speech therapist may be consulted and appropriate intervention strategies initiated. For WSs with hearing loss, use of a hearing aid is recommended when it is possible to deal with figure-ground problems arising from amplification of background, aversive sounds. Teaching of speech (lip) reading may also be effective. WSs are generally skilled at reading facial cues. They are often able to develop speech reading easily.

For tongue-tie, careful surgical cutting of the frenum (cord under the tongue) is recommended. With the physician's approval, this may be done as soon as possible after birth. When delayed until after speech is acquired, articulatory re-education is often necessary.

C. Treatment of Hoarseness

For problems involving a "hoarse, husky voice," voice therapy may be provided with the referral of a physician, in particular, an otolaryngologist (ear-nose-throat specialist). Sometimes, physicians prescribe a diet of "vocal rest," although hoarseness in WSc seems to have special properties (e.g., metallic harshness, deep quality, and occasional nasality) that distinguish it from typical hoarseness.

"Voice mirror" devices and other visual displays of voice qualities may prove useful in the treatment of vocal problems in WSc. In such cases, improving oral mobility, ear training, voice placement, and breath control may be helpful.

Hoarseness in WSs is best treated by a SLT who is trained in the specialized techniques required for voice management with other groups of children.

IV. INTERVENTIONS FOR PROBLEMS OF SEMANTICS

Whereas most WSs display relative strengths in their knowledge of word meaning and taxonomic categories, they tend to have problems with word finding, certain semantic relational terms, and some aspects of figurative language. These problems can be addressed with interventions appropriate for WSs.

A. Interventions for Word-Finding Problems

For problems of word-finding, SLTs can use structured therapy, formal instructional programs, mediational strategies, and control mechanisms.

Examples of WSs' imprecise use of vocabulary often pop up in conversation with them. Sometimes they seem to know a word intuitively but lack its more subtle features and accurate usage (Scheiber, 2000). Geschwind (1972) referred to this kind of word finding difficulty as "mild dysnomia."

Structured Therapy

As a first step, word knowledge must be assessed to determine whether WSs' difficulty involves word finding or their unfamiliarity with the word. Picture arrays may be used to test whether WSs are able to select the picture that matches the word named by the SLT. Asking WSs to label the pictures reveals whether they themselves are able to produce the word. Confrontation naming or rapid fire questioning should be avoided because it usually intensifies WSs' word-finding problems.

A good place to begin is by discussing the special interests of the individual WSc and encouraging more precise selection of words where warranted. Interventions designed to improve word recall may be used to provide practice and assist in identifying the particular words likely to cause problems. In applying the technique of sentence completion, the therapist provides the first part or stem of the sentence, like "I want to eat ___," for the WSc to complete (Wiig & Semel, 1984, pp. 271–274). Type of sentence frame and response specificity may be manipulated, for example: "You can put the book on ___," "You can ride on ___," "My favorite TV show/movie is ___," or "Winter is colder than ___."

In cases where WS word-finding problems reflect limitations in vocabulary, especially spatial, temporal, quantitative, or dimensional terms, techniques designed to facilitate the WSc's use of semantic relational terms are advised.

Formal Instructional Programs. Several types of published programs may be useful in treating WSs' word-finding difficulties. These include the *Word-Finding Intervention Program* (German, 1993), and the Clinical Language Intervention Program (CLIP; Semel & Wiig, 1982; CLIP-*Semantic Worksheets*, Semel & Wiig, 1991).

Mediational Strategies

In cases involving recall problems, WSc may be encouraged to employ repair strategies, such as use of appropriate cues (Levine, 1993; Wiig & Semel, 1984, pp. 263–267). These may include phonetic cues (e.g., "a br-, brush, no, comb"), rhyming cues ("kid," "hid"), phonemic cues (i.e., word starts with a certain letter, or sounds like "x") (Levine, 1973), visual imaginal cues (i.e., it looks like "x"), serial cues (e.g., Monday, Wednesday, no, Friday), and functional cues (i.e., it is used for "x"). Semantic association cues ("it's like a broom," it's a shovel) may be especially helpful. Sometimes retrieval may be aided by shadowing, that is, by echoing verbal input, or self-cueing by subvocally repeating the speaker's last words or question.

Control Mechanisms

Another approach is to try to reduce WSc's level of stress so it is easier for them to locate a target word. They can be encouraged to ask for additional time to respond (e.g., "Give me a minute," or "I'll have to work on that," or "That's a new one on me. I guess I'll have to look it up"). They may also ask the speaker to repeat what was said. Simply acknowledging not knowing an answer (e.g., "I really don't know the name of it," "Don't know—I've never seen one") can take some of the onus from being pressured to respond.

Both strategies, asking for extra time and admitting not knowing an answer, can ease word-finding problems that reflect difficulty in recalling or accessing a known word, as well as those involving limitations in vocabulary, especially spatial, time, and quantitative terms (Lucas, 1980, p. 178).

Judicious use of humor is another approach that is useful for reducing WSs' self-consciousness about their word-finding problems. For example, the SLT or other adult could analogize by relating the difficulty in finding a word to catching a butterfly with a net, dramatically pairing the "swishing" of the net with the catching of the word that got away. Many WSs appreciate humor that is literal, concrete, or slapstick, and enjoy "hamming it up" (Scheiber, 2000).

B. Interventions for Semantic Relational Problems

Inadequate knowledge of semantic relational terms may be addressed through the use of barrier tasks in structured therapy, formal instructional programs, and naturalistic uses of functional activities. These may be of help in the development of cognitive skills, like classification, as well other language skills.

Structured Therapy

The standard barrier task involves placing three to five or more items of special interest to WSc on a table in front of the individual, a duplicate set on the other side in front of an adult (i.e., speech therapist, parent or instructor), and a barrier in the middle of table so the child cannot see the other person's items or their placement.

Training may begin once it is determined that the WSc knows the names of the objects and understands the barrier task. In training spatial terms, for example, the therapist or instructor gives a spatial instruction to the WSc and performs the corresponding object placement, such as "Put the cat *under* the table." Then they view each other's display and the WSc is given feedback. Other spatial terms and opposites that may be administered include "up–down," "on–off," "over–under," "on–in–under," "above–below," "in front of–in back of."

If pretraining of contrastive concepts, such as "in–on," is required, then demonstration of the concept is best accomplished through the use of objects that may refer to both terms, like a table with a drawer or a box with a lid (Messick, 1994). Ordinarily, terms should be introduced in their usual order of acquisition, such as "in–on," "under–next to," then "back–front," except when a certain spatial term is particularly relevant for the WS individual. It may be appropriate to teach a child who is preoccupied with the lining up of objects the terms "front–back" at a relatively early stage. These instructional methods can accommodate other kinds of semantic relations (i.e., temporal, sequential, and inclusion concepts) by using terms like "before–after," "first–second," "all–some," and so on. Task difficulty may be adapted by varying the number of objects and their similarity.

As the WSc becomes familiar with the task, roles may be reversed so that the WSc instructs the SLT, parent, or instructor as to how to move the object(s).

Language Intervention Programs. Instructional programs provide another way to help WSc comprehend the subtle nuances of relational terms. Programs that focus on barrier tasks include *Make-it-Yourself Barrier Activities* (Schwartz & McKinley, 1987) and *Barrier Games for Better Communication* (Deal & Hanuscin, 1991). The *Clinical Language Intervention Program* (*CLIP-Semantic Worksheets*, Semel & Wiig, 1982) and *CLIP-Semantic Worksheets* (Semel & Wiig, 1991) to offer activities designed to improve WSs' expression and understanding of synonyms and antonyms as well as a variety of terms, including causal, temporal, spatial, quantity, and familial relationships. Another useful program featuring these terms is *Conversations with Conjunctions* (May, 1994).

Naturalistic Activities

Active participation in structured household activities can provide an ideal medium for strengthening WSs' language skills.

Kitchen Tasks. Relational concepts and terms may be objectified within the context of performing kitchen tasks. Showing the child that water becomes hot and boils when it is put on the stove can help the child acquire temporal, sequential, and causal concepts. For example, "*If* we heat water on the stove, *then* it boils." Similarly, using a recipe calls for a certain ordering of steps that may be verbalized as they are performed (CLIP-Preschool, Semel & Wiig, 1997).

Table Games. Likewise, simple board games may help WSc learn language concepts at home and at school. Spatial terms (e.g., "up–down," "across–in front of–behind," and "diagonal") are used in games like tic-tac-toe. In learning to play games, WSc usually require individual instruction taught slowly in a series of very small steps apart from the rest of the family or classmates.

C. Interventions for Problems of Figurative Language

Whereas many WSc are able to appreciate concrete metaphors, similes, and use them adequately (Bertrand et al., 1994a), WSc often have a tendency to overuse cliches and idioms. They may also profit from help in interpreting abstract forms of figurative language.

Structured Therapy. The SLT may assist in developing WSs' use of metaphors. For example, the therapist may present a metaphor (e.g., "My car is a lemon") and ask which of the following sentences conveys its meaning better: "My car tastes like a lemon," or "My car is sour like a lemon." Sometimes figurative language, like "she fell apart," needs to be explained. WSc tend to be very concrete in their use of words.

Overuse of cliches by WSc should also be monitored. Alternative ways of expressing the intended meaning may be suggested and practiced. This includes withholding the cliche or other response until an appropriate word or sentence can be produced.

Intervention activities to help improve the comprehension and use of figurative language by WS individuals may be found in CLIP (Semel & Wiig, 1982) and the *CLIP-Semantic Worksheets* (Semel & Wiig, 1991). Other intervention programs include *Saying One Thing, Meaning Another* (Spector, 1997), *Cartoon Cut-Ups* (Hamersky, 1995), and *Figurative Language* (Gorman-Gard, 1992).

Finally, it should be noted that although the focus here is on the problems in semantics faced by many WS individuals, their semantic abilities in other areas such as vocabulary, taxonomic categories, creative use of words and analogies, and appreciation of semantic associations should not be overlooked (see Table 2.1, p. 36). These abilities underlie or contribute to the efficacy of many of the intervention approaches suggested for dealing with their difficulties in this (semantics) and other areas.

V. INTERVENTIONS FOR PROBLEMS OF SYNTAX

Although many WSs become syntactically adept by late childhood, they are usually deficient when compared to normal age-mates and vulnerable to certain morphosyntactic problems. Some of their syntactic problems are relatively minor, while others may undermine conversational flow, informational exchange, and test performance. Some children pick up grammar like sponges, others are stumped by verb uses and other grammatical rules (Scheiber, 2000).

One way of addressing these kinds of problems is to include syntax in WSs' treatment programs. Proper use of syntactic constructions may be assisted through the use of structured therapy (Scheiber, 2000) and naturalistic, step-by-step applications of that therapy.

Typical problem areas include pronominalization or using personal pronouns correctly, wh-questions, inflections (e.g., plural nouns, past tense verbs), and complex sentence forms (i.e., compound and embedded sentences). Many interventions used with other children are applicable to treating WSs' problems with syntax.

In group intervention programs, WSs can sometimes serve as models to children with more severe syntactic problems who need help in learning how to express their basic needs and ideas. This can help to boost WSs' self-image and provide additional reinforcement for their treatment efforts.

A. Interventions for Pronominalization

Failure to use the correct forms of personal pronouns violates grammatical rules and may disrupt the flow of speech (Bellugi, Marks et al., 1988). This can make it difficult to follow what a WSc is trying to say in a sentence like: "John hit Susie real hard and then . . . he [she] cry and told her mother that she [he] hit her."

In treating WSs' pronoun problems, it is generally advisable to introduce personal pronouns in the order used for learning disabled children (Wiig & Semel, 1984, pp. 226–228)—that is, first, singular pronouns agents (i.e., "I," "you," "he," "she"), then plural agent pronouns (i.e., "we," "they"), next pronouns as objects and possessives (i.e., "him," "his"), and so on.

Confusions of gender and number may be clarified by using props (e.g., dolls, puppets, and objects) in dramatic depiction of sentence structures. Pretraining WSc with the props and their names is often necessary. Once pretraining is completed, the WSc can be asked to participate in intervention activities by using props to enact actions. For example, the SLT says: "This is Mary. *She* picks up the book." [WS is asked to do it] "Mary gives the book to Larry. *He* gives *it* back to *her*. *She* puts *it* on the table." [WS does it] . . .

Usually a SLT's repertoire includes other ways of clarifying the use of personal pronouns. These may be supplemented by formal instructional programs, such as *CLIP-Syntax Worksheets* (Semel & Wiig, 1990b) and *CLIP–Morphology Worksheets* (Semel & Wiig, 1990a). In addition, WSs often have problems in understanding the rapid pronoun shifts that often take place in conversation (e.g., "It's the green one"). A useful intervention program for improvement in pronoun usage is *Syntax Modules: Pronoun* (Wilson & Fox, in press).

B. Interventions for Wh-Questions

Although most WSs are able to generate and comprehend many question forms, some may have particular difficulty with wh-questions (Scheiber, 2000; Semel, 1988). This can interfere with WSs' ability to converse, acquire information, and perform adequately in instructional, educational, and testing situations. SLTs can assist WSs with such problems in several ways.

Pretraining on the Concept of Questions. Some WSc may need to have the concept of "questions" explained, in other words, that questions are used to obtain information. Explanations may also be needed: For example, "People may ask you questions to find out what you want or more about your problem." Demonstrations of how to answer questions that begin with "wh" may be useful.

Identification of Wh Words. A prerequisite to answering wh-questions is knowing what kind of information is being requested. SLTs may help WSs distinguish between the various forms of wh-questions (i.e., "what," "when," "where," "which," "why," and "how"). This may be done by presenting referent statements and asking what type of wh word would be relevant in that context. For example, WSc could be asked whether the words "in the house" tell about "where" or "when," whether the word "tomorrow" tells about "where" or "when," and so on (Wiig & Semel, 1984, pp. 467–468).

Question Simplification. Another approach is to circumvent use of difficult wh forms through the use of question simplification (Semel, 1988; Wiig & Semel, 1984, pp. 468–469). That is, simply rephrasing a troublesome question by substituting the common carrier: "what + modifier." In fact, comprehension of wh-questions within school settings can be markedly improved by using this device, for example:

"who"	"*what* person"
"which"	"*what* name"
"where"	"*what* place"
"when"	"*what* time"
"how"	"in *what* way"
"why"	"*what* reason"
"whose"	"*what* person"

Question Elicitation. Practice with question forms may be provided by presenting scenarios or statements that the WS individual uses to request information. For example, the SLT or other adult can make a statement to which the WSc responds with a question:

"Please get my glasses for me." [Where are they?]
"Grandma's coming to visit." [When is she coming?]

The instructional program *Language Intervention Activities* (Semel, 1982a) provides additional activities that may help improve use of wh-questions.

Monitoring Wh Problems. In addition, SLTs, parents, teachers, and others can become aware of the way in which WSs respond when they cannot understand a question. They may react by saying "What?", "What did you say?", or "You want me to tell you the name of this?" Such statements can serve as cues to help identify the types of Wh-questions that may need paraphrasing (i.e., "what + modifier"). They may also be used to probe WSs' understanding by inquiring, "Did you understand the question?", or "What did I ask you?" Having WSs repeat what they thought was the question can provide clues about whether the question was understood.

Other programs dealing with intervention of wh-questions are: *Request* (Daly & McGlothlin, 2000) and *WH-Questions* (Collins & Cunningham, 1982).

In any case, WSs cannot be expected to answer questions they cannot comprehend. Determining whether this is so is a necessary prerequisite for any of these treatment options.

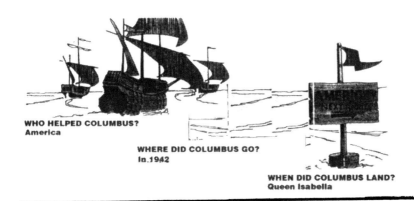

WHO HELPED COLUMBUS?
America

WHERE DID COLUMBUS GO?
In 1942

WHEN DID COLUMBUS LAND?
Queen Isabella

CHANGE	TO	
WHO	➔ WHAT PERSON?	➔ WHAT PERSON HELPED COLUMBUS? Queen Isabella
WHERE	➔ WHAT PLACE?	➔ WHAT PLACE DID COLUMBUS DISCOVER? America
WHEN	➔ WHAT TIME?	➔ WHAT YEAR DID COLUMBUS LAND? In 1492

C. Interventions for Morphosyntactic Problems

The morphosyntactic problems of WSs should be dealt with as needed. One useful, formal instructional program, *Syntax It Is* (Atkins, 1992), provides 12 amusing, illustrated stories that feature storytelling to address a variety of morphosyntactic problems. This is typically effective with older WSc.

Suggestions for dealing with specific morphosyntactic problems are described below.

Plurals and Past Tense. As a rule, overgeneralization of irregular noun plurals and past tense verbs are WS errors that may sound strange but they do not disrupt the communication process. It is apparent that the child is substituting a regular form for an irregular form and the listener can easily reinterpret "felled" to mean "fell" or "fallen."

Repeating and expanding the erroneous form is advisable, however, because it indicates that the listener understood the WS individual while providing a corrected, expanded model of the target form (e.g., "You say your 'feet' hurt"). This is an effective use of naturalistic techniques.

Verb Forms. A potential issue for intervention includes distinctions of duration and time in verb forms like the progressive (e.g., "walk-*ing*"), auxiliary (e.g., "*was* walking" or "*will* walk"), and modal ("*can* walk" or "*may* have walked").

In presenting such distinctions, use of concrete symbols like size or color cues can help to distinguish the tense forms of verbs, that is, actions taking place in the present versus the past or future. The irregular forms of past tense verbs and plural nouns may be illustrated pictorially (e.g., a boy who "fell" down, or a pair of "feet") and the accompanying speech sound printed in large letters next to the picture (e.g., "e" as in "egg" for "fell," "eee" as in "squeek"). Semantic associations may also be used to indicate the connection between target word and its pronunciation.

Comparatives and Prefixes. Interventions can include instruction on proper use of the comparative and superlative forms of adjectives (e.g., "small*er*," "big*gest*") and the meaning of prefixes (e.g., "*un*do, *re*do). Concrete techniques of depiction involving the use of objects, simple commands, and directed questions are best suited for WSs. See Wiig and Semel (1984, pp. 452–455), the CLIP-Syntax Worksheets (Semel & Wiig, 1990b), and the *CLIP-Morphology Worksheets* (Semel & Wiig, 1990a) for extensive intervention materials for dealing with comparatives and prefixes.

Prepositions. Confusions involving prepositions are directly related to difficulties with particular kinds of semantic relational terms, specifically, those denoting spatial, directional, and temporal relations. Treatment approaches are similar to those suggested for semantic relational terms (Wiig & Semel, 1984, pp. 220–222; *CLIP-Syntax Worksheets*, Semel & Wiig, 1990b; and *CLIP-Morphology Worksheets*, Semel & Wiig, 1990a). These references include demonstrations that use physical objects, actions, and verbal commands in structured therapy and naturalistic activities. Other materials and programs for the teaching of prepositions to WSs should be considered, for example, the *Flip Book for Individualizing Pronoun and Preposition Practices* (Hollingsworth, 2000) and *Making Sense with Syntax* (Krassowski, 1998). Other programs that may be useful are *Swim, Swam, Swum* (Wilson & Fox, 1998-R) and *CLIP-Syntax Worksheets* (Semel & Wiig, 1990b).

D. Interventions for Problems With Complex Sentences

In cases where difficulties in understanding and using compound and embedded sentences seriously impede performance, interventions may be employed.

Complex Sentences. Use of subordinating conjunctions, such as "because," "since" (i.e., cause–effect relations); "when," "after," "before," "until" (temporal relationships); and "although," "if" (conditional relationships) are often in need of therapy. A variety of interventions described in Wiig and Semel (1984, pp. 470–477) can be simplified and adapted to WSs. Improving WSs' use of subordinating conjunctions can have the added benefit of increasing their ability to draw conclusions, interpret analogies, make inferences, and produce summary statements.

Problems with comprehension of complex sentences may be addressed through analysis and synthesis of conjunction deletions. Practice in coordinating conjunctions with deletions can be provided by presenting a series of related sentences that the WSc is asked to interpret with help as needed, for example:

"The girl watched TV," "The girl came home," so, "The girl watched TV since she came home."
"The boy drank the water because he was very thirsty."

Additional practice can be provided by presenting incomplete sentences and having WSs select an appropriate conjunction ("and," "but," "or"). Materials such as *Connect a Card—Building Sentences with Conjunctions* (Fendall, 2000) and *Conversations with Conjunctions* (May, 1994) may be helpful.

Embeddings and Relative Clauses. Instruction in the use of complex sentences (relativization or embedded relative clauses, center-embedded or right-branched) may need to be greatly simplified for WSs. One technique is the resolution or analysis of complex sentences into their component parts or propositions (see Wiig & Semel, 1984, pp. 476–478; also Semel & Wiig, *CLIP-Syntax Worksheets,* 1990b).

E. Additional Techniques

Although the interventions described previously are almost exclusively structured therapy, the principles and applications may be adapted to the naturalistic approach. Within the ebb and flow of everyday conversation and activities, parents, teachers, and others can respond to WSs' spontaneous misuse of pronominalization, verb forms, or prepositions by asking for clarification and providing the appropriate form. Similarly, noncomprehension of wh-questions or complex sentences can be dealt with by responding with simplified, explanatory statements. This provides a good model of correct production, as well as assuring WSs that their statements are understood, although in need of correction.

Thus, both functional activities and language feedback can be applied to the typical problems that most WSs have with syntax. Other WSs who are more language impaired will require methods used for early language acquisition.

VI. INTERVENTIONS FOR IMPROVING LANGUAGE PRAGMATICS

Pragmatics refers to the use of language in real-life situations such as social conversation (Scheiber, 2000). It is by far the most difficult area of language for most WSs once they have progressed beyond the period of language delay. In many cases, unexpected strengths in language pragmatics are also revealed. This reflects partly the way in which their socioemotional and maladaptive behaviors impact the functional aspects of language pragmatics, namely, ritualizing, controlling, and feeling, and partly the way in which the cognitive limitations of many WSs influence the informing functions.

Interventions for the problems of language pragmatics listed in Table 2.3 are presented in the order presented earlier, except for deletion of three areas of relative strength. Because of the need for assistance in this area, interventions for pragmatic language use and social skills may be usefully included to become part of the WSc's individual educational profile (IEP; Scheiber, 2000).

A. Interventions for Problems With Ritualizing Functions

Inappropriate Greeting Behaviors

Most WSc need specific help in learning to refrain from greeting and conversing with almost every new person they meet. Simply asking WSs to stop behaving in this way is usually ineffective. This must be dealt with from both a language and behavioral perspective.

Mediational Strategies. Frequently, a prerequisite for dealing with inappropriate greeting behaviors is helping WSc become more aware of the social role differences of various kinds of people, such as strangers, acquaintances, service people, professionals, friends, and family members. Pointing out variations in people encountered in the street, school, restaurant, bus, or store can help to sensitize WSs to these distinctions.

Suitable forms of greeting can be modeled and imitated by WSc. This should begin with identification of those situations in which greeting behavior is appropriate. Then it may be extended to other contexts. Usually WSc need to be told to attend to and imitate the modeled speech and behavior. This must be explained before, during, and after the behavior is modeled.

Reenacting a situation like a greeting problem in the classroom or the neighborhood can provide the context to role-play alternative ways of communicating. Mock situations where compulsive greeting is inappropriate can be portrayed, videotaped, repeatedly watched by the WSc, and critiqued by both child and adult. Instructing WSc to act out various kinds of encounters in dramatic improvisation or with puppets can also be effective, especially if the behavior is depicted in an exaggerated and humorous fashion.

Predetermined signals or cues like the shake or nod of the head, or withdrawing an outstretched arm may be used to indicate whether a WS should use or withhold a certain behavior or form of speech modeling feedback. Considerable practice may be needed to shape greeting behavior (Scheiber, 2000; Semel & Rosner, 1991a, 1991b).

Training WSs to show self-restraint through use of "self-talk" is more difficult, although some WSs can be trained to do so. After determining that they understand that other people may become angry or disappointed when they call out a greeting to a stranger, WSs may be instructed to repeat to themselves: "I cannot speak up now. It will make (teacher/mother/others) angry."

Discussing why uncontrolled greeting behavior is inappropriate or disruptive is a necessary part of all mediational techniques. Appealing to WS's sense of fairness that not everyone can greet visitors may sometimes be effective. Discussion of the potentially dangerous consequences of unrestrained greeting behavior may be best postponed until the WS is older.

Control Mechanisms. Direct instruction is required when WSs feel compelled to speak to strangers in public places, the street or elevator, or to visitors in the classroom. In these and other situations, WSs need to be told emphatically that they must not approach and greet every person they encounter.

Inappropriate greeting behavior can sometimes be dealt with by giving WSs specific assignments for welcoming people. This procedure is called "rechanneling." In the classroom, WS students can be given the assignment of "official class greeter" in which they are permitted to greet people on a specified list but no others. Other roles WSs can assume include class historian or classroom host/hostess. This provides them with appropriate opportunities for them to greet others, but within specified limits.

Social pressure may be exerted by expressing how unhappy one becomes when the WS individual repeatedly engages in undesired behavior, like "getting out of your seat to say hello to everyone that comes into the classroom."

Correcting inappropriate greeting behavior is a difficult task requiring much repetition and practice. Do not underestimate the amount of effort it takes to improve this behavior. Intervention for greeting behaviors may be found in *CLIP-Pragmatics Worksheets* (Semel & Wiig, 1992a).

Inappropriate Requests for Attention

Uninhibited calling out in group situations, like a classroom, group meeting, or programmed event, is often inappropriate and disruptive to teachers and students alike. Like the compulsive greeting behavior of WSs, inappropriate calling out involves impulsivity and it can often be handled with control mechanisms and mediational strategies.

Control Mechanisms. At the most basic level, WSs can be told that this type of behavior is annoying or disturbing to others and it will not be tolerated. It is important for teachers and other adults to set definite limits and provide specific rules in an authoritative manner, for example:

"The rule here is that you must raise your hand before you talk out."
"Now it is my turn to talk and your turn to listen."
"I'll call on you if you hold that question until I'm finished."

Direct instruction may be necessary when the behavior occurs, such as:

"You're calling out. You need to think about your behavior. Go to the time-out table and think about it."

Mediational Strategies. Explaining why calling out is annoying can be particularly effective with some WSs. They may be told, for example, "I know you have lots of interesting things to say and good questions to ask, but we all can't talk at once. If everybody spoke at once, we would not be able to hear what anybody is saying. Only one person can talk at a time in this class."

Demonstration, dramatization, and discussion, as well as signals or cues, can be useful. In some cases, WSs can be helped to self-monitor their tendency to call out by engaging in "self-talk."

Formal Instructional Programs. Providing organized instruction in how to request attention in acceptable ways may be helpful. Worksheets illustrating alternative ways to call for attention are included in the pragmatics worksheets of CLIP (Semel & Wiig, 1992a).

Reinforcement. Whatever the mechanism, WSs should be promptly reinforced whenever they engage in appropriate behavior, like remembering to raise their hand to ask permission before speaking out. Being allowed specific time to talk is an important element when reinforcing WSs for curtailing their intense desire to call out.

B. Interventions for Problems With Informing Functions

Talkativeness

Often, problems of verbosity can be dealt with by identifying the factors involved, applying control mechanisms, and reducing related problems in the areas of topic relevance, turn-taking, and persistent questioning.

Analyzing and discussing situations under which WSs are able to curb excessive talk may help. Identifying the strategies and conditions under which the problem is exacerbated or reduced may provide insight into how this problem can be handled.

Direct measures for managing verbosity are often needed. Parents and teachers can provide specific time periods for listening to WSc (Levine, 1993) when they can "hold the floor." This can be an essential part of managing this problem.

Alternatively, daily periods of required silence can be imposed in which WSs must remain quiet and listen to others, for example, during storytelling or certain lessons. WSs usually need to receive direct, explicit instructions as to what times are inappropriate for talking. Friendly jibes, gestural, or verbal reminders may be used to persuade WSc to allow others to talk. It is important to reinforce WSs at times when they are appropriately quiet. A broad smile at the WS youngster can be particularly effective reinforcement.

Topic Relevance

WSs seem able to maintain a topic of conversation and make relevant comments under certain conditions. Whether or not the condition is right may depend on several factors, including the subject of the conversation, the person to whom they are speaking, the listener's response, the amount of noise in the auditory surround, and how determined the WS person is to talk. SLTs, educators, psychologists, and family members can work together to identify the circumstances and situations that affect each WS individual.

In addition, "off target responding" may reflect several types of difficulties. These may include not attending selectively to verbal input and its context, or poor identification of the common referent in a conversation or question–answer exchange (i.e., the people, objects, actions, locations, events and their relationship). Other factors may include poor understanding of the basic semantic relations needed to establish joint references (i.e., agent, action, object), and the nature of speaker–listener roles in conversation and question–answer exchange (Lucas, 1980, p. 167). WSc may also have difficulty recognizing that someone is trying to end a conversation and may overlook signals from others, such as looking around the room, shifting from foot to foot, or showing a facial expression of impatience or boredom (Scheiber, 2000).

Structured therapy is usually needed to help develop topic maintenance skills and awareness of a listener's desire to end a conversation. Many problems of topic relevance reflect WS difficulties in topic closure, that is, using semantic boundaries as cues for ending a topic or conversation. SLTs can help WSs become more aware of linguistic markers that indicate semantic boundaries and function as cues for the topic under discussion and what was said (Lucas, 1980).

Sample conversations can be presented and WSs may be asked to judge whether the speakers stayed on topic. Conversational starters may be used to introduce a topic to which WSs respond, such as "My favorite time in school is when ____." Use of carefully defined topics and close-ended questions can help WSs stay on target (Lucas, 1980, p. 68).

Role-playing or discussing a particular situation, such as preparing a meal or getting on a bus, may help generate topic-specific speech. Video and audio recordings of the conversation or role-playing exchange may be played and critiqued. Listening to paragraphs or sentences for an inappropriate word or phrase is also useful (Hoskins, 1996).

Alternatively, storytelling methods may be used to elicit integrated kinds of statements. In the sequence story task, for example, the SLT presents a series of pictures and asks WSs to tell a story about each picture. These statements can be shaped and judged in terms of their use of sequencing, semantic information, and appreciation of listening–speaking roles (Lucas, 1980, p. 168).

The SLT or other adult may also tell a story, which the WSc is then asked to retell. Stories may be real, imaginary, or a nonfiction account from a book. Language level and content should be appropriate and of interest to the WS individual. Also, roles may be reversed and the WS individual may be asked to tell a familiar story with specific instructions to avoid undue elaboration.

Monitoring, correcting, and constructively critiquing WS's rendition of a repeated or self-generated story are critical parts of this procedure. Excessive verbiage and story diversions must be pointed out. The WS individual should be asked whether these are related to the story, then told to repeat the story without adding superfluous items. Taping WS's statements, discussing ways to curtail excess verbiage, and retaping the new rendition can be very helpful.

SLTs and other adults may also pose structured questions about routine activities, like "What did you eat for lunch today?", and then evaluate the answers (see "Answering of Questions," p. 95). Narrow topics and closed questions, such as "How did you get here today?", can elicit statements to be monitored and corrected when the reply is excessively long, stumbled, or rambling (Lucas, 1980).

SLTs may also use reasoning to explain the need for topic relevance, such as saying, "When you're talking with someone, it is important to pay attention to what the other person says and to keep talking about the same thing. You can keep the conversation going longer by talking about the same topic. It is not a good idea to suddenly start talking about something else."

Supplementing these strategies with techniques such as taping, replaying, and critiquing a child's output in conversation, as well as role playing, storytelling, or teaching WSs to self-administer reminders (e.g., "Remember to stay on topic") may be particularly helpful. Useful intervention strategies may be found in Hoskins (1996).

Topic Perseveration

Topic persistence or talking endlessly about conversational topics of intense interest may occur in response to conversational or task demands that exceed the abilities of the WS individual (Lucas, 1980). Topical persistence may also serve as a way of gaining the attention of others.

A constructive way of dealing with the problem of topic persistence is re-ducing the complexity of task demands, that is, task management. Helping WSc expand their conversational repertoire and areas of interest is also ef-fective (Levine, 1993; Semel, 1988; Semel & Rosner, 1991b). Another approach is to limit the amount of time or provide specific time slots for WSs to talk about their favorite topics (Levine, 1993). Ignoring WSc's repetitious chatter about a particular topic is also recommended (Udwin & Yule, 1998b).

Alternatively, engaging in structured activities in naturalistic settings can provide a topic for conversation and help to reduce irrelevant chatter. Television, videotapes, or other media offer opportunities for WSs to report on items of interest that have a clear focus, such as sports events, educa-tional programs for children, news summaries, or weather reports. Oppor-tunities to display their language skills can also help WSs develop an im-proved self-image (Hoskins, 1996).

Daily reading aloud to WSc is an excellent way to develop their listening skills and provide interesting topics for conversation. Talk may have to be slowed down, information fed in short units, and distractions kept to a mini-mum. Such measures may help to overcome problems in tracking auditory information and following a course of thought.

Turn-Taking

Parents, teachers, and SLTs can help WSs deal with problems of medi-ational strategies and naturalistic approaches may be useful in dealing with WSs' problems of turn-taking often exhibited during conversational ex-change. Parents, teachers, and SLTs may also help with related problems of turn-yielding, trying to "hog the floor," or refusing to give up their turn.

Conversational skills may be enhanced by using natural situations, such as the dinner table or snack time, to help WSc acquire or sharpen some of the pragmatic skills necessary for two-way exchange. This includes limiting talk to one person speaking at a time, listening courteously to others, offer-ing and following directions, and conversational turn-taking/turn-yielding.

Providing concrete demonstrations of the problem behavior, appropri-ate modes of turn-taking/turn-yielding, and discussing the distinction is crit-ical. Sometimes, the reasons why poor turn-taking/turn-yielding behavior is unacceptable must be demonstrated and explained over and over again: It is rude, unfair, and confusing.

Modeling, role playing, puppetry, playacting, or improvisational dramati-zation are useful techniques. Hand puppets, which are easy to manipulate, can be made from old socks or paper bags. By adding a very large mouth or a very small mouth to each puppet, the stage is set for humorous enact-ment of turn-hogging, turn-waiting, and turn-yielding.

Concrete analogies can also help WSs understand the concept of turn-taking/turn-yielding. Explaining, for example, that conversation is like playing ball: Only one person can have the ball at a time, the ball is passed from one person (speaker) to the other (listener), turns are taken, and play stops when one player drops the ball, when it goes out of bounds, or when both players finish playing and put the ball away.

Answering of Questions

Difficulty in answering questions can reflect various problems. Diagnosing the source of the difficulty is the first step. Providing appropriate practice opportunities with the use of structured questions is another.

Input Problems. A precondition for being able to answer questions appropriately is being able to comprehend what is being asked. Sometimes WSs require assistance in distinguishing the various forms of wh-question words. Rephrasing the question into a "What" format can be helpful (see the earlier section, "Interventions for Problems of Syntax").

At other times, problems in understanding the semantics or meaning of the question may interfere. In such cases, WSs may stumble, not answer at all, or be "off target."

Ability to answer questions depends, too, on the WSs' level of information. If the WSs are unfamiliar with the subject of the question, they should be encouraged to simply admit that by saying, "I don't know that," or "I don't remember that right now." Many WSs will need to be told repeatedly that it is all right to respond in this way. Depending on the WS individual, self-instructional routines may be used as aids (e.g., "I must remember to say, 'I don't know' ").

In many cases, WSs are familiar and knowledgeable about the subject in question but they still may have difficulty giving an acceptable answer. Often they need assistance in learning how to process questions more efficiently by rehearsing the question to themselves, or asking the person to repeat part or all of the question.

Output Problems. At times, problems with word finding or retrieval undermine WSs' ability to answer appropriately in a reasonable time. WSs may stumble, go "off target," or use conversational distractors when they are unable to locate the answer they want (see the section, "Interventions for Problems of Semantics"). Similarly, question format or response mode may undermine WSs' ability to perform. Questions requiring long or sequenced answers may trigger irrelevant responses like changing the subject, using empty placeholders, or circumlocutions.

Some demands of answering questions may be reduced by presenting sentence frames and asking WSs to insert a target response in the frame. Rephrasing the question to permit a one word answer, use of forced choice methods, or nonverbal responding may be helpful.

In formal testing situations, use of conversational distractors—like changing the topic, flattering, or questioning the examiner—may indicate difficulty with question content, phrasing, or response mode. If possible, question type and response mode should be modified to accommodate these problems. Extensive cueing and "testing-of-limits" procedures may be used in posttest sessions to better determine WSs' ability limits.

Structured Questioning. Guided practice in the answering of questions can be provided by asking WSs to respond to questions about a recently presented story. Question type and difficulty can be adjusted to fit the needs of the individual and the material.

Factual questions, such as "Who-Did-What-When-Where-To Whom-How," address the essential elements: "Who was in the story?", "What happened to her?", and "Where did it happen?" This strategy may be applied to both single sentences and analysis of a paragraph or story. It often helps to improve comprehension.

Questions that ask about sequential events in the story, such as "What happened first?" or "What happened next?", may be more difficult to answer. Using a time line that indicates the beginning, middle, and end of the story may help WSs concretize the terms used in the question and formulate their response.

Temporal relations may be another area of difficulty in which focal, concrete questions may provide directed practice in question answering. For example: "When did he know 'X'?" or "Does the story tell about different times of the day?" If the WS individual seems confused, then part of the story may be read again and referred to a time line.

It is important to discuss cause and effect relations because they are often difficult for WSc to grasp. The following sample questions can be used to probe such relations: "What happened before 'X': event 'Y' or event 'Z'?"; "Was 'Y' the cause of what happened to 'X'?"; "Are there other things that happened in the story that may have caused 'X'?"

Evaluative or affective questions can personalize the story and make it more meaningful for the WS individual. Examples include: "Which of the characters did you like best in the story?", "How do you think the characters in the story felt about what happened?", "What would you do if this happened to you?"

Questions that contrast and compare events, characters, or significant items found in the story are also useful. The WS individual may be asked to indicate how certain aspects of the story (persons, objects, animals or locations, actions) are alike or different, and whether the story recalls a movie, television program, or another story. It is not unusual for WSs to refer to similar situations, use clever and original analogies, or concrete idioms and cliches that suggest some insight into the story. These should be reinforced.

Informational Exchange

Problems in providing and requesting information can undermine WSs' ability to communicate effectively in conversational and instructional settings. Focusing on specific speech acts that are likely to cause problems of informational exchange helps address these and related difficulties with topic maintenance. This includes asking for clarification or repetition of information, stating a problem, providing specific information, clarifying the reasons they agree or disagree, and explaining how to perform certain acts. Mediational strategies are well suited for these purposes.

Role playing and pretend play may help WSc use speech acts that are otherwise difficult for them, such as asking a fellow student for directions or clarification and repetition of information (Scheiber, 2000). Structured questioning, discussing, modeling, videotaping, and viewing exaggerated versions of inappropriate behaviors may also aid understanding.

Following Instructions.   Problems involved in following instructions for performing visuospatial constructive tasks (i.e., block building, drawing, or arts and crafts) may be addressed through the use of verbal mediational techniques. Talking the WS individual through each step in the process facilitates the process (see chap. 4, p. 157).

Broader problems in WSs' difficulty in following instructions are addressed in chapter 7, Section II, D, "Poor Adaptability." That section considers multiple, contributing factors to such problems: attentional difficulties, limitations in language and memory capacity, distractibility, uncooperativeness, rigidity, and so forth. Organized intervention in following directions may be found in computer programs, *Following Directions: Left and Right* (Semel, 1997), *Following Directions: One and Two Level Commands* (Semel, 1998), as well as in *Make-It-Yourself Barrier Activities* (Schwartz & McKinley, 1987).

C. Interventions for Problems With Controlling Functions

Because of the value that WSs place on social interaction, it is not surprising that they face various kinds of difficulty in the controlling functions of communication, that is, in influencing and being influenced by others. Intervention approaches for alleviating six types of problems are described next.

Persistent Questioning

The unusual intensity and persistence of WSs' patterns of questioning require special measures. Generally, the first step is to identify the problem.

Identifying the Problem. Because persistent questioning often relates to an anxiety-provoking situation, task, or upcoming event, the source of the anxiety should be ascertained and dealt with in the best possible way. The anxiety may arise from changes in plans or schedule, visits to the doctor or dentist, taking of tests, or being faced with difficult tasks. Suggestions concerning the way to handle such fears and anxieties are discussed in chapter 7, Section II, A.

Control Mechanisms. Many parents and teachers have found direct instruction to be effective in curbing persistent questioning. After having determined that the question had been answered satisfactorily and understood at least once before, limits are placed on the number of times the same question can be asked (Levine, 1993). WSc may be told: "Only one time per question, did you ask that question more than once?" "You just asked me that question. What did I tell you?" Simply ignoring repetitions of the same question is another approach (Udwin & Yule, 1998b).

Other strategies include changing the topic, distracting the WSc with other activities, turning the tables by asking the child the repeated question, or offering a social reward for a 5- or 10- minute period of silence (Levine, 1993).

Mediational Strategies. Dramatization techniques such as tape recording, videotaping, and role playing may help WSs realize how irritating incessant questioning can be to others.

In the long run, however, the most effective approach is teaching WSs self-instructional skills, even though this usually involves providing extensive training and practice opportunities (Semel & Rosner, 1991a, 1991b). Examples of such strategies may include: *self-reminders* (e.g., "They don't like me to do keep asking the same question over and over again. They stop talking to me if I do it, so I'd better stop repeating questions"); *self-monitoring* (e.g., "There I go again, asking the same question"); *self-replies*, or silently reminding himself/herself of the answer to the question (e.g., "They said we would leave right after lunch"); and *self-reinforcement* (e.g., "I didn't annoy them, I answered it myself").

Many WSs seem able to benefit from this type of training, providing those that can with increased flexibility and control.

Conversational Distractors

Changing the subject, talking about a favorite topic, making flattering remarks, and asking the other person questions are some of the ways in which WSs use conversational distractors to avoid difficult topics, tasks, or questions. Although sometimes successful, it is often counterproductive because it can discourage others from conversing with them. It can also interfere with attempts to assess their abilities and provide the help they need in coping with their difficulties.

The first step in dealing with use of conversational distractors is to recognize its occurrence and establish the reasons for its use. These can include WSs' desire to hide their shortcomings, avoid compliance with requests or task demands, bypass failure, or win favor from others.

With problems of task difficulty, efforts can be made to reduce task size and complexity. For example, a task may be divided into small, cumulative subtasks (see chap. 4, Section II, C). Pretraining on the task and use of substitute activities are other options.

Difficulty in answering questions may be addressed by applying interventions suggested for this problem. This includes determining the type of processing problem, providing structured practice in the answering of questions, and altering question type or response format.

Problems of topic difficulty may be dealt with by using SLT techniques, including structured questioning. Use of narrow, focused questions, in particular, may help get WSs back on track.

WSs can also be helped to become more aware of their use of conversational distractors by recalling conversations in which that occurred or using forms of dramatization, like puppetry, to demonstrate the problem. Videotaping and tape recordings may also be helpful.

Flattery and Personalization. Flattery and personalization are typical ways in which WSs seem to attempt to avoid dealing with topics, questions, assignments, or tasks. This can impede communication or be embarrassing to others. Flattering older people or people with status can be inappropriate.

In such cases, direct instruction is important. WSs can be told it is not nice or polite to say these kinds of things. Examples appropriate to this context should be cited. Intervention strategies related to giving and receiving compliments may be found in *Social Star* (Gajewski, Hirn, & Mayo, 1994).

Another approach is to explain that compliments sometimes make "X" feel embarrassed and that person does not know what to say. To help WSs understand the concept "embarrassed," reference can be made to situations in which the WS feels embarrassed or uncomfortable, like failing to perform or complete a task. The same types of direct instruction and reasoning techniques can be applied to situations in which WSs pose inappropriate personal questions to others.

Some WSc will have difficulty understanding the concept of something being too personal to be talked about, but they may be able to understand that people can feel uncomfortable when they do not know what to say.

Finally, SLTs, psychologists, parents, and teachers can use control mechanisms to curtail the overuse of distractors by directly instructing WSs to return to the main topic of conversation or point of questions. They can redirect irrelevant chatter by smiling and saying "I asked you ____," or asking direct, topic-related questions when WSs stray from the topic or use other conversational distractors, such as flattering the other person.

Direct and Indirect Requests

Because indirect requests are not always interpreted as requests, SLTs, parents, teachers, and others should monitor the appropriateness of WSs' reactions to such statements. If an indirect request is not understood as a request (e.g., "The pizza is good" may mean "I'd like some more pizza"), it should be rephrased as a direct statement or request that most WSs can comprehend.

Many WSs may benefit from having the concept of indirect requests explained, as well as practicing how to differentiate indirect from direct requests.

Accepting Restrictions

The concept of restrictions is often difficult for WSs to understand and accept. It is not uncommon for WSs to reject restrictions (i.e., warnings, prohibitions, and denials of permission) by reacting negatively, becoming agitated, or refusing to accept such restraints.

To address these problems, steps must be taken to clarify the concept and its application through a four-step process: explanation, illustration (examples), demonstrations, and discussion.

It is not appropriate to try to deal with WSs' difficulty in accepting restrictions at the time they are being warned, prohibited, or denied permission. More neutral times should be selected. This is also the type of issue where group SLT sessions are especially effective because children may become more aware of their own situation by listening to the problems and solutions of others.

Prohibitions and Warnings. WSs often need to be told to listen carefully when someone is trying to tell them about the importance of heeding warnings and prohibitions.

Example statements may be presented to determine whether the WS individual is able to understand these restrictions and why they should be imposed, for instance:

"Don't cross the street until the light is green."
"Stay right next to me. Don't wander away."

Role playing and discussing situations in which WSc are most likely to receive a warning is also helpful.

Denial of Permission. Similarly, the concept "denial of permission," may need to be clarified. In working with WSs, SLTs, teachers, and other adults may try to clarify this concept by saying something like: "Sometimes, even though you ask for permission very nicely, the answer can be no. . . . There are appropriate/good ways and inappropriate/bad ways to respond when you can't do something. Some ways are better than others."

SLTs and others may also help WSs understand this notion by providing examples of situations in which permission is denied, the reasons why it was denied, and alternative ways of responding. Discussion may be stimulated by referring to common situations involving requests to do something, go somewhere, ask for something like a toy or pet, borrow something like clothing, toys, books, or CDs. Dramatization and videotaping offer other possibilities for exploring this issue.

Avoidance of Responsibility

Consistent with their overwhelming desire to be "loved" and prized as a companion, WSs often have difficulty accepting responsibility or blame for their behaviors, as well as difficulty accepting and expressing criticism. Their feelings can be hurt very easily and they may be unwilling or unable to risk offending others. The four-step process of explanation, illustration, dramatization, and discussion can serve as an outline for addressing these problems.

Accepting Responsibility. The concept of responsibility should be personalized and explained, as should the range of options available in accepting or avoiding it. The SLT can set the scene by personalizing the concept of responsibility and explaining the range of options available in accepting or avoiding it, for example:

"When someone asks you to do something you can say you'll do it or you don't want to do it."

"You could upset someone or they could get angry with you if you are not polite when you tell them that you can't do something."

"Sometimes, you need to accept responsibility even though you don't like it."

Role playing and other mediational techniques may be used to depict situations in which the concept of avoiding responsibility applies, like doing chores or cleaning up their own materials. This includes posing hypothetical situations and scenarios. WSs may also be given alternative ways of responding and then asked to judge whether each indicates acceptance or avoidance of responsibility. Examples could include forgetting to brush your teeth, mail a letter, or take the dog for a walk; leaving the bird cage open; or some other rule-governed activities (see chap. 7). An intervention program that addresses issues of accepting responsibility may be found in *Social Star* (Book 3) (Gajewski et al., 1996).

Prompting, correction, discussion, and reinforcement should accompany and follow each response. Sometimes WSs can generate their own examples of times when they experienced such problems and alternative responses that could be employed.

Accepting Blame. In dealing with the concept of accepting blame, WSs may be told, in effect, that when one is blamed for engaging in wrongdoing, such as forgetting to do something important, or failing to follow rules or transgressing, it is advisable to accept the blame. Otherwise, guilt, anxiety, or a rift in relationships may result. WSs are usually very eager to avoid these consequences.

Explanation, illustration, demonstration, and discussion may be applied in this instance, too.

Accepting and Expressing Criticism. This is another area where WSs may benefit from structured therapy. It is helpful to explain the concept of criticism, in general, through the use of explanation, illustration, demonstration, and discussion.

WSs may also need to be cautioned that it is unwise to become angry when one is criticized because then "everyone becomes upset and no one feels good. . . . It's okay if your feelings are hurt a little, but you shouldn't let the criticism stop you from trying again."

Various ways of responding to criticism may be presented and WSs may be asked to judge which are better: running away, blaming others, changing the topic, refusing to try again, saying to oneself that the person was just trying to help, or trying again (Montague & Lund, 1991).

Role playing the receiving of criticism from teachers, parents, siblings, and peers can be very helpful. Hypothetical situations may provide the basis of valuable discussions, for example, "Georgia was working on her homework when her brother walked by and said, 'That's not how you do it! Don't you know how to do it right?' How could she react? What could she do?"

As with other types of problems, a combination of approaches may be required. The SLT, parent, teacher, or other specialist may provide vignettes and topics of discussion that are applicable to the particular WS individual. Naturalistic settings are especially well suited for dealing with the controlling functions of language pragmatics by establishing prototypical situations in which these types of problems may occur. Real situations also provide the opportunity to monitor the natural occurrence of such problems and provide appropriate feedback for the use of alternative responses, desirable ones like accepting blame or criticism gracefully, and being tactful in their use of such behaviors. Whereas the focus of these pragmatic activities has been how to prevent WSc from being intrusive, demanding, or annoying to others, it should also be the responsibility of the adults (parents and teachers) to protect WSc from the aggression of others.

Organized intervention programs dealing with pragmatics in general are *Pragmatic Language Intervention* (Bliss, 1993), *Ready-to-Use Conflict Resolution Activities for Secondary Students* (Perlstein & Thrall, 1996), *Getting With It* (Frank & Smith-Rex, 1997), *Working with Pragmatics* (Anderson-Wood & Smith, 1997) *Job-Related Social Skills* (Montague & Lund, 1991; and *Let's Talk Inventory* Bray & Wiig, 1987).

VII. INTERVENTIONS FOR IMPROVING DISCOURSE AND NARRATIVE SKILLS

Interventions need not be aimed only at what WSs do poorly. They may also be focused on the enhancement of their language strengths (Scheiber, 2000). Consistent with general practice, evaluation of the discourse and narrative skills of WSs need to precede the use of interventions. Younger WSc, in particular, may need help in learning how to express thoughts and ideas in linguistic units longer than sentences in discourse and narration. Both areas overlap with problems of language pragmatics, especially topic closure.

A. Evaluation

Standard storytelling tasks, like the Frog Story and the Bus Story Language Test (Paul, 1996; Renfrew, 1994), can be used to evaluate the narrative skills of WSs. The Bus Story Language Test (Renfrew, 1994, cf. Paul, 1996) analyzes story output in terms of proficiency level: heap, sequence, primitive narrative, chain, or true narrative. This is based on the number of informational units the examinee uses in retelling the examiner's narration of the Bus Story. Thus, the narrative skills of WSs can be quantified and compared with those of other groups, including youngsters who are language delayed (Paul, 1996). Techniques for quantifying stage of narrative development with the Frog Story are described in the section on narratives in chapter 2, see p. 60.

B. Facilitation of Discourse

Some WSs may need assistance in identifying, describing, and arranging the essential elements of a discourse topic. Selective choice of topics and use of structured questioning can help develop these skills.

WSs seem better able to perform when the topic is broad and the information organized. Appropriate topics include the areas of special interest, such as types of animals, coins, machines, or generalized scripts and event structures (e g , going to the store, attending birthday parties, or eating at a restaurant; Carrow-Woolfolk, 1985, pp. 313–315). See chapter 5, Section II "Curiosity." Descriptions of television programs, movies, or stories are other options. An organized interventional strategy to help WSc focus on a topic may be found in Hoskins (1996).

In addition, questioning can be used to encourage the inclusion and emphasis of relevant information. Pertinent types of questions include factual questions (i.e., "Who," "When," "Where," "How?"), sequencing questions (e.g., "What happens next?"), temporal questions (e.g., "When did that happen?"), and causal questions (e.g., "What caused that to happen?", "Why did it happen?").

These strategies are similar to those suggested for problems of topic relevance and closure (see chapter 3, Section VI, "Pragmatics."

C. Development of Narrative Skills

Learning to understand the requisites of story grammar may help some WSs improve the organization of their stories. Skills that may need to be strengthened include knowing how to specify the events or episodes of the story, describing reactions to those events or episodes, and establishing the story setting (i.e., the time, place, and characters involved in the story; Clark & Clark, 1977, pp. 168–170). This often involves explanation of causal relations, as well as event prediction and resultant outcomes. These issues are relevant to the development of reasoning as well.

Dramatic enactment, improvisation, and puppetry can be encouraged by providing WSs with a story line based on a real life experience or photos depicting an event (Carrow-Woolfolk, 1985, pp. 316–317). Dramatization of a WS story in the classroom can help boost the WSs' self-esteem and sense of participation in school activities. The use of videotaping can further enhance self-esteem.

Once dramatization has taken place, it can be transferred to story form and feedback can be provided through the use of restatement, recasting, and expansion. Thus, tools of the naturalistic approach can be incorporated into interventions used with WS stories or narrations as with other forms of expressive language.

Also, structured questioning can be used to help WSs establish a comprehensive framework for the story, see use *of* structured questioning discussed in chapter 3, Section V, "Syntax," Section VI, "Pragmatics." To further develop story cohesiveness, WSs often need opportunities to identify cause–effect relations, make inferences, and generate alternative outcomes (see interventions for improving discourse discussed earlier).

Formal instructional programs that may be helpful in developing WSs' narrative skills are *Storybuilding* (Hutson-Nechkash, 1990), *Story Making* (Peura-Jones & DeBoer, 1995), *More Story Making!* (Peura-Jones & DeBoer, 2000), and *Step-by-Step Narratives* (Coleman, 1997).

It is also recommended that WSs be reinforced and praised for the storytelling skills they actually possess. As WSs relate their stories, examples of their use of advanced syntax (i.e., compound and complex sentences, appropriate tense markers, and so forth) should be noted so that they become cognizant of their achievements in this area. Using orally told stories for composition and expository writing assignments can help WSs employ their storytelling skills in meeting academic requirements. Selection of topics for storytelling can be extended to curricular content areas of social science, science, language arts, and so forth.

WSs' ability to linguistically encode affect should be reinforced as well. When appropriate, WSs can be told that they are making appropriate use of prosodic features, such as changes in pitch, volume, and stress, and dramatic devices like whispering, exclamatory phrases, and so forth in their storytelling efforts. Examples of their effective use of affective devices may be used as models for other students.

WSs are particularly "needy" for social reinforcement, attention, and praise. Their storytelling skills can help to enhance their self-concept and provide a useful and entertaining contribution to their educational-social environment.

VIII. SUMMARY AND CONCLUSIONS

This chapter presents four types of intervention strategies—structured therapy, mediational strategies, naturalistic methods, and control mechanisms—that are distinct yet complementary in the way they deal with the major problem areas of WS language: delay, speech and voice, semantics, syntax, pragmatics, discourse, and narration.

Basic to all intervention approaches is the role of a speech language therapist (SLT) and structured therapy. Besides having primary responsibility for language assessment and treatment, SLTs usually serve as consultant and guide to parents, teachers, and others in their efforts to promote WSs' language skills. Their use of nonstructured forms of intervention in everyday situations is especially important. This includes mediational strategies, such as labeling, rehearsal, demonstration, dramatization, and self-instruction; naturalistic approaches, such as structured household tasks, play activities, and language feedback; and control mechanisms, especially reinforcement, direct instruction, and rechanneling tactics. Thus, parents, teachers, and other specialists are vital links in the intervention chain, particularly in the area of language pragmatics.

The SLT occupies the dominant position in the treatment of language delay and speech and voice problems in WSs. Treatment of other difficulties of WSs in the areas of syntax, semantics, discourse, and narration may appear to be less important because many of these problems tend to be accommodated within the usual ebb and flow of language exchange, whereas problems of severe language delay or inarticulate speech cannot be overlooked.

Nevertheless, dealing with the less critical aspects of WSs' language problems can have a major impact on WSs' ability to converse easily, share and process information efficiently, use language creatively, and make progress academically and vocationally. Helping WSs become more facile and informed in their use of language may involve assisting them with semantic problems of word finding, relational terms, and figurative speech, and with syntactic problems of personal pronouns, wh-questions, certain inflections, and complex sentence forms. Also, assistance is often sorely needed in restraining some of the undesirable behaviors of WSs in language pragmatics, like compulsive greeting behavior and incessant calling out, and in improving behaviors relating to verbosity, topic relevance, perseveration, turn-taking, persistent questioning, and other functions of language pragmatics, as well as developing their discourse and narrative skills.

It must be further noted that WSs display a wide range of language abilities, deficits, problems, and difficulties. Those individual differences in language, as well as other attributes, must be taken into account in designing therapeutic programs. It is also clear that intervention strategies that are viable for children with other forms of developmental disorder may not be appropriate for most WSs. In keeping with their psycho-educational profile, most WSs tend to be more responsive to verbal mediational techniques, especially dramatization, storytelling, and self-instruction, and to verbal-social forms of reinforcement and social pressure than are many with other forms of mental retardation.

Finally, it must be noted that most WSs are extremely gratifying to work with. They tend to be very cooperative and amenable to treatment. Most importantly, definite signs of progress can usually be observed by SLTs, parents, teachers, and others and attributed to their efforts. Of course, such positive results depend on the severity of the problem, use of suitable techniques, and experienced providers. Through their efforts and those of the WSs involved, the language problems and difficulties of many WSs can be addressed, their language potential developed, and their language skills used to bootstrap performance in other weaker areas.

4

Perceptual and Motor Performance

Most individuals with WS (WSs) are intensely hypersensitive and severely impaired in the areas of perceptual and motor performance. This is apparent in the difficulties they usually face in performing everyday activities that involve visuospatial, motor, and visuomotor skills. Hypersensitivity to certain ordinary sounds plague almost all WSs, and tactile sensitivity affects quite a few. In addition, paradoxical perceptual abilities are often exhibited by WSs within the visual, auditory, and tactile areas of perception.

This chapter deals with the many difficulties and isolated skills of WSs in the areas of visuospatial, motor, and visuomotor integration, tactile sensitivity, and auditory sensitivity. Each area has its own distinct properties, its own specialized forms of clinical treatment, and psycho-educational techniques of intervention.

I. VISUOMOTOR PERFORMANCE

Most WSs are plagued with significant developmental delays and problems in performing many activities of daily life (Udwin & Yule, 1998a). Awkwardness, embarrassment, and even failure may beset their attempts to deal with certain aspects of self-care, using household appliances, participating in sports activities, or differentiating right from left. These are examples of areas of likely deficiency and frustration.

According to parents, 97% of children with WS (WSc) are impaired in drawing, 89% in cutting with a knife, 77% with personal grooming, and 77% in using scissors (Utah Survey, Semel & Rosner, 1991a, 1991b). Many are unable to use zippers, buttons, or snap their pants in order to dress themselves. Tying shoelaces or buckling a belt may be monumental tasks. Most WSc (92%) are reported to have visual perceptual problems (Utah Survey, Semel & Rosner, 1991a, 1991b). Most are severely delayed in learning how to throw and catch a ball; some never develop any degree of proficiency in these skills. Elementary academic tasks like copying simple figures or numbers stymie them, no less learning how to write legibly with ease.

These are visual-spatial-motor acts that require the integration of visuospatial and motor skills. Even though visuospatial and motor skills are interrelated functionally, they are often dealt with separately in the research literature. The present chapter follows that tradition by presenting visuospatial information first, and then motor functioning. This allows visuomotor performance to be examined in terms of its individual components, mechanisms, and disciplines involved in its treatment.

A. Visuospatial Domains

Insight into the visuospatial domains of WSs began with the intense scrutiny and testing of a few WSa (Bellugi et al., 1988b). This has been vigorously pursued in studies of numerous subject groups and tasks, as well as tracked developmentally, compared with other populations, and examined analytically.

The visuospatial domains of WSs encompass the two major areas: visualspatial-integration skills that are used in visuospatial construction and visuomotor tasks (e.g., grooming, dressing, eating, and handwriting); and visuospatial cognition, which is demonstrated in certain visuospatial and face recognition tasks.

Information about the visuospatial domain of WS, its contrasts, components, and mechanisms, is presented here.

Visuospatial Construction Deficits

Visuospatial construction (VSC) refers to the operation of partitioning a visual stimulus into its constituent parts and the inverse operation of assembling separate elements to constitute a whole. Three areas of investigation—drawings, block constructions, and related tasks—demonstrate the quantitative deficiencies and qualitative distinctions of WSs in the area of VSC. Related tasks include puzzle assembly, cube construction, copying designs, and pegboard tests. Table 4.1 presents a summary of research findings.

Drawing Tasks. Severe deficits in the area of drawing are evident in the attempts of WSa (*n* = 3, 11–16 yrs) to draw pictures of familiar objects, such as a bicycle, elephant, or flower, as part of the Boston Diagnostic Aphasia Examination (BDAE; Bellugi et al., 1988b).

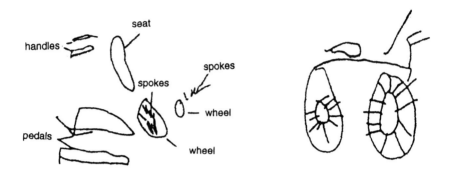

FIG. 4.1. Drawings of a bicycle by same WSc at age 9;7 yrs and 12;11 yrs (Bertrand & Mervis, 1996). From "Longitudinal Analysis of Drawings by Children with Williams Syndrome: Preliminary Results," by J. Bertrand and C. B. Mervis, 1996, *Visual Arts Research, 22*, p. 32. Copyright 1996 by the Board of Trustees of the University of Illinois. Reprinted with permission.

The drawings of WSa tend to be fragmented, significant parts are missing or disarranged, and perspective and spatial organization is inadequate. A house may be depicted as two lines, an adjacent square could be a door, or a series of squares off to the side could represent windows (Bellugi et al., 1988b). Similarly, the freehand drawings of WSc (*n* = 17, 4;10–15;3 yrs) show "a general poverty of contents, stereotypes, scarce observation of spatial relations" (Milani, Dall'Oglio, & Vicari, 1994). Another example of WSs' drawing style is shown in Fig. 4.1.

In contrast, WSs usually produce elaborate, grammatically well-formed descriptions of their poorly executed drawings that clearly describe objects such as a bicycle or elephant (Bellugi et al., 1992). WSa also tend to talk their way through their drawings, for example, saying "It's a line, and a circle. It's a circle, and a line," while drawing a flower (Bellugi et al., 1988b). Verbal mediation of visuomotor tasks turns out to be an effective mode of intervention for WSc (Sabbadini, 1994; Semel, 1988; Semel & Rosner, 1991b; Udwin & Yule, 1998).

Visuomotor Integration (VMI). Drawing difficulties are also evident in WSs' drawing of geometric forms on the VMI, Beery's Developmental Test of Visual-Motor Integration (Bellugi et al., 1988b). Many are able to copy correctly only the two simplest items: straight lines and circles. Even composites of these figures, like a triangle, intersecting lines, or a circle of dots, are often too difficult for WSa. This yields VMI scores in the range of developmentally normal 5-year-olds, even though their language age-equivalent (AE) scores are in the range of 7- to 12-year-olds, and their chronological age (CA) ranges from 11 to 16 years (Bellugi et al., 1988a; see chap. 2). Typically, WSa (*n*

= 10) score significantly lower than DSa (n = 9) on the VMI (Bellugi et al., 1992; Bellugi et al., 1994; Wang, Doherty, Rourke, & Bellugi, 1995).

WSc of school age (n = 30) also perform poorly on the VMI. Most score three standard deviations (SD) below the mean (M) of the norms (Dilts et al., 1990; Morris et al., 1988). In fact, WSc (n = 62, 2–11 yrs) resemble children diagnosed for focal brain lesion (n = 52, 2–11 yrs), especially those with right hemisphere lesions (n = 30) in their marked departure from the findings of a normal population (Beret, Bellugi, Hickok, & Stiles, 1996). Similarly, Italian children with WS (n = 17, 5–15 yrs) score significantly lower on the Beery VMI test than normal controls matched on mental age (Milani et al., 1994). By age 10, DSc generally score higher than WSc on the VMI (Bertrand, Mervis, & Eisenberg, 1997).

Tracing in the VMI Drawing Task. However, allowing WSa to trace stimulus figures markedly improves performance of many WSs. Under tracing conditions, WSa may be able to depict both the external and internal lines of two- and three-dimensional figures they are asked to copy (Bellugi et al., 1988b). This suggests that a WSa's difficulty with drawing tasks reflects problems of visuospatial cognition and motor planning as well as motor movement (Bellugi et al., 1992; Bellugi et al., 1988b; Bellugi, Wang, & Jernigan, 1994).

Block Construction Tasks. Block Design tasks provide another way to assess WSs' spatial cognition and visuomotor coordination. In the Block Design subtest of the Wechsler Intelligence Scale for Children–Revised (WISC–R), subjects are asked to reproduce two-dimensional block patterns using colored blocks that are red, white, or half red and half white. The timed test presents patterns of increasing complexity.

In keeping with their poor performance on drawing tasks, WSa (n = 6, 10–17 yrs) totally fail the Block Design test. DSa (n = 6, 11–18 yrs) also fail, but their error pattern differs markedly from that of WSa (Bellugi et al., 1992; Bellugi et al., 1994; Bellugi et al., 2000). Figure 4.2 depicts the Block Design task (Wechsler) and typical block arrangements produced by WSa and DSa (Bellugi et al., 2000).

Other studies confirm the extreme difficulty WSs have with block construction tasks. On the Differential Abilities Scale (DAS), over one half of WSs (n = 80, 4–47 yrs) obtain the lowest possible score, 88% are in the first percentile, and just 10% score within the normal range of the pattern construction subtest (Mervis et al., 1999).

Likewise, children with WS (n = 73, < 14 yrs, M = 7 yrs) test much lower than their chronological age on another block construction task (Atkinson et al., 2001). For example, WS 8-year-olds perform in the 2- to 4-year-old age

Different Deficits in Block Design for Williams and Downs: (Fractional Attention to Detail in Williams)

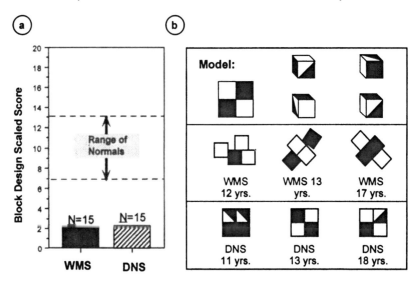

FIG. 4.2. Block design constructions of WSa and DSa (Bellugi et al., 2000). From "I. The Neurocognitive Profile of Williams Syndrome: A Complex Pattern of Strengths and Weaknesses, by U. Bellugi and M. St. George (Eds.), Linking Cognitive Neuroscience and Molecular Genetics: New Perspectives from Williams syndrome. *Journal of Cognitive Neuroscience, 12* (Suppl. 1, p. 19). Copyright 2000 by the Massachusetts Institute of Technology. Reprinted with permission.

range for normal children on this test. Similar construction tasks yield comparable results (Atkinson et al., 2001).

Other Tasks. Other studies substantiate the difficulty that WSs have with visuomotor tasks, either in terms of absolute measures, relative to their own performance in other areas, or that of other groups. On the Reitan pegboard and delayed drawing tests, WSc ($n = 5$, 7–11;6 yrs) score at the bottom of the scale. They are also significantly lower than other types of mentally retarded controls on VM tasks, although they are comparable on language tests (MacDonald & Roy, 1988).

In a similar vein, WSc ($n = 7$, 4;3–8;5 yrs) perform worse on visual perceptual items—such as puzzle assembly, drawing a person, and cube construction—than on other tests of the McCarthy Scales of Children's Abilities, with the single exception of the motor subscale (Bennett, La Veck, & Sells, 1978). They also perform worse than a group of developmentally disabled children on the visual perceptual and motor subscales of the McCarthy, although they do score consistently higher than the others on the subscale of expressive language (Bennett et al., 1978).

Once again, there is a gap between relatively high language skills and abysmally low visual-spatial-motor performance. This is further upheld in the marked contrast between the scores of WSs (n = 16, 7–28 yrs, M = 22;8 yrs) on nonverbal subtests (e.g., pattern construction, matrices, shape sequences) and verbal subtests (e.g., word definitions and category similarities) of the DAS (Jarrold et al., 1998). Interestingly, the advantage of verbal over nonverbal skills increases gradually over the childhood years as a result of greater growth in the verbal domain than in the nonverbal domain. The verbal–nonverbal difference is attributed to the scores of a few of the older WSs (n = 16, 7–28 yrs, M = 16;10 yrs) who are high in verbal skills (Jarrold et al., 1998).

Across studies, visuomotor scores are consistently lower than those in other areas of the DAS. For example, 85% of WSs (n = 37 children, 26 adults) score at the first (lowest) percentile on pattern construction but show relatively high performance on the verbal subtests (Naming/Definitions and Similarities) and the digit recall subtest (Short-Term Memory) of the DAS (Mervis et al., 1999). Scores of WSc (n = 9, 10–20 yrs) on academic achievement tests are significantly higher than their VMI scores on the Beery (Pagon et al., 1987).

Table 4.1 presents a summary of research findings on the visuospatial construction deficits of WSs.

Components of Visuospatial Cognition

In view of the overwhelming evidence of WSs' severe deficits in visuospatial construction, the question arises as to the extent to which visuospatial cognitive factors and/or motor difficulties are implicated in these deficits. Several studies provide at least partial answers.

Motor-Free and Motor Visual Perception Tasks. In order to identify areas of particular vulnerability, a large battery of visuospatial stimulus and motor response tasks was administered to WSs (n = 10, 11–18 yrs, M = 16 yrs) and DSs (n = 9, 11–20 yrs, M = 15 yrs) (Wang et al., 1995). On the VMI, DSs performed significantly better than WSs in copying geometric figures; this is consistent with previous reports. More interestingly, WSs did not differ significantly from DSs on the Motor-Free Visual Perception Test (MVPT), which uses stimulus matching to circumvent the need for motor responding on tests of figure-ground discrimination, spatial relationships, visual memory, visual closure, and visual discrimination (Wang et al., 1995).

The difference in results suggests that WSs are especially vulnerable on tasks requiring eye–hand (fine motor) coordination. Even so, both groups of adolescents, WSs and DSs, performed in the range of pre-school and young school-aged children on the VMI, MVPT, and Gestalt Closure tasks (Wang et al., 1995).

TABLE 4.1
Research on Visuospatial Construction Deficits of WSs

Type of Test or Performance	Result	Source or Reference
Visual Perceptual Problems	WSc 92%	Semel & Rosner, Utah Survey
Impaired in Drawing	WSc 97%	
Problems Cutting with Knife	WSc 89%	
Personal Grooming Prob-		
lems	WSc 77%	
Problems Using a Scissors	WSc 77%	
BDAE: Fragmented Drawings	Many WSa	Bellugi et al., 1988b
Fragmented Drawings	Some WSc	Milani et al., 1994
Verbal Descriptions,	WSa Verbal > Drawings	Bellugi et al., 1992
Object Drawings		
VMI: Copying Geometric	WSa ~ normal 4;11 yr olds	Bellugi et al., 1988b
Figures[#]		
VMI[#]	WSa < DSa	Bellugi et al., 1992, 1994;
		Wang et al., 1995
VMI[#]	WSc ~ DSc	Bertrand et al., 1997
VMI[#]	WS < 3 SD below Normals	Dilts et al., 1990;
		Morris et al., 1988
VMI[#]	WSc ~ FLc	Beret et al., 1996
VMI[#]	WSc < normal MA controls	Milani et al., 1994
Block Design Test (WISC–R)[#]	WSa ~ DSa, both fail	Bellugi et al., 1992, 2000
Block Construction (DAS)	WSs 88% in first percentile	Mervis et al., 1999
Block Construction[#]	WSc AE < CA,	Atkinson et al., 2001
	WSc AE ~ 1/2 CA	
Reitan Pegboard & Delayed	WSc < MR controls	MacDonald & Roy, 1988
Drawing[#]		
Visual Perceptual Subscale,	WSc < MRc	Bennett et al., 1978
McCarthy Scales[#]		
DAS Subtests,	WSs Verbal > Nonverbal	Jarrold et al., 1998
Verbal vs. Nonverbal[#]		
Academic Achievement	WSc Achievement Test >	Pagon et al., 1987
Tests vs. VMI[#]	VMI	

Note: % = percent of subjects; # = subject scores; WSa = WS adolescents &/or adults; WSc = WS children; DS = Down syndrome; "a" = adolescents/adults; AE = age-equivalent score; MA = mental age; CA = chronological age; MR = mentally retarded; FL = focal lesion.

Line Orientation Test. Most importantly, WSs and DSs fail miserably on a spatial, nonmotor test, Benton's Line Orientation Task, and so do DSs (Wang et al., 1995). This task merely requires the subject to select the line with the same angle as a target pair of lines within a display of 11 lines oriented 18 degrees apart. In repeated studies, most WSa are able to complete less than 40% of Benton's Line Orientation Task correctly, many are unable to pass even the practice trials (Bellugi et al., 1990; Bellugi et al., 1988b; Wang et al., 1995). This suggests that the deficit underlying the visuospatial problems of WSs involves basic spatial processing and motor execution.

Simplifying the stimuli in a line orientation task can, however, improve performance. Using a rotatable hand of a wooden mannequin, 55% of WSc (n = 15, 4–14 yrs, M = 9;8 yrs) score within the range of normal controls in matching the angle of a slot oriented at a 0, 45, 90, or 135 degree angle (Atkinson et al., 1997). Still, performance deteriorates markedly when motor components are added by requiring WSc to insert a card in the slot.

Distinctive Processing Style

In dealing with visuospatial tasks, WSs frequently exhibit a particular kind of processing style in which the parts or local elements of the stimulus usually dominate the configurational or global elements that are often lacking or underrepresented. This is evident in their block constructions, freehand drawings, copying of geometric figures, and probably in their visual processing of faces and objects. In contrast, DSa tend to exhibit a configurational or global processing style in which the external outline of a stimulus is usually preserved but internal details are often omitted.

To illustrate, WSa's block constructions tend to contain internal details but may fail to follow the overall configuration of the target design, whereas DSa tend to maintain the overall configuration but may fail to represent the separate parts. Thus, the block constructions of WSa and DSa are usually structural opposites (Bellugi et al., 1992; Bellugi et al., 1994). See Fig. 4.2.

In freehand drawings of objects like a bicycle, WSa typically attend to the features of the figure and fail to represent or integrate the larger outline, whereas DSa often do the reverse (Bellugi et al., 1994; Wang & Bellugi, 1993).

This pattern is further confirmed in the hierarchical figure task in which WSa frequently have difficulty depicting the global level of a two-tiered stimulus like a large "H," but are able to produce the small "Bs" that comprise the "H." On the other hand, DSa may produce the entire "H" shape but fail to depict the smaller "Bs" (Bellugi et al., 1992; Bellugi et al., 1994; Wang & Bellugi, 1993). A sample pattern is depicted here:

```
B     B
B     B
B     B
B B B B
B     B
B     B
B     B
```

Other research suggests, however, that age may play a role in determining WSs' processing style. That is, WSc appear to be less consistent than WS adolescents or adults in their use of a local processing style (Milani et al.,

1994). On tasks such as the VMI, Block Design, and hierarchical design, some WSc apparently favor a global style, others a local style; occasionally, both global and local features are accurately represented. Generally, however, WSc score lower than normal MA controls on visuoperceptual tests, such as the VMI, Raven's Progressive Matrices, (better known as a test of abstract reasoning), and the Block Design test, but not on facial recognition (see later).

Task type may also influence processing style. Reportedly, WSa (n = 13, 18–47 yrs, M = 35 yrs) display "low level" global organization in a perceptual visual search task. That is, they respond faster to a target stimulus when the foils appear massed rather than distributed over the surface of the display. Whether the WSs are responding to the global aspects of the array or to the isolated position of the target stimulus may be questionable (Mervis et al., 1999; Pani, Mervis, & Robinson, 1996). It is clear, however, that WSa (n = 21, M = 30 yrs) produced better block designs when small spaces were inserted between segments of the target stimuli (Mervis et al., 1999).

Table 4.2 summarizes research findings on the components of visuospatial cognition in WSs.

TABLE 4.2
Research on Components of Visuospatial Cognition in WSs

Type of Test or Performance	Result	Source or Reference
MVPT (Nonmotor Visual Perceptual Test)	WSa ~ DSa	Wang et al., 1995
VMI[#]	WSa < DSa	
Benton Line Orientation Task[#]	WSa fail, less than half of test completed	Bellugi et al., 1988b; Bellugi et al., 1990; Wang et al., 1995
Modified Line Orientation Task[#]	WSc 55% ~ normal CA controls	Atkinson et al., 1997
Processing Style: Block Constructions Freehand Drawings VMI, Hierarchical Figures	WSa Local Style, DSa Global Style (All Tasks)	Bellugi et al., 1992; Bellugi et al., 1994
Processing Style: Block Constructions Freehand Drawings VMI, Hierarchical Figures	Some WSc Local Style Other WSc Global Style Some WSc Accurate	Milani et al., 1996
Visual Search Task	WSs Low Level Spatial Organization	Pani et al., 1996
Modified Block Construction Test	WSa, Slightly Separated Blocks > Regular Model	Mervis et al., 1999

Note: % = percent of subjects; # = subject scores; WSa = WS adolescents &/or adults; WSc = WS children; DS = Down syndrome; "a" = adolescents/adults; AE = age-equivalent score; MA = mental age; CA = chronological age.

Face Recognition Abilities

The truly remarkable face recognition abilities of WSs are now well established (Bellugi et al., 1988b; Bellugi et al., 1994; Karmiloff-Smith, 1997; Milani et al., 1994; Udwin & Yule, 1991; Wang et al., 1995), but still a source of amazement and puzzlement. The striking difference between the extremely poor performance of WSa on visuospatial construction tasks and their consistently high level performance on face recognition, discrimination, and memory tasks seems incongruous (Bellugi et al., 2000). For example, the average (median, Md) score of WSa was 80% correct (within the normal range of performance) in the initial study of face recognition (Bellugi et al., 1988b).

The contrast in results cannot be due to differences in response mode (recognition vs. construction) because WSs perform poorly on the Benton Line Orientation Test, a visuospatial recognition test. Task difficulty also does not seem to be the critical factor, although it certainly does affect performance in other situations. In fact, the task requirements of the Benton Facial Recognition Test are rather stringent. Subjects are shown a frontview photograph of a target face and asked to select it from an array of faces, including the target, photographed in three-quarter views or under different lighting conditions. Yet, WSa frequently score within the range of normal adults and children of their own chronological age on this task, besides outperforming DSa by a wide margin (Bellugi et al., 1992; Bellugi et al., 1988b; Bellugi et al., 1994).

Other studies provide further evidence of the special face discrimination skills of WSs (Karmiloff-Smith, 1992, 1997; Milani et al., 1994). Whereas WSc score much lower than normal MA matched children on visuospatial construction and other visuoperceptual tasks, they actually score higher than normally developing children on the Benton Face Test (Milani et al., 1994).

WSs also perform consistently at a comparable level to MA matched normal children on other face recognition tests, even when the models' hair and hairline are obscured by scarves in the photographs (Deruelle, Mancini, Livet, Casse-Perrot, & de Schonen, 1999). One version of the task requires the subject to identify the face that matches the target in emotional expression, gaze direction, lip reading (vowel produced), gender, age, or identity. Under these conditions, both the WSs (n = 12, 7–23;9 yrs, M = 11;11 yrs) and MA controls score significantly lower than CA normal controls. Possibly, the less than normal CA performance may reflect the absence of certain relevant, high contrast cues. Figure 4.3 shows one of the face conditions used by Deruelle et al. (1999, Exp. 1).

On standard face recognition tasks, subjects are shown numerous pictures of unfamiliar faces, which are then intermixed with newly presented pictures of faces. WSc outperform mentally retarded controls in discriminating "old" from "new" pictures of faces, as in the Rivermead Behavioral Memory Test (Udwin & Yule, 1991). WSs (n = 17, M = 19;8 yrs) also surpass

FIG. 4.3. Examples of face stimuli used by Deruelle et al. (1999). From "Configural and Local Processing of Faces in Children with Williams Syndrome," by C. Deruelle, J. Mancini, M. O. Livet, C. Casse-Perrot, and S. de Schonen, 1999, *Brain and Cognition, 41,* 283. Copyright 1999 by Academic Press. Reprinted with permission.

DSs (n = 10, M = 18;5 yrs) on the Warrington Face Memory Test (Bellugi et al., 2000).

Performance on another test of facial recognition, the Mooney Closure Faces Test, confirms the remarkable facial recognition skills of WSa (Bellugi et al., 1988b; Wang et al., 1995). In this test, the stimuli are photographs of faces obscured by shadows and fragmented contours. Nevertheless, WSs (n = 33) perform within the normal range on this test, with 71% correct, and better than DSs (n = 10), with 67% correct (Bellugi et al., 2000; Wang et al., 1995).

Even so, WSs generally do poorly on visual closure tests of nonface stimuli (Bellugi et al., 1988b; Bellugi et al., 1994; Wang et al., 1995). In fact, WSc (n = 22, 4–10 yrs, M = 7 yrs) perform significantly worse on the Visual Closure Subtest of the Illinois Test of Psycholinguistic Abilities (ITPA), an embedded figures test, than children with nonspecific developmental disabilities (Crisco, Dobbs, & Mulhern, 1988). This may reflect difficulty with figure-ground relations, that is, being able to differentiate or extract a target figure from the background, as well as difficulty in being able to use partial, local cues to infer the entire global figure.

Having rejected both response mode and task difficulty as possible explanations of the face recognition abilities of most WSs, two other factors may be considered. One is the special status of faces for WSs. That is, most WSs are absolutely transfixed by human faces from infancy on (Mervis, discussion comment, Wang, 1994). Researchers also note that WS toddlers may become so fascinated with the faces of examiners that this actually interferes with their performance (Jones et al., 2000). Anecdotal reports of parents further attest to the special power of people's faces for WSs. See chapter 5 for information on WSs' "reading" of facial expressions and emotion.

Distinctive Processing Style of Faces. Another possible factor may be that WSs are able to successfully apply their distinctive local processing style to tasks involving human faces: face perception, discrimination, and recognition. At first glance, this is paradoxical, because configural, not feature or local processing, is generally assumed to dominate in face processing tasks. In fact, there is a large body of research suggesting that normally developing individuals tend to respond to faces in a configurational or global manner from infancy on (cf. Deruelle et al., 1999). Other studies suggest, however, that normal children may shift from componential or local processing to configural processing of faces over the school-age years (Mills et al., 2000). There is also the possibility that WSs may adopt a configural style solely when processing faces. This is bolstered by the notion that facial processing involves specialized mechanisms and neural networks (Deruelle et al., 1999).

One way to investigate how people typically view faces is to compare their ability to process faces presented upright (regular orientation) with their ability to process faces presented upside-down (inverted orientation). Presumably, viewing faces in an upright orientation involves viewing them as configural, global wholes, whereas upside-down faces involve "componential" processing in terms of "local" features or parts. If the upside-down condition results in a decrease in performance from that obtained under the normal, upright face condition, then it is inferred that configural processing is typical and the decrease is due to the lack of standard cues. If there is no decrease, then it is inferred that the subject is processing both orientations locally.

Applying this methodology to the Benton Facial Test, WSa ($n = 10$, 10–20 yrs) scored higher than DSa on both the standard and inverted face versions of the test, but the latter difference was not statistically reliable (Wang et al., 1995). Even so, WSs' comments suggested that they were using componential (local) features in face discrimination tasks (Karmiloff-Smith, 1997; Wang et al., 1995).

More convincing evidence of WSs' local processing of faces comes from studies that manipulate the properties of the stimuli to be matched. Comparing WSs' ability to distinguish target from similar pictures of faces and houses presented in upright or inverted fashion, the WSc differed significantly from both MA and CA normal control groups in their response pattern. Whereas the normal groups showed significantly more errors on inverted faces than on inverted houses, WSs' performance did not decrease significantly under conditions of inversion for either faces or houses. This suggests that the normal groups ordinarily respond configurationally to face stimuli and so they are disrupted by the inversion of faces. Apparently, they do not usually process houses configurationally. WSs, instead, seem to process both faces and houses componentially, that is, by local features (Deruelle et al., 1999, Exp. 2).

In a preliminary study that manipulated facial properties, WSs (n = 10, M = 23 yrs) and normal CA controls responded to a matching task of face stimuli requiring mainly configural or componential processing (Karmiloff-Smith, 1997, Exp. 2). Overall, WSs scored almost as high as normal controls, but they responded significantly worse than controls, only at chance, when the stimulus condition presumably required configurational kinds of processing (e.g., when the faces were very similar or certain features were masked that would deter use of a feature comparison strategy). Ongoing research also indicates that WSa respond to local, eye change in pictures of faces as rapidly and accurately as other people, but less so to configural change in feature arrangement (Karmiloff-Smith, Williams Syndrome Newsletter, 2001, *18*(1), p. 3).

Similarly, WSc have more difficulty differentiating target patterns from configural distractors that differ spatially from the target than with feature distractors that differ in shape from the target. In contrast, MA and CA normal controls have greater difficulty discriminating between targets and distractors that differ in terms of features (shape) rather than configuration (spatially). These results are in keeping with WSs' predilection for processing patterns in a local style, and normal controls' predilection for a configurational style (Deruelle et al., 1999).

Object Recognition. WSs' unusual assortment of visuospatial deficits and skills is further evident in their ability to identify objects that appear in atypical perspectives in the Canonical/Noncanonical Views Test (Bellugi et al., 1994; Wang et al., 1995). When objects are presented in their canonical, customary orientation, such as a watering can viewed from the side, they are usually identified successfully by both WSa and DSa. However, when objects are shown in a noncanonical orientation, such as a top down view of a funnel, which may befuddle even investigators who are not familiar with the stimulus pictures, WSa surpass DSa at 76% to 66%, respectively (Wang et al., 1995).

TABLE 4.3
Research on Face Recognition and Related Abilities of WSs

Type of Test or Performance	Result	Source or Reference
Face Recognition Test (Benton)[#]	WSa 80% at Md of normal range	Bellugi et al., 1988b
Face Recognition Test (Benton)[#]	WSa > DSa	Bellugi et al., 1992;
		Bellugi et al., 1994
Face Recognition Test (Benton)[#]	WSc ~ normal MA controls	Milani et al., 1996
Face Recognition Test[#]	WSs = MA controls < CA controls	Deruelle et al., 1999
Face Recognition (Rivermead)	WSs > MR controls	Udwin & Yule, 1991
Warrington Face Memory Test	WSa > DSa	Bellugi et al., 2000
Mooney Closure Faces	WSs ~ normal range,	Bellugi et al., 2000
	WSs > DSs	Wang et al., 1995
Visual Closure Subtest ITPA	WSc < MRs	Crisco et al., 1988
Upright vs. Inverted Faces and Houses	WS = Upright & Inverted, Faces & Houses	Deruelle et al., 1999
	MA & CA Controls Inverted Faces < Upright Faces	
	MA & CA Controls Inverted Houses = Upright Houses	
Local vs. Configural Changes in Faces	WSs < Controls on Configural Change	Karmiloff-Smith, 1997
Local vs. Configural Distractors for Target Patterns	WSc Configural < Local MA & CA Controls, Local < Configural	Deruelle et al., 1999
Object Recognition—Canonical vs. Noncanonical Views	WSa = DSa Canonical WSa > DSa Noncanonical	Wang et al., 1995

Note: % = percent of subjects; # = subject scores; WSa = WS adolescents &/or adults; WSc = WS children; DS = Down syndrome; "a" = adolescents/adults; AE = age-equivalent score; MA = mental age; CA = chronological age.

Table 4.3 summarizes research findings on the face recognition and related abilities of WSs.

Individual Differences and Developmental Trends

So far, the focus has been on the absolute and relative performance of WSs on visuospatial tasks involving construction and cognitive processing, like stimulus recognition and discrimination tasks. Issues of individual differences and age-related trends of performance among WSs are, however, of practical and theoretical interest.

Individual Differences. In contrast to the frequently mentioned individual differences of WSs in the area of language, little has been previously said here on this topic. This reflects the extremely low performance of WSs on standard tasks like drawing, figure copying, block building, and line orientation. The range of scores is typically truncated on such tests.

However, a number of studies reveal variability among WSs in this area. Italian children with WS (n = 17, 5–15 yrs) are reported to show age-related changes in performance and wide variability on various tests of spatial ability, including the VMI, Rey, Block Design, and Hierarchical Stimuli test (Milani et al., 1994). Variability is reported for WSc (n = 18, 9–10 yrs) in their drawing of objects (BDAE) and VMI test performance (Bertrand et al., 1997). Also, there are similar reports for WSs (n = 28, 4;6–38;5 yrs) in the Draw A Person (DAP) test and VMI (Dykens, Rosner, & Ly, 2001).

Developmental Trends. There are, moreover, clear indications of developmental trends toward improvement in WSs' performance on block construction and drawing tasks. Over the childhood years, block building scores on the DAS increase with age (Mervis et al., 1999) and some improvement is shown on a similar block construction task (Atkinson et al., 2001).

Error analyses reveal an age-related decrease in the number of broken configurations in block constructions. WS adults tend to preserve the 2 × 2 arrangement of the blocks in their constructions even when the pattern is incorrect, whereas WSc are likely to make more serious errors (Mervis & Klein-Tasman, 2000).

Comparable results of slight but significant progress are reported in WSs' copying of geometric figures on the VMI (Dykens et al., 2001; Mervis & Klein-Tasman, 2000). These may be contrasted with stronger gains in WSs' drawing of objects and people and WSs' growth patterns in other areas (Bertrand & Mervis, 1996; Bertrand et al., 1997; Dykens et al., 2001; Stiles et al., 2000).

Growth Patterns Across Areas. Distinctions in the growth patterns of WSs and other groups are dramatically conveyed in graphs depicting their performance on tests across major areas of functioning (Atkinson et al., 2001; Bellugi et al., 1999; Jones, Rossen, & Bellugi, 1994).

Figure 4.4 illustrates the growth patterns of WSs (n = 71, 5–30 yrs) on tests of visuospatial construction (VMI), language vocabulary (PPVT–R), and face processing (Benton Test of Facial Recognition) at three age levels: school age, adolescence, and adulthood (Bellugi et al., 2000).

On face processing, WSs perform higher than would be expected at each age level. They score within or near the age range of normals, at or above their own mental age, and significantly higher than a matched group of DSs (7–28 yrs, M = 14;6 yrs).

In contrast, WSs do not excel in measures of early language acquisition (PPVT-R). They are delayed in acquiring vocabulary (PPVT-R) relative to the norms and their own mental age. On a par with DSc at the youngest age level tested, WSc progress at a reasonable rate, leaving DSc behind in their acquisition of vocabulary.

Distinct Trajectories in Cognitive Domains in Williams Syndrome

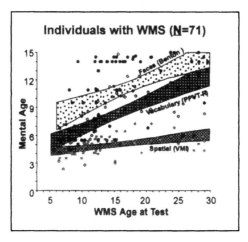

FIG. 4.4. Growth patterns across areas: Face recognition, language, and V-S Construction of WSs and DSs (Bellugi et al., 2000). From "I. The Neurocognitive Profile of Williams Syndrome: A Complex Pattern of Strengths and Weaknesses," by U. Bellugi and M. St. George (Eds.), Linking Cognitive Neuroscience and Molecular Genetics: New Perspectives from Williams Syndrome. *Journal of Cognitive Neuroscience, 12*(Suppl. 1, p. 24). Copyright 2000 by the Massachusetts Institute of Technology. Reprinted with permission.

In line with previous reports in this section, WSs are markedly impaired on visual-spatial-motor tests (VMI) relative to the norms, their own MA levels, and DSs on the VMI. Their acquisition curve flattens out almost completely by adolescence (Bellugi et al., 1999; Bellugi et al., 2000; Jones et al., 1994).

The rate of progress also varies with area: steeper, more accelerated growth for face recognition than for language, a moderate rate for language, and a very shallow rate for visuospatial VMI (e.g., Bellugi et al., 1999).

Another study (Atkinson et al., 2001) reported similar results for the growth curves of WSc (n = 73, 8 mo–13;8 yrs, M = 7;3 yrs) on other measures of visual-spatial-motor integration (block construction, tube construction, and WPPSI–R object assembly) and language. On tests of visuospatial construction, WSc exhibit large delays that become more pronounced with age. The small amount of age-related improvement that occurs tends to be curtailed by an apparent ceiling in performance (Atkinson et al., 2001). Many of the older WSc in this study, at 12 years old, were scoring at the age-equivalent level of 2- to 4-year-olds (Atkinson et al., 2001).

And, once again, the age trends in VSC contrast sharply with the scores of the same WSc on language tests of vocabulary (PPVT–R) and grammar

(TROG). Although WSc show a slower rate of language progress than that of normally developing children, they do not seem to reach a performance ceiling on language measures as they do on visuospatial motor tasks (Atkinson et al., 2001).

Developmental Delay Versus Deviance. Two explanatory models have been offered to account for the pattern of WS results in the area of visuospatial processing: developmental delay and deviance.

The developmental delay interpretation draws on the age-related improvement that WSc show in VS construction tasks and VMI tests (Dykens et al., 2001; Mervis et al., 1999; Mervis & Klein-Tasman, 2000). This improvement can be attributed to an age-related increase in general cognitive ability. Correlations between visuospatial performance and measures of intelligence, CA and MA, are offered as evidence. Pattern construction tasks correlate significantly with CA in WSc (Mervis et al., 1999). VMI scores correlate significantly with MA in WSs (Dykens et al., 2001) and with CA in WSc (Mervis & Klein-Tasman, 2000). WSc also resemble normally developing children in the ordinality or predictability in the types of items passed on the VMI (Bertrand et al., 1997). Visual inspection suggests that WSc's errors involve mainly problems in knowing how to connect two VMI figures at their point of intersection, which is a problem shared by many learning disabled and brain injured children.

WSs' drawings of objects and people provide stronger, although mixed, results regarding age-related advances in VSM ability (Bertrand et al., 1997; Bertrand & Mervis, 1996; Dykens et al., 2001; Stiles et al., 2001).

In drawing objects from the BDAE, WSc (n = 18, 9–10 yrs) produced significantly fewer recognizable drawings and a significantly smaller proportion of major parts of objects than did normally developing children matched individually for CA or MA (Bertrand et al., 1997). Although WSc did not differ significantly from MA matches in the proportion of disorganized pictures, they were more likely to produce seriously disorganized (nonintegrated) pictures than their MA matches (Bertrand et al., 1997). Differences in item difficulty, flower, house, and elephant, from easiest to hardest, are similar to previously obtained results (Bellugi et al., 1988b).

Consistent with a developmental delay interpretation, ability ranged widely among WSc in drawing recognizability, disorganization, and inclusion of parts, with the "parts" measure correlating positively with total score on the McCarthy Scales, an intelligence test (Bertrand et al., 1997).

Importantly, the drawings of younger normally developing children (n = 40, 4–7 yrs) have many of the same characteristics as those of WSc, namely, poor recognizability, omission of parts, and poor integration of components (Bertrand et al., 1997). However, the drawing skills of normal children increase dramatically over the preschool years (see also Stiles et al., 2000). Almost all of the drawings of normal 5-year-olds are recognizable; none of the drawings by children in the 6- or 7-year-old group show disorganization (Bertrand et al., 1997). Comparability is therefore evident in the kinds of pictures that young normal children (4- and 5-year-olds) and WSc (9- and 10-year-olds) tend to produce (Bertrand et al., 1997).

WSs' drawings of people also provide strong support for a developmental model of VSM impairment (Dykens et al., 2001). Although many of the drawings that WSs ($n=28$, 4;6–38;5 yrs, $M = 14;2$ yrs) produced on the DAP test were unrecognizable as people (43%), WSs did not differ significantly from matched groups of individuals with mixed forms of mental retardation or DS on this measure. Almost all subjects in each group were classified as being at the lower stage(s) of drawing development (i.e., scribbles, tadpoles, or transitional), not at the stage of conventional drawings.

In line with the developmental model, MA was significantly related to DAP scores and developmental level in all three groups, and scribblers were chronologically younger than individuals at higher drawing levels (Dykens et al., 2001). However, it was only among WSs that DAP scores were significantly higher than IQ scores on the Kaufman Brief Intelligence Test (K–BIT) and higher than VMI scores. Qualitatively, too, the DAP drawings of some WSs (those at the higher MA levels) far exceed the quality of most WS drawings in the literature in terms of recognizability, completeness, articulation of details, and attractiveness. Nonetheless, the percentage of WSs at that level is not quite a majority; some of the midlevel drawings of people may not be recognizable to some uninformed observers, and the age span of WSs exceeds that of most other studies.

Dykens et al. (2001) attributed the advantage of DAP over VMI and K–BIT IQ scores to the social orientation of WSs, their stronger motivation for drawing people rather than shapes, and more opportunities for practice in drawing figures. Other interpretations are possible, namely, training (see Stiles et al., 2000).

Longitudinal studies of WSc's drawings of objects and persons provide additional support for a developmental interpretation (Bertrand & Mervis, 1996; Stiles et al., 2000). In two longitudinal studies, development is delayed and severely impaired, but there is definite progress that seems to follow a normal course in the drawings produced (Bertrand & Mervis, 1996; Stiles et al., 2000), and in VMI measures of ordinality (Bertrand & Mervis, 1996).

Specifically, a case study of longitudinal improvements in the drawings of a WSc produced between ages 4 and 6 shows an increase in the elaboration of figures, inclusion of objects, combining of features, and placing of people in a context (Stiles, Sabbadini, Capirci, & Volterra, 1996). The effects of intensive training in the drawing of houses, and especially people, are vividly described and illustrated (Stiles et al., 2000). Training in the drawing of people was evidently more successful in terms of the products produced and the generality of training (Stiles et al., 2000).

Developmental change is also dramatically demonstrated in a longitudinal study of six WSc tested at 9 to 10 years of age (T1) and again 3 to 4 years later at 12 to 14 years of age (T2). Drawing tasks included objects from the BDAE (flower, house, elephant), as well as drawing a person, a bicycle, and the VMI test (Bertrand & Mervis, 1996).

Gains were substantial, from 30% to 46%, in the recognizability of the drawings, and there was a decrease in disorganization, from 43% to 19%, for seriously disorganized pictures at T1 and T2. Judges were generally able to distinguish which of a subject's pictures was produced at the older age. Still, more than one half of the drawings of these WSa were unrecognizable, less than one half were organized at T2, and the criteria used for recognizability and organization were rather lenient. Thus, some adolescents with WS may be able to produce recognizable and organized drawings.

Once again, drawing quality seems to be associated with the subject matter: Good drawings are more likely to result when the objects are people or flowers. Houses are a bit more difficult, and the elephant and bicycle more so.

Little is said about the possible effect of training on performance, although it is suggested that WSs may use verbal strategies to improve their performance on VSC tasks (for further discussion, see Stiles et al., 2001).

Comparison of the drawings of WS adults (n = 10, 19–66 yrs) with those typical of WS children also shows an age-related improvement (Hodenius, Holtinrichs, Curfs, & Fryns, 1994). Still, there are limits, because the adults' drawings continue to show "overdoses" of details and poor organization (Hodenius et al., 1994).

Deviance Model. There is also a great deal of evidence that favors a deviance interpretation in that the growth patterns of WSc are highly atypical. Besides marked delay, progress tends to proceed at an extremely slow rate and levels off prematurely. This is evident in the disparity between WS performance and normal development (Atkinson et al., 2001) and in the improvement in brain lesion cases that increases more sharply over the childhood years than that of a matched group of WSc (Beret et al., 1996).

When the quantitative difference between WSs and other groups becomes so extreme, it approaches that of a qualitative difference, that is, deviance. This is evident in the marked age gap between the acquisition of drawing rules, block building, and hierarchical pattern skills by normal children, generally by the end of their preschool years, and the typically immature, often distorted, output of adolescents and adults with WS (Bertrand et al., 1977; Bellugi et al., 2000; Dukette & Stiles, 2001). Furthermore, the mechanism underlying this highly atypical pattern of growth may reflect intrinsic difficulty in dealing with VS integration of forms (Stiles et al., 2000). Besides, a large percentage of WSs produce fragmented, disorganized, unrecognizable drawings. The frequency and conditions under which this occurs (i.e., type of subject matter, population, motivation, practice, amount and type of training) remain to be determined.

More to the point, WSc tend to respond to VS and face stimuli in a very distinctive manner. That is, the facial processing of WSc differs substantially from that of normal MA controls in their response to upside-down faces, objects, and patterns. This suggests that WSs process these kinds of stimuli componentially, not configurally as do normals. They have a distinctive processing style (Deruelle et al., 1999) that favors a deviance interpretation.

There are also indications from neurogenetic studies of WSs suggesting that the brain organization of WSs may be atypical in regard to their perceptual processing of visual stimuli (discussed later).

Table 4.4 presents a summary of research on individual differences and developmental trends in the visuospatial domains of WSs.

Underlying Mechanisms

Amazingly little is known about the mechanisms underlying the visuospatial processing of WSs, despite its critical role in many important areas: self-care, interpersonal relations, schooling, and vocational opportunities. Advances are being made, however, at four levels of biogenetic research.

LIM-kinase I. There are reports that deletion of a particular gene, LIM-kinase 1 (LIMK1, adjacent to the elastin, ELN, gene in band 7q11.23 on chromosome 7), is implicated in the visuospatial constructive impairment of WSs and others with partial characteristics of WS on tasks such as block building, puzzles, and drawing (Frangiskakis et al., 1996; Tassabehji et al., 1996). Subsequent research, however, questions these findings, as several non-WS individuals with substantiated deletions of ELN and LIMK1 show no evidence of visuospatial constructive impairment (Tassabehji et al., 1999).

Advances in genetic molecular analyses of genes in the central area of the common deletion in WSs, WSTF through LIMK1, are showing promise in discovering the genes associated with "subtle defects" in WS cognition (Korenberg et al., 2000).

Dorsal Cortical Stream. There is also evidence that the VSM difficulties of WSs may have a neural basis, specifically, in the dorsal cortical stream, which transmits visuospatial information, the "where" of objects, to the parietal lobe. In contrast, the ventral cortical stream transmits visual identity information, the "what" or recognition of objects and faces, to the temporal lobe (Atkinson et al., 1997).

Importantly, WSc ($n = 15$, 4–14 yrs, $M = 9;8$ yrs) exhibit a dissociation in these forms of neural functioning. They perform similarly to young normal

TABLE 4.4
Visuospatial Domains: Individual Differences and Developmental Trends in WSs

Type of Test or Performance	Result	Source or Reference
Visual Perceptual Tests[#]	WSc Variability	Milani et al., 1996
Drawing: BDAE & VMI[#]	WSc Variability	Bertrand et al., 1997
Drawing: DAP Test[#]	WSs Variability	Dykens et al., 2001
Block Construction[#]	WSc scores increase f) CA	Mervis et al., 1999
	WSc scores increase f) CA	Atkinson et al., 2001
Block Building Errors[#]	WSa < WSc	Mervis & Klein-Tasman, 2000
VMI[#]	WSs scores related to MA	Mervis & Klein-Tasman, 2000
VMI[#]	WSs scores related to CA	Dykens et al., 2001
Face Processing[#]	WSs ~ normal MA	Bellugi et al., 2000
	WSs > DSs	
	WSs Face Task > WSs' MA	
Vocabulary (PPVT–R)[#]	Early Wds: WSc ~ DSc	Bellugi et al., 2000
	Later: WSc > DSc	
VMI[#]	WSs < norms, own MA, DSs	Bellugi et al., 2000
VS Construction Tests[#]	WSc < Norms on VS Tests	Atkinson et al., 2001
Language (TROG/PPVT–R)[#]	WSc > on Lang vs. VS Tests	
Ordinality on VMI[#]	WSc ~ Normal MA matches	Bertrand et al., 1997
Drawings BDAE[#]		
Recognizability	WSc < MA Normal Matches	Bertrand et al., 1997
Major Parts Included		
Seriously Disorganized	WSc > MA Normal Matches	
Drawing Difficulty BDAE[#]	WSc: Elephant > House > Flower	Bertrand et al., 1997
Drawing Parts BDAE[#]	WSc: correlates with Intelligence Test Scores	Bertrand et al., 1997
Drawing Skills BDAE[#]	Increases in Normal Children in Preschool Years, Stages Similar to Drawings of WSc (9–10 yrs)	Bertrand et al., 1997
Drawing Skills (DAP)[#]	WSs ~ MRs (matched, mixed forms), ~ DSs	Dykens et al., 2001
DAP[#]	WSs, MRs, DSs: Scribblers Younger, Others Better Drawers	
DAP, K–BIT, VMI[#]	WSs: DAP > K–BIT, VMI	
Longitudinal Drawing Progress	WSc Case Study	Stiles et al., 2000
Longitudinal Drawing Study	WSc Gains in Recognizability, Organization People & Flowers > Houses > Elephant & Bicycle	Bertrand & Mervis, 1996
Drawings[#]	WSa > WSc	Hodenius et al., 1994
VS Slope of Age Change	WSs: Shallow, Truncated	Atkinson et al., 2001; Beret et al., 1996; Bellugi et al., 2000
Face Processing Style	WSc: Local Style	Deruelle et al., 1999

Note: % = percent of subjects; # = subject scores; WSa = WS adolescents &/or adults; WSc = WS children; DS = Down syndrome; MR = mentally retarded; "a" = adolescents/adults; MA = mental age; CA = chronological age; see text for test identification (e.g., BDAE).

controls on tasks associated with ventral stream function, namely, form coherence and matching spatial orientation, but are acutely impaired compared to normals on tasks involving the dorsal stream, namely, global coherence of motion and visuomotor accuracy (Atkinson et al., 1997). There are further indications that WSs' visuospatial difficulties involve the interaction of dorsal-stream spatial information with frontal control functions (Atkinson et al., 2001).

Cortical Hemispheric Functioning. At the cortical level, studies of the event-related brain potentials (ERPs) of WSs and other groups to facial stimuli (Mills et al., 2000) indicate that WSs exhibit a distinctive way of perceiving faces. This is evident in both the electrophysiological response to face stimuli and its location in the brain.

Unlike normal adults, WSs show an early abnormally small negative response wave at 100 msec and an abnormally large negative wave response at 200 msec to both upright and inverted faces. Responses at these latencies are associated with perception of faces. WSs also exhibit a major negative 320 msec wave for faces that are both upright and inverted. Responses at this latency are associated with face recognition. In contrast, normal adults display ERP differences to matched versus unmatched upright faces at N320. Moreover, this is mainly in the anterior regions of the right hemisphere, whereas WSs do not display this right hemisphere asymmetry or a differing wave pattern at N400 msec for match–mismatch responses to inverted faces (Mills et al., 2000).

These results are supported in a "hairnet" study of brain activity that shows that face processing in WSs occurs mainly in the left side of the brain, not the more typical right side. Moreover, activity is the same for upright and inverted faces in WSs rather than showing the processing changes that typically occur with inversion in other groups (Karmiloff-Smith, WSA Newsletter, 2001, *18*(1), p. 3).

Preliminary data also suggest that WS memory for faces is correlated with an ability to recognize and classify faces. These functions are related to the inferred volume of the inferior frontal cerebrum, but not the volume of seven other cortical regions (Bellugi, Hickok, Jones, & Jernigan, 1996).

In addition, functional magnetic resonance imaging (fMRI) studies suggest that the intact brains of WSs have several distinctive features, including reduction in size of the occipital lobe, the primary and secondary centers of vision in the brain (Reiss et al., 2000).

Neuroanatomical studies of deceased WS brains also reveal cellular changes in area 17 that may be implicated in some of the visual perceptual problems of WSs (Galaburda & Bellugi, 2000). Further research is needed on these issues.

Sensory Level. At the sensory level, WSs ($n = 11$) often display an anomalous condition, monofixation syndrome. This refers to cases in which the individual exhibits peripheral, but not central, fusion of the images of the two eyes (Olitsky, Sadler, & Reynolds, 1997). Based on ophthalmic evaluation, Olitsky et al. (1997) reported that no subject in their study had normal (visual) motor (nonstrabismus) or normal sensory (nonmonofixation) results.

Other aspects of ophthalmic exams and their implications for WS vision and visuospatial processing are discussed in Section II. A.

B. Motor Functioning

Parents, teachers, researchers, professionals, or others acquainted with WS are keenly aware that most WSs have impaired motor coordination. Children with WS (WSc) are described as "awkward," "klutzy," and "poorly coordinated." Delays in motor development, aberrant response patterns, and poor motor planning are common. Anecdotal reports convey the severity of these deficits, as in a mother's description of her 7-year-old WS son's response to catching a ball: "A ball is thrown—one thrusts up the hands. But Terry [her son] would stare at the ball and let it hit him" (Anonymous, 1985, p. 265).

This scenario depicts some of the many problems in motor coordination, reported in 97% of WSc, and problems of apraxia or poor motor planning, reported in 92% (Utah Survey; Semel & Rosner, 1991a, 1991b). Normal motor planning includes establishing the need for an action, formulating a plan for its execution, and executing the action. Information must be organized so the body knows how to move, what it can do, and its position in space (Scheiber, 2000). In WSs, the ability to self-generate previously learned habits, like coloring a circle, is often problematic. Extending prior knowledge to new situations is even more challenging, such as applying skills used in walking down stairs to negotiating a circular staircase. Clinical tests indicate that 71% of WSs ($n = 24$, 2–30 yrs) exhibit both imitative and constructional apraxia (Chapman, du Plessis, & Pober, 1996).

WS difficulties in motor coordination and motor planning tend to impact four areas: gross motor, fine motor, and visual-spatial-motor performance, as well as problems of spatial orientation. Gross motor, spatial, and fine motor problems are discussed later; visual-spatial-motor problems, evident in tasks such as drawing and block construction, were already discussed.

Gross Motor Deficits

Gross motor problems refer to WSs' difficulties with large muscle activities, muscle tone, and proprioceptive input (Doherty, Bellugi, Jernigan, & Poizner, 1989). Generally, WSc have a peculiar stance and gait, poor balance, and extreme difficulty executing simple tasks, such as throwing and catching a ball, carrying a glass of water across the room without spilling, stepping on and off the curb without tripping, and learning how to ride a bicycle (Scheiber, 2000). Motor abilities of WSs are generally considerably lower than expected from their age or cognitive level (Dilts et al., 1990).

Forty-one percent of parents mention poor gross motor coordination as a problem in open-ended interviews (Udwin et al., 1987). This is evident in WSs' gross motor functioning in the following areas: reflexes, early motor development, locomotion, balance problems, problems of spatial orientation, handling sports equipment and participating in sports activities, as well as formal test results.

Reflexes. A reflex is an automatic response to a specific external stimulus (Smith, 1989). Reflexes that are regularly present in nonhandicapped infants may be delayed, absent, or disorganized in WSc.

Three automatic postural reactions are often impaired in children with special needs. These include the righting reaction, which maintains the head in a vertical position and establishes a stable relation with the torso and surrounding space; the equilibrium reaction, which responds to changes in the center of gravity by flexing the head or trunk and extending the arms or legs; and the protective reaction, in which the arms and legs are automatically extended to prevent or break a fall (Ayres, 1981).

Clinical observation reveals that many WSc are significantly delayed or impaired in executing the automatic postural, righting, and protective reactions that most children begin to acquire during their first year.

Early Motor Development. Gross motor coordination is also often delayed or impaired (Dilts et al., 1990). WSc are reported to attain, on average, independent sitting at 11+ months compared to 7 months in normally developing children (Trauner, Bellugi, & Chase, 1989; Shirley, 1933, cf. Hetherington & Parke, 1993, p. 181). Supported walking appears at an average age of 18 months in WSc compared to 11 months in normally developing children (Dodge, 1995; Shirley, 1933).

Motor inefficiency is often exhibited in even the most fundamental skills, such as steering the body without falling or acquiring the skeletal alignment required for standing up straight. Many WSs tend to have difficulty executing the minute movement patterns, adjustments in posture, and shifts in weight needed to perform actions like walking down the stairs or jumping down from a higher plane with ease (Barsch, 1967).

Locomotion. Parents report sizable delays in WSs' learning to walk independently compared to the normative age of 15 months in nonhandicapped children (Shirley, 1933, cf. Hetherington & Parke, 1993). Most WSc learn to walk between ages 2 and $3^1{}_2$ years (Bellugi et al., 1988b; Dodge, 1995), but sometimes not until age 4 (Scheiber, 2000). Reportedly, 18% of WSc have difficulty in walking (Tharp, 1986). Most are cautious about walking on slopes or uneven surfaces (Dilts et al., 1990); and 69% are anxious about walking on different textured surfaces like grass, gravel, or bumpy pavement (Utah Survey, Semel & Rosner, 1991a, 1991b). Walking downstairs is a problem for 64% of WSc (Utah Survey, Semel & Rosner, 1991a, 1991b). Climbing upstairs is a problem for 78% of WSc (Atkinson et al., 2001). Running is difficult for 41% (Tharp, 1986).

Gait abnormalities are exhibited by 70% of WSc (n = 17, 2–8 yrs) and 85% of WSa (n = 7, 12–30 yrs) on tests of walking, running, tandem gait, and stressed gait relative to age-referenced data (Chapman et al., 1996). Clinical tests also indicate that WSa have a higher rate of abnormal responses (76%) than DSa (48%) in running, toe- and heel-walking, hopping, and skipping (Trauner et al., 1989). These may involve problems with balance.

Balance Problems. Many WSc tend to need help in learning how to deal appropriately with sensations of movement and balance. These sensations are under the control of the vestibular and kinesthetic/proprioceptive systems (Barsch, 1967). Eighty percent of WSc are said to have gravitational insecurities (Utah Survey, Semel & Rosner, 1991a, 1991b), and 60% have difficulty with balance (Tharp, 1986).

Jumping, hopping, and skipping are extremely difficult for many WSc, partly because of their problems maintaining balance (Udwin & Yule, 1998b). Parents report that 83% of WSc avoid jumping from a higher place (Utah Survey, Semel & Rosner, 1991a, 1991b). Normally developing children usually acquire single-foot hopping by 6 or 7 years of age (Barsch, 1967), whereas WSc are often delayed. Extended periods of two-footed, immature "hops" are typical before WSc become able to sustain one-footed dynamic balance.

Delays in learning to skip are also typical. After starting with one-sided skipping, WSc attempt bilateral skipping, followed by the rhythmic, bilateral interweaving of the lifting of each side of the body. This is required for complete mastery. Many children with learning disabilities have similar problems with skipping.

As preschoolers, many WSc resist playing on a swing or a seesaw, although they may enjoy being tossed in the air. Many are unable to catch themselves easily enough to recoup their balance if they fall. Some WSc have unexplained aversions to activities involving new movement patterns; some have a history of getting sick in cars, elevators, or airplanes. Paradoxically, many of these children say they enjoy fast-moving carnival rides and roller coasters.

In later years, the balancing problems of WSc can cause delays in learning to ride a bicycle or use roller skates. Nevertheless, eventually, many do learn to ride a bicycle.

Sports Activities. WSc are usually significantly delayed in learning how to throw and catch a ball. Most normally developing children master throwing and catching of a ball by age $6^1\!/_2$ (Barsch, 1967), but 51% of school-age WSc have problems throwing a ball and 67% have trouble catching a ball (Tharp, 1986). Some never acquire these skills at all.

Many WSc throw a ball with one arm without shifting their body weight or making the mandatory trunk rotation and forward glide of one foot. More refined throwing efforts, achieved by synchronizing the position of the arm and thrusting the body while simultaneously stepping forward (Barsch, 1967), are far more difficult movements and seem to be beyond the ability of many WSc (as well as other children with special needs). The cross-diagonal body adjustment required for throwing proficiency (Barsch, 1967) is often never achieved by WSc.

The act of catching a ball requires the child to visually track the flight path of the ball and accurately judge its trajectory. Body weight must be shifted to accommodate body position to the path of the ball and the hands extended to catch the ball (Barsch, 1967). As with learning disabled children, many WSc seem unable to perform the three-dimensional visual tracking and rapid body adjustment necessary to catch the ball (Barsch, 1967). Some WSc are able to catch the ball only when it makes contact with their bodies. At other times, they tend to let the ball go past them. Merely kicking a ball presents a problem for 41% of these individuals (Tharp, 1986).

Formal Test Results. Formal test measures of gross motor skills substantiate the severity of WSc's problems. Toddlers and young children with WS score at the first and second percentile on the Peabody Developmental Gross Motor Scales. Items include tests of balance, locomotion and non-locomotion skills, ball playing, and reflexive behaviors. The age-equivalent (AE) score of the younger subgroup ($n = 18$, < 3 yrs) is 15 months; the AE score of the older subgroup ($n = 21$, 3–7 yrs) is 28 months (Shea, Borton, Allen, & Pober, 1996). The scores are far below their chronological ages.

Similarly, young children with WS ($n = 7$, 4–8 yrs) score significantly lower than children with nonspecific developmental disabilities on the motor subscale of the McCarthy Scales of Children's Abilities, a standardized test of motor skills (Bennett et al., 1978). Items include walking a line, bouncing a ball, standing on one foot, and catching a beanbag.

In another study, all nine subjects, school-age WSc (10–20 yrs), performed at the third percentile level in the gross motor function section of the Bruininks–Oseretsky Test of Motor Proficiency (Pagon et al., 1987).

Subtests include tests of running speed, balance, sequential and simultaneous bilateral coordination of upper and lower limbs, and strength of certain body parts. Thus, there is strong and consistent evidence of severe gross motor deficits in WSc.

Mechanisms. Difficulties in the musculoskeletal system of WSs, including poor muscle tone and possible contractures, may contribute to the gross motor delays and deficiencies characteristic of WSs. Proprioceptive and kinesthetic problems as well as problems of balance are also evident (Dodge, 1995; Shea et al., 1996). Many of these factors are reflected in clinical conditions common to both WSs (see p. 149) and learning disabled children.

Factors involving the central nervous system are postulated as well (Shea et al., 1996). However, surprisingly little is known about the motor cortex, motor cerebellum, and motor pathways of WSs, with the possible exceptions of Atkinson et al.'s (1997, 2001) research on the dorsal cortical stream and the programmatic brain research of Bellugi and colleagues (Bellugi et al., 2000).

Problems of Spatial Orientation

Many WSc are significantly impaired in establishing a directional orientation and in their perceptual organization of space (Kephart, 1960). They seem to have difficulty establishing their own laterality, directionality, and understanding of the phenomenon of mirror image. "Laterality" and "directionality" refer to the child's awareness of left–right and other directional concepts, including relational terms that refer to spatial dimensions like "left–right," "up–down," and "front–back." "Mirror image" refers to the left–right reversal and inversion of the image of an object seen in a mirror (Kephart, 1960).

Most academically achieving children become aware of laterality and directionality by their early elementary school years (Kephart, 1960), but these continue to be problem areas for many WSs throughout childhood and beyond.

Directionality. In normal development, the young child rotates the whole body to explore things on one side or the other and these space-oriented experiences aid in the development of depth perception. That is, the child establishes a three-dimensional representation of space (Barsch, 1967).

Clinical observations reveal that many WSc have difficulty using proprioceptive and kinesthetic cues to determine spatial relationships. The ability to make bodily adjustments is needed in order to meet situational demands, such as shifting body weight so that others can pass by on a crowded bus or to recouperate one's balance on a shifting boat (Barsch, 1967).

Directionality problems may also contribute to the difficulty that WSs have in "finding their way," reported in 36% of WSc, and in "crossing roads," reported in 49% (Atkinson et al., 2001). Difficulty in judging the distance and speed of cars may be another factor affecting WSa's problem crossing roads (Udwin, Howlin, & Davies, 1996).

Laterality. By age 6, most nonimpaired children can differentiate between the left and right sides of their own body. By age 9 or 10, they can usually identify right and left on other people (M. Levine, Brooks, & Shonkoff, 1980, pp. 138–139).

Some WSc seem unaware of the difference between the two sides of their own bodies; they are unable to distinguish their right side from their left, and many have difficulty understanding the verbal concepts "right" and "left."

Parents report that 38% of WSc "do not know their left from their right," and 28% "cannot set a table," which is a task that requires shifting directional focus and reversal and inversion on occasion (Utah Survey, $n = 64$, 4–22 yrs, Semel & Rosner, 1991a, 1991b). Many WSc are unable to comprehend the concept of a mirror image or understand that they project a mirror image of their own body. They also tend to have problems in correctly labeling the contra-lateral parts of their own bodies, let alone being able to automatize right and left responses, or deal with letter reversals like "b" and "d." In these respects, WSc are much like many learning disabled children.

Clinical observations of postadolescent WSs suggest that difficulty with directional concepts, "left" and "right," may continue into adulthood. These are also expressed in problems of "handedness," including hand preference, an area of fine motor performance.

Handedness. Most academically achieving children establish hand preference by age 4 to 6 (Levine et al., 1980). In contrast, handedness usually develops late in WSs. It is often delayed until age 5 to 8 or even as late as age 10 (Bellugi et al., 1988b; Doherty et al., 1989).

On tests of handedness and manual dexterity, WSa often exhibit a lack of strong right-handedness and a tendency toward confused or mixed handedness: The right hand does better on one task, the left hand on another (Bellugi et al., 1988b). Clinical observation suggests that WSc may have a tendency to alternate their hands while performing tasks that require crossing the midline of the body.

WSa also show greater prevalence of left-handedness in daily activities than is usual for people without a family history of left dominance (Bellugi et al., 1988b). Because handedness is an indirect indicator of brain organization, this suggests that the cerebral cortex and other brain centers may be organized atypically in WSs, as discussed in the context of brain mechanism related to face recognition abilities.

Fine Motor Deficits

Fine motor problems refer to difficulties with self-care, use of tools and sports equipment, arts and crafts, writing, and motor overflow. It also includes difficulties with "handedness," already discussed.

According to parents, 94% of all WSc (n = 48, 0–20+ yrs), show fine motor delay (Survey of Midwest Region, Williams Syndrome Association, National Newsletter, 1989, April). As a result, most WSc are severely impaired in carrying out ordinary acts of daily living, including self-care, classroom assignments, extracurricular activities, and pre-vocational tasks.

Activities of Daily Living. WSc are characterized by "poor development in the use of tools for skills in play, self-care, school, domestic care, hobbies and vocation" (Dilts et al., 1990, p. 127). Many of these difficulties were already described in the section on visual-spatial-motor problems. Almost all WSc (90%) are described as deficient in the use of tools (Utah Survey, Semel & Rosner, 1991a, 1991b). According to Morris et al. (1988), "The majority of [WS] children and adolescents [are] unable to tie their shoes easily, cut with a knife, or use a broom" (p. 321). Even in adulthood, 33% of WSa (n = 119, 16–39 yrs, M = 23 yrs) are unable to dress themselves completely without help (Udwin, 1990).

A seemingly simple task such as buttering a slice of bread or making a peanut butter and jelly sandwich can be problematic for most WSc. This is because they do not have the fine motor skills involved in holding a knife, exerting the appropriate amount of pressure, or performing a spreading motion with the knife.

Learning difficulty is common in paper and pencil tasks, like writing and drawing, that rely on fine motor skills (Levine, 1993). Problems with "pencil grasp" occur in over 80% of WSc (Utah Survey, Semel & Rosner, 1991a, 1991b; Tharp, 1986). Even among WSa, writing skills may be affected (Udwin, 1990).

Arts and craft projects, such as pasting, coloring within the lines, and cutting a straight line are often extremely messy, with more paste ending up on the child than on the items intended to be pasted. Functional activities like folding articles of clothing, towels, or sheets are troublesome for most WSs, adults as well as children. Appliance use and routine tasks, such as the turning required in adjusting handles or faucets or combination locks, can be extremely frustrating. Visuospatial deficits in reading dials compound these problems.

Warning signs of fine motor difficulty may be evident in the presence of associated movements, like foot tapping, when the WS individual is performing a fine motor task like writing or tying a shoe (i.e., "motor overflow"). Symptoms of "motor overflow" often include protrusion of the tongue, some drooling, or lip or head movements activated by pencil or hand movement (Levine et al., 1980).

Formal Test Results. The fine motor problems of WSs are extremely serious, at least as serious as their gross motor problems. Among WS infants (*n* = 13), fine motor delay is greater than gross motor delay on the Bayley Scales of Infant Development (Plissart, Borghgraef, & Fryns, 1996a).

In older WSc, fine motor scores are comparable to or worse than gross motor scores on the Bruininks–Oseretsky Tests of Motor Proficiency (Pagon et al., 1987). Fine motor items on the Bruininks–Oseretsky assess the subject's ability to coordinate precise hand and visual movements, and to engage in visual tracking with movements of the arms and hands. Also assessed is hand and finger dexterity and hand and arm speed. Thus, many of these items test both visual-spatial-motor integration and fine motor skills.

Clinical fine motor testing reveals abnormalities in 60% of WSc and 71% of WSa (Chapman et al., 1996). Compared with DSa, WSa exhibit a much higher rate of abnormal responses (53% vs. 33%, respectively) on basic neurological tests of finger–thumb opposition and wrist pronation–supination (Trauner et al., 1989). The fine motor scores of WSs are also lower than expected for their age level or their performance on tests of general ability (Dilts et al., 1990).

Mechanisms. Because many of the skills involved in fine motor difficulties reflect problems with visual-spatial-motor integration, those mechanisms appear applicable to motor difficulties as well. Specifically, genetic (LIM-kinase1), neural (dorsal cortical stream), and sensory (monofixation syndrome) mechanisms, as well as possible deviations in cerebral organization, may be manifested in problems of hand dominance. Clinical problems involving aspects of the visual and motor systems are described on pages 141–142 and 149–151.

Table 4.5 presents a summary of research findings on the various areas of motor functioning in WSs.

II. INTERVENTION APPROACHES FOR VISUOMOTOR PROBLEMS

Aside from being seriously impaired in the various areas of visuomotor performance (i.e., visuospatial construction, visuospatial cognition, gross motor, spatial orientation, and fine motor skills), the deficits of WSs in these ar-

TABLE 4.5
Research on Motor Functioning in WSs

Type of Test or Performance	Result	Source or Reference
Motor Coordination Problems	WSc 97%	Semel & Rosner, Utah Survey
Problems of Apraxia	WSc 92%	
Abnormal Apraxia	WSs 71%	Chapman et al., 1996
Poor Gross Motor Coordination	WSc 41%	Udwin et al., 1987
Independent Sitting	WSc ~ 1 yr	Trauner et al., 1989
	Normals ~ 7 mo	Shirley, 1933
Supported Walking	WSc ~ 18 mo	Dodge, 1995
	Normals ~ 11 mo	Shirley, 1933
Independent Walking	WSc ~ 2–3.5 yrs	Bellugi et al., 1988b; Dodge, 1995
	Normals ~ 15 mo	Shirley, 1933
Difficulty with Walking	WSc 18%	Tharp, 1986
Difficulty with Running	WSc 41%	
Anxious Walking on Slopes, Uneven Surfaces	WSc 69%	Semel & Rosner, Utah Survey
Problem in Walking Downstairs	WSc 64%	
Problem in Climbing Upstairs	WSc 78%	Atkinson et al., 2001
Toe-Walking/ Cerebral Palsy-Type Tightness	WSa 31%	Trauner et al., 1989
Abnormal Gaits	WSc 70%, WSa 85%	Chapman et al., 1996
Abnormal Running, Walking, Hopping, Skipping	WSa > DSa	Trauner et al., 1989
Gravitational Insecurities	WSc 80%	Semel & Rosner, Utah Survey
Difficulty with Balance	WSc 60%	Tharp, 1986
Avoids Jumping from Heights	WSc 83%	Semel & Rosner, Utah Survey
Problems Throwing a Ball	WSc 51%	Tharp, 1986
Problems Catching a Ball	WSc 67%	
Problems Kicking a Ball	WSc 41%	
Difficulty Finding Their Way	WSc 36%	Atkinson et al., 2001
Difficulty Crossing Roads	WSc 49%	
Do Not Know Left from Right	WSc 38%	Semel & Rosner, Utah Survey
Cannot Set a Table	WSc 28%	
Peabody Developmental Gross Motor Scale	WSc AE < CA	Shea et al., 1996
Motor Subscale, McCarthy Scales of Children's Abilities	WSc < MRc	Bennett et al., 1978
Gross Motor Section, Bruininks–Oseretsky Test of Motor Proficiency	WSc third percentile	Pagon et al., 1987
Fine Motor Delay	WSc 94%	WSA, Midwest Region Survey, 1989
Deficient in Tool Use	WSc 90%	Semel & Rosner, Utah Survey
Unable to Dress Self Independently	WSa 33%	Udwin, 1990
Problems with Pencil Grasp	WSc > 80%	Semel & Rosner, Utah Survey

(Continued)

TABLE 4.5
(Continued)

Type of Test or Performance	Result	Source or Reference
Handedness Established	WSc 5–8 or 10 yrs	Bellugi et al., 1988b; Doherty et al., 1989
	Normals 4–6 yrs	Levine et al., 1980
Bayley Scales of Infant Development	WSc Fine Motor Delay > Gross Motor Delay	Plissart et al., 1996a
Bruininks–Oseretsky Tests	WSc Fine Motor Score = or < Gross Motor Scores	Pagon et al., 1987
Finger–Thumb Opposition, Wrist Pronation–Supination	Abnormal Responses, WSa 55%, DS 33%	Trauner et al., 1989
Fine Motor Abnormalities	WSc 60%, WSa 71%	Chapman et al., 1996

Note: % = percent of subjects; # = subject scores; WSa = WS adolescents &/or adults; WSc = WS children; DS = Down syndrome; "a" = adolescents/adults; AE = age-equivalent score; MA = mental age; CA = chronological age.

eas tend to interact and accumulate. The resultant problems, practical and educational, generally call for professional assessment and treatment.

Clinical aspects and treatment of vision, visual functioning, and motor problems are discussed first, followed by suggestions for psycho-educational techniques that may help to address some of the WSs' visual-spatial-motor difficulties.

A. Clinical Aspects of Vision

The overall extent of visuospatial and visual-spatial-motor integration problems of WSc underscores the importance of initiating early, intensive programs of evaluation, treatment, and management of visual functioning. In addition, there are clinical conditions of vision that are intrinsic to the structure and operation of the WS eye.

In other words, clinical aspects of "seeing" include two related areas: vision, or the study of the typical characteristics and disorders of the eye; and visual functioning, which includes visual-spatial-motor (VSM) integration skills. Although the distinction between the sensory or visual aspects and the functional or perceptual (VSM) aspects of seeing is somewhat arbitrary, real differences exist in terms of the types of professionals to be consulted, clinical tests conducted, and treatment orientation.

Information on specialists, clinical conditions, evaluation, and treatment of WS vision is presented next. Interventions for problems involving VSM skills comprise primarily psycho-educational techniques. These are described following the section on clinical aspects of motor functioning.

Specialists

Ophthalmologists. For diagnosis and treatment of eye disorders, an ophthalmologist or medical doctor specializing in vision should be consulted to determine the health status of the eye and its structures. Apropos of the widespread incidence and severity of eye problems, 44% of WSc are reported to have been seen by an ophthalmologist (Morris et al., 1988).

Other Specialists. Parents report that WSc have profited from the services of a number of professionals besides ophthalmologists, pediatric ophthalmologists, and neuro-ophthalmologists. These may also include optometrists trained in developmental vision, specialists trained in orthoptics, occupational therapists with neurodevelopmental training (NDT) and/or sensory integration (SI) training, and physical therapists (WSA Newsletter, 1991, Summer). Adaptive physical education teachers, psychologists, chiropractors, osteopaths, special educators, and instructors are also said to have helped some WSc deal with their visuomotor perceptual problems.

No single profession has a cure for the numerous visual perceptual problems associated with WS. Besides, not all types of specialists may be available, and there may be advantages to choosing professionals who are skilled at providing individually tailored approaches to evaluation and treatment.

Characteristics of WS Eyes

Usually, individuals with handicapping conditions and mental retardation are at a greater risk for vision impairment than the general population. In the case of WSs, obtaining information about their visual structures, conditions, and functioning is of vital importance. At the level of sensory processes, some information about the structures and frequent problems of the eyes of WS children is available, including vulnerability for strabismus and certain refractive errors (Winter, Pankau, Amm, Gosch, & Wessel, 1996).

Stellate Pattern. Clinical reports of the ocular features of WS patients note the frequent occurrence of a stellate or starlike pattern in the iris in about 70% of cases (Greenberg & Lewis, 1988; Jones & Smith, 1975; Winter et al., 1996). Although generally linked to blue eye color, it is often considered part of the facies or features characteristic of WSs (Greenberg & Lewis, 1988; Jones & Smith, 1975; Utah Survey, Semel & Rosner, 1991a, 1991b; Winter et al., 1996).

Strabismus. Strabismus is a condition marked by misalignment of the eyes and eye muscle imbalance (Greenberg & Lewis, 1988). With normal vision, both eyes are aimed at the same target. Strabismus is apparent when one eye fails to look straight ahead. Children with this condition may tilt their heads in an effort to align their eyes, or squint more often.

Many WSs have strabismus. Across studies, the reported incidence ranges from 30% (Greenberg & Lewis, 1988; Jones & Smith, 1975) to 50% (Atkinson et al., 2001; Martin, Snodgrass, & Cohen, 1984; Morris et al., 1988; Pagon et al., 1987; Winter et al., 1996), to 78% (Kapp, von Noorden, & Jenkins, 1995) and 89% (Trauner et al., 1989).

There are several types of strabismus corresponding to the direction to which the misaligned eye points. Among WSc and WSa, the most common type is infantile esotropia (Greenberg & Lewis, 1988; Kapp et al., 1995). In esotropia, the misaligned eye is directed inward, resulting in crossed eyes. Because the eyes point in different directions, two different images are sent to the brain. In the absence of treatment, the child may learn to ignore one image and use only one eye in order to avoid double vision. This phenomenon, known as amblyopia, generally occurs in half of children with strabismus. It usually results in a loss of depth perception and normal two-eyed vision unless treatment is initiated early.

Refractive Errors. WSs are also vulnerable to either of two types of refractive errors: hypermetropic, indicating hyperopia or farsightedness; and myopic, indicating myopia or nearsightedness. In hyperopia, the farsighted visual image is focused behind the retina so that close-up objects look blurred. In myopia, the nearsighted visual image is focused in front of the retina so distant stimuli are difficult to discern. Normally, young children (kindergarten age) are farsighted to some degree; the condition decreases as the eye grows during the elementary school and teenage years.

Refractive errors are reported in about 54% of WSc (Atkinson et al., 2001). The predominant type of error is hypermetropic, or farsightedness, which is diagnosed in 68% of WSs (Greenberg & Lewis, 1988; Winter et al., 1996). Hyperopia (blurring of near objects) is fairly common in WSc (Morris et al.,1988). This condition can produce eye discomfort and strain and interfere with near point tasks such as learning to read, reading a book, and writing.

Myopia, or nearsightedness, may also have a negative impact on WS learning because deficits in accommodation and convergence may cause difficulty in seeing the chalkboard. Such problems may also affect WSc's ability to engage in sports, ball playing games, and other activities that require visual processing, depth perception, and spatial judgments.

Other Conditions. WSc may be susceptible to problems of acuity or sharpness of vision; 36% of WSs tested at less than age normative values on tasks involving matching of letters or preferential looking at patterns of gratings (Atkinson et al. 2001). Evidence of slight clouding of the lens in two WSc (9 yrs) suggests including examination for cataracts with WSs (Winter et al., 1996).

Wherever possible, vision consultations should be made regularly and suggestions, where relevant, should be reported to the school.

Treatment of Eye Disorders

Treatment of Strabismus. Treatment of strabismus is aimed at straightening the eyes and restoring normal binocular, or two-eyed, vision.

Treatment options include surgery to reposition eye muscles, lenses where appropriate, patching of one eye, specific visual training, or orthoptic exercises. During surgery, muscles on the inner wall of the eye that have become tightened are repositioned in order to weaken their pull on the crossed eye. True strabismus is not outgrown. Surgery, if recommended by an ophthalmologist, should be performed in the early years of life to prevent permanent loss of two-eyed vision. Due to the high incidence of strabismus and its effect on the visual abilities of WSc, thorough examination by a qualified ophthalmologist, pediatric ophthalmologist, or neuro-ophthalmologist and developmental optometrist is strongly recommended. The ophthalmologist or developmental optometrist may patch the good eye in order to strengthen or improve vision in the misaligned, amblyopic eye. Patching is most effective when it is introduced early. In older individuals, the brain may not be able to learn to ignore the image perceived by one eye, so double vision may persist. When untreated, early amblyopia may cause irreversible damage.

Treatment of Refractive Errors. An ophthalmologist, or eye specialist, can evaluate vision for refractive errors and prescribe corrective lenses when needed. Younger WSc who are farsighted (hyperopic) may benefit from the use of convex glasses. This may reduce academic problems related to hyperopia or blurring of close objects. Similarly, prescriptive lenses can be used to correct myopia (i.e., nearsightedness), thereby reducing problems with distant vision.

Although corrective lenses may reduce eyestrain by supporting the eye's ability to focus, lenses may not fully restore normal visual acuity. However, detection and correction of refractive errors are prerequisites for assessment of difficulties in functional vision.

Evaluation of Visual Functioning

Research on visuospatial cognition, visual-spatial-motor integration, and the structural aspects of WS eyes all contribute to a "Williamesque" profile of marked deficits and individual differences in those deficits. Evaluation of visual functioning is usually sought after parents, physicians, or teachers observe certain warning signs that warrant formal, professional assessment (Levine, 1997).

Grounds for Referral. Parents and educators may be unsure about the need for clinical evaluation, but certain kinds of informal observations can be helpful in making a decision.

Common signs of deficits in acuity or sharpness of vision include excessive eye strain, holding a book too near or too far away, squinting or blinking to see distant objects more clearly, discomfort or fatigue resulting in reduced comprehension of written material, and errors when copying from a chalkboard. Difficulties in learning to read or an aversion to reading sometimes arise from uncorrected visual problems. Accuracy in judging size, shape, and color is indicative of skill in using monocular visual cues. Distance is best judged using binocular vision.

It is also important to note whether the children use both eyes or turn or tilt their head or the paper so that only one eye is used in viewing an object. This can be indicative of an imbalance in binocular vision (i.e., difficulty in using both eyes for near and distant vision). If so, this may be a sign of strabismus. Inadequate use of both eyes affects various aspects of visual perception, including judgment of spatial orientation, depth perception, visual accuracy, and extent of the perceptual field. This, in turn, may interfere with learning to read and write, as well as other activities of daily living, such as walking down stairs, tying shoelaces, or performing other self-help tasks.

Binocular vision is an important part of learning to read. Problems may be manifested in skipping of lines, losing one's place, and rapid fatigue while reading. Reading requires consistent discrimination of the form, shape, and size of letters and numbers. Writing requires one to reconstruct those patterns while avoiding the reversing, inverting, or transposing of letters, words, or numerals. For these reasons, visual discrimination, or the ability to detect subtle or marked similarities and differences between objects or pictures, should be evaluated, because it may affect learning to read and write.

Clinical experience suggests that WSc often have difficulty directing and controlling their visual attention. Problems may occur in locating items on a page or in a room, in confusing figure and ground relationships, or in focusing on relevant visual information in the presence of competing visual input. They may also have difficulty engaging in self-directed, effective visual processing. This is essential for several kinds of visual processing, namely, visual tracking, or keeping one's eyes on visual targets; visual scanning, or inspecting visual stimuli in an organized, efficient, effective manner;

and visual matching, or perceiving relevant differences between visual stimuli. Deficient visual processing can be especially burdensome when performing near-point tasks and classroom work (e.g., comparing prefixes and words).

Clinical Assessment. Vision specialists, including developmentally trained optometrists and orthoptic technicians, can be useful for assessing functional vision and prescribing remediation for WSc with problems in this area. The patient's acuity or sharpness of vision, eye coordination, binocular vision, peripheral vision, perceptual accuracy, and speed are evaluated. Visuomotor control is noted, as are eye tracking movements, near and distant vision, visual fields and visuospatial perception.

Generally, the vision specialist explores eye coordination, including the ability to perform rotations, fixations, and convergence. Binocular vision is checked for evidence of double vision, discrepancy between near-point and far point vision, and the child's ability to follow a moving target. The vision specialist also checks the patient's ability to perform adequate "accommodative rock," the change in focus required to adapt from far- to near-point vision, like shifting from looking at a page in a book on the desk to looking at the chalkboard and then at the page again. This is often a major problem for WSc.

Formal Tests of Visual Perception. Tests of visual perception are especially important for WSc, because they can help to identify the nature of the child's visuoperceptual problems and point in the direction of much needed intervention. Testing should be preceded by an ophthalmologic examination to rule out structural problems with the eyes and the need for important medical intervention. Tests of visual perception should evaluate various aspects of visuoperceptual processing and types of abilities. Several psycho-educational tests may be useful with WSs.[5]

---

[5]Psycho-educational tests that are particularly useful for testing the visual functioning of WSs include the Beery Developmental Test of Visual-Motor Integration (VMI) (Beery, 1982), which tests the drawing and copying of geometric forms; the Motor-Free Visual Perception Test (MVPT; Colarusso & Hammill, 1972), which avoids use of motor components in the testing of stimulus matching, figure ground discrimination, spatial relationships, visual memory, visual closure, and visual discrimination; and the Frostig Developmental Test of Visual Perception (Frostig, Maslow, Lefever, & Whittlesey, 1964), which tests visual-perceptual skills that are crucial for WSs, such as eye-motor coordination and figure ground perception.

Other tests include the Revised Visual Retention Test (Benton, 1963; Sivan, 1992), which contains Benton's tests of face discrimination and spatial orientation; subtests from Ayres' (1989/1991) Southern California Sensory Integration and Praxis Tests; and the Bender Visual Motor Gestalt Test (Bender, 1938).

Visual Training Programs

Many parents report that participation in a visual training program markedly improved their WSc's visual functioning. Training programs aim to increase children's ability to process and interpret what is seen by helping them use their eyes more efficiently (Frostig & Horne, 1964; Stiles et al., 2000).

Administered by visual specialists, such as optometrists and orthoptic technicians, visual training programs emphasize discrimination of form, contour, relative position, and relative size. Particular attention is also paid to hand–eye coordination. Activities to improve visuomotor coordination and eye movement control are prescribed. To promote visual tracking in multiple directions (e.g., vertically, horizontally), WSc may be asked to focus their eyes on different parts of the room. They may also be asked to look at designated points and objects, pictures, letters, or words, as rapidly as possible. Visual scanning "games," conducted by the specialist, special educator, or parent, can provide additional practice.

Visual training activities do not purport to teach children how to read and there is some controversy about their value. There is a great deal of anecdotal evidence, however, concerning the helpfulness of visual training programs in teaching WSc how to use their eyes more effectively and efficiently. This is consistent with the belief that learning how to attend and direct the eyes onto targets are prerequisites for many kinds of common visuospatial tasks, including reading, writing, and dealing with numbers.

Qualified Professionals. Readers should be cautioned about the hazards of incompetent professionals and the critical importance of selecting adequately trained and experienced specialists. There are reports of misdiagnosis and disregard of symptoms, such as a 7-year-old WS boy who was diagnosed as farsighted only, even though his left eye turned noticeably outward when he looked at nearby objects. Clearly, he showed symptoms of both accommodative and convergence insufficiency, that is, lack of adaptation of the curvature of the lens in response to changes in distance and difficulty in joint focusing of the two eyes. Although the boy's eyes responded positively to subsequent training in eye convergence, nontreatment had worsened his poor eye–hand coordination and academic problems before his difficulties were properly diagnosed (Anonymous, 1985).

Clinical Conditions and Visual Functioning

Although the relation between the structural conditions of WSs' eyes and their VSM deficits is of vital importance, little research has been conducted on this topic. However, a preliminary study reports a number of clinical conditions in WSc (n = 75, 18 mo–13 yrs). About 50% are said to have common pediatric visual abnormalities, including poor visual acuity (i.e., sharpness of vision), strabismus, stereo vision deficit, and marked refractive errors (Atkinson et al., 1996; Atkinson et al., 2001). There is also some evidence that monofixation syndrome, or poor binocular central fusion, occurs in 55% of WSs (n = 11). This may be a contributing factor to strabismus (Olitsky et al., 1997).

Importantly, the occurrence of such conditions does not seem to correlate with the severity of WSs' visuospatial deficits, which are often inherent in problems of visual functioning (Atkinson et al., 1996; Atkinson et al., 2001). The investigators hypothesize, instead, that such visuospatial difficulties are related to deficits in the development of specific cortical pathways (Atkinson et al., 1996), possibly impairment in the dorsal stream that leads to the parietal lobe (Atkinson et al., 1997) or frontal control functions (Atkinson et al., 2001).

In any event, all individuals with WS should be screened periodically by an ophthalmologist from infancy on because of the frequency of strabismus and refractive problems. Assessment of functional visual problems is also advised.

B. Clinical Aspects of Motor Performance

The gross motor, fine motor, and related difficulties of most WSs interfere with many aspects of their lives. To help address these problems, specialists should be consulted as required for evaluation of motor functioning, screening and examination of clinical conditions, and therapy. These clinical aspects of motor performance are discussed later. Other approaches involving use of psycho-educational techniques are also described in Section C, along with strategies that may help in dealing with various kinds of related visuospatial and visuomotor problems.

Specialists

WSs may be able to benefit from the services of many kinds of professionals who are trained and skilled in treating various aspects of motor problems. These may include neurologists, orthopedists, physiatrists (doctor of physical medicine and rehabilitation, MD), physical therapists, occupational therapists, and specialists in adaptive physical education, special education, gymnastic coaching, athletics training, cranio sacral massage therapy, and dance therapy. There are also reports of chiropractic treatment dramatically improving the postural alignment and motor coordination of WSc.

WSc should be referred to an orthopedist (bone specialist, MD), physical therapist (PT), or occupational therapist (OT) for formal evaluation if they show signs of poor motor skills. Physical therapy (PT) and occupational therapy (OT), in particular, offer treatment programs that are generally very helpful to WSc (Scheiber, 2000; Udwin & Yule, 1998b; Williams Syndrome Association Newsletter, 1995, Vol. *12*(2), pp. 7–10).

Physical therapists (PTs) assess, monitor, and treat problems involving body and muscle strength, endurance, motor efficiency, balance and coordination, postural alignment, motor skill acquisition, and progressive deformities (Dodge, 1995). Occupational therapists (OTs) assess functioning and treat problems involving use of the upper extremities, especially the hands. Visuospatial, motor, and general sensory-integration problems may be addressed by OTs as well, not just the "occupational" types of fine motor skills implied by their title (Levine et al., 1980). That is, OTs "can help with skills needed for the job of living" (Scheiber, 2000, p. 47).

According to the WSA Checklist Survey, 40% of WSc receive physical therapy and 43% attend occupational therapy (Semel & Rosner, 1991b). A more recent survey cites higher rates for children with WS (*n* = 112, < 9–16+ yrs): 71% for physical therapy, 87% for occupational therapy (Grejtak, WSA National Newsletter, 1996, Fall, pp. 6–8).

Some WSc receive sensory integration therapy (SIT) instead of, or in addition to, occupational therapy (Weeks & Smolarok, WSA National Newsletter, 1997, *14*(1), Spring, pp. 12–13; WSA National Newsletter, 2000, *17*(4), December, p. 15). Sensory integration is a therapeutic approach introduced by occupational therapists (Ayres, 1972). It focuses on how the sensory information of all systems is processed: tactile, vestibular, proprioceptive, visual, auditory, olfactory, and gustatory (American Occupational Therapy Association).

Referral for PT, OT, or LT or SLT is often made through a qualified physician, physiatrist, or family doctor. Therapy of this type may be conducted within a school system, private home, special summer camp, hospital, or university clinic.

As with problems of vision, it is important for parents, teachers, and others involved with WSs to be informed and selective in choosing a specialist or team of specialists to provide an appropriately aggressive intervention program for the motor difficulties of the WS individual. There are encouraging reports of the benefits of starting early in working with a coordinated team of OTs, PTs, and SLTs (Scheiber, 2000).

Unfortunately, some professionals are unacquainted with Williams syndrome and unaware of how they can contribute in treating WSs. In such cases, the therapist should receive pertinent information about the syndrome and the particular individual to be treated.

Assessment of Motor Functioning

Assessment of motor functioning is advised at critical or transitional periods of development in infancy (3, 6, 9, and 12 mo; 2 and 3 yrs), periodically throughout the school-age years, and as indicated by frequent monitoring during adolescence and adulthood (Dodge, 1995). Guidelines for health supervision of WSs also recommend evaluation and treatment of orthopedic issues and problems throughout life (American Academy of Pediatrics, 2001).

Grounds for Referral. Deficits or anomalies in gross motor functioning involving reflexes, early motor development, locomotion (walking, running, walking down stairs), posture, other gross motor skills (e.g., hopping, skipping, jumping), and sports activities (e.g., throwing or catching a ball) are grounds for referral.

Likewise, difficulty performing many of the eye–hand motor activities of daily living, such as grooming and dressing, handling tools and utensils, educational assignments, or arts and crafts projects may indicate the need for professional evaluation and intervention.

Types of Examinations. Professionals usually conduct their own examination and tests depending on their field of expertise and the clinical conditions that they treat. Therapists usually conduct standard and ancillary tests of motor functioning, interviews of parents, teachers, and relevant others, and clinically observe the WS individual.

Clinical Tests for Gross Motor Problems. Gross motor problems can be screened by physicians and therapists using clinical tests, such as tests of eye–upper limb coordination (e.g., tossing or catching a ball), body position sense and balancing regulation (e.g., standing on one foot), multilimb coordination, and complex motor organization like hopping on each foot successively (Levine et al., 1980).

PTs' examination for gross motor problems includes careful study of the musculoskeletal system (i.e., skeletal muscles, tendons, joints, and bones of the body), which controls body posture, stability, and mobility, as well as study of the vestibular, proprioceptive, and kinesthetic systems (Dodge, 1995).

Problems with posture, that is, scoliosis, should be evaluated with x-ray tests administered and evaluated by an orthopedist.

Clinical Tests for Fine Motor Problems. Screening items for fine motor skills may include effectiveness of pincer grasp (e.g., thumb–forefinger grasp), manual dexterity, finger dexterity, and rate control (e.g., tapping rate), as well as skill in performing daily living activities and certain fine motor tasks.

Clinical conditions associated with fine motor problems are evaluated by examining finger awareness or localization (i.e., finger differentiation and/or finger agnosia), ability to perform rapid hand alternation movements, apposition of fingers and finger–thumb, laterality, and consistent eye–hand (ipsilateral) preference (Levine et al., 1980). Critical components of fine motor skills, like grasp and release, are observed (Bailey & Wolery, 1989), as well as the ability to translate verbal directions into motor responses, praxia or motor planning, and the sequencing of motor responses. OTs, like PTs, also evaluate and treat vestibular, proprioceptive, and kinesthetic systems.

Tactile sensitivity to touching, being touched, pressure, texture, and temperature should be tested, and the presence of tactile defensiveness or oversensitivity to certain forms of sensory stimulation should be diagnosed. Overreactivity, rather than underreactivity, is the more common difficulty of WSs (Dilts et al., 1990; Plummer, 1994; see also WSA National Newsletter, 1991 Summer, pp. 16–17; WSA National Newsletter, 1995 Summer, pp. 8–10). The presence of associated movements (i.e., "motor overflow") should also be noted (Levine et al., 1980).

Formal Tests of Motor Skills. Professionals may use standard psychoeducational tests of gross motor and fine motor skills, as well as clinical tests or examinations in assessing and diagnosing the motor problems of WSs.[6]

Clinical Aspects of Gross Motor Functioning

Several conditions involving gross motor functioning are often reported in WSs: muscle tone disorders, contractures, radial-ulnar synostosis, hallux

---

[6]Tests that measure both gross motor and fine motor skills include the Bruininks-Oseretsky Test of Motor Proficiency (Bruininks, 1978) and the Peabody Developmental Gross Motor Scales and Fine Motor Scales (PDMS-2, Folio & Fawell, 2000). The motor subscale of the McCarthy Scales of Children's Abilities (McCarthy, 1972) is useful for evaluating gross motor performance. The Purdue Perceptual Motor Survey (Roach & Kephart, 1966) may also be used.

For assessing fine motor skills, the Developmental Test of Visual-Motor Integration (VMI; Beery, 1982), the Developmental Test of Visual Perception (Frostig et al., 1964), and the Sensory Motor Integration and Praxis Tests (Ayres, 1991) may be particularly helpful in revealing the problems of WSc.

Subtests of some intelligence tests may also provide useful information, including, the Perceptual-Performance scale of the McCarthy Scales of Mental Abilities (McCarthy, 1972), relevant items from the Stanford–Binet (4th ed.; Thorndike, Hagen, & Sattler, 1986), the Leiter International Performance Scale (Leiter, 1948), and some of the Performance scale subtests of the WISC–III (Wechsler, 1991). The Kaufman tests for children, K-ABC (Kaufman & Kaufman, 1983) and K-BIT (Kaufman & Kaufman, 1990) are often advised for WSc. These tests can be administered by trained professional psychologists, testing specialists, or educators with special training.

valgus, postural problems, and vestibular and kinesthetic difficulties (Dodge, 1995).

Muscle Tone Disorders. Muscle tone deficits are often evident in WSc and these may contribute to their gross motor problems. Muscle tone, the degree of tension in the muscles of the body at rest, is required for the development of gravitational stability, normal body posture, balance, and movement (Smith, 1989). It may be gauged by the resistance of muscles when an individual's arm or leg is moved through a normal range of motion. In muscle tone disorders, the degree of resistance in the muscles may be either too much (hypertonic) or too little (hypotonic).

Many WSc seem to have poor or low muscle tone, or *hypotonia*, that is, soft, underdeveloped flabby muscles that do not allow controlled motion of the joints, accompanied by flaccid posture. Low muscle tone is fairly common in WS infants (Dodge, 1995). It is also evident in 41% of WSc (*n* = 17, 2–8 yrs; Chapman et al., 1996).

Other WSc have the contrasting muscle problem, excessive muscle tone, or *hypertonia*. This is marked by hard, stony muscles, resistance to movement, tight joints that permit only a limited range of motion, and awkward or rigid posture. Such abnormal muscle tone is often associated with delays in the acquisition of developmental milestones of motor skills, atypical posture, and atypical movement patterns. Hypertonia appears in 85% of older children and adults with WS, but in just 29% of younger WSc (Chapman et al., 1996). Thus, there appears to be an age shift in muscle tone disorders in WSs from mainly hypotonia in childhood to hypertonia in adolescence and adulthood.

Contractures. Joint limitations or contractures are also common in WSs; the overall incidence is approximately 50% (Dodge, 1995; Hagerman, 1999). Joint limitations affect the strength, coordination, and quality of movement patterns. These are permanent muscular contractions that may occur in the wrist, elbows, hands, hips, knees, and ankles of WSc and adults. They may be accompanied by leg pains and cramps (Dykens, Hodapp, & Finucane, 2000). Caused by muscle fiber disorder or fibrosis of the tissues supporting the muscles of the joints, it tends to become more prevalent with age (Morris et al., 1988).

Radial-Ulnar Synostosis. Radial-ulnar synostosis or fusion of the lower arm bones (radius and ulna) is sometimes found in WSs. It limits their ability to turn the palm upward and rotate the lower arm. This can greatly affect a person's ability to manipulate objects, engage in bimanual play, and perform activities of daily living (e.g., those required in eating and dressing).

Hallux Valgus. Hallux valgus, or problems involving displacement of the big toe, is another common musculoskeletal deviation in WS. It has been reported that in 78% of WSs, the big toe may be displaced under or over the surrounding toes. This can contribute to difficulties in the ability to balance oneself in an upright, erect position. It may also result in pain while standing or walking (Dodge, 1995).

Postural Problems. Postural position difficulties and various types of spinal deformity are also widespread in WSs. Lordosis, or swayback, is anterior concavity in the neck (cervical) or lower back (lumbar) areas, and is found in 38% of WSs. Kyphosis, or humpback, is posterior convexity in the thoracic (chest) region, and is found in approximately 20% of WSs. Scoliosis, a C-curve or lateral curvature of the vertical spine, is found in 12% of these individuals (Dodge, 1995).

The typical posture of WSs consists of a slightly crouched stance with increased hip and knee flexion, heels often off the floor, kyphosis with head held forward, internal rotation of the lower extremities, pelvis tipped forward with lumbar lordosis and protruding abdomen, and so forth (Dodge, 1995).

Vestibular and Kinesthetic Difficulties. In combination, the vestibular and kinesthetic-proprioceptive systems help to provide appropriate balance for the individual, both against gravity and during movement. They also provide internal awareness of the body's position in space during movement. The vestibular apparatus is located adjacent to the inner ear; it controls the sense of gravity and acceleration through space. Kinesthesis originates in the joints, tendons, and muscles. It is stimulated by movement, and it provides information about touch, being touched, and body position (Schoenbrodt & Smith, 1995).

WSc often present vestibular and kinesthetic problems.

Treatment of Gross Motor Problems

PT or OT should be consulted when WSc are delayed or impaired in motor functioning. Aside from treating muscle tone disorders and contractures, therapists generally focus on improving WSs' postural and gravitational stability, and the ease, speed, and accuracy with which they perform a variety of motor acts.

Treatment of Muscle Tone Disorders. WSc who are found to have hypertonia should be treated aggressively with physical and/or occupational therapy designed to increase their range of motion and motor competence. Untreated hypertonia can lead to muscle contractures and permanent joint deformities. It is often accompanied by postural abnormalities such as kyphosis (hunchbacked condition) and lordosis (forward curvature of the spine). These problems are usually more responsive to treatment early in life before they become more severe. In most cases, PT treatment of hypertonia may have to be maintained throughout life to prevent curtailment of function.

Treatment of Contractures. Physical or occupational therapy can sometimes prevent or reduce the severity of contractures by treating associated problems of joint movement and rotation flexibility. Splints may sometimes be used by therapists to reduce the effects of excessive muscle tone and prevent contractures. Assistive or adaptive devices may be employed to maximize independence in activities of daily living.

Treatment of Proprioceptive, Spatial Problems. Many WS youngsters need help learning to interpret and use proprioceptive input (stimuli arising from within). This is reflected in their clumsiness and significant problems with spatial orientation. A qualified therapist can provide proprioceptive stimulation either passively, through a range of motion exercises, or actively, with traction and joint compression. Skilled OTs may also be able to help develop WSc's proprioception through vestibular stimulation. This can help to improve motion, posture, and muscle tone. Therapists with advanced neurodevelopmental training (NDT) or sensory integration (SI) training can also assist with the problematic automatic reflex responses of WSc.

Sensory Integration Therapy. OTs with advanced training in SI have a repertoire of techniques for remediating some of the motor problems of WSs. These can include gross motor and fine motor problems as well as difficulties with tactile defensiveness (see Section III, "Tactile Defensiveness").

A mother's description of her WS son, his motor difficulties, and his treatment activities provides a vivid account of SI techniques (Anonymous, 1985). At 7 years of age,

> Terry exhibited poor motor planning and infantile motor responses. . . . For example, he had trouble holding up his head and extending his arms while lying on his stomach. If his eyes were closed and he was to identify the spot where a person touched him, he might point to one [eight] inches away. He did not respond normally to motion.

> The sensory integration program concentrated not on passive repetition, but on the child's developing a repertoire of appropriate, spontaneous motor responses to what he saw, felt heard, touched, or what touched him. . . . To learn to hold up his head and thrust his arms for protection, Terry rode on his stomach on a padded scooter board. He would careen down a ramp toward a wall of cardboard boxes. What must he do to knock them down? Lift up his arms and raise his head. Ten minutes later he would shift to another activity— spinning, or catching a ball thrown to him as he swung on his stomach on a padded swing, or rolling about in a giant cylinder. (Anonymous, 1985, p. 965)

SI therapy is often conducted in a specialized environment containing many types of equipment, including suspended swings and hammocks, scooter boards and inclined ramps, a 5-foot ball for training in recuperation of balance, and positioning or vibrating pillows. Vestibular stimulation may be applied in a rotational, linear, or orbital direction, with the WS child's inner ear receptors positioned vertically, horizontally, or inverted.

Vestibular stimulation may be useful for developing an awareness of body position and location in space needed to maintain stable body posture and perform tasks involving stationary or dynamic positions. Vestibular stimulation also encourages the child to perform isolated or segmented movements of body parts with greater accuracy, such as those required to make appropriate balance and postural adjustments. Finally, vestibular stimulation may facilitate changes in muscle tone and overall movement patterns.

Some parents have noted that vestibular stimulation seems to help their WSc become more aware of their bodies. With increased body awareness, WSc appear better able to develop their motor skills, such as how to position themselves in order to ascend and descend stairs more easily and with less fear. Of course, only a skilled therapist should administer SI and vestibular stimulation.

Therapists may also use tactile stimulation materials, including brushes of various textures, cremes, lotions, oils, and textured fabrics. Others trained in SI may use water activities (e.g., whirlpool bath) and swaddling/wrapping (e.g., rolling body in a blanket) to stimulate tactile responses (Weeks & Smolarok, WSA National Newsletter, 1997, Spring, pp. 12–13). Sometimes, the therapist will decide that it is appropriate to wrap the child with ace bandage wraps or use a vibrating pillow. Highly specialized OTs may use icing or brushing techniques or gentle, passive compression of the joints of the upper and lower extremities. Some parents of WSc are very impressed with the benefits of brushing and compression in calming WSc and increasing their cooperativeness. Nonprofessionally trained personnel, including parents, should not perform brushing, icing, or compression, because there are a number of contraindications for these types of treatment.

Certain activities designed to enhance body awareness and movement exploration skills may be suggested to special educators and parents. Psycho-educational techniques provide other ways of handling certain gross motor problems, such as those involving locomotion or laterality.

Treatment of Fine Motor Problems

An occupational therapist may also be consulted for the evaluation and treatment of problems of fine motor functioning and gross motor problems.

In order to improve fine motor skills, OTs typically help teach WSs activities of daily living, such as those required in eating or grooming, as well as help develop their table-top eye–hand motor skills, and in-hand manipulations skills. Music instruction and therapy is another approach to strengthening WSs' fine motor skills (see chap. 5, Section IV).

In the area of self-care, WS children usually require a great deal of extra assistance in learning good grooming habits. Often, they need help combing and brushing hair, trimming nalls, and polishing shoes. The techniques of good personal hygiene must be systematically taught. Youngsters may need special help to learn how to fold and use toilet paper. Use the mirror to instruct the child about teeth, and how to brush and floss them. Because WS children generally have visual perceptual problems and poor eye–hand coordination, they need special instruction in how to use the shower dial. Hot water must be used carefully to avoid being scalded. Although these skills may seem either trivial or obvious, the failure of WSc to develop them can cause serious problems. Mastery of these skills is also central to the development of independent functioning.

Special devices and training are often employed in helping WSc become more skilled and independent in dressing themselves. OTs may introduce functional aids, such as the Montessori button board with large to small buttons in a graduated vertical series, a zipper board that uses a string to pull the zipper, and velcro for aiding or circumventing tasks such as tying of shoes. Large dolls and doll clothing may be helpful for teaching the skills of dressing. See also Section C for psycho-educational techniques.

Handwriting. OTs also tend to focus on handwriting, a particularly vulnerable area for WSs (see AOTA, Handwriting, at *htp: www.aota.org*). Parents report that 93% of WSc have "difficulties with handwriting," and 58% of the same WS group having "difficulties with reading" (Utah Survey, Semel & Rosner, 1991a).

In handwriting, muscle stability of the hand is needed in order to support finger adjustment and integrate the movement of minuscule muscles and joints. Whereas the fingers of the hand and wrist are largely responsible for the act of writing, the whole upper body, including the shoulders, arms, and torso, is used in writing tasks. The motor demands of handwriting extend beyond the hand and require coordinated use of large segments of the body. Arm rotation and postural adjustment accompany shifts in wrist action that establish an optimal writing position. Balance of the trunk and stability of the shoulder and forearm are required in order to make rapid, coordinated adjustments across the midline of the body. The opposite, nonwriting side of the body is used to help control the writing surface. Also, motor planning is required in order to anticipate and activate the minute adjustments involved in pencil grasping and the concomitant movement patterns required for letter formation (Scheiber, 2000).

Almost all WS children are plagued with handwriting problems. Even after they have learned to write, their letters tend to be poorly formed, crowded together, and extend off the line and the edge of the paper. The handwriting of most WSc is striking in its illegibility, poor spatial features, and painstaking effort. With the addition of pressure to perform or multiple processing demands, the act of handwriting becomes almost insufferable to many WSs.

Preparing WS children to write involves providing them with and teaching them how to use appropriate materials.

Most WS children need to be shown how to hold a pencil correctly. Use of a tripod "pencil-grip" or other type of built-up pencil is one way to deal with pencil problems (Udwin & Yule, 1988, 1989). Another way is to use pens and thin "Flair"-type magic markers instead of pencils; smooth, flowing movements are more difficult to make with pencils.

Use of lined paper is essential in order to help WS youngsters write more legibly and produce letters and numbers more uniform in size. Raised lines may provide additional positional cues. A slant board, slanted from 11 to 20 degrees, is also suggested for writing, drawing, and reading material (Grejtak, 1996a).

Because of their poor motor coordination skills, many WS children may need special instruction in learning how to erase. Erasing problems may be eased by providing specialized materials, like a wet sponge as a chalkboard eraser or magic tablets instead of paper and pencil. Allowing WSs to place parentheses or a circle around errors rather than having to erase them is another option. Supervised practice in erasing may also be helpful.

Poor paper position often contributes to WS children's difficulties in writing. The most frequent error is slanting the paper sometimes as much as 90 degrees, perhaps in an attempt to compensate for visuomotor bias. Holding the paper in a straight, rigidly set vertical position is another type of error. Proper hand posturing and slant of the paper are critical for WS students.

WSc are often left-handed. Efforts to comply with teaching procedures for right-handed children sometimes result in their writing with an awkward slant and "hooking" their hand around. Holding the pencil at least one-half inch above its sharpened part allows left-handed children to see what is being written and may help them avoid "hooked" writing. Demonstrating and reinforcing correct left-handed pencil and paper position is important. Special penmanship materials are available for left-handed writers.

Providing supportive furniture, with a chair and writing desk/table that is adjusted to the child's height, may help WSc sit more comfortably and write better. This may mean arranging more comfortable seating, making sure that the WS child's body is properly supported by placing a block or book under the feet, or furnishing a special, oversized rectangular desk with a recessed seating area in the middle and a large top surface to rest elbows. Proper positioning of the body, correcting poor posture, and orienting the writing paper correctly often aids the learning process. These measures and use of special materials like pencil grips, lined paper, and a slant board may be particularly important in dealing with fine motor related problems, such as the "motor overflow" shown by some WSc.

Finally, it should be noted that use of tape recorders, typewriters, computers, or "peer" note-takers offer the invaluable option of bypassing the demands of handwriting while still allowing WSs to perform assigned tasks in many situations (Grejtak, 1996c; Lenhoff, WSA National Newsletter, 1997 August, Vol. *14*(2), 8; Udwin & Yule, 1998a, 1998b).

C. Psycho-Educational Techniques

Parents, teachers, special educators, and others can play a pivotal role in developing WSs' visuospatial, motor, and VSM skills by seeking professional evaluation and treatment when advised. They may also help to facilitate WSs' development in these areas by employing certain psycho-educational techniques. These may include verbal mediation, task management, naturalistic activities, and control mechanisms.

These are complementary approaches in which clinicians and professional specialists, particularly those in the fields of education and psychology, often serve as initiators and advisors in the use of psycho-educational techniques by parents, special educators, teachers, and others involved with WSs. Although it may be unrealistic to expect major improvement from the use of such techniques, some observable benefits can be obtained.

Verbal Mediational Techniques

Verbal strategies capitalize on the language abilities and predilections of WSs to promote their visual-spatial-motor skills. Verbal mediational strategies may be used to address WSs' problems with VSM tasks, motor performance, visuospatial cognition, and spatial orientation.

Verbal Mediation of Visual-Spatial-Motor Tasks. The extreme difficulty that most WSs experience in drawing and copying figures, block building, and other assembly construction tasks may be reduced by encouraging
them to use verbal mediation techniques, specifically, to label stimuli, stimulus features, motor acts, and the sequence of acts or task components.
Physical demonstration of the relation between stimulus elements and motor acts should accompany the verbal description.

Verbal Mediation of Drawing. Instructing WSa to associate parts of a
picture with verbal cues and verbalize the sequence of drawing parts of the
illustration may markedly improve performance (Bellugi et al., 1988a;
Semel, 1988; Udwin & Yule, 1998a; Volterra et al., 1994).

To illustrate verbal mediation, consider the task of teaching a very young
WS child how to draw a simple form, like two lines in the shape of an "L"
(Sabbadini, Discussion comment from Wang, 1994). First, the WSc is shown
the examiner's stimulus model, a large figure of an "I" or straight line with a
distinctive mark like a large green concentric dot at the top and a red dot at
the base of the vertical line. Each part is pointed out and verbally labeled.

Next, the child repeatedly draws the line with a finger, and then later
with a pencil while the examiner labels the parts of the stimulus and guides
the child's motor movements. After practice trials in which the motor guidance is no longer provided, the examiner administers verbal instructions,
like "Start at the green dot," "Go straight down the street to the red dot,"
and "Stop at the red dot." These verbal instructions function as verbal mediators or intervening steps between the stimulus model and the WSc's
drawing of the "I."

At the early stages of therapy, repeated practice with dots and verbal instructions may be necessary and progress may be slow (Stiles et al., 2000).
Type of subject matter may influence rate of learning and amount of generalization. Training on drawing of houses and people, in particular, is more
productive than that achieved with geometric forms (Stiles et al., 2000).
Coaching the WSc to add specific facial features, the person's body, and objects to drawings of people seemed to aid the process (Stiles et al., 2000).

Stencils of geometric forms, figures, objects, or animals may also be presented, and WSs may be asked to trace the outline, name the parts, and
then identify the entire figure as it emerges from the outline. Letters of the
alphabet may be copied, traced, named, and provided by semantic cues
(Udwin & Yule, 1998a). Other materials, such as pipe cleaners, playdough,
or clay, may also be used to construct figures or letters that can be labeled
and described.

Semantic Associations for VSM Problems. Semantic associations involve using verbal cues to make connections between items easier to understand and remember. For example, the letter "o" can be described as a

big round juicy orange. A meaningful verbal analogy can help to concretize the concept needed to perform the task.

This may also be applied to tasks of folding (i.e., folding of paper, clothes, towels, and other material). These are problematic even for many older WSc. Most are unable to line up the edges of the objects correctly or exert enough pressure to make the critical crease in the proper place.

In teaching WSs how to fold, verbal labels are attached to each element: the item, its parts, and the act of joining the parts. A critical aspect of the process is to use semantic associations to describe the task of taking hold of the corners, aligning the edges, and joining the corners. Mediators may include such phrases as "make the corners kiss," "make it into a box," "make a sandwich," or "take the ear of the rabbit (corner) and put it on top of the other ear" (Semel, 1988). Verbal analogies and other mnemonic associations also may be used to simplify visuospatial assembly or construction tasks.

Once mediational techniques have been established, some WSs may be trained to extend their use to rehearsal and self talk. Usually this requires a great deal of additional practice and instruction.

Verbal Mediation of Motor Functioning. Verbal mediation may also be used to improve performance in tasks that require response differentiation, motor planning, coordinated movement, spatial orientation, and gross motor and fine motor skills (Udwin & Yule, 1998a, 1998b).

Verbal Mediation of Modeling and Imitation. Modeling and imitation can help WSs to acquire gross motor skills like jumping and skipping and fine motor skills like buttoning or holding a spoon. Adding mediational cues during teacher input and the child output or imitation of motor acts can markedly improve WSs' ability to develop these skills.

WSc can be instructed to describe aloud each component body part, object, and action while it is being demonstrated and while it is being performed. Thus, movement patterns can be established, practiced, and maintained by talking WSs through the processes of modeling and imitation.

To avoid confusion, modeling should be done from a nonmirror image position with the child whenever possible. It is important to sit or stand beside the child rather than facing each other. The same is true in presenting drawings or illustrations of target behaviors.

Verbal Instructions for Motor Acts. Verbal instructions and commands can be used to direct WSc to perform gross motor activities, like running or "Stand on tiptoes," and to instruct fine motor movements like opening and closing hands or playing finger games. Of course, it is necessary to determine first whether the children are familiar with the terms for body parts and actions. Names of less frequently used words for body parts—like "waist," "wrist," or "ankle"—may need to be taught directly.

Verbal Mediation of Visuospatial Cognition. Use of verbal labels may help WSs engage more thoroughly in visuospatial analysis, thereby increasing their ability to process configurational wholes and deal with visual figure ground relations.

For example, verbal mediation may be used to help WSs discriminate between visually similar stimuli. In "matching to sample" and visual matching tasks, a target stimulus is presented along with some variants; the subject is asked to name, describe, and compare the features of each stimulus, and to determine whether they are identical, similar, or different than those of the target. Verbally describing the relation between two objects in terms of attributes (e.g., size, shape, quantity, direction, distance, or color) may help WSs process visual information more efficiently.

Various types of simple matching tasks can be presented ranging from single to multiple items, and from simple items (e.g., objects or pictures) to more complex items (e.g., letters, numbers, or words). For example, letters can be matched with letters in a different case (i.e., upper case, lower case) or in words. Confusable letter pairs—such as "b"/"d," "p"/"q," "u"/"n," or "t"/ "f"—may be more easily differentiable by labeling or color coding their distinctive features (Rosner & Pochter, 1986).

In fact, systematic comparison is a prerequisite to learning how to read, write, and do arithmetic. Other tasks like switching channels on a television set, telling time, operating a dial, or using a vending machine also require making feature comparisons and determining matches and mismatches.

Verbal Mediation for Problems of Spatial Orientation. Fortunately, verbal mediational techniques may be applied to WSs' problems with directionality, sequentiality, and spatial relational terms. For example, WSc may be asked to turn in a specified direction toward certain objects, a particular spot relative to themselves, or to point up or down. Alternatively, WSc can be instructed to "act out" verbal commands that feature spatial and directional terms (e.g., "Put the book __," "Put the 'X' on the desk/in your desk/ under the desk") or to use toys and doll houses to stimulate directional movement patterns that can be verbally described. Talking software is available to help develop this skill.[7]

---

[7]Semel, E. (1997). *Following directions: Left and Right* [Computer program]. Winooski, VT: Laureate Learning Systems. (Talking software for special needs for the Apple II series, Macintosh and PC).

Speech language therapists can be consulted to help deal with problems involving semantic relational terms or be asked to incorporate such terms in their therapy program.

Verbal-Spatial-Motor Games. Concrete, physical activities are helpful ways to establish a better understanding of spatial and directional terms. An obstacle course can be constructed out of the school room or play furniture and the child asked to follow verbal instructions to "walk" around particular obstacles or in particular directions, such as "over," "behind," "under," and "in front of."

Motor awareness can be accentuated by constructing a tunnel out of materials like pillows or cushions with a toy as a reward at its end (Scheiber, 2000). Blankets may be draped over furniture and the WSc instructed to go "into" the tunnel, crawl "to the end" of the tunnel, or "stop" at certain points. In this way, WSc can receive both verbal input and kinesthetic feedback from their guided movements. They can also learn the "feel" of spatial relational terms through motor learning that simplifies and concretizes spatial concepts, along with the appropriate verbal labels.

Verbalization of Travel Routes. Practice using verbal descriptions of travel routes may help WSs find their way and become more familiar with directional terms. Practice finding their way accompanied by written instructions help those WSs who are able to read (Udwin & Yule, 1998a, 1998b).

WSs may be asked to enact with words and pantomime how to get from their home to school or work, from school or work home, from home to visit a friend or relative, or go to a store. This may involve learning to identify clearly visible landmarks (e.g., a movie theater or distinctive storefront) as a point of reference and associating the designated spot or place with appropriate interventions.

Task Management Techniques

Intervention strategies involving task management include manipulation of the environment, as well as analysis and modification of visuospatial and motor tasks that are difficult for WSs to perform.

Manipulation of Visual Context. Most WSc are highly distractible; many have problems with figure ground relations. Optimizing performance often requires controlling the visual environment in which WSs work. Sufficient lighting, preferably with glare reduction, should always be used. Light should be indirect and its source located so that the work surface is free of shadows. Extraneous visual stimuli should also be minimized for WSc who are easily distracted visually (see chapter 7, Section II, B on "Distractibility," p. 310).

Using visual cues to highlight and simplify target stimuli may also be productive. Salient visual cues, such as borders, grouping, and figures of different size or color can be used to emphasize key elements in a display. Attaching a picture or name placard to the child's school locker can help the child remember its location.

Task Management of Visual-Spatial-Motor Problems. Task analysis provides the insights needed to establish a program of task management. It is a valuable technique to use in attempting to minimize the vision-related problems, motor-related problems, and VSM problems of WSs. Each step of a task is scrutinized, along with the number and complexity of the steps and the instructions.

Simplification of tasks requiring VSM integration is usually helpful and often necessary. Difficulty in performing activities of daily life, such as grooming and dressing, may be reduced by establishing a routinized order of subtasks and providing a series of pictures that depicts each step. Verbal cues may be added (Udwin & Yule, 1998b). Problems with tying shoes or buttoning shirts may be handled by modifying the clothing, for example, by substituting velcro fasteners for shoe laces, buttons, or zippers (Levine, 1993).

Walking Down Stairs. Use of task analysis may ease the fearsome difficulty of walking down stairs. Sometimes it is helpful to instruct WSs to look straight at the stairway wall and hold onto the stair railing, initially with both hands. Glancing at the corner of the stair rise or placing masking tape at the edge of each step are other ways of coping. In addition, PTs and OTs may be able to provide considerable assistance in this area.

Ball Handling. Learning to play ball is usually a difficult and frustrating task for WS youngsters. Training in basic ball handling, readiness skills, and specific, sequential instruction in catching can be helpful. This may begin by rolling a large rubber ball toward a child seated on the floor with legs apart. Initially, it is helpful to roll the ball to only one side, then the other side of the child's body. Later on, the ball can be rolled to the child's midline.

Once these skills are acquired, ball games may be introduced (see "Active Games and Sports," p. 164).

Task Management of Laterality Problems. Difficulty in establishing laterality and differentiating right from left may be reduced by using salient cues and memory aids (mnemonics) to help the WS individual distinguish the two sides. For example, a bracelet can be placed on one hand, a ring on the other. Or, an "R" can be marked on one hand, and an "L" can be marked in another color on the other hand. The WS individual may also be shown how the left hand forms on "L" when the thumb is extended outward while viewing the back of the hand. Both the meaning and the use of such cues must be carefully explained.

A computer program for children, *Following Directions: Left and Right* (Semel, 1997), can be used to help develop left–right discrimination in WSs. The program presents self-correcting activities designed to improve differentiation of left and right in the person, in objects, and the direction of objects relative to the person. More advanced exercises dealing with reversals and mirror images are part of the program that WSs seem to enjoy.

Activities for Promoting Visuospatial Cognition. Clinical experience indicates that many WSc are deficient in the use and control of visual attention. Although WSc usually make excellent and appropriate eye contact with people, they often have difficulty directing their eye gaze onto other types of targets, especially complex visual stimuli. Attempts to focus attention on tasks like puzzles, studying a workbook, looking at the chalkboard, or reading a book can be extremely frustrating, because the eyes and thoughts of WSs are often elsewhere.

Parents, caregivers, teachers, and other professionals can provide opportunities for WSs to develop their visual attention skills. Usually this involves using task analysis to devise activities that provide experience in skills basic to visuospatial cognition, that is, visual tracking and visual scanning. This is a type of task engineering.

Visual Tracking. Use of coordinated eye movements (Stiles et al., 2000) may be encouraged by providing practice in visual tracking (i.e., focused viewing of a moving target). This may involve an apparently simple task like watching fish in a goldfish bowl or tropical fish in a fish tank. It may also include various kinds of ball or other games, such as watching a tennis game or ping-pong game from "center court," or playing ball or simple marble games. All involve viewing an interesting, moving target.

Visual Scanning. Visual scanning refers to the ability to systematically examine visual stimuli in order to accurately identify and discriminate such stimuli efficiently. Most normally developing children acquire these kinds of automatic eye movement patterns over the early childhood years. Many WSs can benefit from informal activities designed to help improve their visual scanning skills.

WSs can be asked to skim through magazines or newspapers to find selected bits of information, such as specific objects or colors. A page in a book, newspaper, or magazine may also be scanned for a particular word or letter.

Naturalistic Activities

Naturalistic activities refer to structured use of practical experiences and informal activities to promote the development of VSM skills.

Functional Activities for VSM Deficits. Structured, functional activities (e.g., kitchen tasks, games, sports, and arts and crafts) provide WSs with opportunities to develop their VSM skills within a social, informative context. Such activities offer immediate, concrete feedback concerning whether performance is successful or improvement is needed, and afford the opportunity to interact with family, neighborhood children, peers, and others in projects or activities.

As a general rule, tasks need to be presented in small incremental, cumulative steps that take task difficulty and the need for guided instruction into account.

Kitchen Tasks. Many kinds of kitchen tasks require eye–hand coordination: using a rolling pin to prepare dough or a cookie cutter to cut out shapes like letters or geometric forms; crushing graham crackers for a pie crust; snapping beans; using a vegetable peeler, egg beater, or can opener; and grating, slicing, or chopping foods.

Play Activities. Playing selected games may help to develop certain aspects of VSM integration. Working on simple puzzles necessitates attending to visual-tactile shapes and searching the array of unused pieces for a likely candidate to complete the picture. A special family "puzzle" table provides companionship and assistance.

Certain games, such as flashlight tag, encourage visual tracking and eye–hand coordination. In flashlight tag, an adult shines a light at various locations in a darkened room and WSc are asked to "catch" the adult's beam with their light. Roles can be changed so the WSc is the spotter and the adult is the catcher.

Visuospatial construction skills may be developed in many play contexts, such as using toys with interchangeable parts (e.g., stackable animal blocks), doll houses that include toy furniture and people that can be arranged along with verbal commentary, and toy construction kits depicting houses, fire stations, farms, and so forth. These materials may serve to entertain as well as to provide a verbal mediational context for visuospatial construction and creative storytelling.

Motor Games. The child's awareness of body parts and types of movement can be cultivated by playing games like "Simon Says" and "Hoky Poky." Both games provide opportunities for following verbal commands, imitating body positions, and differentiating the left and right sides of the body.

Interest in performing motor acts may be encouraged by instructing WSc to do "finger play" or pantomime familiar actions, such as driving a car or school bus, directing traffic, and swatting flies, or to enact verbal associations like reaching up to touch the stars or reaching over the ocean.

Music may be incorporated into motor activities like balancing, ball play (Udwin & Yule, 1998a), or playing "statues" to music to help improve balance (Scheiber, 2000).

Physical Exercise. With medical permission, parents, teachers, and others can introduce informal active games and sports as a way of providing gross motor activities and practice (Udwin & Yule, 1998a, 1998b). Engaging in active warm-up exercise prior to starting academic class assignments may help to limber up and relax WSs (Scheiber, 2000).

At a simple level, WSc may be encouraged to practice various walking or running movements, such as walking like a "Raggedy Ann" doll or a bear on all fours. Adding music or rhythmic beats while WSc walk, run, hop, skip, or jump capitalizes on their musical interests and talents.

Active Games and Sports. Having WSc participate in backyard games (e.g., volleyball, tetherball, badminton, or croquet) may encourage coordination of large muscles. "Street games" like "Giant Steps," "Follow the Leader," "Mother May I," "Capture the Flag," "Tag," and "Kick the Can" may make for enjoyable hours and facilitate important lessons in teamwork, following directions, and strategic thinking.

Once certain skills are acquired, ball games may be used to help improve VSM coordination. Batting or hitting a ball suspended from a pole (Tether or Marsden ball) can provide visuomotor practice without the pressure of group play. Adjusting or lowering the hoop may help to reduce basketball difficulty. Giving children their own ball offers additional opportunities for practice and decreases peer pressure. It also avoids problems in having children line up for turns with the group's equipment and eliminating those who miss the basket.

Coordination and control of body movements may be enhanced by introducing sports that emphasize body rhythm and use of all extremities (e.g., running, swimming, dance, and special gymnastics; MacDonald & Roy, 1988). When approved of by their medical doctors, WSs join aerobics and stretching classes and enjoy learning how to dance. Jazzercise is also very popular. Supervised use of playground and gym equipment, active games, and sports are good for developing motor skills and social contacts.

Arts and Crafts. Simple, structured arts and crafts and carpentry projects represent alternative, interesting ways to provide opportunities for
WSs to develop fine motor skills. Even those with few fine motor skills are
able to make a stylish, respectable looking ceramic tile ashtray, use playdough, or fingerpaint.

Under careful supervision and with emphasis on safety, WSs may be
taught to use certain types of tools and appliances, including a hammer,
screwdriver, saw, paint brush or roller, spray paint, and tape measure.
Competence in such areas may provide background for the development of
vocational interests and skills.

Suggestions for other types of projects may be obtained by consulting
professionals who work with children with developmental delay: occupational therapists, adaptive physical educators or optometrists, or vocational
counselors. Resources, including books, may also be available from organizations like the Association for Retarded Citizens (ARC; see Appendix).

III. TACTILE SENSITIVITY

For many WSs, tactile stimulation is a valuable source of data about what
they can reach out and touch, and what makes contact with their bodies.
One of six major senses, touch, along with vision, audition, taste, smell, and
vestibular/kinesthesis, has its own physiological, neuroanatomical, and behavioral properties. It can provide information about the pressure, size, locus, shape, hardness, texture, and temperature of tactile stimuli.

For many, but not all WSs, tactile stimulation is an important sensory
channel that may be relatively intact or in need of enhancement (Scheiber,
2000; Semel, 1988). Used either unimodally (singly) or multimodally (in combination with other sensory modes), it can enable WSs to explore and encode the identity and characteristics of an almost unlimited number of stimuli including objects, animals, people, geometric figures, and symbols (e.g.,
letters and numerals). Thus, haptic perception (being touched) can sometimes help some WSs compensate for their visuospatial deficits. This may
be accomplished by adding tactile stimulation along with kinesthetic and
proprioceptive cues in teaching motor and academic skills. For others, tactile sensitivity can be a curse.

A. Tactile Defensiveness

Unfortunately, tactile sensitivity has a negative side for those WSs who suffer
from "tactile defensiveness," that is, extreme sensitivity and aversion to tactile stimuli that are not usually bothersome to most other people (Scheiber,

2000; Semel, 1988). A soft silky blanket or a fuzzy stuffed animal may not be perceived as cuddly, instead it may seem abrasive to such children.

Parental reports indicate that 41% of WSc and 33% of WS infants (n = 113, 0–3 yrs) show signs of tactile defensiveness (WSA Checklist Survey, Semel & Rosner, 1991a, 1991b). This may be an underestimate because the term is often unfamiliar to parents at the time they enroll in the WSA. According to Ayres (1991), a leading occupational therapist/researcher, from 5% to 10% of the general population of American children are affected by sensory integration problems, which include tactile defensiveness (WSA National Newsletter, 1991 Summer, p. 13–15).

Tactile defensiveness is a multifaceted problem that complicates the lives of many WSs and their families (Scheiber, 2000; Semel, 1988). A defensive response may be set off by a parent's light touch on the arm, a pat on the back from another child, the rubbing of pants against the child's legs, or pressure from a chair against the body. When WSs are affected by tactile defensiveness, it may be evident throughout their bodies in vermiform or wormlike motions of entire segments or limbs of the body as they squirm away from being touched. In other cases, tactile defensiveness may be more localized. For some WSc, it may also be accompanied by deficits in tactile perception.

Aversion to Routine Activities. Tactile defensiveness is often apparent in WSc's extreme resistance to various kinds of grooming care, such as face washing, hair combing, teeth brushing, mouth rinsing, bathing, haircutting, clipping fingernails, and so forth. Having their faces or corners of their mouths wiped with a napkin bothers some WSc. Others resist having the "sand" removed from their eyes. Applying sunscreen or lip ointment may be traumatic; some WSc find soap bubbles in the tub disturbing. Intense aversion to medical and dental visits is common.

Problems with Texture. Many WSc seem to avoid letting anything they perceive to be irritating touch their bodies (Scheiber, 2000; Semel, 1988). Some are reportedly bothered by the "feel" of new clothes, fuzzy shirts, short socks, and turtle neck sweaters. Irritation from a tag on the back of a shirt may be severe enough to require removing the label. Rough or scratchy fabric in clothing may be strenuously avoided; soft textured clothing, long sleeves, long pants, and high socks are usually strongly preferred. Many WSs dislike coarse terry cloth towels. Walking barefoot on certain textured surfaces (e.g., grass, dirt, or sand) may force some WSs to halt in their tracks and cry.

Oral Sensitivity and Eating Problems. Various kinds of problems associated with the oral cavity are also noted (Scheiber, 2000; Semel, 1988). Some WSc continue to put objects in their mouths way beyond the preschool years, the point when most children have outgrown this habit. Other WSc avoid touching food with their lips (see chap. 2, Section II, A, Oral–Motor Problems).

A "strong gag reflex" is evident in 59% of WSc (WSA Checklist Survey, Semel & Rosner, 1991a, 1991b). Interestingly, there is a statistically significant relation in the WSA Checklist data between occurrence of a strong gag reflex and the presence of tactile defensiveness (41%, WSA Checklist Survey, Chi Square (1) = 5.13, p = .02).

Sometimes severe gag reactions are triggered by very specific kinds of conditions. In certain youngsters, touching food with both hands or the lips can trigger the gag response, but it will not occur if the same youngsters touch the food with only one hand. To avoid unpleasant oral contact, WSc may devise clever techniques, such as using their teeth to remove food from a fork or spoon rather than using their lips. To eat foods such as bread, they may fold the bread in half and take a bite out of the center without using their lips. The remaining portion is usually not eaten.

Food texture appears to be critical to food aversions. Some WSc will not accept food that is crunchy, very firm, or mushy. Crackers may be avoided completely. Other WSc may be unwilling to eat foods that have more than one texture, such as strawberries or granola in yogurt. For many, cookies cannot contain any nuts, raisins, walnuts, or marshmallows. If so, they will be painstakingly removed by the child. For others, all carrots or celery must be filtered out of chicken soup. Sometimes noodles are acceptable, but rice is not tolerated.

Many parents report that their WSc will eat peanut butter—smooth, unchunky peanut butter—without leaving a trace. For reasons that are not understood, peanut butter is the most widely accepted food among WSc. Spaghetti is the second most accepted food.

Fifty-eight percent of parents describe their WSc as "Picky Eater/Self-Imposed Diet" on the WSA Checklist Survey (Semel & Rosner, 1991a, 1991b). In this respect, WSc (n = 70, M = 9;2 yrs; n = 53, M = 14;6 yrs) exceed a matched group of mentally retarded children in being known as "fussy eater" and exhibiting "food fads" (Einfeld et al., 1997; Einfeld, Tonge, & Rees, 2001).

Classroom Issues. Teachers, too, must face the confusing, manifold aspects and implications of tactile defensiveness. In the classroom, such youngsters may not be able to tolerate sitting on a hard-surfaced chair for long periods of time. During play, some WSc avoid mud or sand and dislike getting dirty. Certain arts and crafts materials may be irritating and should be avoided: finger paints, paste, and pipe cleaners. Standing in line with other children may also bother some WSc. When touched by another child, they may recoil, or scratch or rub the spot.

Other Child Groups. Individuals with other forms of developmental disorder may also show many characteristics of tactile defensiveness. Children with learning disability, autism, and Fragile X syndrome may exhibit "tactile defensiveness" and unusual sensitivity to oral stimulation; scratchy materials, including grass; standing in line with other children; aversion to being handled; as well as vestibular, kinesthetic, and proprioceptive problems (Schoenbrodt & Smith, 1995).

Mechanisms. Experts in sensory integration view tactile sensitivity as an essential component of dysfunction in sensory integration, along with difficulties in the vestibular and proprioceptive systems. Each system may be under or overreactive to stimulation. Disorders in sensory integration are believed to cause a number of behavioral problems. These may include oversensitivity or undersensitivity to stimuli in the environment, hyper-(high) or hypo- (low) activity level, impairment in gross motor and fine motor functioning, speech and language delay, distractibility and impulsivity, and academic difficulties (Weeks & Smolarok, 1997, WSA National Newsletter, Spring, 14, April, pp. 12–13).

Aside from sensory integration theory and treatment, mechanisms underlying deviations in tactile sensitivity appear to be unexplored. At the present, there is a paucity of research dealing with the somatosensory centers at the cortical and subcortical level of WSs.

B. Interventions for Tactile Defensiveness

Clinical approaches, task management, and psychological support may be used to help address problems of tactile defensiveness in WSs. Interventions may also benefit those WSs who have difficulty processing tactile stimuli (Libera, WSA Newsletter, Fall 1993, *10*(4), pp. 24–26). Children with these problems need direct, supportive assistance in order to learn how to differentiate tactile stimuli and organize tactile sensory input. Hyperreaction to tactile stimuli may also make it difficult for a youngster to develop in-hand manipulative and fine motor skills, as well as eye–hand coordination (Ayres, 1981).

Clinical Approach

The first step in clinical treatment is to determine the range and severity of symptoms in the particular WS individual.

Assessment. A qualified occupational or physical therapist may conduct an evaluation using standardized tests, such as the Sensory Motor Integration and Praxis Tests (Ayres, 1989/1991), as well as structured observation and clinical interviews (WSA National Newsletter, 1991 Summer, Vol. *8*, p.

16–17). Assessment may include investigating the presence of avoidance behaviors described earlier.

Treatment. Where there are deficits in the integration and processing of tactile input, a sensory integration (SI) trained OT may be able to help WSc become more tolerant of tactile stimulation (WSA National Newsletter, 1991 Summer, Vol. *8*, p. 16–17). This may involve use of a special technique, gradual desensitization, in which graduated tactile stimulation is applied to various areas of the body, including legs, shoulders, forearms, hands, and face. The WSc's aversion to being touched or handled may be lessened by the therapist's use of various massage techniques, such as brushing or firm rubbing with or without lotions, oils, or cremes as appropriate. Some motor activities and vestibular stimulation may also be helpful.

Gentle, but firm, stroking of the arms, legs, and—eventually—the face with the hands may be gradually tolerated. Then, daily, regular use of lotions may be introduced. Using somewhat firm rather than soft strokes or allowing the child to apply the lotion may be helpful. In very gradual stages, a soft brush may be used. Most WSc will accept "deep touch" better than light touch, and coarse texture better than soft texture (Weeks & Smolarok, 1997, WSA National Newsletter, Spring, *14*, April, p. 12–13).

With the help of a well-trained SI therapist, it is possible to expand the child's acceptance of textured foods and stimulation of the body surface. Experience with walking barefoot on varied textures (e.g., a carpet, rice, shaving cream or styrofoam bubbles) may be provided (Weeks & Smolarok, 1997). Therapists may also use water activities and procedures like erasing chalk marks placed on the child's body (Weeks & Smolarok, 1997). Many of the techniques SI therapists use to treat WS problems of motor functioning, such as vestibular stimulation, are applicable to tactile defensiveness.

Some speech language therapists (SLTs) are also trained to treat oral-motor problems of WSc (see chap. 3, "Language Interventions and Treatment"). Months of daily oral stimulation using graduated desensitization may be required before the WSc will accept foods containing multiple textures. Care needs to be taken in the way a napkin is used to wipe or stimulate the mouth area.

As tactile stimulation may have a cumulative effect, the therapist should continually monitor the child's delayed and diffused reactions to tactile stimulation, including stimulus rejection.

Task Management

Adjusting the physical environment may markedly reduce certain forms of sensory-motor irritation. This involves identifying the basis of the child's tactile defensiveness, such as discomfort from the seat of a school desk or the rubbing of slacks or dresses against the calves of the legs. Appropriate steps may then be taken to alleviate or eliminate the source of discomfort, like placing a soft pillow on a chair or classroom seat, providing knee socks to reduce friction from clothing, or removing clothing labels that may touch the back of the neck or other body parts.

Aversion to washing may be eased by allowing the child to apply a warm washcloth. Parents may be creative, too, in handling troublesome eating habits. One mother deals with her child's refusal to eat more than the center of a piece of bread by cutting each slice of bread into three longitudinal strips and giving her WSc one section at a time (Anonymous caller, personal communication, Williams Syndrome Hotline, June 1998).

Parents also note that WSc sometimes show an intriguing shift in their reaction to certain stimuli that had caused tactile defensiveness. Once a stimulus that was abhorrent becomes tolerable, it often becomes pleasurable and sought-after.

Comments

Unfortunately, the issue of tactile defensiveness is often overlooked in the writings of researchers, clinicians, and reviews of WS. Except for comments of parents and those working most directly with them, the topic of WS tactile defensiveness is usually neglected. This situation needs to be rectified.

Regarding treatment of problems of tactile defensiveness, although it may be time consuming and require a great deal of patience, progress can be made through reassurance, rechanneling, and appropriate programs of intervention.

Finally, individual differences in all aspects of tactile defensiveness must be recognized. Among WSc who show tactile defensiveness, the severity and range of symptoms differ considerably. Some WSc respond negatively to only one or two forms of stimulation, like irritation from pants touching the leg, or having corners of the mouth wiped. Whereas problems of oral sensitivity may be associated with tactile defensiveness, other WSc may be just picky eaters. Some kinds of aversions (i.e., avoidance or dislike of certain foods) may occur independently of tactile defensiveness.

In addition, many children with WS seem unaffected by tactile defensiveness. For these WSc, the tactile channel may be exploited, instead of avoided, in play activities, arts and crafts, and especially in academics where touching, tracing, and producing three-dimensional, tactually salient letters, words, and numbers may help them compensate for their visual-spatial-motor integration deficits.

IV. AUDITORY SENSITIVITY

The devastating nature of auditory hypersensitivity is vividly conveyed by the mother of a WS boy:

Terry stiffened and sobbed [when he heard a buzz saw]. In church, . . . the congregation clapped from the last song and he stiffened again and cried. He looks as though he's in pain. His body quakes and he rocks back and forth. . . . Time and again we carried him sobbing away from a clapping audience. A food blender on high speed, Pavarotti hitting a high note on television sent him into that rigid terror. (Anonymous, 1985, p. 967)

The most striking auditory feature of WS is hypersensitivity to certain sounds, accompanied by unexpected strengths in music and phonological memory (Arnold et al., 1985; Lenhoff et al., 1997; Semel, 1987). Auditory hypersensitivity or hyperacusis is defined as a "consistently exaggerated or inappropriate response . . . [to sudden onset of unexpected background sounds] that are neither intrinsically threatening nor uncomfortably loud to a typical person" (A. J. Klein, Armstrong, Greer, & F. R. Brown, 1990, p. 339). The reaction can be "severe enough . . . to make it impossible to travel in town, or to perform household chores in the presence of the child" (Martin et al., 1984, p. 60).

Auditory hypersensitivity is important to discuss because of its severity and centrality in the WS profile. Associated issues of auditory processing skills, as well as problems with auditory figure–ground perception, are also examined. Clinical aspects of audition, auditory perception, and processing are noted, followed by suggestions for interventions that may help WSs cope better with their auditory hypersensitivity and figure–ground problems. Related topics of musicality and phonological memory are dealt with in chapter 5, "Specific Aptitudes."

A. Auditory Hypersensitivity

Parents are to be credited with alerting researchers and physicians to the intensity and frequency of auditory hypersensitivity in WSc and underscoring the observations of others (Bellugi et al., 1988b; Semel, 1988). Research surveys indicate that almost all WSs (i.e., approximately 90%) have or have had this problem (Klein et al., 1990; Semel & Rosner, 1991a; Van Borsel, Curfs, & Fryns, 1997). Approximately 12% of WSs ($n = 65$, 1–28 yrs, $Md = 8$ yrs) are reported to "outgrow" auditory hyperacusis (Klein et al., 1990)— some in their early years, others as late as 22 years of age (Van Borsel et al., 1997). About 50% of WSa are said to experience significant problems with hypersensitivity to sounds (Udwin, Howlin, & Davies, 1996).

Most WSs ($n = 82$, 2–46 yrs, $M = 14$ yrs) show a strong interest in sounds and are sensitive enough to be able to detect a specific sound in a noisy environment (Van Borsel et al., 1997). They seem to be unusually sensitive to nearly imperceptible sounds in the distance and have a compulsion to investigate what is making the sound (Semel, 1988).

Types of Stimuli. Although there is no set list of the specific stimuli that may trigger hypersensitivity, certain kinds are mentioned frequently by parents. These include the sounds of machines and sudden noises (e.g., power saw, lawn mower, vacuum cleaner, pneumatic drill, balloon burst, thunder, exploding fireworks, hand clapping) (Arnold et al., 1985; Klein et al., 1990; Udwin & Yule, 1996; Van Borsel et al., 1997). Aversive sounds are often described as "loud," "high-pitched," and having "sudden onset" (Klein et al., 1990; Semel, 1988; Van Borsel et al., 1997). Sometimes the offensive sound is very specific; for example, a WSc may be very disturbed by the sound of a certain music box or the ring of a particular telephone, but may be unaffected by other sounds (Semel, 1988).

Interestingly, noises that consistently irritate WSs may later become a source of fascination (Doherty et al., 1989). This is reported in 79% of WSc (Utah Survey, Semel & Rosner, 1991a, 1991b). There are accounts of a shift from "hate" to "love" for the sounds of machines, vacuum cleaners, and lawn mowers.

Reactions to Offensive Sounds. The most typical reaction of WSs to aversive sounds is to put their hands over their ears (Klein et al., 1990; Semel & Rosner, 1991a, 1991b; Udwin & Yule, 1996; Van Borsel et al., 1997). This is shown in 90% of WSc (Utah Survey, Semel & Rosner, 1991a, 1991b). Other frequently reported responses include crying (68%), cringing (65%), running away (35%), making verbal remarks about the sound (35%), hysteria (5%), and rocking back and forth (3%) (Klein et al., 1990). WSs can become so distracted by sounds that they ignore other activities (Van Borsel et al., 1997).

Other Child Groups. In keeping with clinical observation, WSc exceed a mixed group of mentally retarded children in being hypersensitive to sounds and music (Gosch & Pankau, 1994b). WSc ($n = 70$, $M = 9;2$ yrs) are also more likely than matched mentally retarded controls to cover their ears and avoid particular sounds (Einfeld et al., 1997). This difference persists in a follow-up study 5 years later (Einfeld et al., 2001).

Clinical observation also suggests that the auditory hypersensitivities of WSc differ somewhat from those of children with other types of developmental disability. Unlike the auditory perceptual problems of children with learning disability, the hypersensitivity of WSc is most often triggered by the sudden and abrupt onset of background sound. Unlike the frenetic responses of autistic children, WSc typically cease all activity and seem compelled to identify the source of the sound. According to Marriage and Turk (1996), the unusual reactions of WSs to sound and other stimuli differ from those of children with Fragile X, idiopathic learning disability, and Down syndrome.

Mechanisms. At present, there is no evidence to support the notion that auditory hypersensitivity is associated with certain sensory or structural properties of the WS ear (see later). Moreover, auditory hyperacusis is not related to either ear infections (otitis media) or attention deficit hyperactivity disorder (ADHD, a behavioral disorder; Meyerson & Frank, 1987; Van Borsel et al., 1997).

Interestingly, neurophysiological studies (Neville, Holcomb, & Mills, 1989) implicate a cortical mechanism, auditory hyperexcitability, as possibly associated with WSs' auditory sensitivity. There is also preliminary evidence that WSs exhibit a neurochemical imbalance in which their serotonin level is low, which may operate as a central mechanism affecting both their auditory hypersensitivity and their hyperreactivity to certain stimuli, such as particular kinds of odors and visual input like spinning objects (Marriage, 1994; Marriage & Turk, 1996).

B. Auditory Processing Skills and Figure–Ground Problems

The auditory perceptual processing of WSs shows strengths and limitations. The proficiencies are well known, the deficiencies less so, possibly because of their being overshadowed by the interrelated and more acute condition of auditory hypersensitivity.

Auditory Processing Skills

The proficiencies of many WSs are seen in their ability to attend to, identify, interpret, and remember auditory information. This is reflected in their highly developed vocabulary, typically an area of strength, and excellent phonological memory (Levine, 1993; Mervis et al., 1999). As a rule, WSs tend to perform better on auditory rather than visual tasks (e.g., Crisco et al., 1988). Teachers, too, report that most WSc respond better to material presented in the auditory versus the visual mode. The unusual aptitude of WSs for music and their gift for learning foreign languages are other indications of their auditory capabilities (see chap. 5, p. 235).

Auditory Figure–Ground Problems

On the other hand, clinical experience indicates that a number of WSs have problems of auditory figure–ground perception: that is, difficulty in trying to separate out and listen to the signal (i.e., "figure") of the message, instead of the irrelevant or "background" noise (Wiig & Semel, 1976, p. 88).

Besides being adversely affected by sudden, loud background noise (i.e., auditory hypersensitivity), many WSs have the related problem of auditory figure–ground deficiency. Of recent interest to speech and hearing experts, this condition refers to problems in the ability to process speech, due to the presence of ambient noise that would not ordinarily undermine the average person's listening (American Speech-Language-Hearing Task Force on Central Auditory Processing Consensus Development, ASHA, 1996).

Acoustic Interference. In such cases, WSs may become badly distracted by the presence of "normal" background sound, acoustic reverberation, room "echo" (Bellis, 1996; Chermak & Musiek, 1997), or other speech (i.e., "competing acoustic signals" and "degraded" acoustic signals) (ASHA, 1996). A cogent example is that of a talented, 14-year-old WS boy who walks into a large ballroom to perform and is

> mildly overwhelmed . . . [by] simply too much noise and too many people for him to focus on a single conversation. Most people with Williams syndrome are auditorily distractible and have trouble focusing in a crowd. He goes from person to person but seems a little 'spacey;' having trouble focusing on a real conversation. (Levine & Wharton, 2000, p. 368)

Competing messages, confusing auditory signals, and impaired sound clarity can disrupt WSc's ability to understand or remember what a speaker is saying (Scheiber, 2000).

Auditory Discrimination and Memory. Auditory figure–ground problems are also apparent in the difficulty some WSs have in detecting subtle differences in sounds, words, and sentences whether in a noisy or quiet environment (Bellis, 1996). This is often observed when these WSs are learning phonics or sounding out words.

Noisy places, poor noise suppression, people who speak unclearly, people with a pronounced accent or a regionalism different from local speech, or people who cover their mouths and muffle their speech can cause WSs to miss important sounds or signals. Confusions may occur between similar sounding words or messages, such as "other" and "discover," or "I ran into the bike" instead of "I rented the bike." Certain words may become so distorted that the WS individual blocks them out. Directions or task instructions may be misperceived as strings of meaningless sounds or garbled words that do not make sense.

Auditory Closure. Auditory closure is a related, common problem of WSs involving difficulty in predicting or filling in missing elements of spoken messages in the presence of competing sounds. This exacerbates WSs' auditory figure–ground problem, because most people are able to infer missing or ambiguous information from speech context and can make auditory closure. This option is often unavailable to WSs, so they may not be able to compensate for distortions that routinely occur due to rapid or muf-fled speech or normal background sound. Auditory closure problems may also take the form of impaired, slurred, or rapid speech on the part of WSs.

Variability and individual differences exist, however, in the extent to which WSs exhibit auditory figure–ground deficiencies. Some WSs may not experience these problems at all, others only in unfavorable circumstances, and a few may be quite handicapped by them.

It should also be noted that this condition may be found among children with other types of handicapping conditions, such as learning disabilities, ADD, autism, and nonverbal learning problems.

C. Clinical Aspects of Audition and Auditory Processing

Reflecting the current body of knowledge, information on the clinical as-sessment, diagnosis, and treatment of disorders of audition and auditory processing is presented next.

Auditory Hypersensitivity. Despite intense interest in auditory hyper-sensitivity, little is known about the auditory capabilities of WSc except that their audiometric tests are often normal (Martin et al., 1984; Meyerson & Frank, 1987). Audiological assessments of WSs show no indication of any consistent peripheral auditory pathology (Marriage, 1994). Neither "stape-dial or acoustic nerve damage or cochlear and vestibular impairment" has been associated with Williams syndrome (Meyerson & Frank, 1987, p. 259).

Nevertheless, hypersensitivity should be evaluated by an audiologist (Klein et al., 1990) and assessed with an audiological battery. This usually includes tests of reflex threshold, loudness increment, and ultra-high fre-quency sensitivity; signal-to-noise ratio tasks may also be useful (Meyerson & Frank, 1987). Examination often reveals that the hearing of WSc is well within the normal range.

Specialists. Other specialists, besides audiologists, may be called on for auditory diagnosis and treatment. Otolaryngologists and otologists are consulted for the medical aspects of auditory problems, like otitis media, myringotomy, or hypersensitivity. Speech language therapists (SLTs) or au-diologists can provide auditory desensitization or other training when rec-ommended (see later). Otolaryngologists, otologists, or audiologists can review clinical findings (e.g., the audiogram of the patient's loudness threshold for tones or other sounds at multiple frequencies) and suggest various kinds of treatment, including ear devices or hearing aids.

Ear Disorders. A sizable number of WSc, approximately 40%, appear to have ear-related medical problems (Klein et al., 1990; Trauner et al., 1989). Morris et al. (1988) estimated that 38% of WS infants have chronic problems with otitis media during the first year of life. Over 50% of WSs, infants to adults, are reported to have many episodes of otitis media and/or use of eartubes (Klein et al., 1990; Van Borsel et al., 1997).

Several investigators have linked recurrent ear infections early in life to subsequent auditory and verbal deficits (Klein et al., 1990) and auditory attentional difficulty (Feagans, Kipp, & Blood, 1994).

Tests for Auditory Processing Deficits. Several formal tests are suitable for evaluating the auditory perceptual capabilities of WSs. All involve target speech and competing messages. The Competing Sentences Test (CST) (Willeford & Burleigh, 1994, p. 153) consists of simple sentences presented dichotically: the target sentence to one ear, the competing sentence to the other ear. The listener is asked to repeat the sentence heard in the target ear only and ignore the competing sentence.

Other tests use competing background noise or speech to study this phenomenon. Administered by an audiologist or SLT, these tests include the SCAN-C (Keith, 1999), the Goldman–Fristoe–Woodcock Test of Auditory Discrimination (Woodcock, 1976), and the Flowers–Costello Test of Central Auditory Abilities (Flowers, Costello, & Small, 1973).

Ear Devices. Certain types of ear devices may be helpful for auditory hypersensitivity, some for auditory processing deficits. Options include use of filtered ear protectors (Meyerson & Frank, 1987), headphones (Scheiber, 2000), earplugs that block out extraneous sounds (Van Borsel et al., 1997), earmuffs, and ear protectors that reduce sounds by 5, 20, or 40 decibels. Ear phones may be used to deliver classroom instructions or taped lessons. This may also improve WSs' ability to focus attention.

More recently, caution is advised in the use of earplugs previously recommended (e.g., Udwin & Yule, 1988) due to concerns that such devices interfere with normal hearing of important sounds like speech (Marriage, 2001; Udwin & Yule, 1998b). Earplugs should therefore be used sparingly, over brief periods of time. They are, perhaps, most useful when there is considerable background noise that cannot be controlled (i.e., on an airplane trip; Marriage, 2001). A case study of a young WSc with acute hypersensitivity, resulting in highly disruptive and aggressive behavior as well as obvious signs of pain due to the intensity of the sound input, demonstrates the therapeutic value of using earplugs under these conditions (O'Reilly, Lacey, & Lancioni, 2000).

Resistance to wearing ear devices may be handled by placing them in a play context, that is, instructing WSs to imagine that they are assuming the role of an astronaut, pilot, or telephone operator. Oftentimes, this can appeal to their interest in dramatization.

Amplification Devices. Use of a mild-gain amplifier may be especially helpful for dealing with problems of auditory figure–ground processing in certain WSs. The amplifier increases the volume of the desired signal thereby improving the quality of voice input without causing an increase in the volume of background noise. Another option is to use a low amplification tube, such as a funnel attached to a flexible plastic tube, or an empty cardboard paper towel roll or a stethoscope. The approximately 10 decibel amplification without distortion that this simple device provides could produce just enough "auditory magnification" to help the WS discriminate sounds that are so difficult for many WSers to distinguish easily during a phonics or reading lesson. This procedure works particularly well on a one-to-one basis.

Auditory Training. Therapists may use communication systems that increase the signal-to-noise ratio in earphones to provide auditory training. Use of an auditory trainer or similar device can sometimes facilitate listening during therapy sessions. In some cases, it can also aid the child's listening when being read to or given instructions. It can be especially helpful for WSc with attention deficits and disordered auditory processing. In other cases, it can have the opposite effect due to the possible amplification of background sounds.

Some parents are considering another technique called auditory integration training (AIT), which is being used by Alfred Tomatis (1978) and his student, Guy Bernard, to treat auditory-related problems in children with developmental disabilities (e.g., autism and dyslexia) through structured listening to filtered music. Its applicability to children with WS is yet to be determined and the American Speech Language Hearing Association (ASHA) has issued warnings as to its merits. In fact, import of AIT equipment has been banned in the United States "pending further investigation of its use and efficacy" (Schoenbrodt & Smith, 1995, p. 90).

Clinical Treatment with Noise Generators. A more credible approach involves the use of noise generators to reduce auditory hypersensitivity (Marriage, 2001, WSA National Newsletter, V. 18(1), pp. 4–6). Adapted from a technique used by audiologists for adults with hyperacusis and management of tinnitus, noise generators are embedded into an open ear mold, through which masking sounds are carefully modulated to provide attenuation of troubling sounds, while still allowing important sounds like normal speech to be heard. Care is taken in adjusting the volume of the masking (background) sound and the amount of time it is used. Although the mechanism by which aversive sounds become tolerable is not yet known, this technique is reported to have been successful in treating a number of WSc in England (Marriage, 2001). This form of treatment may be investigated by consulting professionals in hyperacusis at a local hospital, clinic, or child development center. Further information on the numbers of WSc served and their treatment outcomes would be helpful.

Behavioral Desensitization Training. School-age children may profit from a structured program of carefully planned exposure to sounds they consider intrusive, such as a doorbell or telephone ringing, a vacuum cleaner whirring, a blender running, a fire crackling, steam hissing, sirens, airplanes, helicopters, or bird calls. Controlled, organized listening experiences can help some WSc adapt to environmental noises and learn to process several sounds simultaneously, such as a voice against a low frequency background noise (Marriage, 2001).

Parents and teachers can also arrange situations in which WSc are able to exert control over aversive noises, such as clapping their hands or turning a machine on and off (Semel & Rosner, 1991a, 1991b; Udwin & Yule, 1998a, 1998b; Van Borsel et al., 1997). A more systematic approach involves making tape recordings of sounds that are particularly troublesome to WSc, such as school bells. Allowing the WSc to regulate the volume of the tape recorder gives the child a sense of control and aids in the child's accommodation to the sound (Levine, 1993; Meyerson & Frank, 1987; Udwin & Yule, 1998b; Van Borsel et al., 1997).

A Developing Listening Skills Program (Semel, 1982b) provides sound desensitization and activities for listening enhancement. The tapes included are designed to teach WSc to listen for particular environmental sounds and identify their meaning, instead of being overwhelmed by them. They familiarize children to common auditory stimuli, such as sounds heard at night, restaurants, airports, zoos, and construction sites. Initially, WSc may need reassurance and comforting while listening. Voice stimuli are added later in the program to help WSc learn to ignore background sounds and follow directions.

Treatment for Auditory Figure–Ground Problems. Auditory figure–ground problems may be addressed more directly by seeking the services of an experienced SLT. In conjunction with use of ear devices, desensitization training, and other clinical treatment programs (e.g., noise generator), the SLT can administer treatment designed to improve critical aspects of auditory figure–ground perception that typically impede the auditory processing of certain WSs. This should include interventions to deal with the following problems: auditory discrimination in quiet and background noise, auditory closure in quiet and background noise, and following directions in quiet and background noise.

As with the treatment of hyperacusis, clinical treatment should be supplemented by psycho-educational intervention approaches.

Hearing Loss. It should also be noted that there are a few WSc who suffer from actual hearing loss in one or both ears. A survey of WSs in Belgium and the Netherlands (Van Borsel et al., 1997) reports permanent hearing loss in 10% of WSs. There is some suggestion of an age-related increase in hearing problems. A study of adults with WS reports that almost all had a perceptive hearing loss and/or serious hearing problem (Hodenius et al., 1994).

Treatment of Hearing Loss. WSc tend to face the same types of speech and language difficulties as other individuals with hearing loss. However, they differ in an important respect, because they are usually extremely resistant to being fitted with a hearing aid. This may be a reaction to the amplification of extraneous background noises often caused by hearing aids, because WSs are generally extremely troubled by such sounds. For some WSc, protests over hearing aids may be related to tactile defensiveness (see Section III on p. 165).

In cases where hearing loss is progressive, it may be wise to provide speech/lip-reading lessons, speech therapy, and auditory training.

D. Psycho-Educational Interventions for Auditory Sensitivity

Because of the serious distress caused by auditory hypersensitivity and the disruption of functioning caused by auditory processing problems, it is important to try to find effective ways of dealing with these conditions. This may be difficult because they tend to be triggered by commonplace kinds of sounds and situations.

Besides consulting professionals for diagnosis, evaluation, and treatment of clinical problems as already suggested, several kinds of psycho-educational techniques may be helpful in managing or reducing the severity of WSs' problems of auditory sensitivity. These include use of environmental controls, task management (compensatory) strategies, verbal mediational techniques, and control mechanisms.

Environmental controls are applicable to both conditions, and task management techniques mainly to problems of auditory processing, whereas verbal mediational techniques and control mechanisms are best differentiated by type of condition. These interventions straddle the boundaries between specialists, parents, teachers, and others involved with WSs. Advice of specialists, like audiologists and speech language therapists, is helpful in some cases, mandatory in others.

In any event, becoming cognizant of the reality of hyperacusis for most WSs is a prerequisite to other approaches for that condition. That is, it is vitally important to recognize that WSs are not merely pretending to be bothered by certain sounds or seeking attention; they are suffering from an identifiable condition. It is also important to understand that many of the intervention approaches described in this section, clinical and psychoeducational, are complementary and are best applied in combination with others (Marriage, 2001; Semel, 1988; Semel & Rosner, 1991b, 1994). Similarly, it is becoming increasing clear that some WSs are vulnerable to auditory processing deficiency, a real and verifiable substantiated disorder (ASHA, 1996), for which certain clinical and psycho-educational approaches may be of real benefit. One program which can be helpful in the treatment of auditory processing problems is the Semel Auditory Processing Program (Semel, 1995R). SAPP is a systematic, a highly structured small-step teaching program which features developing the mastery of sound-symbol correspondence. It can be used to help reduce the many auditory-processing confusions that children encounter in dealing with the inconsistencies in language.

Environmental Controls

Controlling the auditory environment is usually a very helpful way of handling problems of auditory hypersensitivity and reducing problems of auditory processing deficiency. Selecting household appliances with low noise levels (Klein et al., 1990) and restricting the use of appliances with disturbing noise qualities when the WS individual is present can temporarily relieve these problems (Meyerson & Frank, 1987; Van Borsel et al., 1997).

In the classroom, it may be helpful to seat the WSs in a location that minimizes exposure to disturbing sounds and away from windows and doors. Using sound absorbing materials, like draperies, curtains or shades, upholstered furniture, pillows, carpeting and acoustic ceiling tile is also helpful. Open classrooms should be avoided. Warning WSs a bit in advance about predictable sounds like hourly bells or fire drill signals, or adjusting their volume or pitch, may also reduce their shock value (Levine, 1993; Semel, 1988). This can be tricky, however, because telling them too far in advance may cause unnecessary anxiety. Reducing the level of noise in the workplace may be necessary for those WS adults who suffer from hypersensitivity to noise and may suffer panic attacks or aggressive outbursts in response to discomfort caused by sounds (Udwin & Yule, 1996).

Being allowed to leave the room or situation where there are highly aversive sounds is an option that should be made available when necessary (Marriage, 2001; Udwin & Yule, 1998a, 1998b).

Task Management

Whereas environmental controls are designed to attenuate background noise, task management strategies are the inverse; they are designed to accentuate the signal so that WSs with figure ground processing problems may be able to extract relevant input from the background noise more easily.

Several measures may assist in this regard. These include having the speaker and listener placed in a face-to-face view of each other. This is particularly important when making special announcements, giving instructions, introducing a new topic, or making changes in an assignment or program. Attention should be focused on the speaker by making eye contact, calling the WS individual by name, using physical proximity, and smiling directly at the WS individual.

Often, watching the speaker's face can help the WS individual "fill in the blanks" of a voice message that may be distorted or incompletely heard. Also, the smaller the distance between the speaker and listener, the better the signal-to-noise ratio.

Other useful hints are for the speaker to speak slowly, clearly, loudly enough, and use short, simple, easy-to-understand sentences, especially when giving directions. To encourage better listening, key words may be emphasized by varying volume, intonation, rate, stress, or inserting a long pause.

Verbal Mediation for Auditory Hypersensitivity

For problems of auditory hypersensitivity, recognition of the sound and reassurance by adults are the primary techniques; self-instructional strategies are useful with some older or more capable WSs.

Acknowledgment, Reassurance, and Explanation. Use of a three-step process is basic to the application of verbal-mediational strategies for auditory hypersensitivity (Marriage, 2001; Semel & Rosner, 1991a, 1991b; Udwin & Yule, 1998a, 1998b). First, the adult should acknowledge the occurrence of annoying sounds and offer reassurance (Udwin & Yule, 1998b). For example, "Boy, that sure is a loud noise," "I know it hurts your ears," "Let's try to make it easier for you," or "Would you like to put on your head phones?" Second, the adult may assist the child in identifying the source of the sound. Third, the adult should explain that the sound is the result of something happening or working (e.g., "the blades of the fan make a humming sound when they go around and cool the air"). Often the WSc is comforted by having the sound identified and its presence confirmed (Van Borsel et al., 1997).

Signals, Rehearsal, and Self-Talk. Once the WSc responds positively to the three-step process described previously, other strategies for dealing with auditory hypersensitivity may be introduced.

Parents and teachers can use affective signals, like a smile, nod, wink, "OK" gesture, or shorthand verbal cues to indicate that they are aware of the WS child's distress.

Rehearsal may be incorporated into the process by encouraging WSs to repeat the reassuring statements and explanations offered by adults (e.g., "It's only a fan").

Some WSs may be taught to use "self-talk" to deal with their auditory hypersensitivity. Several forms of self-talk may be helpful: self-reminders (e.g., "I know that sound." "It's only a fan."), self-encouragement (e.g., "Try to block it out." "I can do it."), self-instruction (e.g., "I know what is making that noise." "I can look for it later."), and self-reinforcement (e.g., "I did it; I am not so afraid of that noise anymore."). These techniques are applicable only to certain individuals with WS.

Verbal Mediation for Auditory Processing Problems

Verbal mediational techniques for auditory processing problems may be divided in terms of who carries out the strategy: parents, teachers, and other adults, or WSs themselves.

Adults' Monitoring of Auditory Processing Problems. Adults, parents, teachers, and others should routinely monitor WSs' comprehension and repeat information and instructions as needed. Periodically, they should check on WSs' understanding by having the person repeat what was said or answer relevant questions about the topic. Corrections should be made as necessary by rephrasing, making modifications, and re-monitoring.

WSs' Identification of Problem and Request for Clarification. It is important for WSs to become aware of their auditory perceptual problems by having them pointed out, and in particular, the conditions under which they occur. This will usually require use of demonstration and dramatization techniques, and it may be successful with only more cognitively able WSs.

Once this is accomplished, however, WSs may be able to explain their figure ground problems to others and ask for modification of conditions that exacerbate their problems. For example, they could learn to say: "I don't hear so well when there is a lot of noise going on," or "When there is a racket outside, I can't hear a word you are saying," or "I work best in a quiet place so I need to be seated away from noise."

WSs may also be encouraged to ask others for feedback about their performance, such as, "Did I get those instructions right?" and request clarification when they have difficulty hearing what others are saying. They can ask a speaker to talk more slowly, louder, or to repeat or provide additional information. These are repair strategies similar to those recommended for problems with the pragmatics of language, in particular, information exchange.

Control Mechanisms for Auditory Hypersensitivity

Reinforcement. WSc should be strongly rewarded for responding positively to their parent's or teacher's statements or their own self-talk. Most WSc value personal, verbal, and affective forms of reinforcement (e.g., verbal praise, affective positive signals, personal approval) more than most types of tangible, concrete reinforcement (e.g., candy or tokens) (see chap. 3).

Accommodation. Unfortunately, some WSc have such extreme levels of acoustic distress that they are unable to be helped by the palliative measures described earlier. These WSc children appear to require accommodation on the part of their parents and teachers. This may include allowing and accompanying the WSc to search for the source of a bothersome noise. Some parents report that they routinely take their WSc on a tour of restaurant noises before seating the child at the table. This can enable the family to dine amiably instead of having to attend repeatedly to the child's auditory hypersensitivity.

It is also important to note that failure to deal constructively with WSs' auditory hypersensitivity may result in endless parent–child and teacher–child struggles. When WSs are frequently overwhelmed by uncontrollable hypersensitivity, they can become so unmanageable that family members and teachers are no longer able to reach them.

Control Mechanisms for Auditory Processing Problems

The primary form of control mechanism for WSs who have acquired the verbal mediational strategies suggested is self-reinforcement.

Self-Reinforcement for Auditory Processing. WSs may also reinforce themselves for taking positive steps in avoiding intrusive noises and asking speakers to adapt their speech to facilitate their comprehension. The following are examples of self-talk: "I got the message even though it was noisy in there." "I am learning to be a good listener."

As the skills of self-regulating listening behavior develop, WSs can learn that their successful listening experiences are not based on "luck" alone and they can control their listening success.

On the other hand, the consequences of untreated auditory processing problems are unnecessary failure, frustration, and limitations in WSs' potential for success and mastery. It is also a shame for WSs to be deprived of an area, language skills, in which they hold the potential for success.

V. SUMMARY: PERCEPTUAL AND MOTOR PERFORMANCE

Of the four areas represented in this chapter, two—visual-spatial-motor (VSM) and motor functioning—reflect severe deficiencies in performance. The others, tactile sensitivity and auditory sensitivity, reflect overreactivity to common stimuli that do not usually bother other people.

Visual-Spatial-Motor Problems

Generally, WSs have a unique combination of VSM deficits and skills. Their drawings of common objects are often unrecognizable; simple designs like a triangle or diamond are copied poorly, global stimuli are frequently minimized, block constructions are extremely primitive, and spatial orientation tests are often failed. Yet, the same WSs exhibit remarkable skill in their recognition of unfamiliar faces and identification of objects viewed in unusual perspectives.

WSs frequently exhibit the clinical disorders of strabismus and refraction errors (farsightedness and nearsightedness), which are usually diagnosed and treated by ophthalmologists. Qualified vision specialists and formal tests of visual perception may also be helpful in evaluating visual functioning and providing suitable interventions. Although eye problems, if present, need corrections, there does not seem to be any causal link between the structural visual characteristics of WSs and their VSM deficits.

Motor Problems. Almost all WSs suffer from severe deficits in motor development, motor planning, and gross and fine motor functioning. Difficulties are common in performing everyday activities, such as eating, grooming, tool use, sports, writing, and arts and crafts. Gross motor functioning is impacted by problems of spatial orientation, whereas fine motor performance is impaired by deficits in visuospatial functioning. Problems of spatial orientation are reflected in difficulties with laterality, directionality, and handedness, among others.

Professional evaluation of WSs' motor functioning is strongly recommended because of the prevalence and severity of their motor problems. Difficulties involving the musculoskeletal, kinesthetic, and vestibular systems are common; these may include problems of muscle tone, contractures, proprioception, posture, and balance, as well as problems of spatial orientation, directionality, and laterality.

Almost all WSs require treatment in order to lessen or avoid the worsening of motor problems, such as joint limitation or contractures, postural abnormalities (kyphosis, lordosis), and loss of muscle function. Besides physicians, OTs, PTs, and sensory integration therapists with advanced training can often provide expert evaluation and specialized treatment.

Interventions for VSM Problems. In addition, three types of psycho-educational techniques may be helpful with the VSM integration problems associated with WS: (a) verbal mediation to aid visuospatial construction, motor functioning, visuospatial orientation, and visual processing; (b) task management to help optimize visual input, improve motor performance, and reduce confusions of laterality; and (c) naturalistic activities to provide experience with visual tracking and scanning, and functional activities, like kitchen tasks, to provide practice using VSM skills.

Untreated VSM problems may accompany or lead to serious educational consequences for WSs, such as difficulties in learning to read and write as well as many kinds of physical, perceptual, and social consequences.

Tactile Sensitivity

Tactile defensiveness is less often reported, occurring in approximately 40% of WSs, than problems of auditory hypersensitivity, motor functioning, and VSM integration. WSs differ in their ability to use tactile stimulation as a valuable source of sensory information and in the severity of their problems with tactile sensitivity.

Tactile defensive reactions can range from annoyance to aversion, from extreme distress to debilitation. Reactions may be triggered by many kinds of stimuli, including certain clothing, grooming activities, walking surfaces, types of chairs, oral stimulation or foods, or even visits to dentists or physicians.

In treating tactile defensiveness, specialists in occupational and sensory integration therapy can evaluate the condition and administer treatment. Psycho-educational techniques, mainly environmental controls, may help to alleviate the severity of the symptoms.

Auditory Sensitivity

Almost all WSs experience auditory hypersensitivity for at least some part of, and usually throughout, their lives. Triggered by everyday sounds, such as household machines, airplanes, thunder, or audience applause, the response can be annoyance, aversion, or so overwhelmingly intense that it dominates everything else. There is little evidence of structural abnormalities of the ear or audiometric anomalies to account for WSs' hyperacusis. Other aspects of WSs' auditory sensitivity can be constructive; this is indicated in their musicality and use of auditory processing in learning to read and spell. A related problem, auditory figure ground deficiencies, is less well studied, but interference from observations of everyday ambient noise or nearby conversations may interfere with WSs' ability to understand what the speaker is saying or to answer questions appropriately.

5

Specific Aptitudes

Beside their unusual aptitude for language, most WSs have an impressive aptitude in four other areas: sociability, curiosity, memory, and musicality. As with language, each is central to the phenotype and daily lives of most WSs. These are islands of considerable skill, unexpected in individuals with limited cognitive abilities and numerous behavior problems (see chap. 6).

Each area is characterized by its own kind of paradoxical properties, both problems or limitations and abilities or talents that may be used as "Access" channels to help WSs realize their potential. Interventions are needed to maximize the capabilities and address the problems of WSs in these areas.

This chapter describes the positive and problematic aspects of each specific aptitude and suggests intervention approaches relevant for each area: sociability, curiosity, memory, and musicality.

I. SOCIABILITY

Most individuals with WS (WSs) exhibit an intriguing mix of social attributes. They tend to be exceptionally friendly, outgoing, and sensitive to the feelings of others. Yet, they often exhibit problems of overfriendliness, poor peer relations, oversensitivity, and difficulty in understanding higher level concepts of social cognition. Such contradictions challenge the assumption that sociability is a unitary trait. They also underscore the need for interventions to address the social difficulties and build on the social skills associated with WS.

A. Social Orientation

Typically, parents, teachers, professionals, and even casual observers are struck by the social nature of most WSs. Beuren (1972) described WSc as "very active and always happy," "charming characters . . . very different from many other mentally retarded children" (p. 47). Other professionals portray them as "friendly . . . socially disinhibited," having an "outgoing social nature," "exuberant enthusiasm," "a strong social orientation," and a "sense of the dramatic" (Dilts et al., 1990; Levine, 1997; MacDonald & Roy, 1988; Udwin et al., 1987; von Arnim & Engel, 1964). Similarly, parents describe WSc as: "kind, friendly and outgoing, sensitive and caring" (WSA National Newsletter, 1989, April, p. 31); "loving, joyful, with a great sense of humor" (WSA National Newsletter, 1994, Vol. *11*, Winter, p. 25); and "very cute and sweet . . . the happiest little boy you could ever meet" (WSA National Newsletter, 2000, Vol. *17*, p. 27).

Surveys of parents support these observations. Almost all WSc (95%), are said to be "unusually friendly," 98% "initiate conversations with others easily," and 88% "seek to engage in and develop conversations with others" (Utah Survey, Semel & Rosner, 1991a, 1991b).

On a general measure of "Sociability," parents rate WSc (n = 15, 4–18 yrs, M = 9;6 yrs; n = 41, 4–8;11 yrs) higher than on almost all other subscales of the Vineland Adaptive Scale (Greer et al., 1997; Mervis et al., 2001). Within Sociability, WSc are rated higher on items related to interpersonal skills than items related to play/leisure or coping skills (Mervis et al., 2001). This mirrors the deficits WSc typically show in the area of gesture/symbolic play versus the development of language skills (see chap. 2).

Composite response measures also indicate marked sociability in WSs compared to that of other groups. For example, parent ratings of Global Sociability are significantly higher for WSa (n = 20, M = 19 yrs) than for matched groups of DSa, AUTa, or normal CA controls (n = 15) (Jones et al., 2000, Exp. IV). WSa also exceed these groups on all three components of this measure: the tendency to approach others, be approached by others, and empathize with or comment on others' emotional states (Jones et al., 2000).

Similarly, WSc (n = 204, 1–12 yrs) score higher on "Approach," a dimension of temperament, than the norms for normal control children (Tomc, Williamson, & Pauli, 1990). This is found very early in life, in fact, from age 1 on (Tomc et al., 1990). Also, WSs (n = 13, 10–50 yrs, M = 22 years) score higher than matched MR controls on Approach in a study using the Dutch adaptation of the Parents Temperament Questionnaire for Children (Plissart, Borghraef, Volcke, Van Den Berghe, & Fryns, 1994).

Even as toddlers, most WSc (n = 22, 15–58 mo; n = 14, 25–31 mo) are irresistibly attracted to opportunities for social interaction (Jones et al., 2000, Exp. II, Jones et al., 1996). WS toddlers tend to use social engagement devices like eye contact, smiling, and focusing on other people's faces from a very early age (Jones et al., 1996; Jones et al., 2000). Almost all WSc (92%; $n = 25$, < 34 mo) are reported to stare intensely at the geneticist during an evaluation, compared to none of the contrast group (Mervis & Klein-Tasman, 2000). Prelinguistically, these tendencies can be so strong that they interfere with WSc's performance (Jones et al., 2000). In fact, many stare at the examiner's face or eyes to obtain information while performing perceptual motor and other laboratory tasks. Although social referencing can be a distraction in some contexts, it can have adaptive value in other situations by providing signals of a threat of danger or feedback of performance. This quality sets them apart from autistic children, who rarely engage in eye contact.

"Attention-Seeking" is another attribute strongly associated with WS. In line with this, WSs ($n = 35$, 14–50 yrs, $M = 24;6$ yrs) are rated significantly higher than matched groups of PWa or MRa on items such as "enjoys being a show-off," "often initiates interactions," and "never goes unnoticed in groups" on the Reiss Profiles (Dykens & Rosner, 1999).

Within the childhood years and 5 years later as adolescents, WSc ($n = 70$, $M = 9;2$ yrs; $n = 53$, $M = 14;6$ yrs) score significantly higher than MR matched controls on "overly attention-seeking," as well as "overaffectionate" and "inappropriately happy or elated" on the Developmental Behavior Checklist (Einfeld et al., 1997; Einfeld et al., 2001). Whereas the typical "happiness" of WSs is usually endearing and uplifting to others, it may also appear to be a bit "too much." Levine and Wharton (2000) provided the cogent example of a WSa commenting on a very gloomy day that the snow is "making all different colors of the rainbow in the trees! It's like SHINY RAINBOWS on the trees" (p. 367).

Similarly, "Agreeableness" is a personality dimension on which WSc ($n = 28$, 2;9–19;6 yrs, $M = 9;4$) are rated higher than PW children ($n = 39$) or boys with Frag X ($n = 32$). They are even comparable to age-mates in regular school on this dimension (Curfs, van Lieshout, deMeyer, Plissart, & Fryns, 1996; van Lieshout, deMeyer, Curfs, & Fryns, 1998). This provides further evidence of the considerable warmth, empathy, and trusting nature of most WSc.

Along the same lines, teachers generally rate WS students ($n = 58$, first-, third-, and fifth-graders) favorably on scales of social skills (Levine & Castro, 1994). In fact, ratings of WSc on the Social Initiation scale of the Teacher Rating of Social Skills (TROSS) are higher than the norms for all contrast groups: academically achieving children as well as children with learning disability, behavior disorder, and mixed forms of mental retardation. On the Cooperation scale, WS students are comparable to the norms for academically achieving children and superior to those for three special needs groups. It is most unusual for children with a developmental disorder to score similarly to normally developing children.

This is reflected in the written comments of teachers, such as reporting that a WSa has "the best personality of any kid—'special' or 'normal' that I have ever met" (WSA National Newsletter, 1989 November, pp. 34–35). Clinical observation, too, indicates that the personal charm of most WSs is hard to match.

Table 5.1 presents a summary of research studies dealing with the WSs' social orientation and overfriendliness.

B. Overfriendliness

As a rule, WSc are trusting, gullible, and insatiable in their quest for social interaction. They are described as "uninhibited in their dealings with adults." Typically, they greet strangers or acquaintances "like old friends" (von Arnim & Engel, 1964). They tend to speak easily with adults, sometimes in an inappropriately familiar manner. They may hug, kiss, or pat even casual acquaintances, but not so frequently as observed in the "aligning" type of Down syndrome. This can be embarrassing to parents, and potentially dangerous when extended to strangers. It is also closely related to their frequent lack of constraints in the pragmatics of language, such as compulsive greeting behavior, improper use of flattery, wheedling favors that are often denied others, and asking personal questions (see pp. 48–49 and p. 55).

On a more positive note, overfriendliness may be intrinsic to WSs' sociability, apparent in their lack of shyness, good stage presence while performing in public, and sense of humor. Thus, overfriendliness is a significant core feature of the WS profile (Mervis et al., 1999).

In open-ended interviews, 64% of parents and teachers spontaneously mention the "marked friendliness [of WSc] toward adults, including strangers" (Udwin et al.,1987). All of the WSc (n = 5, 7;3–11;6 yrs) observed in another study (MacDonald & Roy, 1988) were said to be friendly, loquacious, and socially disinhibited. Compared to children with nonspecific forms of mental retardation, WSc (n = 19, 4–10 yrs) are noted for being overfriendly, exhibiting no reserve, tending to follow a stranger without hesitation in the rating responses of parents on Achenbach's Child Behavior Checklist (Gosch & Pankau, 1994b).

Likewise, personality ratings for WSs reveal a strong tendency toward "social disinhibition" and difficulty in modulating interactions (Dykens & Rosner, 1999). WSs are also said to display an "overaffectionate" nature in childhood and adolescence (Einfeld et al., 1997; Einfeld et al., 2001).

In fact, WSa (n = 26, M = 24 yrs) are significantly more likely to say that they would be willing to approach and strike up a conversation with an unfamiliar individual than normal MA or CA matched controls (Cassady, Bellugi, Reilly, & Adolphs, 1997; Jones et al., 2000, Exp. III). Interestingly, WSa

TABLE 5.1

Social Orientation and Overfriendliness in WSs: Summary of Results

Type of Behavior or Test	Frequency or Result	Source or Reference
Unusually Friendly	WSc 95%	Utah Survey
Initiates Conversations Easily	WSc 98%	
Engages, Develops Conversations Easily	WSc 88%	
Vineland Adaptive Scale[#]	WSc Sociability > Daily Living Skills	Greer et al., 1997; Mervis et al., 2001
	WSc Interpersonal Skills > Play/ Leisure or Coping Skills	Mervis et al., 2001
Global Sociability[#]	WSa > DSa, AUTa, Normal CA Controls	Jones et al., 2000
Approach[#]	WS > Norms NH	Tomc et al., 1990
	WS > Controls MR	Plissart et al., 1994a
Stared at Examiner's Face[#]	WSc > CA Normal Controls	Mervis & Klein-Tasman, 2000
Reiss Profiles[#]:		
Attention Seeking	WSa > PWa, MRa	Dykens & B. Rosner, 1999
Often Initiates Interactions	WSa > PWa, MRa	
Never Goes Unnoticed	WSa > PWa, MRa	
Developmental Behavior Checklist[#]:		
Overly Attention Seeking	WSc & WSa > MRc and MRa	Einfeld et al., 1997,
Overaffectionate	Controls	Einfeld et al., 2001
Inappropriately Happy or Elated		
CA Child Q–Set	WSc ~ Normal CA Controls >	Curfs et al., 1996
Agreeableness[#]	PWc, Frag X boys	van Lieshout et al., 1998
TROSS:		
Social Initiation[#]	WSc > Norms NH, LD, BD, MR	Levine & Castro, 1994
Cooperation[#]	WSc ~ Norms NH > LD, BD, MR	
No Fear of Strangers	WSc 98%	WSA Midwest Region, 1989
No Fear of Strangers	WSc 96%	WSA Checklist Survey
Friendly, Socially Disinhibited	WSc 100%	MacDonald & Roy, 1988
Child Behavior Checklist[#]:		
Overfriendly	WSc > MRc	Gosch & Pankau, 1994b
No Reserve	WSc > MRc	
Follows Strangers	WSc > MRc	
Self-Report[#]: Willing to Approach, Converse with Other People	WSa > Normal MA, Normal CA Controls	Cassady et al., 1997; Jones et al., 2000
Parental Separation Task[#]: Anxiety	WSc < Normal CA Controls	Jones et al., 2000
Overfriendliness[#]	WSa < WSc	Finucane, 1996; Gosch & Pankau, 1996b
	WSa 100% Problem on Job	Davies et al., 1997

Note: % = percentage frequency; # = mean amount; WSc = WS children; WSa = WS adolescents or adults; DS = Down syndrome; AUT = autistic; N or NH = normally developing; MR = mentally retarded; PW = Prader–Willi syndrome; Frag X = Fragile X syndrome; LD = learning disabled; BD = behavior disorder.

seem to be more easily influenced by obvious cues, like smiling (a powerful incentive and stimulus for WSs in many contexts), than by more subtle cues, like furrowed eyebrows (Jones et al., 2000, Exp. III).

Unlike most children, WSc seldom "cling" to parents or show "stranger anxiety." Over 90% of WSc are said to display "No Fear of Strangers" (WSA National Newsletter, 1989 April, pp. 21–22; WSA Checklist Survey, Semel & Rosner, 1991a, 1991b). Even WS infants are unlikely to show stranger anxiety (<25%) (WSA Checklist, Semel & Rosner, 1991a, 1991b), and WS toddlers (n = 22, 15–58 mo; n = 14, 15–31 mo) are less likely to be troubled by a laboratory Parental Separation Task than are normal CA controls (Jones et al., 2000, Exp. II). This contrasts markedly with the number and intensity of other fears and anxieties in most WSs (see chap. 6). It seems likely that sociability is a domain-specific, specialized skill of WSs (Karmiloff-Smith, 1992).

In adulthood, 73% of WSa are still overfriendly and lack restraint with strangers despite repeated warnings (Udwin, 1990). Parents and caregivers report overfriendliness as a major concern; some WSa are not allowed to go out alone. Still, 100% of employers of WSa (n = 21) mention overfriendliness as a problem on the job (Davies, Howlin, & Udwin, 1997). According to parents and caregivers, 59% of WSa (n = 70, 18–39 yrs) are "physically over-demonstrative," 10% made reports to the police of sexual assault, and another 10% made allegations of sexual assault that were unreported to the police (Davies, Udwin, & Howlin, 1998). Even so, overfriendliness is less often reported for WS adults than children (Finucane, 1996; Gosch & Pankau, 1996b).

Table 5.1 presents a summary of studies on the social orientation and overfriendliness of WSs.

Dealing With Overfriendliness

Most WSs need extensive training in learning socially acceptable ways of interacting with other people and using self-protective measures (Dykens & Rosner, 1999). This is strikingly apparent in the classic example of a WS youngster who after painstaking, carefully presented instruction on the importance of not speaking to strangers began pleasantly asking everyone she encountered, "Are you a stranger?"

The need for human contact seems to be so overwhelming that it tends to override everything else. The extra attention that WSs often receive from people who think that overfriendliness is "cute" may also reinforce this behavior (Udwin & Yule, 1998a, 1998b).

Although difficult to overcome, the overfriendliness of WSs may be addressed by applying certain psycho-educational techniques or seeking professional treatment when necessary.

Psycho-Educational Techniques

Psycho-educational techniques are among the most effective approaches when teaching WSs how to behave appropriately with others. They include providing social instruction and encouraging appropriate social behavior through the use of verbal mediation strategies and control mechanisms.

Social Awareness Instruction. Most WSs do not understand that people differ in terms of their social role and type of relationship, such as parent, family member, close family friend, casual acquaintance, professional (teacher, therapist, physician, nurse), employee, or service person (bus driver, secretary, clerk). They may also need help differentiating between levels of certain relationships, such as parent–child, best friend–self, teacher–student, or doctor–patient. Such concepts are a prerequisite to understanding why individuals respond differently to different kinds of people.

Social training also includes explaining how people differ in their interpersonal characteristics, for example, what kinds of functions they typically serve or what is special in the way they behave toward the WS individual. Other useful forms of training include observing people in real-life situations, modeling appropriate forms of behavior, or employing other kinds of dramatization techniques (Levine, 1993; Semel, 1988; Udwin & Yule, 1998a, 1998b).

Once WSs have become aware of such distinctions, they may need to be taught how to behave appropriately in a circumscribed situation with different kinds of people—for example, how to greet different kinds of people (i.e., family members, friends, neighbors, authority figures, acquaintances, or strangers). Generally, instruction should start with the most familiar and proceed to the less familiar. Having mastered one situation, WSs may then be taught how to greet or interact appropriately with various kinds of people in other settings. (See Semel & Wiig, 1992.)

Verbal Mediational Techniques. Mediational strategies, such as modeling, role play, videotaping, and dramatization are extremely useful ways to demonstrate, differentiate, and explain alternative ways of behaving to WSs (see also Udwin & Yule, 1998a, 1998b). Puppets or stories about an imaginary child may be used to illustrate the dangers that may result from speaking to strangers or going away with them (Scheiber, 2000). Asking structured questions or having WSc retell the story may help to concretize its message. Identifying peers and others whose behavior is appropriate may also be helpful.

Importantly, the WS individual should be urged to enact and verbalize the rationale for acceptable kinds of behavior. Explicitness, dramatization, rehearsal, repeated instruction, and reminding are often needed. Of course, individual differences also affect WSs' ability to use various techniques. Some are unable to acquire or generalize desired behavior even after extensive training. Others can be taught self-instructional social skills, such as saying with self-talk, "I won't talk to him because he's a stranger, I don't know him . . ."

Control Mechanisms. Regardless of approach, WSc must be discouraged from approaching or welcoming the advances of strangers. Direct instruction using clear, unambiguous statements is often necessary (e.g., "don't talk to strangers," "you don't know that person, don't hug him"). A strong position must be taken with this problem. Lapses must be censured, and appropriate behaviors should be reinforced (Udwin & Yule, 1998a, 1998b). Instruction is often necessary, too, in learning how to act appropriately with acquaintances and familiar people. Hugging and kissing should be discouraged; WSs must be told that such behavior is unacceptable, except with family members. The recipients of WSs' attention should also be advised that they should communicate to WSs the inappropriateness of their overfriendly behavior. Udwin and Yule (1998a, 1998b) stressed that it is never too early to start to restrain this tendency to approach strangers.

It is also extremely important to help WSs identify the behaviors of others that may be potentially harmful to them or illegal. This includes situations that may involve or lead to abuse, drugs, molestation, sexual exploitation, or rape. WSs should be taught to recognize and avoid contacts, verbal as well as physical (e.g., touching), which may bring about uncomfortable feelings or are considered taboo. In such circumstances, they should know how to report a suspicious, potentially harmful situation or actual incident to a trusted adult. Some parents say they deal with this problem by "never let[ting] him out of my sight" (Anonymous, Williams Syndrome Hotline, Sept. 1999).

Treatment by Professional Specialists

In cases in which parents or teachers are unsuccessful in teaching WSs appropriate behaviors, a professional specialist may be able to help. Educational specialists, child psychologists, speech language therapists, counselors, or special education teachers are among the professionals who may be able to provide suggestions, guidance, or assist in establishing and administering an intervention plan on an individual basis. Sometimes modification of an ongoing approach is necessary in type of reward, method of training, or type of explanation used in a particular case. In severe cases, it may be advisable for a team of professionals to work together in addressing an issue, such as the danger of consorting with strangers.

Occasionally, WSc are unresponsive to verbal-social techniques, SLT, and psychological therapy even when adjustments are made to fit the needs of the individual child. In such cases, behavior modification methods may be helpful (see chap. 3, p. 74).

C. Peer Relations

Aside from family, peers provide the major influence for the socialization of most normally developing children. Over the childhood years, peers be- come increasingly important as models, referents, and reinforcers of social behavior, that is, they serve as the arbiter of social rules and yardstick by which most children gauge their behavior and themselves.

Age Trends in Peer Relations

With WSs, amount and type of interest in peers usually varies markedly over the course of development. Typically, young children with WS do not seek social companionship from age-mates. Many prefer solitary and paral- lel play to interactive play (Arnold et al., 1985). Eighty-three percent are said to be "rather solitary," and 64% prefer adults over other children (Udwin et al. 1987).

During the school years, interest in peers and problems with peer rela- tions often appear (Dilts et al., 1990; Levine, 1993; Tharp, 1986; Udwin & Yule, 1998b). Parents report that 71% of WSc have difficulty in making and keeping friends their own age, 41% antagonize children their own age (Utah Survey, Semel & Rosner, 1991a, 1991b), 56% have problems with other chil- dren (Tharp, 1986), and 35% are "not much liked" by peers (Udwin et al., 1987). Many prefer normal, younger children instead of same-age peers (Tharp, 1986). Compared to a matched group of mentally retarded children, WSc are more likely to be rated high on items like "does not mix with own age group" and "prefers adult company" (Einfeld et al., 1997; Einfeld et al., 2001). Reportedly, both WSs and PWs have more difficulty with rejection and fewer friends than a matched group of mentally retarded individuals (Dykens & Rosner, 1999).

On the other hand, a sizable percentage of WSc may not have these kinds of peer problems. In fact, there is a significant minority, 30%, who are not reported to have difficulty with peer relations (Utah Survey, Semel & Rosner, 1991a, 1991b). Udwin and Yule (1998b) reached a similar conclusion, namely, "many children and adults [with WS] are popular and well-liked. . . . [They can] establish warm and caring friendships both within and outside their immediate families . . . (p. 7).

Yet, many WSc eagerly seek peer contact and friendship. In fact, WS stu- dents are rated as high as academically achieving students and higher than children with learning disability, mental retardation, and behavior disorder on the Peer Reinforcement scale of TROSS, that is, the extent to which they reinforce other students (Levine & Castro, 1994). Nonetheless, few are successful in fulfilling their desires for an active social life. Many WSc ($n = 20$, 6;8–14;4 yrs) express "feelings of loneliness . . ." (Bailly et al., 1994).

In adulthood, problems of poor peer relations and loneliness tend to persist or become more severe (Udwin & Yule, 1998b). A majority (67%), of WS adults (WSa) are said to be extremely limited and isolated socially from disabled as well as nondisabled people of their own age (Udwin, 1990). In fact, parents rate adolescents and adults as more seclusive and less extroverted than WSs of childhood age (Curfs et al., 1996; Gosch & Pankau, 1996b). This is consistent with age trends showing decreasing extroversion with age in the general adult population (McCrae et al., 1999).

However, new information and a change in attitudes and school policy toward people with special needs, including WSc, may make it less likely for them to experience social isolation within the school context. Advice to employees may also reduce the social problems of WSa on the job (Udwin et al., 1996).

Factors Affecting Peer Relations

WSs' difficulty with peers may often stem from problems of immaturity. Parents report that 81% of WSc have difficulty in playing age-appropriate games and using sports equipment (Utah Survey, Semel & Rosner, 1991a, 1991b). Poor visual-spatial-motor skills and cognitive deficits may affect their ability to participate effectively in team sports or interact appropriately in other play activities.

Problems following certain pragmatic language rules, such as topic maintenance, relevance, being able to accept criticism, accepting responsibility, expressing anger, being tactful, and turn-taking may also contribute to communication difficulties with peers. This can be a real turn-off for peers; adults are usually more accepting and forgiving of deviations in following conversational rules.

Likewise, WSc ($n = 6$, 4–12 yrs) are often relatively weak in skills involving social reciprocity (Bregman, 1996; Udwin & Yule, 1998b) and may have difficulty understanding the special nature of peer relations (Dykens & Rosner, 1999). Because WSs may be overly eager to strike up friendships and social contact, they have a tendency to come on too strong with age-mates (Dykens & Rosner, 1999). Behavior problems of excessive anxiety and fears may also undermine WSs' attempts at friendship (Dykens & Rosner, 1999).

Tension with peers may further reflect the difficulty that WSs may have in expressing negative feelings to peers. Afraid of being rejected or unskilled in knowing how to object tactfully to a peer's behavior, WSs may just "clam up" or feel angry and alienate the peer by making remarks that are not very tactful (see chap. 2, Pragmatics of Language).

In addition, some WSs engage in irritating forms of behavior that may contribute to their being rejected, such as "social crowding" (i.e., standing uncomfortably close to another person), wheedling favors, bossing others, or being a poor loser (Scheiber, 2000; Udwin & Yule, 1998a, 1998b).

Table 5.2 presents a summary of research studies dealing with peer relations.

Improving Peer Relations

In view of the disconnection experienced by many WSs between their desire for social interaction and friendship and their actual circumstances (much too often, of disappointment, isolation, rejection, and vulnerability), there is a great need to provide WSs with social skills training (Dykens & Rosner, 1999). Interventions that may help WSs establish and maintain peer relations heavily depend on the use of psycho-educational techniques to

TABLE 5.2
Peer Relations of WSs: Summary of Results

Type of Behavior or Test	Frequency or Result	Source or Reference
Rather Solitary	WSc 83%	Udwin et al., 1987
Prefer Adults to Peers	WSc 64%	
Difficulty Making, Keeping Friends	WSc 71%	Utah Survey
Antagonizes Other Children	WSc 41%	
Problems with Other Children	WSc 56%	Tharp, 1986
Not Liked by Other Children	WSc 35%	Udwin et al., 1987
Devlopmental Behavior Checklist[#]:		
Does Not Mix with Age Group	WSc > MRc	Einfeld et al., 1997;
Prefers Adult Company	WSc > MRc	Einfeld et al., 2001
	WSa > MRa	
Reiss Profiles[#]:		
Rejection, Fewer Friends	WSs & PWs > MRs	Dykens & B. Rosner, 1999
TROSS[#]:		
Reinforces Other Students	WSc ~ NH, WS > LD, BD, MR	Levine & Castro, 1994
Isolated, Limited Socially	WSa 67%	Udwin, 1990
More Seclusive, Less Extroverted	WSa > WSc	Curfs et al., 1996; Gosch & Pankau, 1996b
Problems Playing Age-Appropriate Games	WSc 81%	Utah Survey

Note: % = percentage frequency; # = mean amount; WSc = WS children; WSa = WS adolescents or adults; N or NH = normally developing; PW = Prader–Willi syndrome; MR = mentally retarded; LD = learning disabled; BD = behavior disorder.

develop social awareness, reduce inappropriate behavior, and provide opportunities for social interaction.

Differentiating Social Behaviors

Social Awareness. Many WSs need to become more aware of the special requirements of friendship in order to strengthen their contacts with peers. Mediational strategies similar to those suggested for controlling overfriendliness are helpful here. In particular, puppetry, storytelling, and improvised dramatization may be used to enact the frustrating, unsuccessful, and inappropriate encounters that WSs often experience with peers.

Language Functions. WSs must also learn that conversational topics and emotional forms of expression may need to be adapted to fit the type of person involved. Speech language therapists can play a vital role in helping WSs learn to make such pragmatic distinctions (see chap. 3, pp. 99–103). They may also help WSs learn how to express negative feelings in an appropriate manner.

Assistance with conflict resolution with peers is provided in some special community college-level programs that offer training in independent living skills as well as academic content (WSA National Newsletter, 2000 April, *17*(1), 16). Some valuable tips on how to resolve conflicts with friends include defining the problem, reactions and feelings to it, and finding solutions such as compromising and negotiating (cf. PACE Program Curriculum, National Louis University, Evanston, IL; 847/475-1100, ex. 2670).

Control mechanisms, such as direct instruction and differential reinforcement of appropriate responses (verbal–social rewards) and inappropriate responses (reprimands, negative reinforcement), are also of value in helping WSs realize the special nature of peers and adherence to conversational rules with peers.

Reinforcing Appropriate Peer Conduct

It is extremely important that WSs be made aware of their tendency to engage in certain annoying forms of peer-directed behavior like manipulating, bossiness, social crowding, and being a poor loser. They may also need help in learning how to better control those tendencies. Parents and teachers are advised to be honest, direct, and give feedback in a noncritical way when WSc do things that "turn people off" (Scheiber, 2000). They may also explain to others that WSs may say or do things that may be embarrassing or upsetting, but this is usually due to their lack of social inhibitions, not maliciousness (Udwin & Yule, 1998a).

Wheedling. Some WSs overuse their ability to curry favors from adults, like getting an extra ice cream cone or riding next to the bus driver, without understanding that this can alienate their peers. They should be made aware of the connection and the unfairness of obtaining special favors should be explained to those who can understand such reasoning. It should also be noted that many WSs have been observed to want to adhere to strict ethical standards of conduct.

Bossiness. In handling bossiness, it may be helpful to tape-record or videotape samples of WSs' objectionable behavior, discuss the tapes with them, and re-tape new vignettes with goal appropriate behaviors. Alternatively, placing WSs in a small group that works toward a common goal may avert bossy behavior (Putnam, Pueschel, & Gorder-Holman, 1988, p. 89). Even so, some WSc seem to be inherently "bossy," such as the WS youngster who assumed the role of director and "bossed" other, nonhandicapped students while a play was being performed! (Anonymous, Williams Syndrome Hotline, Dec. 1999). Sometimes, WSs' families and teachers need to have a sense of humor to deal with these behaviors. They may also need to help WSs modulate their overenthusiasm for social contact and their tendency to come on "too strong" with peers (Dykens & Rosner, 1999).

"Social Crowding." Some WSs have a tendency to invade the personal space of others by standing very close to them, literally "breathing down their necks" (Scheiber, 2000). This can be extremely annoying to peers and needs to be controlled. Dramatizing the unpleasantness of social crowding through videotaping, role playing, puppetry, and improvisational play, may help WSs understand why it should be curtailed (Udwin et al., 1996; Udwin & Yule, 1998a, 1998b). For example, a role-playing actor could cry out, "Please move, I can't make a step without bumping into you or stumbling on your big feet."

Some, but not all, WSc respond favorably to explanations about how most other children do not want to have their personal space invaded. An "arms length" is a convenient yardstick for WSc to use in gauging the appropriate amount of personal space for most people. Control mechanisms of direct instruction and reminders are often necessary regardless of strategy. At times, the WS child may need to be moved gently when crowding others.

Poor Losers. The popularity of some WSs may be further jeopardized by their intense need "to win" compounded by their difficulty with turn-taking/turn-yielding and delay of gratification. Thus, they may become known as "poor losers."

To address this problem, it helps to start by conducting one-to-one play sessions with an adult. Numerous play sessions are usually required with the adult prepared to lose frequently, especially at the beginning. Repeated coaching in turn-taking and game playing with various family members may help the WSc become more self-confident, proficient, and willing to sometimes lose. Then, play opportunities with a single peer, preferably a slightly younger peer, can be introduced. Finally, several carefully selected peers can be included in supervised playing of games familiar to the WSc.

Providing Opportunities for Peer Interaction

Many WSc are able to deal better with peers in highly structured situations than in free-play contexts (Udwin & Yule, 1998a, 1998b). Inviting other children to play supervised games at the homes of WSc is one approach. Taking the WSc and a potential friend to outings (e.g., movies, sport events, or picnics) may provide an enjoyable context with a structured situation for social interaction (Udwin & Yule, 1998a, 1998b).

Pairing WSc with classmates to work on a specific project may stimulate social interaction both outside and inside the classroom (Levine, 1993). Teachers and parents may cooperate in encouraging this type of interaction. Sometimes these pairings may fail, other times they may succeed.

Older and Younger Peers. A broad range of children may be considered for friendship building of WSs: older and younger children, and children with and without special needs (Levine, 1993).

When establishing social contacts with younger children, it helps to start by compensating for problems of immaturity and provide playmates more compatible than are age-mates. Older peers may be suitable, too, if they are willing to assume a mentor role and use less stringent standards than with same-age peers. Sometimes, close supervision or termination of "older peers" may be necessary if it appears that the WSc is being taken advantage of or abused.

Formally Organized Groups. As WSc mature, parents and teachers can encourage WSs to participate in organized groups, such as religious groups, community groups, choirs, music, or hobby clubs that feature their "special" interest (e.g., coin or stamp collecting; Udwin & Yule, 1998a, 1998b). Many parents testify to the tremendous benefits church programs can provide for WSc, for example: "One of the best things I ever did for my son was to get him involved with our church and the youth groups" (WSA National Newsletter, 2001 Fall, Vol. *18*(3), p. 27). Health and fitness programs, activities of the Association of Retarded Children and Adults (ARCA), and the Special Olympics are often well suited for many WSc. These groups sponsor events or trips that can offer enjoyable and valuable experiences for some WSs.

Music and arts programs are another attractive option for WS young-sters and adults with these interests and talents (see later section, "Musi-cality"). Inspired by the success of the annual music and arts summer pro-gram for WSs at Belvoir Terrace, Lenox, Massachusetts (see later section, "Musicality"; and WSA National Newsletters, e.g., 2000, *17*(4), pp. 20–21), many music, arts, and camping programs suitable for WSs are being estab-lished. These may be found throughout the United States (Michigan, Blue Lake Music Therapy Camp; Minnesota, Friendship Ventures at Edenwood Camp; Texas, Music Therapy Program in San Antonio), as well as in Europe (e.g., Spain, Ireland; WSA National Newsletters, 1998 December, Vol. *15*(3), p. 18; 2001 Fall, Vol. *18*(3), pp. 20–21).

Special organizations such as the Summit Summer Travel program, City Tours (WSA National Newletter, 1992 Spring, Vol. *9*(1), p. 13) and Able Trek Tours provide travel opportunities for older WS individuals and other dis-abled groups. (See Appendix for current information.) These have been evaluated favorably in WSA newsletters. For older WSs, classes in the local high school evening program, community college or local YMCA/YWCA provide other opportunities for social interaction and general stimulation.

Opportunities for postsecondary education suitable for some WSs are expanding. Besides PACE, 13 programs are available scattered throughout the United States (see WSA National Newsletter, 1997 Summer, Vol. *14*(2), pp. 20–22).

Formally Organized Social Programs. Articles in the WSA National Newsletter provide information about several formal social programs, in-cluding "Best Buddies" and "Circle of Friends."

The "Best Buddies" program matches college students with disabled people in the community to visit and attend organized functions together, like picnics or sports events (WSA National Newsletter, 1991 (2), Summer, pp. 22–23; see Appendix). "Circle of Friends" uses the concept of social net-working to inform small groups of academically achieving youngsters of the social isolation of a WS classmate and motivate them to include the WS stu-dent in a specially formed social circle (WSA National Newsletter, 1994 Spring, Vol. 11, 5–6). Both programs include many elements that are essen-tial for encouraging peer success for WSs, that is, supervision, structure, service orientation, and interesting activities.

Kindred Peers. Individuals with WS or other forms of developmental dis-ability can often serve as compatible companions, or "kindred peers," for WSs. This is especially true during the years of adolescence and young adulthood when opportunities for peer interaction become more limited as achieving age-mates often become preoccupied with more intimate rela-tionships and the school years draw to a close.

As there are usually few WSs in a local community, they eagerly await WSA sponsored social events and meetings to be with other WSs. With increasing age, greetings between WS youngsters become more enthusiastic, and interaction becomes more positive and sustained. They appear to be almost magnetically drawn to each other. At large public events, such as the Special Olympics, parents report that WSa tend to end up "hanging out" together. Young adults with WS seem to realize that they are better understood and accepted by WS peers with their own kinds of difficulties, but others with special needs may help to fill the void.

Parents of WS youngsters are often eager to provide opportunities for companionship, including exchange visits with other teens and young adults with WS through inquiries in the WSA Newsletter (e.g., WSA National Newsletter, 1991 Fall, Vol. 8, p. 19). Regional groups and meetings are another way in which families can establish contacts and find a companion for their WS child. Formally organized groups for children or people with special needs, like ARCA or a camp for exceptional children, provide another option (discussed earlier).

Peer Alternatives. Peer substitutes can provide social contact and access to activities of interest for WS youngsters and young adults. "Tutors" of various types may be employed to instruct or supervise individuals with WS in areas of interest or need, including academic subjects, computer use, sports (e.g., swimming, horseback riding), topics of special interest, arts, crafts, music, and dancing. Thus, longings for "friendship" may be assuaged by employing an older, more mature, normally developing high school or college student to serve as a tutor or companion.

Elderly persons may also serve as mentors, friends, or volunteers to help individuals with special needs. Senior citizen organizations are one source of information for such contacts for "grandparent" substitutes. In addition, some WS youngsters routinely visit the elderly in nursing homes (see the next section).

D. Empathy

People close to WSs are often amazed by their incredible sensitivity and compassion for the mood, feeling, and concern of others—that is, their empathy (Semel, 1988; Semel & Rosner, 1991a, 1991b). Sometimes, they seem almost psychic with their uncanny knowledge and responsivity to the feelings and circumstances of others (Semel, 1988; Semel & Rosner, 1991a, 1991b). Siblings of WSs attest to these tendencies: for example, "You [WSa] care about your family, You hate when they're upset. You always want to help us, To you we're all in debt" (WSA National Newsletter, 1991 January/February, p. 28); or "She is always so sympathetic . . . knows when to give a great big hug or great big kiss" (WSA National Newsletter, 1995 Spring, Vol. *12*(2), Spring, p. 26).

Parent surveys confirm these impressions: One survey reported that 98% of WSc have "strong empathy for the feelings of others" (Utah Survey, Semel & Rosner, 1991a, 1991b), and another reported a figure of 75% (WSA Survey, Midwest Region, WSA National Newsletter, 1988, pp. 21–22).

Parent ratings of "empathy" are higher for WSc than children with Prader–Willi (PWc) or Fragile X syndrome (Frag Xc) (Curfs et al., 1996), and WSs score higher than either PWs or MRs on items such as "feels terrible when others are hurt" (Dykens & Rosner, 1999). On the empathy component of the Experimental Sociability Questionnaire, WSs are rated significantly higher than normal (CA) controls or DSs. Not surprisingly, AUTs are rated lower than either group on this component, that is, the ability to empathize with or comment on other's emotional states (Jones et al., 2000, Exp. IV).

These characteristics are demonstrated in a research study that used a "staged" facsimile of a minor "accident" to compare the empathic responses of WSc (*n* = 10, 6;11–10;11, *M* = 8;4 yrs) and PWc to the feigned pain of a familiar examiner. The results are clear-cut: WSc exhibited significantly greater empathy than the PWc, evident in considerably more comforting behavior, expressions of sympathy and help, and overall concern for the "pained" examiner. Although the groups were comparable in the amount of attention paid to the examiner, the PWc tended to display peculiar positive affect and laughter in contrast to the appropriate affect and concern expressed by the WSc (Tager-Flusberg & Sullivan, 1999).

On an anecdotal level, WSs are known to exhibit many of the classic forms of prosocial behavior, such as wanting to be helpful and share with others. WSs also tend to root for the underdog and be concerned about issues of social and moral injustice, like fairness and equitable treatment. They are generally committed to high moral standards and strenuously opposed to antisocial, risky forms of conduct, such as using drugs or engaging in promiscuous behavior.

Social Cognition

Reports of the unusual sensitivity of WSs to the moods, feelings, and concerns of others raise questions about whether their responsivity constitutes an automatic reaction to cues emitted by another person or the ability to infer the emotions and thoughts of others. Within the research literature, the term "theory of mind" refers to the ability to "see inside" the mind of another person and deduce that person's perceptions, emotions, and thoughts.

The research studies reported investigate WSs' ability to understand the emotions and thoughts of others, a requisite to true insight into the concerns of others, that is, to possess a "theory of mind."

Understanding of Emotions. Consistent with their skill in face recognition, WSc (*n* = 12, 9–23 yrs) score very high on discrimination of emotional expressions (happy/sad) on schematic faces. Performance is at a level similar to that of mental age (MA) matched normal controls and children with autism (Karmiloff-Smith et al., 1995, Exp. 1). The WSc are also comparable to normal controls, frequently 100% correct, and vastly superior to children with autism in being able to use a character's directional gaze to infer what the character desires or intends ("Which candy does he want?"/will he take?) (Karmiloff-Smith et al., 1995, Exp. 1).

WSa (*n* = 13, *M* = 27;3) also exceed a matched group of PWa, but are lower than normal CA controls, on an "Eyes Task" in which subjects are asked to choose the verbal labels that accurately described the expression shown by pairs of eyes extracted from magazine photographs (Tager-Flusberg, Boshart, & Baron-Cohen, 1998). Test stimuli and items were not simple; they included perceptual states (e.g., noticing you–noticing someone else), attitudinal states (e.g., interested–not interested, or sympathetic–not sympathetic), and emotional states (e.g., attraction–repulsion) (Tager-Flusberg et al., 1998). Yet, approximately one half of the WSa scored within the range of normal controls in selecting the correct term that matched the mental state of the target stimulus, that is, they were responding significantly better than chance.

In contrast, WSc (*n* = 22, 4;6–8;7 yrs, *M* = 7;2 yrs) did not differ significantly from matched groups of PWc or MRc on an "emotion matching" task in which the children were shown black and white photographs of faces depicting four common, labeled emotions (i.e., happy, scared, angry, sad) and asked to sort the photos to match the emotions of previously presented targets (Tager-Flusberg & Sullivan, 2000, Exp. 3). Although the groups performed quite well, especially on the "scared" and "happy" pictures, WSc did not show the advantage predicted in the social perceptual area of "theory of mind."

The contrast between the results with that of Tager-Flusberg et al. (1998) may be due to the much younger age of the WSc in the Tager-Flusberg and Sullivan (2000) study and its use of a sorting task rather than a forced choice verbal label procedure. In any event, it is inconsistent with other research showing WSs' keen appreciation and elicitation of emotional responses in others.

In addition, WSs are often able to infer the emotional responses of protagonists depicted pictorially in story vignettes even when standard cues of emotion, like voice intonation and facial expression, are deleted (Reilly et al., 1994; Singer, Delehanty, Reilly, & Bellugi, 1993). In fact, WSa (*n* = 14) are comparable to mental age matched normal child controls (*n* = 30) and significantly better than DSa (*n* = 8) in inferring emotions. Thus, their understanding of emotions seems to contrast markedly with their other cognitive abilities (Reilly et al., 1994). There are limits, however, to this "emotional understanding" because WSc (*n* = 7, 7–11 yrs) are poorer than younger normal children (*n* = 25, 5–7 yrs) in providing explanations of their responses (Singer et al., 1993).

Understanding Mental States. When it comes to the ability to think about someone else's mental activities, most WSs might be expected to have extreme difficulty because of the abstractness of the task. Surprisingly, there is considerable evidence to suggest that WSc possess the basics of "theory of mind," or the ability to think about someone else's mental activities. For example, young WSc (*n* = 20, 3–8 yrs, *M* = 5;9 yrs) produce words that refer to mental states, such as "thinking," "understanding," "believing," and "wishing" spontaneously in their language samples (Kelley & Tager-Flusberg, 1994).

False Belief Tasks. Experiments employing simple "false belief" tasks provide further evidence of the ability of WSs to differentiate their thoughts from those of others (Karmiloff-Smith, 1992; Karmiloff-Smith et al., 1995, Exps. 2 & 3).

One standard task, changed locations, consists of showing the subject and another observer (child or doll) a particular event, like placing a cake in the pantry or candy in a basket. Then, while the observer is not watching or is out of the room, the location of the target object is changed (e.g., the candy is put in a box). Next, the subject is asked where the observer would look for the target. Another standard task, "unexpected contents," consists of showing subjects a standard, packaged object, like a pencil case, that contains unexpected contents like candy (not pencils). Then, the subject is asked what another child who has just entered the room would think was in the box.

By about age 4, normally developing children typically pass these basic "false belief tasks," which differentiate what the subject was shown from what was seen or would be seen by another observer. That is, they are able to distinguish their own knowledge from the mental state of the observer, which contrasts with younger children, who typically report what they themselves saw, not what they know the observer saw.

There is strong evidence that WSc are able to pass these kinds of false belief tasks. In fact, 94% of WSc give the correct answer and use mental state terms like "think" to explain the behavior of the other, hypothetical child. In contrast, few AUTc (about 29%) succeed on such first-order theory of mind tasks (Karmiloff-Smith et al., 1995, Exps. 2 & 3). Apparently, there may be limits, however, in terms of IQ (not less than 50; Karmiloff-Smith, 1992), and age (older than 4;5 years; Tager-Flusberg, Sullivan, & Zaitchik, 1994).

In particular, children with WS (n = 22, 4;6–8;7 yrs, M = 7;2 yrs) perform quite poorly on apparently simple false belief and even simpler "explanation of action" tasks that test subject's ability to explain a character's actions by using terms that refer to desire, emotion, or cognition (Tager-Flusberg & Sullivan, 2000, Exps. 1 & 2). Surprisingly, WSc did not perform any better than PWc or MRc on either task. In fact, their average scores were actually lower—although not significantly lower—than the other groups.

The discrepant results between studies (Karmiloff-Smith et al., 1995; Tager-Flusberg & Sullivan, 2000) are attributed to age and task differences: namely, positive results are more likely with older children and with tasks that used examiners (people), not props and toys, to enact the change in location of objects in the false belief tasks.

Higher Level Concepts. According to subsequent studies, some WSs (31%–88%) are able to pass second-order theory-of-mind tasks in which the ability to comprehend a person's thoughts about another person's thoughts is tested through the use of stories (Karmiloff-Smith et al., 1995, Exps. 5 & 6). In contrast, none of the subjects with AUT were able to pass the second-order tasks, even though many had considerably higher IQs than the WSs. These tasks usually require the intelligence of normal 7- to 9-year-olds to unravel the erroneous suppositions a character has about another character's thoughts; although both have correct information, one thinks the other has wrong information.

Comparing these results with WSs' performance in other areas, it appears that most WSs exhibit their highest level of competence in three areas: language skills, face processing, and theory of mind (Karmiloff-Smith et al., 1995).

Other research does not support this contention. Specifically, WSc (n = 22, 8.17–17.25 yrs, M = 11.58) do not exceed matched groups of PWc and MRc in another study using second-level belief stories to test subject's abilities in the area of theory of mind (Sullivan & Tager-Flusberg, 1999).

In addition, older WSc (10–17 yrs) usually have difficulty with higher level theory of mind concepts, such as traits, moral commitment, friendship, and self-concept (Tager-Flusberg, Sullivan, Broshart, Guttman, & K. Levine, 1996). Thus, they show significant impairment in their understanding of abstract social cognitive constructs, although their performance is quite comparable to the comparison group of PWc and, interestingly, closely related to their IQ levels.

This is consistent with anecdotal comments of researchers suggesting that WS adolescents and adults may have particular difficulty detecting the truthfulness of others. This type of behavior involves operating on two levels: manifest and latent (Bertrand et al., 1994a).

There are also reports that some WSs may have difficulty "reading" nonverbal cues such as "facial expressions, gestures, posture, and tone of voice" (Scheiber, 2000). The apparent inconsistency between these and reports of WSs' sensitivity to the feelings of others deserves further scrutiny. That is, one hears rather frequently about WSs having high levels of cognitive awareness regarding the thoughts and feelings of others and some insight into their own emotionality. As an example, a parent describes how a WS teenager apologized for acting angrily at home, and explained that she had been stressed at school with "I'm just trying to deal with things" (WSA National Newsletter, 1995 Winter, Vol. *12*(1), 12). In this respect, WSs tend to differ from most children with other forms of developmental disorder.

Overview. Examination of the previous research studies suggest that results differ as a function of three dimensions: (a) the complexity or reiterative nature of the concept or task being tested, with better performance, of course, on simpler concepts and tasks; (b) the cognitive domain being tested, with WSs tending to perform better on tasks involving affect and direct person perception and relations rather than abstract, hypothetical stories; and (c) the age and intelligence of the WS is very important. This is an area in which true individual differences are clearly apparent. It is also an area that draws on WSs' strengths in other areas, such as face recognition, interest in faces and emotional expressions (a important trait even in toddlers), and strengths in expressive language, affect, prosody, and vocabulary (Dykens & Rosner, 1999).

Table 5.3 summarizes studies on empathy and social cognition in WSs.

Oversensitivity

The strong empathic tendencies of most WSs may also have negative implications. If WSs see someone in obvious distress, like a child crying on the way to school, they may become totally absorbed and unable to carry on with another activity. They also tend to worry about potential problems or disasters involving injury, illness, or harm affecting people they care about (e.g., parents, siblings, other family members). This may even extend to acquaintances and people unknown to them (Udwin & Yule, 1988). Such worries can take on the features of perseverative, obsessive-like fears or anxieties (see Chap. 6, "Maladaptive Behaviors").

These kinds of overreactions may arise at least partly from cognitive limitations in their ability to differentiate between unlikely possibilities and likely possibilities, like a plague infecting their town versus one individual exposed to measles contracting the disease. It may also reflect limitations in WSs' ability to alleviate another person's distress. They may be unable to determine the cause of the distress, or lack the physical, intellectual, or practical resources needed to remedy the situation.

TABLE 5.3
Empathy and Social Cognition in WSs: Summary of Results

Type of Behavior	Freqency or Result	Source or Reference
Strong Empathy for Feelings of Others	WSc 98%	Utah Survey
Empathetic of Others	WSc 75%	WSA Midwest Region, 1989
Empathy[#]	WSc > PWc, Frag Xc	Curfs et al., 1996
Reiss Profile: Feels Terrible When Others Are Hurt[#]	WSs > PWs, MRs	Dykens & B. Rosner, 1999
Experimental Sociability Questionnaire: Empathy[#]	WSs > DSs, Normal CA Controls > AUTs	Jones et al., 2000
Empathic Response to Feigned Accident[#]	WSc > PWc	Tager-Flusberg & Sullivan, 1999
Discrimination of Emotions[#]	WSc > Normal MA Controls & AUTc	Karmiloff-Smith et al., 1995
Directional Gaze to Infer Desires, Intentions[#]	WSc > Normal MA Controls > AUTc	Karmiloff-Smith et al., 1995
Eye Task: Judging Eye Expressions[#]	WSa > PWa, WSa < Normal CA Controls WSs 50% in Normal Range	Tager Flusberg et al., 1998
Emotion Identification, Matching Task[#]	WSc ~ PWc, MRc	Tager-Flusberg & Sullivan, 2000
Infer Emotional States: Story Vignettes[#]	WSa ~ Normal MA Controls > DSa	Reilly et al., 1994; Singer et al., 1993
Explain Emotional States[#]	WSa < Normal MA Controls	
First-Order False Belief Task[#]	WSc 94% > AUTc 29%	Karmiloff-Smith, 1992; Karmiloff-Smith et al., 1995
Simple False Belief Task: Explanation of Action[#]	WSc ~ PWc, MRc	Tager-Flusberg & Sullivan, 2000
Higher Level, Second-Order Theory of Mind Tests[#]	WSc 31% - 88% Pass, > AUTs 0%	Karmiloff-Smith et al., 1995
Second-Level Belief Stories	WSc ~ PWc, MRc	Sullivan & Tager-Flusberg, 1999
Higher Level Theory of Mind Concepts: Traits, Friendship[#]	WSc ~ PWc	Tager-Flusberg et al., 1996

Note: % = percentage frequency; # = mean amount; WSc = WS children; WSa = WS adolescents or adults; N or NH = normally developing; LD = learning disabled; BD = behavior disorder; MR = mentally retarded; AUT = autistic; DS = Down syndrome.

Dealing With Oversensitivity

When WSc become disturbed or distracted by the problems of others, it is generally advisable to try to "strike a balance" between providing comfort and making too much fuss about it (Udwin & Yule, 1988). It is usually helpful to acknowledge their concern and assure WSs that, if possible, appropriate steps will be taken to deal with the problem.

In dealing with realistic concerns and worries, it is best for adults to try to help WSs address the problem, such as encouraging students to prepare for a test. In contrast, unrealistic worries or anxieties, such as concern that a healthy parent is dying may be played down or approached with other techniques used to reduce WSs' fears and anxieties (see chap. 7, "Intervention Approaches for Maladaptive Behaviors," pp. 304–305).

In addition, it is generally helpful to support the efforts of WSs to aid a crying or distressed person and to discuss these events with them. They may be asked how they would feel if the same thing happened to them, or what steps could have been taken to avert the incident or relieve the problem. Commending WSs for their prosocial concerns can promote this behavior and boost their self-esteem. For some WSs, sensitivity and concern for others may serve as the basis for vocational and volunteer opportunities.

E. Capitalizing on Social Skills

Aside from its value as a personality attribute, sociability is a valuable WS asset for promoting their development. It lays the groundwork for verbal-social interventions, various kinds of application in the classroom, and opportunities for possible employment.

Types of Interventions

Affective Control Mechanisms. The intense desire of WSs to please others is undoubtedly related to the extremely high value they place on social rewards. These may include verbal approval (e.g., "It really pleases me when you do 'X'"), praise (e.g., "Good job"), nonverbal signs of approval (i.e., broad smile, body language, gesture, knowing wink), or being granted time to socialize with other people.

Likewise, sensitivity to the emotions of others and desire to spare them pain may account for the potency of negative, social reinforcement. These may include statements of personal disapproval or displeasure, such as "I'm really hurt when you do that" or "I am very angry that you did . . . ," or nonverbal, affective signals, like a frown, raised eyebrow, or shake of the head. Especially effective when trying to reduce undesirable behaviors, nonverbal cues have the further advantage of being able to be used discreetly without disrupting other activities.

Clinical experience also suggests that socially based rewards may have greater incentive value for WSc than for many other child groups, including the nonhandicapped, learning disabled, autistic, or ADHD children.

Mediational Strategies. The social and verbal predilections of most WSs may account, at least in part, for the unusual effectiveness of mediational strategies in formal instruction and behavior management. That is, there may be a link between the ease with which WSs identify with others and their responsivity to role playing, modeling, and dramatization (i.e., puppetry, storytelling, improvised dramatization). It may also account for WSs' responsiveness to reasoning, especially when it specifies how certain actions or behaviors can affect or harm other people as well as the WSs themselves.

Self-instructional strategies also draw on the verbal-social proclivities of WSs as they epitomize the internalization of the behaviors, explanations, beliefs, and wishes of others.

Although children with other forms of developmental disability, such as children with ADD, autism, learning disability, and other forms of mental retardation are said to benefit from self-talk or "cognitive behavior modification" (Schoenbrodt & Smith, 1995), most WSs are responsive to such training. This may be attributable to their language skills and deep-seated desire to please others.

Classroom Applications

In the classroom, WSs' greatest asset may be their ability to charm and win over teachers (WSA National Newsletter, Fall 1993, Vol. 10, pp. 22–24). Their verbal–social skills may also be used as a learning resource and access to school activities (Levine, 1993).

For example, WSs' talent for dramatization considering age and IQ, may be used to enact episodes, events, or tales involving historical figures. This may be particularly useful in the social studies and language arts. Their verbal–social talents may also be applicable to assignments involving interviewing various people, such as fellow students or local leaders on a variety of topics. WSs may even be given the opportunity of reporting their findings to their own class, other classrooms, or even the entire school in an assembly.

In addition, WSs' sense of humor and skill in performing may be a valuable asset in being asked to participate in theatrical and musical activities. It may even bring success and attention—real ego-boosters—to WSs, many of whom tend to be show-offs (Dykens & Rosner, 1999).

Vocational Opportunities

On a more practical level, WSc's social skills and empathy can form the basis for service-oriented forms of employment and volunteer activities, such as nurse's aide, work in a retirement home, preschool teacher and assistant, hospital volunteer, or assistant to workers with animals. Depending on their cognitive level and behavioral maturity, some WSs may be able to be taught simple first aid and safety measures. Others may be able to assist in the bathrooming needs and feeding of those unable to help themselves.

WSa are often particular favorites of residents in nursing homes (WSA National Newsletter 1991 January/February, Vol 8(1), 17).

II. CURIOSITY

The inquisitiveness of most WSs is distinctive in its intensity, directness, and specificity. Similar to other aptitudes, it has both positive and negative features. On the positive side, most WSs show intense interest in specialized topics. This can be a definite asset. On the negative side, many WSs develop obsessive attachments to certain objects or topic perseverations that interfere with their ability to function adequately (Udwin & Yule, 1998a, 1998b).

Although narrower in scope than other aptitudes, curiosity typically dominates many aspects of WS life. Parents report that literally all WSc (97%) show "intense inquisitiveness" (Utah Survey, Semel & Rosner, 1991a, 1991b). Moreover, WSc are significantly more likely than MR controls to be described as "obsessed" and "preoccupied with an idea or activity" (Einfeld et al., 1997). The term "obsessive" is often ascribed to both PWs and WSs (Dykens & Rosner, 1999).

Both aspects of WSs' curiosity, positive and negative, are discussed next, followed by interventions for dealing with them.

A. Types of Curiosity

Specialized Interests

Clinical experience indicates that many WSs become intensely interested in and then avidly pursue a specialized topic. Their information on the topic can be surprisingly detailed and comprehensive.

One WSc is an expert on flags and knows the flag of almost every country. His descriptions are so informative that people unfamiliar with flags are able to use them to select the correct one from a large array of flags. Another WSc specializes in coins and knows the denominations of many nations. Other specialties include types of plants and their phyla, certain kinds of animals and their taxonomy, large machines, and so forth.

Areas of special interest mentioned in profiles of WSc include: "firetrucks, firearms, trains, photography" (WSA National Newsletter, Fall 1993, 10, 24–26); dinosaurs, Indians, and the martial arts (WSA National Newsletter, Fall 1993, Vol. 10, 26–28); books about science, space, and American Indians; and collections of anything that is small (WSA National Newsletter, Winter 1994, p. 25). The list of special interest areas is lengthy, varied, and may even include famous people (Udwin & Yule, 1998b).

Interestingly, topics of major interest may shift over time for a particular WS individual. New topics can emerge, and old topics may lose their strength.

Object Attachments

On the negative side, the inquisitiveness of some WSc is evident in intense, almost obsessive interest in certain kinds of items. Parent surveys indicate that almost half of WSc (46%) are "fascinated by fans, motors, toys that spin" (WSA Checklist Survey, Semel & Rosner, 1991a, 1991b), 44% "show a curiosity about shiny objects" (Utah Survey, Semel & Rosner, 1991a, 1991b), and 35% are fascinated with "spinning objects" (WSA Midwest Region, WSA National Newsletter, 1989 April, pp. 21–22). In open-ended interviews, 52% of parents and teachers mention that WSc are fascinated/preoccupied "with particular items or topics, e.g., machinery, electrical gadgets, trains, refuse, babies" (Udwin et al., 1987).

A few WSs fixate on objects such as doorknobs, brass buttons, or metallic wallpaper, whereas others are preoccupied with tiny objects that open easily. Still others are fascinated by the movement of objects or objects that make certain sounds. Some WSc become spellbound by the opening and closing of a door.

Whereas most normally developing infants are fascinated by shiny, moving objects, their interest generally fades by mid or late infancy. In contrast, the object fixations of WSc often persist throughout childhood and beyond (Finucane, 1996; Levine, 1993; Semel, 1988; Semel & Rosner, 1991a, 1991b; Udwin et al., 1987).

The intensity of some of these fixations is unusual, too. Parents describe how WSc stare transfixedly, as though almost hypnotized, at rotating objects like a phonograph record or the spinning motion of a washing machine, clothes dryer, or music box. Some consider this to be a defining characteristic of WS (Lenhoff, Discussion comment, Wang, 1994). Similarly, Mervis reported that WS toddlers typically respond to a toy car by spinning its wheels instead of pushing the car, which is the dominant response of most other children (Mervis, Discussion comment, Wang, 1994).

Table 5.4 presents a summary of research studies on various aspects of the curiosity of WSs.

Comparison with Autism

Like WSs, autistic (AUT) youngsters also become captivated by certain types of information. With AUTs, however, these tend to be more fragmented and obscure than the specialized interests of WSs. For example, AUTs are known to focus on visuospatially bound input, like patterns or puzzles, or numerical items, like the addresses of juvenile courts (Frith,

TABLE 5.4
Curiosity in WSs: Summary of Results

Type of Behavior	Frequency or Result	Source or Reference
Intense Inquisitiveness	WSc 97%	Utah Survey
Obsessed, Preoccupied with Idea or Activity[#]	WSc > MRc	Einfeld et al., 1997
Fascinated by Fans, Motors, Toys that Spin	WSc 46%	WSA Checklist Survey
Curiosity of Shiny Objects	WSc 44%	Utah Survey
Fascination with Spinning Objects	WSc 35%	WSA Midwest Region, 1989

Note: % = percentage frequency; # = mean amount; WSc = WS children; MR = mentally retarded.

1989, p. 112). Typically, the special interests of WSs exceed those of AUTs in breadth and depth of knowledge.

AUTs resemble WSc, too, in their fascination with shiny objects, small parts, wheels, toys, and objects that can spin (Sattler, 1988; Schoenbrodt & Smith, 1995). Differences exist, however, in the intensity of their object preoccupations; those of AUTs' tend to be more overwhelming and all consuming than those of WSs. Along the same lines, WSc often interact with other people while manipulating their special object(s), whereas AUTs tend to become overwhelming and all-consuming, never making eye contact. Some AUT engage in "self-spinning," going round and round. This is not usually observed in WSc.

Distinctions between these conditions become blurred, however, in the few individuals who have dual diagnosis of WS and AUT (see chap. 6, pp. 282–283).

B. Managing Object Attachments

Dealing with the object attachments of WSc is usually difficult because the objects are often commonplace, like tiny, shiny, or spinable things, and the attachments can be extremely intense. Although such fascination is resistant to change, some of the following suggestions may be helpful. Fortunately, the strength of object fixations tends to decrease with age (Finucane, 1996).

Environmental Controls. Physically removing items of special interest wherever possible is the most direct approach. It is particularly important to eliminate such items from the child's room, desk, classroom, testing room, and rooms used for family activity because they are an absolute distraction for many WSc.

Control Mechanisms. With some WSs, direct, explicit instructions to refrain from focusing on the obsessive object or activity may be effective. Consistency, firmness, repetition, and patience are usually required. Displays of anger or exasperation should be avoided because such attention often encourages the undesired behavior. In some cases, it may be possible to re-channel the child's fixation by making the operation of punching out dots from colored paper into a socially acceptable behavior, for example, using them for making greeting cards.

Diverting attention from the obsessive, perseverative object or topic is also recommended (Levine, 1993; Udwin & Yule, 1998a, 1998b). Role play, stories, discussion, and small group projects may be used to teach alternative topics (Levine, 1993). New activities and interests may be introduced and played together with the WSc (Udwin & Yule, 1998b). The preoccupation should be brought under control early, before it gains ground.

In other cases, parents have found their child's involvement to be so overpowering that they try to accommodate it by allowing the child to have structured, supervised contact with the object of attachment. Trying to eliminate a firmly established item or topic of preoccupation may cause considerable anxiety and distress. Instead, it may be better to try to limit the preoccupation by allowing a circumscribed amount of time for the WS individual to be involved with it (Udwin & Yule, 1998a, 1998b). A fixed amount of time, such as 10 minutes every day, may be set aside for engaging in the obsessive activity or interest topic, but only if the WS individual controls the preoccupation at other times (Udwin et al., 1996; Udwin & Yule, 1998a). Gradually, the amount of time set aside for the object or topic of focal interest may be reduced.

Behavior Therapy. Sometimes, behavior modification techniques may be required when other approaches have failed. However, even when adjusted for WSs, it is not usually the treatment of choice. It is commonly used for children with ADHD or autism.

Treatment for Other Preoccupations. Related kinds of preoccupations, namely obsessions and perseverations, may require other sorts of interventions. (These are described in the section on "Topic Perseveration" in chap. 3. Also see "Intervention Approaches for Language Problems," and material on "Obsessions" included under "Emotional Disorders" in chap. 6). Cases of obsessive compulsive disorder that meet the psychiatric criteria for the disorder and those with severe obsessive symptoms should be treated by qualified mental health professionals. Speech language therapists may help WSs learn how to handle their tendency to overuse their area of special interest to the point where it begins to dominate their choice of conversational topics and bores or alienates peers and others, even family members (see chap. 3, pp. 93–94).

C. Capitalizing on Special Interests

The specialized interests of WSs often need to be honed to be used to full advantage. This may involve providing encouragement, as well as materials and resources appropriate to the WS's level of knowledge, cognitive skills, and type of interest area.

For example, a WSc who is fascinated with plants may be helped to collect specimens, and classify or group plants into simple perceptual categories, like size, color, or shape. Real or pictured exemplars can be added, and characteristics and simple conceptual categories can be identified (e.g., plants, trees, and flowers). As the child accumulates information from books and other sources, more advanced methods of classification can be developed by establishing hierarchies (i.e., nested phyla). Interest in plants may be extended into related areas, such as gardening, landscaping, attending garden shows, or visiting an arboretum.

Other kinds of collections, based on coins, flags, rocks, and so forth, provide similar kinds of intellectual opportunities and practical applications. With proper support, adults with WS are "able to channel preoccupations into appropriate activities, such as collecting Elvis memorabilia or attending concerts of favorite singers" (Finucane, 1996).

Once developed, topics of special interest may be used to promote the classroom learning, social relations, and avocational and vocational opportunities of many WSs.

Applying Specialized Interests

Classroom Learning. Many educators advocate capitalizing on topics of special interest by using them as a focal point for the curriculum and assignments of WSs or to reward desirable kinds of behavior (Levine, 1993; Semel, 1988; Udwin et al., 1996; Udwin & Yule, 1998a, 1998b). Specialized topics may be read about and written about, used as examples in arithmetic, and provide the context for studying material in the social sciences and other sciences. For example, interest in plants and flowers may be utilized in the counting of objects in arithmetic, spelling the names of various plants, or composing stories with plants or flowers as the main focus.

Social Relations. The specialized interest areas of WSc may also be used to facilitate appropriate kinds of social interaction with peers and adults (Scheiber, 2000). There are clubs, collectors, hobby groups, and professional meetings associated with many areas of interest (e.g., coin merchants, stamp collectors).

In the absence of organized groups, parents and teachers may assist WSs in locating peers or adults with shared interests and arranging supervised meetings at home or in the school.

Special interests may also provide a lifelong hobby or avocation to share with others. Knowing that one has expertise can provide personal satisfaction and bolster one's self-esteem.

Vocational Opportunities. Special interests can sometimes be encouraged, expanded, and developed into areas of employment or volunteer work. For example, interest in plants may be extended to gardening or landscaping jobs as an assistant, interest in pets or animals to work in a pet store or horse barn, interest in machines to auto detailing, and so forth.

In seeking employment, vocational assessment and vocational placement specialists can be useful sources of guidance and information. Because many counselors may be unfamiliar with WS and its uneven ability profile, they may need some orientation in order to be able to offer realistic advice.

III. MEMORY

"Memory" is the storehouse of past experiences and accumulated knowledge. It can include a glimpse of a scene, a name, a face, personal information (name, address, date of birth, names and characteristics of family members and friends), a building, the layout of a room, or a pattern of floor tiles. It may also be knowledge about how to ride a bicycle, change a light bulb, bake a cake, add and subtract numbers or fractions, read and analyze a text, map, formula, or graph, or recall a poem or melody.

In keeping with the variety of types of memory, opinions vary widely as to the memory capabilities of WSs. A clinical researcher noted "uncanny memory skills" (Frank, 1983), but 43% of parents complain of "memory problems" (Tharp, 1986). On the other hand, parents and teachers frequently note WSc's verbal imitative skills (Udwin et al., 1987) and excellent memory for words, phrases, stories, and tunes. The accuracy and detail with which they often remember events, faces, voices, poems, songs, prayers, jokes, limericks, and even object location seems remarkable. On the other hand, WSs tend to forget recently presented material, including instructions, facts, and descriptive and explanatory information. Recall of symbols, such as phonemes, letters, and written words, is often impaired with the result that learning to read may be labored.

In line with these differences, parents, teachers and others sometimes distinguish between short-term memory and long-term memory in WSs. For example, parents report that 98% of WSc have "good long-term memory," whereas 80% of the same WSc are said to have "poor short-term memory" (Utah Survey, Semel & Rosner, 1991a, 1991b). Other parent surveys indicate poor STM for approximately 50% of WSc (WSA Survey, Semel & Rosner, 1991a, 1991b; WSA Midwest Region Survey, WSA National Newsletter, 1989 April, pp. 21–22). The discrepancy in results may reflect uncertainty about the terminology, although individual differences may play a role.

In the research literature, short-term memory (STM) refers to a brief retention event that usually lasts less than 30 seconds between input and output. Long-term memory (LTM) refers to a retention task that extends beyond short time intervals. This may include memory for symbols (i.e., alphabet and words, numbers and number facts), motor skills (i.e., riding a bicycle, driving a car), and personal situations and events (i.e., birthdays, holidays, lost objects, old friends, former residences). STM is supposedly transient and limited in size, and LTM is rather permanent and almost unlimited in size.

Variations in mode of stimulus input and response output—auditory, visual, verbal, tactual, and/or kinesthetic—may also affect performance. Other factors affecting memory include type of task, material to be remembered, and specificity of instructions to remember, explicit or implicit.

Laboratory studies of WSs' memory abilities, STM and LTM, are described next, and information on the effects of mode, type of memory task, and other factors is provided. These are summarized in Table 5.5. After reviewing the research literature, the discussion turns to suggestions for the improvement of WSs' memory functioning and ways to utilize their memory strengths.

A. Short-Term Memory

The immediate memory span test is probably the most widely used measure of memory functioning and one of the earliest tests of children's intelligence. Item lists of increasing length are presented at a rapid rate, one item at a time. Span is determined by the longest list the subject can accurately recall in correct order. WSs' memory span has been tested with both verbal and visuospatial types of material with disparate results.

Verbal STM

Items used in studies of WSs' verbal STM are primarily digits. Only a few studies have used words, nonwords, or sentences.

Digit Memory Span. WSa performance is consistently strong on tests of digit span. Adolescents with WS ($n = 9$, $M = 13$ yrs) score significantly higher than DSa on the digit subtest of the WISC–R (Wang & Bellugi, 1994). Like-

TABLE 5.5
Short-Term Memory Studies of WSs: Summary of Results

Type of Behavior or Test	Frequency or Result	Source or Reference
Good Long-term Memory	WSc 98%	Utah Survey
Poor Short-term Memory	WSc 80%	WSA Checklist Survey
Poor Short-term Memory	WSc ~ 50%	WSA Midwest Region, 1989
Digit Span[#]	WSa > DSa	Wang & Bellugi, 1994
Digit Span[#]	WSs > MRs	Mervis et al., 1996
Digit Span > DAS[#]	WSs	Mervis et al., 1996
Digit Span > Verbal WISC–III[#]	WSc	Finegan et al., 1996
Backward Digit Span[#]	WSa > DSa	Wang & Bellugi, 1994
Digit Span[#]	WSc ~ Norms N (MA Match)	Vicari et al., 1994
Auditory Sequencing Test[#]	WSc ~ Controls MRc	Crisco et al., 1988
Word Span > Verbal WISC[#]	WSc	Finegan et al., 1996
Sentence Span > Verbal WISC[#]	WSc	
Digit Span[#]	WSc Increase (f) Age	Mervis et al., 1999
Phonological Memory: Learning Nonwords[#]	WSc > Controls N (MA Match)	Karmiloff-Smith et al., 1993
STM Word Lists:		
Phonologically Similar[#]	WSc ~ CA Normal Controls Dissimilar > Similar List	Vicari et al., 1994
Word Length Effect[#]	WSc ~ CA Normal Controls	
Word Frequency Effect[#]	WSc < CA Normal Controls	
Corsi Block Span[#]	WSa < DSa	Wang & Bellugi, 1994
Corsi Block Span[#]	WSc < Norms N (MA Match)	Vicari et al., 1994
Visual Sequencing Test[#]	WSc < Controls MRc	Crisco et al., 1988
Corsi Block Span[#]	WSc < DSc	Jarrold et al., 1999
Digit Span[#]	WSc > DSc	
Corsi Block Span[#]	WSa < MLDs, Normal Nonverbal, MA Controls	Jarrold et al., 1999
Digit Span[#]	WSa ~ MLDs, Normal Nonverbal MA Controls	
Rivermead Behavioral Memory Test: Face Recognition[#]	WSc > Controls MR	Udwin & Yule, 1991
Warrington Recognition Memory Test: Faces	WSs > DSs	Bellugi et al., 2000

Note: % = percentage frequency; # = mean amount; WSc = WS children; WSa = WS adolescents or adults; DS = Down syndrome; N or NH = normally developing; MR = mentally retarded; MLD = mildly learning disabled.

wise, WSs (*n* = 50, 4–46 yrs) exceed mentally retarded individuals of mixed etiology on the digit span subtest of DAS (Mervis et al., 1999).

Digit span also tends to surpass performance on tests of general intelligence. This is evident in the difference between WSs' (*n* = 40, 3–34 yrs) digit span and total IQ scores on the DAS (Mervis et al., 1999), and the difference between WSc's (n = 15, 6–14 yrs) digit span and composite scores on the verbal scale of WISC–III (Finegan, Smith, & Meschino, 1996).

WSa have a clear advantage over DSa on backward recall tests (Wang & Bellugi, 1994). As this test requires recalling items in reverse order from that used in presentation, it is assumed to measure "working memory," or a person's ability to operate mentally on information. Interestingly, WSs' backward recall, that is, their working memory, is related to their performance on language comprehension tests (Wang et al., 1997).

During the childhood years, however, digit span appears to be unexceptional. Young Italian children with WS (n =16, M CA = 9.41, M MA = 4.6) are comparable to MA matched normal children on digit span, neither significantly better nor worse (Vicari, Pezzini, Milani, Dall'Oglio, & Sergo, 1994; Vicari, Brizzolara, Carlesimo, Pezzini, & Volterra, 1996). Likewise, WSc (n = 22, 4–10 yrs, M = 7 yrs) are comparable to, not higher than, controls with nonspecific disabilities on digit tests of auditory sequencing (Illinois Test of Psycholinguistic Abilities; Crisco et al., 1988). Perhaps young WSc are at a disadvantage because they are less familiar with numbers. Alternatively, there is a maturational component of memory span.

Consistent with this interpretation, digit span on the DAS shows an age-related increase over the course of childhood (n = 57, 4–17 yrs), which is maintained in adults (n = 30). In fact, over two thirds of WSs in this study score in the normal range (Mervis et al., 1999).

Other Verbal STM Tests.   Preliminary findings of WSc suggest that their word span, the longest list of unrelated words they can correctly recall, and their immediate sentence recall (Sentences Repetition subtest of the Clinical Evaluation of Language Fundamentals–Revised, CELF–R) are higher than expected from their verbal IQ (WISC) scores (Finegan et al., 1996).

Phonological Memory.   Even more outstanding are reports of WS's phonological memory skills evident in the ease with which French-speaking WSc (n = 10, 9–21 yrs, IQ = 51–67) learn pseudo-words like "bicron" and "spodine" as the names for pictures of fictional animals and objects (Karmiloff-Smith, Grant, & Berthoud, 1993). In fact, WSc are significantly better than normal children matched on mental age in repeating the nonce words correctly on their first try. They also tend to make fewer learning errors than the controls (10% vs. 80%), even though they were outperformed by controls on a morphosyntactic test of generalization of gender language rules.

Even so, WSs are usually quite poor in recalling phonemes that are presented separately, such as "b-e-t"–"b-a-t"; "b-i-t"–"b-u-t." Perhaps the auditory similarity of the vowels and the visuospatial similarity of the letters interfere with learning. This can be a major problem for WSs in learning to read.

Sensitivity to phonological similarity in STM recall of word lists is also evident in the comparable recall of WSc (n = 12, M = 9;11) and normal CA controls (n = 12, M = 5;2) on lists composed of acoustically similar or dissimilar two-syllable nonwords; both groups recalled the dissimilar list better than the interference list (Vicari, Carlesimo, Brizzolara, & Pezzini, 1996b). Word length, or number of syllables per word, also affected the groups similarly, but word frequency (high vs. low frequency words) had a lesser effect on WSc than normal controls (Vicari et al., 1996b). This is attributed to "impaired access to lexical-semantic knowledge" and overreliance on phonological memory in WSc (Vicari, Carlesimo, et al., 1996a). Alternatively, the lesser importance of word frequency may reflect the atypicality of WSs' semantic networks in which secondary, less frequent associations of words have more efficacy in WSs than other groups (Bellugi et al., 2000).

Visuospatial STM

In contrast to their performance on verbal STM tests, WSs usually score at the bottom of the scale on visuospatial tests even when the test is designed to mirror the digit span task procedurally.

Visuospatial Span. A visuospatial analogue of the digit span test, the Corsi Block Task, consists of nine identical small black boxes, corresponding to the nine numbers used in digit span tests. The examiner touches a specified number of the boxes in random order and the subject is asked to duplicate the act in the same order.

In marked contrast to their digit span abilities, WSs are consistently outperformed by comparison groups on the Corsi Block Task: WSa score significantly lower than DSa (Wang & Bellugi, 1994); WSc score lower than matched normal MA controls (Vicari et al., 1994). WSc also perform significantly worse than mentally retarded matched controls on the visual sequencing (span) subtest of the Illinois Test of Psycholinguistic Abilities (ITPA), although they are superior to controls on the auditory sequencing (span) subtest of ITPA (Crisco et al., 1988).

Opposite Patterns of Verbal and Visuospatial STM Results. Combining the separate results already reported, there is a double dissociation between the verbal, digit span and visuospatial, Corsi block results of WSa and DSa: WSa are superior to DSa on digit span; DSa are superior to WSa on the Corsi Block Task (Wang & Bellugi, 1994). This pattern is essentially replicated in Italian WSc except for the similarity in digit span between WSc and controls (Vicari et al., 1994).

It is further supported by comparisons of digit span and Corsi task performance in WSa (n = 16, M = 16;10 yrs, all < 18 yrs), DSc (n = 25, M = 12;7), and a group with moderate learning difficulties (MLD; n = 17, M = 12;6 yrs). The latter was added to determine whether the dissociation between STM results in WSa and DSa may be attributed to differences in general learning patterns (Jarrold, Baddeley, & Hewes, 1999, Exp. 1). In keeping with previous results (Wang & Bellugi, 1994), once adjustments were made for differences in group characteristics, there was a double dissociation between the verbal and visuospatial memory span scores of WSs and DSs.

In another STM study, WSa (n = 16, M = 17;5 yrs) did not differ significantly from either MLDs (n = 16, M = 13;1 yrs) or normally developing mainstream children MSc (n = 16, M = 5;3 yrs) on digit recall, but they were significantly worse than either control group on Corsi block recall (Jarrold et al., 1999, Exp. 2). On a spatial-nontemporal STM pattern test, WSa were worse than MLDs, but not MSs.

Based on the relation between WSa's STM and their MA, verbal and nonverbal MA, the investigators conclude that the nonverbal abilities of WSs are "in some way the consequence of a deficit in visuospatial memory" rather than the reverse (Jarrold et al., 1999, p. 648). Perhaps WSs are especially impaired by the sequential spatial and/or temporal aspects of VS STM tests, which impact the fundamental quantitative, relational deficits of WSs evident in their problems with semantic relational terms, numbering, dimensionality, seriation, and transitivity.

Face Recognition. In contrast to the impaired VS span results, most WSs excel on STM tests of face recognition. Consistent with previously cited reports of excellent face discrimination (Bellugi et al., 1994; Milani et al., 1994; see chap. 4, p. 117), WSc (n = 20, 6;6–14;6 yrs, M = 10;5 yrs) outperform a matched group (verbal IQ) on the face recognition STM subtest of the Rivermead Behavioural Memory Test (Udwin & Yule, 1991). Similarly, WSs outperform DSs (n = 17, n = 10) on the Warrington Recognition Memory Test of face recognition (Bellugi et al., 2000).

Table 5.5 presents a summary of parent surveys and research studies on WSs' STM.

B. Long-Term Memory

Although studies of LTM are more limited than those of STM, research indicates, once again, marked effects of stimulus mode and type of task on WSs' memory abilities. WSs' LTM performance tends to be much better when the material is verbal and semantically relevant, rather than visuospatial, visual-spatial-motor, or noncontextual in nature.

Verbal LTM Tasks

Immediate Free Recall. Methodologically, immediate free recall bridges the gap between STM and LTM as it involves a single presentation of a list of unrelated words, usually at a 2-sec rate. Typically, list length exceeds memory span, and the subject is asked to immediately recall the words in any order. The task also serves as a bridge between two forms of memory processing: recall of the final, recency items that presumably involves phonological STM, and recall of items from the initial (primacy) and middle sections of the list that supposedly involves transfer from STM to LTM through the use of strategies like rehearsal (Rosner, 1972).

Interestingly, WSc (n = 16, M = 10;1 yrs) are comparable to MA matched controls (n = 16, M = 5;5) in recalling the last few, recency list items, but they are much worse than controls in recalling the initial or primacy items of the list (Vicari et al., 1996a). This supports previous findings suggesting that WSc are proficient in phonological (STM) memory for common words, whereas they appear to be impaired in the use of rehearsal (i.e., the process by which items can be transferred from ST to LTM). Furthermore, WSc may be more vulnerable to interference in that early list items are superseded by later ones, and less likely to be influenced by the temporal distinctiveness of initial items in the list.

Free Recall Learning and Delayed Recall. Free recall (FR) learning examines subjects' ability to acquire a list of items over a series of alternating study and test trials (Rosner, 1970, 1971). In FR of unrelated words, WSc (n = 12, 11–19 yrs) do not differ significantly from MA matched children (n = 12, M CA = 6 yrs) in the number of items recalled over five learning trials, but WSc tend to recall less than controls (Vicari et al., 1994; Vicari, Bellucci, & Carlesimo, 2001). Similarly, WSc do not differ significantly from matched controls in amount of item loss over a 15-minute delay (Vicari et al., 1996a; Vicari et al., 2001). Differences in favor of MA matched controls were shown, however, in another study of WSc's (n = 16, M = 10.12) free recall (Vicari et al., 1996a).

Recognition Item Tests. WSc also differ from MA matched controls in the previous study on only certain aspects of item recognition (Vicari et al., 1996a; Vicari et al., 1994). When asked after a 30-minute delay to discriminate between "old," previously presented items, and "new," intermixed foils, WSc are as skilled as controls in identifying old items, but they are much worse than the others in rejecting foils (Vicari et al., 1996a). This suggests that WSc are particularly vulnerable to interference, that is, they have problems distinguishing new from old items or in censoring irrelevant responses.

Category Free Recall. In researching the category free recall of WSs, that is, their memory for semantically related information, several studies have used the California Verbal Learning Test–Children's Version (CVLT-C). Its 15-item word list is composed of members of common categories (e.g., fruits, toys, and clothes) arranged randomly in the list (Delis, Kramer, Kaplan, & Ober, 1995).

According to Wang (1992), WSa exceed DSa in both the number of items recalled and amount of clustering or the grouping of items by category at output. Clustering involves recalling items from the same category sequentially (e.g., "grapes," "apple," "hat," "shirt"), rather than nongrouped by category (e.g., "grapes," "hat," "apple," "shirt") (Bellugi et al., 1994). This finding suggests that WSa appreciate, at least implicitly, the semantics of category members.

This is supported by studies of category production showing that many WSs are able to name at least as many category items as individuals of comparable mental age (Bellugi et al., 1994; Carey et al., 1993, 1994; Scott et al., 1994; Volterra et al., 1994) and their knowledge of category properties is comparable, as well, to that of normal MA controls (Carey et al., 1993, 1994; Johnson et al., 1994).

Metamemory. Metamemory refers to knowledge about memory. This includes knowledge about one's own memory ability, as well as general factors that affect memory performance and use of memory strategies. Preliminary findings from research interviews of WSa (n = 11, 16–32 yrs) suggest that they operate at the level of normal 4-year-olds in the area of metamemory (Bertrand, Mervis, Armstrong, & Hutchins, 1994b). For example, although 86% of WSa appear to understand the relation between amount of study time and learning of new material, only 36% seem to understand that a time delay between input and output would affect their ability to remember (Bertrand et al., 1994b). Insight into memory strategies is particularly lacking. Even though 71% spontaneously sorted pictures by category, none of the WSs could explain why this would help them remember (Bertrand et al., 1994b).

Paired-Associate Learning. On the other hand, WSa are said to show remarkable skill in paired-associate learning (PAL) in which item pairs are presented and the subject has to learn to respond with the second response item of the pair when the first stimulus item is presented (Wang, 1992).

This is demonstrated in the ease with which WSa memorized a list of 20 capital-country pairs (e.g., "France?–Paris", "Senegal?–Dakar," "Nicaragua?–Managua," "Saudi Arabia?–Riyadh," "Ecuador?–Quito," "Australia?–Canberra"; Karmiloff-Smith, 1992). An unusual feature of this learning is its rote-like nature in that item familiarity did not seem to affect performance and learning was almost entirely unidirectional, from stimulus to response, rather than bidirectional, or from response to stimulus, as well. This has definite implications for teaching WSs because PAL resembles real-life tasks like learning vocabulary or spelling lists.

Short Story Recall. Finally, the excellent retention of short stories by WSc should be noted. That is, WSc (n = 20, 6;5–14;5 yrs, M = 10;4 yrs) tend to surpass controls matched individually on age, sex, and verbal IQ on both immediate and delayed recall tests of a short story read aloud by the examiner (Udwin & Yule, 1991).

Visuospatial LTM

Unlike their relatively good performance on verbal LTM tasks, WSs' performance on most visuospatial LTM tasks is markedly impaired.

For example, WSc perform markedly worse than normal MA controls on both the copying and delayed recall of composite geometric figures on the Rey Figure Form B, a spatial LTM test (Vicari et al., 1996a). In addition, WSc's memory of the Rey's Figures decayed significantly more during the delay interval than that of the controls, when recall was calculated as the percentage of the subject's copying score.

Consistent with previous reports of visuospatial deficits (chap. 4, p. 110), WSc also perform poorly on the item location subtest of the Rivermead Behavioural Memory Test (RBMT) in which subjects are asked to reduplicate the random arrangement of six discs on five successive trials (Udwin & Yule, 1991). On the fifth trial, WSc perform much worse than mentally retarded matched controls (M = 3.5 vs. M = 5.0 items) (Udwin & Yule, 1991).

On the other hand, the same WSc remember visuospatial route information as well as MA matched controls (Udwin & Yule, 1991). This unexpected result is attributed to WSc's ability to verbally encode the spatial task. It provides further support for the viability of using WSs' verbal skills to help them compensate for their visual-spatial-motor deficits (see chap. 4, p. 157).

Implicit and Explicit Memory Systems

LTM is further differentiated into two systems: implicit memory and explicit memory. *Explicit memory* refers to declarative memory for what has been experienced, learned, or acquired—like memory span, FR, personal history, or almost all of the research tasks already described. It involves consciously trying to remember information. In contrast, implicit memory refers to changes in current performance that reflect previous experience or information of which the individual is not conscious or aware. In simple terms, implicit memory involves how, or memory for procedures (like previous experience with stimulus items), skills (motor or perceptual), and habits (e.g., conditioning).

Evidence for this distinction is based partly on research on amnesiac patients, Huntington's disease, Alzheimer patients, and developmental studies of age-related changes in ability in tasks involving explicit memory versus little developmental change in tasks involving implicit memory. There is also evidence that different brain structures may be involved in the two memory systems (Vicari et al., 2001; Wang, Cass, Bellugi, & Tzeng, 1996).

The study of WSs' implicit memory is motivated partly by interest in determining how WSs would perform under the conditions of implicit memory, that is, without conscious attempts to remember or draw on existent memories, and on tasks that examine different aspects of memory than those reported earlier. In addition, centers in the brain related to implicit memory are somewhat preserved (cerebellum) or nonpreserved (basal ganglia) in WSs (Vicari et al., 2001).

Initial studies suggest a double dissociation between the explicit and implicit memory of WSa and DSa (Bellugi et al., 1994). WSa were at a disadvantage relative to DSa in pursuit rotor learning (i.e., learning to keep a stylus on a rotating disk), an implicit memory task, whereas they outperformed DSa on free recall, an explicit memory task (Bellugi et al., 1994).

However, WSa ($n = 7$) had an advantage over DSa ($n = 7$) in implicit sequence "learning," that is, their reaction time (RT) to a randomly ordered series of colored dot locations decreased more than that of DSa when a nonrandom sequence was introduced (Wang et al., 1996). These preliminary results are intriguing because they imply that rotor pursuit learning and implicit sequence learning may represent dissociable functions, whereas studies of neurological patients suggest that both forms of learning are either impaired or preserved because both are affected by the basal ganglion (Wang et al., 1996).

Studies of Down syndrome children reveal that they perform similarly to MA matched normal controls on a broad range of implicit memory tasks, visual and verbal, procedural learning, and repetition priming, although markedly poorer than controls on explicit memory tests (Vicari et al., 2001). Interestingly, these implicit memory tasks presumably tap different parts of the brain: basal ganglia and cerebellum for visuomotor and cognitive skills; associative neocortex and posterior hemispheric regions in repetition priming (Vicari et al., 2001).

Previous studies report relative preservation of cerebellar size in WSs compared to that of DSs, and atrophy of basal ganglion structures in WSs. To further complicate matters, recent MRI research reports a decrease in the neuronal marker N-acetylaspartate in the cerebellum of WSs.

How then would WSc be expected to perform on various tasks of implicit memory that presumably implicate these particular parts (i.e., basal ganglia and cerebellum) of the brain? In contrast to other groups, WSc (n = 12, 11–19 yrs) exhibit fractionation on implicit memory tasks. They are comparable to normal MA matched controls on repetition priming tasks in which pre-exposure to target stimuli facilitates their recognition of Fragmented Pictures, as well as their production of target words on the Stem Completion test. On the other hand, WSc are inferior to controls and markedly impaired in an absolute sense on both procedural learning tasks: Tower of London puzzle and Serial RT test.

In trying to solve the Tower of London puzzle, WSc seemed unable to engage in cognitive planning or conceptual learning: They were substantially worse than controls in the initial block of trials and failed to show improvement in the second trial block. On the serial reaction task, WSc's decrease in RT seemed to result from practice with the task rather than reacting to the shift in conditions from a random series of colored circles to an ordered series, one of which was the target to which the subject responded. Once the random set was reintroduced, the normal MA controls showed a large increase in RT, indicating that the previous pattern had been implicitly learned, whereas the WSc did not show this rebound effect. Interestingly, the WSc responded similarly to controls on the two explicit memory tasks: FR and recognition of the items in the FR list.

The contrast between these results and those previously reported for DSc suggests that the procedural learning deficit of WSc is not a "mere expression of a global cognitive impairment affecting mentally retarded people but, rather, . . . a peculiarity of this particular etiological group" (Vicari et al., 2001, p. 673). Importantly, note that WSc exhibit a split or fractionation between procedural learning and repetition priming within the area of implicit memory, as well as the more customary split between explicit and implicit memory. In contrast to the usual difference in WS performance on verbal versus visuospatial STM and LTM tasks, WSc were relatively unimpaired on both types of priming tasks, verbal (Stem Completion) and visuoperceptual (Fragmented Pictures), although verbal skills may have mediated picture (visual) recognition.

In reference to other groups, WSc's results most resemble those of Huntington dementia patients, which implicates the basal ganglia and not the cerebellum as a major factor in the implicit memory functioning of WSs (Vicari et al., 2001). In any event, the pattern of results shown by WSc is distinct from that shown so far by other groups of mentally retarded individuals, as well as that of neurological patients or normally developing children. Once again, this indicates that WSs are characterized by fractionated patterns of behavior that occur both within and between areas. It also implies that the interventions most appropriate for WSs may differ substantially from those most applicable to other groups.

Table 5.6 presents a summary of research findings on WSs' LTM, which includes studies of explicit and implicit memory.

TABLE 5.6
Long-Term Memory Studies of WSs: Summary of Results

Type of Behavior or Test	Frequency or Result	Source or Reference
Immediate Free Recall Primacy[#]	WSc < Normals (MA Match)	Vicari et al., 1996b
Immediate Free Recall Recency[#]	WSc ~ Normals (MA Match)	
Word Recognition[#]	WSc ~ Normals (MA Match)	
Distractor Word Errors[#]	WSc > Normals (MA Match)	
Free Recall Learning[#]	WSc < Normals (MA Match)	
Free Recall Loss with Delay[#]	WSc ~ Normals (MA Match)	
Immediate Free Recall[#]	WSa > DSa	Wang, 1992
Category Free Recall[#]	WSa > DSa	Bellugi et al., 1994a
Category Free Recall Clustering[#]	WSa > DSa	
Metamemory: Effect of Study Time	WSa 86%	Bertrand et al., 1994a
Effect of Delay	WSa 36%	
Sort by Category	WSa 71%	
Understand Sorting Helps	WSa 0%	
Short Story Recall[#]	WSc > Controls MR	Udwin & Yule, 1991
Short Story Delayed Recall[#]	WSc > Controls MR	
Rey Figure Form B, Spatial LTM: Copying Test[#]	WSc < Normal MA Controls	Vicari et al., 1996a
Loss on Retention Test[#]	WSc > Normal MA Controls	
Rivermead Behavioral Memory: Learning Spatial Location of Disks[#]	WSc < MRs Matched Controls	Udwin & Yule, 1991
Learning Visuospatial Route[#]	WSc ~ MRs Matched Controls	
Implicit Procedural Memory: Learning Pursuit Rotor Task[#]	WSa < DSa	Bellugi et al., 1994
Implicit Serial RT Task[#]	WSa > DSa	Wang et al., 1996
Implicit Memory Tests:[#]	DSc ~ Normal MA Controls	Vicari et al., 2001
Visual & Verbal Implicit Tests	DSc ~ Normal MA Controls	
Procedural Learning	DSc ~ Normal MA Controls	
Repetition Priming	DSc < Normal MA Controls	
Explicit Memory FR		
Implicit Memory Tests:[#]		
Repetition Priming	WSc ~ Normal MA Controls	Vicari et al., 2001
Fragmented Pictures—Visual Stem Completion—Verbal		
Procedural Learning Tower of London Puzzle Serial RT	WSc < Normal MA Controls	

Note: % = percentage frequency; # = mean amount; WSc = WS children; WSa = WS adolescents or adults; DS = Down syndrome; MR = mentally retarded; N or NH = normally developing; MR = mentally retarded; DS = Down syndrome.

C. Improvement of Memory

Although the research studies reported so far reveal certain generalities about WSs' memory strengths and deficits, the preliminary nature of many of these findings and the wide variability among WSs in memory functioning suggest that individual evaluation of WSs' memory abilities may often be warranted. Professionals from a number of fields, such as school psychologists, child psychologists, psychometricians, and special education and learning disability specialists may be helpful in selecting, administering, and interpreting memory tests.

Several standardized tests of aptitude and ability contain subtests that may be helpful in providing information about WSs' memory abilities: namely, the Detroit Test of Learning Aptitude (DTLA), the Stanford–Binet, and the McCarthy Scales of Children's Abilities. Other tests that may be informative include the Rivermead Behavioural Memory Test (Udwin & Yule, 1991), the California Verbal Learning Test–Children's Version (CVLT–C) (Delis et al., 1995), and several memory subtests of CELF–R (Semel et al., 1987). Informal observation may also be useful, such as noting WSs' ability to recall a story, poem, movie, television program, or what "Simon Says."

Following evaluation, parents and teachers may consider introducing interventions to help strengthen WSs' memory skills. Based on clinical experience and the memory literature on various normally developing and developmentally delayed groups (Brown, 1975; Campione & Brown, 1977; Hayes & Rosner, 1975; Kail, 1984; Kail & Hagen, 1977; Rosner, 1971; Wiig & Semel, 1984), three intervention approaches are suggested for use with WSs: optimization of input information, application of memory strategies, and facilitation of response output.

Optimizing Input Information

A prerequisite to memorization is understanding the information, activity, event, or situation to be retained. Knowledge of the content area should be determined and steps taken to familiarize WSs with relevant information before presenting material, such as instructions, facts, spelling words, explanations, or a story. Visual attention may be directed where needed by highlighting key elements (i.e., color coding or underlining letters, words, and numbers) or grouping items that are to be associated and remembered together (i.e., presenting a numeral along with the corresponding number of objects).

In following directions, the amount of material may need to be reduced and the language simplified (see chaps. 2 and 3). Often, this involves using task analysis and procedures of task management to ensure that the material is relevant, familiar, simplified, and modally appropriate.

For most WSs, it is particularly important that the material to be memo-rized is interesting and understandable. Information that is meaningful (i.e., related to a topic of special interest, favorite activity, important event or holiday) is remembered better than isolated or seemingly irrelevant items. Tasks that demand rote memorization and exact reproduction of nonde-script or artificial information should be avoided wherever possible. If re-quired, as in learning the three R's, the material may be presented in an in-teresting or relevant context. Clinical researchers note that the "attentional problems" of WSc ($n = 20$, 6;8–14;4 yrs) impinge on their memory perform-ance, which markedly improves when "emotionally charged" material is in-troduced (Bailly et al., 1994).

Items should also be easily distinguishable and logically sequenced. Ma-terial that exceeds WS's memory span may be divided into subcomponents and presented as "bits" or personalized elements that WSs are more likely to retain. After the separate parts are learned, items can be recombined and memorized as an entire set. This is particularly important when WSs do not understand material to be memorized, such as the pledge of allegiance to the flag.

Modal preferences or learning styles should also be taken into account. Many WSs perform better when material is presented in an auditory, verbal mode or when visual stimuli are supplemented by auditory-verbal input (e.g., naming). This is particularly true when learning the basics of reading, writing, and arithmetic. Adding tactile-kinesthetic input to visual or vi-sual–auditory stimuli through the tracing of letters, words, numbers, or process signs can be helpful for many WSc (but not those with tactile defen-siveness; see chap. 3 and 4).

Promoting the Use of Memory Strategies

Three types of memory strategies are generally effective with most indi-viduals: rehearsal, elaboration, and organization (Campione & Brown, 1977; Hagen & Stanovich, 1977; Hayes & Rosner, 1974; Kail, 1984; Ornstein & Haden, 2001; Rosner, 1971; Wiig & Semel, 1984). These are forms of verbal mediation. Some WSs may use memory strategies spontaneously, others may be trained to do so, and still others—the majority—require the imposi-tion of conditions designed to stimulate the use of strategies.

Rehearsal. Rehearsal means literally to "re-hear" or restate previous in-formation by repeating the input over and over again, like a phone number or street address. Most WSs are excellent candidates for use of rehearsal as a memory strategy. This is consistent with their well-known verbal/phono-logical skills and successful use of rehearsal as a psycho-educational strat-egy (see pp. 67, 182–183).

Verbal rehearsal may make it easier for WSs to remember visuospatial and visual-spatial-motor information, areas in which they are usually severely deficient. For example, confusions about how to find one's way from place to place may be reduced by helping WSs verbally label and rehearse significant landmarks and turning points as well as the entire visuomotor sequence. Along the same lines, WSa may be helped to better manage the use of equipment (i.e., vending machines, pay telephones, or tape recorders), with less frustration and embarrassment, by encouraging them to verbalize and rehearse key components of the task.

Verbal rehearsal may also be used to facilitate WSs' learning of various types of lists. This includes free recall learning in which small item groups can be rehearsed together; paired-associate learning in which each item pair can be repeated several times; and serial learning in which the entire item sequence or an item subset can be rehearsed repeatedly. These strategies are particularly helpful when rote learning is involved.

In any case, the optimal number of items that can be rehearsed together must be determined. A rule of thumb is to use the individual's memory span, which is usually two to three items for most WSc. Longer lists may be segmented into small units, and pausing between item groups may facilitate rehearsal as well as the initial learning of the items. The rehearsal process should be repeated, practiced, reiterated, and monitored for correctness.

Elaboration. Clinical observation suggests that many WSs benefit from the use of "concrete" associative cues, verbal analogies, and metaphors in the classroom and other contexts. In teaching how to write the letters of the alphabet, the WS student may be instructed, for example, that " 'O' is like an orange," "an 'X' is like crossed arms," and "let the light shine through the loop of an 'l.' " Some WSs may be able to learn to generate their own semantic associations. Music may offer "hooks" to aid memorization by providing auditory structure as well as mnemonics.

Many tasks involve trying to remember unrelated item pairs or items that have little apparent relation to each other or the context. In such cases, most normally developing children and adults spontaneously generate meaningful links between items that are difficult to associate with each other or recode an unmemorable item into a more distinctive form.

Recoding can involve emphasizing or modifying the properties of an item, such as adding color or substituting a memorable word for a neutral stimulus item, for example, the word "twin" could be recoded as "two" and "win." Similarly, the item pair "book"–"tree" could be transformed into the sentence, "A book is hanging from the tree," or a visual image of the connection. Both forms of elaboration usually facilitate the paired-associate learning of most normally developing children, and also mentally retarded individuals when connectors are provided for them (Campione & Brown, 1977).

Finally, associative cueing can help WSs remember and prepare for real-life events. Concrete, external cues are helpful in reminding WSs about forthcoming events, activities, or to take certain items, such as placing an invitation in a prominent place, or an item to be taken to school or a party near the door.

Organization. Many kinds of memory tasks require individuals to exceed their immediate STM span that places a strain on their memory. Organizing items into groups, or "chunks," can help to reduce memory load and facilitate item retrieval (Rosner, 1971). Groupings are based on some form of shared similarity, such as category membership, visual similarity (size, color, shape), phonetic or auditory similarity, functional relations (i.e., things to dig with or cut with), coordinated or associated items (e.g., bread and butter, smoke and pipe), or event-related items (e.g., things to take to a picnic, or see and do at the circus) (Rosner & Smick, 1989). Grouping may also help to emphasize the similarity of items, like parts of speech, letters of the alphabet, number of syllables, and things you like.

Organizational strategies are effective in learning or remembering lists of items, such as grocery lists, lists of classmates, spelling lists, lists of chemical elements, or kinds of machines, tools, or animals and their attributes. The versatility and wide applicability of organizational schemes attest to their usefulness.

Regarding WSs' use of organization, research reveals that many are able to take advantage of category relations within free recall lists and sorting tasks (Bellugi et al., 1994; Bertrand et al., 1994b; Wang, 1992). This is especially true when items from the same category are blocked or appear contiguously, not randomly, during list presentation. Informing WSs of the particular categories represented in the list, either before list presentation or presenting items along with their category name, may also help to accentuate the categorical nature of the material and help them remember.

Clinical experience suggests that organizational strategies may aid WSs' retention efforts in many instructional contexts, such as learning the letters of the alphabet, word families, and the structural rules of English in learning to read and write. Number grouping aids—such as an abacus, beads, flannel boards, number lines, or the manipulation of toy objects—may be used to help WS students learn arithmetic facts, principles, and computational skills.

It is most unlikely, however, that WSs would be able to transfer organizational strategies from trained material or situations to new ones (Campione & Brown, 1977).

Facilitating Response Output

The memory output of WSs may be improved by using techniques of task management. This includes selection of appropriate modes of response, use of retrieval cues, and providing appropriate feedback and incentives.

Response Options. With WSs, choice of response and testing mode may be critical to obtaining an accurate estimate of their capabilities.

Because most WSs are likely to have visuomotor deficits, tasks requiring fine motor skills and eye–hand integration should be avoided unless the purpose of the test is to evaluate those skills. When retention is the central concern, WSs should be evaluated with response channels that are relatively intact. For most WSs, this means using verbal responses.

Alternative forms of responding (i.e., use of a typewriter, computer, or calculator) may be introduced to help reduce WSs' handwriting problems. Changing test format so that the amount of writing is limited to filling in the blanks, one word response, short answer, multiple choice answer, or underlining or circling items may also be helpful. Response selection methods, such as recognition or forced choice, tend to be less difficult for WSs than response production methods, such as recall, reproduction, reconstruction, or reenactment of stimulus items. Item choice methods have the further advantage of helping to circumvent WSs' problems in word finding and answering of questions. Simple tests can be made more challenging by increasing the number or similarity of foils.

Retrieval Cues. Generally, the use of relevant retrieval cues markedly increases the amount of information most individuals can recall. For example, subjects recall significantly more category items when cued with the name of each category during testing than merely being asked to recall all list items. Performance may also be improved by re-presenting cues administered during input, such as "What are the green/big/circus or school items on the list?" (Rosner & Smick, 1989).

Clinical observation indicates that many WSs may benefit from the use of cueing. In the classroom, for example, providing the initial sound of a word or a rhyming word may help WSs recognize a written word or handle a word-finding problem (see chap. 3).

Response Feedback. Problems of motivation and uncertainty about adequacy of performance can undermine the learning, retention, and evaluation of most WSs in the classroom, as well as in other contexts, including formal testing, and family and group situations. Most WSs need appropriate incentives and benefit from feedback that is immediate, informative, and constructive whenever possible.

Because of WSs' sensitivity to criticism and fear of failure, correct responding and improvement should be emphasized when commenting on WSs' performance. This may involve modifying standard grading practices because just putting an "X" on an incorrect response can be devastating to many WSs. Instead, self-correcting didactic materials may be used for instruction, and answer keys and self-correcting guides may be useful for evaluating one's own performance. Informing WS students of their errors in a constructive, noncritical way is an art. Finally, use of personalized forms of verbal-social rewards is vital to the teaching of WS students. An encouraging smile, in particular, seems to motivate WSs to try again to get the correct answer.

D. Capitalizing on Memory Skills

Many WSs possess memory strengths that may be used to their advantage in educational and social applications.

Educational Applications. Generally, the phonological rote memory and verbal LTM skills of many WSs may be used as a focal point in formal learning situations that would otherwise overtax their academic capabilities. Ability to memorize rote information may be applied in learning how to read and spell as well as in content areas. Arithmetic is the exception because memorization of number facts and calculation routines may be futile unless WSs are able to understand to some extent the underlying principles of mathematics, such as the one-to-one correspondence between numerals and quantities.

Within learning contexts, many WSs may be able to apply their verbal LTM skills to help them remember various types of information (e.g., dates, events, or stories). It may also be used to help expand their knowledge of special interest topics by adding facts and information. In areas such as social studies, sciences, and language arts, WSs' well-established ability for face recognition and their spongelike retention of socially relevant information and events may be a real asset. Most WSs are interested in, and are able to recount in detail, personal attributes, what was said by whom and where, what they were doing, and so forth.

Similarly, various kinds of classroom assignments can draw on the language skills of WSs (Udwin & Yule, 1998a). They may be asked to memorize and recite poems or stories or recount past events. Many WSs also seem to have a talent for learning foreign languages. Providing opportunities for them to learn, practice, and "show off" these strengths can be educationally and socially rewarding.

In addition, the WSs' ability to remember jokes, poems, and stories may be put to advantage by having the individual perform in school programs or those of other organized groups. Most WSs are "natural" performers, seem to have little or no stage fright, and thoroughly enjoy "hamming" it up (Dykens & Rosner, 1999).

Social Applications. Memory skills may also be used to compensate for shortcomings and promote social interaction in other situations. Within the family, the WS individual may be asked to remember and report on significant information, such as a travel route, weather update, or team scores. Foreign language skills can come in handy when ordering food in an ethnic restaurant. Anniversaries and birthdays of family members and friends can be included in WSs' storehouse of functional information.

LTM skills may also be used, with assistance, in preparing a photo album of family members and special events. Sorting the snapshots, arranging them chronologically, and pasting them in albums can provide opportunities to practice visuomotor skills and cognitive operations like classification and seriation. Developing a dialogue associated with the scrapbook may provide interesting topics for conversation (see Wiig & Semel, 1984) and enhance WSs' social interactions with family, friends, and neighbors.

Another application draws on the often reported remarkable memory of many WSs for prayers and hymns. Participation in religious ceremonies is a personally meaningful and socially relevant way to apply their language, memory, and musical abilities. The impressive musical skills of many WS individuals are described next.

IV. MUSICALITY

Musical proficiency matches, if not exceeds, the unusual language skills associated with WS (Don, Schellenberg, & Rourke, 1996, 1999). Lauded by parents, clinicians, and educators, musicality is the fourth "specific aptitude" of WSs, and a prominent part of the WS profile. Parents deserve major credit for recognizing the latent musical talent of many WSs (e.g., "Bravo Gloria," PBS Television program, 1988, cf. Lenhoff & Lenhoff, WSA National Newsletter, 1993, *10*(3), 8–10; also, Semel, 1989; Tharp, 1986) and the potential of using that talent to further their development. The intensity of interest, natural flair, and appreciable musical achievements of many WSs go far beyond what would be expected from their competence in other areas.

Parent surveys report that 86% of WSc remember songs easily, 87% like to sing, and 71% have musical talent (Utah Survey, Semel & Rosner, 1991a, 1991b). "Love of music" is reported in more than 90% of WSc in other surveys (Midwest Region WSA National Newsletter, 1989 April, pp. 21–22; WSA Checklist Survey, Semel & Rosner, 1991a, 1991b). Researchers are confirming that WSs are "more engaged with musical activities than others" (WSA National Newsletter, 2001, *18*(3), 9).

As with other specific aptitudes, WSs' musicality is subject to certain limitations. Generally, WSs are unable to read music notation and they may be limited in the particular instruments they can play due to their fine motor deficits (Lenhoff, Perales, & Hickok, 2001).

On the other hand, many WSs possess unusual musical skills and the good fortune to have families and others who are dedicated to cultivating those skills.

A. Recognition of Musical Talents

The first significant sign of national recognition of WS musicality was a
news segment of "All Things Considered" on National Public Radio (December 19, 1994) featuring the "Williams Five," a group of WSa who live within a
20 mile radius of each other in Orange County, California (WSA National
Newsletter, 1994 Spring, Vol. *11*, p. 13). Aside from demonstrating their remarkable musical talents in singing, playing musical instruments, and composing, the program included interviews with members of the "Williams
Five," a few of their parents, and Nancy Goldberg, director of Belvoir Terrace, a highly rated music and arts camp. Having observed the musicality of
several dozen WSs in a special camp session, Goldberg summarized her impressions as follows: "All [of] the WS campers showed amazing talent. Their
ability to hear and recall music is much greater than my gifted [nonhandicapped] campers, even my music majors." Although individual variability
in WSs' musicality is now well established, the extent of the musical ability
of many WSs continues to amaze researchers, musicians, and the general
public as it is further revealed in research studies and special media programs (WSA National Newsletter, 2001 Spring, 18(2), 27).

Several television specials have demonstrated WSs' unusual aptitude for
music and presented important information about other features of WS. For
example, the television program "60 Minutes" (host Morley Safer, October
19, 1997) contrasted the singing expertise of Gloria Lenhoff, who knows
1,000 songs and sings in over 20 languages, with her inability to add 5 and 4.
The gifted rock n' roll piano playing and spontaneous composing of Michael
Williams contrasts with his inability to walk outside his own house without
getting lost. Likewise, the lovely singing of Meghan Finn, who studies music
in college, contrasts with her inability to distinguish her left from right. A
television documentary by Dr. Oliver Sacks, "Don't Be Shy, Mr. Sacks" (Part
4 of the "NOVA" four-part series, "The Mind Traveler," on PBS) presented vignettes of WSs engaged in a variety of activities, and commentaries by
Sacks and other investigators. "Inside Edition," "Nightline," and "Chronicle"
are examples of television documentaries and "news magazine" shows that
have featured segments on WSs' musicality (WSA National Newsletter, 2001,
18(2), 30).

Many of the significant segments from "60 Minutes" and Sacks' special
are captured in a videotape, "Williams Syndrome: A Highly Musical Species"
(EOPI, 1996),[8] which includes comments of researchers, Ursula Bellugi and
Colleen Morris, and parents and WS campers attending the 1995 one-week
program at Belvoir Terrace. Performance highlights include Gloria learning

---

[8]The videotape, "Williams Syndrome: A Highly Musical Species", is available through the
WSA (PO Box 297, Clawson, MI 48017-0297); other videotapes about the musicality of WS and related topics may also be ordered from WSA.

a difficult piece "with the expertise of a Juilliard student." A young WS man is shown receiving piano instruction and having the piano "under his control." Another young WS man follows complex interactive and separable two-handed rhythm instruction in drumming by "locking into" the instructor's eyes rather than watching his hands or drumming motions. Still another segment features a WS composer and singer of country blues ballads who accompanies himself on the piano or guitar.

In fact, establishing the one-week music and arts summer program at Belvoir Terrace for WSs was a major factor in the recognition and development of WSs' musical talents. Through the efforts and commitment of parents (especially Sharon Libera and Howard Lenhoff), Director Nancy Goldberg, her dedicated staff, and WSA support, the WS music and arts camp has flourished since its founding in August 1994.

As a result of the camping experience and the encouragement of parents, camp staff, other music instructors, the WSA, and other organizations, many WSs continue to receive musical instruction and participate in music activities in their communities (e.g., WSA National Newsletter, 1995 Summer, Vol. *12*(3), 17; WSA National Newsletter, 2000 April, *17*(1), 12). A number of WSc and WSa perform in musical groups, ensembles, or special productions offered by community music schools, school music programs, adult education centers, or churches (WSA National Newsletter, 2000 April, *17* (1), 12). Some WSs participate in organizations that focus on people with special needs, such as "Potential Unlimited." Others participate in "regular" school groups and compete in regional contests (WSA National Newsletter, 1999 June, Vol. *16*, 3). In fact, the musical achievements of WSs are heralded so frequently by the press, special programs, performances, and awards that the WSA Newsletter has initiated a regular column called "Show Stoppers" (WSA National Newsletter, 1999 September, Vol. *16*(3), 18–19).

The accomplishments of WSs have also served to pique the curiosity of researchers and musicians about the nature of WSs' musicality, its extent, and the proficiency level of WSs' musical abilities.

B. Research on WSs' Musicality

Although research on WSs' musicality is in its early stages, a few papers provide important information about their abilities in the areas of melody, rhythm, and absolute pitch. The qualitative reports and impressions of researchers, professional musicians, music instructors, and child educators provide further insight into the special nature of WSs' musical talents.

Laboratory Studies

Musical proficiency is demonstrated in the ability of WSc (n = 10, 8–13 yrs, M = ~11 yrs) to discriminate between melodic pairs as well as rhythmic pairs in the Tonal and Rhythm subtests of Gordon's "Primary Measures of

Music Audition" (Don et al., 1996, 1999). Actually, they perform at a level comparable to their scores on the Peabody Picture Vocabulary Test–Revised (PPVT–R). This suggests that WSs' musical abilities are a match for their highest scoring area of language skills (see chap. 2, p. 24).

Rhythmic Abilities. A production test of WSs' ability to copy or repeat verbatim rhythmic segments provides further evidence of their "uncanny sense of rhythm" (Levitin & Bellugi, 1998). Presented with a graduated series of one- and two-measure rhythmic patterns, ranging from simple to difficult rhythms, slow to rapid tempo, WSc (n = 8, 9–20 yrs, M = 13;5 yrs) from the 1996 music and arts camp are comparable to a normal younger comparison group (n = 8, 5–7 yrs) in correctly reproducing the patterns clapped by the experimenter on two thirds of the trials. In fact, the WSc are more likely than the other group to produce completion patterns on trials in which they were incorrect (Levitin & Bellugi, 1998). This suggests, once again, that music is a special skill for many WSs.

The relation between WSs' rhythmicity, aptitude for language, and immediate memory is currently being investigated, as is the relation between fine-grained timing mechanisms in the brain and vulnerability to hyperacusis (Boucher, 1999, September, *16*(3), 3).

"Perfect" Pitch. The very rare ability of "perfect" pitch, exhibited by only approximately 1 in 10,000 people in the general population, is a highly specialized gift that has been informally noted and attributed to WSs by a number of clinicians, researchers, and musicians (e.g., Goldberg, NPR, December 19, 1994; Lenhoff, 1996; Scheiber, 2000; Semel, 1988). It refers to the ability to accurately identify by name and produce the pitch of musical notes. Thus, on hearing a note or notes played singly, as chords, or in a song, a person with perfect, absolute pitch can name the notes, and being given the names of notes, could sing or play the proper sounds on a musical instrument.

A recent study (Lenhoff et al., 2001; WSA National Newsletter, 2001 September, *18*(3), 7) substantiates previous impressions of absolute pitch (AP) in a small, selected sample of WSs (n = 5, 13–43 yrs). Presented with a large sample of random single notes, both "natural" and "accidental" (sharps and flats) from several octaves, the WSs averaged 97% correct! Presented with dyads and triads of natural notes played together, the WSs were once again almost perfect (M = 98%) in their naming of the notes. Preliminary testing of relative pitch or the relation between pitches revealed talent in this area too. Despite some difficulty in explaining the task and adapting it to the participants' production skills, performance still averaged 85%. In addition, all except one of the participants demonstrated considerable skill in retention of the notes and names of the notes from previously learned songs, as well as the ability to transpose the melodies into different keys. Scores for this task ranged from 63% to 98% correct (*M* = 86%).

As remarkable as these results are, so too is the atypicality of the musical background and response mode of the WS participants. None could read music, the mean IQ of the four with available test results was 58, and all scored within the mildly retarded range (51–69). Also, the names of certain notes were recently acquired for at least one WS individual. To accommodate that difficulty, she was given the reverse AP task of singing notes that were named. Her scores were over 90% correct on the AP task, 90% on RP production, and 98% correct on the retention and transposition task.

The musical skill of the five participants varied. Only one had started musical instruction before age 6, yet all had perfect pitch. This contrasts with the general view that music instruction should begin within the critical period from 3 to 6 years of age in order to develop AP. The present AP results provide another example of the singularity of some of the characteristics of WS.

The frequency with which AP is present in the general population of WSs, however, will not be easy to determine. The requisite ability for testing AP, knowing the names of notes, even though the WS person may be unable to read music, is very uncommon to say the least. The present results reported suggest, however, that the present WSs who possess that skill also exhibit AP, and other advanced musical abilities. One of the investigators estimates that 30% of WSs may have the ability to develop absolute pitch (WSA National Newsletter, 2001, Fall, *18*(3), 7).

Brain Imaging Research. In addition, results of a brain imaging study of four WSs are consistent with previous reports that many WSs have absolute or relative pitch (Bellugi et al., 1996; Hickok, Bellugi, & Jones, 1995). Similar to professional musicians with absolute pitch, the WSs showed leftward asymmetry of the planum temporale area in the auditory cortex (Schlaug, Jancke, Huang & Steinmetz, 1995). Because asymmetry of the planum temporale area is associated with language processing, this provides further evidence for the notion that the language and musical skills of WSs may be related neuroanatomically. This is also consistent with the link between language and musicality reported by Don et al. (1996, 1999).

Qualitative Information

Instructors' observations at the Williams Syndrome Music and Arts Camp at Belvoir Terrace provide compelling testimony to WSs' musical skills. According to Lenhoff (1996): Many WS individuals seem to have a relatively long attention span for musical activities, perfect or relative pitch, an "uncanny" sense of rhythm, the ability to learn songs in foreign languages with near perfect accents, and the ability to retain music, words, and melodies for many years though most do not read music. A number of the WS musically gifted improvise and compose lyrics, and virtually all love performing.

These are almost exactly the attributes of "music aptitude" ascribed to "musically talented" individuals by Dr. Haroutounian, a faculty member of piano at George Mason University (WSA National Newsletter, 2000 April, *17*(1), 12–13).

Some of the qualitative impressions of Levitin, a trained musician and researcher at Stanford University, bear on these points (Levitin & Bellugi, 1998; WSA National Newsletter, 1997 Fall, *14*(3), 15–17). He reported that WSs often display an unusually high degree of engagement or involvement with music and tend to play music with a great deal less self-consciousness than most normal music campers or other nonhandicapped individuals. Although WSs may sometimes lack technical expertise in playing musical instruments (e.g., the clarinet, piano, drum set, or guitar), their musical motor skills seem much better developed than would be expected from the poor coordination shown in everyday tasks like handwriting or using eating utensils (Levitin & Bellugi, 1998; WSA National Newsletter, 1997 Fall, *14*(3), 15–17).

In any event, previous studies of WSs' musicality and musical abilities should be extended to further research areas. Larger samples of WSs studies are needed to extend previous research findings (Bellugi et al., 1996; Don et al., 1996; Levitin & Bellugi, 1998). This includes investigating WSs' ability to discriminate tones, melodies, and rhythms; play instruments by ear; imitate, learn, and recall songs; read music; compose tunes and lyrics. The effects of differences in cognitive ability and age level upon WSs' responsiveness to music training should also be studied as well as the effectiveness of various forms of music training. Many of these and other topics including musical ability and interest, the relation between emotion and music, musicality, and the brain, are being addressed in the ongoing research program of Bellugi and colleagues (Bellugi, Rose, Doyle, Levitin et al., WSA National Newsletters, 2001 Spring, *18*(2), 5).

Adding musicality to the standard test batteries used with WSs is being also considered, although the methodology may still need to be worked out (WSA National Newsletter, 1995 Winter, *12*(1), p. 17). This is particularly meaningful in view of the individual variability evident in WSs' musicality (Nancy Goldberg, cf. videocassette, 1996; Reiss, Schader, Shute, Don, Milne, Stephens, & Williams, WSA National Newsletter, 2001 Spring, *18*(2), 27). Referrals for musical assessment of WSs is apparently available by contacting the Williams syndrome clinic at Children's Hospital in Boston, or Suzanne B. Hauser, Chair of the Music Therapy Department at Berklee College of Music (1140 Boylston Street, Boston, MA 02215) (Scheiber, 2000, p. 35).

TABLE 5.7
Musicality of WSs: Summary of Results

Type of Behavior	Frequency or Result	Source or Reference
Remembers Songs Easily	WSc 86%	Utah Survey
Likes to Sing	WSc 87%	
Musical Talent	WSc 71%	
Love of Music	WSc 91%	WSA Checklist Survey
Love of Music	WSc 94%	WSA Midwest Region, 1989
Discrimination of Tonal or Rhythmic Pairs[#]	WSc ~ WSc PPVT–R	Don et al., 1996, 1999
Music Audition[#]	WSc Music Audition ~ WSc PPVT–R	Don et al., 1996, 1999
Reproduction of Rhythmic Patterns[#]	WSc ~ Normals (MA Match)	Levitin & Bellugi, 1998
Absolute Pitch[#]	WSs 97% (M)	
Relative Pitch[#]	WSs 87% (M)	Lenhoff et al., 2002
Recall & Transposition[#]	WSs 86% (M)	
Asymmetry of Cortical Planum Temporale Area[#]	WSs ~ Professional Musicians	Bellugi et al., 1996

Note: % = percentage frequency; # = mean amount; WSc = WS children; WSa = WS adolescents & adults; N = normally developing; MA Match = matched on mental age; M = mean value.

Personal observation suggests that WSs' musical skills, although surprisingly high, may tend to fall short of the virtuosity exhibited by musically gifted children, including those with other forms of developmental disabilities, like idiot savants and some youngsters with autism (Sacks, PBS NOVA documentary, 1995), although most autistics with musical gifts are unable to attain professional status (Frith, 1992). On the other hand, the ultimate level of musical proficiency that talented WSs may be able to achieve under conditions of optimum instruction and encouragement is not yet known.

In the meanwhile, it is clear that most WSs receive tremendous personal and social satisfaction from their involvement with music. As one WS camper explained at the 1995 music and arts camp, "Music is like soup because I drink it down, it makes me feel all warm inside, and I have a really big spoon" (quotation paraphrased, EOPI videocassette, 1996). Perhaps Oliver Sacks was correct in describing WS as "a musical species" (EOPI videocassette, 1996).

Table 5.7 presents a summary of parent surveys and research studies on WSs' musicality.

C. Developing Musical Aptitudes

Based on the preceding accounts of WSs' musicality, it seems clear that every effort should be made to promote the musical interests and talents of WSs. Whereas music generally enhances the quality of life of most people, this is especially true for WSs because of the obstacles and problems they often face in areas other than music. With music, however, they may derive praise and pleasure.

Music in the Early Years

Early Musical Interests. The age at which musical interests seem to emerge varies among WSs. Often it is observed early in life. The playing of music can soothe WS infants during bouts of colic, lengthen their attention span, and help them become more focused (Scheiber, 2000; WSA National Newsletter, 1993 Spring, 10–11; WSA National Newsletter, 1994 Spring, 7). There are reports of a WSc singing a nursery rhyme before being able to talk, and another of an individual composing a song with a haunting melody, structure, and harmony before being able to read (Scheiber, 2000). Some WSc show sustained interest in music and play an instrument like the piano from age 5 on. In others, it may appear in the grade school years, and with still others, not until puberty (WSA National Newsletter, 1993 Summer, pp. 8–10).

Young WSc should be encouraged to sing and perform with family and friends (Lenhoff & Lenhoff, WSA National Newsletter, Spring 1994, *11*(2), p. 7). They should be provided with simple rhythmic instruments, like the tambourine, wooden sticks, castanets, maracas, rattles, bells, gourds, or even rhythmic clapping. Some WSc develop a repertoire of pieces that they may be able to recognize or sing by the time they are 4 or 5 years old (Lenhoff & Lenhoff, 1994).

As WS children mature, parents should provide experiences that encourage their musical development (Lenhoff & Lenhoff, 1994). WSc should be exposed to different kinds of music by having access to a radio, tape recorder, and musical toy instruments (e.g., a wooden xylophone, drums, shakers, or horns; Scheiber, 2000). Attending concerts or musical theatre or movies, joining musical groups such as choirs, or watching television specials pertaining to music, are other ways for them to access the musical world (Lenhoff & Lenhoff, 1994).

Other "hands-on" kind of experiences may include being taught to listen more critically to musical selections to identify for pertinent details of form, instrumentation, sounds; echo clapping, chanting, and body percussion; and call and response clapping and singing (Haroutounian, WSA National Newsletter, 2000 April, *17*(1), 12–13).

Music Lessons

Readiness for Music Lessons. Once WSc display musical interest, their talents should be encouraged and developed through adapted music lessons. Some prerequisites for determining when to start regular music lessons include the ability to follow instructions and remember information from one lesson to another, and some degree of fine motor control and co-ordination (Coleman, WSA Newsletter, December, 1998, *15*(3), p. 18).

Types of Music Instruction. It is also important to take care in selecting the type of musical instruction and the appropriate music teacher (Gold-berg, WSA National Newsletter, 1995, Winter, *17*; Lenhoff & Lenhoff, 1994).

Adapted music lessons focus on teaching musical skills to individuals with cognitive deficits. Some WSs may benefit from this approach, others from regular forms of music education that provide more opportunities for peer interaction.

A number of WSc have benefited from instruction with the Suzuki method, which emphasizes auditory learning through listening to tapes and imitating music played by others (WSA National Newsletter, 1994 Fall, p. 16; Stambaugh, 1996). Some 7-year-olds with WS may be ready for short lessons with this method. Typically, reading of music is postponed until after aural and instrumental skills are acquired.

Regardless of type of music instruction, the teacher should try to ana-lyze and break down skills into smaller units that a WS individual can mas-ter (Coleman, 1998). Other important characteristics include patience in dealing with unpredictable behaviors and a slower rate of progress than usual, frequent use of positive (socially oriented) reinforcement, and expe-rience in teaching students who are unable to read music but can learn to play "by ear." A good "fit" in terms of personality and acceptance of WS qualities is very important.

In any event, undue pressure to succeed should be avoided (Lenhoff & Lenhoff, 1994).

Guidelines for Teaching Music. Inspired by the experience of instruct-ing WSs at Belvoir Camp, Stambaugh (1996) wrote a "how-to-do-it" article for music instructors. It describes the musical skills commonly displayed by WSs, such as exceptional pitch discrimination, ability to sing in English and other languages or play songs just heard, and long-term retention of melodies.

Physical characteristics of WSs that may affect instruction are also noted. Specifically, their full lips may interfere with playing certain instru-ments (i.e., flute, clarinet, and French horn), and their limited rotation of the wrist, forearm, and fingers may interfere with use of standard hand po-sitions in playing instruments like the guitar.

Popular areas of instruction with WSs include singing and voice lessons and percussion instruments (drums, etc.), which are relatively easy for them to play. The accordion, autoharp, and guitar are also popular. Chords can be played on the accordion by just pressing buttons. The piano is excellent at all ages. Many WSs pick out melodies by ear, sing along with their playing, and like to improvise. Drums bring out a surprising sense of rhythm in some WS youngsters. The trumpet may be appropriate for high school age students and older. Interestingly, some WS teenagers have excellent note-reading abilities.

Behavioral difficulties often associated with WS are also mentioned (e.g., hyperacusis, poor motor coordination, emotionality, and limited understanding of spatial concepts and mathematics). Behavioral management advice is also included. Music teachers are advised to address students by name, use eye contact, and use short sentences when giving verbal instructions. Frustration build-up should be avoided, over-excitement modulated, and conversational distractors dealt with briefly. WSs who are fascinated by the mechanics of musical instruments should be allowed some time for exploration, for example, by pressing the keys, strumming the string, and so on.

Music Camps and Programs

Since its inception, the Belvoir Terrace WS music and arts camp has offered WSs a singular opportunity to pursue "a week of enrichment centering on music, a week of enjoyment finding friends, [and] a future of fulfillment through achievement in the arts" (WSA National Newsletter, 1995, Winter, pp. 18–19). Camp activities usually include musical theater, dance movements, chorus, dramatics, rhythm, private lessons in voice and instruments (piano, drums, etc.), painting, ceramics, swimming instruction, games, campfire storytelling, talent shows, and skits. To attend, WSs are presumed to show some interest and talent in music or the arts and be capable of living in a camping environment without constant parental supervision.

In its first year, 1994, there were 37 campers, from age 9 to 45 years (Stambaugh, 1996). In 1998, enrollment increased to 55 campers, two thirds of which were returnees, and added activities included five bands, a local recital, attendance at musical events, and a bevy of media persons representing newspapers, cable news, feature news programs, French public television, independent documentary, and photo journalism (WSA Newsletter, 1998 September, *15*(2).

Enrollment remains at about 57 WS campers and the camp continues to offer a varied music-arts program with expanded opportunities for public performances, and visitors interested in writing or producing programs about WS. Professors from nearby universities also were guests for a special program about Belvoir, the forthcoming Berkshire Music Academy, and WS (WSA National Newsletter, 2001 September, *18*(3), 20).

The success of the WS camp program at Belvoir Terrace has inspired the establishment of other music camps and programs in the US as well as in other countries.

"Music and Minds" is an educational, 12-day, annual residential program for young WS adults held at the University of Connecticut in Storrs since Summer 1998. Under the auspices of the Department of Educational Psychology (Dr. Sally Reis), the Neag Center for Gifted and Talented Development, the Allied Health and Music Departments, the program offers campers classes in chorus, dance, music, and computers, instrumental or voice lessons, mathematical instruction based on music, with an emphasis on fractions, as well as social enjoyment, and opportunities for researchers to study WSs' special traits (WSA National Newsletter, 1998 Fall, *15*(2), 16; WSA National Newsletter, 2001 Spring, *18*(2), 27).

Another music program for WSs held its initial session at the University of the Incarnate Word (UIW) and the Institute for Music Research at the University of Texas at San Antonio in June 1999. Activities include "group sings, music therapy, private lessons, movement/dance, games, and arts and crafts . . . sing-a-long, karaoke night, jazz concert, disco dance, and camper's talent show" (WSA National Newsletter, 1999 June, *16*(2)).

Music camp opportunities for younger WSc are also being offered. The Blue Lake Music Camp for WSc from ages 3 to 10 held its first session in September 2001 at Muskegon, Michigan. Twenty families attended the weekend program where the WSc had contact with one of four music therapists besides receiving half-hour daily sessions in percussion, choir, tone chimes, music, and movement, as well as piano lessons and art activities (WSA National Newsletter, 2001 September, *18*(3), 21).

"Friendship Ventures at Edgewood Center" in Eden Prairies near Minneapolis, Minnesota, is a traditional residential and day camp with a strong music component that is open to WSc, their siblings, other family members, and friends. As of August 1999, the British Columbia Lions Society is offering a 1-week WS camp that has a music component developed by the Canadian Association of Williams Syndrome (CAWS).

Ireland also initiated a WS music camp in summer 2001. Staff included a staff member, who was a piano teacher, from Belvoir Terrace. Once again there was tremendous enthusiasm and benefits from the camp experience (WSA National Newsletter, 2001 September, *18*(3), 21).

Other camps and special educational programs suitable for WSs can be accessed through the Association of Retarded Children and Adults (ARCA) or "Resources for Children with Special Needs" (WSA Newsletter, March 1999, *16*(1), 17).

Postsecondary Education

Some WSs have been fortunate enough to be selected to attend "High Hopes," a college of music for handicapped persons, located in California. Students at the college include persons who are blind, mentally retarded, and otherwise handicapped. They occasionally travel throughout the country giving performances; some perform solo or in small groups.

In addition, the Williams Syndrome Foundation (WSF) and WSA have formulated plans to establish the Berkshire Hills Music Academy (BHMA), a private 2-year certificate program in South Hadley, Massachusetts. Its mission includes an educational component, "comprehensive training in music, essential academics, social, vocational, and independent living skills," as well as a vocational component, "preparation for careers in areas such as music therapy, recreation, human services and music related careers" (WSA Newsletter, March 1999, *16*(1), 24). Applications are being accepted for the school as of spring 2000 (WSA National Newsletter, 2000 April, *17*(1), 15). The Berkshire Hills Music Academy has now opened its doors, as of September 23, 2001, to 14 students with WS (age 18–28), many with experience at Belvoir Terrace. Future class size is expected to reach 50 students, with the program continuing to emphasize essential academic skills in reading and math, developing independence skills, and increasing proficiencies in music (WSA National Newsletter, 2001 September, *18*(3), 19).

Along the same lines, the Lili Claire Foundation plans to build in Las Vegas a performing arts center and vocational training school for adults with Williams syndrome. Established to honor the memory of Lili Clare, other projects planned by the Foundation include a television center (TV studio), family center, diagnostic center, children's video library and children's book library (WSA Newsletter, June 1999, Vol. *16*(2), 14). The Lili Claire Foundation holds annual fundraising events, offers programs and services at the Family Resource Center at UCLA (University of California, Los Angeles), Life Skills Center at UNLV (University of Nevada, Las Vegas), and supports the Emergency Medical Outreach Fund (WSA National Newsletter, 2001 September, *18*(3), 19).

D. Music as a Resource

As with other specific aptitudes, "Musicality" can be used to enrich the lives of WSs in numerous ways, namely, through educational, socioemotional, and vocational applications.

Educational Applications

Music captures the attention of WSc and helps them stay on task. Music, songs, and rhyme seem to "speed up the learning process" (Udwin & Yule, 1998a) in learning basic information. This includes the times of day (getting up, meals, bath, bedtime), days of the week, months, and seasons of the year (WSA National Newsletter, 1988, Vol. *6*, pp. 15–19), as well as their own addresses and phone numbers (WSA National Newsletter, 1993 Spring, Vol. *10*, pp. 10–12). Music and tunes may be used to help establish routine, rule-governed patterns of behavior, like washing one's hands before dinner (Udwin et al., 1996); songs may be used to help build vocabulary and teach words in foreign languages (Scheiber, 2000). Participation in musical activities may even be used as a reinforcer in certain circumstances.

In the classroom, a lesson with music at its core is more likely to be attended to, learned, and remembered than other kinds of instruction. Learning of alphabetic letters may be aided by associating a specific musical note or tone with each letter name. WS students who are "hooked on phonics" seem to be helped by setting rules of reading to music or rhyme, for example, "C" is pronounced as an "S" sound before "e," "i," and "y," as in "celery," "city," and "icy." Likewise, spelling of words or word families may be aided by including rhyming words in spelling exercises.

In the learning of arithmetic, counting songs, rhymes, and rhythm are effective ways to help WS students establish the relation between numerals and their corresponding quantities. Examples include the song "One-Two Buckle Your Shoe," and the common mnemonic rhyme "twen-ty, thir-ty, for-ty," and so forth. Number facts may be learned more easily by reciting groups of facts in songlike form or chants, like the series of addition or multiplication tables. As already mentioned, the "Minds and Music" summer camp is conducting a pilot program in using music to teach fractions to WSs (WSA National Newsletter, 1998 Fall, *15*(2), 16; WSA National Newsletter, 2001 Spring, *18*(2), 27; Scheiber, 2000).

Similarly, musical knowledge may be used to improve WSs' knowledge of semantic relational concepts and syntactical concepts of comparative and superlative. Differences in tone, melody, or rhythm that most WSs easily recognize may be used to "bootstrap" their understanding of general, relational concepts like "high," "low"; "above," "below"; "soft," "loud"; "before," "after"; "first," "second"; "many," "few"; "faster," "slower"; "same," "different"; and "all," "some." This is a vitally important area in which the application of music can make a real difference.

In addition, WSs' attraction to and familiarity with music may be used as a point of entry in studying history, geography, science, and so forth. Learning songs, such as "Davey Crockett," "Robert E. Lee," or "John Henry," can be a vehicle for WS students to learn about these well-known persons and the historical times in which they lived. Geography is much more exciting when WS students can sing a song of the country they are studying, like "The Mexican Hat Dance;" traditional songs in foreign languages, like "Frere Jacques"; or songs associated with cities like "Chicago," "New York," "San Francisco," and "St. Louis."

More advanced students may be asked to write musical compositions or lyrics that relate to a curricular topic or current event. Some may warrant being presented to the WS student's class or the entire school, particularly if music is part of a holiday program.

In summary, music can provide alternative ways for WSs to satisfy academic requirements and participate in school activities (Grejtak, 1996a). Many WSc are "mainstreamed" in music and are well accepted in that setting (WSA National Newsletter, 1994 Winter, p. 25).

Socioemotional Applications

Social Relationships. Unlike other areas of peer contact, like athletics and arts and crafts, where WSc are at a severe disadvantage, music provides an excellent opportunity for WSs to interact in contexts where they are competent and can contribute to the group. Most can hold their own in singing groups and choirs. Some can even play in a school orchestra or band. Thus, musical activities or groups provide a structured, supervised environment and an arena for peer interaction. Nonschool contacts with older and younger people with like interests or similar skill in music can further widen their social circles.

WSc often relish the role of performer and have no trepidation about appearing in front of schoolmates, music club peers, fellow musicians, or the community. This is one way in which WSs can experience success, receive praise for their accomplishments, and inspire other WSs (Udwin & Yule, 1998a). The father of one of the "Williams Five" reports that his daughter's "greatest pleasure is performing" (WSA National Newsletter, 1993 Summer, pp. 8–10).

Relieving Emotional Tension. Music can also serve as a relief from stress and frustration (Scheiber, 2000). Teenagers and young adults with WS often turn to music to seek refuge from emotional tension by singing, playing an instrument, or listening to music (Levine, 1994). Music therapist Marilyn Leeseberg reported that some WSa are able to compose songs with words that reflect their moods and can help release feelings of anger. Likewise, through improvisation, WSs may be able to express emotions of which they were unaware (Scheiber, 2000). Music may also be a source of self-regulation, which can help WSs mobilize their strength to control negative behavior (Levine, 1994). Other ways of using relaxation methods, including music tapes, to relieve feelings of anxiety and tension are discussed in chapter 7, p. 305.

At a more formal level, music therapy employs music and music-related strategies to promote WSs' mental health and general efficacy. Board certified music therapists are trained to help individuals achieve cognitive, physical, and emotional goals through a variety of music strategies rather than providing music instruction per se (Coleman, 1998).

A related type of formal program, eurhythmics, focuses on enhancing body awareness and coordination of body movements by developing the individual's spontaneous response to music. Sometimes the application can be less standardized, with music being used to stimulate body movement, coordination, and expression.

Programs of music therapy, however, are increasingly of interest to parents of WSs. Parents are being advised to consider including music therapy in their WS student's individual educational plan (IEP) (Coleman, 1998). The WSA national office states that "music therapy may be very helpful to young children in overcoming delays and to older children as an aid to learning and stress reduction" (WSA National Newsletter, 2001 September, *18*(3), 15). Parents or members of the student's IEP team may make requests for music therapy assessment. The assessment determines whether therapy interventions (individual, group, or consultative) would be "effective in assisting the child to attain his or her existing IEP goals" (Warlick, Director-U.S. Department of Education, cf. WSA National Newsletter, 2001 September, *18*(3), 15).

Vocational Opportunities

As the musical talents of WSc become better recognized and developed, the practicality of musically related forms of employment may also be examined (e.g., working in a music store in a nonsales capacity). At the very least, it would seem that WSs would value working in an environment that affords opportunities to listen to music. Importantly, both the Berkshire Hills Music Academy in Hadley, Massachusetts, and the Lili Claire Performing Arts Center in Las Vegas plan to include vocational components that involve training and placement in the performing arts and music-related careers (WSA Newsletter, March 1999, *16*(1), 16, 24). These programs should clarify and offer opportunities for WSs in music-related occupations.

In addition, recreational and leisure activities involving music, including volunteering to perform in children's hospitals, senior citizen residential homes, or nursing care facilities, may be of great value for both the WS performer and the audience. Whereas the extent to which WSs may be able to function in a professional capacity in music is not yet known, the personal satisfaction and enjoyment that music can provide in the way of joy, pleasure, and a big boost to self-esteem cannot be overrated.

V. SUMMARY: SPECIFIC APTITUDES

Like their aptitude for language, the four specific aptitudes of WSs—sociability (social skills and empathy), curiosity, memory, and musicality—are deeply embedded in the WS profile (see chap. 2). Distinguished from the more general language aptitude by their specificity, these aptitudes are both similar to, yet different from, each other in certain ways.

Central to each area is its positive features. Friendliness, pleasantness, sensitivity, and empathy are major characteristics in the area of sociability; intense inquisitiveness and special interests stand out in the area of curiosity. Strengths in verbal short-term memory, free recall, and facial recognition predominate the area of memory; talents for singing, playing musical instruments, pitch discrimination, and memory for music are common in the area of musicality.

Each area has its difficulties as well. Overfriendliness, poor peer relations, and overconcern about others are some problems associated with sociability. Obsessive interest in ordinary objects and certain topics are negative aspects of curiosity; deficits in visual-constructive memory, procedural memory, and short-term memory for certain kinds of information pose problems in the area of memory. Constraints in the ability to read music and play some kinds of musical instruments are negative aspects of WSs' musicality.

These deficiencies reflect, in turn, limitations in WSs' cognitive ability and behavioral control. Difficulty in differentiating between various kinds of social roles and relationships, and in curbing uninhibited modes of behavior, may contribute to WSs' problems of overfriendliness and poor peer relations. Difficulty in differentiating between reality and conjecture, and the ability to take effective action are factors in problems of overconcern. Hypersensitivity to certain kinds of sensory-perceptual stimuli may underlie WSs' tendency to become overattached to various objects or perseverate on selected topics of interest. Limitations in working memory, general knowledge, and the ability to inhibit irrelevant responses may contribute to memory problems. Deficiencies in coding and use of symbol systems may underlie difficulties in the ability to read music.

Fragmentation or dissociations are found within several areas. This is evident in the dissociation between friendliness and success with adults and WSs' disinterest or ineptness with peers, between their sensitivity and understanding of others, and the difficulty they often show in respecting the private space of peers. Within the area of memory, there are dissociations shown between WSs' skills in some areas of short-term memory like digit span, but not others like visuospatial span, and between strengths in phonological memory as in learning nonwords but not in learning to read phonologically similar words. There are WS strengths in remembering semantically salient items like poems and in their ability to retain long passages and songs for many years, which contrasts with their inability to remember certain kinds of information for even a few minutes. And the ability of some WSs in composing, transposing, retaining, and performing music is at odds with their difficulty in reading music and playing certain instruments.

Across areas, the special aptitudes also differ in the frequency and intensity with which they appear. Virtually all WSs display marked friendliness and empathy, inquisitiveness, certain kinds of phonological memory skills, excellent face recognition, good semantic memory, and story recall. Almost all WSs are said to love music; the majority seem relatively talented musically, and some exceptionally so. Other characteristics seem to be less regular in their occurrence, such as problems with peer relations, overattachment to objects or topics, certain memory skills, and special giftedness in music.

Intervention approaches for the four areas also share both commonalities and differences. For problems of sociability and curiosity, the psycho-educational strategies of social cognition, verbal mediational techniques, and control mechanisms usually dominate alternative types of interventions. Consultation with professional specialists is another option. Interventions in the area of memory frequently rely heavily on task management techniques for assisting in the processing of input, facilitating response output in areas such as following directions, and increasing the use of memory strategies. In the area of music, interventions center on cultivating the musical aptitudes of WSs and encouraging their participation in musical activities to provide structured socialization with peers and personal satisfaction.

In addition, the aptitude strengths of WSs may be applicable to promoting their development in other ways. Social skills and empathy may contribute to the effectiveness of using social rewards and verbal mediational strategies with WSs, as well as providing them with access to social activities and vocational and avocational options.

With proper training and supervision, WSs may be able to handle service-oriented positions (e.g., aide in a nursing home, child center, or hospital). Likewise, the topical interests of WSs may provide opportunities for related fields of study, adaptation to classroom assignments and the curriculum, as well as participation as a volunteer in school and community programs. Such interests may also facilitate social contacts, provide lifelong leisure activities, and become the catalyst for basic level jobs in horticulture, landscaping, grooming shops, pet stores, or hobby stores. Memory skills can be put to use in the classroom and home through applications that provide the opportunity for WSs to assume the role of historian or commentator on particular topics. Finally, music is a prime example of using a specific aptitude as a resource for promoting the personal, cognitive, social, educational, and vocational and avocational potential of WSs. It is an access behavior par excellence.

For many children with WS, life literally begins after 3:00 p.m. Once the school day is over, WSc are able to join other family members in recreational and daily activities (i.e., library, sports activity, parent's office). Unlike children with other forms of developmental disorder, who may be uncontrollable or physically atypical, WSc are often able to "blend in" with average children. For those WSs who are unable to participate or profit from such interactions, other types of social group experiences should be provided through ARC, Special Olympics, or fitness clubs, dance groups, and choir classes. In fact, most WSs may profit from such experiences.

By carefully fostering these special aptitudes, WSs may be able to realize their academic potential, expand their social, recreational, and vocational opportunities, improve their ability to handle frustration, and enhance their self-esteem.

6

Maladaptive Behaviors

Unfortunately, WSs often exhibit various kinds of behavior problems that affect their ability to function and live up to their potential. Unlike the problems described in previous chapters, the behavior problems of WSs are not usually offset by positive features. As one parent remarked, "It's like having a 4 year old child for 20 years [or more]."

The present chapter deals with six specific types of behavior problems. It also discusses four forms of behavior disorder and their relation to WS, including: (a) general behavior disturbance, (b) autism, (c) attention deficit hyperactivity disorder, and (d) emotional disorders.

Issues of intervention are addressed in the next chapter.

I. TYPES OF BEHAVIOR PROBLEMS

Although there are many ways in which the behavior problems of WSs can be classified, six problem areas tend to predominate in the reports of parents, teachers, clinicians, and researchers. These include fears and anxiety, distractibility and attentional problems, impulsivity, poor adaptability, low frustration tolerance, and atypical activity.

Other problems, such as compulsions, perseveration, aggression, and withdrawal, can be subsumed under these topics. Each of the six types of behavior problems is examined next.

A. Fears and Anxieties

Although some childhood fears and anxieties are part of normal development, those of WSc tend to be unusually pervasive, intense, and persistent, even past the childhood years. For many WSs, the world is a frightening place (Bailly et al., 1994), full of fears and anxieties that may be triggered any time by threatening or disturbing stimuli, or by anticipation of potential distress. Case studies describe some of the typical emotional states of WSs (von Arnim & Engel, 1964): "filled with anxiety," "very self-concerned"(Case 3); "anxiety and insecurity appears whenever he has to encounter small obstacles . . ." (Case 5).

Prevalence of Fears and Anxieties

Survey studies support the case studies. "Exaggerated worrying qualities" is evident in 81% of WSc (Utah Survey, Semel & Rosner, 1991a, 1991b); also 70% of WSc are rated as "worried," and 64% are "fearful" on Rutter's Parents' Questionnaire (Udwin et al., 1987). These are significantly higher rates than those of matched controls (Udwin & Yule, 1991). Based on psychiatric interviews, over half of WSs ($n = 51$) are classified as "worriers" or "excessively worried about the future," with 96% having marked, persistent anxiety-producing fears (Dykens et al., 2000).

WSc are rated higher than MR matched controls on the Anxiety subscale and the item "tense, anxious, or worried" on the Developmental Behavior Checklist (Einfeld et al., 1997; Einfeld et al., 2001). Comparisons with other groups underscore the high levels of fear and anxiety typically shown by WSs. For example, WSc exceed the norms for nonhandicapped, mentally retarded, and clinic patients on the "worry and anxiety" scale of the Personality Inventory for Parents (PIC) (Levine & Castro, 1994). Similarly, WSs are rated higher than PWs and MRs on the item "has many fears" (Dykens & Rosner, 1999). Even in adulthood, WSs are said to exhibit high levels of anxiety; of those in job situations, 90% are reported to have problems with anxiety (Davies et al., 1997). Nearly all WSa are described by parents as being "anxious," and 73% are said to exhibit anxiety (Davies et al., 1998).

The almost universal nature of WSs' fears and anxieties is widely acknowledged, although the intensity of reaction varies. Some WSs may be on "edge," uneasy, or worried, whereas others may be beset with phobias and panic states (Scheiber, 2000).

Types of Fears and Anxieties

The fears and anxieties of WSc may be reactions to a host of stimuli, events, and situations. These may include natural or imagined disasters, changes in schedule or plans, certain kinds of animals, sensory stimuli, motor tasks, new experiences, and the possibility of failure. Many WSs worry excessively about people's health and safety, including their own (Dykens et al., 2000; Scheiber, 2000). Concern about arguments and being teased may reflect WSs' social sensitivities (Dykens et al., 2000; Scheiber, 2000).

According to Isabelle Delga, a practicing child psychiatrist, the perceptual-motor aspects of WSc's fears and anxieties set them apart from those of other children (personal communication, Paris, June 1991). Problems of visual-spatial-motor performance, auditory hypersensitivity, tactile defensiveness, and gravitational insecurities constantly challenge the ability of WSs to carry out daily functions without emotional cost (Dilts et al., 1990; Udwin et al., 1987).

WSc are often frightened and anxious about performing motor or eye–hand tasks, such as riding a bicycle or catching a ball, as well as drawing, coloring, pasting, cutting, and writing tasks (see chap. 4, "Perceptual and Motor Performance"). Visuospatial confusions may contribute to problems of spatial orientation and fear of getting lost.

Acute distress and anticipatory anxiety about sudden, unexpected sounds like bells, machines, and applause afflict most WSs. Thunderstorms can be absolutely terrifying. These reactions, and their intensity, distinguish WSs from individuals with learning disability, DS, and Frag X, who have these problems to a lesser degree (Marriage & Turk, 1996)

Most WSc can be devastated by unexpected changes in routine or schedule that seem commonplace or merely inconvenient to others (Semel & Rosner, 1991b; Vaal, 1994). Some adults with WS also show these fears and anxieties (Udwin, 1990). Their excessive worrying and obsessive behavior can be very difficult to deal with (Plissart, Borghgraef, Van Den Berghe, & Fryns, 1994a).

Fear of new experiences is reported for 38% of WSc in one survey (Midwest WSA Region Survey, WSA National Newsletter, 1989 April, pp. 21–22), and for 47% of WSc in another (WSA Checklist Survey, Semel & Rosner, 1991a, 1991b). Anxiety about changes in plans and problems of rigidity are shown by other child groups with mental retardation, as well as those with learning disability (LDs), autism, and ADD (Schoenbrodt & Smith, 1995).

Another widespread problem is "fear of failure." In open-ended interviews, 34% of parents and teachers spontaneously mentioned that WSc are "overanxious to please" and need constant reassurance that they are performing satisfactorily (Udwin et al., 1987). Unfortunately, anxieties and fears about motor tasks, disrupted routines, and academic inadequacy may become so acute that they control WSc' ability and willingness to perform (Tharp, 1986). They may even avoid initiating certain tasks. Many children with learning disabilities are also likely to fear failure.

WSs often display fear of commonplace situations, like visits to the doctor or dentist, receiving shots or injections, having a haircut or fingernails trimmed, exposure to certain animals, and potential health risks threatening their own welfare and that of others. Spontaneous comments of parents and teachers indicate that over 36% of WSc display "undue anxiety," evidenced by crying easily or worrying over imagined disasters and unfamiliar situations (Udwin et al., 1987).

This wide range of fears and anxieties is not only manifested by WSs as a group, it is also commonly exhibited by WSs as individuals. Fifty percent or more of WSs ($n = 46$) are reported to have 41 different fears (sic) compared to only 2 fears for individuals in a matched control group (Dykens et al., 2000). This may account for many of the problem behaviors of WSs.

Emotionality

Difficulty in modulating emotions is another significant feature of WSs' fears and anxieties. This intensity is evident in the way they show "extreme excitement when happy," "tearfulness in response to apparently mild distress," and "terror in response to apparently mildly frightening events"(Levine, 1993). WSc also tend to be emotionally labile, that is, to show instability or fluctuations of emotion (Levine, 1993; Vaal, 1994). Emotional lability and nervous excitement are evident in WS adolescents and adults as well (Finucane, 1996). People with special needs are generally more vulnerable to problems of fear and anxiety than most others (Levine, 1994).

Along the same lines, research on temperament indicates that WSc and WSa are more likely to display extremely strong, intense emotional reactions than evident in the norms for normal children or the ratings for a matched group of mentally retarded adults (Plissart et al., 1994a; Tomc et al., 1990).

On the personality factor "emotional stability," WSc are rated lower than normally developing children but comparable to children with PW and Frag X syndrome (Van Lieshout et al., 1998; Wiegers et al., 1994). Sixty-four percent of WSs are reported to be "labile" (cf. Dykens et al., 2000, p. 125). WSc are also more likely than matched MR controls to be rated high on the item "inappropriately happy or elated" (Einfeld et al., 1997; Einfeld et al., 2001; also see chap. 5, Section I A, p. 189).

Levine (1994) attributed the high emotionality of many WSs to several factors. These include difficulty tuning out extraneous noxious sounds, distressing sights, or tactile stimulation. Once an emotional response is triggered, it often accelerates in intensity with little likelihood that WSs will be able to modulate, terminate, or habituate to the response. WSs often perpetuate and "relive" unpleasant, fearful, and anxiety-provoking experiences from the past (Scheiber, 2000). Some perseverate on these experiences for a long time.

Table 6.1 presents a summary of research studies dealing with the fears, anxieties, and emotionality of WSs.

TABLE 6.1
Research on Fears, Anxieties, and Emotionality of WSs

Type of Behavior	Frequency or Result	Source or Reference
Exaggerated Worrying	WSc 81%	Semel & Rosner, Utah Survey
Worried; Fearful	WSc 70%; 64%	Udwin et al., 1987
	WSc > Norms N	
	WSc ~ Norms MR	
Fearful[#]	WSc > MA Controls	Udwin & Yule, 1991
Worriers	WSs 50%	Dykens et al., 2000
Worried about the Future	WSs 57%	
Anxiety-Producing Fears	WSs 96%	
Anxiety Subscale[#]	WSc > MR Controls	Einfeld et al., 1997, 2001
Tense, Anxious, Worried[#]		
Worry & Anxiety[#]	WSc > Norms N	Levine & Castro, 1994
	WSc > Norms CL	
Many Fears[#]	WSs > PWs, MRs	Dykens & B. Rosner, 1999
Anxious on the Job	WSa 90%	Davies et al., 1997
Anxiety	WSa 73%	Davies et al., 1998
Fears New Experiences	WSc 47%	Semel & Rosner, Utah Survey
	WSc 38%	WSA Regional Survey
Multiple Fears (Md)	WSs ((41 fears) > Controls (2)	Dykens et al., 2000
Anxious & Frightened[#]	WSs > LD, DS, Frag X	Marriage & Turk, 1996
Emotional Intensity[#]	WSs ~ Controls MR	Plissart et al., 1994;
		Tomc et al., 1990
Emotional Stability[#]	WSc < Controls N;	Wiegers et al., 1994;
	WSc ~ PW, Frag X	Van Lieshout et al., 1998
Labile	WSs 64%	Dykens et al., 2000
Inappropriately Happy or Elated[#]	WSc > MR Controls	Einfeld et al., 1997, 2001

Note: % = percentage frequency; # = mean amount; > /< = significantly more/significantly less; ~ = similar, not significantly different; Md = median value; NORMS = norms or previous sample; Controls = subject group; N = normally developing; MR = mentally retarded; CL = clinic group; LD = learning disabled; DS = Down syndrome; PW = Prader–Willi; Frag X = Fragile X syndrome; WSc = WS children; WSs = individuals with WS, children and adults.

WSs' equanimity may also be undermined by their desperate need for total predictability and stability, which is impossible to achieve under even the best of circumstances. Dilts et al. (1990) interpreted the insecurity, anxiety, and perseverative worrying of WSc as another manifestation of their "hyperreactivity."

All segments of the population become more vulnerable to emotional problems during adolescence, including people with special needs. In fact, many WS youngsters become "moody and more aware of their differences" as they enter adolescence (WSA National Newsletter, 1993 Fall, 10, 24–26). Concerned parents of adolescents and young adults with WS have used the WSA National Newsletter to reach out to other parents who may have observed the "onset of anxiety or [deep] depression" in their WS offspring (e.g., National Newsletter, 1993 Summer, Vol. 10, 21).

More serious kinds of emotional disorders that may meet the criteria of pervasiveness, severity, and disruptiveness required for diagnosis of psychiatric behavior disorders are discussed later in Section II, Part D, Behavior Disorders.

B. Distractibility and Attentional Problems

Distractibility, poor concentration, and attentional problems are at the core of behavioral disturbance in WS. They predominate in frequency and severity over many of the other behavior problems of WSs (Frank, 1983; Udwin & Yule, 1991).

Distractibility is similar to attentional problems in that both involve difficulties with concentration. But, there are differences as well. Perceptual factors like auditory hypersensitivity, tactile defensiveness, visual impairment, and the presence of objects of special interest play a major role in triggering this problem in WSs. In contrast, "poor attention" is usually task dependent or situationally determined in WSc. Thus, these two types of difficulty, distractibility and poor attention, tend to be stimulus and task related, respectively. Both may disrupt performance and interfere with learning in many ways. WSc may become so preoccupied with irrelevant stimuli that they become oblivious to the assigned task.

Research on Distractibility

The universality of distractibility and poor concentration is evident in parents' reports: 100% of WSc are described as distractible and as having concentration problems (Utah Survey, Semel & Rosner, 1991a, 1991b). Parents identify distractibility as the "primary behavior problem" of WSc on Achenbach's Child Behavior Checklist (CBCL), a measure of behavioral disturbance (Dilts et al., 1990), and 100% of parents report that older WSc "can't concentrate or pay attention" on the CBCL (Pagon et al., 1987).

Certain objects seem to be especially distracting for WSs, although the particular type varies with the individual. Parents report that WSc often overrespond to background auditory stimuli (e.g., running motors, engines, vending machines, refrigerators and freezers, airplanes, helicopters, cars, trucks, and fire engines). The subtle noise or regular movement of a ceiling fan or a moving object entrances some WSc. Many seem compelled to search unfamiliar places for the source of unusual sounds or devices. Sudden noise and movement distract most WSc. Shiny items (e.g., chrome, copper pennies, and silver buttons) are objects of fascination for some. Ordinary objects with colorful designs or unusual shapes may captivate still others (see chap. 5, "Curiosity," p. 212).

Commonplace kinds of stimuli that others disregard easily can completely overwhelm individuals with WS. Background stimulation, visual or auditory, can impact critically their ability to learn, their sense of well-being, and the quality of family life.

The distractibility of WSc also tends to exceed that of other groups. WSc are rated higher on "distractibility" than the norms for nonhandicapped children in studies of temperament (Tomc et al., 1990). They also score higher than the norms for nonhandicapped children, mentally retarded children, and clinic children on the Distractibility-Activity-Coordination scale of the Personality Inventory for Parents (PIC) (Levine & Castro, 1994). Likewise, WSc are rated significantly higher on "poor concentration" than a comparison group of mentally retarded children on Rutter's Parent's Questionnaire Scales (Udwin & Yule, 1991). Although learning disabled children and other groups of neurological impaired individuals display distractibility and attentional problems, WSc seem to be more vulnerable to these problems than most children with developmental disorders, with some exceptions (e.g., autistic children and those with ADHD).

In adulthood, "poor concentration" and "distractibility" are among the most frequently cited difficulties of WSs, although they are somewhat less common than in childhood (Finucane, 1996). These difficulties are noted in over 60% of WS adults (Udwin, 1990), and are rated high by parents on standardized questionnaires (Borghgraef et al., 1994), with 90% of WSa having problems with distractibility while working on the job (Davies et al., 1997). These difficulties are disruptive to the lives of 69% of WSa, who need "considerable supervision to stay on task" (Davies et al., 1998).

Research on Attentional Problems

Most WSs have problems maintaining a satisfactory level of attention and appear to have difficulty knowing what to do next, which is closely associated with their distractibility and poor concentration. Parents report that 97% of WSc have difficulty paying attention, and 88% pay attention to the "wrong aspect of situations" (Utah Survey, Semel & Rosner, 1991a, 1991b). This is often associated with messy and careless work habits, wasting time, and failure to complete tasks. WSs seem to resist paper and pencil work; they would rather talk to others. So do many children with learning disorders.

Comparatively, WSc are rated significantly worse than MRc, matched controls, on "short attention" at two age levels ($M = 9;2$ yrs, Einfeld et al., 1997; and $M = 14;8$ yrs, Einfeld et al., 2001).

Interestingly, parents and teachers frequently mention that WSc tend to exhibit marked fluctuations in their level of attention. That is, attention is often limited except when WSs are involved in an area or activity of special interest. A cogent example is depicted in Oliver Sack's television program, "The Mind Traveler" (PBS, September 15, 1998) in which Heidi, an 8-year-old with WS, responds quite differently to various displays in an aquarium. She shows a total lack of concentration when viewing the cuttlefish, which contrasts with her total absorption when feeding barnacles during the same visit.

Direct observation of WSc and DSc substantiate these findings. Half of the WSc compared to none of the DSc have difficulty staying on task and remaining seated during a neurological examination (Trauner et al., 1989). In a similar vein, WSs are rated lower than a matched group of mentally retarded subjects on the item "likely to continue an activity until it's finished" (Plissart et al., 1994). Interestingly, both groups are said to show a "variable level of concentration or persistence in activities" on the same Parents Temperament Questionnaire (Plissart et al., 1994).

Likewise, one half of a small sample of WSs are said to exhibit "significant problems with attention and concentration" based on parents' ratings on the CBCL and Conner's Abbreviated Questionnaire (Bregman, 1996). Another study reports that 87% of WSc display attention problems of borderline clinical significance on the CBCL (Greer et al., 1997).

Clinical researchers such as Vaal (1994) and Levine (1993) asserted that WSc have problems with inattention, a short attention span, and distractibility. But, it is also important to note that most WSc lack the pervasiveness of distractibility and inattention exhibited by children clinically diagnosed as having ADD (Wender, 1987), unless the WSc also have ADD (see Section II, "Behavior Disorders").

Table 6.2 summarizes research studies on WS distractibility and attentional problems.

C. Impulsivity

Many WSc act suddenly or impetuously without considering the consequences of their actions (e.g., such as dashing out into the street without looking, leaving their seats in the classroom without permission, calling out to other students in class, displaying compulsive greeting behavior, not waiting for an entire question to be asked before trying to respond, calling out answers, continually interrupting conversations, and wandering about). These actions are annoying and troublesome indicators of WS impulsivity. WSs often act before they can think things through.

The ability to inhibit or hold back responding at will is usually acquired gradually over the childhood years. In individuals with WS, this form of socialized behavior may be significantly delayed or impaired. Consistent with their problems of distractibility and poor attention, many WSs have difficulty curtailing and controlling their internal impulses. Thus, impulsivity is an outward manifestation of the internal, uncontrolled distractions and the uninhibited, unrestrained patterns of WS behavior. It may also reflect difficulty in understanding the relation between cause and effect (see Section D, "Rigidity").

TABLE 6.2
Research on Distractibility and Attentional Problems of WSs

Type of Behavior	Frequency or Result	Source or Reference
Distractible	WSc 100%	Semel & Rosner, Utah Survey
Concentration Problems	WSc 100%	
Can't Concentrate or Pay Attention	WSc 100%	Pagon et al., 1987
Poor Concentration	WSa 60%	Udwin, 1990
Distractibility on the Job	WSa 90%	Davies et al., 1998
Curious About Shiny Objects	WSc 44%	Semel & Rosner, Utah Survey
Difficulty Paying Attention	WSc 97%	Semel & Rosner, Utah Survey
Short Attention	WSc > MRc	Einfeld et al., 1997; Einfeld et al., 2001
Pays Attention to Wrong Aspects of Task	WSc 88%	Semel & Rosner, Utah Survey
Problems Staying on Task	WSc > DSc	Trauner et al., 1989
Significant Problems with Attention and Concentration	WSs 50%	Bregman, 1996
Attention Problems	WSc 98%	Greer et al., 1997
Persistence/Concentration[#]	WSs ~ Controls MR	Plissart et al., 1994
Distractibility[#]	WSc > Norms N	Tomc et al., 1990
Distractibility/Activity[#]	WSc > Norms N WSc > Norms CL	Levine & Castro, 1994
Poor Concentration[#]	WSc > Controls MR	Udwin & Yule, 1991

Note: % = percentage frequency; # = mean amount; > /< = significantly more/significantly less; ~ = similar, not significantly different; NORMS = norms or previous sample; Controls = subject group; N = normally developing; MR = mentally retarded; CL = clinic group; DS = Down syndrome; WSc = WS children; WSa = WS adults; WSs = WS children and adults.

Nevertheless, impulsivity in WSs has been neglected as a research topic, despite its disruptive and detrimental effects. Although mentioned occasionally by some clinical researchers (e.g., Meyerson & Frank, 1987), this is usually within the context of discussing WSs' problems with concentration (Udwin & Yule, 1988, 1989), rule-governed behavior, and possible involvement with ADHD (Dilts et al., 1990).

Research on Impulsivity

Not all WSc are characterized as impulsive. But, parents report that 71% of WSc show "inappropriate impulsive behaviors," 77% have difficulty waiting for attention, and 52% have difficulty with turn-taking behaviors (Utah Survey, Semel & Rosner, 1991a, 1991b). Similarly, 75% of WSs are identified as "impulsive" (Dykens et al., 2000). PWs and WSs are said to share the personality characteristic "impulsivity" (Dykens & Rosner, 1999).

Interestingly, teacher ratings of WS students on the Schoolroom Social Performance scale of Teacher Rating of Social Skills (TROSS-C) that meas-

TABLE 6.3
Research on WS Impulsivity

Type of Behavior	Frequency or Result	Source or Reference
Impulsive	WSc 71%	Semel & Rosner, Utah Survey
Difficulty Waiting for Attention	WSc 77%	Semel & Rosner, Utah Survey
Difficulty with Turn-taking	WSc 52%	
Impulsivity	WSs 75%	Dykens et al., 2000
Schoolroom Social Performance (i.e., Impulse Control)[#]	WSc < Norm N, ~ LD, BD, MR	Levine & Castro, 1994
Impulse Control Problems	WSa	Finucane, 1996

Note: % = percentage frequency; # = mean amount; > /< = significantly more/significantly less; ~ = similar, not significantly different; NORMS = norms or previous sample; Controls = subject group; N = normally developing; LD = learning disability; BD = behavior disorder; MR = mentally retarded; WSc = WS children; WSa = WS adults; WSs = WSc children and adults.

ures "controls impulses" and "paying attention" are lower than that of regular students but comparable to those of students with other kinds of special needs (Levine & Castro, 1994). Also, some adults with WS are said to be subject to "impulse control" problems, a severe form of impulsivity (Finucane, 1996).

Table 6.3 presents a summary of research on WS impulsivity.

D. Poor Adaptability

Many WSs have difficulty adjusting to the constraints and demands of their physical, social, personal, educational, or vocational world. Most seem limited in their ability to adapt to changing conditions in various aspects of their lives: activities, schedules, and plans, as well as their own needs and goals. This rigidity is a problem area for many WSs (Levine, 1993). It is also apparent in the obsessive compulsivity of some WSs and the common difficulty of many in following instructions. This inflexibility often places WSs at a distinct disadvantage in numerous situations.

In many ways, the "impulsivity" and "rigidity" of WSs are opposite sides of the same coin. Impulsivity is characterized by lack of restraint and inadequate control over internal impulses, whereas rigidity is characterized by lack of flexibility. With impulsivity, the problem is one of response suppression; with poor adaptability, the problem is a failure of response mobilization. In both cases, the underlying problem is difficulty in response management and response systems.

Resistance to Change

As life involves continual change, the everyday functioning of WSs is repeatedly challenged by both minor and major shifts in conditions. Problems of rigidity and feelings of anxiety may be triggered by a lack of structure, disruption of established routines, plans, or schedules, or the presence of new, complex, or unfamiliar situations (Levine, 1993; Semel, 1988; Tharp, 1986; Vaal, 1994).

Seemingly minor changes in a class schedule, new chores at home, or cancellation of a trip may trigger acute anxiety and upset. Even commonplace situations like running out of supplies of toothpaste, cereal, raisins, or toilet paper can throw WSc into a tizzy. They may become anxious, fearful, tense, confused, angry, recalcitrant, noncompliant, and sometimes even nonfunctional. As with brain-damaged individuals, the least little thing—a slight incident, minor failure, or frustration—can set off a catastrophic response as though this ordinary situation were cataclysmic (Goldstein, 1948). To compound matters, when notified about an unanticipated change in plans, WSs tend to worry that the new plan will "go wrong."

One mother paints a vivid picture of how the world appears to a young WS boy and his family (Anonymous, 1985):

> The world about him made no sense to him. . . . To help him grasp a sense of order we made an effort to live more predictably and to speak precisely. . . . One did not say . . . "Time for dinner, wash your hands." We guided him, concretely, through each step. . . . We had to learn to focus on one thing at a time. . . . We lived in slow motion. (pp. 964–965)

Parents report that over three fourths of WSc (77%) have "difficulty handling changes in routine," and 84% show the related problem of difficulty in understanding cause–effect relations (Utah Survey, Semel & Rosner 1991a, 1991b). This problem plays a role in WSc's impulsivity, because it obscures the relation between acts, such as interrupting or not sitting still, and the consequences of those acts.

Problems of rigidity are also reported in studies of WS temperament. WSs are rated lower than the norms for nonhandicapped children on measures of adaptability, such as resistance to change, difficulty in adapting quickly to new demands, and slowness to adapt (Tomc et al., 1990).

Compared to other syndrome groups, however, WSs are at less of a disadvantage (Plissart et al., 1994). Parent ratings of adaptability tend to be lower for WSs than for a matched group with various syndromes, but the difference is insignificant and both groups are said to show "variable adaptability to new or changed situations" (Plissart et al., 1994a). WSs share with PWs being upset by changes in routine to a similar degree that exceeds, however, the reactions of MRs (Dykens & B. Rosner, 1999). Children with learning disability also tend to have problems with rigidity, as do individuals with autism.

Rigidity persists at the adult level. Work supervisors report that 71% of WSa employees "dislike changes in routine" (Davies et al., 1997).

Obsessive Compulsive Behaviors

WSs also tend to engage in various kinds of obsessive compulsive behaviors: compulsive greeting behavior, compulsive talking, compulsive need to identify source of sudden background sounds, obsessive watching of spinning objects, listening to (or watching) motors, fixating on specific objects and topics of special interest, and obsessive interest in the health and welfare of self and others. Other kinds of obsessive compulsive behaviors are described in later sections, namely, a compulsion to fidget (e.g., move to and fro, side to side), a compulsion to engage in self-injurious behaviors (SIBS; e.g., picking at cuticles or scabs), and a tendency to perseverate.

WSc are rated significantly higher than MRc on the item "obsessed, preoccupied with an idea or activity" at grade school age (M = 9;2 yrs, Einfeld et al., 1997), but the difference is not reliable when the subjects are retested 5 years later (Einfeld et al., 2001). Other studies suggest that 43% of adults with WS exhibit "preoccupations/obsessions," and 20% engage in compulsive behaviors (Davies et al., 1998).

In group sessions concerning the problems of adolescents and adults with WS, parents often exchange information about the compulsive tendencies of their WSs. This can include anecdotes about the ritualistic routines of some WSs, such as cracking of knuckles and other habit patterns. Parents generally agree that once young people with WS begin to exhibit a behavior, like rubbing their legs or lap, or a response pattern in connection with a certain activity like getting dressed, the routine will often become elaborated and ritualized. As one mother explained: "Once she [WS young adult] gets started, you just can't stop her." Perhaps these driven forms of behavior serve to reduce WSa's anxiety.

More severe kinds of obsessive compulsive behavior may constitute a type of clinical condition (see section II. D, "Emotional Disorders").

Difficulty in Following Directions

Following directions is a difficult task for many children with WS. Parents attest to such problems and so do teachers. In fact, 87% of WSc are said to "have difficulty following directions" (Utah Survey, Semel & Rosner, 1991a, 1991b).

The reason why this occurs merits further consideration, because parents and teachers often interpret WSs' failure to conform as a sign of negativity, disobedience, or recalcitrance. Instead, WSs' failure to carry out the directions, commands, or instructions of another person may reflect a variety of factors. These may include problems with language comprehension, auditory processing problems, distractibility, inattention, or sometimes refusal to cooperate. Problems in understanding the task, its sequence of steps, or inability on the part of the WS individual to carry out the instructions or task may also deter performance. "Failure to listen" is more understandable and treatable after realizing that this is because the message simply did not register due to interference from other sounds or stimuli. The particular cause or causes must be determined on an individual basis.

It should also be noted that children with ADHD have difficulty following directions (Schoenbrodt & Smith, 1995). However, their difficulties seem to reflect maladaptive forms of response more so than in the case of WSc, whose problems often center on language comprehension. In fact, many WSc are extremely eager to please and will follow instructions if they are able to do so.

In any event, there is a great deal of evidence from the comments and observations of parents and clinicians and results of research studies to indicate that many WSs are prone to problems of rigidity. Perhaps their deep-seated craving for stability and reliance on others is based on their need to establish some sense of continuity and patterning in their lives.

In view of WSs' cognitive difficulty in understanding cause–effect relations and other fundamental concepts, as well as their susceptibility to intense emotional reactions, it is no wonder that many have problems with response mobilization. Under such conditions, the world is a scary, unpredictable place for many WSs. Even in adulthood, the need for order and planning persists (Lenhoff comments, Levine & Castro, 1994).

On the other hand, developmental or chronological age may play a role in determining the kinds of change that an individual with WS may encounter, the resources available for handling change, and the types of intervention that may be effective for the individual.

Table 6.4 presents a summary of research on problems of poor adaptability in WSs.

E. Low Frustration Tolerance

In general, WSc are seen as docile, gentle, and very polite. But, they can become extremely upset and respond excessively if their wishes are denied or they are faced with minor kinds of change or unpleasant situations. The following are descriptions of how WSs react to stress: "They're on a short leash," "when he makes a mistake, he tears the paper up," "he has a tight spring," and "any little thing going wrong can set her off."

Von Arnim and Engel (1964) offered insight into WSc's vulnerability to frustration:

> The children are hypersensitive to feelings of frustration, which may arise either because their motor disability prevents them from carrying out their plans and designs or because their friendliness is not returned by others as

TABLE 6.4
Research on Problems of Poor Adaptability in WSs

Type of Behavior	Frequency or Result	Source or Reference
Difficulty with Changes in Routine	WSc 77%	Semel & Rosner, Utah Survey
Difficulty Seeing Cause–Effect Relations	WSc 84%	Semel & Rosner, Utah Survey
Adaptability[#]	WSc < Norms N	Tomc et al., 1990
Adaptability[#]	WSs ~ MR Controls	Plissart et al., 1994
Upset by Changes in Routine[#]	WSs ~ PWs > MRs	Dykens & B. Rosner, 1999
Dislike Changes in Routine	WSs 71%	Davies et al., 1997
Obsessed/Preoccupied with an Idea or Activity[#]	WSc > MRc	Einfeld et al., 1997
Preoccupations/Obsessions	WSa 43%	Davies et al., 1998
Compulsive Behaviors	WSa 20%	
Difficulty Following Directions	WSc 87%	Semel & Rosner, Utah Survey

Note: % = percentage frequency; # = mean amount; > /< = significantly more/significantly less; ~ = similar, not significantly different; NORMS = norms or previous sample; Controls = subject group; N = normally developing; MR = mentally retarded; PW = Prader–Willi; WSc = WS children; WSa = WS adults.

expected. Their amicable manner will not bear much strain and soon gives way to outbursts of temper [sic] or moments of despair. (p. 375)

Contributing to the stress and low frustration tolerance of WSs are multiple factors, such as internal discomfort (e.g., thirst, tactile defensiveness, upset stomach), denial of a request, and feelings of vulnerability, inadequacy, and helplessness. Many WSc are easily upset by criticism and quickly frustrated by failure or the anticipation of failure. With various deficiencies and thwarted desires, it is no wonder that WSs tend to "fly off the handle," "retreat," or "go through the motions" when their best efforts are merely obstacles to the success they crave. Learning disabled children also tend to have significant problems with low frustration tolerance.

Parental ratings of temperament reveal that WSc have a lower "threshold to arousal" (i.e., are more likely to be aroused by low intensity stimuli) than the norms for nonhandicapped children (Tomc et al., 1990). On the personality item "overreact(s) to frustrations and mishaps," WSc are rated higher than academically achieving children but comparable to children with Prader–Willi and Fragile X syndrome (Wiegers et al., 1994). "Low frustration tolerance" is attributed to WSs and PWs to a similar degree and both groups are lower than MR controls on frustration tolerance (Dykens & B. Rosner, 1999). In adulthood, 62% of WSa are said to exhibit a "low threshold for annoyance compared to others" (Davies et al., 1998).

Although WSs may differ in the form of their particular response to frustration, three response patterns dominate the descriptions and remarks of parents, teachers, and clinicians. These include outer-directed, or "fight," responses; inner-directed, or withdrawal, responses; and perseverative responses.

Outer-Directed Responses

The most conspicuous and frequently mentioned response of WSs to frustration is temper tantrums (e.g., Semel, 1988; Tharp, 1988; Udwin & Yule, 1998a, 1998b). According to child specialists (i.e., psychologists, psychiatrists, educational specialists), tantrums are indicative of high levels of stress and a low threshold for tolerating frustration. Other forms of outer-directed responses include aggression and "acting out."

Temper Tantrums. Parents report that 69% of WSc have temper tantrums when frustrated. The tantrums of 65% are said to be triggered by particular situations, like being denied permission or by a change in plans (Utah Survey, Semel & Rosner, 1991a, 1991b). Another study indicates that the incidence of tantrums in WSc, 61%, exceeds that of a previously tested sample of children with mental retardation (Udwin et al., 1987). Yet another study finds that WSc tend to be more likely than MRc to have tantrums (74.3% to 59%), but the difference is not significant (Einfeld et al., 1997). Even this trend is not present 5 years later (Einfeld et al., 2001).

Across studies, the frequency of temper tantrums ranges between 48% and 74% in WSs (Dykens et al., 2000). Still, a considerable number of adults with WS display temper tantrums (39%), although this is generally less than in WSc (Udwin, 1990).

"Acting Out." The presence of other types of externally directed responses is also noted (Udwin et al., 1987). Several "antisocial" items on Rutter's Parent Questionnaire yield rather high frequencies, namely, 48% of WSc are said to be "destructive," 59% are "disobedient," 48% "fight," 30% tell "lies," and 16% are "bullies" (Udwin et al., 1987). However, these frequencies do not differ significantly from those of MRc, except for one antisocial item, "Destructive." Teacher ratings of the same WSc show that only 12% are rated "destructive" on Rutter's Teachers Questionnaire (Udwin et al., 1987).

Other studies report the presence of such behaviors in some WSs, but not in a consistent majority. "Disobedience" is said to range between 32% and 60% of WSs in various studies (Dykens et al., 2000). WSc do not differ significantly from MRc in the frequency of "lies" (12% vs. 8%), and they are actually lower than normal controls on "obstinate" and "lies" (Gosch & Pankau, 1994b). "Antisocial" forms of behavior, including "lies," "steals," "hides," and "lights fires" seldom occur in WSc, with no significant difference between them and MRc (Einfeld et al., 1997; Einfeld et al., 2001).

Aggression. The situation regarding "aggressivity" in WSc is also problematic. In contrast to their generally noncontentious demeanor, WSc are rated higher than the norms for children referred to clinics on some items of the "unsocialized combative" scale of the PIC (Levine & Castro, 1994). For example, one third of WSc are said to have "trouble with aggression," or "may sometimes hit." There are also individual accounts of WSc engaging in aggression, such as a teacher reporting that a 12-year-old WS girl "beat up" on another student who had made minor insulting remarks.

Levine (1994) attributed these behaviors to problems of impulse control rather than to WSc having a major issue with aggression. However, a few WSc are known to shift from "smiles" to "snarls" under seemingly minor circumstances; they are prone to become agitated and exhibit frequent, intense "meltdowns," the reasons for which are being investigated (Levine & Wharton, 2001).

There is no question, however, that some WSs show aggressive forms of behavior. Between 25% and 47% of WSs are described as "fights, aggressive" (Dykens et al., 2000). Yet, WSc do not exceed MRc on such behavior. No group difference between WSc and MRc is obtained on items such as "hits other children" (Gosch & Pankau, 1994b), or the Disruptive subscale of behaviors that include "kicks, hits" (Einfeld et al., 1997). Similarly, WSs are rated significantly lower than PWs or MRs on "Vengeance" or "mean spirited" (Dykens & Rosner, 1999).

Along the same lines, WSa display little in the way of disturbing behavior compared to adults with other forms of mental retardation (Borghgraef et al., 1994; Plissart et al., 1994a). In fact, WSa tend to be rated lower on "aggressive behavior" by parents and caregivers than normed scores on a standardized questionnaire (Borghgraef et al., 1994).

Developmentally, external-aggressive behavior generally decreases in frequency over the childhood years: The incidence is less in WSa than in WSc, although the frequency of other emotional problems, such as depression, increases with age (Gosch & Pankau, 1996b).

Still, problems of aggression persist in some WSa: Thirty-eight percent are reported to have problems of "anger management" while on the job (Davies et al., 1997). Parents and caregivers report that 41% of WSa display anger at least three times a week, 10% hit out physically at least once, another 10% deliberately break objects, and 4% are known to rip clothes or tear paper when angry (Davies et al., 1998). Thus, a minority of WSs at both age levels, WSc and WSa, have serious problems with aggression.

TABLE 6.5
Research on Low Frustration Tolerance of WSs: Outer-Directed Responses

Type of Behavior	Frequency or Result	Source or Reference
Low Threshold of Arousal[#]	WSc > Norm N	Tomc et al., 1990
Overreacts to Frustrations and	WSc > Nonhandicapped	Wiegers et al., 1994
Mishaps[#]	WSc ~ PWc & Frag Xc	
Low Frustration Tolerance[#]	WSs ~ PWs > MRs	Dykens & B. Rosner, 1999
Low Threshold for Annoyance	WSa 62%	Davies et al., 1998
Temper Tantrums	WSc 69%	Semel & Rosner, Utah Survey
Certain Stimuli Trigger Tantrums	WSc 65%	Semel & Rosner, Utah Survey
Tantrums	WSc 61% > Norms MR	Udwin et al., 1987
Tantrums[#]	WSc ~ MRc	Einfeld et al., 1997; 2001
Temper Tantrums	WSs 48%–74%	Dykens et al., 2000
Tantrums	WSa 39%	Udwin, 1990
Destructive, Disobedient,	WSc 48%, WSc 59%,	Udwin et al., 1987
Fights, Lies, Bullies	WSc 48%, WSc 30%, WSc 16%	
Destructive[#]	WSc > Norms MR	Udwin et al., 1987
Disobedient	WSs 32%–60%	Dykens et al., 2000
Lies[#]	WSc ~ MRc	Gosch & Pankau, 1994b
Obstinate; Lies[#]	WSc < N Controls	Gosch & Pankau, 1994b
Antisocial Behavior	WSc ~ MRc	Einfeld et al., 1997, 2001
Aggression[#]	WSc > NHc & CLc	Levine & Castro, 1994
Fights, Aggressive	WSs 25%–47%	Dykens et al., 2000
Hits Other Children	WSc ~ MRc	Gosch & Pankau, 1994b
Disruptive Behaviors[#]	WSc ~ MRc	Einfeld et al., 1997, 2001
Vengeance, Mean-Spirited[#]	WSs < PWs, MRs	Dykens & B. Rosner, 1999
Mixed Disturbed Behaviors[#]	WSa ~ MRa	Plissart et al., 1994
Aggression[#]	WSa ~ MRa	Borghgraef et al., 1994
External Aggressive Behavior	WSa < WSc	Gosch & Pankau, 1996b
Anger Management Problems	WSa 38%	Davies et al., 1997
Frequently Angry	WSa 41%	Davies et al., 1998
Hits Out, Destroys Objects	WSa 10%, WSa 10%	Davies et al., 1998

Note: % = percentage frequency; # = mean amount; > /< = significantly more/significantly less; ~ = similar, not significantly different; NORMS = norms or previous sample; Controls = subject group; N = normally developing; NH = nonhandicapped; PW = Prader–Willi; Frag X = Fragile (X) syndrome; CL = clinic patients; MR = mentally retarded; WSc = WS children; WSa = WS adults.

Nevertheless, the percentage of WSs with outer-directed forms of behavior is generally less than the frequency with which WSs exhibit fears and anxieties or distractibility and attentional problems.

Table 6.5 presents a summary of research on the low frustration tolerance of WSs and its manifestation in outer-directed forms of response.

Inner-Directed Responses

Inability to deal with frustration may be reflected in immature types of behavior, such as being peevish, "out of sorts," "on edge," touchy, cranky, or thin-skinned. These are forms of irritability, inner-directed ways of expressing frustration. More common in WSs than withdrawal responses, irritability at its extreme may be regarded as a sign of depression (*Diagnostic and Statistical Manual of Mental Disorders, DSM–IV*, APA, 1994). Worries and anxieties are often classified as "internalizing" kinds of maladaptive behavior (Dykens et al., 2000), which may be exacerbated by frustration. Withdrawal is most frequently observed in WSs as refusal to perform or risk failure. These also may be viewed as acts of passive or inward aggression.

Irritability. Generally, WSs are rated high on "irritability." For example, a significantly higher percentage of WSs are rated as "irritable" by parents and teachers on Rutter's Questionnaires than the norms for mentally handicapped youngsters. On the item "fussy," the raters disagree: Teachers but not parents rate WSc significantly higher than the normed percentage for MRc (Udwin et al., 1987).

Likewise, WSc are rated significantly higher on "irritability–immaturity" (i.e., more irritable, less mature) than a group of academically achieving children, but not higher than PWc or Frag Xc on the California Child Q-Set (Van Lieshout et al., 1998; Wiegers et al., 1994). The incidence of "irritability" in WSs ranges between 62% and 68% in various studies (Dykens et al., 2000). WSs and PWs also score similarly but higher than MRs on other kinds of inner-directed behaviors, for example, on the items "highly sensitive to rejection" and "low tolerance for teasing" (Dykens & B. Rosner, 1999). Along the same lines, parents describe 78% of WSc as "confused or seems in a fog" on the CBCL (Pagon et al., 1987).

In adulthood, WSa are rated as less tearful, quarrelsome, and impertinent than WSc on the CBCL (Gosch & Pankau, 1996b). On the other hand, 21% of WSa are said to show "irritability" (Davies et al., 1998), and 57% show "intolerance of others" on the job (Davies et al., 1997).

Self-Injurious Behaviors. Internally directed aggression in the form of "self-destructiveness," is occasionally mentioned in WSs (e.g., Meyerson & Frank, 1987). Unfortunately, some WSc have a tendency to engage in self-injurious behaviors (SIBS), such as picking their cuticles, sores, or scabs on their hands and other body parts. Levine (1993) noted "rocking, nail biting, or skin picking" as WS behaviors that may pose problems in the classroom and home and undermine the health and well-being of the child. Stereotyped motor movements like rocking are observed in about one half of WSa (Davies et al., 1998) (see Section F, "Atypical Activity"). SIBs may also be viewed as a form of atypical activity.

At times, the SIBs of some WSs may be so severe as to require medical attention to treat destructive sores, lesions, harmful abrasions, wounds, or bruises.

This type of self-abuse has been documented in a few WSa. Parents and caregivers observed that 21% of WSa engage in "skin-picking" (Davies et al., 1998).

Perseverative Types of Response to Frustration

Clinical observation indicates that WSc sometimes respond to frustrating conditions by perseverating or repeating the same response or response pattern. Sometimes this involves repetition of a specific response or response pattern that was once—but is no longer—appropriate. Oftentimes, the response is applied inappropriately in various situations. This is particularly the case in classroom or testing situations.

Von Arnim and Engel (1964) described the case of a 7-year-old WS boy (Case 4) who performed quite well on vocabulary items, but "tended to perseverate" when he was unable to solve "Similarity" problems on the same test (Wechsler Individual Scale, an early version of the WISC R).

Perseveration is not unique to WSs; it is often seen in other populations, such as autistic, brain-injured, learning disabled, and language-impaired individuals (including aphasic children and adults). Some researchers speculate that these youngsters may have various types of organic brain disorder, and perseveration may be a neurological sign.

WSs are more likely to show perseveration when they are fatigued or unable to cope with the task, situation, or its requirements. Sometimes perseveration is a defense against doing something that WSs view as odious or the required response is beyond the person's capability. Difficult tasks may also induce inner-directed responses, like "failure to try" and passive resistance.

Language perseveration of phrases, cliches, and topics of special interest may arise when the WS individual is "at a loss for words" or feels pressured to "keep the conversation going." These kinds of perseveration may be related to WSs' problems with word finding or language structure. Some WSc are reported to repeat words and phrases over and over again, and to engage in such behaviors significantly more so than MRc (Einfeld et al., 1997). This tendency decreases over a 5-year period so that WSc no longer differ significantly from MRc in this regard (Einfeld et al., 2001). WSc are at borderline levels of statistical significance in their tendency to exhibit perseveration as one kind of Thought Problem on the CBCL (Greer et al., 1997).

Repetition of a formerly correct motor response is also observed, such as in setting the table. In handwriting, the perseverative responding of WS students may be so strong that they actually go "off the page" when practicing the writing of difficult letters, like the cursive form of "f."

Some WSc perseverate in writing the number sequence "1, 2, 3, 4, 1, 2, 3, 4, 1, 2, 3, 4." This may be due to a particular difficulty in writing the numeral "5." Error repetition may also occur in motor tasks, as in trying to learn to tie one's shoelaces or copying a pattern or design. Some WSc line up toys endlessly without ever playing with them, thus demonstrating another way in which perseveration can manifest itself. Sometimes WSc exhibit stereotypic motoric responses by compulsively "spinning" or "twirling" objects or watching motors revolve. Thus, perseveration may be another manifestation of the rigidity and lack of flexibility described earlier.

Although there is little in the way of research or anecdotal reports regarding the perseverative tendencies of WSs, such responses do occur and should be noted. Although less obvious than temper tantrums or irritability, "blind" repetition or random, aimless repetitive responding may be warning signs of frustration and inability to cope with the task or situation. It may signal the need to modify or discontinue the task to be performed.

Perseverative tendencies may also negatively bias the evaluation of WSc. That is, perseverative responding may be interpreted as an indication of serious limitations in ability, more so than is really the case, rather than a possible sign of growing frustration.

Table 6.6 presents a summary of research on the low frustration tolerance of WSs and the inner-directed and perseverative ways in which it may be exhibited.

TABLE 6.6
Low Frustration Tolerance of WSs: Inner-Directed and Perseverative Responses

Type of Behavior	Frequency or Result	Source or Reference
Irritable	WSc > Norms N, Norms MR	Udwin et al., 1987
Irritability/Immaturity[#]	WSc > Controls N	Wiegers et al., 1994
	WSc ~ PWc & Frag Xc	Van Lieshout et al., 1998
Irritability	WSs 62%–68%	Dykens et al., 2000
Confused, in a Fog	WSc 78%	Pagon et al., 1987
Tearful, Quarrelsome	WSa < WSc	Gosch & Pankau, 1996b
Irritability	WSa 21%	Davies et al., 1998
Intolerant of Others on the Job	WSa 57%	Davies et al., 1997
Skin-Picking	WSa 21%	Davies et al., 1998
Perseverates on Words and Phrases[#]	WSc > MRc	Einfeld et al., 1997
	WSc ~ MRc	Einfeld et al., 2001
Perseverative Thought Problems[#]	WSc at Borderline Significance	Greer et al., 1997

Note. % = percentage frequency; # = mean amount; > /< = significantly more/significantly less; ~ = similar, not significantly different; WSa = WS adolescents &/or adults; WSc = WS children; NORMS = norms or previous sample; Controls = subject group; N = normally developing; MR = mentally retarded; PW = Prader–Willi; Frag X = Fragile X syndrome.

F. Atypical Activity

For the most part, WSs seem composed, subdued, and relatively inactive. There are, however, some WSc who seem to be constantly "on the go," and "set in motion." These youngsters bustle around a room looking at things, sometimes touching objects and, whenever possible, talking as they move about. They never seem to "tone down." Others are tireless in performing aberrant physical acts, like rocking, picking cuticles or scabs (SIBs), or hand-rubbing. Still others appear restless, "antsy," "on pins and needles," troubled, anxious, and agitated.

These are some of the types of atypical activity often associated with WS, namely, excessive restlessness and fidgeting, overactivity and hyperactivity, ADD or ADHD and "wandering."

All involve outward expressions of internal energy or stimulation that are difficult for the individual to modulate or control. All are maladaptive forms of behavior, serious to differing degrees. Some are merely troublesome, others can interfere with the normal functioning of WSs and those around them.

The status of many of these forms of atypical activity is still unclear, due partly to lack of systematic research and partly to problems of terminology. Clinical and scientific use of these terms often differs from the popular meanings of the same words, and sometimes even the clinical/scientific use of terms can vary with the specific test or investigator.

In this context, "restlessness" refers to continuous moving about, "fidgeting" refers to stereotypic motor patterns, "squirmy" means wiggly kinds of movements made while seated or standing, and "overactivity" and "hyperactivity" refer to excessive motion or movement patterns. "Hyperactivity" is also a form of behavior disturbance defined by the occurrence of certain behaviors (e.g., items on the hyperactive scale of Rutter's Questionnaires), as well as a symptom of the clinical condition ADD or ADHD (discussed in the next section).

Qualitative descriptions and research studies dealing with each of the following types of atypical activity are presented next: restlessness, fidgeting and stereotyped movements, "wandering," and overactivity and hyperactivity. Table 6.7 summarizes the research findings.

Restlessness

The literature on WS contains a number of references to high activity and "restlessness" in WSc and WSa. "Restlessness" literally means the absence of rest. It is used to describe people who are "continuously moving" or "discontent" (*Merriam-Webster's Deluxe Dictionary*, 1998). WSc may display roaming or roving behaviors in the classroom. They want to walk around. They have trouble staying in their seats.

TABLE 6.7
Research on Atypical Activity in WSs

Type of Behavior	Frequency or Result	Source or Reference
Activity[#]	WSc > Norms N	Tomc et al., 1990
Restless and Undirected	WSc ~ MRc	Gosch & Pankau, 1994b
Restlessness	WSa 60%	Udwin, 1990
Rocking, Twirling, or Finger Twisting Behaviors	WSc 62%	Semel & Rosner, Utah Survey
Twitches & Mannerisms[#]	WSc > Controls MR	Udwin & Yule, 1991
Picking, Biting Lip, Peeling Fingernails	WSc 40%	Levine, 1994
Repetitive, Stereotyped Movements	WSa 37%	Davies et al., 1998
Wandering	WSc 76%	Semel & Rosner, Utah Survey
Wandering Often	WSc 30%	Semel & Rosner, WSA Survey
Wanders Aimlessly	WSc > MRc	Einfeld et al., 1997, 2001
Overactivity	WSc 26%	Semel & Rosner, Utah Survey
Hyperactivity	WSc 30%	
Hyperactivity	WSc 35%	WSA Midwest Region, 1989
Hyperactivity	WSc 51%	Tharp, 1986
Hyperactivity	WSc ~ MRc	Gosch & Pankau, 1994
Cannot Sit Still	WSc ~ MRc	
Hyperactive	WSc 67% ~ 98th Percentile N	Dilts et al., 1990
Hyperactive	WSc 87%	Arnold et al., 1985
	WSc > Norms N & Norms MR	
Problems Modulating Activity Level	WSs 50%	Bregman, 1996
Situational Hyperactivity	WSc 52% > Norms N > MR	Arnold et al., 1985
Pervasive Hyperactivity	WSc 35% > Norms N > MR	
Hyperactive	WSc 72%	Udwin et al., 1987
Situational Hyperactivity	WSc 35% > Norms N > MR	Udwin et al., 1987
Pervasive Hyperactivity	WSc 37% > Norms N > MR	
Hyperactivity[#]	WSc ~ Controls MR	Udwin & Yule, 1991
Hyperactivity Cutoff	WSc ~ Controls MR	
Overactive[#]	WSc 71%	Einfeld et al., 1997
	WSc > MRc	
	WSc ~ MRc	Einfeld et al., 2001
Active Restless	WS Children > WS Adults	Gosch & Pankau, 1996b

Note: % = percentage frequency; # = mean amount; > /< = significantly more/significantly less; ~ = similar, not significantly different; WSa = WS adolescents &/or adults; WSc = WS children; NORMS = norms or previous sample; Controls = subject group; N = normally developing; MR = mentally retarded.

Parent ratings of temperament indicate that WSc generally show "higher activity" than nonhandicapped children (Tomc et al., 1990). However, WSc do not differ significantly from MRc on items like "restless" (Gosch & Pankau, 1994b). At the adult level, over 60% of parents mention "restlessness" as an area of behavior difficulty in WSa (Udwin, 1990), and "restlessness" is among the behavior difficulties noted most frequently on a standard questionnaire (Borghgraef et al., 1994).

Fidgeting and Stereotyped Movements

Many WSs are likely to engage in various types of stereotypic motor routines. In other words, they are "fidgety," and seem to be apprehensive, agitated, or "all keyed up."

Typical kinds of motor routines of WSs include rubbing their hands over their thighs; shifting their body weight to and fro, to the right or left, most often forward or backward; and finger twisting, finger tapping, or foot swinging. WSs can exhibit these motor patterns in the context of other activities, even while engaged in conversation or another task. It is not clear whether fidgety movements serve any purpose, except for release of excess energy, or possible relief of pressure on tactually sensitive areas.

Other WSs tend to be "squirmy" and have difficulty in sitting quietly. They appear jittery, "rattled," or "all shook up." Occasional twitching can occur, as do other mannerisms like picking at cuticles and fingernail sores or biting a top lip (SIBs). Twirling certain kinds of favored or shiny objects is another form of repetitive behavior sometimes seen in WSc (see chap. 5, section on "Curiosity," and Section E in chapter 6, "Perseverative Responding" (pp. 270–271).

Survey studies suggest that many, but not all, WSc display unusual motor habits. Parents report that 62% of WSc engage in "rocking, twirling, or finger twisting behaviors" (Utah Survey, Semel & Rosner, 1991a, 1991b). Likewise, WSc are rated significantly higher than a matched group of mentally retarded children on "twitches and mannerisms" on both the Parents' and Teachers' Rutter's Questionnaire (Udwin & Yule, 1991). Levine (1994) noted that approximately 40% of WSc exhibit mannerisms, such as picking or biting their top lip, peeling fingernails, and so forth. Fidgeting may be part of the rigidity and compulsivity exhibited by some WS teens and adults. Among adults with WS, 37% are said to engage in "repetitive, stereotyped movements" without any specific goal and without permission (Davies et al., 1998).

Some autistic and other severely retarded individuals engage in finger flapping, play with particles of dust in the air, perform other peculiar gestural motions, and tend to be frequently "on the go." Contrasts with WSs are discussed later in Section II, part B.

Wandering

Wandering is another inappropriate activity sometimes displayed by WSc. This refers to their leaving home, classroom, or a certain location, seemingly inadvertently and going around and about, unaccompanied and without permission.

Wandering is evident in WSc in both the Utah Survey and the WSA Checklist sample (Semel & Rosner, 1991a, 1991b). Responses to the Utah

Questionnaire indicate that 76% of WSc show wandering behavior. Similarly, 30% of parents in the WSA Checklist sample checked that their WSc "wanders from home often" (Semel & Rosner, 1991a. 1991b). WSc are significantly more likely than MRc to "wander aimlessly" according to parents' reports over a 5-year period (see Table 6.7).

When asked about this wandering behavior, parents usually state that these are nonpurposeful lapses. Sometimes they seem to result when WSc absentmindedly pursue unusual sounds. Some parents mention odors or unusual sights as stimuli for wandering. Others are unable to determine what triggers their child's wandering episodes.

Although parents of WSc recognize wandering as a major problem, it has not been adequately addressed in the research literature. Wandering is usually benign in purpose, but it can be troublesome, scary, and sometimes dangerous in its consequences (as it is in Alzheimer's disease). Concerns over a child's wandering tendencies can often control the entire household and lifestyle of a family because they must be on 24-hour alert as to the whereabouts of the WSc.

Overactivity and Hyperactivity

The hyperactive child is often unable to settle down for a quiet time to do anything for more than a few minutes. The child is hardly ever still and may roam around aimlessly. They are always "on the move."

Some WSc are often set into motion by certain stimuli, such as noises, shiny objects, novel events, or clutter in the environment. Tactile defensiveness, internal urges, environmental pressures, biochemical changes, and neurobiological mechanisms may also contribute to overactivity in WSs.

Survey Studies. According to parents, 26% of WSc show "high levels of overactivity," and 30% show "hyperactivity" (Utah Survey, Semel & Rosner, 1991a, 1991b). Two earlier surveys indicated that 51% (Tharp, 1986) and 35% of WSc show "hyperactivity" (Midwest Region Survey, WSA National Newsletter, 1989 April, pp. 21–22). Overt motor hyperactivity tends to decrease with age, so it is generally less in WSa than WSc (Finucane, 1996).

Rating Studies. The frequency of hyperactivity in WSs is generally higher in studies using rating scales and questionnaires than in surveys or single item measures. For example, parents identified 63% of WSc ($n = 19$, 4–10 yrs) as hyperactive on the CBCL (Gosch & Pankau, 1994b). Although higher than the 47% frequency for MRc, the difference on that item is not statistically significant. There is also no difference between groups on "cannot sit still"; the frequency for both WSc and MRc is 42% (Gosch & Pankau, 1994b). Similarly, 67% of WSc score at the 98th percentile or higher on the Hyperactivity scale of the CBCL for parents (Dilts et al., 1990). One half of

WSs are said to exhibit significant problems in modulation of activity level based on responses to the CBCL and Connors Abbreviated Questionnaire (Bregman, 1996). Across studies, the frequency of hyperactivity in WSs ranges between 63% and 71% (Dykens et al., 2000), a narrower range than reported earlier.

Moreover, 87% of WSc meet the criterion for hyperactive on Rutters' Questionnaires, with 52% classified as "situationally hyperactive" (i.e., hyperactive on either the Parents' or Teachers' Questionnaire) and 35% classified as "pervasively hyperactive" or hyperactive on both Questionnaires (Arnold et al., 1985). These levels exceed those obtained for previously tested groups of nonhandicapped children and mentally retarded children (Arnold et al., 1985). Other studies confirm the high rates of hyperactivity for WSc on Rutters' Questionnaires (Udwin et al., 1987), although WSc do not score significantly higher from MRc in those studies (Udwin & Yule, 1991). Similarly, WSs do not exceed other groups, PWs and MRs, in hyperactivity in Dykens and B. Rosner's (1999) study (Dykens et al., 2000). Whereas significantly more WSc were identified as "overactive" than MRc controls when tested at age 9 (71% to 46%; Einfeld et al., 1997), scores for both groups declined with age, and the groups did not differ significantly when retested 5 years later as adolescents (Einfeld et al., 2001).

Thus, there is variation across studies in both the frequency with which WSs are classified as "hyperactive" and the predominance of hyperactivity in WSs compared to other groups. Age level undoubtedly affects the results. WSa (> 20 years) are less likely to be rated "active restless" on the CBCL than are WSc (< 10 years) (Gosch & Pankau, 1996a). Individual differences in interpretation of the terminology may also play a role, as do group differences among WS samples and control groups. Finally, several measures of hyperactivity, such as the hyperactivity subscale of the CBCL and Rutter's Questionnaire, are based on the scores of collections of items. Many items that comprise the subscales reflect some of the well-established characteristics of WS (i.e., distractibility, inattention, and social difficulties), or several types of atypical activity (i.e., like restless, squirmy), rather than focusing mainly on overactivity in the sense of continual, aimless "running around."

Table 6.7 presents a summary of research on the atypical activity of WSs.

Finally, it should be noted that parallels have been drawn between the profile of WS and the neuropsychological pattern of "nonverbal perceptual-organizational-output disability" (Dilts et al., 1990). The latter refers to an inferred pattern of right hemispheric brain dysfunction in which children are impaired in spatial, perceptual, and social functioning (Rourke, 1988; Rourke & Fiske, 1988). Dilts et al. (1990) also suggested that high scores on Achenbach's Hyperactivity scale may be related to the diagnosis of ADHD. There may be distinctions, however, between use of the term "hyperactivity" or "pervasive hyperactivity" and the set of clinical symptoms defined as ADD/ADHD in the *Diagnostic and Statistical Manual of Mental Disorders* (*DSM-IV*) of the American Psychiatric Association (APA, 1994). These distinctions are discussed later.

II. TYPES OF BEHAVIOR DISORDERS

Besides considering WSs' behavior problems as separate types, they may be viewed as an aggregate of symptoms or a general condition of behavior disturbance. Examining the levels and types of general behavior disturbance in WSs is useful information because it can provide a frame of reference for comparing WSs with other subject groups and a standard for evaluating the status of behavior disturbance in individuals with WS.

There is also increasing evidence that some WSs exhibit specific kinds of behavior disturbance—namely, autism, ADHD, and emotional disorders. The clinical criteria for these conditions, the incidence and characteristics of these conditions in WSs, and how they compare with those of other patient groups are described later, after the discussion of general behavioral disturbance and related issues.

A. General Behavioral Disturbance

Measures of general behavior disturbance are based on composite scores of responses to all items on standard questionnaires. Studies of many kinds of subject populations are often used to establish cutoff scores that distinguish individuals who are at risk for developing or displaying various forms of emotional-behavioral difficulty from those that have less extreme scores and display varying degrees of those problems. Typically, WSs score high on such measures, so that a rather large percentage of WSs may meet the criteria of being considered at risk for difficulties.

Evidence of General Behavioral Disturbance

Across various studies, between 52% and 85% of WSc score at or above the cutoff point for being identified as potentially "disturbed" based on ratings on Rutter's Questionnaires for Parents and Teachers (Arnold et al., 1985; Udwin, 1990; Udwin et al., 1987; Udwin & Yule, 1991). Questionnaire items (31 items for parents, 26 for teachers) ask about problem behaviors, such as physical symptoms, emotionality, social difficulties, antisocial and neurotic types of behavior, reaction to school, and hyperactivity.

The rate of behavior disturbance for WSc is consistently higher than the rate for nonhandicapped children (NHc), although not necessarily higher than normative data from mentally retarded subjects or matched groups of

TABLE 6.8
Research on General Behavioral Disturbance in WSs

Type of Behavior	Frequency or Result	Source or Reference
Behavior Disturbance (Parent)	61% WSc > Norms N	Arnold et al., 1985
	WSc ~ Norms MR	
Behavior Disturbance (Teacher)	52% WSc > Norms N	
	WSc ~ Norms MR	
Behavior Disturbance (Parent)	80% WSc > Norms N	Udwin et al., 1987
	WSc > Norms MR	
Behavior Disturbance (Teacher)	67% WSc > Norms N	
	WSc > Norms MR	
Behavior Disturbance (Parent)	85% WSc ~ Controls MR	Udwin & Yule, 1991
Behavior Disturbance (Teacher)	80% WSc > Controls MR	
Neurotic/Antisocial (Parent)	WSc 30%/17%	Arnold et al., 1985
Neurotic/Antisocial (Teacher)	WSc 35%/13%	
Neurotic/Antisocial (Parent)	WSc 39%/30%	Udwin et al., 1987
Neurotic/Antisocial (Teacher)	WSc 26%/21%	
Total Behavior Problem Score[a]	WSc 61% > MRc 41%	Einfeld et al., 1997
	WSc > MRc	Einfeld et al., 1997, 2001
Difficult Temperament	WSc > Norms N	Tomc et al., 1990
Difficult Temperament	WSa ~ MRa	Plissart et al., 1996

Note: NORMS = norms or previous sample; Controls = subject group; N = normally develop-ing; MR = mentally retarded; N = normal; WSc = WS children; WSa = WS adults.

mentally retarded children (MRc) (Arnold et al., 1985; Udwin & Yule, 1991; Udwin et al., 1987). Sometimes the ratings for WSc are significantly higher than that of a comparison group of mentally retarded children, other times the difference is not statistically significant. Table 6.8 presents a summary of findings concerning the general behavioral disturbance and behavioral adjustment of WSs.

Interpretation of these data must take into account, however, that Rutter's Questionnaires are a screening device, not a "foolproof" measure of general behavior disturbance. In fact, 40% of the children with scores above the cut-off point for behavior disturbance did not have that diagnosis confirmed in further tests and interviews in Rutter's Isle of Wight study (Rutter, 1982).

Antisocial and Neurotic Subtypes. Rutter's Questionnaires also provide information about whether an individual's overall behavior disturbance is primarily antisocial or neurotic in nature by comparing responses to these item sets (Rutter, Cox, Tupling, Berger, & Yule, 1975). The antisocial set con-tains items pertaining to stealing, destruction, disobedience, lying, and bul-lying. The neurotic set contains items pertaining to school tears, excessive worries, and fears; also, there are items covering stomach aches and sleep-ing difficulties on the parents' questionnaire, or items like miserable/un-happy on the teachers' questionnaire.

In keeping with previously cited findings on WSc's behavior problems, WSc are more likely to display neurotic kinds of behavior disturbance than antisocial symptoms in terms of mean scores on the two different sections and the number or percentage of WSc who are classified as each type. In contrast, comparison groups tend to be distributed almost equally between the two types (Arnold et al., 1985; Udwin et al., 1987; Udwin & Yule, 1991).

Individual items that show group differences in these and other item sets recall the areas of special difficulty for WSc: fearfulness, worries, somatic difficulties, problems with concentration, fidgeting, and peer relations. Frequently reported problems of eating, wetting, aches, and pains (Udwin & Yule, 1991; Udwin et al., 1987) should be noted, as well as the impact and severity of sleeping problems on WSs and their families (Gosch & Pankau, 1994). This can reach crisis proportions when parents crave even one night of decent sleep. Sleeping disturbances persist in WS adulthood, with 21% experiencing sleep problems; these are disruptive in another 4% of WSa (Davies et al., 1998).

Establishing these as areas of marked difficulty demonstrates the uniqueness of the WS profile and the importance of taking these differences into account in rearing, teaching, and treating WSs. Here, too, there are some marked variations across WSc in the patterns of behavior displayed. Notably, a small minority of WSc occasionally exhibit intense and sudden anger or outbursts of aggression and tantrums that may be directed toward family members or destruction of property (Levine & Wharton, 2001). Typically, the child is very sorry after the outburst. Such "meltdowns" in normally "sunny" WSc are attributed to anxiety, immature coping mechanisms, and frequent frustrations as a result of their inadequate skill to process, edit, and inhibit their response (see the earlier section on low frustration tolerance).

Other Questionnaires. On the whole, the dominant pattern of CBCL difficulty is substantiated in studies using other measures of behavior disturbance, namely, the Developmental Behavior Checklist (DBC) (Einfeld et al., 1997; Einfeld et al., 2001), and the CBCL (Bregman, 1996; Dilts et al., 1990; Pagon et al., 1987).

More to the point, the Developmental Behavior Checklist yields a Total Behavior Problem score with a cutoff standard of 46, which is indicative of "major behavioral and emotional disturbance" (Einfeld et al., 1997; Einfeld et al., 2001). Consistent with previous findings of Udwin, Yule, and colleagues, WSc show a significantly higher frequency than MRc for major behavioral disturbance (61.4% vs. 40.7%). Likewise, the Total Behavior Problem scores of the two groups, WSc ($M = 57$) and MRc 42 ($M = 42$), indicate greater behavioral disturbance for WSc (Einfeld et al., 1997). These differences are sustained in a 5-year follow-up study, with the Total Behavior

Problem scores of both decreasing over time, but the WSc continue to score significantly higher than controls on this measure (Einfeld et al., 2001).

WS Adults. The profile of behavior disturbance in adults with WS is generally consistent with that of WSc (Udwin, 1990). Parents report "restlessness, poor concentration, irritability, attention-seeking behaviors, excessive worrying, fearfulness, and frequent complaints of aches and pains" in over 60% of the WSa studied (Udwin, 1990). Temper tantrums and eating/sleeping difficulties are reported less frequently than in WSc, but are still found in 39% and 47% of adult cases, respectively (Udwin, 1990).

Remarkably similar results are obtained in a study of WSa conducted in Belgium and the Netherlands (Borghgraef et al., 1994; Plissart et al., 1994b). Based on parents' responses to a standardized questionnaire of behavioral problems (Storend Gedragsschaal), WSa seem to "show little disturbing behavior in comparison with other mentally retarded subjects" (Borghgraef et al., 1994). The most frequent behavioral difficulties are: "restlessness, poor concentration, attention-seeking behavior, and complaining," which are the same difficulties, for the most part, as those reported by Udwin (1990). Within a work context, principal supervisors of WSa report distractibility (90%), among other types of problems (Davies, Howlin, & Udwin, 1997). Thus, most of the difficulties of WS childhood persist into adulthood with some moderation of frequency and severity.

Related Behavioral Problems

Temperament. Measures of temperament, or "behavioral style," also indicate that WSs often have "difficult" temperaments (Plissart, Borghgraef, & Fryns, 1996; Tomc et al., 1990). Based on how they are rated on dimensions, such as "approach," "intensity," and "adaptability," WSc and WSs are classified as "easy," "slow to warm up," or "difficult." Even by age 3, significantly fewer WSc were perceived as "easy" compared to norms for normally developing groups of children (Tomc et al., 1990). In the grade school years, only 7% of WSc were rated as "easy," 3% were rated as slow to warm up, 37% were rated "difficult," and the majority, 53%, were viewed as somewhat difficult (Tomc et al., 1990).

As adults, WSs are judged to be more difficult than a matched group of MRc, but the difference is not statistically significant. In fact, both groups are within the range of scores of a normative sample of mentally retarded individuals (Plissart et al., 1996b).

Thus, despite their charm and winning ways, WSs can be difficult to handle. This is not surprising, given their profile of problems presented in this and previous chapters.

Adaptive Behavior Problems. Besides the evaluation of problem behaviors, the extent to which WSs can function adequately in everyday life is of concern. Measures of adaptive behavior deal specifically with this aspect as they assess how well the individuals function in their environment (Mervis & Klein-Tasman, 2000).

A number of studies have established that WSc tend to score lower on measures of adaptive behavior than matched groups of MRc on the Vineland Social Maturity Scale (Gosch & Pankau, 1994b) or norms in the areas of Independent Functioning and Self-Direction on the AAMD Adaptive Behavior Scale (Arnold et al., 1985). Across areas of functioning, WSc consistently test lower on Self-Care Skills and Independence than Socialization or Communication, except for Motor Skills when that is included, as previously noted (Greer et al., 1997; Mervis et al., 2001). Although adaptive measures correlate with mental ability, increase with age, and do not lag increasingly behind the norms over the grade school years, descriptive accounts of WSc's performance leave little doubt of difficulties in the area of self-care. Early studies indicate, for example, that most WSc "need supervision in eating, toileting, and dressing" (Arnold et al., 1985).

In adulthood, many WSa develop the skills necessary for self-care, but this varies across different studies. A case study of 10 WSa (18–48 yrs, $M =$ 26;5 yrs) reports that all patients "cared for their own needs," cook and shop by themselves, use public transportation with supervision, and enjoy and participate in sports (Lopez-Rangel, Maurice, McGillivray, & Friedman, 1992). All had various supervised jobs, including volunteering, sheltered workshops, clerk in offices or music shop, and student; all except two lived at home, and led active, although limited, lives (Lopez-Rangel et al., 1992).

In contrast, a larger sample of WSa ($n = 70$, 19–39;9 yrs, $M =$ 26;8 yrs) is more constrained in their functioning: 27% are nonindependent in toileting, 45% in washing, 47% in dressing, and between 80% and 94% are dependent on others for preparation of food and domestic chores. Daytime occupations and leisure activities also seem more limited (Davies et al., 1997). Differences in intelligence and other abilities and use of appropriate interventions and training opportunities are some of the factors that may account for the striking contrast in accounts.

B. Autism

A minority of WSs appears to exhibit serious kinds of behavior disorder, whereas many others seem prone to less severe versions of these conditions. In fact, a very small number of WSs have been diagnosed for pervasive developmental and psychiatric disorder, in the form of autism, although its exact frequency and specific symptoms are still in question.

Although WS is a very different kind of disorder than autism (AUT), they are related in at least two ways: (a) The prototypic profiles of WS and AUT overlap in several aspects; and (b) there is evidence that dual diagnoses of WS and AUT occasionally occur.

Clinical Criteria of Autism

Autism is a "pervasive developmental disorder," that is, a childhood disorder that affects multiple spheres of functioning, namely, language, attention, perception, reality testing, and motor activity (Sattler, 1988, pp. 629–636). The incidence of autism in the general population is estimated to be 1 in 1,000 births (Schoenbrodt & Smith, 1995), which is more frequent than the estimated frequency of WS (i.e., 1 in 20,000–30,000).

The psychiatric criteria for the diagnosis of autism require marked difficulty in three areas: aberrant social relations, such as avoidance of eye-to-eye gaze and lack of sharing of interests, social, or emotional reciprocity with other people; extreme language impairment, such as significant delay and stereotyped use of language; and obsessively reiterative behavior, such as preoccupations, strict adherence to nonfunctional routines, and stereotyped motoric acts (APA, 1994).

Dual Diagnosis of WS and Autism

Based on the diagnostic criteria of AUT and the presence of several "defining" features of WS, such as certain facial features, mental retardation, and supravalvular aortic stenosis, a very small number of individuals have been diagnosed as having both autism and WS. These are presented as case studies in several articles (Gillberg & Rasmussen, 1994, n = 4 in Sweden; Gosch & Pankau, 1994a, n = 2 cases in Germany; Reiss, Feinstein, Rosenbaum, Borengasser-Caruso, & Goldsmith, 1985, n = 2 in USA).

Excerpts from these cases highlight some of the features of AUTs and their similarity and dissimilarity with the features of WS:

"From age 2 years she would throw extreme tantrums if every wish was not obeyed."

"Whenever upset, frightened, or happy she would tiptoe, and flap her hands."

"She would get stuck on some detail, 'contemplating' a red line or a particular sound for hours." (Case 1, Gillberg & Rasmussen, 1994)

"An unbelievable visual memory and would always be able to get back to a particular place . . . even when normal adults would have problems with this."

"His main interest was in shiny objects at which he would stare for many minutes at a time."

"He would rock back and forth while holding the keys before his eyes."

"One of his favorite pastimes would be to find a good vantage point on the floor where he would lie down to observe the ceiling lamp out of the corner of his eye while flapping his hands." (Case 3, Gillberg & Rasmussen, 1994)

"As an infant he rarely made eye contact. The mother remembered that the boy looked 'through' her or at the wall." (Case 1, Gosch & Pankau, 1994a).

"His parents described him as being uncontrollable, with a tendency to 'destroy everything.' " (Case 2, Gosch & Pankau, 1994)

These and the other few cases of dual diagnosis (total n of cases = 8) demonstrate an abnormality and difficulty with language, lack of verbalization, and avoidance of social interactions that are distinctly different, quite the reverse, from those typically displayed by WSs. Also, the unusual repetitive motor patterns, spinning of objects, intense preoccupations, and excessive "acting out" evident in these case studies go way beyond that shown by most individuals with WS.

Determining the Link Between WS and Autism. The joint occurrence of WS and AUT in these few cases could reflect either an actual linkage between disorders or merely "chance" co-occurrence, like random throws of dice producing an extremely rare event.

To determine which is the case, a sample of WSc with suspected symptoms of AUT ($n = 32$) are being studied (Levine, Pober & Miranda, 1996). In addition, the expected incidence of AUT in the general population (i.e., 7 in 10,000 subjects) is being compared with the obtained number of cases of AUT among WSs. Evidence of a link would be found if the obtained incidence in WS exceeds the incidence of 1 or 2 cases per 10,000 expected by chance (Levine et al., 1996). Based on present findings, it seems quite possible that there is some genetic, biochemical, and/or neuroanatomical link— perhaps dual in nature—between these two disorders. There is also the possibility that these joint occurrences are mediated by the fact that "both involve mental retardation" (Dykens et al., 2000).

Feature Comparisons of WS and Autism

Aside from a few cases with dual diagnoses, the prototypic profiles of WSs and AUTs show marked similarity in certain features but significant differences in others. For example, language and sociability are relative strengths in most WSs, whereas most AUTs are extremely deficient in these areas. They are often unable to speak in their early years. Likewise, visuomotor construction is an area of substantial accomplishment for most AUTs and extreme incompetence for most WSs. In contrast, discrimination of faces is a bona fide skill for WSs and a deficit for most AUTs. In areas where there are similarities, such as fixations on objects or topics and certain kinds of behavior problem, such as overactivity or stereotyped motor patterns, the behaviors of AUTs are usually much more extreme than those of WSs.

It should also be noted that WSs and AUTs display similarities and differences in other areas, namely neurobiological features (e.g., size of neocerebellar vermis, serotonin level), genetics, and the efficacy of various forms of intervention (e.g., behavior modification).

Table 6.9 compares the prototypical features of WS described in this book with those of individuals with autism (APA, 1994; Frith, 1989; Harris, 1995b; Schoenbrodt & Smith, 1995). It brings the prominent features of each into sharp relief, but it necessarily glosses over certain findings and individual differences.

C. Attention Deficit Hyperactivity Disorder (ADHD)

Although attentional difficulties and overactivity have long been recognized, clinical descriptions and definitions of these disorders have evolved over the years (Harris, 1995b). This is illustrated in the changes in terminology in various editions of the American Psychiatric Association's *Diagnostic and Statistical Manual* (DSM) (Harris, 1995b; Sattler, 1988), ranging from "minimal brain dysfunction" (MBD) and hyperkinetic reaction (*DSM–I*, APA, 1968, cf. Harris, 1995b), to attention deficit disorder (ADD) with and without hyperactivity (*DSM–III*, APA, 1980, cf., Harris, 1995), and finally, attention deficit hyperactivity disorder (ADHD) (*DSM–III–R*, APA, 1987).

Currently, ADHD is the most common diagnosis of children referred to psychiatric clinics. Estimates for ADHD range from 1% to 14% of the total

TABLE 6.9
Typical Features of WS and Autism

Characteristic	WS	Autism
LANGUAGE SKILLS & PROBLEMS		
Language Delay	Yes	Significant and Prolonged
Syntax	Good	Poor
Semantics	Good	Poor
Speech Intelligibility	Good	Poor
Pragmatics	Variable	Poor
Nonverbal Communication	Good	Poor
Metaphor/Irony	Variable	Poor

(Continued)

TABLE 6.9
(Continued)

Characteristic	WS	Autism
PERCEPTUAL-MOTOR PERFORMANCE		
Auditory Hypersensitivity	Yes	Yes
Visuospatial Construction	Poor	Good
Facial Discrimination	Good	Poor
Motor Skills	Poor	Fair to Good
Tactile Defensiveness	Yes	Yes
SPECIFIC APTITUDES		
Sociability	Good	Poor
Empathy	Good	Poor
Social Cognition	Good	Poor
Eye Gaze/Contact	Good	Poor
Social Style	Friendly	Aloof
	Affectionate	Passive
	Charming	Odd
Physical Contact	Craves	Avoids
Responses to Being Held	Cuddles	Waxy Flexibility
Focal Topics of Interest	Yes	Yes
Object Fixations	Moderate	Extreme
Object Parts	Sometimes	Extreme
Spins Objects	Sometimes	Extreme
Shiny Objects	Sometimes	Extreme
Memory	Variable	Specific
Musicality	Good	Uneven: Good
BEHAVIOR PROBLEMS		
Anxieties & Fears	Yes	Yes
Phobias	Yes	Yes
Distractible	Yes	Yes
Attentional Problems	Variable	Extreme
Impulsivity	Yes	Yes
Rigidity	Yes	Extreme
Low Frustration		
Tolerance	Yes	Extreme
Tantrums	Yes	Extreme
Aggression	Variable	Extreme
Self-Destructive	Variable	Extreme
Obsessive Compulsive	Variable	Extreme
Withdrawal	Variable	Extreme
Perseveration	Variable	Extreme
Atypical Activity	Variable	Extreme
Fidgeting	Some	Extreme
Hand Flapping	Little	Yes
Rocking	Some	Extreme
Running About	Some	Yes

population, probably from 4% to 5% of school-age children (Schoenbrodt & Smith, 1995). It is well known that children with learning disabilities are sometimes hyperactive, some with, some without, the diagnosis of ADHD.

The present *DSM–IV* criteria for Attention Deficit Hyperactivity Disorder (ADHD) refer to three subtypes: Attention Deficit Hyperactivity Disorder, Predominately Inattention Type; Attention Deficit Hyperactivity Disorder, Predominately Hyperactive-Impulsive Type; and Attention Deficit/Hyperactivity Disorder, Combined Type. These differ in their emphasis on attentional versus hyperactive symptoms. Additional criteria involve age level and severity of symptoms: that is, presentation of symptoms by age 7 and for at least 6 months to a degree that is maladaptive and inconsistent with developmental level (APA, 1994).

ADHD in WSc and WSa

ADHD in WSc. Although children with WS commonly display some of the key features of ADHD (i.e., short attention span, distractibility, and restlessness), there is still some question as to whether they demonstrate the constellation and severity of symptoms warranting the formal diagnosis of Attention Deficit Hyperactivity Disorder (ADHD; Finegan, Sitarenios, Smith, & Mesehino, 1994).

This question was addressed by using a reliable measure of ADHD, DuPaul's ADHD scale, to compare parent and teacher ratings of WSc (n = 17, 5–14 yrs, M = 8 yrs) with those of a matched child group (Finegan et al., 1994). The scale contains 14 items based on *DSM–III–R* criteria, such as: "often fidgets with hands or feet or squirms in seat," "difficulty remaining seated when required to do so," "easily distracted by extraneous stimuli," "difficulty awaiting turn in games or group situations," "often blurts out answers to questions before they have been completed," "has difficulty sustaining attention in tasks or play activities," and items that focus on the attentional properties of ADHD (Sattler, 1988, p. 623; WSA National Newsletter, 1992 Summer, Vol. 9, 10).

Parent ratings indicate that 24% of WSc and 47% of comparison subjects meet the criterion for ADHD, that is, a score of "2" or greater on a 4-point scale ("0" = "not at all" to "3" = "very much") for at least eight items. The difference is statistically significant: WSc are significantly less likely than controls to be classified as ADHD. Teacher ratings show little difference between groups, with 35% of WSc and 31% of the comparison group meeting the criterion for ADHD. Interestingly, this is comparable to the previously reported incidence of "pervasive hyperactivity" in WSc on the Hyperactivity scale of Rutter's Questionnaire (35%: Arnold et al., 1985; 37%: Udwin et al., 1987).

Thus, the ADHD rate for WSc is about four times higher than the 6% rate for the general population of children, although WSc do not have a higher rate of ADHD than children with other kinds of dysmorphic conditions (Finegan et al., 1994). Because many of the behaviors on DuPaul's ADHD scale are typical of WSc, the reason why relatively few met the criterion for ADHD is probably due to the lesser severity of these behaviors in WSc versus those diagnosed with the disorder.

In any event, it is essential that a comprehensive evaluation be carried out to establish a diagnosis of ADHD with its pervasive behavioral symptoms (Scheiber, 2000). The evaluation should be carried out by someone aware of the characteristics of Williams syndrome so that the diagnosis can also reveal whether the WSc is mainly inattentive, or hyperactive and impulsive, or a combination of both.

The evaluation usually includes an in-depth interview with parent and child, an interview with the child's teacher, a complete questionnaire about behavior, and a number of formal tests to pinpoint the interventions a child may need (Scheiber, 2000).

ADHD in WS Adults. It is noteworthy that 46% of WSa ($n = 15$, 18–49 yrs, $M = 29$ yrs) received a diagnosis of ADHD based on clinical judgments of phone interviews with parents and caregivers (Brewer et al., 1996). This compares to the approximately 30% of WSc reported earlier (Finegan et al., 1994). The higher incidence for WSa may be due to differences in age level, differences between sample populations as the WSc were recruited from WSA families and the WSa were clinic patients, and the type of test or criteria used for diagnosis. It also differs markedly from results obtained in structured interviews of parents in which the rate of reported "overactivity" in WSa is 7%; none of the sample showed "Disruptive" overactivity (Davies et al., 1998).

Clinical Contrasts Between ADHDc and WSc

Whereas ADHDc and WSc tend to share certain kinds of problem behaviors (e.g., overactivity, distractibility, inattention, and aggression), they usually differ in the frequency, intensity, and manner in which those behaviors are expressed. Differences between ADHDc and WSc are manifest, too, in the areas of sociability, social cognition, and use of medication.

Regarding "overactivity," ADHDc are typically described as constantly and incessantly in motion, unable to stay with any one activity for very long (Wender, 1987). Although some WSc are frequently "on the move," their activity usually involves searching for special interest items, such as unusual noises, a motor, fan, or novel or shiny objects. Once the item is located, then the WS child's attention and actions are typically riveted on that object.

WSc are usually distracted by specific things, such as unusual, sudden environmental noises, shiny objects, novel items, or unexpected movements, whereas distractibility in ADHDc tends to be pervasive and generalized. Deficits in task organization and completion usually involve cognitive limitations in the case of WSc, in contrast to problems of self-regulation in ADHDc.

Likewise, WSc and ADHDc usually display different forms of inattention. The major difficulty of hyperactive children is in staying on task (i.e., sustaining attention), not in extracting relevant information (i.e., selective attention) (Hetherington & Parke, 1993). In contrast, WSc often have problems identifying the relevant aspect of tasks or situations, but not in staying on task when it is suited to the child's level of achievement or area of special interest. Whereas ADHDc appear to have little stick-to-itiveness, many WSc have been observed to be able to concentrate on special interest topics, watch television or a movie, or listen to music or a story for long periods of time.

Contrasts are further evident in the area of aggression. Over 60% of ADHD children (ADHDc) are said to have problems with aggression or oppositional behavior, whereas most WSc are unlikely to have problems with aggression; they may occasionally strike back but not to intentionally harm another person (Barkley, 1990; Barkley, WSA National Newsletter, 1989, Vol. 7, pp. 15–17). A notable exception is the small minority of WSc who manifest occasional bouts of aggression: lashing out at family members, sometimes destroying property, a real "meltdown" (Levine & Wharton, 2001; see Section I, Part E, "Low Frustration Tolerance," for information on aggression in WSs).

There are further marked differences in the area of sociability. Whereas WSc are known for overfriendliness and social disinhibition, sociability is not a dominant trait of ADHDc (Wender, 1987) or children with "nonverbal perceptual-organizational-output disability," that is, right hemispheric brain dysfunction of children who are differentially debilitated in spatial, perceptual, and social functioning (Rourke, 1988; Rourke & Fisk, 1988).

There are contrasts in social cognition, too. Social perception, or the ability to interpret facial expressions, and role-taking, or the ability to comprehend another person's point of view, are areas of weakness in children with ADHD, but relative strengths for children with WS (Harris, 1995; and see chap. 5, p. 204).

Finally, use of medication has been less often advised in research articles or book chapters pertaining to WSc than in those on ADHD, where medication is emphasized as a treatment of choice (e.g., Hetherington & Parke, 1986; Wender, 1987).

TABLE 6.10
Comparison of WS and ADHD

Problem Behavior or Other Feature	WSs	ADHDs
Distractiblity	Yes	Yes
	Stimulus Based	Pervasive
Attentional	Variable	Yes
Problems	Selective Attention	Sustaining Attention
	Sustaining Attention	
Impulsivity	Yes	Yes
Overactivity	Variable	Extreme
	Stimulus Related	Generalized
Aggression	Variable	Yes
Task Completion	Yes	Yes
Problems	Cognitive	Self-regulation
	Self-regulation	
Sociability	Excellent	Poor
Social Cognition	Good	Poor
Social Perception		
Faces	Good	Poor
Role-Taking	Good	Poor
Use of Medication	Low	High

Table 6.10 summarizes the similarities and contrasts between WSs and ADHDs already discussed.

D. Emotional Disorders

At times, most people show signs of sadness, feeling blue, isolated, or depressed, but this is distinct from acute "clinical depression," a psychiatric disorder defined in terms of a list of criterial symptoms in the *Diagnostic and Statistical Manual of Mental Disorders* (*DSM–III–R*, APA, 1987; *DSM–IV*, APA, 1994). In contrast with the layman's descriptions of "being depressed," or "feeling down," the diagnostic criteria for major depression include having a "depressed mood most of the day, nearly every day"; "markedly decreased interest or pleasure in all or almost all activities most of the day, nearly every day"; "feelings of worthlessness or excessive or inappropriate guilt"; and "recurrent thoughts of death."

Similarly, the occasional experience of "anxiety" as a signal of impending danger or threat of danger is different from the persistent state of free floating anxiety that is not centered on any particular situation or object, that is, the manifestation of an "overanxious" disorder.

Research on Emotional Disorders of WSa

Although the behavior problems of WSs have been known for some time, the presence of more severe conditions has been recognized only recently. Stimulated by some parents' reports of severe emotional problems in WSa, two telephone interview surveys on WSa clinic patients are completed, others are in progress (Brewer et al., 1996; Brewer, Levine, & Pober, 1995; Levine, 1994). Pursuing a long-standing program of research on WS, a larger study of WSa ($n = 70$, 18–39 yrs) uses structured personal interviews with parents and caregivers to obtain information on the behavioral and emotional difficulties of WSa (Davies et al., 1998). As a result, it is now well established that some WSs exhibit clinical symptoms, such as phobias, depression, anxiety disorder, and obsessive compulsive disorder (OCD) (Brewer et al., 1996; Brewer et al., 1995; Davies et al., 1998; Levine, 1994), as well as ADHD.

Table 6.11 presents a summary of research on behavior disorders of WSa.

The initial telephone interview study of WSa clinic patients ($n = 14$, 20–49 yrs, $Md = 25;6$ yrs) revealed that parents reported that 79% (11 of 14) had some emotional problems (Brewer et al., 1995). Of these, 21% (3 of 14) had a formal clinical diagnosis: anxiety disorder, depression, or compulsion disorder. The remaining three WSa were said to have anxious periods but no emotional problem; this was attributed to their having received a great deal of support and acceptance from their family, school, or work environment.

These findings were followed-up in another telephone interview study that used a standardized questionnaire based on the *DSM–III–R* to elicit information from parents about the emotional problems of their WSa ($n = 15$, 18–49 yrs, $M = 28;6$ yrs) (Brewer et al., 1996). Based on a qualified clinician's scrutiny of the responses, six types of psychiatric conditions were identified. These include (along with percentage of WSa with a definite plus probable diagnosis of the disorder in parentheses) simple phobias (100%), ADHD (73%), dysthymia (low positive mood or affect, 53%), depression (33%), overanxious disorder (33%), and obsessive compulsive disorder (33%).

The most commonly reported emotional problem in Brewer et al. (1996) is simple phobia. It is also high in Davies et al. (1998) study where 41% of WSa were reported to have phobias that were disruptive to them or others, and another 16% have phobias that were not disruptive. Disruptive phobias were so intense that they prevented the WSa from engaging in activities, such as attending social gatherings because of their fear of balloons (Davies et al., 1998). Anticipatory anxiety and worry about sudden, unanticipated noises like sirens, doorbells, and fire alarms are particularly noteworthy (Bregman, 1996). Likewise, Brewer et al. (1996) noted that the worries [of WS adults] tend to focus primarily on environmental triggers (e.g., loud sounds, novel or unexpected future events). This is consistent with the ob-

TABLE 6.11
Research on Behavior Disorders in WSs

Type of Behavior	Frequency or Result	Source or Reference
Dual Diagnosis WS & AUT	8 Cases	Gillberg & Rasmussen, 1994; Gosch & Pankau, 1994a; Reiss et al., 1985
ADHD (Parents' Ratings)	WSc 24% < 47% Controls MR	Finegan et al., 1994
ADHD (Teachers' Ratings)	WSc 35% ~ 31% Controls MR	
	WSc ~30% > 6% Norms N	
ADHD		
Definite/Probable Diagnosis	WSa 46%/WSa 27%	Brewer et al., 1996
Overactivity		
Disruptive/Reported	WSa 0%/WSa 7%	Davies et al., 1998
Emotional Problems	WSa 79%	Brewer et al., 1995
Formal Psychiatric Diagnosis	WSa 21%	
Dysthymia		
Definite/Probable Diagnosis	WSa 33%/WSa 20%	Brewer et al., 1996
Mood Disturbance	WSa 10%/WSa 10%	Davies et al., 1998
Disruptive/Reported		
Depression		
Definite/Probable Diagnosis	WSa 0%/WSa 33%	Brewer et al., 1996
Phobias, Simple		
Definite/Probable Diagnosis Phobia	WSa 100%/WSa 0%	Brewer et al., 1996
Disruptive/Reported	WSa 41%/WSa 16%	Davies et al., 1998
Overanxious Disorder		
Definite/Probable Diagnosis	WSa 13%/WSa 20%	Brewer et al., 1996
Anxiety		
Disruptive/Reported	WSa 16%/WSa 73%	Davies et al., 1998
Obsessive Compulsive Disorder		
Definite/Probable Diagnosis	WSa 13%/WSa 20%	Brewer et al., 1996
Preoccupations/Obsessions		
Disruptive/Reported	WSa 50%/WSa 43%	Davies et al., 1998
Compulsive Behaviors		
Disruptive/Reported	WSa 9%/WSa 20%	Davies et al., 1998

Note: WSa = WS adult; Dysthymia = feelings of despair; Definite/Probable Diagnosis = terms used by Brewer et al. (1996) to classify results; Disruptive/Reported = terms used by Davies et al. (1998) to classify results.

servations of Delga cited before (see Section I,A "Fear and Anxieties," p. 254).

Another commonly reported emotional problem is anxiety (Brewer et al., 1995; Brewer et al., 1996). This is consistent with reports of "undue anxiety" in WSc (e.g., Udwin et al., 1987) and, in WSa, a 73% rate of reported anxiety and another 16% displaying anxiety that was disruptive (Davies et al., 1998). It is also consistent with a preliminary study in which one fourth of WSs (6 WSc, 4–12 yrs, and 2 WSa, 23 and 33 yrs) met the criteria for anxiety disorder on the CBCL and Conner's Abbreviated Questionnaire (Bregman, 1996).

"Mood disturbances" that include sadness and depression are reported in 10% of WSa, and another 10% were said to have disruptive mood disturbances (Davies et al., 1998). These are related to the clinical conditions of dysthymia (feelings of despair) and depression evident in 53% and 33%, respectively, of WSa clinic patients (Brewer et al., 1996).

Consistent with Levine's (1994) assessment of WSa's problems, Brewer et al. (1996) interpreted the "chronic depressive symptoms of dysthymia [to] feelings of despair at not fitting in as well as hopelessness about their inability to alter the future."

In keeping with previous accounts of obsessive compulsive behaviors (see p. 263), 13% of WSa clinic patients received a definite diagnosis of obsessive compulsive disorder, and another 20% received a probable diagnosis of this disorder (Brewer et al., 1996). Distinguishing between the two aspects of such problems, preoccupations or obsessions with topics of special interest are more prevalent in WSa (43% are reported to have the problem), and 50% have problems severe enough to be considered disruptive. In contrast, compulsive behaviors have a 20% report rate and there is a 9% report rate of disruptive compulsive behaviors (Davies et al., 1998).

In establishing the clinical diagnoses of all of these and other psychiatric conditions, the key criteria are severity, pervasiveness, and disruptiveness.

As for the reliability of the reported incidence and severity of clinical disorders in WSs, this is still open to question. For example, Finucane (1996) concluded that most WS adolescents and adults ($n = 12$) "are not affected by serious emotional disturbance, [though] some may be prone to problems related to mood and impulse control disorders." These are the problems pinpointed by Brewer et al. (1995, 1996) and Davies et al. (1998). Another study reports that most WSa ($n = 11$, 17–66 yrs, $M = 37$ yrs) show little in the way of disturbing behavior compared to other mentally retarded subjects based on parents' and teachers' ratings on a standardized questionnaire (Borghgraef et al., 1994). Closer analysis reveals, however, that two of six WSa display "mixed" behavioral problems involving extreme worrying and obsessive behavior (Plissart et al., 1994b).

Regardless, the size of samples in several of these studies is small, use of control groups with which to compare the incidence and symptoms of clinical disorders in WSa is lacking, and the criteria for diagnosis are often vague. There is a fine, but critical line between WSs being diagnosed with fears versus phobias, compulsions or preoccupations versus obsessive compulsive disorder, frequent unpleasant feelings of anxiety versus an overanxious disorder, and feeling out of sorts versus manifesting a full-blown depression. There are also enormous implications to the care, restrictions, and opportunities provided for WSs as a result of their type of diagnosis. In both cases, interventions are required, but with maladaptive behavior problems, psycho-educational techniques predominate, with clinical or psychiatric disorders, the services of qualified mental health professionals are required for diagnosis and treatment. A certain percentage of WSa in the studies already cited received help from mental health professionals. According to Davies et al. (1998), 21% of WSa in the study had seen either a psychiatrist (7%), clinical psychologist (9%), both, a counselor, or hypnotherapist. Most of the WSa in the Brewer et al. (1996) received counseling or psychotherapy (10 of 14). In Brewer et al. (1995), 71% of WSa received weekly counseling with a social worker or psychologist. Serious cases must receive expert professional help. Sometimes it is difficult to make contact with professionals who have had clinical experience with both the type of disorder involved and patients with developmental disabilities, let alone WS.

At the same time, it should be kept in mind that research on both aspects of WSa's behavior, behavioral adjustment, and disorders is needed to clarify the status of emotional and psychological areas of WS functioning, which may reflect the kinds of variation obtained in studies of WSs' adaptive behavior.

Nevertheless, anecdotal reports and articles by parents and family members in the WSA National Newsletter are replete with examples of WSs living semiindependently, attending school or work programs, involved in paid, volunteer, or sheltered workshop jobs, and engaged in sports activities, music, or other leisure pursuits, albeit with tremendous amounts of support, guidance, and assistance from their parents, families, communities, and organizations. Although only some adolescents and adults with WS may be able to attain this level of competence, neither are all, or even most, WSs doomed to a life of psychiatric illness or serious behavior disturbance as adults. With appropriate interventions, treatment, educational management, and support from various people, agencies, and organizations, many individuals with WS may be able to live relatively active, satisfying lives.

III. SUMMARY AND CONCLUSIONS

This chapter presents research and commentary on general behavior disturbance, certain kinds of clinical disorders, and six types of behavior problems in WS individuals: fears and anxieties, distractibility and attentional problems, impulsivity, poor adaptability, low frustration tolerance, and atypical activity. All are maladaptive behaviors that interfere, in differing degrees, with the personal, social, educational, and vocational development of WSs.

The six types of behavior problems of WSs are synthesized into two basic categories of features that underlie such problems. Following this section, information on the types of behavior disorders displayed by WSs is summarized.

A. Basic Features of Behavior Problems

There appear to be two major features intrinsic to the specific behavior problems of WSs: high reactivity and low self-regulation. These basic features are present in each of the six types of behavior problems.

High reactivity is manifested in WSs' fears and anxieties by their emotional intensity, lability, and overreaction to certain stimuli. It is manifested in WSs' distractibility and attentional problems by their overresponsiveness to irrelevant stimuli, in their impulsivity by unrestrained responding to internal and external stimulation, and in their poor adaptability by overreacting to ordinary changes in plans, schedules, and situations. It is also apparent in WSs' low frustration tolerance by their overreaction to commonplace obstacles, such as denials, changes, or failure; and in WSs' atypical activity by exhibiting unrestrained or excessive forms of motor activity, like squirming, rocking, or wandering around without a defined destination.

Likewise, *low self-regulation* is evident in each type of behavior problem: in WSs' anxieties and fears by their difficulty in handling or restraining their emotional reactions; in WSs' distractibility and attentional problems by their difficulty in filtering out or ignoring irrelevant stimuli and focusing on relevant stimuli; in WSs' impulsivity by being unable to restrain these impulses; in WSs' poor adaptability by having difficulty accommodating to change and following instructions; in WSs' low frustration tolerance by their tendency to engage in acting out, inner directed, or perseverative types of responses; and in WSs' atypical activity by their difficulty in restraining or withholding extraneous forms of activity.

Furthermore, these two basic features, high responsivity and low self-regulation, are complementary in their impact on WSs' behavior problems. High reactivity reflects a quick trigger or intensified level of response to stimulation and low self-regulation reflects WSs' inability to take the necessary steps to control these excesses. Instead of being able to manage their overresponsivity, many WSs are overwhelmed by it. On the other hand, without a predisposition toward overreactivity, WSs might better be able to rally their resources and exert executive control. Low self-regulation together with overreactivity and some of the core features of WS (i.e., perceptual–motor difficulties and cognitive limitations) may form the basis for the specific behavior problems described earlier.

Underlying Mechanisms

Commonalities exist among the six types of WS behavior problems in terms of underlying mechanisms. Across many of the forms of maladaptive behavior, *perceptual–motor difficulties* and *cognitive limitations* are contributing factors. This is evident in the area of fears and anxieties where auditory hypersensitivity, gravitational insecurities, tactile sensitivity and defensiveness, difficulties with visuospatial processing and orientation, and reluctance to engage in motor activities and academic tasks are integrally related to the extreme emotional intensity of most individuals with WS. These types of stimuli and deviations in sensory-perceptual-motor functioning may also impact WSs' distractibility, impulsivity, poor adaptability, low frustration tolerance, and atypical activity patterns as well.

Cognitive limitations in terms of level of general "intelligence," ability to reason, engage in abstract thought, draw inferences, generalize, and comprehend cause–effect relations can severely restrict the capability of WSs to handle information. This impacts directly on problems of rigidity. It also contributes to WSs' problems in other areas: not realizing that many of their fears are unrealistic or the reasons why internal urges and irrelevant external stimuli should be suppressed or ignored; the consequences of their actions; the difficulty in understanding directions and how to comply with them. Most WSs are unable to comprehend the undesirability of their behavior problems without a great deal of assistance.

B. Types of Behavior Disorders

Aside from the six specific types of behavior problems, some WSs manifest a pattern of general behavior disturbance, a few show signs of clinical disorders: autism, ADHD, and emotional problems.

General Behavioral Disturbance

Whereas the six types of behavior problems involve specific types of response or response patterns, behavior disturbance is indicative of a more general level of behavior difficulty, defined by the particular test and items used to measure that difficulty.

On Rutters' Questionnaires, WSc are significantly more likely to meet the criterion for behavior disturbance than nonhandicapped children. Compared to the norms for mentally retarded children, or control groups of mentally retarded children, WS children are higher in frequency in some studies, not others. WSs' elevated rates of behavioral disturbance appear for the most part to reflect their areas of behavioral vulnerability, such as fears and anxieties, irritability, poor concentration, atypical activity, and poor peer relations, as well as physical problems with sleeping, stomach aches, and wetting. High rates of behavior disturbance in WSc, often significantly higher than that MRc or norms for the NH, are also evident in studies using other questionnaires, such as the CBCL and Developmental Behavior Checklist (Einfeld et al., 1997; Einfeld et al., 2001) and measures of temperament (Tomc et al., 1990).

Clinical Disorders

There are also indications that a few WSs exhibit clinical disorders, although their prevalence and severity are not yet determined. In regard to the relation between WS and autism, most WSs share some of the critical characteristics of autism, such as significant delays in the acquisition of speech and language, patterns of agitation and overactivity, and stereotyped, repetitive tendencies, although this is usually much more severe in individuals diagnosed as autistic than in those identified as WS. A very few individuals are reported to have met the diagnostic criteria of both WS and autism and display a mixture of these characteristics. Dual diagnoses of WS and AUT have been identified in a very few cases that seem to display a mixture of characteristics.

Other types of clinical conditions reported in WSs include depression, simple phobias, ADHD, overanxious disorder, and obsessive compulsive disorder. These occur in notable percentages of WSa in several studies and deserve further study to determine the overall incidence and severity of these conditions in WSs. In the meanwhile, it appears that most WSs do not have serious emotional or activity difficulties, but many may exhibit behavioral problems and clinical-like symptoms that warrant attention.

Anecdotal reports of parents and others suggest that more than a few WS teenagers and adults with WS are functioning at a relatively high level in terms of living semiindependently and being vocationally or avocationally involved with a great deal of support, guidance, and aid from family, community, and organizations. Some of these individuals are receiving assistance for their socioemotional and attentional problems.

CHAPTER

7

Intervention Approaches for Maladaptive Behaviors

WSs are often at the mercy of overwhelming fears and anxieties, frustrating demands, inordinate distractibility, uncontrollable impulsivity, and acute resistance to change. In many cases, they have little in the way of resources to help them withstand these pressures. Because of the high frequency of behavior problems and occasional clinical disorder, most of the families of WSs live under unstable and stressful conditions. Parents, teachers, and others are often troubled by WSs' inappropriate behavior and their continual need for attention and supervision. Few caretakers can avoid feeling discouraged, at least at times, by their lack of control over WSs' maladaptive behavior.

One of the major reasons for working actively to resolve or minimize the behavior problems of WSs is the effect they may have on family, teachers, classmates, neighbors, and those in the workplace. The maladaptive behaviors of WSs may also lead to their rejection or ostracism. This would be difficult for any person to accept, but it can be devastating to WSs because of the high value they place on social contact and approval. It is also essential to provide specialized kinds of treatment for those WSs who exhibit the severe behavior problems or behavioral disorders sometimes associated with WS. Clearly, it is important to address the various forms of maladaptive behavior that WSs may demonstrate.

The next section provides a brief overview of evaluation and diagnosis of the various forms of maladaptive behavior displayed by WSs. This is followed by extensive discussion of interventions that may be applicable to each of the six types of behavior problems associated with WS (see chapter

6). Then, the discussion shifts to the treatment of behavior disorders that are sometimes manifested by individuals with WS.

I. EVALUATION AND DIAGNOSIS
OF MALADAPTIVE BEHAVIORS

Some behavior problems exhibited by WSs are relatively easy to identify. Others can be extremely difficult to distinguish. Identification usually proceeds from specific habits, forms of behavior, or responses of the WS individual to the underlying problems described in chapter 6, such as distractibility or low frustration tolerance.

Although this sounds simple, it may not be so in practice. Life can be very fluid, with one event or experience flowing into the next without the opportunity to distinguish or label it, and the behaviors themselves may cover the gauntlet. For example, "impulsivity" may be inferred from a number of different behaviors, such as interrupting others, continually jumping out of one's seat, running up to "greet" strangers, or dashing into the road.

Specific behaviors may also be examined in terms of how they are related to other types of behavior or symptoms. This can reveal the pervasiveness of the behavior, whether something is "seriously wrong," and whether it represents part of a larger pattern of behavior. Some symptoms cluster together as groups or types of disturbance, like neurotic or antisocial disturbances, or clinical disorders like ADHD, depression, anxiety, or occasionally autism. These problems require clinical specialists familiar with WS to make in-depth formal evaluation, diagnosis, and recommendations for treatment.

Sometimes it is difficult to locate professionals who are qualified to treat the psychological and psychiatric problems of individuals with developmental disability. Specialization in both behavior problems and developmental disorders is not too common. Referrals may be obtained, however, by contacting the University Affiliated Programs for People with Disabilities. This organization operates a number of clinics that can provide referrals to therapists in the region or staff on site (Levine, 1994). Contacting a regional WSA official is another alternative (Levine & Wharton, 2001). The Appendix includes a list of WS clinics that can be used for evaluation, treatment, or referral. Professionals unfamiliar with WS may benefit from receiving background information and relevant literature on the syndrome.

In evaluating and diagnosing WSs' behavior, professional specialists often interview parents, teachers, and the WSs in order to clarify the types of maladaptive behaviors and other characteristics displayed by the individual (Sattler, 1988). Standardized tests may also be administered to help with the diagnosis.[9]

These may provide insight into patterns of internalization, neuroticism, hyperactivity, sociability, approach, soothability, and so forth, some of which can be inferred from test results. Several tests may be used to provide an index of the WS individual's level of general behavior disturbance. Questionnaires for parents and teachers concerning WSs' temperament and personality may be particularly revealing. Often, they provide insight into both strengths and weaknesses in the socioemotional functioning of WSs. The entire pattern of results should be considered in order to recognize the co-occurrence of various problems, patterns, and factors. Tests designed to identify specific kinds of clinical disorders are important tools when the diagnosis of such conditions is at issue.

Another factor to be taken into account is the order in which behavior problems should be addressed. In designing of intervention strategies, the issue of priority often arises because WSs usually exhibit various kinds of problems that may be difficult or inadvisable to deal with all at once. Several factors may be considered in making such decisions, such as how troublesome the behavior is for the WS individual and others. The relative severity of the problem compared to the behavior of those individuals who are normally developing individuals or individuals with other forms of developmental disability (e.g., DS, Prader–Willi, or Fragile X) are additional factors. There are also concerns regarding the availability of resources for dealing with those particular kinds of problems.

Here, too, the advice of clinical professionals can be valuable in designing a coordinated program of intervention, as well as being a major part-

---

[9]Tests appropriate for identifying the behavior problems and disturbances of WSs include several mentioned in chapter 6, namely: Rutter's Questionnaires for Parents and Teachers (Schachar, Rutter, & Smith, 1981; Udwin, Yule, & Martin, 1987); Achenbach's Child Behavior Checklist (CBCL) (Achenbach, 1978; Achenbach & Edelbrock, 1979, 1981); the Teacher Rating of Social Skills (TROSS–C) and the Personality Scale for Parents (PIC) (cf. Levine & Castro, 1994); Conners' Rating Scales-Revised (CRS-R, Conners, 1996); and questionnaires of temperament (cf. Tomc et al., 1990) and personality (California Child Q–set, cf., Curfs et al.,1996; Wiegers et al., 1994).

In addition, the *Diagnostic and Statistical Manual of Mental Disorders* (*DSM–III–R* or *DSM–IV*) of the American Psychiatric Association (1987, 1994) provides guidelines for diagnosis of clinical disorders, the AAMR's test of Adaptive Behavior and Functional Living Skills (ABS–S:2, Lambert, Nihira, & Leland, 1981) and the Vineland Adaptive Behavior Scales (Sparrow, Balla, & Cicchetti, 1984) can provide information on how well the WS individual functions in various situations.

Sometimes, tests that focus on behavioral disturbance or particular types of psychiatric disorder, such as autism or ADHD are needed (Finegan et al., 1994). Finally, items from nonstandarized questionnaires like the Utah Survey or WSA regional surveys can offer insight into certain modes of responding.

ner in its operation. Professionals may also be asked to assume responsibility for monitoring the program and suggesting modifications when
warranted.

II. INTERVENTIONS FOR BEHAVIOR PROBLEMS

As each of the six types of behavior problems mentioned in chapter 6 is
characterized by various kinds of response patterns, a wide range of interventions is provided for each type of behavior problem: fears and anxieties,
distractibility and attentional problems, impulsivity, poor adaptability, low
frustration tolerance, and atypical activity.

A. Interventions for Fears and Anxieties

Providing relief for the fears, anxieties, and worries of WSs is often difficult
because of the nature of these concerns. Many center on common daily
events—sudden loud noises, changes in plans, unfamiliar situations, walking
down stairs. Others involve unavoidable situations (e.g., thunderstorms,
earthquakes, and hurricanes), or hypothetical fears about potential disasters (e.g., the health and safety of themselves and others).

On the positive side, many of WSs' concerns are predictable from past
occurrences, which helps to make them more amenable to certain intervention approaches. These may include verbal mediation strategies, control
mechanisms, environmental controls, problem analysis, stress reduction
techniques, and professional treatment.

Verbal Mediation Strategies

Verbal mediation strategies, such as those described next, may be useful in dealing with general anxiety and particular fears often displayed by
WSs.

Reassurance. Often the physical presence and reassurance of a trusted
person may ease the intensity of WSs' anxieties, fears, and worries. Praise
and encouragement are usually ineffective.

Providing comfort and reassuring WSs that "I'll stay with you during the
storm" may help to reduce their fear of thunderstorms. Engaging in joint,
symbolic action, such as "Let's listen for the thunder together and each
time we hear the thunder we will clap our hands" may also help. In role
playing, the child may be encouraged to produce loud sounds similar to
thunder (see chapter 4, p. 181).

In new or unfamiliar situations where many WSs become fearful and anxious, they may be comforted by the presence of a familiar person, toy, or object (Arnold et al., 1985).

On the other hand, dealing with WSs' fears and anxieties can sometimes get out of hand. Clinicians often recommend striking a balance between providing comfort and not making too much of a fuss about a WSc's fears (Udwin & Yule, 1988). Spending only a few minutes each time a topic is raised serves to acknowledge the child's anxieties and provides support without letting these anxieties get out of hand or be used as a major attention-getting device (Udwin & Yule, 1988). Levine (1994) suggested setting aside a particular time of day for dealing with the WSc's worries.

Dramatization. Stories, role playing, pretend play, and puppetry may be used to dramatize anxiety-provoking situations and relieve tension (Levine, 1993; Semel & Rosner, 1991a, 1991b). Verbal labeling during the enactment can help to clarify elements of the situation and explain the sequence of events.

For example, a therapist, parent, educator, or others can role play a visit to the doctor's office for a physical examination or by using a toy doctor's kit to playact the examination. After the child has practiced being the patient, roles can be reversed. Puppets provide opportunities for WSc to reenact such scenarios on their own once they have become familiar with the routine. Asking the WSc to describe the situation and the actions involved in his own words can supply valuable verbal cues for the child to use during the actual appointment.

"Social stories" is another application of dramatization in which illustrations that depict a situation are presented. The WS individual is asked to tell or write stories about the problem that are then connected with possible solutions to the problem (Scheiber, 2000).

Explanation. Many WSs can be calmed if a trusted adult takes time to discuss situations that are anxiety provoking, like the status of someone's health, a parent's forthcoming trip, or an unfamiliar dog or activity. In the case of thunder, WSc may be told that the noise is caused by a fight between hot air and cold air, or that lightning comes before the thunder. Using a meaningful concrete analogy to explain things can be extremely useful. It is also helpful to have the child repeat the explanation aloud and rehearse it silently.

Self-Instruction. Some WSs may be able to learn to monitor their own emotions and apply the requisite strategies, such as self-monitoring, self-reminding, self-enactment, and self-reinforcement, saying—"Boy, I feel better now," or "I did it myself" whenever appropriate.

Teaching WSs to use "stock phrases" in times of stress may help them transform emotions into verbalizations. The following are examples of some stock phrases: "I can do it," "no trouble," "simple as pie," and "easy does it."

Control Mechanisms

Verbal-Social Rewards. Verbal-social rewards can be extremely important when WSs need encouragement in situations involving physical or mental stress.

Immediately before or during a visit to the doctor, the WS individual can be told how happy the doctor and/or parent will be if he or she is cooperative. Other promised rewards may be a cute bandage, or the treat the doctor will offer because the WSc made her or him happy. Worries should be played down but not disregarded. Social incentives may be used to help motivate WSs to participate in painful procedures like giving blood samples, for example, "We'll be so proud of you, when you ____ ." (Levine, 1994)

Humor. A novel approach, well suited for WSs, is to exploit their sense of humor in difficult situations to reduce stress. When WSs are particularly anxious about some unpleasant situation, reference to an absurdity, silly mistake, or ironic aspect of the situation can help to defuse the threat and provide a better chance for coping with the problem. Verbal humor and witty remarks seem to be particularly helpful, but WSs vary among themselves as to what they consider to be funny—in the way of comedy routines, films, comics, jokes, irony, and so on. Being aware of what "tickles" various individuals can be used to help them untangle their emotions and regain their equanimity (Scheiber, 2000).

Wit on the part of WSc and their ability to appreciate humor in threatening situations offer further evidence that WSc tend to differ from most other groups of mentally retarded individuals.

Environmental Controls

Environmental controls are usually helpful in dealing with anxieties concerning changes in plans and novelty.

Predictable Environment. Generalized anxiety and specific fears, particularly about changes in plans, may be reduced by providing a stable, organized environment and being prepared with contingency plans for unanticipated events and unscheduled changes in routines, plans, or activities. Structured daily routines and activities that adhere to a predictable schedule are helpful strategies. Alterations to schedule and plans should be minimized. For use of prearranged options, see the section, "Interventions for Problems of Poor Adaptability," later in the chapter.

MY DAY

Today is _____ Month _____ Day _____   Today's weather is _____

Things to do Today	Morning	Afternoon	Evening
People to visit			
Grandparents	☐	☐	☐
Neighbors	☐	☐	☐
Friends	☐	☐	☐
Workers	☐	☐	☐
	☐	☐	☐
Pet Care			
Feed the pets	☐	☐	☐
Give pets water	☐	☐	☐
Clean out cages or litter	☐	☐	☐
Take to dog out for a walk	☐	☐	☐
Let the cat out	☐	☐	☐
Brush pets	☐	☐	☐
	☐	☐	☐
Places to go			
Party	☐	☐	☐
Holidays	☐	☐	☐
Movie	☐	☐	☐
TV Show	☐	☐	☐
Bike riding	☐	☐	☐
Music Lesson	☐	☐	☐
Horseback riding	☐	☐	☐
Ball game	☐	☐	☐
Library	☐	☐	☐
Play outside	☐	☐	☐
Play inside	☐	☐	☐
	☐	☐	☐

Along the same lines, events like doctor's visits should not come as a complete surprise. Some preparation, but not too far in advance, may mitigate anxiety (Levine, 1994). Premature discussion may heighten anxiety.

Problem Analysis

Many WSs are able to benefit from discussion aimed at identifying their fears and anxieties and how these may be eased. This is a form of metacognition, or thinking about one's own thoughts, feelings, or emotional state.

Identifying "Worries." The parent or teacher may begin by saying one
of the following:

"Let's try to figure out what you were worried about when __.
Were you afraid that *'X'* will happen, or were you scared about *'Y'*?"
"Are you worrying about something that you can do nothing about?"
"Is this a worry about things that are imaginary or things that could actu-
ally happen?"
"If it actually could happen, what would take place, and what is the worst
case?"

Of course, pauses should be inserted between questions to give WSs sufficient time to think about the answer rather than responding "off the top."
    The timing of problem analysis is also important. It should not take place
while the WS individual is feeling anxious or when anxiety-provoking situations arise. Instead, discussion should be delayed until tension is reduced.

Addressing "Worries." Sometimes metacognition can be used to help
address WSs' "worries" and anxieties. For example, the WS individual can
be asked: "What kinds of things make you feel less scared?" This can provide cues as to how to proceed.
    It is often possible to identify concrete ways in which the WS person's
concerns may be eased. This may involve, for example, helping the WS individual prepare for a trip or exam, encouraging the person to practice an assignment, or helping the person to find a lost object. In dealing with task-
related fears, WSc can be told exactly what behaviors may be expected of
them (Semel & Rosner, 1991b). Verbal mediational "stock phrases" are also
helpful.
    When confronting real worries that exclude the possibility of construc-
tive action, the WS individual may be comforted by being told "Think positively," "Don't expect the worst," or "Just do your best." These phrases are
examples of the use of verbal mediation to help bridge the gap between
emotions and events. These and other phrases like "I will be so happy when
this is over" can be suggested for use as "self-talk."
    WSs may also be reassured by being told that "something like that hap-
pened to me when I was [about your age], but you can see that I'm still here
and getting along just fine." For worries involving other people, it is sometimes helpful to say something like: "It's up to other people to face their
worries just like we are taking care of your own worries right now."
    Regarding unrealistic worries, WSs may be advised that: "It's a waste of
time to worry about things that won't happen for a long time or may never
happen." Explaining in detail the philosophy of "one day at a time" may

help ease the WS individual's concerns. Repeating this phrase at appropriate times can be a powerful aid.

For more extreme worries about unreal situations or objects, the WS person may be reassured by having his or her feelings acknowledged and being told: "Worrying makes you very tense. Let's agree to talk about your worries for a certain amount of time and then do something else." Udwin and Yule (1998a, 1998b) recommend addressing such fears as early as possible in the child's life.

Although many WSs can work together on problem analysis with an adult (parent, teacher, or other professional), some are unable to do so. Other measures are more appropriate for them. To whatever degree the parents and teachers agree to verbally comfort the child, time limits should be placed on discussion of a WSc's anxieties. Reserving a specific time of day for "worry time" is also useful as it can postpone repeated requests for talking/dealing with such topics. In this way, the WSc is discouraged from obsessing and discussion of worries or using it as an unlimited attention-getting device (Udwin & Yule, 1998a, 1998b).

Stress Reduction Techniques

Stress reduction techniques may be useful in handling generalized anxiety, task anxieties, and unidentified worries. This may involve use of relaxation techniques and helping WSs achieve a more positive view of life and their place in it.

Relaxation Techniques. Parents of some WS teens and adults support the use of relaxation techniques to help control their WSs' emotional problems and stress level (Levine, 1994). Techniques mentioned include meditation, yoga, biofeedback, exercise, focused breathing, repeating a common phrase like a mantra, taking a walk, going into the jacuzzi, rubbing stones, manipulating silly putty, rolling Chinese chime balls, listening to audiotapes of relaxation exercises, among others.

Preparing tape recordings of material that is particularly pleasing for the individual, like a certain kind of music or recounting a previously successfully managed experience of a feared situation, can be very effective. One family uses a Walkman during airplane flights to help a WS youth handle his fear of flying (Anonymous Caller, personal communication, Williams Syndrome Hotline, Jan. 1999). A few parents report having used positive imagery with their WSc (see section on "Behavioral therapy," later). This is related to concrete imagery (see section on "Explanation").

Positive Experiences. A more general kind of verbal-social reward, incorporating experiences of social success in usual routines, may be effective in alleviating the overall level of tension and anxiety of WSs (Levine,

1994; Semel, 1988; Semel & Rosner, 1991b). Participation in activities that
draw on the special aptitudes of WSs, like singing in a chorus, can lift their
general mood and boost their self-esteem. Feeling better about themselves
may help WSs cope more effectively with their fears and anxieties and
other forms of maladaptive behavior.

Professional Treatment

Treatment by appropriate professionals (e.g., psychiatrists, psychologists, social workers, and counselors) is advised for cases involving acute
fears and deep anxieties, specific phobias, and other emotional disorders.
Behavior modification, desensitization, and mental imagery procedures
may be adapted to treat certain fears of WSs. Treatment of fears and anxieties related to auditory hypersensitivity and perceptual–motor activities
may require other approaches, namely, speech and language therapy, treatment by an educational audiologist, or physical, occupational, or sensory
integration therapy (see chap. 4).

Psychotherapy. According to Levine (1994), WSa with emotional difficulties are often responsive to both group psychotherapy and individual psychotherapy. Early detection and treatment of WS individuals with problems
of anxiety and emotional difficulty is advised (Brewer et al., 1995). In psychotherapy, some WSs may be able to gain insight into how they typically
react to stress. A psychotherapist may also be able to help boost their self-
esteem, and decrease their feelings of anger, frustration, anxiety, or sadness (Scheiber, 2000).

Medication. Likewise, certain medications have been found to be helpful in relieving the severe anxiety and depression of some WS individuals
(Brewer et al., 1995).

A great deal of background information is needed in regard to use of
medication for WSs, in particular for WSc. The key is always to be fully informed about the effects of any medication, and to coordinate its use with
other forms of intervention. (Scheiber, 2000).

In the use of psychotherapy, too, background information is invaluable
in deciding whether, how, and where a WS individual may benefit from or
require psychotherapy.

The applicability of psychotherapy and medication to WSs' problems of
emotionality and other kinds of behavior disorders is discussed more extensively in Section III, "Clinical Treatment for Behavior Disorders of WSs"
(pp. 341–355).

There are two particular forms of therapy, however, that are especially
appropriate in treating many of the specific fears and anxieties associated

with WS: desensitization and mental imagery. These are briefly described next.

Desensitization Training. With desensitization, a behavioral therapist trains the phobic person to tolerate increasingly closer contact with the feared stimulus. The person is taught methods of physical relaxation and applies these methods to ease the tension when stimulus strength is intensified.

Consider the treatment of a person's phobic reaction to dogs. The child is initially placed at a distance from the feared animal but as close as can be tolerated. While the child practices relaxation, proximity to the dog is gradually increased until a pre-established goal of close association and fear avoidance is achieved, for example, petting or picking up the animal if this can be done safely. WSs need to realize that not all dogs are friendly. The person's approach responses can be positively reinforced, as in the adapted forms of behavior modification suggested for WS individuals.

Mental Imagery. Mental imagery, a more cognitive type of behavioral therapy, may also be helpful. The therapist instructs the patient to imagine or pretend that certain anxiety-provoking situations are taking place. Instructions are introduced gradually, sometimes accompanied by reassurance or stress management techniques like deep breathing, until the patient is able to handle more intense kinds of imagined and then real experiences with the feared stimulus or situation, aided by concrete imagery.

In concrete imagery, the WS's response pattern and its consequences are concretely depicted. Simple step-by-step illustrations of the problem and the tasks involved in its solution are provided. Other examples of the problem are related to it for further discussion and possible applicability. Related verbal analogies can help to concretize the situation for the WSs. This process can be very beneficial for some WSs.

B. Interventions for Distractibility and Attentional Problems

Distractibility is a focal problem for most WSs in terms of frequency and severity. It also affects almost all areas of their lives: interactions with parents and peers (e.g., difficulty in following directions, topic discontinuity); learning in the classroom and other settings; performing adequately in group activities or on the job (see chap. 6). Fortunately, a variety of measures may be used to help WSs control their distractibility and decrease their attention problems. These may include control mechanisms, verbal mediation strategies, problem analysis, environmental controls, task management, and professional treatment.

Control Mechanisms

Several types of control mechanisms may help to moderate the distractibility and attention problems of WSs. Attending behaviors should be rewarded; "off task" behaviors either should be redirected or ignored (Levine, 1993). Remember an old directive given to teachers about positive reinforcement, "catch the child being good," and then comment favorably on the desired behavior. Direct instruction is another approach, and behavioral contracts yet another. Clear and concise instructions help the child to understand what is expected; regular prompting reminds the WSc to stay focused (Udwin & Yule, 1998a, 1998b). In some cases, inattentiveness may occur because the task is too difficult. If this seems to be the case, a somewhat simpler assignment may be substituted.

Reinforcement.   Positive, verbal–social reinforcement may enable WSs to concentrate on and complete assigned tasks. Parents and teachers should reward WSs when they avoid engaging in distracted behaviors, such as paying attention to objects of special interest, background noises, or other children. Improvement in attending to instructions, focusing on a task, or organizing task materials may also be reinforced. Using a chart to plot "on task" performance may help to concretize and motivate these efforts.

Other strategies include making rewards contingent on paying attention for increasing periods of time (Udwin & Yule, 1998a, 1998b) and providing an appropriate reward for task completion.

Occasional use of negative reinforcement is also recommended. Parents and teachers are often amazed at how well WSs respond to statements of personal disappointment or disapproval, such as, "It really makes me sad when you _____."

Direct Instruction.   WSc often require repeated direct instruction (e.g., "look at the paper") and reminders (e.g., "keep on working") in order to concentrate on the task at hand. Such statements should be made in a firm, supportive manner, using an authoritative style. Standing close and smiling directly at the WS individual can help to refocus attention.

Another way to increase WSs' concentration is through individualized instruction (Udwin & Yule, 1988, 1989). This tends to provide organizational support, helps WSs focus on the task, and satisfies their need for attention. Direct eye contact is important, especially when giving directions. Regular prompting may help remind the student to stay on task (Udwin & Yule, 1998).

Behavioral Contracts.   Some educators find it helpful to draw up a behavioral contract with a particular student. If the child is not familiar with the concept of a "contract," then she or he can be told. It is like a promise that two people make to each other." Part A of the contract usually stipulates behaviors that the student agrees to control, such as "I will pay attention" or "I will finish my work"; Part B establishes the predetermined form of reinforcement, for example, "If I do all spelling assignments, I will be able to go to lunch with my teacher." If the procedure of a "token economy" is used, it may be appropriate to say something like, "If I earn ____ (certain number of smiling faces or tokens) by ____ (a certain date), then I will be allowed to ____ (visit the school secretary)." In Part C, students can state their intention, such as, "Next time, I will not ____ (a certain type of behavior)."

The contract is signed by both student and teacher to signify their agreement with its terms. If students are unable to read the contract, then it can be read to them. Contracts can be very effective with certain WSs.

Verbal Mediation Strategies

In applying verbal mediation, it is important to label the distracted behavior as it occurs and contrast it with the desired behavior. This may help make WSs more aware of their problems and better able to discuss them. If the WSc seems really unaware of his or her distracted behavior, a videotape may help to clarify it. Videotaping another student, or the WS individual, while concentrating on a task may demonstrate dramatically the contrast between focused and distracted behaviors.

Dramatization. Puppetry, humor, and social stories are alternative ways of bringing the situation to life and depicting the negative consequences of inattention: Nothing can be accomplished when an individual is preoccupied with extraneous stimuli. (See Section A, "Interventions for Fears and Anxieties," p. 301, for further discussion.)

Self-Instruction. Self-instruction may have impressive results in improving WSs' efforts to concentrate (Semel & Rosner, 1991b; Udwin & Yule, 1988, 1989). In particular, pretaught "stock phrases" may be used to help WSs monitor their own behavior. (See Section A, for more detail.)

Environmental Controls

WSc are usually more likely to pay attention in settings that are quiet and free from distraction (Udwin & Yule, 1998a). Providing for their physical comfort is also important. Although some of the restrictions described here may seem unduly demanding, they are often necessary. They may be slowly reduced over time.

Visual Distractions. In the classroom, the WSc's desk should be cleared of all materials that are not in use (Semel, 1988). A solid-colored desk top may be helpful. Other visual distractions should be eliminated wherever possible by removing or covering unnecessary stimuli, clutter, or items that divert attention from the task at hand (Semel, 1988). This includes objects of special interest (Levine, 1997).

Wall colors that are light in tone and subdued, but not drab, seem to help attention problems. Various shades of green seem to enhance visual perception, hence the use of the color green for chalkboards. Lighting is best when it is free of glare and there are no shadows on written material.

Key information in instructional materials can be emphasized by limiting, wherever possible, the number of items or problems per page, deleting items that are extraneous or confusing, and eliminating blurred copies. A clipboard can help keep papers and desk space organized.

Some WSs can become completely distracted by the clothing worn by teachers, examiners, and other individuals. Shiny earrings, a jangling bracelet, dangling necklace, tossing of the hair, or a floral pattern on a necktie or dress can mesmerize WSs. When dealing with WSs, professionals should consider dressing in solid colors, plain patterns, with few details in their clothing. To further reduce WSs' distractibility, a teacher or examiner may be advised to tie up hair that is long and swishy or tuck it under the collar while teaching or testing WSs.

Auditory Distractions. Auditory distractions should also be minimized (Levine, 1993; Semel & Rosner, 1991a, 1991b). Intrusive sounds may be muffled through the use of noise reduction earmuffs or noise abatement hard hats for children such as those worn by construction workers, or other ear protector devices. Drapes and carpeting, furniture, acoustic ceiling tile, and insulation boards often help to deaden outside noises and sharp piercing sounds. Simply shutting a window may effectively reduce some extraneous noise. Loud bells ringing to signal a period change in school can be extremely aversive to some WSc (see chap. 4, Section IV). The occurrence of disturbing or sudden sounds should be minimized by such measures as turning down the volume on the telephone. When it is necessary to use a loud appliance, the child can be warned and invited to help turn it on (Scheiber, 2000).

Tactile Defensiveness. Tactile defensiveness also may contribute to the WSc's difficulty in paying attention. Annoying tactile stimuli, like a stiff desk chair or irritating clothing, may intrude on the WSc's attention. An occupational therapist should be consulted for severe problems of tactile defensiveness (see chap. 4, Section III).

Location in the Classroom. Seat placement is one of the most valuable tools for combating distractibility in the classroom. Many WSc concentrate better when they are seated near the chalkboard or close enough to the teacher to establish frequent eye contact. Proximity to noisy, busy hallways or windows with interesting views should be avoided. It may be helpful to face the child's desk toward the wall and out of the sun's glare (Grejtak, 1996a).

Seat selection should be determined mainly by the needs of the individual WSc. For some, this means being placed a bit away from all children, for others, being placed near a few "role model" children or "buddies." For still others, placement should be distanced from the most disruptive children. Most profit by sitting near or in front of the teacher. Many WSc are distracted by their classmates' actions. Some may begin to imitate them. Naturally, this should be discouraged when negative acts are imitated.

Proximity to "traffic" patterns or routes to other areas in the classroom may also be disruptive to WSc. Often a controlled workspace, separate work area, or cubicle can help to reduce distractions. A study carrel, or "learning office," with clearly defined boundaries and few visual and auditory distractions may be helpful for seat work. Furniture should be attractive but not distracting, and functionally arranged to be safe and barrier free (see chap. 4). It is also important to plan a "time-out" area as WS individuals often require significant personal space. Short periods of work interspersed with frequent breaks may be necessary (Levine, 1997; Udwin & Yule, 1998a).

Posture Patterns. A traditional attending posture, such as "eyes on teacher, feet on floor, hands on desk, seat up straight," may be helpful for some WSc. For others, it can be obstructive (see chap. 4).

Often the attending pattern of WSs may be quite different from the standard model. Some WS individuals show associated movements; they may tend to tilt their heads as if to view the material better, and their tongue may protrude from the corner of the mouth with some drooling while they are engaged in near-point tasks like writing, drawing, coloring, and cutting. A few exhibit head bobbing when engaged in other motor activities. Others may find it helpful to lie on the floor, as it seems to enhance visual perception. Still others work well in a rocking chair. Such habits may be similar to, or consist of, neurologic "soft signs" like motor "overflow."

Attempts to alter these patterns may sometimes have the unintended effect of reducing the WSc's ability to pay attention or perform fine motor tasks. Unless they interfere with class management, efforts to discourage such mannerisms should be discontinued, at least temporarily.

Task Management

Task management is a powerful way to address the distractibility and attention problems of WSs. Concentration may be markedly improved by dividing each task into small steps, each with a verbalized goal and illustrations presented in the proper sequence. In many cases, the goal for the entire task can be specified and repeated aloud by the WS individual. Directions for each step should be given immediately before it is to be performed and repeated as needed. Off-task behaviors should be redirected or ignored (Levine, 1993). Tasks need to be structured and predictable, yet varied to prevent boredom from repetitive drill.

Standards of acceptable performance should be established beforehand and adjusted to the WS's ability. Task completion should be achievable within the time limits agreed on in advance. Short work periods are optimal (Udwin & Yule, 1998a, 1998b). Under these conditions, the WS individual may be held accountable for finishing the assignment.

Levine (1993) recommended using a high success, high motivation curriculum. This may involve allowing WSs some voice in selecting study content and classroom activities. Attention may be enhanced by including hands-on learning tasks, incorporating pictures into the required material (Levine, 1997), and their considerable musical skills where appropriate. Permitting frequent breaks and some flexibility in the amount and distribution of work time also may be helpful.

Attention Needs. Because most WSs show wide intraindividual fluctuations in attention, the attention pattern of the individual should be determined and utilized whenever possible. New materials should be presented when attending behavior is at its highest, material review in periods of low attention. As WSs are typically less attentive before lunch and at the end of the school day, unfamiliar or challenging material should not be taught during these times.

Other conditions affecting attention behaviors should be identified when possible. For example, relationships with other children may be significant. The teacher's energy, enthusiasm, and proximity may also affect the WS's efforts to attend.

Modality Effects. Likewise, attending behavior may be improved by acknowledging the modality strengths and weaknesses of the WS individual. This entails teaching new material through the most intact sensory channel and reviewing material with less favored channels. Most WSs learn better with auditory input than with other modes, although some WSs learn better visually. Generally, most learn best with multimodal input in which visual or auditory channels are supplemented by tactile-kinesthetic stimulation (except in cases of tactile defensiveness). The WSc's natural verbosity may be used to advantage to teach motor skills by encouraging the youngster to talk through tasks (Udwin & Yule, 1998a, 1998b).

Adapting Content. The characteristics of the material should also be taken into account. It should be appropriate in content and difficulty. Concentration is generally improved when materials are related to the student's area of special interest, or relevant activities and events like holidays (Udwin & Yule, 1988, 1989).

As children with WS are frequently preoccupied with or fascinated by a particular subject, incorporating WSs' topic of special interest into the curriculum may increase the child's interest and motivation to learn. This is especially so when perceptual exercises, reading, and writing assignments are involved (Udwin & Yule, 1998a).

Using rewards related to WSc's obsessive interests, such as time with a particular toy, or permission to watch construction work, can be a powerful incentive for concentrating on less interesting tasks. It is advised that this be done after the child has spent a specific period of time working on assignments, for example, 5 to 10 minutes. Work time may be increased from 5 to 10 to 15 minutes in length; longer periods of work may include 2-minute breaks (Udwin & Yule, 1998a, 1998b).

Caution must be exercised when appealing to a WSc's preoccupations. Excessive dwelling on them may lead to unhealthy obsessions. This may be curtailed by introducing new interests for the child and establishing boundaries for engaging in preoccupations.

Work Partners. An optimal buddy, work partner or work setting may also maximize the WSc's ability to concentrate. The type of partner depends on the particular child. Some WSc work best alone, others do better with a particular buddy or helpful peer, and still others succeed with a teacher's aide (Levine, 1993). An aide can help the WSc to stay focused on the task at hand (Scheiber, 2000). It may also be beneficial to arrange for a note-taker for the child, or to provide help with verbal instructions or picture cues on an assignment (Scheiber, 2000).

Instructional Devices. Many kinds of instructional assists can be provided to enlist attending behaviors. Class materials may be kept organized by using color coding. Notebooks can have color-coded dividers and pockets for loose papers. Spiral bound paper notebooks with color coded dividers or plastic tabs are usually preferable to loose leaf paper. Tape recorders, calculators, computers, magnifiers, study guides, and answer keys are instructional aids that may improve the ability of WSs to focus on assigned tasks. Such equipment may work best with older WSc, and should not be too complex. More than one instructional aid at a time may prove distract-ing. It is important that these devices be included in the WS student's In-structional Educational Plan (IEP).

External "Clocks". Some WSs are able to benefit from using an external time keeping device to monitor their time on task. The device can be an egg timer, digital clock, or large clock with an easy-to-read minute hand. Any will do, as long as the WS individual is able to relate changes in the device to changes in time. Once the expected time for task completion is specified and its relation to the time indicator of the device is understood, work on the task can begin. Timers that use bells or other sounds should be avoided if it is troublesome to the individual. Music boxes may be more useful.

Problem Analysis

Working together with an adult, some WSs can be helped to become more aware of their attention problems and better able to deal with them.

The teacher, parent, or supervisor can broach the subject by saying something like this: "Let's talk about what kinds of things keep you from do-ing your work. Is it ___ or ___?" This can be followed by exploring ways in which the WS individual may be helped: "Would it be helpful if we do this ____ or that?" "What kinds of things could you do to help yourself?"

Professional Treatment

Finally, "consultation with a behaviorist familiar with positive behavior management approaches" may be effective in reducing WSs' distractibility problems (Levine, 1993, p. 4). Adapting behavior modification methods for use with WSs is usually required. This includes using rewards that are opti-mal for the WS (Udwin & Yule, 1988, 1989).

In some cases, medication prescribed by a physician is used to stabilize the attention of WS individuals (Levinson, 1994), especially when inatten-tion is accompanied by other behavior problems or is part of a behavior disorder. Parents and teachers should be informed about the possible ef-fectiveness and side effects of different medications, and realize that "Medi-cation should not be used alone, as a magic bullet, but as part of a fuller program of behavior management" (Scheiber, 2000, p. 65). For further dis-cussion of the use of medication for distractibility and other maladaptive behaviors of WSs, see Section III. B, Psychopharmacology (p. 351).

In any case, people must understand that WSs really suffer from distractibility and attention defects. They are not merely being recalcitrant or disobedient when they are inattentive.

C. Interventions for Problems of Impulsivity

For their sake and that of others, WSs must be helped to control their tendency to act on internal urges and engage in disruptive or dangerous activities. Experience indicates that several types of interventions may help curb WSs' impulsivity, namely, control mechanisms, verbal mediational techniques, logical consequences, problem analysis, relaxation techniques, and professional treatment.

Control Mechanisms

Impulsive behavior usually requires use of control mechanisms, many of which can be effectively combined with verbal mediation.

Direct Instruction. Verbal directives are often effective in bringing unacceptable behavior under control, especially when they are expressed in an authoritative style that implies strong disapproval. Examples are: "Stop that! Hey, I said stop that right now;" or "Don't hug that person, you don't know him/her." Likewise, the WS individual may be told: "Talking out when someone else is speaking is not allowed. Now it's (X's) turn," or "____ (child's name), hold that question; I'll get to it when we're finished with ____." Asking WSs to repeat what was said establishes whether it was understood.

Parents, teachers, and others must try to avoid statements that convey anger, hostility, rejection, or sarcasm even when their patience is completely exhausted by WSs' continual outbreaks, interruptions, or other impulsive behaviors. Overly critical, condescending, shaming, or insulting remarks are counterproductive and can weaken an already fragile ego. These kinds of "put-down messages" can have a destructive effect on WSs' self-esteem and the person's relationship with the WS individual. Usually, it is better to be gentle but firm, and even to employ humor to calm the child (Scheiber, 2000).

Examples of negative, put-down statements that should be *avoided* are: "You should be ashamed of yourself and how you behaved"; "I don't know what is wrong with you, that was a dumb thing to do"; "Are you deaf or something?".

A more effective strategy is to establish and use a mutually determined system of cues to inform WSs that they are engaging in behavior that must be stopped. Cues may include nonverbal signals such as eye contact, facial expressions, finger gestures, or saying the child's name and lightly touching the child to make contact (Scheiber, 2000).

Reinforcement. Impulsive behavior must not be positively reinforced, unwittingly or unintentionally, especially by excessive scolding. Frequent scolding can reinforce bad habits, because it is a form of attention giving.

Instead, the WS individual must come to realize that disruptive behavior has negative consequences. Consistent use of negative reinforcement may help discourage disruptive behavior in the long run.

Parents and teachers should establish clear-cut consequences for misconduct and convey those consequences to their WSs. It is also important to follow through with these warnings by taking appropriate action, such as removing or reducing privileges, imposing time-out in the classroom or the WS's room at home, or reducing time for recess, special interests, or watching television. See page 319 for the use of "logical consequences."

Parents, teachers, and other adults may also appeal to the WSs' desire to please by expressing their displeasure with the individual's antics. Useful statements are: "It makes me unhappy when you do that," or "It hurts me to see you like that." When interfering behaviors do occur, it is usually better to avoid use of punishment and instead employ verbal reinforcement, positive facial cues, or systematic withdrawal of adult attention. Ignoring WSs' misbehavior may be effective because it does not gratify their intense need for attention (Borghgraef et al., 1994; Udwin, 1990).

Along the same lines, positive forms of behavior should receive verbal-social rewards (Udwin & Yule, 1988; 1989). These "good" WSc behaviors may include sitting quietly, waiting patiently, or refraining from quarreling, tattling, bullying, or interrupting. In addition, peer pressure can be used as both a positive and negative reinforcer. Peers can be asked to ignore undesirable forms of responding and to look pleased or express pleasure when the WS individual successfully engages in waiting and turn-taking behaviors. Peers can also serve as models of good behavior for WSs to imitate.

Rechanneling Tactics. Sometimes diversionary tactics can be helpful. For example, providing opportunities for WSs to talk at other times may reduce problems of uninhibited "calling out." Most WSs respond enthusiastically to open-ended questions, such as, "Who has something to share about a holiday vacation/day at school?" After listening to the response, the teacher or parent can help bring the talk to a logical conclusion, smile, and then say, "Now, it is time for you to listen and it is someone else's turn to speak."

Likewise, disruptive forms of behavior can sometimes be curtailed by introducing substitute forms of acceptable behavior. For example, compulsive greeting behavior can sometimes be deterred by asking a WSc to serve as the official class or family "greeter." In that role, the WSc is able to greet selected people who enter the classroom or family home.

Behavioral Contracts. Alternatively, objectionable forms of impulsivity can be dealt with by using a behavioral contract that can be written, oral, or both (for further discussion, see Section B, "Interventions for Distractibility and Attention Problems," p. 308). Examples of behaviors the WSs may agree to control are: "I don't say hello to strangers in my class," "I raise my hand for permission to talk," "I don't talk while others are talking."

Verbal Mediation Strategies

Verbal Rehearsal and Self-Talk. Once desired behaviors have been demonstrated, explained, and understood, WSs may be taught to verbally rehearse the target forms of newly acquired information, such as, "I must not play with matches; I could hurt myself." Likewise, some WSs can use self-instructed reminders and stock phrases once they have been carefully trained in the use of the strategy. (For further discussion, see Section A, pp. 301–302).

Another example of this application is having a WSc learn to say something like: "If I talk when the teacher is explaining a lesson, then the teacher will be angry. I don't want the teacher to be mad at me, so I won't talk now"; "If I raise my hand to ask a question, then the teacher smiles at me and explains what I want to know. So, I better just raise my hand and wait until she calls on me."

Rule-Governed Behavior. In the long gradual process of development, WSc are required to learn and internalize specific rules and limitations that are externally imposed. Society, the home, the school, and the community set forth the requirements of these rule-governed behaviors. Because it is expected that members of society will follow these "rules," they need to be explicitly taught, repeatedly practiced, and incorporated into the individual's behavioral repertoire so that they can be accessed almost automatically. Unfortunately, WSc tend to have difficulty adhering to rule-governed behaviors (Anonymous callers, personal communication, Williams Syndrome Hotline, 1998, 1999, 2000).

Some of the rule-governed behaviors which WSc are often slow to acquire are: (a) obtaining teacher permission before calling out answers or making comments in class; (b) adhering to following safety regulations for car passengers and street crossing; (c) or using dressing, hygiene, and toileting routines; (d) selecting appropriate, clean clothing; (e) playing with and storing toys properly; (f) performing regularly assigned household chores; (g) using shopping carts properly; (h) applying good table manners and behaving appropriately in a restaurant; and (i) adhering to bedtime rituals among others.

In addition, WSs often have problems with punctuality or use of time, for example, in the following situations: (a) time to come to the table for meals, or return home from visiting neighbors; (b) time to engage in special interests; (c) time to listen to tapes, view television and select programs; (d) time to work on homework assignments; and (e) time to turn in teacher assigned papers (Anonymous callers, personal communication, Williams Syndrome Hotline, 1998, 1999, 2000).

Applying Verbal Mediation to Rule-Governed Behaviors. There are several ways to bring WSs' problems with rule-governed behaviors under better control through the use of verbal mediation strategies.

For example, reminding WSs of the rule-governed behavior before there are problems with it may be helpful. Comments such as the following may be used: "Remember, be back soon; we eat at 6:00 PM"; "Remember, the TV is to be turned off by _ o'clock"; "Remember, you must put on your PJs and then brush your teeth."

Verbal mediation can help develop bridging activities that clarify the relation between the behavior and its consequences. Expected rule-governed behaviors can be discussed so that the WSc knows exactly what behaviors are required and which ones are to be avoided. Concrete analogies and reasoning can be used in the discussion to foster increased understanding of rule-governed behaviors.

The use of verbal mediation can help remind the WSc to adhere to a specific rule-governed behavior by setting a brief time limit. A surprisingly simple but effective behavioral control to help WSc comply with issued directions is for the teacher or parent to say something like this:

"I am going to count to three. If you are not _____ by the time I say three, you will not be allowed to _____ (visit the new construction site)."

"One, one and a half, two, two and a quarter, two and a half, two and three quarters . . ."

Fortunately, many WSc comply before the number three has to be uttered (Anonymous callers, personal communication, Williams Syndrome Hotline, 1998, 1999, 2000). Of course, the adult must be prepared to follow through on the consequence or this technique loses its value.

Verbal prompts may be used to help the WSc conform, including reminders like: "You know that you are not supposed to _____." WSc's attempts to comply with prescribed procedures should be verbally reinforced. Others may be informed, in front of the WSc, about occasions when rule-governed behaviors were successfully employed.

To facilitate verbal mediation of rule-governed behaviors, role-playing, videotaping and tape-recording for discussion, demonstration, review, and repetition may be very helpful.

Whereas some WSc are able to use self-instruction, others need regular supervision in the form of direct instruction, repeated explanation, and directed rehearsal to guide their behavior.

It should also be noted that verbal mediation strategies are most suitable for rule-governed behaviors, whereas control mechanisms, specifically time-out methods, work best with acting-out behavior (see Section II. E., pp. 328–329).

It is important to identify alternative patterns of behavior like withdrawal, irritability, and passive aggression as a failure to observe rule-governed behavior when that is the case. Using verbal mediation and dramatization to explain and encourage the use of rule-governed behaviors may help WSs deal with this problem.

Logical Consequences. Discussion and the use of logical consequences that are directly related to the misbehavior may be useful for certain WSs. This type of strategy has some of the elements of behavioral control plus some elements of verbal mediation. It is different from direct punishment in that the consequence of the misbehavior is a logical extension or outcome of the transgression and discussion is an integral part of the process. It is most aptly described by the principle of "the punishment should fit the crime."

In using this procedure, care needs to be taken that angry feelings, threats, or warnings are not issued. There should not be any yelling or put-down messages. Instead, the logical consequence of unacceptable behavior is conveyed in a friendly voice and positive attitude. Elements of moral judgment should not be presented, so the consequence is not related to experiences in which the behavior might have occurred in the past. This technique is not designed to make the child feel guilty or "bad" but simply to foster a better way to behave.

One example of the use of logical consequences addressed a recurring problem with a WSc who failed to pick up her clothes and put them in the hamper even after reminders that only clothes in the hamper would be washed on washday. When it was time to go out the next day and the child did not have any clean clothes, her parent explained, in a direct and assertive way, "You didn't put your dirty clothes in the hamper as I told you to do. You'll have to wear your old dirty clothes that smell." After several such reinforcements, using logical consequences, the WSc learned to put the dirty clothes in the hamper (Anonymous caller, personal communication, Williams Syndrome Hotline, June 1999).

Another example of logical consequences was applied when a parent told her son that the family would eat dinner at 6 o'clock, but he failed to return home on time from visiting the next-door construction site. In a quiet, friendly voice, his mother explained, "You did not come home on time; you're late again. You'll have to wait until we finish dinner, then you may eat by yourself" (Anonymous caller, personal communication, Williams Syndrome Hotline, Feb. 1998). No punishments, no threats, no yelling, coaxing, lecturing, or reminding is ever used when implementing such tactics. The WSc is left to experience the logical consequences of his actions and choices. In this particular case, the procedure helped the WSc learn to avoid irresponsible behavior and pay attention to the time he was supposed to be home (Anonymous caller, personal communication, Williams Syndrome Hotline, Feb. 1998).

Impulsive forms of behavior may often be curbed by verbal labeling, dramatization, and explaining the undesirable consequences of the behavior that the WS individual should try to control. With WSs, it is important to explain the negative effects of each form of impulsive behavior, and the specific cause–effect relations involved in each case. One must be attentive to the amount of time spent discussing such behaviors, or the WSc may quickly perceive that his undesirable behavior gets him additional adult attention (Levine, 1997).

Such discussions may be helped along by WSs' sociability and empathetic nature. For example, the etiquette of turn-taking and turn-yielding may be justified by saying that other children want a chance to be first, too. The need to curtail interrupting in class or calling out to people may be explained by pointing out that this is disturbing to the teacher and other students. The strategy of "logical consequences" is a follow-up and depends on verbal mediation techniques.

Problem Analysis

Working together with an adult, some WSs may be able to discuss their disruptive behavior or tendencies in a rather objective way. This may include deciding which problems should be worked on, the order in which they should be addressed, and by whom.

Stress Reduction Techniques

Some parents of teenagers and adults with WS report that deep breathing and other relaxation techniques may provide a "breather" (Levine, 1994; Scheiber, 2000). This can help some WSs to regroup and gain better control over their impulsive tendencies. (See Section II. A, for other relaxation techniques, p. 305.)

Professional Treatment

Sometimes adapted forms of behavior modification may help WSs who are unreceptive to verbal, interactive techniques and cannot be reached with positive and negative reinforcement contingencies.

In other cases, WSs may benefit from being referred to a clinical or behavioral psychologist or educational specialist for treatment of impulsivity.

This specialist may work directly with the WSc, but also may enlist the co-operation of parents to extend and reinforce the effects of individual treatment sessions.

In addition, specific problems of impulsivity may require specialized forms of treatment. For example, it may be helpful to consult a speech language therapist (SLT) to help deal with problems of calling out or incessant talking that are not amenable to the usual psycho-educational techniques.

The management of WSc can be difficult for caregivers. Unfortunately, there is no magic spell that will suddenly cure problems associated with impulsivity. However, patience, persistence, and good sense go a long way.

D. Interventions for Problems of Poor Adaptability

WSs' poor adaptability is exemplified by problems of rigidity and difficulty in following directions. Although these kinds of problems are still being investigated, steps may be taken to deal with them. For problems of rigidity, intervention strategies may include use of environmental controls, task management, and verbal mediation.

Difficulty in following directions may be addressed by using problem analysis to determine why the individual with WS is not responding positively to the instructions, directions, or commands of others and then applying appropriate measures. Professional treatment may be sought for serious cases of both kinds of poor adaptability.

Interventions for Problems of Rigidity

For problems of rigidity, suggested types of interventions may include environmental controls, task management, and verbal mediation strategies.

Environmental Controls

A structured, routinized lifestyle is often helpful in easing problems with rigidity typically displayed by WSs. Life events that affect the WS individual, directly or indirectly, need to be controlled when possible.

Providing stability in WSs' lives means establishing a strict schedule and sequence of daily routines such as waking up, washing and brushing, breakfast (Levine, 1993; Scheiber, 2000). It also means avoiding whenever possible changes in plans or activities. A regular route and standard order should be used for transportation, day care, school, lessons, and appointments, and preestablished warning signals can be used to mark routine transitions in the schedule (Levine, 1993). The aim is to minimize unexpected change (Levine, 1993; Semel, 1988).

Disruptions in daily routines may also be avoided by maintaining reserve supplies of items such as shoelaces, toothpaste, peanut butter, and toilet paper, and replacing items before the supply runs out. This helps to eliminate a tantrum or the need for unplanned shopping trips that can disrupt activities and routines. It is also helpful to have an extra set of clothing ready when one set becomes unwearable because it is wet, torn, dirty, misplaced, or in the wash. Such stop-gap measures can be used to teach WSs how to deal with small "emergencies." It provides a model of how to use fall-back measures to solve problems and reduce stress.

Procedures for handling possible mishaps can also be arranged, like designating the appropriate person to notify in case the WS individual misses a bus, is late, or is absent. Sharing contingency plans with WSs can help to reduce their anxiety.

Clearly, the need for environmental structure and a predictable, routinized lifestyle places stringent demands on others to accommodate to the unusual needs of WSs. Although it may seem unfair to alter the circumstances of an entire family or classroom in order to serve the needs of one WS person, experience has shown that this is sometimes necessary within reasonable limits. Most parents and teachers opt for stability and manageability, believing that it more than compensates for the inconvenience caused by accommodating to such needs.

Task Management

Generally, it is important to provide WSs with planning tools, adequate preparation time for future events, and information regarding the nature of future events. This involves use of task engineering, a kind of task management.

Planning Aids. Levine (1993) advised using planning devices that are appropriate for WSs' age level. Job charts can be used to list the jobs, chores, or responsibilities that WSs are expected to perform at home (e.g., make the bed, hang up clothes, put dirty clothes in the hamper, help set the table, help clear the dishes) or at school (e.g., water plants, erase the chalkboard, hand out paper). For preschool-age WSc, illustrations can be used to depict schedules and daily routines. Placing pictures of upcoming events and holidays on the proper dates of a wall calendar may help some WSc understand the time involved in preparation before the event.

Daily calendars and event planners can be used with older children and WS adults (Levine, 1993; Scheiber, 2000) to indicate appointments, special occasions, chores, and activities for each day. Weekly and monthly calendars, digital watches, and date books can help the older WS individual understand what to expect and plan for anticipated or routine changes in activities (Semel & Rosner, 1994).

MY JOBS

ME	mon	tues	wed	thurs	fri	sat	sun
Wash my face and hands	☐	☐	☐	☐	☐	☐	☐
Brush my theeth	☐	☐	☐	☐	☐	☐	☐
Put toothpaste away	☐	☐	☐	☐	☐	☐	☐
Take a bath/shower	☐	☐	☐	☐	☐	☐	☐
Hangup towels and washcloth	☐	☐	☐	☐	☐	☐	☐
	☐	☐	☐	☐	☐	☐	☐

MY ROOM							
Pick up toys	☐	☐	☐	☐	☐	☐	☐
Make Bed	☐	☐	☐	☐	☐	☐	☐
Hang up clothes	☐	☐	☐	☐	☐	☐	☐
Put dirty clothes in laundry	☐	☐	☐	☐	☐	☐	☐
Put clean clothes away	☐	☐	☐	☐	☐	☐	☐
	☐	☐	☐	☐	☐	☐	☐

MEALS							
Wash face and hands	☐	☐	☐	☐	☐	☐	☐
Help set the table	☐	☐	☐	☐	☐	☐	☐
Clear the table	☐	☐	☐	☐	☐	☐	☐
Wash the dishes	☐	☐	☐	☐	☐	☐	☐
Clean up after snacks	☐	☐	☐	☐	☐	☐	☐
	☐	☐	☐	☐	☐	☐	☐

SCHOOL							
Do homework	☐	☐	☐	☐	☐	☐	☐
Help make lunch	☐	☐	☐	☐	☐	☐	☐
Get money ready	☐	☐	☐	☐	☐	☐	☐
Get bus pass ready	☐	☐	☐	☐	☐	☐	☐
Get notes for teacher ready	☐	☐	☐	☐	☐	☐	☐
Return library books	☐	☐	☐	☐	☐	☐	☐
	☐	☐	☐	☐	☐	☐	☐

CHORES							
Take out the trash	☐	☐	☐	☐	☐	☐	☐
Put back the trash cans	☐	☐	☐	☐	☐	☐	☐
Put bike away	☐	☐	☐	☐	☐	☐	☐
Sweep	☐	☐	☐	☐	☐	☐	☐
Vacuum	☐	☐	☐	☐	☐	☐	☐
Dust	☐	☐	☐	☐	☐	☐	☐
Wipe	☐	☐	☐	☐	☐	☐	☐
	☐	☐	☐	☐	☐	☐	☐

"Warning Time." Determining the best way to prepare or warn the WS individual of anticipated change or a new situation is often problematic. The responsible adult must determine the optimum time for the particular individual to be informed. For some, advance explanation can minimize distress; for others, announcing change far in advance may provoke unnecessary anxiety and persistent questioning about the forthcoming change (Levine, 1993).

For those who respond well to verbal reasoning, the best time may be just far enough in advance for the WS individual to have the opportunity to relay the information to others. Role play and rehearsal allows verbally skilled WSs to further process the situation by explaining it to others.

New Situations. Foresight and preparation can help WSs adjust to new situations and experiences, such as a new school, community, summer camp, trip, or even a honeymoon (WSA National Newsletter, 1994 Fall, Vol. *11*, 27–28). This requires parents, teachers, and others involved with WSs to analyze the situation and make proper arrangements for the change. For example, WSs may be given the opportunity to visit a new school, acquire unfamiliar words (e.g., "departmentalized" schedule, first period, home room, study hall), and become acquainted with one or two key people, like a friendly peer and a person in authority who is cordial and cooperative. It is also helpful for WSs to be allowed to go through an abbreviated school day. At home, WSs can dramatize and practice what it would be like to enter the new situation.

A mother's report of the wedding and honeymoon of her 25-year-old WS son and his mentally handicapped bride provides a vivid example of planning for life experiences (WSA National Newsletter, 1994 Fall, Vol. *11*, 27–28). The groom's parents visited the honeymoon site in advance, checked everything out and made pre-paid reservations for transfers, transportation, and admission fees. The young couple were taught how to charge meals to their room. Hotel staff were even asked to help get the couple ready for the airport shuttle for the trip home. By planning out details in advance, the WS individual's parents avoided unnecessary stress and anxiety on everyone's part.

Verbal Mediation Strategies

Although environmental controls and task management can help to decrease the amount of unnecessary change, some change is inevitable. Verbal mediation strategies may then be called on to help WSs understand the nature of the change.

Reassurance. Attempts to alleviate a WSc's concerns about change through the use of reassurance or sympathetic acknowledgment of the child's disappointment and worries are usually unsuccessful. Nevertheless, staying in close proximity to the WS individual while discussing the need for a change in plans can provide emotional support and encourage discussion.

Dramatization. Modeling, role playing, storytelling, social stories, and puppetry can be used effectively to depict the need for change and the benefits of adapting to it. Portraying a situation with exaggerated dramatization can appeal to the WSs' sense of humor and help them see their unreasonableness in resisting change.

Explanation. Coping effectively with change may be aided by the use of explanation and rehearsal. This means explaining why a change has occurred and discussing the consequences of failing to adapt to that change. For example, helping a WSc deal with cancellation of a family picnic because of rain may involve reminding the child of the original plan and taking the plan to its current conclusion. That is, explaining that holding the picnic in the rain would result in everyone and everything getting wet. Rehearsal may be introduced once the explanation is understood.

Problem Analysis for Failure to Follow Directions

For difficulty in following directions, problem analysis may offer insights into the factors involved and ways to approach them. Failure to carry out the directions, commands or instructions of another person may reflect problems of language comprehension, memory difficulty, performance limitations, inattention, distractibility, or refusal to cooperate. Although parents and teachers may attribute the noncompliance of WS individuals to disobedience or recalcitrance, other factors are usually involved. Whenever possible, this should be determined through the use of problem analysis.

Language Comprehension. With WSc, instructions may need to be adjusted or modified to the child's level of comprehension. This may require reducing the number of steps in the sequence of instructions, using simple forms of grammar, words that are familiar and relevant, and avoiding or clarifying the use of spatial, temporal, and quantitative terms. Modulation of pitch, volume, and intonation may be used to emphasize important points. SLTs can help with these issues (see p. 97).

Other Factors. Problems in following directions may also stem from other factors. Attentional problems may be eased by employing attention-getting devices, such as saying the person's name. Distractibility problems may be handled by reducing extraneous stimuli, response problems by reducing task difficulty or providing pretraining in performing the task.

Following directions also often involves making a shift in one's activity, mood, or situation. As with other problems of poor adaptability, WSs may have difficulty mobilizing themselves to make such changes. In such cases, explaining the reason for the instructions or forewarning the individual of the forthcoming shift may ease the transition.

Professional Treatment

In cases of extreme negativity or recalcitrance in following directions, the services of a psycho-educational therapist, speech therapist, learning specialist, clinical psychologist, social worker, or other trained mental health specialist may be sought to help deal with this problem. Similarly, professional help may be warranted for serious cases of rigidity especially when problems in the parent–child or teacher–child relationship are involved. See Section III. A, Psychotherapy, pp. 344–346.

E. Interventions for Low Frustration Tolerance

The low frustration tolerance of many WSs often manifests itself in a pattern of general hyperreactivity and three subtypes of response: (a) externalization—tantrums, hitting, lashing out; (b) internalization—withdrawal, performance inhibition, self-destructive behavior; and (c) perseveration—repetitive, off-target, irrelevant responding.

Both general and specific measures are needed to deal with the varied types of WS reactions to frustration. This may involve selecting from among the following six types of intervention strategies: a) control mechanisms; b) verbal mediation strategies; c) problem analysis; d) stress reduction techniques; e) task management; and f) professional treatment.

However, prevention of low frustration tolerance is perhaps the best antidote. Difficulty in coping with too many failures and too much criticism can weaken frustration tolerance. Developing ego-strength and bolstering self-esteem is a vital intervention strategy when it is based on the WS individual having earned some real success or mastery of certain skills, as well as having effectively dealt with some inevitable failures. Adults in the WS individual's environment who provide encouragement and consolation as needed can contribute a great deal to neutralizing the low frustration tensions of many WSs.

Control Mechanisms

Control mechanisms of differential reinforcement, rechanneling tactics, direct instruction, and behavioral contracts may be effective for a variety of responses to frustration.

Differential Reinforcement. Positive responses to frustrating situations should be rewarded whenever possible. Examples of such responses are refraining from tantrums, avoiding withdrawal, resisting perseveration, and utilizing realistic responses to failure.

Tantrums. Outbursts may be resolved by treating them in a firm, consistent manner, such as paying no attention to the child until the tantrum is over, physically removing the child, or imposing a time-out period (Udwin & Yule, 1988, 1989). Exceptions to these measures must be made when the tantrum is damaging the WSc, others, or valuable property. In any case, parents, teachers, and others should be wary of "giving in" to a tantrum and granting what the child wants. This merely reinforces the "bad" behavior. Methods for use of time-out and advantages of this approach are discussed below.

Rechanneling Tactics. Misbehaviors often occur when WSs are unoccupied or during times of transition, such as when entering the classroom, changing classes, or waiting for an appointment, meeting, lesson, or performance to begin.

To avert problems before they occur, the teacher or parent can reduce "waiting times" and provide WSs with interesting tasks they can work on alone. Proximity control in which the parent or teacher stays next to the WSc can facilitate use of cues to elicit good behavior, using a nod of the head, a raised eyebrow, a hand signal, a smile or a frown (Scheiber, 2000).

When the situation in the classroom becomes too stimulating or the WS individual gets out of control, it may be useful to offer instruction that has an active component. Periods of time-out during instruction, or periods of time away from on-task activity, may also be helpful.

Sometimes a "think about it" chair at school or home can assist in calming a WS individual. While sitting in this chair, a telephone may be used, with permission, to dial a story, request information, or speak with a valued person, or a computer may be used to obtain information or play a game.

Sometimes, SIBs such as picking at cuticles or sores can be dealt with by using rechanneling tactics. WSs may be instructed to reach for a straw, piece of gum, or another appropriate replacement when they feel their fingers going into their mouths. Likewise, peeling or picking at cuticles or sores can be redirected into more socially acceptable responses like shredding paper or peeling bark off sticks (Levine, 1994).

Direct Instruction for Anger Control. It is extremely important for parents and teachers to be direct, firm, and assertive in dealing with WSs' anger. While being responsive and sympathetic to the child's feelings, restrictions must be placed on overt aggression or other outer-directed kinds of behavior, like lashing out at siblings, parents, or friends who frustrate them. In other words, adults do need to set firm limits or boundaries on acting-out behavior.

Although parents and teachers may themselves become frustrated by WSs' behavior, they need to "keep their cool" and avoid expressing anger, hostility, or sarcasm (see also "Impulsivity," p. 315). That is, negative comments and put-down messages such as the following should be *avoided*: "I never saw a child in [my class/our family] who was as lazy as you"; "You never listen to what I say"; "Stop that or you'll be really sorry."

Instead, WSs may be told in a firm voice, for example, "Don't talk to me like that. I am very unhappy when you talk that way. It upsets me and embarrasses me."

Permissiveness toward aggression, including verbal aggression, can undermine WSs' effectiveness, especially with peers or in employment settings. As with other children, allowing even minor and occasional forms of aggression toward mother, teacher, sibling, or peers encourages the use of more severe forms. Using aggression to "let off some steam" does *not* lessen future aggression; instead, it encourages it. Unbridled expression of anger in the form of aggression, destructiveness, or violence should not be tolerated.

Adults need to set firm boundaries on the WSs' minor occasional misbehavior—like verbal expression of anger and defiance—without being too punitive or hostile. Otherwise, there is the risk that this could ultimately inhibit their ability to assert themselves when it is necessary and appropriate to do so. Striking an optimal balance between excessive permissiveness and overly severe punishment can be a real balancing act. This is especially so when WSs engage in "acting-out," externalizing kinds of aggressive behaviors.

Dealing With "Acting-Out" Behaviors. There are certain situations in which WSs may demonstrate serious impulsive, "acting-out" kinds of behaviors as opposed to those that are rule-governed. Levine and Wharton (2001) reported that some WSc have been known to lose their temper and become extremely angry with family members or teachers. Such outbursts tend to begin quickly, subside quickly, and be followed by regret. Fortunately, such outbursts tend to decrease with age (Levine & Wharton, 2001).

Examples of impulsive, "acting-out," aggressive behaviors that some WSc have been known to display are temper tantrums, talking back, mocking adults, name calling, making faces, and loud screaming or yelling. Other forms of aggressive, acting-out that WSs may occasionally exhibit are slapping, hitting, pinching; scratching; biting or kicking; hair pulling, pushing, choking, spitting; teasing others; making verbal threats or threatening gestures; mistreating or hurting people or animals; and grabbing, throwing, or destroying their own property or the property of others (Anonymous callers, personal communication, Williams Syndrome Hotline, 1998, 1999, 2000).

Time-Out Procedures. The maladaptive, egocentric, impulse-driven behaviors of WSc can be annoying, irritating, or injurious to others. Although they may not occur frequently, when they do arise, "time-out" procedures have been found to be helpful. Time out has the potential to put an abrupt stop to these unacceptable behaviors, and break the cycle of negative interaction that often ensues.

In effect, time out provides an immediate consequence that can be linked to the WSc's misbehavior. When implementing time out it is important to use only a few words and a few seconds to direct the child to the time-out place. For example, "Go to 'time out' now"; "No screaming." Note that prolonged argument and discussion merely "rewards" the WSc with extra attention.

It is also important to indicate the amount of time to be spent there. In general, the time-out period should last approximately 1 minute for each year of the WSc's age. The place selected for time out should be a very boring environment, such as isolation in a separate room with the door closed (not a closet), or a corner with no toys. Procedures to be followed in time out must be carefully specified, such as "You may not bring toys to time out," and no one is allowed to talk or play with the child. Although this handling may be difficult to enforce, it should be stated and every effort made for compliance.

After the time-out period is ended, there should be discussion of the reason for time out. The WSc may be asked: "Why were you sent to time-out?", and related questions. Correct answers should be reinforced, inadequate responses followed by explaining the rationale for the procedure and having the WSc repeat this aloud, then silently, then once again aloud before being allowed to resume other activities.

Unless WSc develop self-control, they risk the deleterious effects of social rejection. Consequently, firm handling by parents and teachers is vital. Teachers are often challenged to find ways to help WSc modify these impulsive behaviors so that the academic work of the WSc becomes commensurate with their ability, and other students in the class are not hindered by these antics.

"Acting-Out" Between Children. Impulsive, acting-out, aggressive behaviors of WSc can seriously affect sibling and peer relationships. It can also discourage friendships with other children.

When the WSc and a sibling or another child have a fight with each other, most often both children have played a part in the altercation. Discussion about "who started it" and efforts to be fair are often useless. An alternative strategy is to use time out for both children in separate locations. A time limit of about the average of both their ages might be appropriate.

When the time-out period is over, the issues that caused the problem should be discussed. Both children may be asked, for example, "How could you two have handled this in a better way than fighting?"

When posing questions of this kind, the children should be encouraged to give acceptable answers or to be questioned and coached until they do.

Verbal mediation and self-talk strategies may be cited as possible ways of handling aggressive behavior.

Altering behavior is difficult and requires patience, practice, and cooperation. In trying to influence WSs' behavior, it is important to speak in a positive, assertive manner with minimal belittling or criticism. Being friendly, nonjudgmental, calm, and smiling a lot is often more effective than hitting, yelling, and punishing. Recognizing efforts to comply and positively reinforcing various accomplishments is also an effective behavioral control.

Internalizing. Internalizing responses, such as refusing to try, becoming stubborn, resistant, or retreating from a situation physically or mentally, may be countered by encouraging WSs to "stick with it." Willingness to work through a situation should be rewarded, when appropriate, by offering praise ("good job"), general approval (nods, smiles), or other rewards (smiley face stickers). In school, where WSc are especially vulnerable to failure, it is important for the teacher to try to establish a warm and positive relationship. Pleasing the teacher can motivate WSs to work up to capacity and help them become more accepting of themselves.

In the treatment of self-injurious behaviors (SIBs), rewards such as a broad smile or a sticker of a smiley face may be helpful if granted for each time period (e.g., 2, 5, 10 minutes or an hour) in which the WSc refrains from self-injurious forms of behavior like picking at cuticles, sores, or scabs (Levine, 1993). The length of the time period depends on the WS individual's age, developmental level, and so forth. Providing scheduled reinforcement may help WSs become more aware of their own behavior and the need to inhibit their self-destructive behaviors in the future.

SIBs most likely occur as a result of attention difficulties, impulsivity, and developmental or learning disabilities. Some clinicians advise not dwelling excessively on such behaviors, but reminding them instead not to engage in such behaviors (Levine, 1997).

Empathetic appeals may also be effective in sensitizing WSs to how SIBs affect others. For example: "It hurts me when I see you hurt yourself"; "Let's work together to help you stop hurting yourself."

Behavioral Contracts. Simple behavioral contracts that specify desired behaviors such as "I will finish my work," or "I will control my temper" can be drawn up and signed by teacher and student even if the WSc is unable to read. See Section II B, "Distractibility and Attentional Problems" (p. 308).

Verbal Mediation Techniques

Often, WSs can be "talked out" of engaging in certain kinds of unacceptable behavior by discussing the likely consequences of their actions.

Externalizing Responses. Sometimes it is possible to divert the "fight" energy of WSs into constructive channels by reasoning. Discussing the apparent cause of their frustration, suggesting more effective ways to deal with it, and explaining why this is so are all potentially helpful tools (see "Problem Analysis," on p. 332).

Dramatization may be used to portray the unacceptable behaviors of WSc in an exaggerated, humorous way that can help them recognize the grossness of their behavior. It can also be used to help WSs realize the value and importance of maintaining a positive attitude. Role play, puppetry, social stories, videotaping, and speech–language therapy may also assist with related problems of language pragmatics involving denial, such as a WSc becoming angry because he or she was refused permission to visit a dangerous construction site. In addition, many WSs are able to use humor to view their own lapses more objectively, saying something like this to themselves, "Oops, there it [the anger] goes again, just because I couldn't do that. It isn't the worst thing that can happen."

Internalizing responses may also take the form of failure to conform to rule-governed behaviors. This is one way that some WSs cope with frustration.

Perseveration. Persistent perseveration, that is, repetitious behavior with no adaptive value, is difficult to remediate. However, it may sometimes be managed through the use of preestablished signals, such as a raised eyebrow, a shake of the head, or a puzzled expression, to communicate disapproval when the WS individual engages in this type of behavior. A light touch or use of humor may soften reminders saying, for example, "Oops! There you go again," when the perseverative response recurs.

Because perseveration is often unconscious, it may be wise to provide tangible evidence of perseverative responding by presenting videotapes, school papers, tape-recordings of persistent verbalizations, and so forth. As WSc may focus on a single subject of interest, thus limiting conversational topics, alternative topics should be developed so they can participate more ably in discussions (Levine, 1997).

Self-Instructional Skills. Some WSs may be taught to cope by using self-talk techniques like the self-use of humor suggested before. This approach is especially useful in reducing overall tension or inner responses to frustration. It usually involves teaching WSs to self-administer a series of coping statements during each phase of a stressful event (Meichenbaum, 1977; cf. Frank, 1988, p. 209).

Problem Analysis

It is very important for parents, teachers, and other professionals to be sensitive to WSs' emotional state and be able to recognize when WSs are upset and anxious.

In the ordinary flow of life, WSc often feel frustrated and angry toward parents, teachers, or others. It is helpful to try to identify and alleviate the specific factors that irritate WSc.

Failure and Denials. Adults need to be encouraging and supportive of WSs and empathetic with their fears of failure and abandonment. Real or imagined criticism or rejection from teachers, parents, or other significant people can be devastating to the oversensitive WSc. Therefore, special care must be taken when evaluating performance. For example, criticism should be interspersed with positive comments.

In cases where ordinary denials of permission produce extreme frustration, it may be helpful to foresee the situation or be tactful in expressing the denial. Refusal is necessary in some circumstances, especially when the request involves irrational demands like those revolving around an obsessive interest or unrealistic wish.

Coping Mechanisms. Parents, teachers, and others involved should analyze how WSs cope with frustration and identify ways in which they can be soothed or calmed down.

A useful strategy is to help the child to "reflect back" on his feelings by saying, "You seem really upset about. . . . Would you like to tell me about it?" This can often get behind the reasons for the child's acting-out behavior.

A meta-cognitive approach can be used by asking the WS individual to respond to questions, such as: "Do you get upset when you can't ____?"; "What do you do to help yourself not get upset?"; "How can we help you not get so upset?"

Such discussion may be guided by asking focused questions about the WS individual's use of specific techniques that are often effective with other WSs, namely: "When you're upset, do you seek: assistance and comfort from adults; a calm, quiet, place; peer support; or music to listen to or play?"

The next step is to determine whether the WS individual can be encouraged or taught to use adaptive coping strategies to reduce tension build-up and irrational modes of responding. WSs may need to learn specific procedures for seeking assistance to avoid loss of behavioral control when frustrated. Alternatively, parents and teachers may be prompted to monitor such situations and offer help when needed.

Analysis of SIBs. In dealing with self-injurious behaviors it is sometimes helpful to try to determine why the WS individual is engaging in this action. If the motivation is to gain attention, then ignoring the behaviors, whenever possible, may reduce their occurrence. This may be particularly effective in cases where the warnings, pleading, and urging of parents have exacerbated, not decreased, the problem.

With help, some WSs may be able to identify what triggers SIB responses. This may entail meta-cognitive analysis in which the WS individual is asked a series of questions addressing why or when the behavior is exhibited and what steps can be taken to better deal with the behavior.

If a decrease in the behavior is noted, then the WS individual may use verbal interactive techniques to inform others, adults, siblings, the family cat, a pet fish, a picture of a pet on the school desk, "I didn't do it!!"

SIBs can be a very difficult problem to deal with. Visits to the doctor are often necessary.

Stress Reduction Techniques

Bolstering self-esteem is an important way to help WSs overcome their low frustration tolerance. Relaxation techniques may offer another way to reduce tension (Schelber, 2000).

Bolstering Self-Esteem. Developing the talents of WSs and encouraging them to participate in extracurricular activities in which they can shine is perhaps one of the best ways to enhance their self-esteem. Involvement in suitable activities, hobbies, and clubs that can provide opportunities for social interaction and a context for sharing topics of special interest is another (see p. 200). Participating in appropriate performing arts, theatre, music, choir, and religious groups who make provisions for persons with special needs, as well as Special Olympics, can also boost WSs' sense of self-worth. With a doctor's permission, WSs often enjoy engaging in sports activities that may include swimming, skating, bicycling, and horseback riding. This gives the WS individual a heightened sense of power and control.

Relaxation Techniques. Another approach is to help WSs develop a repertoire of acceptable behaviors that can enable them to avoid losing control in a temper tantrum or other provocative act. For many WSs, listening to music is this type of activity; for others, it would include immersing themselves in a topic of special interest (see earlier section, "Problem Analysis").

Task Management

Realistic goals can be established by dividing complex tasks into subtasks of short duration for WS individuals. Simplifying task demands, reducing the difficulty of the required response, or structuring the response with cues so that the WS individual is more likely to succeed at the task may be helpful in reducing tension and inappropriate ways of responding to stress. Perseveration may be one way in which WSs try to defend themselves from failing or acknowledging their inability to perform satisfactorily. Presenting tasks at the appropriate cognitive level may be effective, but it may be necessary to prepare "back up" measures in case the troublesome behavior recurs.

Professional Treatment

Various kinds of professionals may be consulted to help deal with the varied forms of behavior that WSs may exhibit in response to frustration.

Speech Language Therapy for Overreactivity to Denials. One common cause of general tension is overreactivity when parents and other adults deny requests. This may be addressed by consulting speech language therapists (SLTs) trained in handling problems of language pragmatic behavior. They may be able to help WSs learn to respond appropriately to denials and express their own requests in an acceptable manner (see chap. 3, pp. 100–101).

OT/PT or SIT for SIBs. Sometimes, self-injurious behaviors may be considered a manifestation of tactile defensiveness. That is, resistance to soft touch or pressure in some WSs may be accompanied by the need to experience "deep or forceful" stimulation, even though the amount of pressure or stimulation goes beyond acceptable or healthy bounds. The amount of damage they impose can be extremely harmful. PTs and OTs with extensive experience in tactile defensiveness may be able to help WSs with these problems.

Medical Treatment of SIBs. In cases where the self-destructive behavior is very damaging and inflicts injury (e.g., bleeding cuticles or sores), a physician should be consulted.

Adapted Behavior Modification. In cases where temper tantrums are frequent and extreme, adaptations of behavior modification may be appropriate for those unreachable by other means. This may also help inhibit episodes of SIBs when the habit is severe.

Such programs are generally developed under the auspices of a trained behavior therapist (e.g., child psychologist or learning specialist). The program formalizes the use of rewards, like a smile or pat on the back, to deter undesirable behavior. Specific behaviors and rewards are identified as well as the schedule for dispensing desired reinforcements for having successfully refrained from engaging in target behavior. A token economy, in which tokens are dispensed and saved for a "real" reward, may be used with some WS individuals to lengthen the periods of good behavior.

Psychotherapy. Different methods of psychotherapy, including cognitive therapy and desensitization may be useful with WSs who have major difficulties handling stress. Because the overreaction and loss of control exhibited by some WSs may reflect underlying problems of anxiety and underdeveloped coping mechanisms, interventions for extreme cases of "acting-out" should be integrated into a larger therapy plan that may include, for example, the use of medication and play therapy (Levine & Wharton, 2001; see Section III. A, p. 347).

F. Interventions for Atypical Activity

It is extremely important for WSs to receive the help they often need in order to control motor behaviors that are extraneous or excessive.

Many kinds of atypical activities are observed in WS individuals (Anonymous callers, personal communication, Williams Syndrome Hotline, 1998, 1999, 2000). Some of these include: rubbing thighs; restless, jittery, constant fidgeting; repeatedly getting out of one's seat; tipping one's chair; rocking or swaying "to and fro"; twirling objects; shuffling feet; tapping foot, finger, pencil, or other objects. "Wandering" is also reported: around the classroom without permission, around the house, and unexpectedly from the home or a store, the park, fair grounds, etc. Restless sleep may be considered as another kind of problem with atypical activity.

In order to deal with the various forms of WSs' overactivity, six intervention strategies are suggested as being possibly effective with such problems. This may include use of: control mechanisms, verbal mediation strategies, environmental controls, task management, problem analysis, and professional treatment.

Control Mechanisms

Overactivity may sometimes be decreased through the use of differential reinforcement, rechanneling tactics, direct instruction, and behavioral contracts.

Reinforcement. WSs' activity problems may be addressed by identifying target behaviors that need improvement and rewarding those that approximate that goal (Arnold et al., 1985). Target behaviors may include refraining from: (a) disturbing others by making noises, hovering over them, or talking to them; (b) displaying restless, jittery behaviors and constant fidgeting; and (c) indulging in annoying habits, such as shuffling feet, tapping chair, tapping foot or finger, pencil, or other objects.

Staying in close proximity to the individual with WS can provide security and reduce the tendency for aimless motion. Smiling directly at the WS individual can serve as an excellent motivator. The child should also be rewarded for sitting still, listening and concentrating. Udwin and Yule (1998a, 1998b) suggested gradually increasing the required period of time that the child is expected to remain focused before being rewarded. This may start with 1 or 2 minutes and gradually work up to 5, 10, even 15 minutes. Having a behavioral consultant set up this program can benefit both the child and the adults responsible for carrying out the program.

Rechanneling Tactics. When an overactive WSc begins to become disruptive, it may be helpful to make eye contact, and say something to divert the child, or give the WSc something to think about. For example: "We don't do that in this class, but we're going to the gym in two minutes," or "In three minutes, we are going to the library." Asking relevant questions, such as "Are you sitting where you are supposed to be?", may also be helpful.

Providing opportunities for active WSs to move about or make postural adjustments can help to reduce tension and discharge energy. Suggestions include: introducing a stretch break or exercises after completing a long, sedentary task; providing seat cushions for tactile defensive WSc; and permitting the WSc to straddle a chair or use a rocking chair if this helps to curtail unnecessary motor activity. Permitting WSs to move about while carrying out assigned tasks, such as passing out paper, books, or watering the plants, erasing the chalkboard may also serve the purpose of sublimating unfocused activity.

It is also helpful to provide personal space, avoid crowding, and permit a certain amount of fidgeting if it does not disturb others. A teacher can arrange opportunities for WSs to leave the classroom (with a classmate) on predetermined assignments when they begin to show signs of unnecessary activity. If the WSc is able to, taking a message to another teacher can provide a change in environment and an opportunity to visit with others while on the errand.

Active games are other ways to help channel extra energy and reduce various forms of atypical activity. Going through a classroom arranged obstacle course or a game of "Simon Says" can be helpful. Ball handling games offer excitement, enthusiasm, and organized action patterns as well.

Alternatively, the teacher or other adult can introduce movement activities at the end of a task or game by saying, for example: "We have done such a great job, let's give ourselves a great big hug or a pat on the back, or round of applause." "Three cheers—hip, hip, hooray—raise your hands."

Direct Instruction. It is important for teachers and parents to be direct and assertive in stating behavioral goals for WSc, such as saying "There will be no getting out of seats in this class (or your seat in this room); sit down in your chair."

Preventive cues and signals may be used to help a WSc refrain from disruptive behaviors like rocking, walking about, rubbing legs, and so forth. Examples of gestures that may be effective yet discreet include: "thumbs up"; tapping the WSc lightly on the forehead or chin; or shaking one's head "NO!"; Providing a "traffic signal" with a red, yellow, and green light to indicate that the child should stop or monitor his/her own behavior is another, dramatic use of cues.

Behavioral Contracts. Teachers may find it helpful to establish simple behavioral contracts that specify activity-related behaviors to be expected of WSc. (For further discussion and examples of behavioral contracts, see p. 308, this chapter).

Verbal Mediation Strategies

WSc are usually responsive to verbal methods of intervention, such as explanations about why overactivity and fidgeting are undesirable forms of behavior. This is a positive, distinguishing feature of many WSs.

It is helpful for parents and teachers to identify and clearly label inappropriate and appropriate behavior as it occurs when this can be done tactfully without negative consequences (see below). Dramatization of inappropriate behavior through stories, pantomime, puppetry, videotaping, and role play can be used to concretely depict the objectionable aspects of a behavior.

In using explanation, WS individuals usually need to be told exactly why they should try to curtail excessive movements, like fidgeting, rocking, or wandering around the room. The discussion might include concrete examples of how other people have been annoyed, disturbed, or distracted by such behaviors and how such actions may interfere with the WS's performance. The use of meaningful, concrete analogies may also be helpful.

In any event, intensive intervention is best done on a one-to-one basis. Teachers, in particular, may need to be careful about repeatedly labeling a WS student's behavior as inappropriate in the middle of the class. By focusing the attention of the entire class on the WSc's troublesome behavior, the student may be made to feel conspicuous or shamed even though this was not the teacher's intent. Of course, if the WSc is actually disrupting the class, the classroom teacher must do something to curtail the behavior but it is usually wise to overlook minor misbehavior, like squirming. Too many admonishments may make the child the scapegoat or target of ridicule by classmates. It may also unintentionally reward the WS child's undesirable behaviors. Teachers may therefore find it necessary to steer a fine course between not overlooking serious misbehavior and being over-zealous about correcting small deviations.

Environmental Controls

Reducing Distractions. Simplifying the surroundings of the WSc by removing objects of intense interest or distracting power is often an effective way to curtail overactivity. The presence of distracting stimuli—visual, auditory, tactual, or focal objects—may trigger the extraneous movements of some WSc (see section, "Distractibility and Attentional Problems," pp 310–311).

"Wandering." Some parents deal with the worrisome problem of WSs wandering unexpectedly from home or other places by never letting their WSc out of their sight. Others use less restrictive controls.

If the problem is serious, then it might be useful to enlist the cooperation of neighbors, telling them about the WSc's tendency to roam and asking them to phone the family if the child is seen. In one instance, the mother handed out flyers to neighbors, local merchants, postal workers, and trades people describing her child's problem, along with a photo of the youngster, the family's address and phone number, and instructions about what to do if the child was seen wandering around the neighborhood. She even informed the local police station about her youngster's problem (Anonymous caller, personal communication, Williams Syndrome Hotline, Sept. 1998).

Another approach involves instructing the WS individual to always leave some personal object like his or her bicycle near the road or place that is visited. This can provide clues as to the WSs' whereabouts. A simple technique that sometimes works is to ring an unusual sounding bell, a chime, or a noise-maker as a prearranged signal or inducement for the child to return home. One parent tried tying a tiny bell to the child's ankle so that the child could be more easily located after wandering off (Anonymous caller, personal communication, Williams Syndrome Hotline, Dec. 1998).

Providing identification bracelets or tags for WSc can be extremely helpful (WSA National Newsletter, 1988 November, Vol. 6(2), p. 26; Lenhoff, WSA National Newsletter, 2000 April, Vol. 17(1), p. 3). ID tags purchased from the WSA or store-bought bracelets or neck tags can be engraved with vital information, such as the name, address, home phone number, city, state, and zip code of the WS person. It should include the phone numbers of several people whom the WS person knows and trusts, and the medical ID, "Williams Syndrome." Information about the WS person's school, place of employment, care center, or other organization can also be helpful. Fingerprints or footprints can be used as permanent forms of identification.

Even though wandering behavior seems to be on "automatic pilot," it may still be amenable to some psycho-educational techniques when combined with the use of environmental controls. For example, the WS individual may be taken around an unfamiliar place and shown its layout, the location of important places, and major landmarks. These can be verbally labeled. This approach may be used when visiting a theme park, fair, and so forth, or to place boundaries on the neighborhood area within which the WS individuals may travel on their own.

At all times, upon entering a situation, a predetermined place to meet if one is lost should be explicitly pointed out to the WS individual. Examples of such places are: under the clock; in front of the security office at the zoo; the store manager's office; at the box office of a movie theatre; at the entrance to the fair grounds, etc. The WS individual may be asked to repeat and rehearse these instructions and relay them to others when help is needed. Use of "walkie-talkie" devices or giving the WS individual a whistle to use when lost are other ways to ease the fears of WSs and their families. Parents may also use a whistle to signal the WSc to come to them.

Restless Sleep. Many WS individuals struggle with sleeping problems. Difficulty falling asleep or staying asleep has frequently been reported (Udwin & Yule, 1998a, 1998b). Some children have such severe sleeping difficulty that parents take turns keeping watch for hours every night (Anonymous callers, personal communication, Williams Syndrome Hotline, 1998, 1999, 2000). However, two families have reported successful solutions. One parent found the use of a waterbed very helpful. The parents of another youngster settled their WSc in his bed, provided him with tool catalogues, books about his special interest and headphones for music, and began enforcing a "stay in bed" rule. The child was then able to entertain himself and the parents managed to normalize their own sleeping patterns (Anonymous caller, personal communication, Williams Syndrome Hotline, Sept. 1998; July 1999).

These approaches may not work with all WS individuals. Other suggestions for handling WSs' sleep problems include establishing a fixed routine for preparing and settling in bed. This may include reading a story, singing a song, saying a poem, or providing a favorite toy, book, or catalogue. The child should be told firmly that it is time to go to sleep and that you will be leaving the room. Keeping a light on, or using a dimmer switch that can be gradually faded, may help to ease the WS's fears (Udwin & Yule, 1998b). It is important to be consistent in not answering calls or cries, not going back into the bedroom, and if the child gets out of bed, insisting that he or she goes back to bed after making sure that nothing is wrong.

Staying in bed should be rewarded with praise or with concrete reinforcements, such as taking the child out to breakfast, calling grandma and telling her about this happy development, or placing stars or stickers on a bedtime chart each morning that the child's bedtime behavior had improved (Udwin & Yule, 1998b).

Regardless of the approach that is used, parents must above all else be consistent and assertive in enforcing bedtime rules. Otherwise, neither the WSc nor the parents will get enough sleep.

Task Management

Using task management to structure tasks also lessens the excessive motor responses of WSs. This is most critical when new information is being introduced or important tasks assigned. Reducing the length of time the WS individual is required to "sit still" may be helpful, because pressure from the chair may stimulate tactile defensiveness and the need to squirm. Likewise, the amount of time spent on near-point, difficult tasks (e.g., reading, cutting, handwriting) may be monitored and adjusted as needed to lessen "flight responses" (wanting to run) and unwarranted motion.

Problem Analysis

Sometimes, meta-cognitive strategies can be used to encourage WSs to consider and comment on their own overactivity. Parents, teachers, or other professionals may point out a particular form of undesirable activity that the WSc displays, ask why the behavior is shown, and what can be done to reduce or restrain that behavior. This is similar to the approach described for problems of low frustration tolerance (see p. 332).

Adults can help WSs explore ways in which they may gain better control, such as focusing their eyes when listening, using ear plugs or earphones while reading, or pushing the ball of the foot down hard on the floor while writing. Alternative ways to deal with overactivity through the use of time-out and rewards, are discussed in the section on "Control Mechanisms" (pp. 336–337).

Professional Treatment

Several forms of treatment have sometimes been of assistance in dealing with WSs' activity problems.

Behavior Modification. A behavior modification approach is recommended in certain situations where the behaviors are extremely troublesome or harmful to the WS individual or to others. In such cases, adapted forms of behavioral modification programs have sometimes been helpful. This approach may be most applicable to individuals with a dual diagnosis of WS and autism. Such cases are relatively rare.

Cognitive Behavior Therapy. Another treatment approach, cognitive behavior therapy, teaches self-control and problem solving to help individuals gain skills in self-regulation and achieve better control of their behavioral excesses (Harris, 1995b). Administered or supervised by a therapist, this approach may be best suited for WSs who are able to benefit from discussion and self-instructional techniques.

Occupational Therapy. Because tactile defensiveness can sometimes be a major factor in WSs' overactivity, especially with their fidgeting and squirming, it may be helpful to consult an OT for evaluation and treatment. In addition, OTs may be able to provide general assistance because problems of atypical activity often involve difficulties with motor functioning and eye–hand coordination tasks. There is also a potential difficulty with processes of sensory integration.

Medication. Medication is sometimes used with WSs for problems of distractibility, poor attention, and/or atypical activity and, most particularly, with cases that present several of these symptoms. This combination of symptoms is related to the diagnosis of hyperactivity based on measures of behavior disturbance (see pp. 286–289). Medication is sometimes prescribed for overactivity, and quite frequently for cases of ADD and ADHD; for further information, see Section III. B on Psychopharmacology (p. 351).

III. TREATMENT OF CLINICAL DISORDERS OF WSs

The clinical disorders associated with WS differ in many respects from the six types of behavior problems already discussed. Generally, the clinical disorders of WSs are more severe, pervasive, and dysfunctional than WSs' behavior problems. Comparatively, behavior problems are rather specific and perceptible as symptoms, like distractibility, whereas clinical disorders are broader, more deep-seated, and personalized as diagnostic conditions. Developmentally, behavior problems tend to show continuity across the childhood and adult years, whereas clinical disorders seem to be associated with certain age periods, notably, emotional disorders seem to become more evident during adolescence and early adulthood.

Although the majority of WSs exhibit many behavior problems in varying degree, a smaller percentage are vulnerable to clinical problems, in particular, ADHD or emotional–mood disorders. Sometimes this may appear to be a matter of degree, or drawing an apparently fine line, as in the difference between "overactivity" and ADHD, or feelings of anxiety and generalized anxiety disorder. This underscores the importance of consulting professionals for the critical issues of evaluation, diagnosis, and therefore, the treatment of what may seem to the layman to be rather similar types of conditions.

In fact, guidelines for the health care supervision for children with WS recommend "formal evaluation for attention-deficit hyperactivity disorder, anxiety, or both and discussion of treatment options" for WSc (5–12 yrs), and screening of WS adolescents (13–18 yrs) for generalized anxiety disorder (American Academy of Pediatrics, 2001).

Thus, the therapeutic approaches associated with these two categories of maladaptive behavior, behavior problems, and clinical disorders, tend to differ. In the case of clinical disorders, treatment usually shifts in emphasis from the use of psycho-educational techniques of behavioral management for specific problems to broader, more generalized issues and internalized conflicts. Treatment options for clinical disorders include use of psychotherapy and related forms of therapy as well as certain kinds of medication (i.e., psychopharmacology).

In addition, many of the forms of psycho-educational intervention described earlier are applicable to clinical disorders and may be used advantageously in combination with psychotherapy and medication. In fact, multiple kinds of treatment are often recommended. For example, a panel of experts on WS health care suggests considering various treatment options for anxiety, namely, counseling, relaxation techniques, and medications (American Academy of Pediatrics, 2001).

The reverse also holds, that is, specialized forms of treatment are sometimes applicable to WSs' behavior problems. For fears, anxieties, and low frustration tolerance, the use of desensitization (i.e., gradual exposure to aversive stimuli), mental imagery (i.e., guided imaging of difficult situations), and psychotherapy are options. Sometimes, adapted forms of behavior modification may help to control problems of distractibility, impulsivity, and atypical activity. Cases of severe anxiety, distractibility, or overactivity may respond favorably to certain kinds of medication.

At the same time, there are distinctions in the orientation, emphasis and efficacy of intervention approaches that focus on psycho-educational strategies versus clinical treatment. It is therefore reasonable to focus here on the types of clinical treatment used to treat WSs' clinical disorders. In fact, it is heuristically worthwhile to distinguish between the use of psychotherapy and other mental health techniques, on the one hand, and the use of psychopharmacology or medication, on the other hand.

These treatment approaches are discussed next with the cautionary note that very little research has been conducted thus far as to their use or effectiveness with WSs. Nevertheless, it is important to share whatever information is available.

A. Psychotherapy

Since the late 1980s, clinical researchers have recommended that WSs be seen by psychologists [and mental health providers] in addition to various kinds of physicians, OTs, PTs, SLTs, and so forth (Morris et al., 1988).

Yet, little is known about the actual number of WSs who have received various forms of psychotherapy or mental health treatment. Information about their other characteristics (i.e., age, previous level of adjustment), types of specialists consulted, treatment received, and treatment outcome compared to that of WSs with similar diagnoses and little or no formal treatment is sparse. Comparative studies on the incidence of clinical disorders, types of treatment employed, and treatment effectiveness in various developmentally disabled or normally developing groups are also unavailable.

Reports that do exist suggest, however, an underutilization of mental health specialists by many WSs who might have benefited from their services. For example, 15% of WSc ($n = 112$) in one study (Grejtak, 1996c) are said to have received or were receiving counseling services; related forms of therapy, such as music therapy, social skills or play therapy are also reported (Grejtak, 1996c). Information on the problem behaviors or behavior disorders of these WSc is not included, and the age level of the sample, predominately elementary school age, may account for what seems to be a low rate.

Studies of WS adults present a mixed picture (Brewer et al., 1995; Davies et al., 1998). On the one hand, only 21% of WSa ($n = 70$, 19–39;9 yrs) had contact with mental health professionals, seven with a psychiatrist, eight with a clinical psychologist, even though many had serious problems: 41% had phobias serious enough to restrict their activities, another 41% showed frequent displays of intense anger, 19% low mood or depression, another 10% marked mood swings (Davies et al., 1998).

This contrasts markedly with the 71% rate of weekly counseling sessions of another sample of WSa ($n = 14$, 20–49 yrs, Md = 25;6 yrs) with a social worker or psychologist (Brewer et al., 1995). The majority of these WSa, 79%, were said by their parents to have some emotional problems, 21% were formally diagnosed for a clinical disorder (anxiety disorder, depression, compulsion disorder; Brewer et al., 1995).

Many of the clinical disorders associated with WS may be treated through psychotherapy or counseling of varying kinds, including individual, group, and family therapy as well as cognitive psychotherapy. Providing support and treatment in periods of particular vulnerability, like adolescence and early adulthood, is important. This seems to be an especially difficult time for WSs. Perhaps they do not have the resources necessary to handle the ordinary run-of-the-mill problems and transitions of young adulthood. Possibly they only then become truly aware of their limitations and the unlikelihood of their being able to lead a "normal" adult life. These concerns may be exacerbated by their more restricted access to everyday life as their school years end. Unfortunately, information about the developmental antecedents of WSs' maladaptive behavior and comparative studies of their clinical problems is generally lacking with a few exceptions (e.g., Einfeld et al., 2001).

Nonetheless, a wide range of treatments may be applicable to WSs depending on the case, problem, and resources of the individual in question. Generally, WSs are best served by interventions that are explicit and concrete, verbally oriented, and socially interactive. The minority of "nonverbal" individuals with WS usually requires other forms of treatment, such as behavior management, communication and social skills training. However, those WSs who have serious, refractory kinds of behavior problems and certainly almost all with a clinical disorder should be referred to clinical specialists for psychological or behavioral treatment. Reference has repeatedly been made to the advisability of consulting a professional for serious behavior problems in diverse areas, ranging from language (e.g., greeting behaviors, topical perseveration, prolonged language delay), to perceptual–motor performance (i.e., hyperacusis), sociability (overfriendliness), as well as clinical disorders.

However, little has been said about the special issues and problems usually involved in applying psychotherapeutic techniques to WSs. Just as adaptations are usually needed in applying behavior modification methods to WSs, so too there are certain considerations that therapists should generally be aware of in treating WSs with psychotherapy. Drawing on Harris' (1995) framework of issues involved in applying psychotherapeutic methods to treatment of developmentally disabled individuals, preliminary guidelines for use of psychotherapy with WSs are provided next. This is followed by description of various forms of therapy that may be particularly suitable for WSs, and the types of therapists that may be able to deal with their mental health problems.

Psychotherapy Guidelines for WSs

Extending guidelines for the use of psychotherapeutic techniques with the developmentally disabled to WSs (Harris, 1995b), six guidelines for therapists to consider are presented next.

1. *Special consideration of WSs' characteristics.* It is important for therapists to match their therapeutic interventions with the WS's cognitive and developmental level and individual characteristics. The therapist needs to continually assess whether the patient understands what has been said. This may be initially difficult for the therapist because of the uneven profile of abilities and problems often exhibited by WSs.

Initial sessions may focus on allowing WSs to express and distinguish their various feelings before attempting to relate those feelings to particular situations. Some WSs may not yet have enough insight to describe their own behavior accurately or may be too defensive to admit certain problems to the therapist.

2. *Directive approach.* A directive approach is advised in order to address the fundamental problems and pertinent issues of the patient. The rationale for the patient's therapy should be explained along with the procedures that the therapy sessions would follow. Limits need to be set as to the types of behavior allowable in therapy sessions, such as aggression, destructiveness, and, particularly in the case of WSs, overfriendliness and overaffectionate behavior among others.

It is also very important for WSs to receive reassurance, social approval, and encouragement for their use of effective modes of behavior. Asking WSs to consider alternative ways in which they could have handled a problem may improve their problem-solving abilities and begin to provide a repertoire of effective strategies for different situations.

For example, psychotherapy may help WSs who suffer from severe anxiety to become more aware of the thoughts and situations that tend to trigger their anxiety, and to learn to react in more positive ways. Cases of extreme anger can be dealt with similarly by helping WSs with such problems to become more aware of situations that trigger their "fight" response and assist them in learning more effective ways of dealing with their anger.

3. *Flexibility.* Flexibility is needed in the range of treatment options considered and selected. For example, techniques such as play therapy may be introduced (see later). There may also be a need to accommodate to some of the problem behaviors and defenses common to WSs.

Incessant talking about day-to-day happenings, comments about other people, events that have taken or will take place, activities, or physical states may be handled by asking how the WS individual *feels* about these matters. The reverse is also a useful strategy, that is, countering excessive centering on feelings, disturbing experiences, or emotions by having the therapist inquire about the *facts* of the situation. Reflecting the feelings and statements of WSs by commenting or restating more precisely what the WS has said, may help to promote a sense of being understood, accepted, and objectification of WSs' emotions.

Frequent topic changes or the opposite, topic perseveration may be handled by bringing the conversation back to an earlier point. Direct questions may aid the process. Use of metaphors may help to clarify the relation in nonthreatening ways between important elements in WSs' lives, such as understanding the connection between their behavior, feelings, and certain situations.

4. *Family involvement.* Throughout treatment, the family and others integrally involved with the WS individual may need to be included in the therapeutic process. At the least, they are needed to provide background information on the patient and update the effects of therapy. Oftentimes, they are needed to serve as co-therapists and to offer continuing support: "Working with the patient in isolation may be futile . . . because disabled individuals are so dependent on others for care" (Hurley, 1989; cf. Harris, 1995b, p. 495).

In addition, family members often need assistance in accepting the condition of their WS children and learning how to deal realistically and effectively with it. Family therapy is an approach that may deserve consideration.

5. *Therapist attitude.* Issues regarding the therapist's attitudes toward working with disabled patients may need to be addressed. It is important for the therapist to accept the "reality, chronicity, and permanence of the patient's limitations" (Harris, 1995b, p. 495).

In accepting WS patients at their actual level and encouraging positive steps, the therapist should avoid "infantilizing" and overprotecting the patient. Dependency is already an issue for many WSs. Likewise, WSs are usually acutely aware and sensitized to the negative reactions of others to them.

Generally, the success of therapy with WSs depends on the ability of the therapist to establish an emotionally meaningful "therapeutic alliance." This usually involves building trust and rapport over time.

6. *Issue of developmental disability.* Finally, the general issue of developmental disability and the specific condition of WS must be examined, probed, and clarified (see also American Academy of Pediatrics, 2001). WSs may feel uncertain about how they are different and why they provoke particular kinds of responses from others. Experiences with stigmatization and WSs' reactions to them should be examined. Other topics that often need to be addressed include social skill training for facilitation of peer relations and prevention of abuse and exploitation. Finally, because many WSs are almost always under the direction and supervision of various people, agencies, and organizations, they may need help in learning that they can have some choices, as well as where, how, and when to realize them. There is a delicate balance between allowing WSs to exercise their skills and independence and providing the assistance they need to promote their development and their safety.

Related Forms of Therapy

WSs frequently benefit from group therapy as well as individual psychotherapy (Levine, 1994). Some may profit from receiving both types of therapy at the same time. Others from family therapy. Because of their verbal fluency, sociability, and empathy for others, group therapy may be the treatment of choice for some, an adjunct form of therapy for others.

Group therapy may help WSs realize that other people have problems similar to theirs, and to become cognizant of the reactions of others to those problems. Alternative methods of coping may be concretely depicted and the possible consequences of these options discussed. "Brainstorming" may be used in group therapy when several participants have similar needs or problems and they share solutions that other participants may generate.

Caution must be taken, however, in the type of group to which WSs are assigned. Because of their suggestibility and propensity toward imitation, placement in a group with aggressive, antisocial types of individuals is inadvisable. In general, a "controlled" mix of patient types in the group is preferable.

Types of Therapy. Whereas many individuals with developmental disabilities have a great deal of difficulty in identifying with the verbal, introspective process of therapy, this is usually less of a problem for most WSs due to their language skills, love of talking, and general eagerness to share personal information and their reactions with others.

Although little published research is available, clinical experience suggests that the following four approaches may be particularly applicable to treating some of the clinical problems of WSs: play therapy, psychodrama, bibliotherapy, and assertiveness training.

Play Therapy. One form of psychotherapy widely used with children is play therapy. Despite the good expressive language skills of most WSc, they may still find it difficult to talk directly about certain problems and feelings. They may reveal these or work them through more easily in a play therapy situation. Children are sometimes able to verbalize or dramatize in nonverbal ways important feelings, fears, resentments, and needs which they cannot readily express in other settings. The particular medium should be considered, too, as being of interest to the WSc, for instance, use of dolls, play "construction" kits, paints, clay, or games, among others.

Psychodrama. Psychodrama is another variant of psychotherapy that may be particularly useful for some WSs, as it offers the advantages of dramatization, such as story telling, listening, and enactment, along with group therapy methods. Generally, patients are assigned certain roles to enact a problem situation, then roles are reversed, so the problem is experienced from several perspectives as different surrogates.

Of course, it is vital for the therapist in all forms of treatment to be sympathetic and knowledgeable in treating individuals with developmental disability, and ultimately with WS (Levine & Wharton, 2001).

Bibliotherapy. Another variant of traditional therapy, bibliotherapy, uses carefully selected stories, fictional or nonfictional, to help individuals gain better insight or perspective on a problem. Story selection is critical to success.

As the realm of children's literature is vast, a specialist in this area or in library science can be helpful in locating materials that may provide appropriate role models for WSs. The stories may be read by or to the WS individual.

Bibliotherapy may draw on the high level of auditory skills and empathic understanding of most WSs for other people's feelings. Techniques for handling problems successfully may be vividly portrayed in stories and used to encourage WSs to emulate such strategies. "Reframing" a situation in fictional or biographic form may help WSs realize that others have faced similar problems and managed to deal with them effectively.

Assertiveness Training (AT). Although most WSs are very articulate, they can have problems asserting themselves. Some WS individuals have difficulty standing up for their rights. Others have problems coping with denial of their requests. Still others have difficulty saying "no" to unreasonable demands. Many of these kinds of problems can be helped with language therapy that focuses on the pragmatic use of language (see chap. 3, pp. 100–103).

Some WSs with clinical disorders may, however, become too aggressive, overbearing, or demanding when trying to assert themselves. Others are too submissive, too meek, or too reticent in making requests. Neither approach is usually advisable. Those who are too passive often become victims. Those who are too aggressive tend to antagonize or alienate others. Understandably, persons who start out as too inhibited in asserting themselves properly can end up so frustrated that they become very angry and aggressive.

Assertiveness training is often helpful to persons with such difficulties. It can provide guidance and practice in being able to tell others where they stand and what they need in a firm, direct manner without appearing belligerent, discourteous, or aggressive. When appropriately modified, assertiveness training may be of value in helping certain WSs learn how to assert themselves in a variety of situations.

Other Approaches. Within the realm of psychotherapy, other choices exist. Anger management is another approach that may be particularly valuable for those few WSs who are prone to "meltdowns" (Levine & Wharton, 2001). Cognitive (mental imagery) therapy and desensitization training are alternatives already discussed in connection with behavior problems, such as fears and phobias.

Besides psychotherapy of the traditional verbal type, some WSs may benefit from behavioral management procedures, particularly those WSs who are not verbally skilled or predisposed, or who have intransigent symptoms.

More generally, WSs may benefit from art and/or music therapy. WSs often enjoy listening to or playing music. Certain types of music may be very relaxing for WSs who are highly anxious, angry, or agitated.

Types of Therapists. Different types of therapists may be appropriate for treating certain WSs, depending on the category of behavior disorder, and the experience, training, and supervision of the mental health providers as well as their availability. The specialists suitable for providing therapy to WSs may range from psychiatrists and clinical psychologists with a specialty in developmental disorders, to mental health providers in social work, learning disability specialists, special educators and counselors including pastoral counselors and nurse practitioners. The more serious the disorder, the greater the need for experienced, knowledgeable, insightful, and sympathetic therapists.

Less Traditional Approaches. There has been some interest in considering alternative modes of therapy involving nutrition or avoidance of certain foods or chemicals for conditions like autism, DS, and ADHD, but the benefits of such programs have yet to be substantiated; many are in disrepute, with few advocates. There are some individuals within the WS community, however, who believe that certain symptoms of WS may be related to the nutritional and biochemical aspects of WSs' diet.

Contributing to these beliefs is the established success in treating infants born with phenylketonuria (PKU) with dietary restrictions. Other more directly involved factors for WSs include the hypercalcaemia exhibited by many WS infants (i.e., inability to properly digest milk and milk products), physicians' instructions to restrict the use of vitamin D for WSs (American Academy of Pediatrics, 2001), and the well-known picky eating of most WSs. More pertinent to the treatment of behavior disorders in WS is the use of psychopharmacology.

B. Psychopharmacology

Until several years ago, medication was seldom recommended or used as treatment for the behavior problems of WSs. This is no longer the case (e.g., Dykens et al., 2000; Hagerman, 1999; Levine, 1994; Levine & Wharton, 2001; Levinson, 1994; Scheiber, 2000). Moreover, clinical disorders in WSs were not widely recognized or formally treated. This also has changed with the more frequent mention of clinical disorders in WSc and WSa (see chap. 6, p. 296).

Generally, studies in the 1980s either made no mention of treatment, or if it were mentioned, only a few WS were said to have received medication, such as stimulants, and sometimes there was improvement (Pagon et al., 1987). For example, only 12% of WSc (n = 25, 4–16 yrs) in Morris et al.'s (1988) study were being medicated for hyperactivity, all with Methylphenidate (Ritalin) or another drug. Two others had been previously treated for hyperactivity, one with pentobarbital and diphenhydramine, one with Thorazine (Morris et al., 1988).

TO DRUG OR NOT TO DRUG? THAT IS THE QUESTION
NO—WHICH ONE IS THE QUESTION

STIMULANTS
Ritalin   ---------------------Methylphenidate
Dexedrine   ---------------------Dextroamphetamine
Adderall   ---------------------Dextro and Levoamphetamine salts
Cylert   ---------------------Pemoline
Tricyclic Medication
Tenex   ---------------------Guanfacine
Clonidine patch (TTS2)-----------Catapres

Parent surveys confirm the infrequent use of medication. Only 13% of parents who joined WSA between 1983 and 1990 (WSA Checklist Survey, Semel & Rosner, 1991a, 1991b) indicate that their WSc (n = 111, 4–19 yrs, M = 8;6 yrs) "takes medication for behavior and attention problems (e.g., Ritalin, Cylert, amphetamines)". Written comments on the survey range from neutral reports of having used some form of medication to negative remarks (e.g., "On Ritalin for one week, had him taken off; it put him in a stupor"; "Caused seizures") to a positive report (see later).

Warnings about possible adverse effects of Ritalin in three WSc appeared in Biescar (1987, WSA National Newsletter, Vol. 5, p. 7), but no additional cases were reported. However, care was advised to confirm the diagnosis of ADD plus monitoring and adjusting Ritalin dosage (or other drugs) in WSc (WSA National Newsletter, 1988 April, Vol. *6*, 9). More recent reservations about the use of medications in adults with WS center on some parents' concern that medication is an insufficient treatment (Davies et al., 1998).

Still, clinical experience reveals that medication like stimulants can sometimes help young people with WS (Levine, 1994). Some parents report substantial improvement of attentional/activity kinds of problems. One WS student, using Ritalin, improved so dramatically in speech, writing, organization, and attention that school authorities could tell when medication had not been taken (WSA Checklist Survey, Semel & Rosner, 1991a, 1991b, 1994). Other medications, besides stimulants, are being recommended for various kinds of behavior disorders in WSs, including ADHD, mood disorders, depression, anxiety, and obsessive-compulsive disorder. For example, 4 out of 15 WSa (21%) who regularly attend a clinic were prescribed medication for their anxiety disorders: Prozac (n = 2), Elavil (n = 1), and Zoloft (n = 1) (Brewer et al., 1995).

A number of clinician–researchers have also suggested that certain medications, when properly selected and prescribed by a physician familiar with WS, may significantly improve the functioning of WSs with troublesome forms of behavior disorder. This includes the small, special group of WSc, the "snarlers," who otherwise become completely out of control at certain times (Levine & Wharton, 2001).

When and if medications should be used with WSs, and under what circumstances, is a critical issue in treating WSs. The next section provides guidelines for the use of prescription drugs with WSs followed by a summary of research studies on the efficacy and side effects of various kinds of medication.

Psychopharmacological Guidelines for WSs

Helpful guidelines and advice on the use of medication for WSc's behavior problems are provided by Levinson (1994), a pediatrician and father of a WSc (WSA National Newsletter, Winter, 1994, Vol. *11*, p. 3). Pointing out that "distractibility, poor impulse control, and problems with focusing attention are [part and parcel of WS]" (p. 3), Levinson stated that stimulants like Ritalin and Dexedrine have been used to treat people with attention problems for some time. He explained, "It is my experience that many kids with WS will benefit from such medication." He cautioned, however, that "we don't know in advance which WS children will be helped by the use of such medication, and we won't know until we try it. As for whether it's dangerous to try the medication, no, if used and monitored appropriately by a physician familiar with the use of such medication and when good communication exists between parents and doctor, parents and teacher, parents and therapists" (p. 3).

Levinson (1994) also reminded parents and others that use of medication will not bring about a miracle, and it "never replaces the continuing need for us as parents and for all professionals who interact with our children to evaluate and intervene in our children's behavior. Keep an open mind, don't be afraid to try something under the auspices of professionals who know what they are doing" (p. 3).

Types of Specialists. As for procedures for identifying a suitable professional for advising and supervising WSs' use of medications, Levinson (1994) recommended contacting a pediatric neurologist or child psychiatrist for selection, prescription, and monitoring of psychotropic drugs. Pediatricians differ widely in the extent of their experience with psychotropic medication. Some are experts in this area, others have little or no experience or training in psychopharmacology. One needs to inquire about the physician's familiarity with such medication and with WSs.

Other options for locating a qualified physician to consult regarding medications for WSs is through referral by a clinical psychologist, social worker, or the clinics for WS (see Appendix).

Monitoring Medication Effects. People involved with WSs—such as physicians, parents, teachers, supervisors, and therapists—must assist in monitoring the effects of medication and its dosage. This requires teamwork and coordination. Setting up a chart or log to record times and amounts of medication administered, significant behaviors and their times of occurrence may help with the task of keeping detailed, accurate notes. These should be regularly shared with the physician prescribing the medication.

Procedures used to evaluate drug effectiveness may include daily teacher ratings, weekly parent ratings, and direct observations of behavior on high and low demand tasks (Power, Blum, Jones, & Kaplan, 1997). It is also important to monitor any side effects that may arise, adjust dosage when necessary, and sometimes to try another kind of medication for optimum effectiveness. Prescribing proper levels of medication for WSs is a highly complex activity, both an art and a science.

Although no single pharmacological agent has proved to have universal efficacy for all of the maladaptive behaviors sometimes shown by WSc, Levine and Wharton (2001) listed several medications that have been of benefit to some of them. In addition, Hagerman (1999) provided a review of the psychopharmacological literature on the use of medication with WSs. The next section offers a brief summary of that research literature.

Research on Psychopharmacological Treatment of WSs

Research indicates that medication is sometimes appropriate in cases of WS that involve ADD or ADHD (Power et al., 1997) as well as cases involving anxiety or depression (Hagerman, 1999). In evaluating drugs, both their main effects and side effects need to be considered.

For ADD and ADHD symptoms, Hagerman (1999) identified two broad categories of drugs: stimulant and tricyclic medications.

Stimulant Medications for ADD and ADHD. Stimulants used for ADD and ADHD include: Ritalin (methylphenidate), Dexedrine (dextroamphetamine), Adderall (dextro and levoamphetamine salts), and Cylert (pemoline).

So far, placebo controlled trials of stimulant medication, specifically Ritalin (methylphenidate) have been carried out in a small sample, six cases, of WSs (Bawden, MacDonald, & Shea, 1997; Power et al., 1997). Four of the six children had a positive response to methylphenidate in both behavioral ratings and neuropsychological testing. Some were less quarrelsome, impulsive, and moody during the methylphenidate trial period than during a placebo period. In two of the cases (7 & 8 yrs), a 5-mg and a 10-mg dose were compared, and both boys did better with a 10-mg dose (Power et al., 1997). Neither anxiety nor stereotypical behavior appeared to worsen on stimulants. Four of the six patients had cardiac disease (Power et al., 1997), but cardiac complications were not mentioned in this report.

Stimulant side effects can include cardiovascular stimulation, which can elevate heart rate and blood pressure. Therefore, these signs must be watched closely in patients with WS. Hypertension is usually a contraindication for the use of stimulants (Barkley, 1990, cf. Hagerman, 1999).

Appetite reduction, which often occurs when taking stimulants, can interfere with weight gain and height growth. WSs tend to be "picky eaters" and their short, lean stature is already a problem for some with this syndrome even in the absence of medication. Thus, physical growth should be followed closely in children with WS. In addition, Hagerman (1999) reported that higher doses of stimulants may worsen anxiety, which is also an important issue for many WS patients. With ADD and ADHD, the paradoxical effect of stimulant drugs is such that a common reaction is lethargy. Should this occur, it may indicate that dosage needs to be reduced, or medication stopped.

Other stimulants that may be helpful include dextroamphetamine (Dexedrine) and Adderall. To date, only one controlled study has been published documenting the efficacy of Adderall use in 30 non-WS children with ADHD (Swanson et al., 1998). The study reported a prolonged duration of action with improvement in attention, behavior, and math performance in non-WS patients with ADHD on Adderall. Both Dexedrine spansules and Adderall tablets are longer acting and can be given in the morning.

Adderall had up to $6\frac{1}{2}$ hours of effect with the 20-mg dose, as compared to roughly 4 hours for methylphenidate, which means it may not be necessary for the WSc to take medication during school hours.

Pemoline has recently been associated with rare cases of acute hepatic failure. Because of such potential liver problems, Hagerman (1999) recommended that the other stimulants should be tried first for treatment of ADHD in WS before pemoline is considered.

Tricyclic Medications for ADD and ADHD. Stimulants generally do not prolong cardiac conduction nor lead to arrhythmias at higher doses, but tricyclic medications can cause these kinds of cardiac complications, and they should be avoided in patients with cardiac disease.

Tenex (guanfacine) or catapres (Clonidine) may also slightly prolong nodal (heart) conduction, although arrhythmias are rare. Hagerman (1998) reported that these drugs may be used in patients with WS, after consulting a cardiologist, because they lower blood pressure and also treat hyperactivity. However, they do not seem to improve attention problems as well as the stimulant medications.

Medications for Treating Anxiety or Depression. Although no controlled studies have been reported as yet with WSs, Hagerman (1998), Levine and Wharton (2001), and Pober and Dykens (1996) reported that the use of psychopharmacologic approaches for the treatment of anxiety or depression can be beneficial for some WSs.

Selective serotonin reuptake inhibitors (SSRIs) (e.g., Prozac, Paxil, Zoloft) have been used in both normal and developmentally disabled children and adults for treatment of anxiety and depression (Brewer et al., 1995). Anecdotal information suggests that WS patients with either anxiety or depression respond well to SSRI's (Pober & Dykens, 1996) and without serious side effects (Hagerman, 1998). Further studies with larger samples should be conducted to verify these results.

In addition, Gustafson and Traub (1997; cf. Hagerman, 1999) reported that an 18-year-old male with WS was successfully treated with a Clonidine patch (TTS2) in addition to nifedipine in sustained release for hypertension.

General Evaluation on Use of Psychopharmacology for WSs

Based on personal observation of WSc, it appears that pharmacological treatment may be best reserved for cases in which other methods have been tried and failed, or used along with psycho-educational and other approaches. In fact, medication sometimes facilitates a difficult child's responsivity to other forms of treatment which may eventually replace the use of medication (Semel & Rosner, 1991b). Levine (1994) also suggested using medication while other techniques are being introduced.

Others recommend multimodal intervention, including modifications at school, and carefully monitored medication for the treatment of ADD and ADHD symptoms and anxiety or depression (Hagerman, 1999). Similarly, Scheiber (2000) advised that experts in ADHD recommend a multifaceted approach to intervention with an accent on behavior management, rewarding the child for desired behavior. An effective treatment plan may include classroom modifications, behavior modification, parent training, counseling, and medication. Harris (1995b) put it succinctly when he stated that optimal treatment programs are multiple modalities of treatment.

At present, there is a serious lack of relevant, reliable information on the medications that have been used with WSs, and for what conditions, and with what effects. Clearly, there is a need for programmatic research in this area.

Meanwhile, it is important to bear the following in mind:

1. Different pharmacological agents, even within the same "class", may differ in their main effect and side effects.
2. Different children may need differing dosages of the same drug.
3. Although some WSs may benefit substantially from a given medicine, others may show no improvement or even negative reactions.
4. Even a drug that brings about a favorable behavioral response may still induce undesirable physical effects on WSs.
5. Both psychotropic and mood-elevating drugs often have a substantially different effect on adolescents and adults versus their effect on children.

In many cases, however, appropriate choice and application of medication have been of great benefit. In other cases, not so favorable a result has occurred.

IV. SUMMARY AND CONCLUSIONS

To treat the multitude of maladaptive behaviors associated with WS, six major types of behavior problems and their variants, as well as some cases of clinical disorder, numerous kinds of intervention approaches are presented to help WSs and others closely involved with them to deal more effectively with these difficulties. A multiplicity of interventions is required in order to address the wide range of maladaptive behaviors exhibited by WSs and individual differences in their behavioral adjustment and other characteristics.

Consistent with the distinction drawn between types of behavior problems and clinical disorders, interventions may be differentiated into two
classes, psycho-educational strategies and clinical treatments, although
many clinicians and researchers are becoming increasingly aware of the importance of considering a variety of approaches. In dealing with anxiety
problems, for example, these may include use of specific serotonin reuptake
inhibitors (SSRIs) or moclobemide, psychological interventions, behavioral
parenting skills training (i.e., modeling, behavioral relaxation, desensitization, and positive self-statements), and social skill training (Einfeld et al.,
2001). For the most part, these are similar to the psycho-educational approach suggested throughout this book.

Psycho-Educational Approaches

The six psycho-educational techniques presented here—verbal mediation, control mechanisms, problem analysis, environmental controls, task
management, and stress reduction—draw on the verbal, social, and other
strengths associated with WS. Although undoubtedly not an exhaustive list
of interventions that may benefit WSs, it represents those found helpful
with the WSs we have observed.

Although these psycho-educational interventions are somewhat related
and overlapping, each of the six makes its own contribution. Verbal mediation aims at behavioral enhancement, control mechanisms at behavioral
control, problem analysis at behavioral analysis, environmental controls focus on managing external conditions, task management on procedures, and
stress reduction on regulating affect.

There are also commonalities among them. Three of the six—verbal mediation strategies, control mechanisms, and problem analysis—feature *verbal interactive techniques*. All involve verbal communication, social exchange, and the verbal–social predilections of most individuals with WS.
They are designed to concretize and clarify the distinction between appropriate and inappropriate forms of behavior. They also attempt to increase
WSs' understanding and insight about their maladaptive behavior and provide support for them in trying to control such behavior through verbal–social means.

In contrast, the psycho-educational approaches of "environmental controls" and "task management" rely on externally imposed measures to remove extraneous stimulation, give predictability, and simplify the tasks and
activities of WS individuals. In addition, stress reduction may be included
as it often involves using environmental resources to help reduce the tensions of WSs. Together these three comprise "*external strategies*," which
seek to provide organization, reduce situational complexity, decrease external demands, and remove irrelevant stimuli from the environment.

It is interesting to note that all six forms of psycho-educational approach are applicable to the six types of behavior problems described in Section II. Thus, they may be applicable to both the problems of high reactivity and low self-regulation associated with WS.

Clinical Treatment

Finally, use of "specialized treatment" constitutes its own category as an intervention approach though it can be used as an adjunct or complement to either or both of the foregoing categories of intervention strategy: verbal interaction techniques and external strategies. It draws on qualified specialists to treat both types of core behavior problems, high reactivity and low self-regulation.

In particular, the focus of clinical treatment discussed in Section III is on psychotherapy and its variants and on psychopharmacology (see p. 342). These forms of "clinical treatment" involve consultation, evaluation, diagnosis, and therapy by professional specialists, especially for cases of chronic behavior disturbance, clinical disorders, or pervasive developmental disorder. Specialists may also contribute to treatment of the basic behavior problems of WSs, sometimes in a supervisory role for appropriate use of psycho-educational techniques, sometimes through prescriptions for medication.

Psychotherapy. Various psychological treatments are discussed which may be applicable to WSs, depending on the case, problem, and available resources. Many of the behavior problems characteristic of WSs can be treated through individual and group therapy as well as cognitive psychotherapy, behavioral management, adapted behavior modification, anger management, or pastoral counseling. Providing support and treatment in periods of particular vulnerability, like transitions, adolescence, and early adulthood, is also important. Intensive psychotherapy by a psychologist, psychiatrist, or other qualified mental health provider is generally reserved for refractory types of problems.

As for mental health treatment, its form depends on the type of problem, its severity, and the area of expertise of the particular professional. Generally, WSs are best served by interventions that are explicit and concrete, verbally oriented, and socially interactive. Several of the psychotherapeutic approaches described in Section III draw upon WSs' language skills and empathetic strengths. These may include: play therapy, bibliotherapy, family therapy, assertiveness training, and psychodrama, among others. These have their parallels in the verbal interactive forms of psycho-educational intervention, namely verbal mediation, control mechanisms, and problem analysis.

Guidelines for the use of psychotherapy with WSs suggest ways to accommodate to the needs and characteristics typical of WSs and the kinds of behavior problems and clinical disorders associated with them. Those who lack the verbal–social skills of most WSs may require other forms of treatment by experienced specialists, such as adapted behavior modification, play therapy, perhaps medication depending on their type of problem.

Psychopharmacological Treatment. In terms of the advisability of using psychopharmacological agents for WSs, that depends on the type of behavior problem and resources available for prescribing and monitoring the use of medications. Generally, qualified professionals, preferably pediatric psychiatrists or physicians with experience with the psychopharmacological treatment of developmentally disabled individuals, should be consulted. Both the main effect and side effects of medication should be noted as well as the WS individual's own response to the medication. Adjustments in dosage and type of medication may be necessary; age and other characteristics of the individual should be taken into account. Caution is advised in extending drugs used with adults to use with WSc.

Research on the use of psychopharmacological drugs with WSs is sparse, but positive results are cited for certain types of stimulants with some WS cases of ADD and ADHD, and the use of selective serotonin reuptake inhibitors (SSRIs) (e.g., Prozac, Paxil, Zoloft) for treatment of some WS cases of anxiety and depression.

It is important to recognize that the purpose of medication is to improve WSs' ability to function and their quality of life. It is not to sedate them so they are easier to handle. Instead, medication may be most valuable when it is used to promote WSs' receptiveness to other forms of treatment, like psychotherapy or adapted behavior modification, or in conjunction with psycho-educational techniques, such as control mechanisms, verbal mediation, task management, and stress reduction strategies. In certain ways, medication is an extension of the external strategies of psycho-educational intervention, namely, environmental controls, task management, and stress reduction techniques. Multiplicity in approach is becoming the byword for many clinical researchers.

In cases of severe behavior disorder, however, the balance often shifts from the emphasis on psycho-educational approaches toward the efficacy of clinical treatment by mental health professionals and medication.

There is reason to hope that future advances in the fields of biogenetics, biochemistry, and genetic engineering may eventually provide treatments for the symptoms of WS and even the syndrome itself, that we can only dream of now.

8

Summary and Conclusions

Just as a forest is more than a lot of trees, a person is more than a collection of behaviors.

Whereas previous chapters examined the behavioral characteristics of WSs within the separate areas of functioning—namely, language, perceptual-motor performance, specific aptitudes, and behavior problems—this chapter provides an overview of those characteristics. It focuses on the prototypical and associated features of WSs and the specificity of those features to WS. Related issues are the interconnections of features and the genetic and brain mechanisms associated with them.

Approaches to intervention are also considered from a broader perspective. Whereas previous chapters recommended techniques for dealing with the problem-specific difficulties and special skills of WSs, the present chapter provides general intervention guidelines that are applicable across specific areas.

Finally, the chapter discusses possible trends in the future study and treatment of WS. Suggestions for improvement in the care delivery systems of WS conclude the chapter.

I. BEHAVIORAL CHARACTERISTICS OF WS

What are the essential elements of WS behavior? How can the prototypical and associated features of WS be distinguished from the previously noted vast array of items, characteristics, dimensions, factors, and categories, comments, impressions, and clinical observations? Two basic criteria have been applied in order to identify the critical features of WS: the frequency with which WSs exhibit a particular feature, and the consistency with which it is reported across research studies, subject samples, and by individuals familiar with WSs. The significance of a feature for WSs compared to other groups is also considered.

By definition, prototypical features are exhibited by the vast majority of WSs, associated features by a significant subset, rather than by most WSs. Prototypical features are supported by an extensive body of research, associated features are less thoroughly researched.

A. Prototypical and Associated Features of WS

Aside from behavioral features, WS is characterized by physical features (e.g., medical conditions and facial characteristics), and developmental problems (e.g., limitations in mental ability) that are prototypical of WSs in these areas (see chap. 1; also, Bellugi et al., 2000; Mervus & Klein-Tasman, 2000).

In order to identify the prototypical and associated behavioral features of WS, each major area described in this book is re-examined below.

Language Skills and Problems

Language ability is one of the more striking behavioral features of WSs partly because it tends to surpass their performance in other areas (see chap. 2). Although recent studies indicate certain language problems, relative strengths in vocabulary, category concepts, and grammar are generally evident, at least by middle or late childhood (Bellugi et al., 2000; Mervis & Klein-Tasman, 2000). Research, therefore, justifies assigning prototypic status to their language strengths. Associated features include clear articulation, effective prosody, and creative storytelling ability. Although they occur in most WSc, these are less clearly established as prominent features of WS language skills.

On the negative side, WSs are said to show verbosity, excessive use of tangential speech, persistent questioning, and topic perseveration. Aside from these prototypical language flaws, additional difficulties in the social uses of language (i.e., pragmatics) are often noted, namely, compulsive greeting of strangers, calling out, and circuitous answering of questions. These are classified as associated features.

Restricted use of certain complex language forms in syntax and semantics also qualifies as an associated, negative feature. This includes difficulty with some morphosyntactic forms, complexly embedded and nested syntactic constructions, most semantic relational terms, especially those involving spatial and temporal concepts, as well as problems with word-finding and figurative speech.

Delay in early childhood acquisition of language is another prototypical feature of WSs, along with marked variability in the eventual level of their language proficiency and severity of language problems.

Perceptual-Motor Performance

Severe difficulty with most visuospatial (VS) and visual-spatial-motor (VSM) tasks, including drawing and spatial construction, are prototypic of WS. Extended developmental delay and severe impairment in motor functioning, both gross and fine motor, is characteristic of most WSs. Interestingly, VS deficits are not limited to tasks with a motor component; they occur, too, on tests requiring only comparative visual judgments, such as "which stimulus line is longer" (Bellugi, 1994). The prototypic proficiency of WSs on facial discrimination and recognition tasks is all the more striking given their abysmal performance on seemingly similar VS tests and the consistency of their proficiency across age levels and various types of facial processing tasks (Bellugi et al., 2000).

Auditory hypersensitivity to certain environmental sounds is another prime example of a prototypical feature. It is displayed by most WSs and confirmed repeatedly in parental surveys and laboratory tests.

On the other hand, tactile defensiveness is an associated feature. It is reported less frequently, often in less than half of WSc, and it is not as extensively researched as most prototypic features.

Specific Aptitudes

Each of the four specific aptitudes discussed in chapter 5 has its own collection of distinctive features.

Sociability. Marked sociability is a hallmark of WS. Most parents report that their WSs are unusually friendly, initiate conversations easily, show no fear of strangers, and exhibit strong empathy for the feelings of others (see chap. 5). These reports are supported by ratings of WSs on social dimensions, like Approach, Empathy, Non-shyness, and People-Oriented (Dykens & B. Rosner, 1999; Jones et al., 2000; Mervis & Klein-Tasman, 2000; Tomc et al., 1990). Item analyses, too, reveal that WSs are rated high on "feels terrible when others hurt," "often initiates interactions," and "never goes unnoticed in groups" (Dykens & B. Rosner, 1999).

These findings indicate that sociability, empathy, and overfriendliness are integral features of WS. The classification of "poor peer relations," is less certain. On the one hand, the incidence is markedly lower than that of other social attributes. On the other hand, parents and professionals often mention peer problems. Poor peer relations is therefore classified as an associated feature.

Similarly, the status of social cognition or "theory of mind" in WSs is equivocal. Initial reports of skill on "false belief" tasks have been challenged by recent findings. On the other hand, research supports earlier findings of emotional sensitivity (Tager-Flusberg & Sullivan, 2000). Until the disparity in results is resolved, "theory of mind" and "social cognition" should not be included as basic features of WS.

Curiosity. "Intense inquisitiveness" is a prototypic feature of WS due to its high frequency and consistent citing as a feature, but the evidence is more qualitative than quantitative. On the positive side, intense interest in specific topics or types of objects (e.g., coins, insects, flags) is often reported. This associated feature may be manifested by WSs asking questions, seeking information, mentors, and investing emotionally in the topic. Reports of inappropriate focal attachments to objects with certain properties (e.g., fans, motors, or spinning objects) are rather limited, generally occurring in less than 50% of WSc. These qualify as negative, associated features.

Memory. Generalizations regarding the quality of WS memory are even more problematic than those of other areas. This reflects distinctions in performance related to the type of memory tested (i.e., STM vs. LTM), stimulus mode (verbal vs. VS), and type of material (story recall vs. recall of academic facts).

Digit recall, a form of auditory STM, is generally recognized as an area of WS strength. The reliability of these findings suggests that auditory STM is a prototypic feature of WSs (e.g., Mervis & Klein-Tasman, 2000). Even here, however, results are strongly affected by type of material, as WSc are observed to exhibit considerable difficulty in learning to read and recall simple word patterns, such as "bet," "bit," "but." This may be attributed to difficulty in blending phonemes, pattern interference, and auditory discrimination. A good memory for the words of songs, prayers, names of people, foreign language vocabulary, melodies, and rhythms, as well as landmarks, is also worth noting.

Not surprisingly, WSs tend to perform poorly on visuospatial memory tasks in both STM and LTM (e.g., Corsi Block test, immediate and delayed copying of block constructions), but very well on memory tests of faces (Bellugi et al., 2000).

WSs also perform well on story recall, in both STM and LTM, and on certain semantically related tasks in LTM (see chap. 5). Much remains to be done in establishing areas of strength and weakness in this domain.

Music. Musicality is well established as a prototypic feature of WSs, most certainly when it comes to enjoyment and involvement with music. Specification of the precise nature of WSs' musical abilities is less certain.

Most WSs demonstrate talent in the area of music, often in singing. Many are able to play a musical instrument with some proficiency, more than a few are able to compose music with some success and surprising productivity. Television accounts of WS have vividly demonstrated their unusually good memory for music and sense of rhythm. Lack of statistical data as to the frequency with which WSs exhibit these talents obscures classifying it as a prototypical feature at the present time. Wide variation among WSs in their degree of musical talent also suggests that this is an associated, rather than a prototypical, feature. Few negatives exist for most WSs in the area of musicality, except for being typically limited in their ability to play certain instruments and read music.

Maladaptive Behaviors

Although many types of behavior problems are attributed to WSs, only two are clearly established as almost universal, namely, distractibility and anxiety/fears (see chap. 6). The remaining four types of behavior problems—impulsivity, rigidity, low frustration tolerance, and atypical activity—are classified as associated features due to their relatively low frequency and general paucity of available research, but there are some exceptions. For example, high scores on the personality item "overreact(s) to frustrations and mishaps" and the item "Tense" (Mervis & Klein-Tasman, 2000) are consistent with reports of low frustration tolerance and a high rate of tantrums.

In addition to these types of behavior problems, some WSs have a tendency to exhibit certain types of behavior disorders, such as general behavioral disturbance, ADHD, simple phobias, depression, obsessive compulsive disorder, and autistic-like behaviors.

Table 8.1 summarizes the present specification of prototypical and associated features by topical area and the positive or negative nature of the feature. Positive and negative refer to the valence ascribed to the feature, where positive denotes an adaptive, favorable attribute or strength, and negative denotes unfavorable, nonadaptive, impairment, or weakness.

B. Analysis Of WS Profile

In identifying the critical features of WSs, several issues emerge, namely, variations in features, interconnections between features, specificity of features to WS, and neurochemical mechanisms associated with the WS profile.

TABLE 8.1
Prototypic and Associated Features of WS by Area

Major Behavioral Area	Positive Prototypic Features	Negative Prototypic Features	Positive Associated Features	Negative Associated Features
Language	Verbal Skills, Vocabulary, Category Concepts, Grammar	Language Delay, Verbosity, Tangential Speech, Persistent Questioning, Perseveration	Articulation, Prosody, Storytelling	Complex Syntax, Semantic Relations, Word Finding, Compulsive Greeting, Calling Out, Indirect Answers
Perceptual-Motor Performance	Face Discrimination, Recognition	Visuospatial Deficits, Gross and Fine Motor Problems, Auditory Hypersensitivity		Tactile Defensiveness, Activities of Daily Living
Specific Aptitudes	Sociability, Empathy, Curiosity, Auditory STM, Memory for Faces, Musicality	Overfriendliness, Visuospatial Memory Deficits	Topical Interests, LTM of Stories, Categories, Music: Singing, Playing, Composing	Peer Relations, Object Attachments, Difficulty Reading Music
Behavior Problems		Distractibility, Anxiety & Fears		Impulsivity, Rigidity, Frustration, Activity, Clinical Disorders: ADHD, OCD, Depression Autism

Variations in Features

In examining the features associated with WS, individual differences among WSs are clearly apparent as well as the fragmentation or inconsistency in types of features subsumed within a single major area.

Individual Differences. Marked differences between WSs are evident in the wide range of scores they exhibit on many characteristics, such as general mental ability, physical stature, language, and specific aptitudes (e.g., musical talent). Even for "universal," prototypical features with a 100% reported rate of occurrence—such as empathy, auditory hypersensitivity, or distractibility—the intensity and pervasiveness of the response may vary. The extreme in individual differences may be found, however, in the existence of specific subgroups of WSs.

WS Subgroups. So far, several distinct subgroups of WSs have been identified in previous chapters. These include WSc who are nonverbal, those with problems in auditory processing, WSs who show symptoms of autism as well as WS, and those who have a diagnosis of ADHD and WS.

There is also the possibility that other subgroups may emerge in the future. These may include WSc who do not show the prototypical facial features or facies associated with WS, even though they may display the vast majority of other physical, medical, and behavioral characteristics. Tactile defensiveness may comprise another subgroup. There is the further possibility that higher functioning WSs (i.e., those who may be classified as learning disabled instead of mentally retarded because they have IQ scores above 85) may constitute another subgroup, or they may represent just the upper end of the IQ distribution for WS. Designation of subgroup status depends on the extent to which other features are implicated and whether there are qualitative as well as quantitative differences involved.

Although each of the four subgroups noted probably contains only a small number of WSs, they have considerable theoretical and practical significance. Theoretically, generalizations about the prototypical profile of WSs are subject to limitations because of these subgroups. Practically, the selection and implementation of interventions are impacted by the specific characteristics of the subgroups. For example, elementary language skills are obviously a requisite for use of verbal mediational strategies.

Feature Fragmentation

Scrutinizing the list of features identified in Table 8.1 shows that most features refer to a particular component, not a general domain, like language. Even within an area, there is not necessarily regularity in WSs' level or type of performance. Instead, some subareas may be better developed, some more problematic or irksome than others.

Within the field of language, for example, WSs tend to be more advanced in grammar than pragmatics. Even within these subfields, there are irregularities. Grammatical correctness is the rule for relatively complex sentence forms like the conditional, passive, relative clause center-embedded nested phrases, and questions, but morphosyntactic errors are customary for other seemingly simple forms, like past tense, verb tense agreement, use of plurals, or personal pronouns (e.g., "felled," "hisself").

Development is also uneven within the subfield of the pragmatics of language. Relative strength in the feeling functions of communications, like making eye contact, affirming the remarks of a speaker, or being influenced by verbal reasoning, contrasts with worrisome problems in other areas, such as compulsive greeting behaviors, inability to stay "on topic," or difficulty in answering questions directly.

In the subfield of semantics, too, relative strength in knowing category concepts, like the members and properties of "Animals," "Clothing," and "Food," contrasts markedly with weakness in understanding semantic relational concepts, in particular, spatial–temporal terms (see chap. 2; also Bellugi et al., 2000).

Disparities are apparent in other areas as well, such as good STM memory for simple verbal stimuli (i.e., digits, words, and sentences), but extremely poor STM for simple visuospatial stimuli or block constructions. Likewise, sociability and friendliness contrasts with poor peer relations; no fear of strangers contrasts with fear of unfamiliar places, changes in routine, and myriad other fears. Along the same lines, problems with distractibility seem inconsistent with the intense concentration WSs often show when dealing with a topic of special personal interest.

Note that simple explanations like complexity or familiarity with a topic or area fail to explain these discrepancies, so other behavioral factors and/ or neurobiological (genotype and brain) mechanisms must be implicated. This argument is further supported by the fact that WS is exemplified by an unusual set of developmental trajectories that follow distinct paths in the areas of language, visuospatial performance, and face discrimination (see chap. 4).

Regardless of "cause," these disparities make it difficult to generalize from one characteristic to another or to make predictions about WS performance even within a single area. Sometimes they obscure the results of standard tests or questionnaires with WSs.

Measurement Problems. Unevenness in the test scores of WSs within and between major areas of the WS profile tends to pose measurement problems. As a result, the overall or total score of a test or even a subtest score may convey an incomplete or inaccurate picture of what it is supposed to measure because it includes items that are both representative and unrepresentative of WS performance. This applies to a wide variety of measures, including those that are intended to evaluate the cognition, language, behavior, ability, temperament, personality, and so forth of WSs.

Part of the problem may be that tests are constructed on the assumption that certain item subsets are complementary and correlative, at least for the general or special population for which they are devised, but this assumption may not hold for the unusual profile of WS. For example, the Hyperactivity scale on Rutter's Questionnaire or Achenbach's Child Behavior Checklist (CBCL) contains a conglomeration of items, some characteristic of WSs, others less so, which obscures conclusions as to how much "running around" WSs are likely to exhibit (see chap. 6).

Thus, analysis of WSs' responses to specific items on standard tests is recommended, often even required, in order to reveal the "true" nature of WSs' behavior. Unfortunately, these analyses are not often performed but, when they are, results can be very revealing.

This is evident in recent research on feature specificity.

Feature Specificity

Specificity refers here to the extent to which behaviors displayed by individuals with a particular syndrome are totally distinct from those of other syndromes (i.e., "total specificity") or whether they overlap partially, by sharing similarities as well as differences, with certain other syndromes (Dykens & B. Rosner, 1999). In the case of WS, there are many instances in which the behaviors of WSs resemble those of other groups but, on closer inspection, differences emerge in how they are expressed. To illustrate, both WSs and individuals with Prader–Willi (PWs) score high on the dimension "Help Others," but the groups differ on certain items. This is an example of partial specificity. Specifically, WSs exceed PWs on "feels terrible when others are hurt," whereas the reverse is true on "strong maternal/paternal feelings" (Dykens & Rosner, 1999).

Clinical observations and experience further attest to the partial specificity of various kinds of behaviors and subject groups with WSs; namely, there is overlap between WSs and individuals with certain forms of learning disability, mental retardation, autism, and ADHD. For example, WSs differ from many other groups in the high value they place on verbal-social rewards, opportunities for social interaction, and social disapproval, as well as the low value many WSs place on material rewards like candy and typical prizes. Most WSs also tend to be more responsive than individuals with other forms of mental retardation to verbal mediational techniques, such as dramatization, storytelling, and self-instruction, as well as concrete analogies and metaphors.

Whereas fearfulness and anxieties are not unique to WSs, what triggers these emotions may be, namely, a change in plans, visuomotor or motor tasks, auditory hypersensitivity, tactile defensiveness, gravitational insecurities, and concern for the welfare of others. On the surface, WSs and children with ADHD both seem to be "overactive," but clinical observation reveals that WSs are more often searching for objects of special interest or attachment instead of apparently being in constant motion. Along the same lines, there are many significant differences and similarities between some WSs and the typical autistic individual (see chap. 6 and Table 6.9).

There are also points of contrast when it comes to treatment. Techniques of behavior modification, even when adapted to WSs, are not treatments of choice as they may be for many individuals with ADHD or autism. Moreover, although medication is sometimes useful, it seems to be less effective with WSs than with other groups, except when these WSs share some of their major attributes.

Feature Cohesiveness

Besides the fragmentation already discussed, the WS profile appears to evince feature cohesiveness, that is, some features seem to "hang together" or cluster in groups both within and across domains. Within the area of visual-spatial-motor skills, for example, problems that impair performance on various kinds of motor tasks may also be implicated in problems of spatial orientation and left–right confusions (see chap. 4). They may also be related to the difficulty many WSs have, across areas, with semantic relational terms, especially those involving quantitative comparisons (e.g., the comparative terms "bigger," "taller," or "larger") or spatial and temporal dimensions (see chap. 2).

Another example of within area cohesiveness involves the consistency with which sociability, approachability, agreeableness, empathy, and openness "hang together" as a factor (see chap. 5). Its counterpart, across areas, may be WSs' excellent performance on facial discrimination tasks (chap. 4), as well as their overfriendliness with strangers and compulsive greeting behavior (language pragmatics, chap. 2). Impulsivity, a type of behavior problem (chap. 6), may also play a role. WSs are rarely described as reserved, distant, cautious, or inhibited.

On a more general level, it seems likely that the various areas discussed in these chapters are linked in certain ways rather than being completely independent of each other. This is consistent with the parallels pointed out earlier, as well as speculations offered throughout the book, but this needs to be tested empirically.

Interconnections Between Behavioral Categories[10]

Until recently, research on the behavioral characteristics of WS has focused almost exclusively on determining the dominant features and dimensions of WS, with a few exceptions. This is unfortunate because further information about interconnections between features may help to clarify the structure of the WS profile and possible linkages between the phenotype (behavioral features) and genotype of WS.

A first step toward determining whether behavioral features are related across behavioral areas is the reexamination of the results of the Utah Survey in which parents of WSc (n = 64, 4–22 yrs) answered 73 items regarding the major areas discussed in this book (Semel & Rosner 1991a, 1991b; see chap. 1).

For present purposes, the items are grouped into the following categories and subcategories: language (skills and problems); perceptual-motor functioning (visuomotor deficits and auditory hypersensitivity); specific aptitudes (social skills including empathy, poor peer relations, and musicality); maladaptive behaviors (fears and anxieties, distractibility, impulsivity, rigidity, and atypical activity); and academic skills, including reading, writing, and mathematics (Semel & Rosner 1991a, 1991b, see chap. 1). Each subcategory contains at least three items; each is coded in terms of its valence as a positive, favorable behavior or a negative, unfavorable behavior.

Tabulating responses for each WSc by item, the items are combined to form categories and subcategories, each with its own score. Even though many items tend to have predominately yes or no responses, the grouping of items produces a range of scores.

The statistical significance of the relation between response categories and subcategories was tested by conducting a series of nonparametric, Kendall Tau correlational tests on the distribution of parents' responses to items in each category and subcategory. Several statistically significant correlations were obtained (p's < .05–.0001), as were some nonsignificant correlations between the constructed categories and subcategories of the Utah Survey.

Figure 8.1 provides a visual representation of the significant correlations obtained between the subcategories of Language, Perceptual-Motor Performance, and Specific Aptitudes, along with the categories of Maladaptive Behavior and Academic Performance. Straight lines represent positive correlations (direct relations) between categories/subcategories, labeled and

---

[10]Material in this section is similar to: Rosner, S. R., & Semel, E. (2001, June). *Williams syndrome: Interconnections between behavioral profiles.* Poster session presented at the annual meeting of the American Psychological Society, Toronto, Canada.

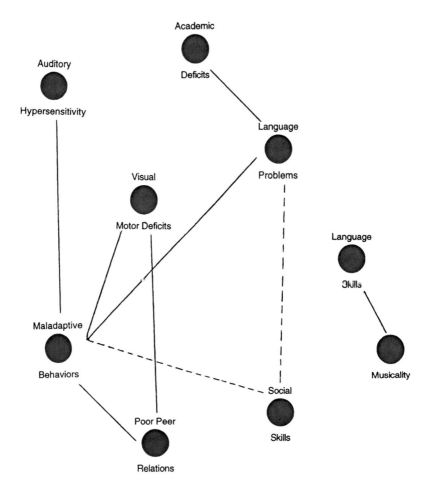

FIG. 8.1. Schematic representation of correlations between topical categories and subcategories of the Utah Survey. – – – = negative correlation – = positive correlation.

depicted by circles; broken lines represent negative correlations (indirect relations) between categories/subcategories.

Results indicate that the frequency of Perceptual-Motor category problem responses by parents is positively correlated with the frequency of Maladaptive category responses by parents ($p < .0001$). This supports Udwin and Yule's (1991) contention that the relatively high rate of behavior problems in WSc is due at least partly to their limitations and deficits in the area of perceptual–motor functioning.

Not surprisingly, the number of Maladaptive category responses of parents is also correlated positively with the number of problem responses in the subcategories Visual-Motor Deficits, Language Problems (i.e., pragmatics of communication, $p < .01$), and Poor Peer Relations ($p < .001$). This is consistent with previous conjectures as to the relation between language problems, such as topic maintenance, turn-taking, answering of questions, topic perseveration and behavior problems (e.g., distractibility, impulsivity, and rigidity). Likewise, it seems reasonable to assert that maladaptive behavior may be a deterrent to peer relations.

Along the same line, there is a negative (inverse) relation between number of Maladaptive Problems and the subcategory Social Skills (and Empathy), $p < .01$, suggesting that WSc who score relatively low in social skills and empathy may also exhibit numerous behavior problems. There is also an inverse relation between Language Problems and Social Skills, such that many language problems, characterized by such behaviors as incessant questioning and topic irrelevance, are associated with impairment of social skills. These results are in line with general findings in the field of child development concerning a linkage between good adjustment and good peer relations, as well as good communication skills (language pragmatics) and sociability. On the other side, poor peer relations is associated with visuospatial deficits ($p < .05$), which is consistent with the notion that difficulty in playing age-appropriate sports and games may interfere with interaction with peers.

More specific to WS, there is a tendency for the subcategory Auditory Hypersensitivity—or oversensitivity to certain ordinary, sudden sounds—to be related to the category Maladaptive Behaviors ($p < .03$). Within this category, auditory hypersensitivity is most strongly correlated with rigidity, characterized by inflexibility, difficulty in adapting to change and in following instructions, as well as distractibility or problems in screening out extraneous stimulation.

Interestingly, the Academic Deficits of WSc are more highly related to Language Problems ($p < .02$) than to other categories or subcategories. Talking out of turn, interrupting, compulsive greeting behavior, poor topic maintenance, word-finding problems, and the inability to answer questions directly are all behaviors that may interfere with or undermine classroom learning.

Finally, the subcategory Musicality is positively correlated with the subcategory Language Skills. This is consistent with the brain imaging research of Bellugi et al. (1996), which suggests that the musical and language skills of WSs may have a common neuroanatomical basis.

Investigation of the interconnections of the topical categories and subcategories from the Utah Survey suggests possible relations between behavioral areas, thereby encouraging efforts to construct questionnaires and conduct studies especially for this purpose. Further research is indicated.

Genetic and Brain Mechanisms

Advances in the fields of the genetics and neurobiology of WS offer insight into the genetic and brain mechanisms of WS and the behavioral features associated with them.

Genotype-Phenotype Research. Research on the WS genotype created a major breakthrough in understanding the cause of WS, namely, that it arises from a microdeletion of DNA in a single copy region of chromosome 7, 7q11.23 (Ewart, Morris, Ensing et al., 1993). Discovery of this specific molecular profile serves as a genetic marker for WS. That is, it is a definitive way of establishing the diagnosis of WS in individuals who exhibit various kinds of physical, medical, and behavioral features of WS that comprise the basis for the usual "clinical diagnosis" of WS.

As such, genotypic research offers two important contributions to investigations of the behavioral features or phenotype of WS. First, it can serve as a screening device for determining that participants in research studies on WS are bona fide members of that syndrome group. More and more, this is used as an index of group membership in studies investigating the cognitive, social emotional, and personality profile of WS (Bellugi et al., 2000; Dykens & Rosner, 1999). It can also be used to differentiate subjects who are erroneously clinically diagnosed for WS; their results can obscure the identification of valid WS features. This is demonstrated in a study of the WS cognitive profile where almost all misdiagnosed subjects did not exhibit the target profile (e.g., higher scores on verbal than on pattern construction tests), whereas the vast majority of other subjects met this and all other criteria of the WS cognitive profile (Mervis & Klein-Tasman, 2000). Advances in the specification of syndromes with related, overlapping features with WS, such as Del (Dp) syndrome (Chilosi et al., 2001), and comparison of these phenotypes with WS, will help to sharpen the profile of WS and reduce the number of false positives in the diagnosis of WS.

A second application of genetic research is investigating the relation between phenotype and genotype, that is, attempting to identify specific genes that are counterparts or contribute to the manifestation of certain behavioral characteristics. Because virtually all WSs who satisfy the criteria for clinical diagnosis of WS exhibit the same genetic marker (Korenberg et al., 2000; Mervis & Klein-Tasman, 2000), it is difficult to find appropriate methods with which to study the relation between genotype and phenotype. One approach is to examine kindreds (blood relatives) of WSs who are assumed to have small deletions in the 7q11.23 region of WS and may therefore exhibit some, but not all, of the behavioral characteristics of WS. By studying a number of kindreds with varying areas of deletion, it may be possible to piece together a genotypic-phenotypic map of WS features (Mervis & Klein-Tasman, 2000).

A more molecular genetic approach involves fine grain analysis of the 1–2 Mb area of deletion of chromosome band 7q11.23 and the immediately surrounding region (Korenberg et al., 2000). A physical map of this region is being developed, including identification of specific genes within the deleted area, breakpoints of the deletion in various subjects, and duplicated regions adjacent to the deleted area. This information has been applied to rather large samples of WSs for whom genetic data and behavioral data are available. Through these efforts, a subset of WSs with smaller than normal deletions has been identified. Matching characteristics of this subset with those of most WSs, it appears that a particular telomeric region (from below gene RFC2 through GTF21) is being tentatively identified as "responsible for a major part of the mental retardation and other features" (Korenberg et al., 2000, p. 101), including facial features of WS. Genes in the region WSTF through LIMK1 (more in the central area of the common deletion) are being "associated with subtle defects in cognition" (Korenberg et al., 2000, p. 102).

Figure 8.2, shows the key regions described above.

Brain Mechanisms. Early investigations of the neural substrate of WS revealed little of major significance. That is, no discernible difference was found in brain structure between the left, language hemisphere and the

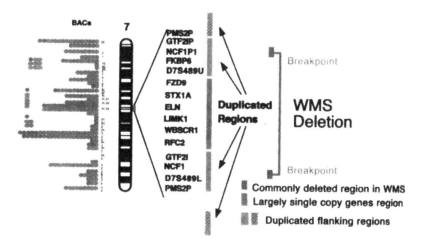

FIG. 8.2. Region of chromosome 7, band 7q11.23, commonly deleted in WSs (Korenberg et al., 2000). From "VI. Genome Structure and Cognitive Map of Williams Syndrome," by J. R. Korenberg, H.-N. Chen, H. Hirota, Z. Lai, U. Bellugi, D. Burian, B. Roe, and R. Matsuoka (2000). In U. Bellugi & M. St. George (Eds.), Linking Cognitive Neuroscience and Molecular Genetics: New Perspectives from Williams Syndrome. *Journal of Cognitive Neuroscience, 12* (Suppl. 1, p. 92). Copyright 2000 by the Massachusetts Institute of Technology, Reprinted with permission.

right, visuospatial (VS) cortical hemisphere to correspond with the well-accepted behavioral contrast between language and VS skills. More recently, the programmatic research of Bellugi and colleagues produced important, although sometimes subtle, results. These point to possible "markers" or definitive brain features of WS. This is based on neuroimaging, high resolution MRI studies of the event-potential responses (ERPs) of WSs and other groups to face and language stimuli (Mills et al., 2000; Reiss, Eliez, Schmitt, Straus, Lai, Jones, & Bellugi, 2000; Schmitt, Eliez, Bellugi, & Reiss, 2001; Schmitt, Eliez, Warsofsky, Bellugi, & Reiss, 2001). Neuroanatomical analysis of the autopsied brains of WSs augment the results (Galaburda & Bellugi, 2000).

For present purposes, the ERP study is most relevant because it indicates that the brain responses of WSs to face and language stimuli are distinct from those of all other groups in both the properties of the electro-physiological response and its location in the brain. This is even more remarkable when we note that face and language functioning are the most "preserved" of WSs' areas of performance, and the better the behavioral performance of WS subjects, the more the results deviated from that of other subjects. Moreover, the processing tasks did not require difficult kinds of behavioral responding. The facial stimuli were photo pairs of men's faces presented sequentially; the subject merely had to judge whether the faces were identical (match) or only similar (mismatch).

Unlike normal adults, WSs showed an early abnormally small negative response wave at 100 msec, an abnormally large negative wave response at 200 msec to both upright and inverted faces, and a major negative 320 msec wave for both upright and inverted faces. In contrast, normal adults displayed ERP differences to matched versus unmatched upright faces at N320, mainly in the anterior regions of the right hemisphere, whereas WSs did not display this right hemisphere asymmetry or a differing wave pattern at N400 msec for match–mismatch responses to inverted faces. Importantly, the ERP patterns of WSs were not observed in two subjects who had a clinical diagnosis of WS but did not have the genetic deletion of WS based on a FISH test (fluorescent *in situ* hybridization).

The MRI study indicates that there may be other possible neural markers for WS, including enlargement of the neocerebellar vermis in the context of an overall smaller brain size, differential development of the paleocerebellum (small) and the neocerebellum (enlarged) in WS, as well as disordered neurons in histology (Bellugi et al., 2000; Reiss et al., 2000). In terms of correspondence with behavioral data, evidence of a greater ratio than usual of frontal to posterior (parietal + occipital) tissue is consistent with the deficits in visual processing associated with the posterior occipital lobes.

Aside from revealing critical differences in brain mechanisms that may help to clarify the neural substrate of WS, the aforementioned research suggests that WS is characterized by an aberrant or atypical neural substrate and type of brain processing, not merely a delay in the development of brain structures and functions.

Evidence of these vitally important genetic and neural mechanisms does not vitiate, however, the marked influence of behavioral characteristics and interventions on the growth and development of WSs. To paraphrase Mervis and Klein-Tasman (2000), behavioral characteristics are manifestations of a developmental process involving cascades of genes, brain mechanisms, and transactions with the environment at all levels, including the kinds of interventions discussed in the next section.

II. INTERVENTION GUIDELINES FOR WS

Having identified the critical features of WS, now consider how to best meet the numerous intervention needs of most WSs as characteristics and interventions are intrinsically intertwined. Because WSs do not conform to customary models of behavior or treatment, WS-oriented, problem-specific types of interventions were suggested for each of the major areas of language, perceptual-motor performance, specific aptitudes, and maladaptive behaviors (see chaps. 3, 4, 5, and 7, respectively). Useful as this may be, general categories and guidelines of WS intervention are needed for brevity and clarity of exposition.

The various types of intervention approaches suggested in previous chapters range in number from the four approaches suggested for language problems to the seven approaches suggested for behavior problems. Although there is some duplication and overlap across topic areas, there are also distinctions; some are relatively minor changes in terminology or applicability, such as "structured therapy" versus "professional treatment," but others involve the addition of other approaches, such as "problem analysis" and "task management."

Building on points of overlap and similarity of function within the previous set of problem-specific approaches, five major categories of behavioral interventions have been established: control mechanisms, verbal mediation strategies, environmental measures, aptitude maximization, and professional specialists. Each subsumes more specific kinds of interventions, as shown in Table 8.3 (p. 383).

Using these five categories as a basis for synthesis and extension of previous recommendations, five guidelines for WS have been developed and are presented next. Although the guidelines are designed to be applicable to most WSs, it is absolutely essential to focus on the WS individual because of the wide variability in degree of expression of so many features of WS and the different environments and resources available to specific individuals with WS.

TABLE 8.2
Relations Between Topical Categories and Subcategories

Target Category	Related Category
Visuomotor Deficits (13)	(+) Maladaptive Behaviors
	(+) Poor Peer Relations
Maladaptive Behaviors (21)	(+) Visuomotor Deficits
	(+) Language Problems
	(−) Social Skills & Empathy
	(+) Poor Peer Relations
	(+) Auditory Hypersenstivity
Language Problems (6)	(−) Social Skills & Empathy
	(+) Maladaptive Behaviors
	(+) Academic Deficits
Language Skills (6)	(+) Musicality
Poor Peer Relations (3)	(+) Maladaptive Behaviors
	(+) Visuomotor Deficits
Social Skills & Empathy (4)	(−) Language Problems
	(−) Maladaptive Behaviors
Auditory Hypersensitivity (5)	(+) Maladaptive Behaviors
Academic Deficits (6)	(+) Language Problems
Musicality (3)	(+) Language Skills

Note: (+) refers to positive Tau correlation between target and related category, (−) to negative Tau correction, .05 < p's < .001. Numbers in parentheses refer to the number of items per category or subcategory.

A. Capitalize on the Use of Control Mechanisms

Understanding the unusual reward system of most WSs is paramount to dealing constructively with them. Knowledgeable use of reinforcement, direct instruction, and re-channeling strategies is basic to strengthening the desirable behaviors and curtailing the undesirable behaviors of most WSs. Reinforcement is also the most effective way of providing WSs with feedback as to the accuracy and acceptability of their behavioral responses.

Effective Rewards. Frequent "doses" of positive reinforcement are vital to encouraging the instruction and behavioral control of most WSs. It can also aid in the acquisition of new behaviors by "shaping" existent patterns of response. Effective incentives for most WSs are whatever they covet, or like to do. Generally, this means verbal praise ("Good Job!"), personal approval ("It really pleases me when you do that"), affirmative signals (big smile, wink, nod), and opportunities for social interaction (e.g., lunch with the teacher). Use of verbal-social reinforcement is recommended for language learning as well as helping WSs deal with certain fears and anxieties (e.g., when facing medical procedures). WSs also tend to respond positively to being rewarded for paying attention or refraining from disruptive or annoying conduct, such as excessive fidgeting.

On the other hand, negative reinforcers are things that WSs would like to avoid. Once again, these are predominantly verbal-social in nature. Representative sanctions include statements of disapproval, particularly personal disapproval (e.g., "That disappoints me, makes me feel bad"); nonverbal negative signals (e.g., prearranged use of head shake, exaggerated frown, waving of the index finger); and planned inattention (e.g., "I can't talk with you when you're having a tantrum"), isolation, or time-out (i.e., brief removal to another, secluded place). Expressions of personal approval and disapproval, especially from a person with whom WSs have a good relationship, are by far the most powerful methods of behavioral control for WSs.

"Acting out" forms of behavior—like tantrums, misconduct, and certain types of impulsivity—are usually best handled with negative reinforcement or direct instruction. Aside from using statements and signals of disapproval, negative consequences for these forms of behavior should be clearly established, related to the deed, and consistently carried out. This includes imposing time-out in the WS's room at home or in the classroom, or temporarily removing certain privileges such as watching television.

Unlike others, WSs are generally less motivated by material rewards like candy or prizes than by verbal-social rewards. Exceptions are certain types of items, books, and other materials pertaining to their topic of special interest (see chap. 5); or participation in activities of value, such as music, sharing jokes, or the opportunity to watch building excavations or motors spinning. Interestingly, stickers of smiling faces also have reward value: Note the special importance of faces and positive affect for many WSs.

Although reinforcement techniques are useful for all children, verbal and nonverbal praise, expressions of personal approval and disapproval, targeted items of special value, and negative reinforcement in the form of planned ignoring are particularly potent for WSs.

In the classroom and other instructional settings, grading and commenting on the performance of most WSs must be done with great care because many suffer from fear of failure, low frustration tolerance, and extreme sensitivity to criticism. Use of personalized verbal–social rewards, self-correcting methods of grading (e.g., answer keys), "errorless" learning as in some computer programs, and informing WSs of their errors in a constructive, encouraging way is of prime importance (e.g., "I'm pleased to see you trying hard. Let's try again this way."). Expressions of anger, hostility, sarcasm, or extreme impatience should be avoided due to their devastating effect on most WSs. Harsh criticism is more likely to result in "avoidance reactions" than increased effort.

Direct Instruction. Brief, precise statements may be required to control the undesirable or dangerous conduct of some WSs. Clear, unambiguous statements may be useful in restraining persistent questioning, overfriend-liness, compulsive greeting behavior, or calling out (e.g., "It is your turn to listen, my turn to talk"). Displays of anger, obtrusive activity, and extreme distractibility may also warrant direct instruction.

Behavioral contracts, in which target behaviors are designated in written or verbal form, and rewards stipulated for refraining from or exhibiting target behaviors, may be helpful for some WS students.

Re-Channeling Strategies. Because many of WSs' most annoying forms of behavior may be very difficult for them to restrain, providing alternative or substitute forms of response may be a viable option. Examples include designating a certain time for a WS student "to hold the floor" instead of calling out, or giving WS individuals something "to think about" when they show signs of excessive restlessness.

Finally, it is important to identify the types of rewards that are effective for the specific WS individual and what kinds of direct instructions and rechanneling tactics, if any, are helpful for that person.

B. Exploit the Power of Verbal Mediation Strategies

Similar to control mechanisms, verbal mediation strategies contribute to both instruction and behavior control but in a more explicative way. Distinct from other categories of interventions, verbal mediation techniques encourage the learning of new responses and insight into social conventions, roles, and rules.

Among the many types of verbal mediation strategies that may be of value to WSs, the following are applicable to a variety of situations: verbal labeling, rehearsal, and explanation; demonstration and dramatization; and self-instruction. Prerequisites for their use, of course, are sufficient verbal skills, social skills, and empathy, as well as general cognitive abilities to provide for the verbalizations, internalization of strategies, behavioral comparisons, reasoning, and generation of strategies that many of these interventions require.

Verbal Labeling, Rehearsal, and Explanation. Verbal labeling refers, of course, to attaching verbal labels to nonverbal components and the relation between them. It is a very powerful device to use in helping WSs acquire early words, process visuospatial (VS) stimuli, and perform VSM tasks, such as drawing, block building, and letter formation in writing tasks. Labeling is also useful for most WSs in identifying and clarifying socioemotional variables including their own internal feelings, emotions, and other behavior problems.

Rehearsal, too, is a potent, all-inclusive type of strategy, especially useful in language learning, memorization, and controlling one's own behavior.

In contrast to rehearsal, or repetition of prior information, *explanation* expands and elaborates on it. Preliminary and follow-up kinds of measures, such as the three-step process used for auditory hypersensitivity and other problems, may be needed (i.e., acknowledgment, reassurance, and explanation). Explanation itself may deal with existing or potential situations or behaviors expected of the WS individual. Once the explanation is understood, having the WS individual repeat it and subsequently rehearse it may help to internalize the explanation. Some WSs are able to extend the process with self-reminders.

Explanation can be a useful tool in dealing with WSs' fears and anxieties and problem behaviors such as impulsivity and overactivity. This may require discussion of topics such as the status of someone's health or a change in plans in order to allay anxieties; or explaining repeatedly, in detail, the reason why each of their impulsive behaviors is unacceptable and the cause–effect relations of each type. Such explanations may be aided by employing demonstration and dramatization strategies, and the use of concrete, familiar analogies, semantic association cues, and metaphors. Of course, explanatory aids must be adapted to the age and comprehension level of the WSc. They should not be too long or complex.

Demonstration and Dramatization. Modeling and imitation are particularly effective techniques to use in teaching WSs various kinds of response patterns in areas as diverse as language learning, motor acts (e.g., jumping down from a high place, holding a fork), and socioemotional strategies (e.g., turn-taking). Instructing WSs to pay attention during the modeling, adding mediational verbal cues, requiring immediate repetition or imitation of the modeled act, and providing feedback and reinforcement for correct performance are essential parts of the procedure for most WSs.

Demonstrating problem behaviors, role-playing, and discussing the distinction between appropriate and inappropriate ways of performing can help WSs understand the difference between them. Of course, the reasons why such behaviors are unacceptable must be illustrated and explained over and over again.

Dramatization techniques can further clarify distinctions between desirable and undesirable forms of response involving behavior problems, such as distractibility, impulsivity, and overreaction to frustration. Combining role play with dramatization techniques can also help WSs act out and deal with anxiety provoking and frustrating situations. Pretend play, storytelling, puppetry, pantomime, photographs, and videotaping are alternative ways of capturing and displaying WSs' objectionable behavior and contrasting it with more acceptable ways of behaving. This is also a way of making WSs more aware of unsuitable behaviors that are "automatic" for them.

Sometimes even these types of strategies need to be preceded by a period of training in "social awareness" or "social instruction" in order to help WSs become cognizant of the different types of individuals they may encounter and suitable forms of communication and social interaction for each type.

Self-Instructional Skills. Some WSs can be taught to use their language gifts to self-administer various kinds of verbal routines, such as self-instruction, self-reminding, self-monitoring, self-coping, self-encouragement, and self-reinforcement. This involves teaching WSs to use their language skills to repeat to themselves the appropriate verbal phrases that others have provided in similar situations. This combines their ability to generate rehearsed versions of the explanations, warnings, instructions, or stress reducing messages that others have provided with the ability to employ them under relevant conditions. It is the strategy, par excellence, for dealing with problems of question persistence (e.g., "There I go again"), overreactivity to stress (e.g., "easy does it"), and difficulty concentrating (e.g., "keep looking").

Use of self-instruction requires training that is situation specific, taught step by step, practiced repeatedly, and explained thoroughly, including a discussion of the benefits. Use of stock phrases facilitates the process (see, e.g., chaps. 3 and 7).

C. Reduce External Pressures and Demands

Attending to external pressures and demands is the requisite role for parents, teachers, and others to adopt in dealing with WSs' problems of overreactivity to certain stimuli and complexities. This usually involves use of task management, environmental controls, and stress reduction techniques.

Task Management

Generally, task management involves both task analysis, to determine the properties of the task, and task simplification, to make it doable for the WS individual.

Task analysis with WSs usually requires identifying the target behaviors involved, dividing a complex task into small, understandable subtasks, practicing one subtask at a time, sequencing the subtasks in a logical order, and combining the subtasks into the whole at the appropriate time.

Task management goes beyond task analysis by attempting to ensure that all aspects of the task are manageable. Limiting the length of the instructions, number of ideas expressed, and minimizing the use of complex grammatical constructions and unfamiliar semantic concepts (e.g., spatial, temporal, or quantitative terms) are important ways of simplifying the instructions. Of course, the rationale for the task, task difficulty, time and mode of presentation (auditory, visual, verbal), spacing of practice sessions, type of response (e.g., verbal, motor), and reinforcement procedures should be considered, if not controlled.

Task management procedures are known to be of value in helping many WSs deal with problems of distractibility, attention control, and task completion. Providing variation in tasks, interesting materials of appropriate difficulty, and shorter work periods are other ways to help WSs stay "on task."

Environmental Controls

How is it possible to deal with the overly distractible, squirmy, and hypersensitive response of most WSs to certain sounds, their surroundings, sometimes to clothing textures, and often to everyday, inevitable changes in schedule or plans? It is almost mandatory to introduce environmental controls, but the rigor with which they are applied may depend on the severity of the WS's problem and the context.

Reduce Perceptual Distractions. Removing potential sources of distraction is the first step. This means providing a neutral, uncluttered environment by controlling extraneous visual stimulation, clutter, and overly "busy" visual furnishings, patterns, clothing, or jewelry. It also means reducing auditory distractions by minimizing exposure to aversive sounds wherever possible by limiting the use of noisy appliances, employing sound muffling devices like heavy curtains or closing the door, and, perhaps, sound desensitization training. For those WSs with tactile defensiveness, the sources of irritation should, if at all possible, be identified and controlled (see chap. 4).

Seat placement is one of the simpler, more effective ways of combating distractibility and overactivity, as is providing personal space. Removing objects of intense interest and attachment is often an effective way of curtailing overactivity. Although sometimes difficult to implement, providing a quiet, structured environment can be extremely useful too.

Regulate Environmental Structure. A structured, predictable lifestyle is frequently helpful in reducing the uncertainties and anxieties WSs often experience in trying to understand and deal with the most mundane kinds of changes in arrangements, schedule, plans, even the foods to be served, or clothes to be worn. Providing a stable, organized environment and contingency plans for unexpected changes in routines, supplies, activities, or projects can help ease the anxieties, fears, and rigidity problems of many WSs (see chap. 7). No one can be completely protected, however, from unexpected or frustrating events, so WSs must also be helped to gradually develop increased frustration tolerance and coping skills.

Stress Reduction

Another way to alleviate some of WSs' problems with anxieties and fears, low frustration tolerance, and atypical activity is through the use of relaxation techniques, such as listening to music, engaging in yoga or meditation, or soaking in a jacuzzi or hot tub.

A more general kind of stress reduction involves taking advantage of the talents and skills of WSs to provide experiences of success, enjoyment, and knowledge of success. This can boost the fragile ego of WSs, help restore their equanimity, and give them the courage or needed encouragement to tackle the next obstacle or challenge.

The specifics of stress reduction depend on the preferences and capabilities of the particular WS individual.

D. Enlist the Services of Qualified Specialists

Because WS is associated with various kinds of medical, clinical, developmental, behavioral, and educational problems, as well as special aptitudes and skills, many types of professional specialists are mentioned throughout the book. These are summarized in Table 8.3. In addition, there are questions concerning how, when, why, and where to consult professionals.

Table 8.3 presents a summary of five major categories of intervention, control mechanisms, verbal mediation strategies, environmental measures, aptitude maximization, and professionals specialists that span the specific areas of functioning discussed in this book. Under each category, cross area variations in the application of the category are listed.

Selection of Specialists. Referrals to specialists often originate with the primary medical physician or therapist of a WS. As a rule, WSs are usually patients of at least one physician at the time of initial diagnosis of WS, if not before. Additional sources for referrals are professionals in allied fields—including psychologists, teachers, educational and clinical specialists, researchers, clergy, experienced leaders of service or specialized organizations (e.g., WSA, ARC), and families of WSs.

It is most important to select highly qualified professionals and avoid those who may be likely to misdiagnose a condition or prescribe question-

TABLE 8.3
Categories of Intervention for WSs

Control Mechanisms	Verbal Mediation Strategies	Environmental Measures	Aptitude Maximization	Professional Specialists
Verbal Reinforcers	Labeling	Task Analysis	Naturalistic Activities	Physicians & Dentists
Nonverbal Signals	Rehearsal	Task Management	Skill Development	Speech & Language Therapists
Social Opportu- nities	Explanation & Discussion	Simplification	Social Applications	Vision Specialists
Valued Items	Demonstration/ Dramatization	Stimulus Controls	Classroom Applications	Specialists for Motor Skills
Desired Activities	Self-Instruction	Stability & Consis- tency	Vocational Options	Hearing Specialists
Direct Instruction	Association Cues	Stress Reduction	Compensatory Measures	Education/Learning Specialists
Re-Channeling	Problem Analysis	Self-Esteem	Remediation	Behavior Problem Specialists
			Resource Utilization	
			Personal Growth	

able, unsubstantiated forms of treatment. Consulting a professional organization or other professionals is one way to learn about qualifications. Licensure, certification, academic degrees, completion of professional exams like "boards," usually but not always, serve as indicators of competence. One would hope that the WS's primary doctor or main therapist is familiar with Williams syndrome or is motivated to learn. Sometimes the "match" between the provider, patient, and family can be an important factor.

Indicators for seeking the services of professionals include the diagnosis of clinical conditions or disorders, significant delays in the acquisition of the milestones of language, motor skills, socioemotional functioning or behavioral control, critical deficits or impairments in important areas like academics, and problem severity. The availability of specialized services and the degree to which problem behavior is considered troublesome are other factors. What bothers one family may not faze another much at all. On a more positive note, development of the aptitudes, interests, and skills of WSs may be a high priority for them and their families, teachers, and others.

Functions of Professionals. In providing interventions, professionals generally serve multiple functions. Among them are providing background information about their field, its orientation, and possible treatment options. Establishing an accurate, comprehensive evaluation of the WS individual through tests, interviews, and review of relevant material is a prerequisite to understanding the individual's condition and the possible need for treatment. Interpretation and discussion of the evaluation is an integral part of the process. Formulation of intervention plans, methods, and the role of key parties in the treatment is also vital.

Treatment may be conducted mainly or solely by the specialist, but often in collaboration with others, like parents and teachers. The professional is also primarily responsible for monitoring the course of treatment, integrating input from others, and modifying the treatment plan as needed after consulting with others. Recommendations for further kinds of treatment, if needed, are also in the province of the specialist.

The number and type of functions a professional assumes varies with the case, the therapist, and a host of other factors. Requests for a second opinion may be made at any point during the process, although it is proper etiquette to inform the primary specialist of this intent.

Types of Professionals. To summarize prior descriptions of specialists frequently consulted by WSs (see Table 8.3), physicians comprise a major segment of essential professionals. Usually the WS is a regular patient of a primary physician, often a pediatrician (MD specializing in children) or a general or family doctor. WSs may also be seen by cardiologists, reflecting the prevalence of heart problems like SVAS, as well as geneticists for WS diagnosis, neurologists for neurological and coordination concerns, and a nephrologist for kidney problems.

Other medical specialists often consulted by WSs include ophthalmologists and pediatric ophthalmologists for disorders of the eye (vision, chap. 4, Section IIA); otolaryngologists and otologists for disorders of audition (hearing) (chap. 4, Section IVC) and hoarse voice (chap. 3, Section IIIC); orthopedists for skeletal (bone) disorders (chap. 4, Section IIB); psychiatrists for behavior disturbances and emotional problems (chap. 7, Section IIA); and more recently, physiatrists (doctor of physical medicine and rehabilitation). The dental problems and abnormalities of most WSs require the general services and sometimes specialized care of dentists and associated specialists.

Nonmedical specialists in a number of fields may also be helpful: for vision, optometrists trained in developmental vision and specialists trained in orthoptics (chap. 4, Section IIA); for gross motor problems and visual-spatial-motor integration skills, physical therapists (PTs), occupational therapists (OTs), and OTs with neurodevelopmental training (NDT) or sensory integration (SI) training, chiropractors, and adaptive physical educators (chap. 4, Section IIB; and for problems of tactile defensiveness, OTs and OTS with NDT and SI training (chap. 4, Section IIIB). Audiologists are consulted for clinical problems and evaluation of audition (chap. 4, Section IVC) and problems of auditory processing, auditory discrimination, and auditory memory may be addressed by speech and language therapists (SLTs) or audiologists. They may also be able to administer auditory desensitization training.

Speech language therapists can be invaluable in dealing with the hardcore problems of language delay, oral-motor difficulties, and facilitating the development and use of syntax, semantics, and articulation. Structured therapy can assist with problems of semantic relations and word-finding in addition to certain problems in the pragmatic use of language.

Because SLT transcends formal boundaries, it may also be used to help improve WSs' communication with peers (chap. 5) and, through the use of verbal mediation, their visuomotor performance on tasks like drawing (chap. 4). In fact, many problems in language pragmatics are amenable to psycho-educational techniques, like verbal mediation, control mechanisms, and naturalistic play, administered by SLTs and/or by parents and teachers, often in collaboration with the SLT.

Within the field of education, psychologists and testing specialists can serve a vital function by conducting a carefully considered assessment of WSs' abilities, aptitudes, academic level, and diagnostic problem areas, where applicable. School personnel, including special education teachers, learning disabilities specialists, as well as experts in curriculum, remediation, music, and physical education may be helpful in providing instruction where needed.

For behavior disturbance, WSs may be referred to an experienced mental health provider. Besides psychiatrists and pediatric psychiatrists, professionals with training in clinical psychology, child psychology, counseling, or social work may be able to provide diagnostic and treatment information and, in some cases, therapy. Specialized treatment is recommended for serious conditions such as ADHD, autistic-like behaviors, specific phobias, acute fears and anxieties, depression, and obsessive compulsive disorder. Treatment may also be recommended for refractory cases of overfriendliness, low frustration tolerance, fearfulness, and atypical activity. In some cases, use of psychotherapy, behavior modification, cognitive therapy, and medication may be helpful (see chap. 7). In less serious cases, parents, teachers, and others may be able to employ psycho-educational techniques successfully, especially with the guidance and advice of experienced professionals.

Depending on the age and interests of the WS, other experts may be enlisted to provide useful services. Examples include specialists in infant stimulation and early childhood programs, play therapy, and self-care skills; tutors for school subjects or computer skills; music or art instructors and therapists; coaches for sports or aerobics; and mentors for WSs' special interests. In adulthood, counselors for issues of sexuality, citizenship, social relations, vocational assessment and placement, independent living, and estate planning may be helpful.

Intervention Plans. In sum, WSs frequently require a multidisciplinary program of interventions in order to deal with their various kinds of clinical conditions, problems, and skills. The first step in planning intervention is to obtain accurate, comprehensive evaluation of the WS individual in the areas of present and potential concern. This usually includes assessment of the individual's physical characteristics, relevant medical conditions, neurological functioning, measures of intellectual ability, and performance in such areas as language, perception, motor skills, socioemotional status, and maladaptive behaviors. Depending on the WS individual's age, appraisal of oral–motor functioning, academic skills, learning style, aptitudes, areas of interest, leisure and vocational activities, and life skills may supplement the evaluation. These should be conducted by qualified individuals who are willing to explain and discuss the results.

The second step in designing an intervention plan is to learn about the possible range of available intervention approaches in light of the overall assessment of the WS individual. Of prime importance is the match between areas that need intervention and the procedures available. Accessibility of resources and professional help, the family situation, care-giving demands, interests and talents of the WS individual, as well as the types of services, schooling, lessons, local and community opportunities, and need to coordinate treatments should be taken into account.

In actuality, intervention plans are not usually as intimidating or overwhelming to formulate or implement as the preceding discussion would suggest. Each of the professions or specialties cited may serve an important need for selected WSs, but a single WS individual is likely to require only a few of them at any particular time in development.

Obviously, no individual with WS could possibly work with all of these professionals for reasons of time alone, even if all services were readily available and cost was no object. Priorities must be set and coordination of services utilized is important.

It should also be recognized that there is some overlap between the responsibilities and expertise of these different professionals. Therefore, a provider or practitioner from any one of a number of professions may be able to assume multiple roles in treating several different types of problems and guiding parents and teachers on a number of issues.

Sometimes, consultation with a specialist in pediatrics, developmental disabilities, learning difficulties, child psychology, counseling, educational management, special education, or a social worker may be helpful in coordinating evaluation results with practical options for treatment programs. Some may be able to help formulate ancillary programs, such as an individualized educational plan (IEP) and additional community or learning resources for WSs.

In some locations, parents of WSs may have difficulty locating any qualified person for certain WS problems. In this situation, the WSA or a university, medical school, or regional WS clinic may be able to offer some information or assistance.

E. Optimize the Potential for Growth

Build on Strengths. As a rule, WSs have strengths in the areas of language, social skills and empathy, topics of special interest, memory abilities, and musicality. Developing these strengths to their full potential is a high priority.

Language functioning may be aided by initiating a program of SLT and stimulating the use of language through verbal media and naturalistic activities. Encouraging appropriate forms of sociability and empathy may help to reinforce and shape WSs' social skills and assist in other forms of intervention. Verbal-social strategies and certain control mechanisms are useful for this purpose.

Specialized interests shown by WSs may be developed and broadened by providing the resources needed to promote the study, research, collecting, classifying, and sharing of prized information. Memory functioning can often be improved by using verbal techniques and mnemonics, including semantic associations, to help WSs remember. Adapting input, introducing memory strategies, and modifying response output may help to enhance WSs' memory functioning, but these must be geared to the particular individual. Musical talents, if evident, may be fostered by providing extensive exposure to music, opportunities to sing and play instruments at an appropriate level of difficulty, access to music lessons, participation in music groups, choir, or chorus, or enrolling in special music and arts programs (e.g., Belvoir Terrace). These must be adapted, however, to the musical abilities of the individual, because there are wide variations in this area too (see chap. 5).

The second priority is taking advantage of the applicability of these special aptitudes and interests in many important areas of WS life, including the classroom, social relations, extracurricular activities, vocational opportunities, recreation, and personal enjoyment. Agreeableness, showmanship, talents, and a good sense of humor can combine to help WSs compensate for the difficulty most have with classroom assignments. Similarly, topics of interest, memory, and musical abilities have a wide range of applications, such as using topical material to motivate studying, applying phonological rote memory skills in teaching WSs how to read and spell, or using music to help teach WSs numerical and quantitative concepts, such as high–low.

Taking into account the preferred mode of learning for a particular individual (auditory, verbal, tactile, visual-verbal, or some combination), the preferred time of day for instruction, and the preferred form of response (oral or forced choice rather than writing) are other ways to accommodate WSs' learning needs (see chap. 5).

Confront Classroom Issues. Whereas specific aptitudes are valuable as compensatory mechanisms in many settings, the problems that WSs often face may require a broader range of interventions. This is generally so in the classroom where WSs are usually confronted with problems of placement, learning readiness, and nonoptimal teaching programs. Such problems may be addressed by applying knowledge of WS characteristics and interventions, along with clinical experience with WSs and other developmentally disabled groups, especially in regard to educational management.

In the case of classroom placement, WSs seldom fit adequately into any standard kind of classroom, mainly because of their unusual ability profile. Full-time placement or mainstreaming in a regular class is appropriate for some WSs. For others, it may be too advanced, although it would provide them with valuable contact with normally developing children whom they often need as models. Part-time mainstreaming may be more appropriate for such youngsters, but this requires deciding which subjects should be mainstreamed and which ones assigned otherwise. Some special education classes may not be very stimulating for WSs unless their unique needs are being met. In classes for children with conduct disorders and behavior problems, they may be vulnerable to other students acting out and even abusing them. Moreover, classes for learning disabled students may be too difficult for most WSs, even though many of the approaches may be consistent with their educational needs. Clearly, the issue of appropriate classroom and grade placement requires careful and often professional judgment because it is a highly individualized decision for each WS.

No matter where the placement is made, the nature of the curriculum and learning programs needs to be scrutinized and considered in relation to WSs' strengths and weaknesses. Because most WSs exhibit learning delays and problems in the use of abstract concepts, extended readiness programs are often a prerequisite to learning even the most elementary kinds of academic skills. Adequate background is usually lacking in at least four essential areas: basic concepts, visuomotor readiness, auditory discrimination training, and language relational terms.

Training in basic concepts includes establishing familiarity with language concepts and auditory and visual discrimination. Activities with large block letters, forms, and numbers (e.g., handling, naming, and tracing the stimuli) provide manipulative and discriminative experience with size, shape, and color, as well as quantitative dimensions and geometric forms. Instruction in basic concepts may also contribute to the development of symbol systems by focusing on the one-to-one correspondence between numerals and number of objects and letters of the alphabet and letter sounds or names.

Criteria that may be used in selecting teaching problems for WSs include program flexibility, stimulus enhancement (e.g., color coding or item grouping), concrete instruction, active learning, built-in success, and realistic program goals. Reading programs that build on the verbal, auditory predispositions of most WSs' are generally more successful than those that emphasize visual or whole word teaching (Grejtak, 1999, WSA Newsletter, *16*(2), 6–9; MacDonald & Roy, 1988; Scheiber & Grejtak, 2000, WSA Newsletter, *17*(4), 6–15; Udwin et al., 1987; Udwin & Yule, 1988, 1989). In arithmetic too, the verbal proclivity of most WSs is reflected in the relative advantage of word problems versus purely computational problems for them in contrast to the greater difficulty of word problems for most students. Learning tools like the computer, tape recorder, and videotape machine provide WSs with the opportunity for repeated practice at their own pace and convenience, a tremendous benefit for remediation. Techniques to aid in the onerous task of handwriting and the learning of mathematics are contained in recent WSA publications (e.g., Scheiber & Grejtak, 2000, WSA Newsletter, *17*(4), 6–15.

Curricular options may also be considered, such as centering instruction on a student's area of special interest or integration of topics (units) of learning.

Maximize Resources. The potential of WSs may be further realized by promoting learning in the home and taking advantage of other resources. Within the home, training in basic skills may be encouraged through functional activities, like kitchen tasks, board games, arts and crafts, and family projects (see chaps. 3, 4, and 5). School instruction may be supplemented by encouraging completion of homework assignments and providing opportunities for practice at home in consultation with teachers and/or other staff. Recognizing the central role of educators, their unique contribution to WS development, and the importance of parent–teacher cooperation is an essential element in stimulating WSs' growth.

Socialization may be promoted by providing opportunities for peer interaction that are appropriate for WS individuals (i.e., familiar, structured situations, or organized outings), and helping them to learn acceptable ways of interacting with others. Independent living skills may be encouraged by providing assistance and instruction in such matters as finances (e.g., spending money, budgeting, banking), grooming and personal hygiene, shopping, and household chores. Preparation for the world of work may begin by developing the specific aptitudes of the WS individual and providing information on potential areas of employment and volunteerism, including personal contact with people in those positions and consultation with a vocational counselor.

Opportunities for learning can also be expanded by maximizing the participation of other people in the life of the WS individual (i.e., family members, mentors, neighbors, group leaders). Community resources (e.g., the library, clubs, and organizations) and media (e.g., books, television, and the Internet) may be used to advantage. In this and other ways, the WSA makes unique contributions by organizing social and professional gatherings for WSs, their families, professionals, and researchers. Besides encouraging contact and sharing between WS families, the WSA contributes by supporting and disseminating advances in the fields of research and treatment, providing support services, and serving as a clearing house for personal, scholarly, and treatment needs.

Finally, the special place of the home and family life should be noted. Aside from offering material and emotional support, the home generally serves as a learning center, recreational center, and planning center for activities out of the home. Parents are also administrators, arranging, scheduling, and participating in medical appointments, and meetings with educators, teachers, and a variety of therapists. Among other responsibilities, this involves keeping track of assessments, reports, and other documents related to their WS child. The condition of WS often requires a combination of activism, protectionism, devotion, and love on the part of parents.

At its best, the home is a sanctuary for WSs where they may receive the nurturing, understanding, acceptance, and affection they so desperately need.

III. FUTURE DIRECTIONS

As the field of Williams syndrome has many facets, so does its future. Developments and advancements are in process in the area of research. They are also emerging in the area of treatment. These trends are discussed next, followed by an examination of the present need for improvement in the care delivery systems of WS and possible future realization of those goals.

A. Research and Treatment

It is often said that "the best predictor of future success is present behavior." If so, then the future of WS research and treatment is guaranteed to be informative and productive. One can only hope that the present momentum of innovation, explication, and discovery will be extended into future gains in our understanding of WSs' behavioral profile, neurobiological mechanisms, and intervention options.

Building on significant progress in identification of the critical behavioral features of WS, further research is needed on a number of issues within specific areas, between general areas, and across subject groups. A first step would be the construction and refinement of questionnaires specifically designed to investigate the special kinds of behavior associated with WS. These may also be used to compare WSs with other syndrome groups, such as DS, PW, autism, ADHD, LD, and MR.

Topics to investigate include WSs' language difficulties with word-finding, semantic relations, and unusual word choice. Another is the contrast between WSs' almost uncanny empathy and social sensitivity to the feelings of others and their lack of insight into behaviors that may antagonize age-mates or endanger their own safety. Ease in recounting or narrating events also contrasts with their apparent difficulty in understanding temporal terms and problems in grasping the connection or relation between events. Other puzzles include the contrast between WSs' visuospatial difficulties and reports of their excellent memory for travel routes, as well as the difference between their generally good immediate memory for words, digits, and short sentences, and rather poor short-term memory for factual, classroom information. Frequent comments and a few substantiated statements about WSs' remarkable memory for stories, poems, hymns, and perhaps movies, should be investigated. WSs spontaneous use of memory strategies and their receptiveness to strategy instruction should also be studied. All of these issues deal with refining the behavioral profile of WSs.

Questionnaires may also examine interconnections among areas. Some of the more intriguing ones to investigate are the relation between language skills, musical ability, and auditory hypersensitivity; the relation between visual and auditory processing problems; and the relation between compulsive greeting behavior, sociability, impulsivity, disinhibition, and constraints in general cognitive ability. The area of academic skills and its relation to behavioral characteristics like language skills and problems, maladaptive behaviors, and visuomotor problems is almost completely unexplored. Other relations hinted at in Section I B, above, should be further tested (see p. 369)

Laboratory studies are also crucially needed to probe and better examine the substance of these behaviors. Questions deserving further scrutiny include clues as to the basis of WSs' unique word choices, their actual visuospatial processing as they view an object figure or the environment, and their blind spots in the area of empathy. It would be interesting to try to understand the phenomenological experience of WSs as they attempt to recount a story or remember a word. Determining the scope and limits of WSs' musical talents is a matter of high priority. Hints already exist, now it is a matter of scoping them out.

On the laboratory front, great strides have been made in establishing the genetic profile of WS. There is also progress in penetrating the nature of the relation between genotype and phenotype. This work holds the promise of producing significant breakthroughs in our understanding of WS. Similarly, studies of the brain mechanisms of WSs—neuroanatomical, neurophysiological, and neurochemical—are in the midst of uncovering distinctive markers for WSs that may be related in the future to their behavioral and genetic profiles.

It is also vitally important to compare WSs with other groups on these behavioral and neurobiological characteristics. That is, to clarify the specificity of these features for WSs and the extent to which they differ or overlap with those of other syndromes. This may reveal much about the uniqueness of WS. It may even provide leads for treatment options. The existence and specification of subgroups is another topic requiring investigation in laboratory studies and questionnaires.

On the applied, treatment side, the present state of knowledge is far murkier and less advanced than that of research on the behavioral and neurobiological aspects of WS. Informational resources are limited to a few published articles, pamphlets, and guidelines, like those recounted earlier and those distributed by the WSA (e.g., Levine, 1993, 1994; Scheiber & Grejtak, 2000, WSA Newsletter, 17(4), 6–15; Udwin & Yule, 1988). Although this material is based almost entirely on clinical experience and observation, rather than empirical data, the high degree of consistency among clinical researchers and professionals in orientation and recommendations attests to its credibility.

Nevertheless, the empirical void in the area of WS treatment options is real and unfilled. A number of conditions remain difficult to treat, among them is auditory hypersensitivity, visual-spatial-motor integration skills, and various maladjustive problems. Certainly, systematic study, or even description, of treatment alternatives would be of value, and even more so, bona fide evaluation studies to determine and compare treatment outcome(s).

There is also the need for progress in the study of WSs' academic skills and ways in which they can be improved. How WSs actually learn to read is itself a puzzle. Investigating the most effective methods by which WSs may be taught to read is of more than theoretical significance. Similarly, the difficulty that WSs experience with quantitative tasks and concepts should be further investigated, as should the ways to help WSs to better comprehend number concepts and operations. Operationalizing what is meant by the need to "concretize" concepts or use "hands on" methods would pay dividends in the teaching of WSs.

Aside from the intrinsic interest in these research and clinical questions, the results of such studies may have important practical and treatment implications. By providing norms and baseline data on the behavioral and educational characteristics of WSs, individual differences among WS may be better measured and conceptualized, including how specific individuals with WS compare with other WSs and how WSs, in general, compare with other groups (i.e., syndrome specificity). Undoubtedly, this would be helpful in planning individual interventions and educational programs and advising professionals of the general tendencies of WSs. It may also lay the groundwork for conducting large-scale evaluation and treatment studies to determine the effectiveness of certain interventions and the relation between types of behavior. An extra bonus is the insight it may offer regarding the interconnectedness of various types of behavior, and the existence and identification of WS subgroups.

Finally, large-scale data banks may aid investigation of the relation between behavioral profiles and the genetic and brain structure and neurochemistry of WSs and other groups. Eventually, it may be possible to find neurochemical or enzymatic interventions that could correct some of the unusual characteristics of WS. In the long term, genetic engineering and the use of "designer genes" may provide a major treatment role in overcoming many significant problems associated with WS.

B. Care Delivery Systems

No one can precisely predict the future, but the outlook for WS should be brighter than it was in the past. A scenario is presented in this chapter showing what is plausible for WS in the years to come. Some statements predict likely developments, based on current trends. Others take the form of suggestions and recommendations of what needs to be done. Still other statements represent hopes, dreams, and wishes that will be difficult but not impossible to achieve. A bit of history is included. During World War II, the U. S. Army had a slogan, "The difficult we do immediately. The impossible takes a little longer." Despite many difficulties, Williams syndrome has already come a long way, and will surely go further. Some changes are already happening, others may take a little longer.

Williams Syndrome Association. Since the Williams Syndrome Association (WSA) was organized in the late 1980s, parents and professionals have forged ahead in making extraordinary advancements in the field of WS. Their efforts have contributed to a "knowledge explosion" about the syndrome, and significantly improved the quality of life of WSs and their families.

The WSA provides many opportunities for group support and encourages parents to network together to overcome problems. Support and encouragement is also extended to the WSs themselves, their siblings, other family members, as well as involved researchers and professionals. In some communities, WSA groups have arranged a meeting place for WSc to become acquainted with each other.

There are 11 regional groups organized throughout the United States. In time, there may be at least one in each state. Currently, there are approximately 10 regional clinics in the United States (see the Appendix). New clinics are scheduled to be opened, and it is likely that in time most states will have one or more comprehensive WS clinics. Ultimately, each major teaching hospital will probably have personnel on its staff qualified to offer services to WSs. The International WSA has chapters throughout the world. New ones are being organized. It is hoped that, in the future, each country will have at least one such group.

The parents and professionals of the WSA have worked hard to obtain and disseminate accurate, interestingly presented information about WS. They have done an effective job in reaching the media and keeping a large number of people informed about developments in WS through publishing a very informative newsletter and providing press releases to community newspapers, radio and television programs, magazines and health publications about WS in general, as well as special events and specific developments in the field.

Medical/Genetic Advances. Advances are being made through the dedicated efforts of parents, teachers, professionals, investigators, and their organizations. Research, systematic planning, and persistence have created new opportunities for growth, development, and satisfaction for WSs and their families. Thanks to the contributions of geneticists from all over the world, including Morris, Jones, Greenberg, Pober, Korenberg, and many others, the thorny issue of diagnosis has been resolved. So has the age at which a diagnosis of WS can be made. In the future, it will be scientifically possible for the diagnosis to be made at birth in virtually every hospital in the world.

On the other hand, the development of better case finding procedures, which would be expedited by a national awareness campaign, are urgently needed. Key professionals such as pediatricians, cardiologists, and nurses, as they become better informed about WS, can lead the way. As more WSc are identified and diagnosed, the chances for obtaining additional funding, appropriate educational management, and medical treatment improve.

Eventually, it may be possible through biochemical research to find neurochemical or enzymatic interventions that could correct some of the unusual characteristics of WS. In the long term, genetic engineering may play a treatment role in overcoming many WS problems.

In the future, the numerous health and feeding problems of the WSc's first year of life, often characterized by severe gastrointestinal difficulties, "colic," and general "failure to thrive," will likely be resolved.

It is possible that certain food substances need to be rigorously excluded from WSs' diet (e.g., milk, which most WSc seem unable to metabolize properly in their early years). As many parents have reported that their child is a "picky-eater," intensive nutrition research may eventually make it possible to develop regimens for WS that could minimize some of their physical and behavioral problems. A striking example of a group where this has been effective is the success achieved with children born with phenylketonuria.

Advocacy. To secure appropriate medical attention and other necessary services, obtain optimum academic achievement and vocational opportunities, and adult living facilities for their grown children, WSA parents have become actively involved in programs for their WS children.

As a result of the WSA efforts, the traditional role of the parent has been redefined. Many parents are now willing and able to act as vigorous advocates for both their children and other WSc. Parents have found creative ways to select, orchestrate, fund, and direct appropriate therapeutic interventions for WSc in many places and in a variety of ways. The work of the WSA has helped to accelerate and augment the academic training of many teachers, therapists, psychologists, researchers, and physicians.

Educational Services for WSs. As a result of the combined efforts put forth by parents, professionals, and scientists, appropriate therapies for WS children—once considered a mere afterthought in educational management—will eventually be mandated.

Presently, however, parents often spend considerable time securing ancillary services, which should comprise the centerpiece of decision making during the early school years. Given more support by various professionals and government agencies, therapeutic interventions can be planned and provided earlier by a more knowledgeable and informed team of parents and specialists working together.

Despite the ever-increasing database of genetic, medical, and psychological research on WS, it has not yet been recognized as a clear-cut medical and legal diagnosis at the federal office of education and the legislative level. There is, as yet, no diagnostic category in Washington specifically labeled for funding Williams syndrome, as there are for other handicapped groups (e.g., the blind, deaf, learning disabled, etc.). Others, too, are proposing the establishment of a specific psychiatric disorder, "Williams Syndrome Behavior Disorder," to be formally included as a psychiatric disorder in the *Diagnostic and Statistical Manual of Mental Disorders* (*DSM–IV*; see Einfeld et al., 1997).

Without such official recognition, little or no federal education funding can be allocated, and consequently, there is a severe lag in direct service delivery for WSc in schools. Parents and professionals have worked hard to obtain public support and funding from federal, state, and local authorities. Specific mandating legislation is still needed to fund programs for WS children and adults. There remains a strong need to monitor and impact legislation, and to intercede when governmental programs and legislation fail to provide needed service delivery to WSs. Other areas of advocacy involve provisions for respite care and facilities and programs for the older and elderly WS adult. The documented lack of respite care for the majority of families caring for adults with WS, and the scarcity of other resources, medical, psychological, and occupational for WSa, speak to the necessity of establishing better care for WSs and those involved with them (Udwin, Howlin, Davies, & Mannion, 1998).

Much has been done by parents and professionals on a volunteer basis to raise funds, but no widespread handicapping condition requiring strong resources and continuous specialized help can be entirely handled by private groups without public funding. This is why skillful and persistent advocacy is essential.

Fifty years ago, little was known about intervention approaches for autism, Down syndrome, cerebral palsy, fetal alcohol syndrome, fragile X, muscular dystrophy, and other disabilities. Dedicated parent organizations and professional associations have worked hard to bring these handicapping conditions to public attention and obtain funding for research, medical services, and mandatory education for them. Cooperative efforts have established these disabilities as accepted medical entities needing special care and educational management.

A considerable amount has been learned about their etiology, medical course, educational needs, and in some cases, prevention. Williams syndrome has a long way to go to reach the funding level of some of these handicapped groups. The history of developing service delivery to these other specialized groups can serve as a model for the future of WS.

Infant Stimulation and Early Childhood Intervention Programs. Today, acceptance and enrollment into early intervention programs from birth to age 3 is available to handicapped or "at risk" children in most states throughout the United States and in some other countries. In the future, depending perhaps on the size of the community, it will be more widely available. Some preschool programs accept WSc and work hard to equip them with the readiness skills needed to prepare them for formal academic learning. Parents and professionals fight hard to enroll WSc into suitable kindergarten programs and early childhood programs, with a moderate degree of success. In the future, with much advocacy, places will be made available for more WSc.

Physical therapists (PT) and occupational therapists (OT) have found ways to increase WSs competence in such areas as self-care, eating and dressing skills, fine motor development, prevention of joint contraction, walking downstairs and ball handling activities. Educators, speech therapists, and language teachers have become interested in cognitive development and language delay. In the future, audiologists will develop ways to reduce the negative impact of auditory hypersensitivity that often plagues WSc.

Elementary School. In years to come, school placement should no longer be such a highly charged emotional issue for parents, psychologists, and school administrators. The specialists concerned will have learned to interpret test results in the light of the unique problems of WS youngsters. Testing procedures can be adapted to allow the time needed by WSc to formulate more accurate and effective responses, to self-correct, and to answer correctly items to which they "know the answer" but are not able to retrieve the information without special cueing techniques by the examiner. Testing the limits and extension testing will help to find ways to teach and reach the WSc. Resulting scores will not be exact equivalents of standard administration scores, but they can illuminate the WS child's potential more clearly.

Teachers will be trained to teach WSc via special in-service programs, so that they will realize that these children can profit from appropriate educational procedures. Such in-service classes can sometimes be taught by knowledgeable and experienced parents (some of whom are also professional teachers), and by professionals with WS experience.

More appropriate educational placements will be possible because schools will understand both the potentials and limitations of WSc, their very special needs, and the different ways they respond to specialized educational techniques in learning such basic academic subjects as the three R's.

The need for one-to-one teaching, or placement in regular classes for some WS children will no longer be challenged by schools. Procedures will exist to enable some WSc to be in a regular school class from which they can profit and share their own unique contributions. Teachers will cooperate by allowing and encouraging WSc to use computers because suitable software will become available for them. Effective home-based educational programs will be developed for parents to use as a means for complementing school-based instruction.

In addition, educational research programs will be established in order to determine effective ways to teach WSs reading, writing, arithmetic, and spelling, and to develop their study habits. Methods are also needed to help strengthen WSs' motor skills and develop their spatial orientation for finding their way about the community. Other priorities include assisting WS in developing better peer relationships, designing better assessment tools, and knowing how to apply their skills in music and language more effectively in learning situations.

On a more general level, the possible benefits of initiating a 12-month educational program to meet the educational and social needs of WSs should be considered. An extended school year may help them maintain and consolidate the skills, knowledge, and appropriate behaviors learned during the regular 9-month school year, preventing the regression often seen during long vacation periods. Such slippage also occurs among normal pupils during a summer vacation, but WSs are less able to afford such losses. A summer program for WSs can also permit coverage of new material and catching up on skills that were lagging during the regular school sessions.

Junior High (or Middle School) and High School. Enriched instructional programs should be developed for WS adolescents. As adolescents strive for independence, their biological drives and the increasing societal pressures (including their peer culture) can have a strong effect. The demands of peer relations (desire to belong to a group), the temptations of sexuality and drugs and alcohol, the increased mobility that comes when normal adolescents acquire a driver's license, and the pressure to make vocational choices all affect WS adolescents too. In future years, because more information will be available, junior high and high schools will be somewhat better prepared for these problems and find more ways of dealing with them. So will parents and siblings of WS teenagers.

As WS adolescents grow into maturity, socialization, basic and functional literacy, citizenship participation, and prevocational training become important in their lives. Later, vocational training and adult living arrangements, preparation for seeking and holding jobs, and learning to manage money come into the foreground.

Greater access to such training may be possible by implementing educational reforms within the school system to develop a functional and practical curriculum. This could include help in practical activities like handling money, performing household chores, cooking, nutrition, and independent travel. For older WSs, this means help in applying for jobs, vocational counseling and training, sex and relationship counseling, and development of avocational interests and skills.

For WSc, cultivation of personal-social skills and special interests as preparation for the world of work begins in the home. Opportunities for the WS child to develop competence cannot be provided too early, and the home will provide multifaceted learning experiences essential to the development of cooperative and independent functioning.

Vocational Opportunities. In the future, career awareness will begin at the kindergarten level, gradually increasing the WS child's exposure to various workers in the community and the contributions that they make. Through the school years, a portion of the regular curriculum can be devoted to career awareness and further exploration in the classroom. Appropriate job fields for WS will be explored early in the curriculum. Special trips, collections, mentoring, or television programs of WSs will be used to encourage further proficiency in a specific topic. In-depth study of various types of occupations will be instituted at an early age, which can have a significant payoff later as career exploration and job preparation become a priority. Areas of special interest or skill can be explored and further developed both at home and in school as a step toward potential employment. But parents must be realistic in their ambitions for their WS children, because many careers are simply not open to them.

Depending on the WS individual's areas of ability, interest, and knowledge, the following types of job-related goals may be considered: food preparation for fast food service; coffee shop worker; farmhand; routine office worker; small motor repairs; janitorial service; pet shop helper; zoo helper;

housekeeping; teacher's aid in early grades; nursing assistant in a nursing home; physical assistant in a school for handicapped children; volunteer work at a hospital; simple computer applications; furniture polisher; carpenter's helper; simple assembly line work; warehouse and stock clerk; packing and handling assistant; construction helper; personal service worker; delivery route worker; grocery bag packer; sweeping, mopping, and polishing floors; animal kennel assistant; grounds maintenance; food service assistant; or plant or tree nursery assistant.

By developing prevocational and vocational training, the employment opportunities for WSs may be enhanced. In providing better employment opportunities for WSs, it is advisable to focus on jobs whose requirements capitalize on the strengths of WSs while not being too demanding in the areas where they are weak.

It is important to identify potential effective job preparation programs and employment options with safety nets, and to develop information on how to coordinate job matching with student skills (i.e., research is needed regarding which jobs dovetail best with WSs ability, knowledge, and interest profiles). It is also important to continue to obtain feedback and establish data files (perhaps in a national registry) concerning how well WSs are placed in various jobs, if they are able to perform successfully, or if they fail to make the grade.

A supplementary need is to provide a continuum of vocational training services aiming toward higher levels of employment, where feasible. These may include school-based programs, community-based training sites, and community-based placement sites.

There is a potential for utilizing state employment services and vocational rehabilitation services for their services in this matter. In some instances, college and university counseling centers may be used for their knowledge of aptitude and interest testing. Parents, agencies, and schools need to maintain a realistic perspective on the work potentials of WSs because of the serious limitations most have in regard to ego strength (including frustration tolerance), degree of social independence achieved, and so forth. WSs should neither be underestimated as potential workers, nor pushed too far or too fast. Demoralizing failure experiences must be avoided whenever possible. Despite this cautionary note, there are some employment options potentially available for WSs, depending on the kinds of job skills developed and the level of an individual's independence and social maturity.

The following are levels of potential work for WSs:

1. Sheltered workshops—At this level, WSs perform relatively simple tasks. Transportation to and from the job site is provided.

2. Supported employment training—This level features a job coach to help develop and improve job skills and adaptive behaviors, such as task

completion, controlling behavioral impulses, concentrating or focusing on the task (resisting distractions), and self-talk reinforcement. The job coach can also help the WSs maintain a good relationship with the employer. At first, transportation to and from the job site may be provided. With time, the goal is independent travel for the WSs.

3. Competitive employment—At this level, WSs no longer need continuing supervision and training (other than that normally provided on the job for all workers). They are able to function fairly independently. A "job coach" might be made available to help if a problem arises. At this level, WSs will travel by public transportation. Keep in mind that only a minority of WSs are likely to reach this high a level.

Residential Options for WS Adults. Various types of living arrangements are needed for adult WSs. Most now live at home with parents. Unfortunately, some are placed in inappropriate residential settings. That is, because such settings typically house people with a wide variety of disabilities, they are not able to focus on the unique needs of a WS adult, and generally contribute little to the WS's growth and development. Also, unfortunately, residential programs are often staffed by workers who are not informed about WSs. Lacking this knowledge, they often use ineffective methods that do not teach skills of independent living.

A more forward thinking plan for WSs in the future provides, especially in metropolitan areas, community residential programs, which may include publicly supported community group homes and/or supervised apartments with a focus on independent skill development. Some of these already exist.

To overcome numerous barriers that prevent WSs from realizing their full potential, it is important for parents, professionals, and organizations to work together to support each other and to insure a brighter outlook for WSs. There is indeed hope for the future.

References

Achenbach, T. M. (1978). The child behavior profile: I. Boys aged 6–11. *Journal of Consulting and Clinical Psychology, 47,* 478–488.

Achenbach, T. M, & Edelbrock, C. S. (1979). The child behavior profile: II. Boys aged 12–16 and girls aged 6–11 and 12–16. *Journal of Consulting and Clinical Psychology, 48,* 223–233.

Achenbach, T. M., & Edelbrock, C. S. (1981). Behavioral problems and competencies reported by parents of normal and disturbed children aged four through sixteen. *Monographs of the Society for Research in Child Development, 46* (Serial No. 188).

American Academy of Pediatrics. (2001). Health care supervision for children with Williams syndrome. *Pediatrics, 107*(5), 1192–1204.

American Psychiatric Association, Committee on Nomenclature and Statistics. (1968). *Diagnostic and statistical manual of mental disorders* (2nd ed.). Washington, DC: Author.

American Psychiatric Association. (1987). *Diagnostic and statistical manual of mental disorders* (3rd ed., rev.). Washington, DC: Author.

American Psychiatric Association. (1994) *Diagnostic and statistical manual of mental disorders* (4th ed.). Washington, DC: Author.

American Speech-Language-Hearing Association (1996). *American Speech-Language-Hearing Task Force on Central Auditory Processing Consensus Development,* ASHA, 1996.

Anderson-Wood, L., & Smith, B. (1997). *Working with pragmatics: A practical guide to promoting communicative confidence.* Eau Claire, WI. Thinking Publications.

Anonymous. (1985). Case history of a child with Williams syndrome. *Pediatrics, 75,* 962–968.

Arkwright, N. (1998). *An introduction to sensory integration.* San Antonio, TX: Communication Skills Builders.

Arnold, R., Yule, W., & Martin, N. (1985). The psychological characteristics of infantile hypercalcaemia: A preliminary investigation. *Developmental Medicine and Child Neurology, 27,* 49–59.

Atkins, P. (1992). *Syntax it is.* Greenville, SC: Super Duper Publications.

Atkinson, J., Anker, S., Braddick, O., Nokes, L., Mason, A., & Braddick, F. (2001). Visual and visuo-spatial development in young children with Williams syndrome. *Developmental Medicine and Child Neurology, 43,* 330–337.

Atkinson, J., Braddick, O., Anker, S., Ehrlich, D., Macpherson, F., Rae, S., King, J., Mercuri, E., Nokes, L., & Braddick, F. (1996, July). *Development of sensory, perceptual and cognitive vision and visual attention in young Williams syndrome children.* Paper presented at the seventh international professional conference on Williams Syndrome, King of Prussia, Pennsylvania.

Atkinson, J., King, J., Braddick, O., Nokes, L., Anker, S., & Braddick, F. (1997, May 27). A specific deficit of dorsal stream function in Williams' syndrome. *Neuroreport, 8,* 1919–1922.

Ayres, A. J. (1972). *Sensory integration and learning disorders.* Los Angeles: Western Psychological Serivces.

Ayres, A. J. (1981). *Sensory integration and the child.* Los Angeles: Western Psychological Services.

Ayres, A. J. (1989/1991). *Sensory integration and praxis tests (SIPT).* Los Angeles: Western Psychological Services.

Bailey, D. B. Jr., & Wolery, M. (Eds.). (1989). *Assessing infants and preschoolers with handicaps.* Columbus, OH: Merrill.

Bailly, L. C., Meljac, C., Calmette, S., & Lemmel, G. (1994, July). *A multi-dimensional approach to cognitive profiles in Williams syndrome.* Poster session presented at the sixth international professional conference of the Williams Syndrome Association, University of California, San Diego.

Barkley, R. A. (1990). *Attention deficit hyperactivity disorder: A handbook for diagnosis and treatment.* New York: Guilford Press.

Barsch, R. (1967). *Achieving perceptual-motor efficiency: A space-oriented approach to learning.* Seattle: Special Child Publications.

Bates, E. (1976). *Language and context: The acquisition of pragmatics.* New York: Academic Press.

Bawden, H. N., MacDonald, G. W., & Shea, S. (1997). Treatment of children with Williams syndrome with methylphenidate. *Journal of Child Neurology, 12*(4), 248–252.

Beery, K. E. (1982). *Revised administration, scoring, and teaching manual for the Developmental Test of Visual-Motor Integration.* Cleveland, OH: Modern Curriculum Press.

Bellis, T. J. (1996). *Assessment and management of central auditory processing disorders in the educational setting: From science to practice.* San Diego, CA: Singular.

Bellugi, U., Bihrle, A., Jernigan, T., Trauner, D., & Doherty, S. (1990). Neuropsychological, neurological, and neuroanatomical profile of Williams syndrome. *American Journal of Medical Genetics Supplement, 6,* 115–125.

Bellugi, U., Bihrle, A., Neville, H., Jernigan, T., & Doherty, S. (1992). Language, cognition, and brain organization in a neurodevelopmental disorder. In G. Megan & C. Nelson (Eds.), *Developmental behavioral neuroscience: Vol. 24. The Minnesota Symposia on Child Psychology* (pp. 201–232). Hillsdale, NJ: Lawrence Erlbaum Associates.

Bellugi, U., Hickok, G., Jones, W., & Jernigan, T. (1996, July). *The neurological basis of Williams syndrome: Linking brain and behavior.* Paper presented at the seventh international professional conference on Williams syndrome, King of Prussia, PA.

Bellugi, U., Lichtenberger, L., Jones, W., Lai, Z., & St. George (2000). I. The neurocognitive profile of Williams syndrome: A complex pattern of strengths and weaknesses. In U. Bellugi & M. St. George (Eds.), Linking cognitive neuroscience and molecular genetics: New perspectives from Williams syndrome. *Journal of Cognitive Neuroscience, 12* (Suppl. 1), 7–29.

Bellugi, U., Lichtenberger, L., Mills, D., Galaburda, A., & Korenberg, J. (1999). Bridging cognition, the brain and molecular genetics: Evidence from Williams syndrome. *Trends in Neurosciences, 22,* 197–207.

Bellugi, U., Marks, S., Bihrle, A., & Sabo, H. (1988a). Dissociation between language and cognitive functions in Williams syndrome. In D. Bishop & K. Mogford (Eds.), *Language development in exceptional circumstances* (pp. 171–189). London: Churchill Livingstone.

Bellugi, U., Sabo, H., & Vaid, V. (1988b). Spatial defects in children with Williams syndrome. In J. Stiles-Davis, M. Kritchevsky, & U. Bellugi (Eds.), *Spatial cognition: Brain bases and development* (pp. 273–298). Hillsdale, NJ: Lawrence Erlbaum Associates.

Bellugi, U., Wang, P., & Jernigan, T. (1994). Williams syndrome: An unusual neuropsychological profile. In S. Broman & J. Grafman (Eds.), *Atypical cognitive deficits in developmental disorders: Implications for brain function* (pp. 23–56). Hillsdale, NJ: Lawrence Erlbaum Associates.

Bender, L. (1938). A Visual Motor Gestalt Test and its clinical use. *American Orthopsychiatric Association Research Monograph* (No. 3).

Bennett, F. C., La Veck, B., & Sells, C. J. (1978). The Williams elfin facies syndrome: The psychological profile as an aid in syndrome identification. *Pediatrics, 61,* 303–306.

Benton, A. L. (1963). *Benton Visual Retention Test* (rev. ed.). San Antonio: The Psychological Corporation.

Beret, N., Bellugi, U., Hickok, G., & Stiles, J. (1996, July). *Integrative spatial deficits in children with Williams syndrome and children with focal brain lesions: A comparison.* Paper presented at the seventh international professional conference on Williams syndrome, King of Prussia, PA.

Berkovitch, M., Pope, E., Phillips, J., & Koren, G. (1995). Pemoline-associated fulminant liver failure: Treating the evidence for causation. *Clinical Pharmacology and Therapeutics, 57*(6), 696–698.

Bertrand, J., & Mervis, C. B. (1996). Longitudinal analysis of drawings by children with Williams syndrome: Preliminary results. *Visual Arts Research, 22*(2), 19–34.

Bertrand, J., Mervis, C. B., & Eisenberg, J. (1997). Drawing by children with Williams syndrome: A developmental perspective. *Developmental Neuropsychology, 13,* 41–67.

Bertrand, J., Mervis, C. B., Armstrong, S., & Ayore, J. (1994a, July) *Figurative language and cognitive abilities of adults with Williams syndrome.* Paper presented at the sixth international professional conference of the Williams Syndrome Association, University of California, San Diego.

Bertrand, J., Mervis, C. B., Armstrong, S. C., & Hutchins, S. S. (1994b, July). *Metamemory in adults with Williams syndrome.* Poster session presented at the sixth international professional conference of the Williams Syndrome Association, University of California, San Diego.

Beuren, A. J. (1972). Supravalvular aortic stenosis: A complex syndrome with and without mental retardation. *Birth Defects: Original Article Series, 8,* 45–56.

Beuren, A. J., Apitz, J., & Harmanz, D. (1962). Supravalvular aortic stenosis in association with mental retardation and a certain facial appearance. *Circulation, 26,* 1235–1240.

Beuren, A. J., Schulze, C., Eberle, P., Harmjanz, D., & Apitz, J. (1964). The syndrome of supravalvular aortic stenosis, pulmonary artery stenosis, mental retardation and similar facial appearance. *American Journal of Cardiology, 13,* 471–483.

Blanche, E. I., Botticelli, T. M., & Hallway, M. K. (1995). *Combining neuro-developmental treatment and sensory integration principles: An approach to pediatric therapy.* San Antonio, TX: Communication Skills Builders.

Bliss, L. (1993). *Pragmatic language intervention: Interactive activities.* Eau Claire, WI: Thinking Publications.

Boehm, A. E. (1986a). *Boehm Test of Basic Concepts-Preschool Version (BTBC-PV).* San Antonio, TX: The Psychological Corporation.

Boehm, A. E. (1986b). *Boehm Test of Basic Concepts-Revised (BTBC-R).* San Antonio, TX: The Psychological Corporation.

Borghgraef, M., Plissart, L., Van Dan Berghe, H., & Fryns, J. P. (1994, July). *Adults with Williams syndrome: Evaluation of the medical, psychological, and behavioral aspects.* Poster session presented at the sixth international professional conference of the Williams Syndrome Association, University of California, San Diego.

Bray, C. H., & Wiig, E. H. (1987). *Let's talk inventory.* San Antonio, TX: The Psychological Corporation.

Bregman, J. (1996, July). *Social, affective, and behavioral impairments in Williams syndrome.* Paper presented at the seventh international professional conference on Williams syndrome, King of Prussia, PA.

Brewer, J., Levine, K., Dykens, E., Bondi, C., Leckman, J., & Pober, B. (1996, July). *Follow-up survey of selected emotional/psychiatric problems in adults with Williams syndrome*. Paper presented at the seventh international professional conference on Williams syndrome, King of Prussia, PA.

Brewer, J. L., Levine, K., & Pober, B. (1995). *Parental survey of psychiatric problems in the adult with Williams*. Unpublished manuscript, Children's Hospital, Boston, MA.

Bromberg, H. S., Ullman, M., Marcus, G., Kelley, K. B., & Levine, K. (1994, July). *A dissociation of lexical memory and grammar in Williams syndrome: Evidence from inflectional morphology*. Poster session presented at the sixth international professional conference of the Williams Syndrome Association, University of California, San Diego.

Brown, A. L. (1975). The development of memory: Knowing, knowing about knowing, and knowing how to know. In H. W. Reese (Ed.), *Advances in Child Development and Behavior* (Vol. 10, pp. 104–152). New York: Academic Press.

Bruininks, R. H. (1978). *Bruininks-Oseretsky Test of Motor Proficiency*. Circle Pines, MN: American Guidance Service.

Campione, J. C., & Brown, A. L. (1977). Memory and metamemory development in educable retarded children. In R. V. Kail & J. W. Hagen (Eds.), *Perspectives on the development of memory and cognition* (pp. 367–406). Hillsdale, NJ: Lawrence Erlbaum Associates.

Carey, S., Johnson, S., & Levine, K. (1994, July). *Two separable knowledge acquisition systems: Evidence from Williams syndrome*. Paper presented at the sixth international professional conference of the Williams Syndrome Association, University of California, San Diego.

Carey, S., Levine, K., & Johnson, S. (1993, March). *Conceptual structure of adults/adolescents with Williams syndrome*. Paper presented at the biennial meeting of the Society for Research in Child Development, New Orleans, LA.

Carroll, D. W. (1986). *The psychology of language*. Pacific Grove, CA: Brooks/Cole.

Carrow-Woolfolk, E. (1985). *Test of Auditory Comprehension of Language-Revised (TACL-R)*. East Aurora, NY: Slosson Educational Publications.

Cassady, C., Bellugi, U., Reilly, J., & Adolphs, R. (1997, April). *Hypersociability in Williams syndrome: Similarities to bilateral amygdala patients*. Poster symposium presented at the annual meeting of the International Behavioral Neuroscience Society, San Diego, CA.

Chapman, C. A., Du Plessis, A., & Pober, B. R. (1996). Neurologic findings in children and adults with Williams syndrome. *Journal of Child Neurology, 10*, 63–65.

Chermak, G., & Musiek, F. (1997). *Central auditory processing disorders: New perspectives*. San Diego, CA: Singular.

Chilosi, A., Battaglia, A., Brizzolara, D., Cipriani, P., Pfanner, L., & Carey, J. C. (2001). Del (9p) syndrome: Proposed behavior phenotype. *American Journal of Medical Genetics, 110*, 138–144.

Clahsen, H., & Almazan, M. (1998). Syntax and morphology in Williams syndrome. *Cognition, 68*, 167–198.

Clahsen, H., & Temple, C. (2002). Words and rules in Williams syndrome. In Y. Levy & J. Schaeffer (Eds.), *Language competence across populations* (pp. 323–352). Hillsdale, NJ: Lawrence Erlbaum Associates.

Clark, H. H., & Clark, E. V. (1977). *Psychology and language: An introduction to psycholinguistics*. New York: Harcourt Brace Jovanovitch.

Colarusso, R. P., & Hammill, D. D. (1972). *Motor-Free Visual Perception Test*. San Rafael, CA: Academic Therapy Publications.

Cole, M. L., & Cole, J. T. (1989). *Effective intervention with the language impaired child* (2nd ed.). Rockville, MD: Aspen.

Coleman, N. (1997). *Step-by-step narratives: Illustrated lessons for telling and writing stories*. Eau Claire, WI: Thinking Publications.

Collins, P. J., & Cunningham, G. W. (1982). *WH-questions*. Austin, TX: Pro-ED.

Conners, C. K. (1996). *Conners' Rating Scales-Revised (CRS-R)*. San Antonio, TX: The Psychological Corporation.

Crisco, J. J., Dobbs, J. M., & Mulhern, R. K. (1988). Cognitive processing of children with Williams syndrome. *Developmental Medicine and Child Neurology, 30,* 650–656.

Curfs, L. M., van Lieshout, C. F. M., deMeyer, R. E., Plissart, L., & Fryns, J. P. (1996, July). *Personality profiles in Williams syndrome.* Poster presented at the seventh international professional conference on Williams Syndrome, King of Prussia, PA.

Daly, G. H., & McGlothlin, S. (2000). *Request.* Eau Claire, WI: Thinking Publications.

Davies, M., Howlin, P., & Udwin, O. (1997). Independence and adaptive behavior in adults with Williams syndrome. *American Journal of Medical Genetics, 70,* 188–195.

Davies, M., Udwin, O., & Howlin, P. (1998). Adults with Williams syndrome: Preliminary study of social, emotional, and behavioural difficulties. *British Journal of Psychiatry, 172,* 273–276.

Deal, J. E., & Hanuscin, L. (1991). *Barrier games for better communication.* Austin, TX: Pro-ED.

Delis, D., Kramer, J., Kaplan, E., & Ober, B. (1995). *California Verbal Learning Test-Child Version (CVLT-Child).* San Antonio, TX: The Psychological Corporation.

Deruelle, C., Mancini, J., Livet, M. O., Casse-Perrot, C., & de Schonen, S. (1999). Configural and local processing of faces in children with Williams syndrome. *Brain and Cognition, 3,* 276–298.

Dilts, C. V., Morris, C. A., & Leonard, C. O. (1990). Hypothesis for development of a behavioral phenotype in Williams Syndrome. *American Journal of Medical Genetics Supplement, 6,* 126–131.

DiSimoni, F. (1978). *The Token Test for Children.* Hingham, MA: Teaching Resources.

Dodge, M. (1995, Spring). Physical therapy concerns and assessment for the child with Williams syndrome. *Williams Syndrome Association National Newsletter, 12,* 8–10.

Doherty, S., Bellugi, U., Jernigan, T., & Poizner, H. (1989, February). Neurobehavioral and neuroanatomical features of Williams syndrome. In U. Bellugi (Chair), *Neural correlates underlying dissociations of higher cortical functioning.* Symposium conducted at the meeting of the International Neuropsychology Society, Vancouver, Canada.

Don, A., Schellenberg, E. G., & Rourke, B. P. (1996, July). *Auditory pattern perception in children with Williams syndrome (WS): Preliminary findings.* Paper presented at the seventh international professional conference on Williams syndrome, King of Prussia, PA.

Don, A., Schellenberg, E. G., & Rourke, B. P. (1999). Music and language skills in children with Williams syndrome. *Child Neuropsychology, 5,* 154–170.

Dukette, D., & Stiles, J. (2001). The effects of stimulus density on children's analysis of hierarchical patterns. *Developmental Science, 4*(2), 233–251.

Dunn, L. M., & Dunn, L. M. (1981). *Peabody Picture Vocabulary Test-Revised.* Circle Pines, MN: American Guidance Service.

Dykens, E. M., Hodapp, R. M., & Finucane, B. M. (2000). *Genetics and mental retardation syndromes: A new look at behavior and interventions.* Baltimore, MD: Paul H. Brookes.

Dykens, E. M., & Rosner, B. A. (1999). Refining behavioral phenotypes: Personality-motivation in Williams and Prader-Willi syndromes. *American Journal on Mental Retardation, 104,* 158–169.

Dykens, E. M., Rosner, B. A., & Ly, T. M. (2001). Drawings by individuals with Williams syndrome: Are people different from shapes? *American Journal on Mental Retardation, 106*(1), 94–107.

Einfeld, S. L., Tonge, B. J., & Florio, T. (1997). Behavioral and emotional disturbance in individuals with Williams syndrome. *American Journal on Mental Retardation, 102,* 45–53.

Einfeld, S. L., Tonge, B. J., & Rees, V. W. (2001). Longitudinal course of behavioral and emotional problems in Williams syndrome. *American Journal on Mental Retardation, 106*(1), 73–81.

Erhardt, R. (Ed.). (1999). *Parent Articles About NDT.* San Antonio, TX: Communication Skills Builders.

Ewart, A. K., Morris, C. A., Atkinson, D., Weishan, J., Stermes, K., Spallone, P., Stock, A., Leppert, M., & Keating, M. (1993). Hemizygosity of the elastin locus in a developmental disorder, Williams syndrome. *Nature Genetics, 5,* 11–16. (WSA Newsletter, Winter, 1994, p. 8).

Ewart, A. K., Morris, C. A., Ensing, G. J., Loker, J., Moore, C., Leppert, M., & Keating, M. (WSA Newsletter, Summer, 1993, pp. 4–5).

Feagans, L. V., Kipp, E., & Blood, I. (1994). The effects of otitis media on the attention skills of day-care-attending toddlers. *Developmental Psychology, 30,* 701–708.

Fendall, P. (2000). *Connect a card—Building sentences with conjunctions.* Eau Claire, WI: Thinking Publications.

Fenson, L., Dale, P. S., Reznick, J. S., Bates, E., Thal, D. J., & Pethick, S. J. (1994). Variability in communicative development. *Monographs of the Society for Research in Child Development, 59* (5, Serial No. 242).

Finegan, J.-A., Sitarenios, G., Smith, M. L., & Meschino, W. (1994, July). *Attention deficit hyperactivity disorder in children with Williams syndrome: Preliminary findings.* Paper presented at the sixth international professional conference of the Williams Syndrome Association, University of California, San Diego.

Finegan, J.-A., Smith, M. L., & Meschino, W. (1996). *Verbal Memory in Children with Williams Syndrome.* Poster presented at the seventh international professional conference of the Williams Syndrome Association, King of Prussia, PA.

Finucane, B. (1996, July). *Behavioral issues in adolescents and adults with Williams syndrome.* Paper presented at the seventh international professional conference of the Williams Syndrome Association, King of Prussia, PA.

Flowers, A., Costello, M., & Small, V. (1973). *Flowers-Costello Test of Central Auditory Abilities.* Dearborn, MI: Perceptual Learning Systems.

Folio, M. R., & Fawell, R. R. (2000). *Peabody Developmental Motor Scales Second Edition* (PDMS-2). Wood Dale, IL: Stoelting Company.

Frangiskakis, J. M., Ewart, A. K., Morris, C. A, Mervis, C. B., Bertrand, J., Robinson, B. F., Klein, B. P., Ensing, G. J., Everett, L. A., Green, E. D., Proschel, C., Gitowski, N. J., Noble, M., Atkinson, D. L., Odelberg, S. J., & Keating, M. T. (1996, July 12). LIM-kinase1 hemizygosity implicated in impaired visuospatial constructive cognition. *Cell, 86,* 59–69.

Frank, K., & Smith-Rex, S. (1997). *Getting with it: A kid's guide to forming good relationships and "fitting in."* Eau Claire, WI: Thinking Publications.

Frank, R. A. (1983, November). *Speech-language characteristics of Williams syndrome: Cocktail party speech revisited.* Poster session presented at the meetings of the American Speech-Language Hearing Association.

Frank, R. A. (1988). Building self-esteem in persons with Down syndrome. In S. M. Pueschel (Ed.), *The young person with Down syndrome.* Baltimore: Paul H. Brookes.

Friel-Patti, S., & Lougeay-Mottinger, J. (1994). Preschool language intervention: Some key concerns. In K. G. Butler (Ed.), *Early intervention II: Working with parents and families. Topics in language disorders* (pp. 137–148). Gaithersberg, MD: Aspen.

Frith, U. (1989). *Autism: Explaining the enigma.* Cambridge, MA: Blackwell.

Fromkin, V., & Rodman, R. (1988). *An introduction to language* (4th ed.). New York: Harcourt Brace Jovanovich, Inc.

Frostig, M., & Horne, D. (1964). *The Frostig program for the development of visual perception.* Chicago: Follett.

Frostig, M., Maslow, P., Lefever, D. W., & Whittlesey, J. R. B. (1964). The Marianne Frostig Developmental Test of Visual Perception, 1963 standardization. *Perceptual and Motor Skills, 19,* 463–499.

Gajewski, N., Hirn, P., & Mayo, P. (1994). *Social skill strategies: Social star (book 2): Peer interaction skills.* Eau Claire, WI: Thinking Publications.

Gajewski, N., Hirn, P., & Mayo, P. (1996). *Social skill strategies: Social star (book 3): Conflict resolution and community interaction skills.* Eau Claire, WI: Thinking Publications.

Galaburda, A. M., & Bellugi, U. (2000). V. Multi-level analysis of cortical neuroanatomy in Williams syndrome. In U. Bellugi & M. St. George (Eds.), Linking cognitive neuroscience and molecular genetics: New perspectives from Williams syndrome. *Journal of Cognitive Neuroscience, 12* (Suppl. 1), 74–88.

Gardner, H., Winner, E., Bechhofer, R., & Wolf, D. (1978). The development of figurative language. In K. E. Nelson (Ed.), *Children's language* (Vol. 1, pp. 1–38). New York: Gardner Press.

German, D. J. (1989). *Test of word finding*. Allen, TX: DLM Teaching Resources. (DLM Teaching Resources, One DLM Park, P.O. Box 4000, Allen, TX 75002.)

German, D. J. (1993). *Word-finding intervention program (WFIP)*. Austin, TX: Pro-ED.

Geschwind, N. (1972). The varieties of naming errors. In M. T. Sarno (Ed.), *Aphasia: Selected readings*. New York: Appleton-Century Crofts.

Gillberg, C., & Rasmussen, P. (1994). Brief report: Four case histories and a literature review of Williams syndrome and autistic behavior. *Journal of Autism and Developmental Disorder, 24*, 381–393.

Goldman, R., Fristoe, M., & Woodcock, R. W. (1970). *Goldman-Fristoe-Woodcock Test of Auditory Discrimination*. Circle Pines, MN: American Guidance Service.

Goldstein, K. (1948). *Language and language disturbance*. New York: Grune & Stratton.

Goodman, J. (1994, July). *Language acquisition in children with Williams syndrome*. Poster session presented at the sixth international professional conference of the Williams Syndrome Association, University of California, San Diego.

Gorman-Gard, K. (1992). *Figurative language*. Eau Claire, WI: Thinking Publications.

Gosch, A., & Pankau, R. (1994a). Autistic behavior in two children with Williams-Beuren syndrome [Letter]. *American Journal of Medical Genetics, 53*, 83–84.

Gosch, A., & Pankau, R. (1994b). Social-emotional and behavioral adjustment in children with Williams-Beuren syndrome. *American Journal of Medical Genetics, 53*, 335–339.

Gosch, A., & Pankau, R. (1996a). Longitudinal study of the cognitive development in children with Williams-Beuren syndrome. *American Journal of Medical Genetics, 61*, 26–29.

Gosch, A., & Pankau, R. (1996b, July). *Personality characteristics and behavior problems in subjects with Williams-Beuren syndrome: A comparison of three different age groups*. Poster presented at the seventh international professional conference on Williams syndrome, King of Prussia. PA.

Gosch, A., Pankau, R., & Stading, G. (1994, July). *Investigation of verbal abilities in children with Williams-Beuren syndrome*. Poster session presented at the sixth international professional conference of the Williams Syndrome Association, University of California, San Diego.

Gosch, A., Stading, G., & Pankau, R. (1994). Linguistic abilities in children with Williams-Beuren syndrome. *American Journal of Medical Genetics, 52*, 291–296.

Greenberg, F., & Lewis, R. A. (1988). The Williams syndrome: Spectrum and significance of ocular features. *Ophthalmology, 95*, 1608–1612.

Greer, M. K., Brown, F. R., Pai, G. S., Choudry, S. H., & Klein, A. J. (1997). Cognitive, adaptive, and behavioral characteristics of Williams syndrome. *American Journal of Medical Genetics, 74*, 521–525.

Grejtak, N. (1996a). *Adaptations and curriculum modifications*. Clawson, MI: Williams Syndrome Association. (Also available at *http://www.williams-syndrome.org/testing.htm*)

Grejtak, N. (1996b). *Connecting the WS cognitive profile to educational strategies*. Clawson, MI: Williams Syndrome Association. (Also available at *http://www.williams-syndrome.org/testing. htm*)

Grejtak, N. (1996c). *Education survey results*. Clawson, MI: Williams Syndrome Association. (Also available at *http://www.williams-syndrome.org/testing.htm*)

Hagen, J. W., & Stanovich, K. G. (1977). Memory: Strategies of acquisition. In R. V. Kail & J. W. Hagen (Eds.), *Perspectives on the development of memory and cognition* (pp. 89–111). Hillsdale, NJ: Lawrence Erlbaum Associates.

Hagerman, R. J. (1999). *Neurodevelopmental disorders: Diagnosis and treatment*. New York: Oxford University Press.

Hamersky, J. (1995). *Cartoon cut-ups: Teaching figurative language and humor*. Eau Claire, WI: Thinking Publications.

Harris, J. C. (1995a). *Developmental neuropsychiatry, Vol. I. Fundamentals*. New York: Oxford University Press.

Harris, J. C. (1995b). *Developmental neuropsychiatry, Vol. II. Assessment, diagnosis, and treatment of developmental disorders*. New York: Oxford University Press.

Harrison, D., Reilly, J. S., & Klima, E. S. (1994, July). *Unusual social behavior in Williams syndrome: Evidence from biographical interviews.* Poster session presented at the sixth international professional conference of the Williams Syndrome Association, University of California, San Diego.

Hayes, D. S., & Rosner, S. R. (1975). The phonetic effect in preschool children: The influence of verbal and rehearsal instructions. *Journal of Experimental Child Psychology, 20,* 391–399.

Hickok, G., Bellugi, U., & Jones, W. (1995, October 13). Asymmetrical ability [Letter]. *Science, 270,* 219–220.

Hetherington, E. M., & Parke, R. D. (1993). *Child psychology: A contemporary viewpoint* (4th ed.). New York: McGraw-Hill.

Hetherington, E. M., & Parke, R. D. (1986). *Child psychology: A contemporary viewpoint* (3rd ed.). New York: McGraw-Hill.

Hodenius, T. M. J., Holtinrichs, J. H. G. J., Curfs, L. M. G., & Fryns, J. P. (1994, July). *Adults with Williams syndrome.* Poster session presented at the sixth international professional conference of the Williams Syndrome Association, University of California, San Diego.

Hollingsworth, B. (2000). *The flip book for individualizing pronoun and preposition practices.* Austin, TX: Pro-ED.

Hoskins, B. (1996). *Conversations. A framework for language intervention.* Eau Claire, WI: Thinking Publications.

Hresko, R., & Hammill, D. D. (1981). *Test of Early Language Development.* Austin, TX: Pro-ED.

Hutson-Nechkash, P. (1990). *Storybuilding: A guide to structuring oral narratives.* Eau Claire, WI: Thinking Publications.

Inamura, K. N. (Ed.). (1998). *SI for early intervention: A team approach.* San Antonio, TX: Communication Skills Builders.

Jargensen, C., Barrett, M., Huisingh, R., & Zachman, L. (1981). *The WORD Test: A test of expressive vocabulary and semantics.* Moline, IL: Linguistic Systems.

Jarrold, C., Baddeley, A. D., & Hewes, A. K. (1998). Verbal and nonverbal abilities in the Williams syndrome phenotype: Evidence for diverging developmental trajectories. *Journal of Child Psychology and Psychiatry, 4*(5), 511–523.

Jarrold, C., Baddeley, A. D., & Hewes, A. K. (1999). Genetically dissociated components of working memory: Evidence from Down's and Williams syndrome. *Neuropsychologia, 37*(6), 637–651.

Johnson, S. C., & Carey, S. (1998). Knowledge enrichment and conceptual change in folkbiology: Evidence from Williams syndrome. *Cognitive Psychology, 37,* 156–200.

Johnson, S. C., Carey, S., & Levine, K. (1994, July). *Dissociations in the conceptual development of people with Williams syndrome.* Poster session presented at the sixth international professional conference of the Williams Syndrome Association, University of California, San Diego.

Jones, K. L. (1990). Williams syndrome: An historical perspective of its evolution, natural history, and etiology. *American Journal of Medical Genetics Supplement, 6,* 89–96.

Jones, K. L., & Smith, D. W. (1975). The Williams elfin facies syndrome. *The Journal of Pediatrics, 86,* 718–723.

Jones, W., Bellugi, U., Lai, Z., Chiles, M., Reilly, J., Lincoln, A., & Adolphs, R. (2000). II. Hypersociability in Williams syndrome. In U. Bellugi & M. St. George (Eds.), Linking cognitive neuroscience and molecular genetics: New perspectives from Williams syndrome. *Journal of Cognitive Neuroscience, 12,* Supplement 1, 30–46.

Jones, W., Lincoln, A., Reilly, J., Grafstein, S., Beret, N., & Bellugi, U. (1996, July). *The use of social engagement techniques in young children with Williams syndrome: A case study.* Poster presented at the seventh international professional conference on Williams Syndrome, King of Prussia, PA.

Jones, W., Rossen, M. L., & Bellugi, U. (1994, July). *Distinct developmental trajectories of cognition in Williams syndrome.* Poster session presented at the sixth international professional conference of the Williams Syndrome Association, University of California, San Diego.

Jones, W., Singer, N., Rossen, M., & Bellugi, U. (1993). Fractionations of higher cognitive functions in Williams syndrome: Developmental trajectories. *American Speech Hearing Association, 35*, 135 (Abstract).

Joyce, C. A., Zorich, B., Pike, S. J., Barber, J. C. K., & Dennis, N. R. (1996). Williams-Beuren syndrome: Phenotypic variability and deletions in chromosomes 7, 11, and 22 in a series of 52 patients. *Journal of Medical Genetics, 33*, 986–992.

Kail, R. V., Jr. (1984). *The development of memory in children* (2nd ed.). New York: W. H. Freeman.

Kail, R. V., & Hagen, J. W. (Eds.). (1977). *Perspectives on the development of memory and cognition.* Hillsdale, NJ: Lawrence Erlbaum Associates.

Kapp, M. E., von Noorden, G. K., & Jenkins, R. (1995). Strabismus in Williams syndrome. *American Journal of Ophthalmology, 119*, 355–360.

Karmiloff-Smith, A. (1992). *Abnormal phenotypes and the challenges they pose to connectionist models of development* (Tech. Rep. PDP.CNS.92.7). Pittsburgh: Carnegie Mellon University.

Karmiloff-Smith, A. (1997). Crucial differences between developmental cognitive neuroscience and adult neuropsychology. *Developmental Neuroscience, 13*, 513–524.

Karmiloff-Smith, A., Grant, J., & Berthoud, I. (1993, March). *Within-domain dissociations in Williams syndrome: A window on the normal mind.* Paper presented at the biennial meeting of the Society for Research in Child Development, New Orleans, LA.

Karmiloff-Smith, A., Grant, J., Berthoud, J., Davies, M., Howlin, P., & Udwin, O. (1997). Language and Williams syndrome: How intact is "intact"? *Child Development, 68*, 246–262.

Karmiloff-Smith, A., Klima, E., Bellugi, U., Grant, J., & Baron-Cohen, S. (1995). Is there a social module? Language, face processing, and theory of mind in individuals with Williams syndrome. *Journal of Cognitive Neuroscience, 7*, 196–208.

Karmiloff-Smith, A., Tyler, L. K., Voice, K., Sims, K., Udwin, O., Howlin, P., & Davies, M. (1998). Linguistic dissociations in Williams syndrome: Evaluating receptive syntax in on-line and off-line tasks. *Neuropsychologia, 36*, 343–351.

Kataria, S., Goldstein, D. J., & Glushnick, T. (1981). Developmental delays in Williams ("elfin facies") syndrome. *Applied Research in Mental Retardation, 5*, 419–423.

Katz, J. (1962). The use of staggered sponderic words for assessing the integrity of the central auditory system (SST). *Journal of Auditory Research, 2*, 327–337.

Kaufman, A. S., & Kaufman, N. L. (1983). *Kaufman Assessment Battery for Children (K-ABC).* Circle Pines, MN: American Guidance Service.

Kaufman, A. S., & Kaufman, N. L. (1990). *Kaufman Brief Intelligence Test (K-BIT).* Circle Pines, MN: American Guidance Service.

Keith, R. W. (1999). *SCAN-C: Test for Auditory Processing Disorders in Children-Revised.* San Antonio, TX: The Psychological Corporation.

Kelley, K. B., & Tager-Flusberg, H. (1994, July). *Discourse characteristics of children with Williams syndrome: Evidence of spared theory of mind abilities.* Poster session presented at the sixth international professional conference of the Williams Syndrome Association, University of California, San Diego.

Kephart, N. (1960). *The slow learner in the classroom.* Columbus, OH: Charles E. Merrill.

Kimmell, G. M., & Wahl, J. (1981). *The STAP (Screening Test for Auditory Perception).* San Rafael, CA: Academic Therapy Publications.

Klein, A. J., Armstrong, B. L., Greer, M. K., & Brown, F. R. III. (1990). Hyperacusis and otitis media in individuals with Williams syndrome. *Journal of Speech and Hearing Disorders, 55*, 339–344.

Klein, B. P., & Mervis, C. B. (1999). Contrasting patterns of cognitive abilities of 9- and 10-year-olds with Williams syndrome or Downs syndrome. *Developmental Neuropsychology, 16*, 177–196.

Korenberg, J. R., Chen, X.-N., Hirota, H., Lai, Z., Bellugi, U., Burian, D., Roe, B., & Matsuoka, R. (2000). VI. Genome structure and cognitive map of Williams syndrome. In U. Bellugi & M. St. George (Eds.), Linking cognitive neuroscience and molecular genetics: New perspectives from Williams syndrome. *Journal of Cognitive Neuroscience, 12* (Suppl. 1), 89–107.

Krassowski, E. (1998). *Making sense with syntax.* Eau Claire, WI: Thinking Publications.

Lambert, N. M., Windmiller, M., Tharinger, D., & Cole, L. J. (1981). *AAMD Adaptive Behavior Scale-School Edition*. Monterey, CA: CTB/McGraw-Hill.

Leiter, R. G. (1948). *Leiter International Performance Scale*. Chicago: Stoelting Co.

Lenhoff, H. M. (1996, July). *Music and Williams syndrome: A status report and goals*. Paper presented at the seventh international professional conference on Williams Syndrome, King of Prussia, PA.

Lenhoff, H. M., Perales, O., & Hickok, G. (2001). Absolute pitch in Williams syndrome. *Music Perception, 18*, 491–503.

Lenhoff, H. M., Wang, P. P., Greenberg, F., & Bellugi, U. (1997, December). Williams syndrome and the brain. *Scientific American, 277*, 68–73.

Levine, K. (1993, Fall). Information for teachers. *Williams Syndrome Association National Newsletter, 10*(4), 3–9. (Also available at *http://www.williams-syndrome.org/teacher.htm*)

Levine, K. (1994, Spring). Educational testing. *Williams Syndrome Association National Newsletter, 11*(2), 3–5.

Levine, K. (1997). *Guidelines for psychological assessment of young children (age 4–12) with Williams syndrome*. Williams Syndrome Association, Clawson, MI. (Also available at *http://www.williams-syndrome.org/testing.htm*)

Levine, K., & Castro, R. (1994, July). *Social skills profile of school-aged children with Williams syndrome*. Paper presented at the sixth international professional conference of the Williams Syndrome Association, University of California, San Diego.

Levine, K., Pober, B., & Miranda, S. (1996, July). *Williams syndrome and autism: Is there a link?* Paper presented at the seventh international professional conference on Williams syndrome, King of Prussia, PA.

Levine, K., & Wharton, R. (2000). Williams syndrome and happiness. *American Journal of Mental Retardation, 105*(5), 363–371.

Levine, K., & Wharton, R. (2001, June). Severe behavioral challenges in some children with WS: When smiles turn to snarls! *WSA National Newsletter, 18*(2), 23–26.

Levine, M. D., Brooks, R., & Shonkoff, J. P. (1980). *A pediatric approach to learning disorders*. New York: Wiley.

Levinson, M. (1994, Winter). The use of medications to modify behavior. *Williams Syndrome Association National Newsletter, 11*(1), 3.

Levitin, D. J., & Bellugi, U. (1998). Musical abilities in individuals with Williams syndrome. *Music Perception, 15*(4), 357–389.

Lopez-Rangel, E., Maurice, M., McGillivray, B., & Friedman, J. M. (1992). Williams syndrome in adults. *American Journal of Medical Genetics, 44*(6), 720–729.

Losh, M., Reilly, J., Bellugi, U., Cassady, C., & Klima, E. (1997). Linguistically encoded affect is abnormally high in Williams syndrome children. *International Behavioral Neuroscience Society Abstracts, 6*, 2–53.

Lucas, E. V. (1980). *Semantic and pragmatic language disorders: Assessment and remediation*. Rockville, MD: Aspen Systems.

MacDonald, G. W., & Roy, D. L. (1988). Williams Syndrome: A neuropsychological profile. *Journal of Clinical and Experimental Neuropsychology, 10*, 125–131.

Marriage, J. (1994, July). *Central hyperacusis in Williams syndrome*. Paper presented at the sixth international professional conference of the Williams Syndrome Association, University of California, San Diego.

Marriage, J. (2001, March). So what can we do about hyperacusis? *WSA National Newsletter, 18*(1), 6–8.

Marriage, J., & Turk, J. (1996, July). *Hyperacusis in Williams syndrome: Part of a global sensory sensitivity?* Paper presented at the seventh international professional conference on Williams Syndrome, King of Prussia, PA.

Martin, N. D. T., Snodgrass, G. J. A. I., & Cohen, R. D. (1984). Idiopathic infantile hypercalcaemia—a continuing enigma. *Archives of Disease in Childhood, 59*, 605–613.

May, C. H. (1994) Conversations with conjunctions. *Assessment and activities for oral language.* Austin, TX: Pro-ED.

McCarthy, D. A. (1972). *Manual for the McCarthy Scales of Children's Abilities.* San Antonio: The Psychological Corporation.

McCrae, R. R., Costa, P. T., Pedrosa de Lima, M., Simoes, A., Osrendorf, F., Angleitner, A., Marusic, I., Bratko, D., Caprara, G. V., Barbaranelli, C., Chae, J., & Piedmont, R. L. (1999). Age differences in personality across the life span: Parallels in five cultures. *Developmental Psychology, 35,* 466–477.

McDade, H. L., & Varnedoe, D. R. (1994). Training parents to be language facilitators. In K. G. Butler (Ed.), Early intervention II: Working with parents and families. *Topics in Language Disorders Series* (pp. 149–160). Gaithersberg, MD: Aspen.

Mayer, M. (1969). *Frog, where are you?* New York: The Dial Press.

Meichenbaum, D. (1979). *Cognitive behavior modification.* New York: Plenum.

Merriam-Webster's deluxe dictionary, tenth collegiate Dictionary (1998). Pleasantville, NY: Reader's Digest Association, Inc.

Mervis, C. B., & Bertrand, J. (1993, March). *General and specific relations between early language and early cognitive development.* Paper presented at the biennial meeting of the Society for Research in Child Development, New Orleans, LA.

Mervis, C. B., & Bertrand, J. (1994, July). *Early lexical development of children with Williams syndrome.* Paper presented at the sixth international professional conference of the Williams Syndrome Association, University of California, San Diego.

Mervis, C. B., & Bertrand, J. (1997). Developmental relations between cognition and language: Evidence from Williams syndrome. In L. B. Adamson & M. A. Romski (Eds.), *Research on communication and language disorders: Contributions to theories of language development* (pp. 75–106). Baltimore: Brookes.

Mervis, C. B., Bertrand, J., Robinson, B. F., Klein, B. P., & Armstrong, S. (1995, March). *Early language development of children with Williams syndrome.* Poster session presented at the biennial meetings of the Society for Research in Child Development, Indianapolis, IN.

Mervis, C. B., & Klein-Tasman, B. P. (2000). Williams syndrome: Cognition, personality, and adaptive behavior. *Mental Retardation and Developmental Disabilities Research Reviews, 6,* 148–158.

Mervis, C. B., Klein-Tasman, B. P., & Mastin, M. E. (2001). Adaptive behavior of 4- through 8-year children with Williams syndrome. *American Journal on Mental Retardation, 106*(4), 82–93.

Mervis, C., Morris, C. A., Bertrand, J., & Robinson, B. F. (1999). Williams syndrome: Findings from an integrated program of research. In H. Tager-Flusberg (Ed.), *Neurodevelopmental disorders: Contributions to a new framework from the cognitive neurosciences* (pp. 65–110). Cambridge, MA: MIT Press.

Mervis, C. B., & Robinson, B. F. (2000). Expressive vocabulary ability of toddlers with Williams syndrome or Down syndrome: A comparison. *Developmental Neuropsychology, 17*(1), 111–126.

Messick, C. K. (1994). Ins and outs of the acquisition of spatial terms. In G. Kathleen Butler (Ed.), *Early Intervention I: Working with infants and toddlers, Topics in Language Disorders Series,* 67–78.

Meyerson, M. D., & Frank, R. A. (1987). Language, speech and hearing in Williams syndrome: Intervention approaches and research needs. *Developmental Medicine and Child Neurology, 29,* 258–270.

Milani, L., Dall'Oglio, A. M., & Vicari, S. (1994, July). *Spatial abilities in Italian children with Williams syndrome.* Poster session presented at the sixth international professional conference of the Williams Syndrome Association, University of California, San Diego.

Miller, J. F. (1988). The developmental asynchrony of language development in children with Down syndrome. In L. Nadel (Ed.), *The psychobiology of Down syndrome* (pp. 167–198). Cambridge, MA: MIT Press.

Mills, D. L., Alvarez, T. D., St. George, M., Appelbaum, L. G., Bellugi, U., & Neville, H. (2000). III. Electrophysiological studies of face processing in Williams syndrome. In U. Bellugi & M. St

George (Eds.), Linking cognitive neuroscience and molecular genetics: New perspectives from Williams syndrome. *Journal of Cognitive Neuroscience, 12* (Suppl. 1), 47–64.

Montague, M., & Lund, K. (1991). Job-related social skills. *A curriculum for adolescents with special needs.* Eau Claire, WI: Thinking Publications.

Morris, C. A. (1994, July). *The search for the genetic etiology of Williams syndrome and supravalvular aortic stenosis.* Paper presented at the sixth international professional conference of the Williams Syndrome Association, University of California, San Diego.

Morris, C. A., Demsey, S. A., Leonard, C. O., Dilts, C., & Blackburn, B. L. (1988). Natural history of Williams syndrome: Physical characteristics. *The Journal of Pediatrics, 113,* 318–326.

Morris, C., Thomas, I., & Greenberg, F. (1993). Williams syndrome: Autosomal dominant inheritance. *American Journal of Medical Genetics, 47,* 478–481. (WSA Newsletter, Winter, 1994, p. 9).

Neville, H. J., Holcomb, P. J., & Mills, D. M. (1989, February). Auditory sensory and language processing in Williams syndrome. In U. Bellugi (Chair), *Neural correlates underlying dissociations of higher cortical functioning.* Symposium conducted at the meeting of the International Neuropsychology Society, Vancouver, Canada.

Olitsky, S. E., Sadler, L., & Reynolds, J. D. (1997, August). Subnormal binocular vision in the Williams syndrome [Condensed Article]. *Williams Syndrome Association Newsletter, 14*(2), 5–6.

O'Reilly, M. F., Lacey, C., & Lancioni, G. E. (2000). Assessment of the influence of background noise on escape-maintained problem behavior and pain behavior in a child with Williams syndrome. *Journal of Applied Behavior Analysis, 33*(4), 511–514.

Ornstein, P. A., & Haden, C. A. (2001). Memory development or the development of memory? *Current Directions in Psychological Science, 10*(6), 202–205.

Pagon, R. A., Bennett, F. C., LaVeck, B., Stewart, K. B. & Johnson, J. (1987). Williams syndrome: Features in late childhood and adolescence. *Pediatrics, 80,* 85–91.

Pani, J. R., Mervis, C. B., & Robinson, B. F. (1996, April). *Low level spatial organization in Williams syndrome.* Poster session presented at the Cognitive Neurosciences Meeting, San Francisco.

Pankau, R., Partsch, C. J., Gosch, A., Oppermann, H. C., & Wessel, A. (1992). Statural growth in Williams-Beuren syndrome. *European Journal of Pediatrics, 151*(10), 751–755.

Pankau, R., Partsch, C. J., Winter, M., Gosch, A., & Wessel, A. (1996). Incidence and spectrum of renal abnormalities in Williams-Beuren syndrome. *American Journal of Medical Genetics, 63*(1), 301–304.

Paterson, S. J., Brown, J. H., Gsodl, M. K., Johnson, M. H., & Karmiloff-Smith, A. (1999). Cognitive modularity and genetic disorders. *Science, 286,* 2355–2358.

Paul, R. (1996). Clinical implications of the natural history of slow expressive language development. *American Journal of Speech Language Pathology, 5,* 9–21.

Perlstein, T., & Thrall, G. (1996). *Ready-to-use conflict resolution activities for secondary students.* Eau Claire, WI: Thinking Publications.

Peura-Jones, R., & DeBoer, C. (1995). *Story making.* Eau Claire, WI: Thinking Publications.

Peura-Jones, R., & DeBoer, C. (2000). *More story making!* Eau Claire, WI: Thinking Publications.

Plissart, L., Borghgraef, M., & Fryns, J. P. (1996a, July). *The early development in children with Williams syndrome.* Paper presented at the seventh international professional conference on Williams syndrome, King of Prussia, PA.

Plissart, L., Borghgraef, M., Van Den Berghe, H., & Fryns, J. P. (1994a, July). *Temperament in Williams syndrome.* Poster session presented at the sixth international professional conference of the Williams Syndrome Association, University of California, San Diego.

Plissart, L., Borghgraef, M., & Fryns, J. P. (1996b). Temperament in Williams syndrome. *Genetic Counseling, 7,* 41–46.

Plissart, L., Borghgraef, M., Volcke, H., Van Den Berghe, H., & Fryns, J. P. (1994b). Adults with Williams syndrome: Evaluation of the medical, psychological, and behavioral aspects. *Clinical Genetics, 46,* 161–167.

Plissart, L., & Fryns, J. P. (1999). Early development (5 to 48 months) in Williams syndrome. A study of 14 children. *Genetic Counseling, 10*(2), 195–196.

Plummer, V. (1994, July). *The use of a sensory integrative approach in promoting functional change.* Poster presented at the sixth international professional conference of the Williams Syndrome Association, University of California, San Diego.

Pober, P. R., & Dykens, E. M. (1996). Williams syndrome: An overview of medical, cognitive, and behavioral features. *Child and Adolescent Psychiatric Clinics of North America, 5,* 929–943.

Power, T. J., Blum, N. J., Jones, S. M., & Kaplan, P. E. (1997). Brief report: Response to methylphenidate in two children with Williams syndrome. *Journal of Autism and Developmental Disorders, 27*(1), 70–87.

Putnam, J. W., Pueschel, S. M., & Gorder-Holman, J. (1988). Community participation of youth and adults with Down syndrome. In S. M. Pueschel (Ed.), *The young person with Down syndrome* (pp. 77–92). Baltimore: Paul H. Brookes.

Reilly, J., Harrison, D., & Klima, E. S. (1994, July). *Emotional talk and talk about emotions.* Paper presented at the sixth international professional conference of the Williams Syndrome Association, University of California, San Diego.

Reilly, J., Klima, E. S., & Bellugi, U. (1990). Once more with feeling: Affect and language in atypical populations. *Development and Psychopathology, 2,* 367–391.

Reiss, A. L., Eliez, S., Schmitt, J. E., Straus, E., Lai, Z., Jones, W., & Bellugi, U. (2000). IV. Neuroanatomy of Williams syndrome: A high resolution MRI study. In U. Bellugi & M. St. George (Eds.), Linking cognitive neuroscience and molecular genetics: New perspectives from Williams syndrome. *Journal of Cognitive Neuroscience, 12* (Suppl. 1), 65–73.

Reiss, A. L., Feinstein, C., Rosenbaum, K. N., Borengasser-Caruso, M. A., & Goldsmith, B. M. (1985). Autism associated with Williams syndrome. *The Journal of Pediatrics, 106,* 247–249.

Renfrew, C. (1994). *Rendrew bus story: Language screening by narrative recall.* Centreville, DE: Centreville School.

Roach, E. G., & Kephart, N. C. (1966). *The Purdue Perceptual-Motor Survey.* San Antonio: The Psychological Corporation.

Roid, G. H., & Miller, L. J. (1997). *Leiter International Performance Scale, Revised.* Wood Dale, IL: Stoelting Co.

Rosenberg, S., & Abbeduto, L. (1993). *Language and communication in mental retardation: Development, processes and intervention.* Hillsdale, NJ: Lawrence Erlbaum Associates.

Rosner, S. R. (1970). The effects of presentation and recall trials on organization in multitrial free recall. *Journal of Verbal Learning and Verbal Behavior, 9,* 69–74.

Rosner, S. R. (1971). The effects of rehearsal and chunking instructions on children's multitrial free recall. *Journal of Experimental Child Psychology, 11,* 93–105.

Rosner, S. R. (1972). Primacy in preschoolers' short-term memory: The effects of repeated tests and shift-trials. *Journal of Experimental Child Psychology, 13,* 220–223.

Rosner, S. R., & Pochter, A. S. (1986). *Children's form reversal errors: Mirror-images and part-matching.* Presented at the annual meetings of the Midwestern Psychological Association, Chicago.

Rosner, S. R., & Semel, E. (2001, June). *Williams syndrome: Interconnections between behavioral profiles.* Poster session presented at the annual meeting of the American Psychological Society, Toronto, Canada.

Rosner, S. R., & Smick, C. (1989, April). *Cueing maintenance of slot-filler and taxonomic categories.* Presented at the meetings of the Society for Research in Child Development, Kansas City.

Rossen, M., Klima, E., Bellugi, U., Bihrle, A., & Jones, W. (1996). Interaction between language and cognition: Evidence from Williams syndrome. In J. H. Beitchman, N. Cohen, M. Konstantareas, & R. Tannock (Eds.), *Language, learning, and behavior disorders: Developmental, Biological, and Clinical Perspectives* (pp. 367–392). New York: Cambridge University Press.

Rourke, B. (1988). The syndrome of nonverbal learning disabilities: Developmental manifestations in neurological disease, disorder, and dysfunction. *The Clinical Neuropsychologist, 2,* 293–330. (Also, APA Address, Division 40)

Rourke, B. P., & Fisk, J. L. (1988). Subtypes of learning-disabled children: Implications for a neurodevelopmental model of differential hemispheric processing. In D. L. Molfese & S. J. Segalowitz (Eds.), *Brain lateralization in children* (pp. 547–565). New York: Guilford Press.

Rubba, J., & Klima, E. S. (1991). Preposition use in a speaker with Williams syndrome: Some cognitive grammar proposals. La Jolla, CA: *Center for Research on Language, 5*, 3–12.

Rutter, M. (1982). Epidemiological-longitudinal approaches to the study of development. In W. A. Collins (Ed.), *The concept of development: The Minnesota Symposia on Child Psychology* (Vol. 15, pp. 105–144). Hillsdale, NJ: Lawrence Erlbaum Associates.

Rutter, M., Cox, A., Tupling, C., Berger, M., & Yule, W. (1975). Attainment and adjustment in two geographic areas: I. The prevalence of psychiatric disorder. *British Journal of Psychiatry, 126,* 493–509.

Sabbadini, L. (1994, July). Comments. In P. Wang (Chair), *Multidisciplinary approaches: Clinicians, educators, and researchers.* Symposium presented at the sixth international professional conference of the Williams Syndrome Association, University of California, San Diego.

Sattler, J. M. (1988). *Assessment of children* (3rd ed.). San Diego, CA: Jerome M. Sattler.

Schachar, R., Rutter, M., & Smith, A. (1981). The characteristics of situationally and pervasively hyperactive children: Implications for syndrome definition. *Journal of Child Psychology and Psychiatry, 22,* 375–392.

Scheiber, B. (2000). *Fulfilling dreams—Book 1. A handbook for parents of Williams syndrome children.* Clawson, MI: Williams Syndrome Association.

Schlaug, G., Jancke, L., Huang, Y., & Steinmetz, H. (1995, May 5). Response to O. Sacks, Musical ability [Letter]. *Science, 268,* 621–622.

Schmitt, J. E., Eliez, S., Bellugi, U., & Reiss, A. L. (2001). Analysis of cerebral shape in Williams syndrome. *Archives of Neurology, 58*(2), 283–287.

Schmitt, J. E., Eliez, S., Warsofsky, I. S., Bellugi, U., & Reiss, A. L. (2001). Corpus callosum morphology of Williams syndrome: Relation to genetics and behavior. *Developmental Medicine and Child Neurology, 43*(3), 155–159.

Schoenbrodt, L., & Smith, R. A. (1995). *Communication disorders and interventions in low incidence pediatric populations.* San Diego: Singular.

Schwartz, L., & McKinley, N. (1987). *Make-it-yourself barrier activities.* Eau Claire, WI: Thinking Publications.

Scott, P., Mervis, C. B., Bertrand, J., Klein, B. P., Armstrong, S. C., & Ford, A. L. (1994, July). *Semantic organization and word fluency in older children with Williams syndrome.* Poster session presented at the sixth international professional conference of the Williams Syndrome Association, University of California, San Diego.

Semel, E. (1982b). *Sound-order-sense: A developmental listening skills program* (SOS). [Tape Recordings]. Townsend, MA: S and J Associates, Inc. Available from P.O. Box 167, Townsend, MA 01489.

Semel, E. (1982a). *Language Intervention Activities.* San Antonio, TX: Psychological Corporation.

Semel, E. (1987, June). *Williams syndrome: Symptoms and management.* Paper presented at the Williams Syndrome Association meeting of Region V, at the Salk Institute, La Jolla, CA.

Semel, E. (1988, August). *Optimal teaching strategies for Williams syndrome children.* Paper presented at the National Meeting of the Williams Syndrome Association, Salt Lake City, UT.

Semel, E. (1995R). *Semel Auditory Processing Program. A Remedial Program for Children* (SAPP). Townsend, MA: S and J Associates. Available P.O. Box 167, Townsend, MA 01489.

Semel, E. (1997). *Following directions: Left and right* (Computer program). Winooski, VT: Laureate Learning Systems. (Talking software for special needs for the Apple II series, Macintosh and PC).

Semel, E. (1988). *Following directions: One and two-level commands* (Computer program). Winooski, VT: Laureate Learning Systems. (Talking software for special needs for the Apple II series, Macintosh and PC).

Semel, E., & Rosner, S. R. (1991a, February). *The behavioral characteristics of children with Williams syndrome: Analysis of the Utah survey.* Report presented to a meeting of the Laboratory for Language and Cognition, Salk Institute, La Jolla, CA.

Semel, E., & Rosner, S. R. (1991b, May). *A study on the significant characteristics and techniques for management of children with Williams syndrome.* Invited Address, Belgium Study Group for the Mentally Handicapped, Brussels, Belgium.

Semel, E., & Rosner, S. R. (1994, July). *Williams syndrome: Paradoxical behavior and interventions.* Paper presented at the sixth international professional conference of the Williams Syndrome Association, University of California, San Diego.

Semel, E., & Rosner, S. R. (1995). Williams syndrome: Paradoxical behavior and interventions. *Genetic Counseling, 6*(1), 162.

Semel, E., & Wiig, E. H. (1982). *Clinical Language Intervention Program (CLIP).* San Antonio, TX: The Psychological Corporation.

Semel, E., & Wiig, E. H. (1990a). *CLIP-Morphology Worksheets.* San Antonio, TX: The Psychological Corporation. Harcourt Brace Jovanovich.

Semel, E., & Wiig, E. H. (1990b). *CLIP-Syntax Worksheets.* San Antonio, TX: The Psychological Corporation. Harcourt Brace Jovanovich.

Semel, E., & Wiig, E. H. (1991). *CLIP-Semantics Worksheets.* San Antonio, TX: The Psychological Corporation. Harcourt Brace Jovanovich.

Semel, E., & Wiig, E. H. (1992a). *CLIP Pragmatics Worksheets.* San Antonio, TX: The Psychological Corporation. Harcourt Brace Jovanovich.

Semel, E., & Wiig, E. H. (1992b). *Clinical Language Intervention Program- Preschool (CLIP-P).* San Antonio, TX: Communication Skill Builders. A division of The Psychological Corporation.

Semel, E., Wiig, E. H., & Secord, W. (1987). *Clinical Evaluation of Language Fundamentals-Revised (CELF-R).* San Antonio, TX: The Psychological Corporation.

Shea, A. M., Borton, D. C., Allen, J., & Pober, B. (1996, July). *Gross motor attainments in Williams syndrome from infancy to seven years.* Paper presented at the seventh international professional conference on Williams Syndrome, King of Prussia, PA.

Singer, N., Delehanty, S. G., Reilly, J. S., & Bellugi, U. (1993, March). *Development of emotional inferences in Williams syndrome.* Poster session presented at the 60th biennial meeting of the Society for Research in Child Development, New Orleans, LA.

Singer-Harris, N. G., Bellugi, U., Bates, E., Jones, A., & Rossen, M. L. (1997). Contrasting profiles of language development in children with Williams and Down syndromes. In D. J. Thal & J. S. Reilly (Eds.), Origins of language disorders (Special issue). *Developmental Neuropsychology, 13*, 345–370.

Sivan, A. B. (1992). *Benton Visual Retention Test* (5th ed.). San Antonio, TX: Psychological Corporation.

Smith, P. D. (1989). Assessing motor skills. In D. B. Bailey, Jr., & M. Wolery (Eds.), *Assessing infants and preschoolers with handicaps.* Columbus, OH: Merrill.

Sparrow, S. S., Balla, D. A., & Cicchetti, D. (1984). *Vineland Behavior Scales.* Circle Pines, MN: American Guidance Service.

Spector, C. C. (1997). *Saying one thing, meaning another.* Eau Claire, WI: Thinking Publications.

Stambaugh, I. (1996, November). Special learners with special abilities. *Music Educators Journal,* 19–23.

Stevens, T., & Karmiloff-Smith, A. (1997). Word learning in a special population: Do individuals with WS obey lexical constraints? *Journal of Child Language, 24*, 737–765.

Stiles, J., Sabbadini, E., Capirci, O., & Volterra, V. (1996, July). *Drawing abilities in Williams syndrome: A case study.* Poster presented at the seventh international professional conference on Williams syndrome, King of Prussia, PA.

Stiles, J., Sabbadini, L., Capirci, O., & Volterra, V. (2000). Drawing abilities in Williams syndrome: A case study. *Developmental Neuropsychology, 18*(2), 213–235.

Sullivan, K., & Tager-Flusberg, H. (1999). Second-order belief attribution in Williams syndrome: Intact or impaired? *American Journal of Mental Retardation, 104*, 523–532.

Swanson, J. M., Wigal, S., Greenhill, L. L., Browne, R., Waslik, B., Lerner, M., et al. (1998). Analog classroom assessment of Adderall in children with ADHD. *Journal of American Academy of Child and Adolescent Psychiatry, 37*(5), 519–526.

Tager-Flusberg, H., Boshart, J., & Baron-Cohen, S. (1998). Reading the windows to the soul: Evidence of domain-specific sparing in Williams syndrome. *Journal of Cognitive Neuroscience, 10*(5), 631–639.

Tager-Flusberg, H., & Sullivan, K. (1999, April). *Are theory of mind abilities spared in children with Williams syndrome?* Poster session presented at the biennial meeting of the Society for Child Development, Albuquerque, NM.

Tager-Flusberg, H., & Sullivan, K. (2000). A componential view of theory of mind: Evidence from Williams syndrome. *Cognition, 76*, 59–90.

Tager-Flusberg, H., Sullivan, K., Boshart, J., & Guttman, J. I. (1997, April). Theory of mind abilities in Williams syndrome: Is there evidence of a spared cognitive domain? In H. Tager-Flusberg (Chair), *Cognitive functioning in Williams syndrome: Contributions to theoretical controversies in child development.* Paper symposium conducted at the biennial meeting of the Society for Research in Child Development, Washington, DC.

Tager-Flusberg, H., Sullivan, K., Boshart, J., Guttman, J., & Levine, K. (1996, July). *Social cognitive abilities in children and adolescents with Williams syndrome.* Paper presented at the seventh international professional conference on Williams Syndrome, King of Prussia, PA.

Tager-Flusberg, H., Sullivan, K., & Zaitchik, D. (1994, July). *Social cognitive abilities in young children with Williams syndrome.* Paper presented at the sixth international professional conference of the Williams Syndrome Association, University of California, San Diego.

Tassabehji, M., Metcalfe, K., Fergusson, W. D., Carette, M. J. A., Dore, J. K., Donnai, D., Read, A. P., Proschel, C., Gutowski, N. J., Mao, X., & Sheer, D. (1996). LIM-Kinase deleted in Williams syndrome. *Nature Genetics, 13* (July), 272–273.

Tassabehji, M., Metcalfe, K., Karmiloff-Smith, A., Carette, M. J., Grant, J., Dennis, N., Readon, W., Splitt, M., Read, A., & Donnai, D. (1999). Williams syndrome: Use of chromosomal microdeletions as a tool to dissect cognitive and physical phenotypes. *American Journal of Human Genetics, 64*, 118–125.

Thal, D., Bates, E., & Bellugi, U. (1989). Language and cognition in two children with Williams syndromes. *Journal of Speech and Hearing Research, 32*, 489–500.

Tharp, E. (1986). *Educational questionnaire results.* Report presented at the Williams Syndrome Association annual board meeting.

Thorndike, R. L., Hagen, E. P., & Sattler, J. M. (1986). *Stanford–Binet Intelligence Scale* (4th ed.). Chicago, IL: Riverside Publishing.

Tomatis, A. A. (1978). *Education and dyslexia.* Fribourg, Switzerland: AIAPP.

Tomc, S. A., Williamson, N. K., & Pauli, R. A. (1990). Temperament in Williams syndrome. *American Journal of Medical Genetics, 36*, 345–352.

Trauner, D. A., Bellugi, U., & Chase, C. (1989). Neurologic features of Williams and Down syndromes. *Pediatric Neurology, 5*, 166–168.

Trott, M. C., Laurel, M., & Windeck, S. L. (1993). *SenseAbilities: Understanding sensory integration.* San Antonio, TX: Communication Skills Builders.

Tyler, L. K., Karmiloff-Smith, A., Voice, K., Stevens, T., Grant, J., Udwin, O., Davies, M., & Howlin, P. (1997). Do people with WS have bizarre semantics? A primed monitoring study. *Cortex, 33*, 515–527.

Udwin, O. (1990). A survey of adults with Williams syndrome and idiopathic infantile hypercalcaemia. *Developmental Medicine and Child Neurology, 32*, 129–141.

Udwin, O., Howlin, P., & Davies, M. (1996a). *Adults with Williams syndrome: Guidelines for employers and supervisors* (pp. 1–5). Williams Syndrome Foundation (UK). (Available at *http://www.williams-syndrome.org.uk/employ.htm*)

Udwin, O., Howlin, P., & Davies, M. (1996b). *Adults with Williams syndrome: Guidelines for families and professionals.* Williams Syndrome Foundation (UK). (Available at *http://www.williams-syndrome.org.uk/fam.prof.htm*)

Udwin, O., Howlin, P., Davies, M., & Mannion, E. (1998). Community care for adults with Williams syndrome: How families cope and the availability of support networks. *Journal of Intellectual Disability Research, 42*(3), 238–245.

Udwin, O., & Yule, W. (1988). *Infantile hypercalcaemia and Williams syndrome: Guidelines for parents.* Essex: Infantile Hypercalcaemia Foundation.

Udwin, O., & Yule, W. (1989). *Infantile hypercalcaemia and Williams syndrome: Guidelines for teachers.* Essex: Infantile Hypercalcaemia Foundation.

Udwin, O., & Yule, W. (1990). Expressive language of children with Williams syndrome. *American Journal of Medical Genetics Supplement, 6*, 108–114.

Udwin, O., & Yule, W. (1991). A cognitive and behavioural phenotype in Williams syndrome. *Journal of Clinical and Experimental Neuropsychology, 13*, 232–244.

Udwin, O., & Yule, W. (1998a). *Williams Syndrome: Guidelines for teachers* (rev.). Williams Syndrome Foundation (UK). Available at the Williams Syndrome Organization UK Web site: *hhtp://www.williams-syndrome.org.uk/teachers.htm*

Udwin, O., & Yule, W. (1998b). *Williams syndrome: Guidelines for parents* (rev.). Williams Syndrome Foundation (UK). Available at the Williams Syndrome Organization UK Web site: *hhtp://www.williams-syndrome.org.uk/parents.htm*

Udwin, O., Yule, W., & Martin, N. (1987). Cognitive abilities and behavioural characteristics of children with idiopathic infantile hypercalcaemia. *Journal of Child Psychology and Psychiatry, 28*, 297–309.

Vaal, J. J. (1994, July). *Diversity in development of Williams syndrome.* Paper presented at the National Family Conference Williams Syndrome Association, San Diego, CA.

Van Borsel, J., Curfs, L. M. G., & Fryns, J. P. (1997). Hyperacusis in Williams syndrome: A sample survey study. *Genetic Counseling, 8*(2), 121–126.

van Lieshout, C. F., De Meyer, R. E., Curfs, L. M., & Fryns, J. P. (1998). Family contexts, parental behavior, and personality profiles of children and adolescents with Prader-Willi, fragile-X, or Williams syndrome. *Journal of Child Psychology and Psychiatry, 39*(5), 699–710.

Vicari, S., Belluci, S., & Carlesimo, G. A. (2001). Procedural learning deficit in children with Williams syndrome. *Neuropsychologia, 39*, 665–677.

Vicari, S., Brizzolara, D., Carlesimo, G. A., Pezzini, G., & Volterra, V. (1996a). Memory abilities in children with Williams syndrome. *Cortex, 32*, 503–514.

Vicari, S., Carlesimo, G. A., Brizzolara, D., & Pezzini, G. (1996b). Short-term memory in children with Williams syndrome: A reduced contribution of lexical-semantic knowledge to word span. *Neuropsychologia, 34*, 919–925.

Vicari, S., Pezzini, G., Milani, L., Dall'Oglio, A. M., & Sergo, M. (1994, July). *Neuropsychological profiles in Italian children with Williams syndrome.* Poster session presented at the sixth international professional conference of the Williams Syndrome Association, University of California, San Diego.

Volterra, V., Capirci, O., Pezzini, G., Sabbadini, L., & Vicari, S. (1996). Linguistic abilities in Italian children with Williams syndrome. *Cortex, 32*, 663–677.

Volterra, V., Sabbadini, L., Capirci, O., Pezzini, G., & Ossella, T. (1994, July). *Linguistic abilities in Italian children with Williams syndrome.* Paper presented at the sixth international professional conference of the Williams Syndrome Association, University of California, San Diego.

von Arnim, G., & Engel, P. (1964). Mental retardation related to hypercalcaemia. *Developmental Medicine and Child Neurology, 6*, 366–377.

Wang, P. (1992, June). The relationship of neuropsychological and neurobiological profiles in Williams and Down syndromes. In U. Bellugi & P. Wang (Chairs), *Two genetic syndromes of contrasting cognitive profiles: A neuropsychological and neurobiological dissection.* Symposium conducted at the meeting of the American Psychological Society, San Diego.

Wang, P. P. (1994, July). Multidisciplinary approaches: Clinicians, educators, and researchers (Chair). Symposium, presented at the sixth international professional conference of the Williams Syndrome Association, University of California, San Diego.

Wang, P. P., & Bellugi, U. (1993). Williams syndrome, Down syndrome, and cognitive neuroscience. *American Journal of Diseases of Children, 147*, 1246–1251.

Wang, P. P., & Bellugi, U. (1994). Evidence from two genetic syndromes for a dissociation between verbal and visual-spatial short-term memory. *Journal of Clinical and Experimental Neuropsychology, 16*, 317–322.

Wang, P. P., Cass, S., Bellugi, U., & Tzeng, O. (1996, July). *Implicit sequence learning in Williams and Down syndromes.* Poster presented at the seventh international professional conference on Williams syndrome, King of Prussia, PA.

Wang, P. P., Doherty, S., Rourke, S. B., & Bellugi, U. (1995). Unique profile of visuo-perceptual skills in a genetic syndrome. *Brain and Cognition, 29*, 54–65.

Wang, P. P., Ennis, K. M., & Namey, T. L. (1997, April). Working memory and language skills in Williams syndrome. In H. Tager-Flusberg (Chair), *Cognitive functioning in Williams syndrome: Contributions to theoretical controversies in child development.* Paper symposium conducted at the biennial meeting of the Society for Research in Child Development, Washington, DC.

Ward, N. (1994, July). *Improving the social use of language (Pragmatics).* Paper presented at the National Family Conference Williams Syndrome Association, San Diego, CA.

Wechsler, D. (1991). *Wechsler Intelligence Scale for Children-III (WISC-III).* San Antonio, TX: The Psychological Corporation.

Wepman, J. M. (1987). *Wepman's Auditory Test, Second Edition.* Los Angeles: Western Psychological Services.

Wender, P. H. (1987). *The hyperactive child, adolescent, and adult: Attention Deficit Disorder through the lifespan.* New York: Oxford University Press.

Wiegers, A., de Meyer, R., van Lieshout, C. F. M., Plissart, L., Curfs, L. M. G., & Fryns, J. P. (1994, July). *Personality profiles of children and adolescents with Williams syndrome compared with other syndrome groups and matched groups in regular school.* Poster session presented at the sixth international professional conference of the Williams Syndrome Association, University of California, San Diego.

Wiig, E. H., Secord, W., & Semel, E. (1992). *Clinical Evaluation of Language Fundamentals-Preschool (CELF-P).* San Antonio, TX: The Psychological Corporation.

Wiig, E. S., & Semel, E. M. (1976). *Language disabilities in children and adolescents.* Columbus, OH: Charles E. Merrill.

Wiig, E. S., & Semel, E. (1984). *Language assessment and intervention for the learning disabled* (2nd ed.). Columbus, OH: Charles E. Merrill.

Willeford, J. A., & Burleigh, J. M. (1994). Sentence procedures in central testing. In J. Katz (Ed.), *Handbook of Clinical Audiology* (4th ed., pp. 256–268). Baltimore: Williams & Wilkins.

Williams, J. C. P., Barrett-Boyes, B. G., & Lowe, J. B. (1961). Supravalvular aortic stenosis. *Circulation, 24*, 1311–1318.

Wilson, M., & Fox, B. (1998-R). *Swim, swam, swum: Mastering irregular verbs.* Winooski, VT: Laureate Special Needs Software.

Wilson, M., & Fox, B. (in press). *Sterling editions: Syntax modules.* Winooski, VT: Laureate Special Needs Software.

Winter, M., Pankau, R., Amm, M., Gosch, A., & Wessel, A. (1996). The spectrum of ocular features in the Williams-Beuren syndrome. *Clinical Genetics, 49*(1), 28–31.

Wolery, M., & Smith, P. D. (1989). Assessing self-care skills. In D. B. Bailey, Jr. & M. Wolery (Eds.), *Assessing infants and preschoolers with handicaps.* Columbus, OH: Charles E. Merrill.

Woodcock, R. (1976). *Goldman-Fristoe-Woodcock auditory skills test battery.* Circle Pines, MN: American Guidance Service.

Appendix

Williams Syndrome Organizations—USA

Williams Syndrome Association (WSA)
PO Box 297
Clawson, MI 48017-0297
Ph: (248) 541-3630   FAX: (248) 541-3631
www.williams-syndrome.org
e-mail: *Tmonkaba@aol.com*

The WSA provides information and emotional support to individuals with the characteristics of WS, their families, and professionals who work with them. It develops programs and services to help build upon the strengths and deal with the challenges of WS, encourages and supports research, and seeks to increase public awareness and understanding of WS. It is a very active organization that serves as a clearinghouse for information and initiates projects designed to enhance the lives of WSs and those associated with them.

WSA Regional Associations—There are eleven WSA regional groups covering the USA: Far West, Northwest, Mississippi Valley, Mid-Atlantic, South Central, Great Lakes, Rocky Mountain, Upper Midwest, Tri-State, Southeast, and New England Region. Each has its own program of activities and events, officers, and state representatives. The WSA National Newsletter, *Heart to*

Heart, regularly includes a list of contact persons and information for the regional associations.

Williams Syndrome Foundation (WSF)
University of California
Irvine, CA 92679-2310
Ph: (949) 824-7259
www.wsf.org
e-mail: *hmlenhof@uci.edu* or *williamssyndrome@hotmail.com*

The Williams Syndrome Foundation is dedicated to improving the lives of young people with WS, primarily through establishing music programs and residential villages. It also serves as a conduit for research and information on WS, specializing in the musicality, cognitive profile, brain and genetic advances of WS.

Lili Claire Foundation
2800 28th Street, Suite 325
Santa Monica, CA 90405
Ph: (310) 396-4355   FAX: (310) 396-2127
www.liliclairefoundation.org
e-mail: *staff@liliclairefoundation.org*

The Lili Claire Foundation is developing programs to benefit individuals with WS and other neurogenetic birth defects. These include a partnership with the UCLA Family Resource Center and establishing a Lili Claire Life Skills Center at the University of Nevada, Las Vegas.

WSA Organizations—International

The Williams Syndrome Foundation—United Kingdom
161 High Street
Tonbridge; Kent TN9 1BX
England
PH: 01732 365152   FAX: 01732 360178
www.williams-syndrome.org.uk/
e-mail: *John Nelson*

Canadian Association for Williams Syndrome (CAWS)
PO Box 2115
Vancouver, BC
V6B 3T5
Canada
Ph: (604) 596-0180
www.bmts.com/~williams

International Williams Syndrome Organization Web Sites

Argentina
Asociacion Argentina de Sindrome de Williams (AasW)
www.welcome.to/aasw (en espanol)

Belgium
Williams Association of Belgium
Users.skynet.be/wsa-bel-be

France
Williams-France/EST (France)
Perso.wanadoo.fr/syndrome_de_williams

Germany
Bundesverband William-Beuren Syndrom (Germany)
www.w-s-b.de

Hungary
www.korb1.sote.hu/williams.html

Israel
Eitan-Israel Association of Rare Diseases (In Hebrew)
www.eitan-rd.com

Spain
Asociacion Sindrome de Williams (A.S.W)
lingua.fil.ub.es/~hilferty/asw.html

Spain, Valencia
ASOCIATION VALENCIANA SINDROME DE WILLIAMS
Personales.jet.es/avsw/

Sweden
www.databasen.se/forening/williams-syndrom/

Other countries with Williams Syndrome organizations, but no current website, include: Australia (Williams Syndrome Support Group of Victoria); Italy (Associazione Italiana Sindrome di Williams (ASW); Japan (Williams Syndrome Association of Japan); New Zealand (Williams Syndrome Association); and Norway (Norsk Forening for WS). Lists are printed regularly in the WSA Newsletter (Heart to Heart) and websites of the WSA and WSF

Williams Syndrome Clinics—USA

The Children's Hospital, Boston
300 Longwood Ave.
Boston, MA 02115
Tammy Hopper-Graham Ph: (617) 355-6501

Cincinnati Center for Developmental Disorders
Elland & Bethesda Ave.
Cincinnati, OH 45229-2899
Dr. Nancy Lamphear Ph: (513) 636-4691

Lutheran General Hospital (Temporarily Discontinued)
1875 Dempster, Suite 325
Park Ridge, IL 60068
Ph: (708) 696-7705

Children's Hospital of Philadelphia
34th St. & Civic Center Blvd.
Philadelphia, PA 19104

Children's Hospital & Health Center (Referrals Only)
Outpatient Department, Children's Way
San Diego, CA 92123
Dr. Fred Rose
Ph: (858) 453-4100, ext 1222 or (800) 434-1034

Children's Hospital of Buffalo
219 Bryant St. Buffalo, NY 14222
Dr. Laurie Sadler Ph: (716) 878-7530

Yale University School of Medicine
New Haven, CT
Dr. Barbara Pober Ph: (203) 737-2754

Spaulding Rehabilitation Hospital
Boston, MA
Dr. Karen Levine Ph: (617) 573-2200 (Outpatient Services)

Schneider Children's Hospital
New Hyde Park, NY
Dr. Joyce Fox Ph: (718) 470-3010

Professional Organizations

American Medical Association (AMA)
515 North State Street
Chicago, IL 60610
Ph: (312) 464-5000, or (800) AMA-3211
www.ama-assn.org

American Music Therapy Association, Inc. (AMTA)
8455 Colesville Road, Suite 1000
Silver Spring, Maryland 20910
Ph: (301) 589-3300   FAX (301) 589-5175
Musictherapy.org
e-mail: info@musk

American Occupational Therapy Association, Inc. (AOTA)
4720 Montgomery Lane
PO Box 31220
Bethesda, MD 20824-1220
Ph: (301) 652-2682
www.aota.org

American Physical Therapy Association (APTA)
1111 North Fairfax Street
Alexandria, VA 22314-1488
Ph: (703) 684-2782 or (800) 999-2782
www.apta.org/

American Psychiatric Association (APA)
1400 K Street N.W.
Washington, DC 20005
Ph: (888) 357-7924   FAX: (202) 682-6850
www.psych.org
e-mail: *apa@psych.org*

American Psychological Association (APA)
750 First Street, NE
Washington, DC 20002-4242
Ph: (800) 374-2721 or (202) 336-5510
www.apa.org

American Speech-Language-Hearing Association (ASHA)
10801 Rockville Pike
Rockville, MD 20852
Ph (Professionals/Students): (800) 498-2071
Ph (Public): (800) 638-8255
www.asha.org
e-mail: *actioncenter@asha.org*

Council for Exceptional Children (CEC)
1110 North Glebe Road, Suite 300
Arlington, VA 22314-1488
Ph: (888) CEC-SPED, or (703) 620-3660
FAX: (703) 264-9494
www.cec.sped.org

The Genetic and Rare Disease Information Center
PO Box 8126
Gaithersburg, MD 20898-8126
Ph: (888) 205-2311
e-mail: *gardinfo@nih.gov*

The Genetic and Rare Disease Information Center is a collaborative effort of the National Human Genome Research Institute (NHGRI) and the National Institutes of Health's Office of Rare Diseases (ORD). It offers access to specialists who can provide accurate, reliable information about genetic and rare diseases to patients and their families.

Learning Disabilities Association of America, Inc. (LDA)
4156 Library Road
Pittsburgh, PA 15234
Ph: (412) 341-1515   FAX: (412) 344-0224
www.ldanatl.org
e-mail: *info@ldaamerica.org*

National Association of School Psychologists (NASP)
4340 East West Highway, Suite 402
Bethesda, MD 20814
Ph: (301) 657-0270   FAX: (301) 657-0275
www.nasponline.org

Psychodrama Training Institute
19 West 34th Street, Penthouse
New York, NY 10001
Ph: (212) 947-7111   FAX: (212) 239-0948
www.psychodramanyc.com

Publications

WSA Publications—Heart to Heart, the WSA Newsletter, contains informative research, treatment, and networking articles on WS for families, teachers, and others. On its web site, WSA lists many publications that appeared in its Newsletter as well as other references and videotapes. Topics include: Information for Teachers; Testing and Evaluation Strategies for Williams Syndrome; Medical Guidelines for Williams Syndrome; Williams Syndrome and the Brain; How to Develop an IEP that Works; Independent Living. Some references may be downloaded.

WSF-UK provides informative guideline pamphlets for parents, teachers, families and professionals, employers and supervisors, and physicians free to its members or for a small charge. Some may be downloaded from its web site.

The *WSF* web site provides lists of references for researchers and the layman, articles that may be downloaded as well as synopses of research and information on WS.

Exceptional Parent Magazine
65 East Route 4
River Edge, NJ 07661
Ph: (201) 489-4111
FAX: (201) 489-0074
www.eparent.com

Exceptional Parent Magazine—is an extremely useful resource for WS parents, teachers, and others.

Scientific Papers—Websites

OMIM—Online Mendelian Inheritance in Man
www3.nobi.nlm.nih.gov/htbin-post/Omim/dispmim?194050

Karen Scarpelli's Williams Syndrome Monthly Medline Alert
www.geocities.com/HotSpring/8172

Support Organizations

The ARC of the United States (Association for Retarded Citizens)
1010 Wayne Ave., Suite 650
Silver Spring, MD 20910
Ph: (301) 565-3842
www.thearc.org
e-mail: info@thearc.org

Idea Partnerships

Provides information about IDEA '97, Individuals with Disabilities Act, which introduced reforms in education for exceptional children. This partnership is a coalition of service providers, administrators, families and advocates, policymakers.
   www.Ideapractices.org

   Families and Advocates Partnership for Education (FAPE)
   www.fape.org

   Provides information about IDEA

Recreation/Enhancement Opportunities

   Special Olympics
   1325 G Street, NW/Suite 500
   Washington, DC 20005
   Ph: (202) 628-3630   FAX: (202) 824-0200
   www.specialolympics.org
   e-mail: info@specialolympics.org

   Best Buddies: National Headquarters
   100 SE Second Street, #1990
   Miami FL 33131
   (305) 374-2233
   www.bestbuddies.org
   e-mail: *LavemeL@BestBuddies.org*

   Best Buddies—Provides opportunities for one-to-one friendships and integrated employment for people with mental retardation.

Tours

   Summit Summer Travel Program/ City Tours
   Mayer Stiskin, PO Box 384, 110-45 71st Road, Suite 1G
   Forest Hills, NY 11375
   Ph: (800) 232-9908 or (718) 268-0020
   www.summitcamp.com
   e-mail: *summitcamp@aol.com*

   Able Trek Tours
   PO Box 384, Reedsburg, WI 53959
   (800) 205-6713, or (608) 346-2311
   www.abletrektours.com

The Guided Tour, Inc. (Adult Vacations)
7900 Old York Rd., Suite 114B
Elkins Park, PA 19027-2239
Ph: (215) 782-1370
www.guidedtour.com

Camps

General Camp Information
www.kidscamps.com

Provides information by type of camp and state.

Edward J. Madden Open Hearts Camp, Great Barrington, MA
(Steve Lasky (866) 275-8633)

Marbridge Summer Camp, Manchaca, TX (Special Needs Camp,
Ages 16-30), Ph: (512) 282-1144, x 413
e-mail: *wchoermann@marbridge.org*

Music/Art Camps

Belvoir Terrace, Lenox Massachusetts
For Application: Contact WSA
For Information: Sharon E. Libera, PhD, Camp Coordinator
139 Taylor St.
Granby, MA 01033
Ph: (413) 467-9381
e-mail: *jlibera@javanet.com*

A one-week music/arts summer program for WSs. Featured in television specials and video-cassettes.

Other music/art camps and programs for WSs include: Blue Lake Fine Arts Camp, Twin Lake, MI; Friendship Ventures at Edenwood Camp, MN; Music Therapy Program, San Antonio, TX; Music & Minds (Neag Center for Gifted Education and Talent Development, University of Connecticut, Storrs, CT 06269-2007, Ph: (860) 486-4826, e-mail: *rms97001@uconnvm.uconn. edu;*); a music camp in Spain, one in Ireland (see WSA for information).

Resources for WS Teenagers and Adults

Housing Resources

The National Housing Center for People with Disabilities
Technical Assistance Collaborative, Inc

One Center Plaza, Suite 310
Boston, MA 02108
Ph: (617) 742-5657   FAX: (617) 742-0509
www.tacine.org/lhousingframe.html
e-mail: info@tacinc.org

Educational Programs

PACE Program Curriculum, National Louis University, Evanston, IL
(847/475-1100, x 2670).

The Berkshire Hills Music Academy (BHMA)
PO Box 407
South Hadley, MA 01075
Ph: (413) 540-9720
www.berkshirehills.org
gregwilliams@berkshirehills.org

Post-Secondary Education Planning Resources

National Clearinghouse for Post-Secondary Education for
Students with Disabilities
www.health-resource-center-org

LDA Book Store ("Directories—Schools/Colleges/Camps")
http://ldanatl.org/store

State Resource Sheets—Education Contacts by State
www.nichcy.org/index.html

PACER—Midwest Regional Center for Educational Advocacy
www.pacer.org/index.html

Future Planning

Estate Planning Booklet, Available from WSA

Author Index

Subject Index

external "clocks" to maintain
  attention, 314
instructional devices, 313, 314
modality effects, 312, 313
work partners, 313
verbal mediation strategies, 309
  dramatization, puppetry, humor,
    stories, 309
  self-instruction, 309
Down syndrome (DS)
language,17-19, 21, 24-27, 31, 32,
  35, 37, 39, 40
motor ability-skills, 132
sociability, 188
visuomotor, 188
Dysnomia
  see Word-finding problems

E

Education
aptitude maximization, 387, 388
aptitude maximization, table, 383
build on strengths, 387, 388
classroom issues, 388, 389
classroom placement, 388
compensation
  classroom applications,
    sociability, 210
  classroom learning, special
    interests, 215
  educational applications, memory
    skills, 233
  educational applications, music
    abilities, 245-247
  story-telling skills, 105
curriculum, 388, 390
instructional devices, modality
  effects, 313, 314
post-secondary education, 245
see also Academic skills
  Appendix, educational programs,
    428, 429
Emotional disorders, 289-307
depression, clinical criteria, 289

dysthymia, 290, 292
mood disturbance, 292
obsessive compulsive disorder
  (OCD), 290, 292
overanxious disorder, 289, 290, 292
phobias, 290
research studies, 290-293
treatment by specialists, 293
Empathy, 202-207
characteristics, 202, 203
dealing with oversensitivity, 208, 209
emotional understanding, 204, 205
false belief tasks, 205, 206
higher level concepts, 206, 207
others' feelings, 202, 203
oversensitivity, 207-209
research summary table, 208
social cognition, 203-207
theory of mind, 203-207
Environmental controls, 310, 380-382
perceptual distractions, aversions,
  160, 161, 166, 172, 213, 310, 381
environmental stability, 302, 303,
  322, 324, 382
stress reduction, 305-306, 333, 382

F

Face recognition, 117-121
Benton Face Test, 117-119
local processing style, 119, 120
Mooney Closure Faces Test, 118
processing styles of faces, 119, 120
upside down faces, 119
Visual Closure Subtest, 118
Facial characteristics, 2-4
Fears and anxieties, 252-257
emotionality, 255-257
prevalence, 253
research summary table, 256
types of fears, 253-255
Fears and anxiety problems, interventions, 300-307
control mechanisms, 302
use of humor to reduce stress, 302

Occupational therapy (OT), 70, 76,
147, 151, 152, 154, 169, 334, 397
Oral-motor problems, 20, 21, 69, 70,
166, 167, 169
Overfriendliness, interventions, 192-194
control mechanisms, 194
professional specialists, 194, 195
social awareness instruction, 193
verbal mediational techniques, 193,
194
Over-reactivity
adaptability problems, 261, 262
auditory hypersensitivity, 171, 172
fearfulness, 255
emotionality, 255, 256
high reactivity, 294
impulsivity, 259-261
low frustration tolerance, 264-271
oversensitivity, others' distress,
207- 209
tactile defensiveness, 165-168
visual distractibility, 310

P

Peer relations, 195-202
characteristics
age trends, 195, 196
difficulties with peer relations, 196-
200
bossiness, 199
expressing negative feelings, 196,
197
immaturity, 196
poor losers, 199, 200
problems with pragmatic language
rules, 196
social "crowding", 199
social reciprocity problems, 196
wheedling, 199
improving peer relations, 197-200
kindred peers, 201, 202
non-agemate friends, 200
organized groups, 200, 201
organized social programs, 201
peer alternatives, 202

promoting social awareness, 198
providing opportunities for peer
interaction, 200-202
research summary table, 197
see also Sociability
Perseveration, 51, 52, 93, 94, 270,
271, 326, 334
Physical therapy (PT), 70, 147, 151,
152, 334, 397
Prader-Willi syndrome (P-W)
adaptability, 262
agreeableness, 189
behavior problems, 299
curiosity, 211
empathy, 203
emotionality, 255
emotions, understanding, 204
false belief tasks, 206
fears, 253
frustration tolerance, 265
hyperactivity, 276
impulsivity, 259
irritability, 269
partial specificity, 367
peers, 195
vengeance, 267
Professional organizations, 424, 425
Professionals, types of specialists, 11,
12, 349, 382-387
auditory specialists, 175
behavior problems, 194-195, 293, 306
clinical disorders, 293
functions of specialists, 383
intervention plans, 386, 387
maladaptive behaviors, 385
motor problems, 146, 147
research specialties, 11
selection of specialists, 382, 383
vision specialists, 140, 144, 145
see also Medical conditions, problems
Occupational therapy (OT)
Physical therapy (PT)
Sensory integration therapy (SIT)
Speech language therapy (SLT)
Professional treatment, types of
treatment, 306, 307, 346